YORK MYSTERY PLAYS

L. TOULMIN SMITH

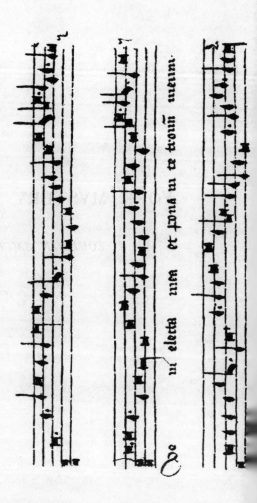

ASHBURNHAM M.S. 137. LEAF 235.

PLATE I.

York Plays

THE PLAYS PERFORMED

BY THE

CRAFTS OR MYSTERIES OF YORK

ON THE DAY OF

CORPUS CHRISTI

IN THE 14TH, 15TH, AND 16TH CENTURIES

NOW FIRST PRINTED FROM THE UNIQUE MANUSCRIPT
IN THE LIBRARY OF LORD ASHBURNHAM

EDITED

WITH INTRODUCTION AND GLOSSARY

BY

LUCY TOULMIN SMITH

NEW YORK / RUSSELL & RUSSELL

FIRST PUBLISHED IN 1885

REISSUED, 1963, BY RUSSELL & RUSSELL

A DIVISION OF ATHENEUM PUBLISHERS, INC.

L. C. CATALOG CARD NO: 63-15180

ISBN: 0-8462-0313-8

PRINTED IN THE UNITED STATES OF AMERICA

CONTENTS.

[An asterisk is affixed to the five Plays which are accompanied by the Towneley parallel.]

NOTE.—It may be useful to rehearse the municipal books belonging to the Corporation of York herein quoted :—

Liber Memorandorum $\frac{A}{Y}$. A.D. 1376–1478.

A Register of deeds, charters, and ordinances, 1371–1577, marked $\frac{B}{Y}$.

Minute or Council Books, *Lib.* III, 1461–1479 ; a volume marked II and IV, 1480–1485 ; *Lib.* V, 1483–1489 ; *Lib.* VII, 1493 ; Book 9, 1503–1519.

A Book marked 25 *H.* 6, containing some fines, fees, and classified payments.

Chamberlain's accounts, Vol. I (the earliest preserved), 11 Hen. VIII ; II, 27 Hen. VIII ; and IV, 1 Elizabeth.

CORRECTIONS.

Page 27, line 153, *read* malysoune *for* malysonne

,,   35, title, *read* et *for* and

,,   95, ,,   50, *read* remened *for* remeued

,, 152, second marginal note, *read* fondlings *for* foundlings

,, 179, ,,   ,,   ,, *read* mite *for* mighty one

,, 179, line 29, *insert* n *in* and

,, 183, ,, 183, *read* caut *for* cant

,, 230, first marginal note, *read* makes game of *for* stakes

,, 295, line   77, marginal note, *read* over-garment *for* shirt

,, 302, ,, 290, *read* mefte *for* meste

,, 321, ,,   32, *read* [chasted] *for* [hasted]

,, 369, ,, 330, *dele* comma *after* Joseph, *insert* comma *after* is

,, 371, ,, 408, *dele* full stop *after* his

,, 384, ,, 199, *dele* comma *after* Satan

,, 398, ,,   57, *read* oure *for* ure

,, 402, ,, 119, *insert* God *before* graunt

,, 403, ,, 147, *read* menne stele *for* mennestele

,, 403, third marginal note, *read* ? action *for* death

,, 430, line 105, *read* thraste *for* thaste

,, 464, ,, 263, *read* Vs to for-do *for* Vs for to do

,, 484, *for* Solomon iii. 8 *read* Solomon iv. 8.

INTRODUCTION.

I.

THE Manuscript volume containing the collection of religious plays, anciently performed on the day of Corpus Christi by the craft-gilds of York, belongs to the Earl of Ashburnham[1], to whose liberal permission the public owes it that this valuable addition to our early dramatic literature is now for the first time printed; and I desire to record here my sincere thanks for the full and free use of the MS. which he has kindly accorded me.

It is not a little remarkable that these long-desired plays have never yet seen the light. Scholars have known since the publication of Thoresby's History of Leeds, that such a collection existed[2], but no one appears ever to have done more than make a cursory examination of it; this was only done by the writer 'L.' in the Gentleman's Magazine, and, more carefully, by the late Rev. Mr. Garnett, of the British Museum, whose opinion on it was printed in the Catalogue of Mr. Heywood Bright's library, after whose sale the late Lord Ashburnham purchased the volume.

PEDIGREE OF THE MANUSCRIPT. The history of the volume is curious. It was the book wherein the plays, performed by the crafts from the fourteenth to the sixteenth centuries with the sanction and authority of the corporation, were 'registered' by the city officers, and it must therefore have belonged to the corporation. It was at one time in the care of the priory of Holy Trinity in Micklegate, at the gates of which was the first station in the circle of performances through the city as early as 1399,—

---

[1] No 137 in the *Appendix* to the Ashburnham Catalogue.

[2] See the Gentleman's Magazine, vol. 54, p. 103; Chester Mysteries, ed. Thos. Wright, Shakespeare Soc. 1843, I. introd. p. i; Halliwell's Dictionary of Old Plays, *s.v. York Mysteries;* The Skryveners' Play, ed. J. P. Collier, Camden Soc. Miscell. 1859, p. 5; W. C. Hazlitt in his edition of Warton's Hist. of English Poetry, 1871, II. p. 224; Le Mistére du Viel Testament pub. par feu Baron J. de Rothschild, Soc. des Anciens Textes français, 1878, I. p. xlvi *note.* It was the last that first directed my attention to the volume.

'at the Trinitie yaits where the clerke kepys the regyster,' we learn from the chamberlain's accounts of 1554 [1]. At the time of the Reformation various attempts were made to amend the book of plays, as is shown both by many notes scattered through its leaves and by notices in the municipal records [2]; but, in spite of these, the plays could not withstand the new spirit of the times, and were discontinued about 1580. What now became of the book of the plays is only matter of conjecture; that it had been customarily kept at Trinity priory accounts for its not being found among the municipal records at this day; yet, after the dissolution of the priory in 1538, the book still remained under the control of the city, the council in 1568, and again in 1579, agreeing that it should be amended and corrected. How long it remained in their hands it is impossible to say, but it seems probable that having been laid aside, it soon fell into the hands of some member of the Fairfax family. Two Fairfaxes had been Recorders of York in the previous century, and many of the family sat on the Council of the North for reform of religious matters through the sixteenth century [3]. In 1599, Sir Thomas Fairfax of Denton (grandfather of the general) was on the Council; not quite a hundred years later, Henry Fairfax, one of his descendants in the Denton line, wrote on a fly-leaf of the York play MS., 'H. Fairfax's book, 1695.' This Henry was son to Henry fourth Lord Fairfax, and grandson to the Rev. Henry Fairfax of the

---

[1] Extracts from the Municipal Records of York, 1843, by Robert Davies, pp. 232, 264 *note*. (This is the work hereinafter referred to as 'Davies.') That the book was kept by a clerk (whether lay or cleric) at the priory does not militate against its being a municipal possession; we know that the chamberlains paid for registering a play as late as 1558, see after, p. 18 *note*; the station before the Trinity gates was exempted from the usual rent due to the corporation, which cannot have been on account of sanctity, for the 'place at the Minster yaite' was charged with a high rent. There was perhaps some connection between the municipality and the priory in the matter of clerks and writing which ensured the immunity enjoyed. We know, from the example of Robert Ricart, town-clerk of Bristol, in the fifteenth century, that relation on this ground between religious bodies and municipalities existed. See Ricart's Kalendar, Camden Soc. 1872, pp. i, v. William Revetour, the chantry priest and keeper of Corpus Christi gild, was at one time deputy town-clerk of York; see after, p. xxx. The other stations for which no rent was paid to the city in 1554, were the Common Hall, a place where 'my Lady Mayres and her systers [i. e. wives of the aldermen] lay,' and the Pavement, a public place in the midst of the city.

[2] Davies, pp. 269, 271-2.

[3] Drake's *Eboracum*, pp. 368, 369.

Denton line, rector of Bolton Percy, and uncle to the parliamentary general, Lord Fairfax. Scholarly tastes and a love of books ran in the family; the old clergyman shared them [1]. General Fairfax saved many manuscripts at the blowing up of St. Mary's Tower, York, in 1644, and fostered the immense industry of Dodsworth. The Plays [2] would perhaps, if one of the salvage, have been included by the general with his legacy to the Bodleian Library in 1671 [3]; but he had other books: and there are the two possibilities,—either that it was rescued from destruction as a curious relic by one of the Denton family in authority during the latter part of Elizabeth's reign, or that it may have been among those preserved from St. Mary's Tower, and have been presented by the general to his uncle Henry. From the time that it came into the possession of the grandson of 1695, the links of ownership are unbroken; a note (presumably in Thoresby's hand) on the back of the fly-leaf inscribed by Fairfax, records that he gave it to Ralph Thoresby,—'Donum Hon. Hen. Fairfax Arm. Rad⁰. Thoresby.' The book accordingly appears in the catalogue of his manuscripts appended by Thoresby to his *Ducatus Leodiensis* [4]. At the sale of Thoresby's collection in 1764, although described as 'a folio volume written upon vellum of Old English Poetry, very curious,' Horace Walpole bought it for only £1 1s. At Walpole's sale the bookseller Thomas Rodd gave £220 10s. for it, and sold it to Mr. Heywood Bright of Bristol in 1842 for £235. At the dispersion of this gentleman's collection, in 1844, Mr. Thorpe bought it for £305 for the Rev. Thos. Russell, and it was afterwards sold to the late Lord Ashburnham [5].

DESCRIPTION OF THE MANUSCRIPT. The MS. consists of 270 leaves of parchment or vellum, of which 48 are blank, bound in the original wooden binding, once covered with leather, which is now much torn and in rather bad condition.

---

[1] His second son Brian was also an antiquary, but his library was sold.

[2] The book is not found in the list of 'my bookes,' at Gilling. of Sir William Fairfax, among inventories between 1590 and 1624. The Fairfaxes of Gilling were the senior line. See *Archæologia* 1883, a paper by Mr. Ed. Peacock, to whom I am indebted for a copy.

[3] Life of the great Lord Fairfax, by C. Markham, 1870, pp. 148, 445; see also Drake's account of the saving of these records, p. 575.

[4] Ed. 1816, p. 73 (third paging).

[5] See Walpole's Letters, ed. Cunningham, 1861, vol. ix. p. 525, appendix; also Thorpe's Sale Catalogue.

The blank leaves at the beginning and the end, of which there are several, have been nibbled by mice. On the first blank leaf at the end are written 'Corpus Cristi playe' twice, and the names 'Thomas Cutler, Richarde Nandicke,' the same names being scribbled many times inside one of the covers. At the end, too, of the Smiths' Play, fol. 89, the initials R. N. are inscribed with the same flourish and late hand. I regret that I cannot find any information as to these names. Among senseless scribbles on another leaf are the names 'John Willson' and 'Willm. Pennell.' The leaves throughout the volume, which are eleven inches high, and eight inches wide, were originally not numbered at the top [1], but were counted at the bottom by the signatures of the quires, like early printed books, being made up in fours (i.e. eight leaves to a quire), A to Z, &, ꝯ, and xxvj to xxxiiij, the whole being preceded by an unsigned quire, which must have been inserted in order to add two omitted plays. Some few of the marks are cut in the binding, especially in the early quires. In five of the quires, viz. B (iv, v), G (iv, v), O (iii, vi), R (ii, vii)[2], & (ii, vii), a pair of leaves has been removed, it would almost seem purposely, for the volume is not in such a loose condition that they could have fallen out; but beyond this the MS. is complete. The handwriting, which is in good condition throughout, is principally that of the first half of the fifteenth century [3], written in one column confined within a ruled margin. The three plays on the inserted quire at the beginning were probably written a few years later than the body of the volume, which began with the Cardmakers' play [4] (III); there is a date, 1583, irregularly written, in a faint ink, on lf. 5 at the end of the first play, but it can have nothing to do with these entries, which are in a hand of a hundred and fifty years earlier. Three pieces were inserted by a hand which we

---

[1] The modern numbering was unfortunately not made on the definite plan of either including or excluding all blank leaves, some are figured, some are not. But a true account can be taken of all the leaves by following the signatures which I have placed in the margin throughout. It is sometimes important, as will be seen.

[2] See pages 37, 195, 199, 236, 242, 335, 341. The passages lost comprised part of the Woman taken in Adultery, the Raising of Lazarus, the Sop given to Judas, and the Lord's Prayer. The losses in G occur in a blank.

[3] See a specimen in the frontispiece, and after, p. xxviii.

[4] The Cardmakers' being the third of the inserted plays is thus given twice over; I have printed from the second or earliest copy: see p. 14.

are able to date at 1558 from the municipal books. The Fullers' play (p. 18), although certainly an old one, had been 'never before regestred' when the chamberlains of that year paid for the omission; the others are—an addition in the Glovers' play (p. 37), and the entire play of the Purification of Mary (p. 433), which may be of later composition than the rest, superseding a play undoubtedly used at an earlier date on the same subject[1]. Quite at the end is a fragment, in a hand apparently of the close of the fifteenth century, of a new play for the Innholders (p. 514). At the head of four blank leaves which immediately follow Play XXII (sign. M iv b) is the following in the hand of the sixteenth century :—

> ' *The vinteners.*
> Loo, this is a yoyfull day,
> Archedeclyne, for me and . .'

showing that here it had been intended to enter the play of the Vintners[2], on the *Marriage at Cana,* which stands in both the early lists at this place in the series, but of which we have now only this first line preserved. A similar blank of five leaves was left after Play XXIII (sign. N v b), at the top of which is written, by the original hand, 'The Ironmongers;' evidently their play, on *Jesus eating with Simon the leper and Mary Magdalene* (Burton, No. 25, see p. xii), had also been meant to be inserted in its right place, but for some reason it was delayed, unfortunately for ever.

Scattered through the volume are frequent small alterations or corrections[3], little *nota* and indications that ' *hic caret*' or ' *hic caret de novo facto,*' all of which are later than the text, most of them in a hand of the second half of the sixteenth century. In three places it is thus stated that the plays have been re-written, but no copy is registered,—' Doctor, this matter is newly mayde, wherof we haue no coppy[4] ;' in numerous others it is pointed out that a new speech is wanting; in one case '*loquela magna et diversa ;*' in another that the text does not agree[5]. Sometimes a line or words

---

[1] See Burton's list, No 17. p. xxi.
[2] No. 22 in Burton's list of 1415. See p. xxii.
[3] There are between forty and fifty, besides those specified further on.
[4] Pp. 93, 138, 177.
[5] See, for example, pp. 120, 121, 199, 239, 312, 426, 472.

omitted in the original are supplied[1]; in three instances the words are glossed to the more modern usage[2]. All these are evidence that the plays underwent careful revision in 1568, when the city council agreed 'that the booke therof shuld be perused and otherwaise amended before it were playd,' in obvious antici- pation of the correction or censure of the reforming Archbishop Grindal. Dr. Matthew Hutton, dean of York, had already this year given his opinion on the Creed Play[3], 'that it shuld not be plaid, ffor thoghe it was plawsible to yeares agoe, and wold now also of the ignorant sort be well liked, yet now in this happie time of the gospell I know the learned will mislike it[4].' The 'Doctor' whom the city officers were eager to assure that so many portions of their favorite plays were 'mayd of newe,' was none other than Hutton himself[5]. In 1575 they desired that the archbishop, who had some of 'the play bookes as perteyne this cittie' in his custody, should 'apoynt twoe or thre sufficiently learned to cor- recte the same, wherein by the lawes of this realme they are to be reformed;' and this evidently not having been done for the Corpus Christi plays, the council returned valiantly to the charge, and, in 1579, before ordering them to be performed, agreed that 'first the booke shalbe caried to my Lord Archebisshop and Mr. Deane to correcte, if that my Lord Archebisshop doo well like theron[6].' Happily this correction was never carried out, as the present state of the book shows; and the plays appear to have never been performed after this time.

Besides these, there are several alterations in the names of the crafts which stand at the head of each play[7]: these are in various hands; one is dated 1553.

The MS. is plain, without ornament or flourish; most of the plays have a space left for a large initial, in but few cases filled up. The rubricator's work consists of the names of the speakers (in which he occasionally made mistakes), a rule between every speech, and a touch upon the initial letter of every line of poetry. In the

---

[1] E. g. pp. 54, 99, 106, 398, 410.   [2] Pp. 31, 43, 131.
[3] Performed every tenth year by the Gild of Corpus Christi.
[4] See the whole of this interesting letter, in Davies' Extracts, &c. pp. 267–8.
[5] He was dean of York from 1567–1589.
[6] Davies, pp. 271, 272.
[7] At pp. 123, 125, 146, 178, 193, 320, 349, 421, 456.

play which began the original book, and must have been the first entered (III. the Cardmakers, sign A-i) are eight large red letters, but these were not continued. The rubricator also added the lines for connecting rimes, usually seen in early MSS. of poetry, throughout the first portion of the book, as far as P. viij, after which they cease. A few other words and original stage directions are also in red. Punctuation of course there is none ; nor are there any marks for the cæsura, perhaps not to be expected at so late a period. In one case only the scribe has collected his *dramatis personæ*, viz. at the end of the twentieth play (p. 171). The stage directions of the MS.[1] are much fewer and less descriptive than those which are found in the Chester and Coventry collections, and of these several were added by the late correcting hand.

DATE OF THE MANUSCRIPT. The book appears to have set out with the intention, a few years after A. D. 1415, of entering all the plays in their due order, at the expense of the corporation[2], with the names of the crafts then performing them. The 'originals' of the plays (see pp. 18, 29) could not be brought in all at once, so the copyist seems to have begun with what he had before him, i. e. the Cardmakers' (III), on the first leaf, forgetting that two others should precede it; he continued, leaving blank spaces where he had not the originals yet to copy from, making occasional errors as copyists will, but on the whole doing his work pretty faithfully till he came to about the middle, when he must either have had several confusing MSS. to work from, involving perhaps alterations and combinations in the plays, or he may have been required to make these himself. This may be the source of the errors and irregularities in the verses which abound in the plays numbered XXVIII to XXXVI, treating of the betrayal, trial, and passion of Jesus. From a few of these blunders it would seem that the scribe wrote partly by ear or from memory, not quite understanding what he was about; and the state of the two leaves of music of which

---

[1] See, for example, pp. 2, 3, 53, 98, 134, 177, 190, 285, 329, 493.
[2] Unfortunately the Chamberlain's Books of York have not been preserved further back than 11 Hen. VIII (1519), so that we are unable to establish this point, and several other interesting details relating to the plays ; but the entry of 1558 on p. 18, and the claim exercised by the city over the book, sufficiently point that way.

copies are given in Plates II and III leads to the same conclusion[1]. Even if of York he was used to the Midland tongue, which affected his copy of the old Northern language of the originals.

To show why 1430–1440 is the probable date of the MS. it will be necessary to go back to the records of the city of York, which yield much information on the history of the plays. Mr. Robert Davies, late town-clerk, gathered more than is to be found elsewhere in the pages 'On the Celebration of the Corpus Christi festival in York' appended to the valuable work already referred to; and Drake, in the appendix to his big folio, 'Eboracum,' prints, incorrectly enough, several important documents relating to the performances. Mr. Riley, in his Report on the Records of York to the Historical Manuscripts Commission, vol. i, p. 109, printed translations of two extracts of interest; beyond these, whatever quotations I give from the municipal books are the fruit of my own researches at York.

Nearly the oldest book the city possesses is the 'Liber diversorum memorandorum[2] Civitatem Ebor. tangentium,' beginning 51 Edward III, A.D. 1376, marked on the cover $\frac{A}{Y}$. In it were enrolled the ordinances of crafts or trade gilds[3], arbitrations in disputes, &c. It is therefore the fitting place in which to find, entered by the hand of Roger Burton the town-clerk himself, a detailed list of the plays and of the crafts who were assigned to perform them, this list being dated A.D. 1415. This is followed by a curious '*Proclamacio ludi*,' and by another list of the plays and crafts, also signed by Burton, but without date[4]. This second list, which reckons fifty-seven plays and gives but the short title of each, does not quite agree with the first one, which reckons fifty-one plays, nor yet with our MS., which contains forty-eight plays. On examination of these discrepancies the MS. is found to agree with Burton's list of 1415 much more than with the second list. The former was treated as the authoritative ' Ordo[5],' for, on examination of the original, the

---

[1] Was it a professional 'notor' who wrote the music out? I think not; it was merely the usual 'scrivener' or 'text-writer' of the whole. See p. xxxix.

[2] The book referred to by Riley.

[3] The charter of the Weavers' gild goes back to Hen. I.

[4] Printed (with but one or two slight inaccuracies) by Davies, pp. 233–236.

[5] A marginal note shows that a similar schedule of the pageants written by

side for the names of the crafts is found to be full of alterations, erasures, and new writing, of differing dates, evidently made to correct the list to the changes among the crafts. For, as business grew, a new craft would spring up, an old one decay and become too poor to produce its play, a new one must take its share; one craft trenching on the trade of another must share its burdens, sometimes two, or even three plays would be combined into one, sometimes a play would be laid aside and the craft to which it had been assigned must join in producing some other. A comparison of different notices and ordinances of the companies relating to the plays explains many of the changes in the list; and as Drake has given a very incorrect translated copy, I here print it from the original, together with a few extracts at the foot which will illustrate the whole.

'*Ordo*[1] *paginarum ludi Corporis Cristi*, tempore Willi. Alne Maioris, anno regni regis Henrici quinti post conquestum Angliæ tercio, compilatus per Rogerum Burton clericum communem, in anno domini millesimo ccccxv^mo.

Tannours [2] ... { (1) **1.**[3] Deus pater omnipotens creans et formans celos, angelos, et archangelos, luciferum et angelos, qui cum eo ceciderunt in infernum.

Plasterers ... { (2) **2.** Deus pater in sua substancia creans terram et omnia que in ea sunt per spacium v. dierum.

Cardemakers { (3) **3.** Deus pater formans Adam de lymo terre, et faciens Euam de costa Ade, et inspirans eos spiritu vite.

the town-clerk was to be officially delivered to the crafts yearly in the first or second week of Lent. See next note.

[1] In the margin against the title in a contemporary hand it is noted, ' Deliberande sunt sedule paginarum subsequenter in forma subscripta Artificiis per vj servientes maioris ad clavam, prima vel ij^a septimana quadragesime annuatim, scribende per communem clericum.' The list occupies fos. 243 v°-245, four pages. Leaves 243-4-5-6 have been all cut by some destroyer, two of them nearly severed in half. Some of the erasures and alterations were evidently made by Burton himself while writing. The writing has in a few places near the beginning been recently tampered with, i.e. re-written on *old* letters in blacker ink. I have compared the handwriting of the Ashburnham MS. with this list and the Proclamation, both of which are by Burton, but it is not the same.

[2] *Barkers* in the Register and in the second list, nearly the same trade.

[3] The black figures refer to the corresponding play in the Register (the text).

b 2

Fullers ... ... $\left\{\begin{array}{l}\text{(4) 4. Deus prohibens Adam et Euam ne comed-} \\ \text{erent de ligno vite.}\end{array}\right.$

Coupers... ... $\left\{\begin{array}{l}\text{(5) 5. Adam et Eua et arbor inter eos, serpens de-} \\ \text{cipiens eos cum pomis ; Deus loquens eis} \\ \text{et maledicens serpentem, et angelus cum} \\ \text{gladio eiciens eos de paradiso.}\end{array}\right.$

Armourers ... $\left\{\begin{array}{l}\text{(6) 6. Adam et Eua, angelus cum vanga et colo} \\ \text{assignans eis laborem.}\end{array}\right.$

Gaunters ...
(Glovers)[1] ... $\left.\begin{array}{l}\\ \\ \end{array}\right\}$ (7) 7. Abel et Kaym immolantes victimas.

Shipwrightes $\left\{\begin{array}{l}\text{(8) 8. Deus premuniens Noe facere archam de} \\ \text{lignis leuigatis.}\end{array}\right.$

Pessoners and
Mariners ...
(Fysshmon-
gers) [2] ... ... $\left.\begin{array}{l}\\ \\ \\ \\ \end{array}\right\}$ (9) 9. Noe in Archa et vxor eius, tres filij Noe cum vxoribus suis, cum diuersis animalibus.

Parchemyners
Bukbynders $\left.\begin{array}{l}\\ \\ \end{array}\right\}$ (10) 10. Abraham immolans filium suum Isaac super altare, garcio cùm bosco et angelus.

Hosyers [3] ... $\left\{\begin{array}{l}\text{(11) 11. Moyses exaltans serpentem in deserto,} \\ \text{Pharao Rex, viij Judei admirantes et} \\ \text{expectantes.}\end{array}\right.$

Spicers ... ... $\left\{\begin{array}{l}\text{(12) 12. [Doctor declarans dicta prophetarum de na-} \\ \text{tivitate Christi futura] [4]. Maria, Angelus} \\ \text{salutans eam, Maria salutans Elizabeth.}\end{array}\right.$

[5] Pewterers
Founders ... $\left.\begin{array}{l}\\ \\ \end{array}\right\}$ (13) 13. Maria, Josep volens dimittere eam, angelus eis loquens [5] vt transeant vsque Bedlem.

---

[1] Written above Gaunters in explanation.
[2] Written above Pessoners in explanation.
[3] According to the following, in 1403 the Hosiers and Drapers joined at one play, in 1415 they were separate ; see No. 48. 'De la pagyne de Moyses et pharao &c., hosyers. Fait a remembre que le viij^me io^r de may lan du regne nostre S^r le Roy henry quart puis le conquest dengletere quart, accorde est & assentu deuaunt le maire de la Citee deuerwyk, les chaumbreleyns & autres bones gentz de mesme la Citee, en la chaumbre de counseil sur le pount de Ouse en Euerwyk, entre les gentz de Draper craft & les gentz de hosyer craft deuerwyk, que touz hosyers que vendront chauuces ou facent chauuces a vendre, ouesque les vphaldres quels vendront drape de leyne desore enauaunt aueront la charge del pagyne de Moyses et Pharao &c., en la Jue de corpore Xpi, horspris les Dubbers et ceux que sount assignez a eux.' (Book $\frac{\text{A}}{\text{Y}}$, fo. 129 v°.).

[4] These words are interlined; they refer to the long speech which I have assigned to a 'Prologue,' pp. 93–98.
[5] These two words are written over an erased line.

Tylers[1] ... ...
(fo. 244.)

{ (14) **14.** Maria, Josep, obstetrix, puer natus iacens in presepio inter bouem et azinum, et angelus loquens pastoribus, et ludentibus, in pagina sequente.

Chaundellers

{ (15) **15.** Pastores loquentes adinuicem, stella in oriente, angelus nuncians pastoribus gaudium de puero nato.

Orfeuers[2] ...
Goldbeters ...
Monemakers

{ (16) **16, 17.** Tres Reges venientes ab oriente, herodes interogans eos de puero iesu, et filius herodis[3] et duo consiliarii et nuncius[3]. Maria cum puero, et stella desuper, et tres Reges offerentes munera.

(quandam)[4] ...
Domus Sci ...
Leonardi ...
(jam Masons)[4]

{ (17) **41.** Maria cum puero, Josep, Anna, obstetrix, cum pullis columbarum. Symeon recipiens puerum in vlnas suas, et duo filij Symeonis.

Marsshals ...

{ (18) **18.** Maria cum puero et Josep fugientes in Egiptum, angelo nunciante.

[1] In the Register these are called Tillethekkers, i. e. tile-thatchers. There are besides the tile-makers for Play XXXIII (36 of the above list).

[2] 'Goldsmythes' is written above 'Orfeuers,' and 'Masons' aside of it. See the text, pp. 123, 126, where the two plays on this subject are given to the Masons and the Goldsmiths. In Burton's second list it is also two plays instead of one, but the first, 'Masons, Herod interrogans tres reges' written in a later hand, tells the same tale of change. This piece finally fell into the charge of the Minstrells. See p. 125.

[3] 'Filius herodis' and 'nuncius' are added in another ink.

[4] Words in brackets added later. This is the only instance in which a religious house—the ancient hospital of St. Leonard's—brought out one of these plays. What caused them to give it up does not appear, but in 17 Edw. IV, 1477, the mayor and common council ordered, 'q^d pagina *Purificationis beate Marie virginis* decetero ludebit annuatim in festo Corpis X^{ti} sicut alie pagine ; & super hoc concordat est quod *Cementarii* istius Civitatis pro tempore existentes portant onera & expensis pagine predicte, et ipsam in bono & honeste modo annuatim ludendam producent. . . Et quod laboratores istius civitatis annuatim decetero, vid. Kidberers, Garthyners, erthe wallers, pavers, dykers, ground wallers with erthe' should pay 13^s. 4^d. in aid of this pageant. The city also granted them aid. This was perhaps the time when the above words were added. The Hat-makers, who were made incorporate in 1493 (Book $\frac{A}{Y}$, fo. 362 v°), must have joined them later. The play itself is one of those registered in or near 1558. I did not perceive that it is out of place till too late to set it in the right order in the text.

Girdellers ...
Naylers ... ...
Sawiers ... ...
{ (19) **19.** Herodes precipiens pueros occidi, iiij^or milites cum lanceis, duo consiliarii Regis, et iiij mulieres deflentes occisionem puerorum suorum.

Sporiers... ...
Lorymers ...
{ (20) **20.** Doctores, Jesus puer sedens in templo in medio eorum, interrogans eos et respondens eis, iiij^or Judei, Maria et Josep querentes eum, et inuenientes in templo.

Barbours ...
{ (21) **21.** Jesus, Johannes Baptista baptizans eum, et ij angeli administrantes.

Vynters[1] ...
{ (22) Jesus, Maria, sponsus cum sponsa, Architriclinus cum famulia sua, cum vj ydreis aque vbi vertitur aqua in vinum.

Feuers ... ...
{ (23) **22.** Jesus super Pynaculum templi, et diabolus temptans eum, cum lapidibus, et ij angeli administrantes, &c.

Couureours ...
{ (24) **23**[2] Petrus, Jacobus, et Johannes ; Jesus ascendens in montem [2] et transfigurans se ante eos. Moyses et Elyas apparentes, et vox loquentis in nube.

Irenmangers[3]
{ (25) Jesus, et Simon leprosus rogans Jesu vt manducaret cum eo ; ij discipuli, Maria Magdalena lauans pedes Jesu lacrimis suis, et capillis suis tergens.

Plummers ...
Patenmakers
} (26) **24.**[4] Jesus, duo apostoli, mulier deprehensa in adulterio, iiij^or Judei accusantes eam.

fo. 244 v⁰.
Pouchemakers
Botellers ...
Capmakers[4]...
{ (27) **24.** Lazarus in sepulcro, Maria Magdalene, et Martha, et ij Judei admirantes.

---

[1] This is one of the plays for which a blank was left, but never filled up, in the Register. See before p. xv.

[2] The words between the figures are written over an erased line.

[3] This play was omitted in the Register, although intended to be entered at first ; see before p. xv.

[4] In the Register the Cappemakers or Cappers have one play combining the subjects of this and the next, 26 and 27. Ordinances of the Cappers were enrolled in 1481 (Council Book, No. II) ; the Hatmakers were incorporate in 1493, and a later note at the side of their entry states that 'This cappers are jonyd together into one company,' 1591 (Book $\frac{A}{Y}$, fo. 362 v⁰), indicating, I suppose, that the two trades had joined. Before this time their names had been added to that of the Cappers in the Register of Plays. See p. 433. It seems strange it should

Skynners ... (Vestment- makers)[1] ...	(28) **25.** Jesus super asinum cum pullo suo, xij apostoli sequentes Jesum, sex diuites et sex pauperes, viij pueri cum ramis palmarum, cantantes *Benedictus* &c., et Zacheus ascendens in arborem sicamorum.
Cuttellers ... Bladesmyth ... Shethers ... Scalers ... ... Buklermakers Horners[3] ...	(29) **26.**[2] Pylatus, Cayphas, duo milites, tres Judei, Judas vendens Jesum.
Bakers ... ... (Waterleders)[4]	(30) **27.** Agnus paschalis, Cena Domini, xij apostoli, Jesus procinctus lintheo lauans pedes eorum; institucio sacrimenti corporis Cristi in noua lege, communio apostolorum.
Cordwaners ...	(31) **28.** Pilatus, Cayphas, Annas, xiiij milites armati, Malcus, Petrus, Jacobus, Johannes, Jesus, et Judas osculans et tradens eum.
Bowers ... ... Flecchers ...	(32) **29.** Jesus, Anna, Cayphas, et iiij^{or} Judei percucientes et colaphizantes [5]Jesum; Petrus, mulier accusans Petrum, et Malchus [5].
Tapisers[6] ... Couchers ...	(33) **30.** Jesus, Pilatus, Anna, Cayphas, duo consiliarii, et iiij^{or} Iudei accusantes Jesum.

have been added to the Masons and Laborers for the *Purification* (see p. xxi, *note* 4). I have found nothing as to the Plummers, who stand for this play in both Burton's lists.

[1] Added later. Old-fashioned people in Yorkshire still remember the vests made of well-dressed skins, often handsomely embroidered.

[2] In 1492 the Blacksmiths and Bladesmiths disagreed, one result of the arbitration before the Mayor was that they no longer contributed their 'paiaunt silver' to the same pageant (Book $\frac{A}{Y}$, fo. 330).

[3] 'Horners' added later; on 31 April, 15 Hen. VII (1500), it was ordered that the Horners 'from nowfurth paying pageant money to be contributory with the cutlers and bladsmyths.' (Book $\frac{B}{Y}$, fo. 194 v°.).

[4] 'Waterleders' added later. In the second list this play, 30, is divided in two, of which the Bakers have one, the Waterleders the other. But the Register agrees with the present in having but one play, assigned to the Bakers, while the Waterleders combine with the Cooks (p. 307).

[5] These words appear to have been re-written in a blacker ink.

[6] The word is here spelt Tapisers, in the other places Tapiters; in the Old

Littesters ... } (34) **31.** Herodes, duo consiliarii, iiij^{or} Milites, Jesus, et iij Judei.

Cukes ... ... } (35) **32.** Pilatus, Anna, Cayphas, duo Judei, et Judas
Waterleders ... } reportans eis xxx argenteos [1].

Usages of Winchester, of a rather earlier date, the same trade is called Tapener. (English Gilds by Toulmin Smith, p. 350.) It is curious that no mention is made by Burton of dame Percula, Pilate's wife, nor of any of the personages in the first scenes, which must have been prominent and popular. A later note in the Register seems to refer to another play for the Couchers (see p. 146 *note*) : it may be that there were two plays on this subject, and that Burton describes the (shorter) one not registered.

The Linenweavers contributed to the Tapiters' pageant, for in 1477 they were discharged of the necessity of doing so (Council Book, Lib. III. fo. 20 v⁰.). But in 1485 they joined them again, laying their own pageant aside (Council Book, II and IV, fo. 74.)

[1] In Burton's second list, there follows, between 35 and 36 of the above, 'Sausmakers, Suspencio Jude.' (Drake erroneously inserts it in the list above.) We learn from two interesting entries that this was a distinct play in which ' Judas se suspendebat et crepuit medius : ' in Play XXXII of the Register, Judas says he will go out and kill himself (p. 314), but there is hardly room to suppose that he does it on the stage, as not the slightest remark is made upon it by succeeding speakers. The following relates to this play (Book $\frac{A}{V}$, fo. 48 b, printed in Hist. MSS. Com. i. p. 109 : unfortunately Mr. Riley gives neither date nor conclusion, and I did not myself see it in the original, but it is probably before 1410):—

' Whereas there was grievous complaint made here in the council-chamber by the craftsmen of the city, the "salsarii" to wit, whom we commonly call "salsemakers," that, although by usage hitherto followed, all the folks of the *salsemaker crafte*, and also of the *candel crafte*, without the Flesshchameles [Flesh shambles], who in their houses and windows sold and exposed Paris candles, did at their own costs and charges together maintain, upon the feast and holiday of Corpus Christi in that city the pageant in which it is represented that Judas Scarioth hanged himself, and burst asunder in the middle, yet now the Pellipers [Skinners] and other craftsmen of this city as well, by themselves and their wives, in great numbers, themselves not being salsemakers, do make and do presume to sell and expose Paris candles in their houses and windows ; yet, upon being asked, they do refuse to contribute to the maintenance of the pageant aforesaid ; therefore unless some speedy remedy shall be applied thereto, and they be made to contribute from henceforth jointly with the Salsemakers, these same Salsemakers will no longer be able to support such pageant.' The play was eventually either suppressed, or a portion was cut out, and we get the remainder as part of our XXXII, not in XXXIII, as might be expected from the next extract.

It is difficult to trace the changes, or the precise dates when they were made, but that the form of the plays was affected by the quarrels among the crafts the following extract shows. It indicates also a reason for the divergences in part of the subject between XXXIII of the Register and 36 of Burton's list above. The play in the Register accords with the agreement of 1422 and with Burton's description of 1415, except that it does not comprise the portion drawn from the Millers' play on the casting lots for the Vestments. Plays XXXIII-XXXV must therefore have been enregistered sometime subsequent to 1422.

' Cum nuper in tempore Henrici Preston maioris [1422], de avisamento consilii camere, pagina de lez Salsemakers ubi Judas se suspendebat et crepuit

Tielmakers ...
Milners [1]
(Ropers,
Seveourz)
Turnours ...
Hayresters ...
Bollers ... ...

(36) **33.** Jesus, Pilatus, Cayphas, Anna, sex milites tenentes hastas cum vexillis, et alij quattuor ducentes Jesum ab Herode petentes Baraban dimitti et Jesum crucifigi, et ibidem ligantes et flagellantes eum, ponentes coronam spineam super caput eius ; tres milites mittentes [2] sortem super vestem Jesu.

To[undours] [3]

(37) **34.** Jesus, sanguine cruentatus, portans crucem uersus Caluariam. Simon Sereneus, Judei angariantes eum vt tolleret crucem, Maria mater Jesu, Johannes apostolus intimans tunc proxime dampnacionem et transitum filii sui ad caluariam. Veronica tergens [4] sanguinem et sudorem de facie Jesu cum flammeolo in quo imprimitur facies Jesu ; et alie mulieres lamentantes Jesum.

medius in ludo Corporis Cristi, et pagina de lez Tilemakers ubi Pilatus condempnavit Jesum morti, et pagina de lez Turnors, Hayresters, et Bollers ubi Jesus ligatus erat ad columpnam et flagellatus, et pagina Molendinariorum ubi Pilatus et alii milites ludebant ad talos pro vestimentis Jesu et pro eis sortes mittebant et ea parciebantur inter se, fuerunt combinate simul in vnam paginam, ceteris predictis paginis pro perpetuo exclusis, que quidem pagina decetero vocabitur pagina condempnacionis Jesu Cristi :—super hoc artifices artium predictarum contendebant inter se de modo solucionis ad paginam. predictam.' Arbitrators were appointed who settled that the Salsemakers and Tilemakers should bear the burden and expenses, 'et ipsam in bono et honeste modo annuatim ludendam producent ; ' the Millers to contribute yearly 10s., and with the others 'in cibo potuque solacia percipiant ; ' the Hayresters to contribute 5s. and one of them ' circueat cum ludo et pagina,' also to share the ' solace.' The shares for reparations to the pageant were also fixed and admonition given that none ' litiget nec aliquam discordiam faciat.' Finally ' quod nulla quatuor artium predictarum ponat aliqua signa, arma, vel insignia super paginam predictam nisi tantum arma cujus hon. civitatis.' (Book $\frac{A}{Y}$, fo. 274 v°. Davies gives a part of this, p. 235 *note*.)

[1] Several changes are apparent in the writing here. The Ropers and Sevours [? Sievors] were added later. As to the Milners, see last note, and p. 320 *note*.

[2] This last subject, which had been that of the Millers' play (see last note but one), is contracted in the Register to a few lines at the end of XXXIV and XXXV ; see pp. 347, 358.

[3] The leaf here is very thin owing to erasure ; a hole is in the middle of this word and an interlineation above it, which may have been Shermen.

[4] This word is doubtful, the above seems to be the right reading. The Play XXXIV in the Register makes one of the Maries perform the office of Veronica ; see p. 343, ll. 184-190.

fo. 245.

Pynners   ...

Latoners   ...

Payntours ...

(38) **35.** Crux, Jesus extensus in ea super terram ; liij^or Judei flagellantes et trahentes eum cum funibus, et postea exaltantes crucem et corpus Jesu cruci conclauatum super montem Caluarie.

Bouchers   ...

Pulters ... ...

(39) **36.** Crux, duo latrones crucifixi, Jesus suspensus in cruce inter eos, Maria mater Jesu, Johannes, Maria, Jacobus, et Salome. Longeus cum lancea, servus cum spongea, Pilatus, Anna, Cayphas, Centurio, Josep [ab Aramathia[1]] et Nichodemus, deponentes eum in sepulcro.

Sellers[2] ... ...

Verrours[3]   ...

Fuystours ...

(40) **37.** Jesus spolians infernum, xij spiritus, [vj] boni et vj mali.

Carpenters ...

(Junours, Cart-

wrightes, Caru-

ours, Sawers)[4]

(41) **38.** Jesus resurgens de sepulcro, quatuor milites armati, et tres Marie lamentantes. Pilatus, Cayphas [et Anna. Juvenis sedens ad sepulcrum indutus albo, loquens mulieribus[4]].

Wyndrawers

(42) **39.** Jesus, Maria Magdalena cum aromatibus.

Broggours ...

Wolpakkers...

(Wadmen)[5] ...

(43) **40.** Jesus, Lucas, et Cleophas in forma peregrinorum.

Escriueners ...

Lum[i]ners ...

Questors[6]   ...

Dubbers   ...

(44) **42.** Jesus, Petrus, Johannes, Jacobus, Phillipus et alii apostoli cum parte piscis assi et favo mellis, et Thomas apostolus palpans vulnera Jesu.

Talliaunders[7]

(45) **43.** Maria, Johannes Euaungelista, xj apostoli, ij angeli, Jesus ascendens coram eis, et iiij^or angeli portantes nubem.

---

[1] ·Later interlineation.

[2] 'Sadellers' is written above.

[3] 'Glasiers' written over.

[4] These passages added later. In 1562 we find that the joyners, carpenters, carvers, wheelwrights, and sawyers were united, and were henceforth quit of paying to the charges of the Ropers' and Turners' pageant. Book $\frac{B}{Y}$, fo. 234.

[5] 'Wadmen' in a later hand. In the Register this play is assigned to the Sledmen : see pp. 421, 426.

[6] 'Pardoners' is written in the same small explanatory hand as before, over 'Questors.' This play is marked for the Scriveners only in both the Register and the separate copy. See pp. 448, 455. As to Luminers, see *Index*.

[7] 'Taillyoures' is written over.

Potters ... ... $\left\{\begin{array}{l}\end{array}\right.$ (46) **44.** Maria, duo angeli, xj apostoli, et spiritus sanctus descendens super eos, et iiij^{or} Judei admirantes.

Drapers... ... $\left\{\begin{array}{l}\end{array}\right.$ (47) **45.** Jesus, Maria, Gabriell cum duobus angelis, duo virgines et tres Judei de cognacione Marie, viij Apostoli, et ij diaboli.

Lynweuers ... $\left\{\begin{array}{l}\end{array}\right.$ (48) Quatuor Apostoli portantes feretrum Marie, et Fergus pendens super feretrum, cum ij aliis Judeis [cum vno Angelo][1].

Weuers of wollen ... ... $\left\{\begin{array}{l}\end{array}\right.$ (49) **46.** Maria ascendens cum turba angelorum, viij apostoli, et Thomas apostolus predicans in deserto.

Hostilers[2] ... $\left\{\begin{array}{l}\end{array}\right.$ (50) **47.** Maria, Jesus coronans eam, cum turba angelorum cantans.

Mercers... ... $\left\{\begin{array}{l}\end{array}\right.$ (51) **48.** Jesus, Maria, xij apostoli, iiij^{or} angeli cum tubis, et iiij^{or} cum corona, lancea, et ij flagellis; iiij^{or} spiritus boni et iiij^{or} spiritus maligni, et vj diaboli.'

A careful study of the foregoing shows, I think, that the Register closely agrees with Burton's list of 1415, as originally written; but that the corrections in the list of the older names to Barkers,

---

[1] This play, founded on a well-known incident in the apocryphal legend of the death of Mary, is the only one all trace of which is wanting in the Register. As the play must have been attractive on account of the behaviour of the impious Fergus from whom it came to be named, the omission is singular, especially as it is included in Burton's second list, ' Masons, Portacio corporis Marie.' The testimony of the records appears contradictory; the earliest I find is in 16 Edw. IV, 1476, when the Lynenwevers are discharged from contributing to the Tapiters pageant because they ' have in þaire propir personnes, comen afore þe saide maire and counsaile, and þere of þaire fre mocion and will have bounden þayme and þayre craft perpetually to kepe bryng forth and place or make to be placed yerely upon Corpus Cristi day a pageant and play called Fergus at þaire propir costes and expenses.' (Council Book III, fo. 20 v°.) In 2 Ric. III, 1485, ' it was determyned that the Tapiters Cardemakers and lynwevers of this Citie be togeder annexid to the bringing furth of the padgeantes of the Tapiter craft and Cardmaker. Soo that the padgeant called Fergus late broght furth by the lynwevers be laid apart.' (Council Book II, IV, fo. 74.) But notwithstanding this it was evidently contemplated that ' Fergus ' might one day be revived, for thirty-two years later, 9 Hen. VIII, in an arbitration between the linenweavers and the woollen weavers, the former agree to pay 5s. yearly to the cutlers on behalf of the woollen weavers, ' vnto suche tyme as the said lynweuers will play or cause to be played the pageant somtyme called vergus pageant ; and then the said lynweuers shall reteyn & kepe the said vs. toward þer own charges for the bringyng furth of the said vergus pageant.' (Minute Book 9, fo. 94 v°.)

[2] This is in a later hand, and written on an erasure. The Innholders, which seems another name for the same business, brought out this play after 1483.

Glovers, Fyshmongers, Goldsmythes, &c. the insertion of the lines for the Prologue in XII, and the amalgamations in our text of Burton's Nos. 26 and 27, and, in XXXIII, of the older plays recorded in the agreement of 1422 (p. xxiv), all point to the period of the Register as a few years later, say from 1430–1440.

The omission of 'Fergus' was probably accidental; it does not affect this point. The manuscript authorities at the British Museum consider the hand-writing to date between 1430–1450. We have no more exact data than these on which to form a judgment or to base a nearer determination of the date of the MS.

The difference in the number of plays (fifty-seven) found in Burton's second list is accounted for thus; of the nine more than in the Register, three are those there omitted, viz. the *Marriage at Cana, Jesus in the House of Simon,* and *Fergus*; in two cases the subjects of two plays are found combined in one of the Register, in two other instances three are combined in one, thus ten plays are reduced to four, making an apparent loss of six.

OTHER PLAYS: MUNICIPAL CONTROL: STATIONS, PROCLAMATION, &c. York was from the fourteenth to the sixteenth centuries a play-loving city, and the performances must have benefited the inhabitants by the concourse of visitors they attracted, who were by no means always of the baser sort. Besides the Corpus Christi plays they had several others. 'Once on a time, a *Play* setting forth the goodness of the *Lord's Prayer* was played in the city of York; in which play all manner of vices and sins were held up to scorn, and the virtues were held up to praise[1].' The play found so much favour that a gild of men and women was founded for the express purpose of keeping it up; among their rules (which contain the usual provisions for mutual help) some of the members were bound to ride or walk with the players through the streets during the play until it was ended, to ensure good order. Wiclif, who died in 1384, advocating the translation of the Bible, refers to 'þe paternoster in engliȝsch tunge, as men seyen in þe pley of York[2].' In 1389 they had no land nor goods 'save the proper-

---

[1] 'English Gilds,' by Toulmin Smith, p. 137, Preamble to ordinances of Gild of the Lord's Prayer.
[2] De officio Pastorali, cap. 15. English Works, ed. F. D. Matthew, E. E. T. Soc. p. 429.

ties needed in the playing of the play,' and a chest to keep them in.   The play itself is now lost, but as it held up the vices to scorn and the virtues to praise, there must have been several divisions or books, perhaps a separate play for each quality; the whole was called the 'play' of the Lord's Prayer, just as the whole collection of our Register was called the 'Corpus Christi playe.'   Canon Raine of York is the fortunate possessor of a compotus Roll[1] of this gild ' Oracionis domini,' dated Michaelmas, 1399, which shows that there were then over 100 members and their wives, and that they possessed rents and receipts amounting to £26 5s. 11½d. Many curious details are entered concerning 'expensis convivie,' reparations, &c., and the purchase of a quantity of cloth, bought to be sold again, every measure and the price paid being carefully set down; but the only gleaning as to the gild-play is that among ' debita vetera' scored off, John Downom and his wife had owed 2s.·2d. for entrance fee, ' sed dictus Johannes dicit se expendisse in diuersis expensis circa ludum *Accidie* ex parte Ric. Walker ijs. jd., ideo de predicto petit allocari.'   In this play we may pre-sume the vice of gluttony was ·'held up to scorn.'

The gild of Our Lord's Prayer went the way of most other gilds at the dissolution, but their play-book seems to have remained in the hands of the Master of St. Anthony's gild (which escaped), for in 1558 it was performed in lieu of the Corpus Christi plays on that festival under care of the officers of St. Anthony's, though at the cost of the city[2].   In 1572 the Master was ordered to bring the book to my Lord Mayor to be perused, amended, and corrected, after which the play was again performed with great state on the Corpus Thursday of the same year.   But alas! on 30 July, 'my Lord Archbisshop of York [Grindal] requested to have a copie of the bookes of the Pater Noster play, whereupon it was aggreed that His Grace shall have a trewe copie of all the said bookes even as

---

[1] My acknowledgments are due to Canon Raine for his kindness in putting this Roll into my hands.

[2] ' Armetson, peynter, shall have for peynting of certeyne canvas clothes for Pater Noster playe liijs. iiijd. of the money gathered of pageant silver.'   ' For-asmoche as the money gathered of the pageant sylver will not amount to the chardge of Pater Noster play by iiijli., it is aggred that my lord mayor shall goe over agayne and reasonably gather of every occupacion chardgeable to the same the sayd some behynde.'   Minute Book, July 1558, quoted in Davies, p. 266 *note*.

they were played this yere.' His Grace was asked for the books in 1575, but they have not been heard of since [1].

In 1408 the gild of Corpus Christi was founded in order to do honour to the feast of that name by a procession, which rapidly became rich and popular [2]; it had nothing to do with the plays performed on Corpus Christi Day, which, as we have seen, were produced by the crafts (with the single exception of St. Leonard's Hospital); but in 1446 [3] William Revetor, a chantry priest, member and warden of the gild, bequeathed to the gild a play called *The Creed Play*, with the books and the banners belonging to it, to be performed through York every tenth year. The play-book must then have been old and long in use, as in 1455 it was so worn and imperfect that the officers of the gild had got it transcribed, and, according to the inventory of gild property made in 1465, it consisted of twenty-two quires (quaternos), whence we may judge that it was of considerable length. It was performed about Lammas tide every tenth year, and five such performances, beginning in 1483 [4] are recorded; the last of these, in 1535, superseded the usual Corpus Christi plays [5], a proceeding to which the crafts in 1545 would not consent. The gild was abolished in 1547, but the books of the Creed play remaining in possession of the Hospital of St. Thomas, the city council tried in 1568 to have it performed again. It was then that the book was sent to Dean Hutton, who, in the letter before referred to, gave 'suerlie

---

[1] See Davies' Extracts, pp. 269, 271.

[2] See 'English Gilds,' p. 141. My father made a natural error (in which Drake preceded him, followed by Skaife and Klein) in confusing the procession of the gild and the Corpus Christi pageants together, and supposing them both to have been brought out by the gild. I take the above particulars as to the Creed play from Davies' Extracts, pp. 257–260, 267, 268, 272 and *note*, to which the reader is referred for fuller information, as well as to Skaife's edition of the Register of Corpus Christi, in which are printed the inventories of the gild. The properties used in the play are also given by Davies, p. 273.

[3] Register of the gild of Corpus Christi, ed. by R. H. Skaife, Surtees Society, 1872, pp. 24, 294.

[4] The performance in 1483 seems to have been an exceptional one, given on 7th September, when Richard III came to York for his second coronation. 'Agreid that the Creid play shall be playd afore our suffreyn lord the kyng of Sunday next cumyng, apon the cost of the most onest men of every parish in thys Cite.' Davies, p. 171.

[5] The Chamberlain's book for 27 Hen. VIII contains two lists of the contributions paid by the pageant-masters of thirty-five companies, though the Corpus play was not played.

mine aduise that it shuld not be plaied,' and we hear of it no more.

Each of these two great plays may, I think, undoubtedly be described in the term, 'ludus in diversis paginis,' applied to the Corpus Christi plays [1]. There was also in York the universally-spread play of St. George, at Midsummer, with its procession [2]; but nothing is known of the local text of this, which was almost surely a single short play.

The plays just mentioned were brought out by or for their respective gilds, or afterwards under the care of the corporation. The Corpus Christi plays were brought out in York, as in every other English town where they are known, by the crafts or trade companies [3], to which they seem to have been regarded as a peculiar adjunct. Archdeacon Rogers' words [died 1595] as to the Chester plays apply here exactly—'the actors and players were the occupacions and companies in this cittie, the charges and costs thereof, which was greate, was theires also [4].' His description of the pageant-scaffold, and of the manner of moving from street to street, performing in turn at each station, may be borne in mind while reading the following notes from the York records, which, if they do not add much that is quite new to our knowledge of the machinery and methods pursued, fill in the picture with several interesting details. It will be observed that they form a near parallel to the similar practices, especially as regards contributions to the pageants and the combination or discharge of crafts, which obtained at Coventry [5]. The control by the municipal officers over the whole of these entertainments comes out perhaps more prominently in the York documents than anywhere else, though there cannot be a doubt from the general relation of the craft gilds to the towns that this was really exercised everywhere.

The earliest notice of the Corpus Christi plays in York yet found is in 1378, when certain fines incurred by the Bakers were

---

[1] 'Quendum ludum sumptuosum in diversis paginis compilatum veteris et noui testamenti,' &c. Preamble to record touching W. Melton, see after, p. xxxiv.
[2] See Davies, p. 263.
[3] There is some doubt about what plays the Coventry crafts produced.
[4] Ormerod's Cheshire, ed. 1810, I. p. 300.
[5] See Thos. Sharp's Dissertation on the Coventry Mysteries, 1825, pp. 8–12.

ordered to go, half to the city chamber, half 'a la pagine des ditz Pestours de corpore cristi.' (Book $\frac{A}{Y}$, fo. 9 v⁰.) From this, as from the next notices, it is apparent that the plays had already been in use for many years; each craft had its assigned pageant to which the members contributed, a certain number of Stations in the city were appointed before which each play in turn was acted; the whole of the plays had to be got through in one day, therefore no craft must take their pageant anywhere else. In 1394 it was ordered by the mayor, bailiffs, and commonalty assembled in the Gildhall that all the pageants should play in the places appointed of old time (*antiquitus assignatis*) and not elsewhere, viz. as it was proclaimed by the mayor, bailiffs, and their officers, and the crafts were to be fined if they did not conform[1]. In 1397 Richard II was at the festival in York, when special preparations were made. He seems to have been placed at the head station at the gates of Holy Trinity, the porter of which received a fee of 4*d.*[2] In 1399 there was still trouble about the stations; the commons petitioned the council that, as they are at great cost about 'le juer et les pagentz de la iour de corpore cristi,' which were not performed as they ought to be on account of there being too many places, the number of these should be limited to twelve. Davies gives the list of these as ordered at this date[3]—probably it was an old order re-affirmed. The same places (described a little differently) are found in an order of 7 June, 1417, which I here copy from Drake[4].

'For the convenience of the citizens and of all strangers coming to the said feast that all the pageants of the play called Corpus Cristi Play should . . . begin to play, first—

At the gates of the pryory of the Holy Trinity in Mikel-gate, next
At the door of Robert Harpham, next

---

[1] Book $\frac{A}{Y}$, fo. 15 v⁰. and Davies, p. 230.

[2] Davies gives an interesting fragment of a Chamberlain's account from which these facts are learnt. The pagina with its painting, clothes, and new banner, and which required eight porters to move it, may refer to a special scaffold for the occasion; it cannot here be the play.

[3] Book $\frac{A}{Y}$, fo. 17 v⁰. Davies, pp. 231, 232.

[4] Eboracum, Appx. xxxii.

At the door of the late John Gyseburn, next
At Skelder-gate-hend and North-strete-hend, next
At the end of Conyng-strete towards Castel-gate, next
At the end of Jubir-gate, next
At the door of Henry Wyman, deceased, in Conyng-strete, then
At the Common Hall at the end of Conyng-strete, then
At the door of Adam del Brygs, deceased, in Stayne-gate, then
At the end of Stayn-gate at the Minster-gates, then
At the end of Girdler-gate in Peter-gate, and lastly
Upon the Pavement.'

In the same year 1417, according to Davies, this restriction was removed, the city allowed free trade in the matter, and ordered that 'those persons should be allowed to have the play before their houses who would pay the highest price for the privilege, but that no favour should be shown[1].' Whether the stations had been actually rented before this date is not seen; in 1478 we note a lease by the corporation of a point at the east end of Ouse bridge for twelve years, and the 'dimissio locorum ludi Corporis Christi,' or the 'Lesys of corpus cristy play' come to be not an infrequent entry in the Chamberlain's Accounts, and a source of income to the city[2]. Davies gives a list of these for twelve places, temp. Hen. VIII, and another for sixteen places in 1554[3]. In 1519 I find a list of fourteen places let to various persons at rents varying from 12d., 2s., 2s. 8d., 3s. 4d., to 4s. 4d. In 1535 these leases brought in nothing because 'Creyd play was then played.'

Of the Proclamation referred to in the order of 1394 above, we have a copy entered by the town clerk, Burton, in 1415, immediately following the schedule of plays. The Mayor, as officer of the king's peace, had this duty, see similar proclamations at Bristol before festive occasions[4]; perhaps the latter part of the announcement may answer to the words of the bane or messenger preceding the Chester plays; in York, too, when the Pater Noster play was given on Corpus Christi day a special 'bayn or messenger' was twice sent round the city to announce it.

---

[1] Davies, p. 241.
[2] Just as at the present day the city of Leipzig lets the booths and the ground on which to erect them in certain places to individuals for the great annual fairs.
[3] Extracts, pp. 241, 264.   [4] English Gilds, p. 427.

' *Proclamacio* [1] *ludi corporis cristi facienda in vigilia corporis cristi.*
Oiez, &c.   We comand of ye kynges behalue and ye Mair and ye
shirefs of yis Citee yat no mann go armed in yis Citee with swerdes
ne with Carlill-axes, ne none othir defences in distorbaunce of ye
kynges pees and ye play, or hynderyng of ye processioun of Corpore Christi, and yat yai leue yare hernas in yare Ines, saufand
knyghtes and sqwyers of wirship yat awe haue swerdes borne eftir
yame, of payne of forfaiture of yaire wapen and inprisonment of
yaire bodys.   And yat men yat brynges furth pacentes yat yai play
at the places yat is assigned yerfore and nowere elles, of ye payne
of forfaiture to be raysed yat is ordayned yerfore, yat is to say xl*s.*
And yat menn of craftes and all othir menn yat fyndes torches, yat
yai come furth in array and in ye manere as it has been vsed and
customed before yis time, noght haueyng wapen, careynge tapers
of ye pagentz.   And officers yat ar keepers of þe pees of payne of
forfaiture of yaire fraunchis and yaire bodyes to prison : And [2] all
maner of craftmen yat bringeth furthe ther pageantez in order and
course by good players, well arayed and openly spekyng, vpon
payn of lesyng of C.*s.* to be paide to the chambre without any
pardon.   And that euery player that shall play be redy in his
pagiaunt at convenyant tyme, that is to say, at the mydhowre be-
twix iiij[th] and v[th] of the cloke in the mornynge, and then all oyer
pageantz fast followyng ilk one after oyer as yer course is, without
tarieng.   Sub pena facienda camere vi*s.* viii*d.*'

The picture of these good folks up at half-past four on a summer
morning ready to act their parts one after another reminds us of
Ober-Ammergau, in strong contrast to the habits of the modern stage.

Up till 1426 the procession of Corpus Christi and the plays had
both been taken on the same day, but in that year (it is entered on
the records [3]) one William Melton of the Minor Friars coming to
the city, in different sermons ' ludum populo commendabat, affirm-
ando quod bonus erat in se et laudabilis valde ;' but for several

[1] This document has been printed by Sharp and Marriott, both from Drake,
who, however, has many inaccuracies in this as in the schedule.   It is here
collated with the original in Book $\frac{A}{Y}$, fo. 245 v⁰.

[2] From here to the end is in a different hand, and written over an erasure.
[3] Book A, fo. 269.   See Davies, p. 243.   Drake gives a translation of the
whole, Eboracum, Appx. xxix.   Melton is styled ' sacre pagine professor,' a description of his status like the familiar S.T.P., but Drake, having pageants in
his head, translates it ' professor of holy pageantry.'

reasons (probably because the sale of indulgences was affected by the non-attendance of the people at church) he induced the people to have the play on one day and the procession on the second, 'sic quod populus convenire possit ad ecclesias in festo.' The people, however, still kept the day of the festival for their play [1].

PAGEANTS AND THE PAGEANT-HOUSES. There is no doubt that at York, as at Coventry, the word pageant was used both for the travelling scaffold on which the play was performed, and for the representation. (Various forms of the word occur, *pachent*, *paiaunt*, *pagende*, *pagyant*, *padzhand*, *padgion*, *paidgion*, *padgin*.) 'Reparations to the pageant' are referred to not unfrequently [2]. Several items for carpenter's work and for painting are found in 1397 (at the visit of Richard II): in 1500, 'the cartwryghts [are] to make iiij new wheles to the pagiaunt [3].' We might have found much illustrative matter in the compotus rolls or account books of the various companies, but unfortunately very few of these are preserved, the Book of the Pewterers, 1599, and the Innholders Ordinary, 1608, do not refer to the play [4]. The Bakers' Accounts [5] from 1584 down to 1835 have, however, been rescued : under date 1584 are the following items as to the pageant-scaffold :—

'Paid to the paidgion maisters for monye that they hadd laid furthe after the makinge vppe o[r] accomptes concerning the playe as folow[th]

Item for ij Iron lamps for the padgion, x*d*.

Item for byrkes and Resshes to the padgion, ij*d*.

Item for ij gallands of ayle, viij*d*.

Item to the laborer for taykinge the clothes vp and doune, and nayles, iiij*d*.

Item to vj*d*. laborers for puttinge the padgion, ij*s*.'

For St. George's play in 1554 there were payments 'for vj yerdes of canves to the pagyant,' and 'for payntyng the canves and pagyant.' There is nothing to show whether the clothes or canvas were used as adjuncts by way of scenery, or for draping some portions of the scaffold. On some parts of the machine were placed the arms of the city, who would not permit the crafts to set their signs instead,

---

[1] Davies, pp. 243, 244, and see *ib.* p. 77.   [2] See pp. xxv *note*, xl.

[3] Davies, pp. 230, 240 ; 239.

[4] I was told that an old compotus roll of the Mercers' company still exists, but I have been unable to get a sight of it.

[5] In the private possession of Joseph Wilkinson, Esq., of York, who kindly lent me the volumes.

see the agreement for combination in 1422 before cited[1]; and indeed the sign of the municipal authority over and recognition of the whole 'Play' was unmistakably given by the use of the banners with the city arms, which were set the previous evening at the stations where the players were to perform[2]. In 1478 the city paid 'pro uno baneȓ. Thome Gaunt pro ludo Corporis Cristi,' and to Margaret the sempstress 3*d*. 'pro emendacione vexillorum ludi Corporis Cristi,' both which were evidently public property[3].

These big movable stages which cost money to make and repair had to be put away carefully while not in use, and the companies hired buildings for this purpose, the memory of which still lingers in the name Pageant Green[4] (now the railway station), near to which there appear to have been several of these houses, in a place called Raton-rawe. Thus we hear of 'le pagent-howse pellipariorum' in 1420[5]; in 1502 'the cookes shall have sufficient and convenient roome for theyr pagiaunt with the pagiaunt house of the baxters ;' and in 1585 the Bakers received 'paidgion rent' of the Pynners and Paynters, while they paid 'to the brigg maisters for the padgion howse' rent, items which continue in their accounts for many years[6]. Among 'fre rentes to be paid yearely' and other 'Rents due' to the corporation, entered in a book dated 1626, are found the following, substantial relics of the old play-loving days:—

Of the Skinners for the pageante howse farme yerely due, xij*d*.
Of the Walkers for an Outeshott, iiij*d*.
Of the Tapiters for their pageante howse, xij*d*.
Of the Tanners for the pageante howse, xij*d*.
Of the Carpenters for their pageante howse, xij*d*.
Of the Bakers for their pageante hówse, xij*d*.
Of the Cordiners for their pageante howse, xij*d*.
Of the Cowpers for an outeshott, iiij*d*.'

---

[1] Page xxv, *note*.

[2] 1399. 'Et ordinatum est quod vexilla ludi cum armis ciuitatis liberentur per maiorem in vigilia corporis cristi, ponenda in locis vbi erit ludus paginarum, et quod vexilla ipsa annuatim in crastino corporis cristi repertentur ad eandem, ad manus maioris et camararie ciuitatis, et ibidem custodiantur per totum annum.' Book $\frac{A}{Y}$, fo. 17 vᵒ. This ordinance was made at the time that the stations were re-declared : see before, p. xxxii.   [3] Davies, pp. 64, 65.

[4] See 'Walks through the city of York,' by Rob. Davies, 1880, p. 130. It is remarkable that in his interesting paper on the Pavement, pp. 245–248, the writer does not allude to the performance of the plays there. See before, p. xxxiii.

[5] Book $\frac{B}{Y}$, fo. 42 vᵒ.   [6] Davies, p. 240.

THE PLAYERS. It will have been noted that the public Proclamation required the crafts to provide 'good players, well arayed, and openly spekyng.' It was a serious matter, and the credit of the city was at stake, no foretaste of Bully Bottom and of Shakespeare's ridicule warned the citizens of their future dis-esteem. It is hardly too much to say that the following law is one of the steps on which the greatness of the Elizabethan stage was built, and through which its actors grew up. It was ordained on 3 April, 1476, by the full consent and authority of the council, ' þat yerely in þe tyme of lentyn there shall be called afore the maire for þe tyme beyng iiij of þe moste connyng discrete and able players within this Citie, to serche, here, and examen all þe plaiers and plaies and pagentes thrughoute all þe artificers belonging to Corpus Xti Plaie. And all suche as þay shall fynde sufficiant in personne and connyng, to þe honour of þe Citie and worship of þe saide Craftes, for to admitte and able ; and all oþer insufficiant personnes, either in connyng, voice, or personne to discharge, ammove, and avoide.

' And þat no plaier þat shall plaie in þe saide Corpus Xti plaie be conducte and reteyned to plaie but twise on þe day of þe saide playe ; and þat he or thay so plaing plaie not ouere twise þe saide day, vpon payne of xls. to forfet vnto þe chaumbre as often tymes as he or þay shall be founden defautie in þe same[1].'

The meaning of this last order is not clear, for each player would have to play as many times as there were stations : can it mean that no player might undertake more than two parts? At the end of the *Play of the Sacrament* (see after, p. lxviii ;) the names of eleven players are given, with a note that ' IX may play it at ease,' showing that some must here have taken double work. In Bale's Kyng John, and in Preston's King Cambyses, several parts could be performed by one actor (Ward's Hist. of Eng. Drama, i. p. 105 ; Thos. Hawkins' Eng. Drama, vol. i. p. 249).

There was no lack of players to call in aid of examination ; a hundred years before my lord Leicester's and the other itinerant noblemen's companies of Elizabeth's time so frequently visited the city[2], we find the players of Donnington, Wakefield, and London visiting York.

[1] Council Book, No. III, fo. 13 v°. ; Davies, p. 237.
[2] See Davies, p. 277.

1446. 'Item Ministrallis in festo Corporis Cristi, xx*s.*
ludentibus in festo natalis domini, viij*d.*
ludentibus in festo circumsisionis, xij*d.*
iij ludentibus de Donyngton, xij*d.*
j ludento de Wakefeld, vj*d.*'

1447. 'iiij ludentibus de London die dominica proxima post fest. Corp.
Cristi, vj*s.* viij*d.*
les ministralls in festo Corp. Cristi, xvij*s.*
ij ludentibus Joly Wat and Malkyn, ij*d.*' [1]

It will not be forgotten that the Towneley plays were performed
in the neighbourhood of Wakefield.

EXPENSES OF THE PLAYS : PAGEANT-MASTERS. It has been seen
that the crafts supplied the players and the pageants, and hired the
pageant houses. To support these expenses each company appointed two 'pageant-masters,' whose duty it was to collect the
contributions of members, spend, and account for them and
the playing-gear, and look after the proper conduct of the play
of their craft. The 'ordinances' of most of the crafts included
one stipulating that members should pay to the support of their
pageant, e.g. the Cutlers' in 1444 and earlier [2], the rate being
often called 'pageant-silver,' while of fines incurred, half was also
to go to the same fund. On the formation of a new company, or on
the combination of old ones, even as late as 1572, it was laid
down that the 'craft shall goo with their pageant throughe the
citie as other occupacons and artificers doeth [3].' The play in
fact so wove itself into the economy of the companies that it
became important to settle how much strangers and non-franchised
men should pay towards it, and his pageant often became a test
of what craft a man belonged to. For one trade was continually
(in the natural course of change) encroaching upon another,

---

[1] From an account-book of classified payments, &c., marked 25 *H.* 6. The
last item, which occurs twice, seems to refer to some inferior representation.

[2] Book $\frac{A}{Y}$, fos. 40, 41. 'Padgin monnye' survived among the *Bakers* till 1771.

[3] The Plaisterers, Book $\frac{B}{Y}$, fo. 237. The '*Musicians* commonly called the
Mynstrells' recorded their ordinances in 1561, choosing masters and two
teachers of the 'said sciens or craft' like any other craft; the members also had to
pay 'towardes the supportation and bryngyng forth of their pageant.' Book $\frac{B}{Y}$,
fo. 230. See after, p. 125.

which engendered jealousies and uncertainty when contributions towards a fixed liability such as the proper pageant came in question. All these difficulties, arbitraments, bye-laws revised and enrolled, were settled in the Mayor's court, hence their entry on the official records of the city. A few of these, given as shortly as possible, may be of interest.

1424, 31 March. *Plasterarii et tegularii domorum.* By arbitration before the mayor it was settled that each man using both trades should be 'in solvendo utrique pagine ipsarum artium;' every workman of the tilers to pay 'ambabus paginis,' 3*d.*[1] The same trade in 1572 ordered that every 'lyme-burner,' a foreigner, shall pay 4*d.* pageant-money.

The Barbours. Foreigners[2] who sell in the city shall be annually contributory to 'paginam barbitonsorum lumenque.' About 1476 from *Glovers* and sellers of 'ynglissh ware' there was to be collected yearly 'to the sustentacion and vphalding of the pagende of the for-saide crafte,' 'of a denysen ij*d.*, and of a straunger iiij*d.*,' excepting men 'selling London ware' and members of the gild of Holy Trinity[3].

Escriveners de Tixt. Davies prints some ordinances of this company without date, referring them to *temp.* Rich. II. In one of these the craftsman incurring a fine 'paiera xx*s.* desterlinges, cest assavoir x*s.* a la chaumbre du counseil et x*s.* al oeps de lour pagyne et lumer appartenaunte a lour dit artifice[4].' As 'Tixtwryters, luminers, noters, turners, and florisschers,' they enrolled new ordinances in 1491; no priest having a salary of seven marks or more might exercise the craft; 'any forein vsing any part of the same craft that cumyth into this citie to sell any bukes or to take any warke to wurk shall pay to the vp-holding of their padgiant yerelie, iiij*d.*'[5]

---

[1] Book $\frac{A}{Y}$, fo. 249.

[2] *Ib.* fo. 72. 'Foreigner' is used in these extracts in the sense of a non-citizen.

[3] Book $\frac{B}{Y}$, fo. 146 v°.

[4] Memoirs of the York Press, by Robert Davies. Westminster, 1868, Introd. pp. 1, 2.

[5] Book $\frac{B}{Y}$, fo. 167: compare the above with No. 44 of Burton's list.

In 1485 the *Girdlers* ordered that all those 'of the church as other' who make things pertaining to their craft ('bokes, claspes, dog colers, chapes, girdilles,' &c.) shall pay double the rate due from a member of the craft towards bringing forth their pageant[1]. This must have been directed against some poor monk or priest who tried to finish off his own book-covers.

The *Lynweuers*, however, by the arbitrament of 1517, were allowed to 'aske, clame, nor take no pageant money or pageant siluer of any foreign straunger that is not freman fraunchesed[2].'

The *Curryours* ordered that 'quilibet servicius in prima leva-cione shoppe' should pay 3*s*. 4*d*. 'pro sustentatione pagine[3].'

For the *Millers* it was ordered (probably before 1400) that all who 'follow the craft called "Mele-makers"' shall pay to the pageant of the millers as they should reasonably agree with the masters of the pageant[4].

Another trade combination was that of the *Pynners and Wyre-drawers* in 1482, those that 'makes pynnes or draweth wyre, or maketh ffisshe-hukes or shobakilles[5],' must join at the pageant of the Pynners[6]; while the following settlement of a discord shows the proportionate charges on master and journeyman, and how the chamberlains acted as temporary trustees.

21 Nov., 1517, *Skinners*, &c. :—

'At whiche day it was agreed that for a peace to be hade betwixt the Skynners and the vestment makers that from hensforth the vestment-makers shall pay yerly to the bryngyng furth of the Skynners pageant, euery maister viij*d*. & euery jenaman iiij*d*., & no more, to be paide w*t*oute denye, yerly, to the chamberlayne handes affore the fest of Wit-sonday, and then the skynners to resceyue it atte chamberlayne handes, and they not to be charged w*t* the repparacons of there pageant[7].'

Shipmen and Mariners. A 'concordia' was made at an early date between 'marinarios et piscenarios de Vsegate,'—'habentes batellos, de modo soluendi ad paginam nauis Noe, ad quam vtraque pars singulis annis fuit et est simul contributoria[8].' And

---

[1] Council Book, Nos. II, IV, fo. 74.

[2] Minute Book 9, fo. 94 v°.

[3] Book $\frac{A}{Y}$, fo. 274.

[4] Hist. MSS. Com. I. p. 109.

[5] Shoe buckles.

[6] Book $\frac{A}{Y}$, fo. 369 v°.

[7] Minute Book 9, fo. 93 v°.

[8] Book $\frac{A}{Y}$, fo. 52 v°.

the Shipmen agreeing on their ordinances in the council chamber, 1479, ordered that a franchised man 'salyng as maister w^t a freman pay yerely ij$d$., and he þ^t salys as a felowe pay jd., to the sustentacion and vpholding as well of the pageant of Noe, as of þe bringing furth and beryng of certan torches before the shryne of corpus xpi, yerely.' And to chuse searchers and pageant master on the 'secound sonday of clene lentyn[1].'

The ordinances of the *Marshals and Smiths* and of the *Armourers* throw light on the functions of the pageant masters, officers whom the *Bakers* continued to choose down to 1611 and 1656[2]. The former, besides ordering them in 1409 to summon the craftsmen, in 1443 ordained 'þat every man of þe said craftes shal be preuy to þe receytes and expense of al money þat shal be receyued to þe said pageantes, as wele pageaunt-siluer as other. And þat þe pageant-maisters of both þe said craftes shal make þair rakenyng and gife accompt euery yere fro nowe furth, vpone Sononday next before Missomerday[3].' The *Armourers* in 1476 agreed to meet yearly on the second Sunday after Corpus Christi day to choose their searchers and pageant-masters for the ensuing year; they also ordered 'that alle the maisters of the same crafte from nowe-furth yerely on Corpus Xpi day in þe mornyng be redy in thair owen propre personnez, euery one of thayme with ane honest wapyn, to awayte apon their pagende maisters and pagende at þe playnge ande settynge furth thair saide pagende, at þe firste place where they shall begyne. And so to awayte apon þe same thair pagende thurgh þ^e cite, to þ^e play be plaide as of þ^t same pagende[4].'

The *Spuriers and Lorymers* in 1493 made a similar regulation, that all the masters of the craft ' shall attend vppon yer paiaunt from y^e maten of play be begune at y^e furst place vnto such tyme as y^e said play be played and finished thrugh the toune at y^e last playse[5].'

Returning to the pageant-masters, it is abundantly clear that they collected the pageant-silver and expended it, for example,

---

[1] Book $\frac{A}{Y}$, fo. 294 v°.   [2] Bakers' accounts, cited before.

[3] See ' Ordinances of the Marshals and Smiths at York ' in the *Antiquary*, March, 1885.

[4] Book $\frac{B}{Y}$, fo. 146.   [5] Council Book, No. VII, fo. 109 v°.

the *Goldsmiths* declared in 1561 that they 'shall yerely make a dewe accompte of the money and of the playing geare vnto thoccupation on St. Dunstan's even[1],' and the lyme-burners were to pay their money yearly when demanded by the pageant-masters (1572)[2].

Burton's list of 1415 and the Register give the *Ostlers* as playing the Coronation of our Lady. The following shows that there must have been a re-arrangement in 1483, when perhaps the new play of which a fragment is written at the end of the Register (see p. 514) was tried. Four men came before the mayor, 'and by the assent of all the Inholders of this seid Cite tuke apon them to bryng furth yerly duryng the term of viij yere then next folluyng the pagent of the Coronacion of our Lady perteyning to the said Inholders, and also to reparell the said paghant; so þᵗ they þᵗ holds Inys and haith no syns pay as wele, and as moche yerely to the reparacion of the said pagent, and brynging furth of the same, as the said Inholders þᵗ haith syns doyth,' i.e. 4*d*. each[3].

II.

COMPARATIVE LITERATURE. It would be out of place here to enter into any disquisition on the history or origin of the religious drama, even in England, which have been treated by various writers[4]; the York Corpus Christi plays step in to a definite period when the drama was already in the hands of laymen and quite apart from liturgical service, although we perhaps get a few glimpses of the former con-

---

[1] Book $\frac{B}{Y}$, fo. 229 v°.

[2] See also the concord between the Marshals and Smiths in 1428: *Antiquary*, as before.

[3] Council Book, No. V, 28 April, 1 Rich. III. The city agreed to aid the Iniholders by 2*s*. a year, which is found in the Chamberlain's accounts of 1522 to have been paid.

[4] It is enough to name the well-known works of Adolf Ebert, and J. L. Klein, for Italy, Spain, and Germany; Mone and Wilken for Germany; D'Ancona for Italy; Sepet and Petit de Julleville for France; Morley ('English Writers'), Collier, Ward, and some chapters in Warton for England. To which should be added 'Early Mysteries and Latin Poems of twelfth and thirteenth centuries,' by Thomas Wright, 1838, an important little volume; W. Marriott's 'Collection of English Miracle Plays,' Basel, 1838; Thomas Sharp's 'Dissertation on the Coventry Mysteries,' Coventry, 1825; Mr. J. O. Halliwell-Phillipps' chapter on the Coventry Mysteries in the fourth edition of his 'Outlines of the Life of Shakespeare,' and the first chapter of W. Kelly's 'Notices illustrative of the English Drama,' 1865.

nection with the church through the houses of St. Leonard and of Holy Trinity[1], through the music attached to the 46th Play, and possibly through the authorship of our plays. Compared with the remains of this kind of literature which still exist on the continent, our islands are poor indeed; and what we have has suffered by fragmentary treatment. The York cycle forms an important contribution to our stock; it is, as a whole, the most complete English collection, the only known full text that we are sure was played by the crafts at the Corpus Christi festival. It may be useful to gather up briefly the places in our country where religious plays are recorded to have been performed, and all the examples of such plays themselves which now remain, for comparison[2]. We thus see that there must have been at least eight or ten cycles of plays dealing with 'matter from the Creation' till Domesday at greater or less length; in such cases as Dublin and Newcastle it is probable that the accounts are fragmentary, and that the names of some parts are lost. Candlemas, Whitsuntide, and the day of Corpus Christi were the favorite seasons, but most of these cycles seem to have been played at Corpus Christi festival[3],—the Chester collection belonged to Whitsuntide. In France the day of Corpus Christi was celebrated with dumb shows, or *mystères mimés*, with the procession; their great dramatic cycles were performed at other seasons, and apparently not with the recurring regularity of ours; the municipalities took them up with zeal and vigour: but the plays do not seem to have become so closely a part of the life of the people as, for instance, in York[4].

On the comparison of the cycles, the unity of design running through them becomes apparent. The subject was always taken from the biblical histories in due order, the greater part from the New Testament and the apocryphal legends connected with it, which were part of the religion and entered into the literature of the middle ages. We note, too, a sense of appropriate calling in the occupations to the subject of the particular play assigned

---

[1] See before, pp. xi, xii, xxi, xxxii.

[2] See Appendix II to this Introduction. Some other notices in topographic works and local records are likely to be found, though I have collected all known to me.

[3] It is not known when the Cornish cycle was performed.

[4] L. Petit de Julleville, 'Les Mystères,' Paris, 1880, tom. i. pp. 198, 351–356.

to each, which must have had some original impulse. Jusserand
and other writers have noticed this incidental fact, which is illus-
trated by the Dublin, Newcastle, and Beverley lists, as much as by
any other. It may be studied in the York collection, which shows how,
amid the shifting of crafts, this fitness was on the whole preserved.

The festival of Corpus Christi was instituted in 1264. The
great poem *Cursor Mundi*, written early in the 14th century, by a
native of the Durham district, was intended, he tells us, for the
honour of Mary (lines 69-120, 23909-20); but whatever impulse
sent it forth, it is impossible not to be struck with the general resemblance, in subject and arrangement, between the *Cursor Mundi*
and the York cycle of Corpus plays[1]. This offers a closer parallel
to that poem than any of the other collections; first, because it is
more perfect and comprehensive; secondly, because it is free from
much of the coarse jocularity and popular incident which were introduced into the Towneley and Coventry plays. Several portions
of the *Cursor* are as dramatic as the limits of a narrative in
couplets would allow, e.g. the legend of Seth and Adam (ll. 1237-
1432), the story of Joseph, the Harrowing of Hell (ll. 17849-
18450), or the Death and Burial of Mary. The York plays, while
cast in a poetic form with skill and power of a higher level than
that of the *Cursor*, take up the course of the biblical history, more
especially of the New Testament, on the same model. Comparison of the several series fills up some of the blanks and gaps which
occur in one or other of them; for example, the seventh play at
Beverley was on 'Adam and Seth,' in its right order, a subject
which occurs in no other plays except the Cornish dramas 'Origo
Mundi' and the 'Creation.' The Chester plays, 23 on Prophecies
and the Fifteen signs of Doom preceding the end of the world, and
24 on Anti-Christ, are both unknown elsewhere among English
plays, though found in the *Cursor*. On the other hand, reference
to the *Cursor* helps to explain points but slightly touched in the
plays, such as the incidents of Judas bursting at his death (see
before, p. xiv, *Cursor*, ll. 16492-16516); and the prophecy of the
Sibyl[2] in the Towneley play 7. The meaning of the 'Prologue

---

[1] Professor Ten Brink remarked on the influence of the *Cursor* on the mysteries,
in 1877, 'Geschichte der Englischen Literatur,' p. 360.
[2] On the Fifteen Signs and the Sibyl see M. P. Meyer's 'Daurel et Beton,'
Soc. des Anc. Textes Franç. 1880, p. xcvii, and references there given.

of prophets ' or ' Processus prophetarum [1],' a play which occurs in the Chester, Towneley, and Coventry sets, also receives light from a comparison with the *Cursor*.

While the general conception of the *Cursor*, which embodied the popular belief of the time, must have had its influence on the composition of the Corpus plays, it must not be forgotten that the same ideas operated on the religious drama abroad. In France the cycles attained great dimensions; in Italy they were not so complete, but the separate plays were more important [2]. In Germany the great extent and influence they reached may be judged, not only by the history of their great cycles, but by the relics which survive to our day in the Passion Play of Ober Ammergau of seventeen parts (founded in 1633), and that of Brixlegg in Tyrol [3] of sixteen parts, comprising the events from the Entry into Jerusalem to the Resurrection and Ascension. No doubt in other places too in Germany and Spain they yet may linger on.

DATE OF COMPOSITION: AUTHORSHIP. Although the date of composition of the York Plays is not known, it may, I believe, safely be set as far back as 1340 or 1350, not long after the appearance of the *Cursor*. The references to them mentioned before in 1378 and 1394, in the latter as ' of old time,' lead to this conclusion, no less than the style of language

---

[1] In York this subject forms a Prologue to Play XII. See p. 93.

[2] I have found nothing in the printed collections of *Sacre Rappresentazioni* resembling our York series. But among the Ashburnham MSS. now sold to Italy there is a fine MS. (Libri 1264), dated 1490, of an Italian play which, preceded by a long Latin poem on the twelve sibyls, begins with a prologue of prophets and the Procès de Paradis, and then, from the Annunciation to the Resurrection, goes through the whole bible and apocryphal story. The whole is written continuously, without break of *giornate*; full and frequent stage directions are given, and the actors are numerous. Several interesting developements might be noted, such as Herod's three sons, the ship with captain and sailors with whom the Magi sail to Herod, the bridging over the time between ' Jesu picolo ' and ' Jesu grando,' the appearance of Sculapio at the sickness of Lazarus, &c. We find here too the porter (named Merlin) who, as at York, denies entry to Judas. The play may be a compilation of others; it is not a mere joining of the separate plays printed by Signor D'Ancona, who has kindly pointed out to me such a one in MS. at Florence.

[3] The writer of the preface to the little play-book of Brixlegg, in 1883, modestly points out the serious object of the players; and he claims that though the religious drama in Germany, even in the middle ages, did not attain such artistic perfection as in Spain, the culture of it has had most important effects in the spiritual education of the people.

and the metre in which they are written. The unknown author, whoever he was, possessed much skill in versification at that period when the old alliteration of the English, altered though it were from its earlier forms, was still popular, yet when the poet had found the charms of rime, and the delights of French verse allured him to take on new shackles while casting off the old. That he belonged to one of the religious houses of the North in the Yorkshire district may well be hazarded, on account of the knowledge of the scriptures, and especially the careful concordance of the narrative from the gospels shown in the plays. The Towneley plays are not only written in the same dialect, but five of them are the same as five of the York plays [1], with certain passages cut out or modified. If, as the editor of that collection suggests (pref. p. x), it is made up partly of compositions from other similar collections, the presence of these five taken from York is explained; as the style of the York collection does not vary to the same extent, this is more likely of the two to be the original source. As far as may be judged from the characteristic titles which are all that remain of the Beverley plays, that collection also resembled the York more than any other, and it is worth comparing the two together. The Beverley title often takes hold of what must have been the prominent feature to the vulgar eye rather than the subject, such as the ' Sleeping Pilate,' ' Deeming Pilate,' ' The Pynnacle,' &c., which helps recognition of the York piece. If the text of the Beverley plays ever turns up, it may be tested in how many places one Yorkshire play-wright had influence.

As a help in the study of the York cycle of plays I subjoin a comparative table of the four English collections [2], adding a B to the York subjects to denote where the Beverley titles (which will be found in Poulson's Beverlac) seem to agree with them.

---

[1] See pp. 68, 156, 372, 396, 497, where the parallel passages are given for the sake of comparison and various readings. For the opportunity of collating these with the original MS. I have to thank the courtesy of the owner, Mr. Bernard Quaritch, of Piccadilly. The Surtees editor did not apparently take count of the losses the MS. has undergone, though he mentions some of them. The signature of the quires shows that 12 leaves at the beginning and 12 between the *Ascenscio* and *Juditium*, besides others, were lost before it was put into the present old binding. The handwriting differs from that of the York MS. entirely, and is rather later, probably of the end of the fifteenth century. Like the York, it must be a copy from older originals.

[2] Appendix I to this Introduction.

SOURCES OF THE YORK PLAYS. These are indicated in the margin of each play [1]. They follow pretty closely the biblical narrative, with however occasional deviations, as in the account of the ten plagues and in some of the quotations in the Prologue of Prophets in Play XII, which do not all agree with the Vulgate. In the subjects from the Old Testament no other apocryphal legends are introduced except those relating to Lucifer and the rebel angels. The exact source of these for our mediæval writers I cannot find, although it is known that they originated in the East among the Iranian legends. The allusion in Noah's words, that the world shall be burnt with fire, may be referable to the same source. M. James Rothschild has shown that the legend of the Fall of Lucifer, unknown to Jerome, was adopted by a Christian writer at the close of the fifth century [2].

The Old and New Testament portions are linked together by a series of prophecies relating to Mary and the Holy Child, all taken from the bible, suggested by Luke xxiv. 27 (Play XII). In other compositions of the kind the prophecies of a sibyl or sibyls as to Jesus are introduced; sometimes, as in the Towneley (9), Chester (6), and in the Italian play (Libri 1264) a story of Octavian the Emperor is added or interwoven with them. The York plays in this respect are more direct and simple, they contain nothing of the kind. Nor do we find, as in other places, much reference to the apocryphal legends (fully dealt with in the *Cursor*) of the birth and childhood of Mary, and of the Infancy of Jesus, the thirteenth play containing nearly all of this subject. Of this one the originals will be found in '*The Gospel of Pseudo-Matthew*,' '*History of Joseph the Carpenter*,' '*Protevangelium or Gospel of James*,' and '*Nativity of Mary* [3].' For one point I have not found any authority, viz. the blossoming of Joseph's rod [4], whereby he was marked out as the husband of Mary; all these works, instead, make a dove to proceed from the rod. Among other sources which may be taken into account as most surely affording inspiration to the writers of these

---

[1] The reader is requested to correct the marginal references to the versicles on pp. 483, 484, according to note 3, on p. 526.

[2] 'Mistère du Viel Testament,' Vol. I, Introd. p. xlii.

[3] The references are made to these books in Migne's 'Dictionnaire des Apocryphes' and B. Harris Cowper's 'Apocryphal Gospels.'

[4] Play XIII. l. 32.

plays, is the *Speculum Humanæ Salvationis*, that very popular religious picture-book of the fourteenth century, the effects of whose influence on pictorial and sculptured art were far-reaching. Who can say indeed whether its curious four-fold groups of types and antitype, of subjects in Old Testament and legendary history brought to bear upon the events of the Sacred Scheme, as well as the similar representations of the earlier *Biblia Pauperum*, may not now be bearing fruit in the tableaux or *Vorbilder* of the Bavarian and Tyrolese plays? In a MS. of the *Speculum* of about 1380, with Italian paintings, at Paris [1], Joseph's rod is depicted like a small tree *full of flowers*, with a dove in the middle, ' Hic disponsatur virgo Maria Josepho ' written above ; the reference Is. xi. 2 showing whence the idea sprang.

The apocryphal *Gospel of James* comes in Play XVII: thence the Bible is followed, with a mention .of Anti-Christ in XXIII (p. 189), till in Play XXVIII. p. 251, the brilliant light from Jesus which strikes back the soldiers seems to have some other source than the fancy of the poet [2]. In XXIX the incidents of Matthew are disarranged in order, as occasionally elsewhere. In Plays XXX, XXXI the *Gospel of Nicodemus* furnishes the Dream of Pilate's wife and other stories. The allusion to the legend of Pilate's name (p. 271) is from a variation of the Abgar-legend (Veronica and Vespasian) among the apocryphal gospels [3]. The story of the Squire who lets 'Calvary locus' (p. 318) and is cheated of his title-deeds, must be of English invention ; but in the next Play (XXXIII), the Trial and Condemnation, much is taken from the '*Acts of Pilate*' (otherwise *Gospel of Nicodemus*), which narrates the miraculous bowing of the standards, &c. In Play XXXIV (p. 339) we have an allusion (the only one, I believe, in the plays) drawn from the fine legend of the Holy Tree, which, having sprung from a seed on Adam's tongue, appears in the histories of Moses, David, and Solomon, till it is finally cut down for the cross [4]; and

---

[1] MS. Arsenal, 593, fo. 8.

[2] Mrs. Jameson (Hist. of our Lord in Art) makes no reference to this incident. I have not besides been able to identify the allusion to Habakkuk, p. 116/137.

[3] See article on Tischendorf's edition in the 'Zeitschrift für deutsches Alterthum,' Berlin, 1876, vol. 20. pp. 168, 186.

[4] The tree-legend, with the oil of mercy, runs throughout the *Cursor*. See also a somewhat different verson in Baring-Gould's ' Curious Myths of the Middle Ages,' pp. 378-384, and authorities mentioned by B. Harris Cowper, ' Apocryphal Gospels,' p. ci.

on p. 343 is a reference to the Vernacle, the third Mary evidently acting as Veronica and showing the kerchief with the impression of the sacred face to the audience [1].

The account of the Crucifixion with its too great realism, the rearing of the cross and hammering of wedges and mortices, will be understood by anyone who has witnessed the actual ceremonies that take place on Good Friday in a Roman Catholic church [2].

For Play XXXVI (Death and Burial of Jesus) the Greek version of the *Gospel of Nicodemus* supplies many incidents; XXXVII, the Descent into Hell (or Harrowing of Hell) is founded on some chapters in the Latin version of the same book (before referred to), to which XXXVIII is also partly indebted. The next six plays follow the biblical narrative, with some inversion, and addition of extraneous matter in XLI, The Purification. The next three, on the Death, Assumption, and Coronation of Mary, find their origin in the two texts of *Transitus Mariæ*, the apocryphal legend, printed by Tischendorf [3], and some versicles from the Song of Solomon. Interwoven passages of scripture and tradition form the groundwork of the final piece, The Judgment Day. It is a singular thing that for the Coronation of Mary there appears to be no written authority, not even in the Arab *Passing of Mary, of St. John* [4], nor the Golden Legend; it is a tradition that has grown up as a corollary to the story of her Assumption—a beautiful ending to her history, which has worked itself into art [5] and the drama. Though (as several Roman Catholic authorities have informed me) there never has been a church festival of the Coronation, the subject was

---

[1] See ll. 184–190, and before, p. xxv. I have omitted to note this in the margin.

[2] The rites which I saw in Malta, together with the pictured religious processions there, helped me vividly to realize much of these plays.

[3] 'Apocalypses Apocryphæ,' Lipsiæ, 1866. That part of the story of the death of Mary which relates the bearing of her body to burial, and the attack upon the bier by the wicked Jew, whose arm thereupon became rigid, seems to have been a favourite; as seen in Burton's list the play was known by the name of the Jew, *Fergus*, the most prominent personage. Why or whence he had this name is a puzzle, but his appellations were various, in the Arab text *Japhia*; in Le Mystère de l'Assomption of 1518, *Isachar* (Migne's Dict. des Apoc. ii. p. 523; *ib.* Dict. des Mystères, p. 160); in *Transitus Mariæ* (Tischendorf's text A) he is *Reuben*; while Mrs Jameson (Legends of the Madonna, p. 318) calls him the high priest *Adonijah*. The *Cursor* (ll. 20719-63, and version in Part v. ll. 611-749) gives no name.

[4] Migne, Dict. des Apocryphes, ii. 506.

[5] Mrs. Jameson's Legends of the Madonna, pp. 328, 329.

brought into at least two plays in England, at York and Beverley. My endeavours to identify the music inserted in Play XLVI have led me more particularly into this enquiry, with this result.

If, as is likely, these endeavours to trace the sources of the text be found defective, I must crave indulgence in a difficult field.

VERSE AND STYLE. The reader will judge for himself, but I believe that, far from meriting the hard words frequently poured on the rudeness of the early plays, these of York will be found to compare favourably in diction, and certainly so in verse, with the better specimens of Middle English Northern poetry. The great variety of metre in the collection, totally unlike the regular verse in which the French mysteries are uniformly written, points to their native growth, and the improbability of their having been translated or introduced from France. The following is a sketch-analysis of the metre. I must leave to those better versed than myself in the interesting study of historic metre to determine how much of it is due to the old Norse and English poetic tradition and how much to the newer Norman French influence[1]. The old Northern poets, who cultivated the art of verse so carefully, undoubtedly left their mark on the Yorkshire composer. The poetry cannot, it must be remembered, be scanned like Shakespeare or Chaucer, or even like the *Cursor*; it must, for the greater part, be read according to accent or stress, the intervening syllables, more or less in number, being slurred or read with a lighter touch. This sort of verse is much like the unbarred music of the same period. Attention may be drawn also to the manner in which the varied metre is adapted to the style of subject to be treated or to the personage speaking; for example, Deus and Jesus invariably speak in grave, dignified verse, while the long, pompous, mouth-filling lines, excessive in the alliterative stress, are put into the mouths of those who, like Herod, Pilate, and Caiaphas, open a play and are meant to make an imposing impression. The original purpose was forgotten when Shakespeare jested at the alliteration and at Herod's brag.

[1] The best and clearest account of old Northern and Teutonic metre is that given by Messrs. Vigfusson and Powell in their splendid work 'Corpus Poeti-cum Boreale,' vol. i. pp. 432-458. Bearing specially on the poetry of the plays, see pp. 433-4, and 450-1. On the mixed character of the verse in the Towneley and Coventry plays, see Schipper's 'Altenglische Metrik,' pp. 226-231.

SKETCH-ANALYSIS OF METRES.

Description of Stanza.	Rimes.	Style.	Plays.
4-lines; of 4 accents...	a b a b	... ...	III.
6-line; 4 ll. of 4 acc., 2 tags.	a a a b a b ...	Much iteration in some of these.	VI, XXII, XXXVIII, XLII.
7-line; 5 ll. of 4 acc., 2 tags.*	a b a b c b c ...	... ...	XIV, XXI, XXV.
8-line; 4 ll. of 4 acc., 4 ll. of 3 acc.	a b a b c d d c ...	Alliterative; many weak endings.	I, XL, XLV.
8-line; 4 accents ...	Alternate ...	A little alliteration.	VIII.
8-line; 3 accents ...	a b a b c a a c...	... ...	XIX.
8-line; 4 accents ...	Alternate ...	Partly alliterative.	XXXIX, XLIII, XLVIII.
9-line; 4 ll. of 4 acc., 5 ll. of 3 acc.	a b a b c d d d c	Alliterative, with a few weak endings.	XXX.
10-line; 2 triplets before a quatrain.	a a b c c b d b d b	... ...	IV.
10 line; ibid.	a a b a a b c b c b	... ...	XXXIV.
10-line; quatrain before 2 triplets. (Stanzas 9–16 of 11 lines.)	a b a b c c b ┐ c c b ┘ a b a b c b c d ┐ c d c ┘	Partly alliterative.	XIII.
11-line; 6 ll. of 4 acc., a tag; 4 ll. of 3 acc.	a b a b c b c d c d c	... ...	V.
11-line; 9 ll. of 4 acc., 2 tags	a b a b b c d b c c d	... ...	VII.
11-line; 8 ll. of 4 acc., a tag, 2 ll. of 3 acc.	a b a b b c b c d c d.	Alliterative (only two regular St.)	XVI.
12-line; 8 ll. of 4 acc., 4 ll. of 3 acc. (In XV, ll. 36–85 are in 7-line stanzas, like above *.)	a b a b a b a b c d c d.	Partly alliterative; iteration in XXXVII and XLIV. X irregular.	X, XI, XII, XV, XVII, XX, XXIII, XXIV, XXVII, XXXV, XXXVII, XLIV.
12-line; ibid.	a b a b a b a b c b c b.	Partly alliterative.	II.
12 line; ibid.	a b a b a b a b c d d c.	Alliterative ...	XXVIII.
12-line; 6 ll. of 4 acc., 2 ll. of 4 syllables, a tag, 3 ll. of 3 acc.	a b a b c c d d e f e f.	... ...	XVIII.
12-line; 4 ll. of 4 acc., 7 ll. of 3 acc., a tag.	a b a b b c b c d c c d.	Alliterative, with prevalence of weak endings.	XXXIII.
13-line; 9 ll. of 3 acc., 3 ll. of 2 acc., a tag.	a b a b b c b c d e e e d.	Alliterative with much iteration.	XXXVI.
13-line; 8 ll. of 4 acc., 4 ll. of 2 acc., 1 l. of 3 acc.	a b a b b c b c d e e e d.	Alliterative, with much iteration.	XLVI.

d 2

SKETCH-ANALYSIS OF METRES (*continued*).

Description of Stanza.	Rimes.	Style.	Plays.
14-line ; 8 ll. of 4 acc., 6 ll. of 3 acc.	a b a b a b a b c d c c c d.	Partly allitera-tive.	IX, XXVI.
16-line ; irregular, the two last lines long with interwoven rimes.	8 lines, a b 8, c d c c c d e e.	Some allitera-tion.	XXXI.

In each of four plays mentioned above, XII, XIII, XV, XXX, two or more forms are found, changing in accordance with the subject.

XXXII comprises three forms of stanza, with alliteration and iteration.

XLVII is various, probably intended to be sung.

XXIX (alliterative) and XLI (of later date) are irregular.

Here then are twenty-two different forms of stanza. They are of two classes, (*a*) the alliterative, in which the metre is determined by accent or stress, not by the number of syllables or feet ; (*b*) determinable by accent or feet, the lines having usually a fixed number of syllables; in this class the alliteration is nearly lost. Both kinds end in rime. Some of the stanzas are very complicated, chiefly in class (*a*). In XL and XLVI is that regular repetition (or iteration) of the last line of one stanza in the first line of the next, dear to the northern poets; and there is a partial but decided iteration of link-words in the same manner in Plays VI, XIV, XXXII, XXXVI, XXXVII, XXXVIII.

In examining the end-rimes the original northern forms, which have often been altered by the later transcriber, account for differences that are not bad rimes or mistakes. Instances are *ropes* and *japes*, 286/387 ; *blowes* and *lawes*, 293/19 ; *rude* and *stroyd*[1], 277/175 ; *unrude* and *hyde*, 423/67–9 ; *haylsing, kyng*, and *yenge*, 100/215, 132/161 ; *reste* and *thirste*, 256/63–5 ; *fore* and *were*, 185/14–6 ; *care* and *sore*, 278/201–5 ; *care* and *more*, 494/94–6 ; *alone* and *agayne*, 237/148–50 ; *handis* and *spende*, 353/122–4 ; and others. In *liste* and *tyte*, 291/533–7 ; *wiste* and *myght*, 290/502, we seem to have only assonance. *Law* when it rimes with *ay*, 285/361–3, should be *lay*, the Norman-French form, as often actually found.

The necessities which the alliterative style imposed caused not only the frequent use of certain phrases which became almost conventional, like 'keen and cold,' 'more and mynne,' 'mengis my

[1] See p. lxxiii.

mood,' ' rede by rawe,' &c., and the recurrence of the *cheville* or fill-gap (word or words used to fill up a line, such as *bedene, on high, not to layne*), but sometimes gave a distorted sense to a word in order to fit a rime or an accent. It is true that something must be allowed for the poetic twist of words, as well as for the turn or shade of meaning peculiar, first, to the northern dialect ; second, to the period of middle English : but in a few cases nothing would explain the use of the word except the requirements of rime and alliteration. The glossary, in which I have had the valuable assistance of Dr. J. A. H. Murray, endeavours to solve these difficulties; while it offers a few conjectural meanings and suggestions in some cases where words appear to be corrupt.

It should be remarked that interjectional and vocative phrases are generally treated as prose, that is, they are outside the verse, which must be measured independently of them [1].

LANGUAGE. A few notes on the dialect, and the normal grammatic forms, will be found in Appendix III. It is unnecessary, therefore, for me to do more than point out several other peculiarities, such as the occasional suppression of the subject of the verb, pp. 277/178, 283/307, 297/146; the frequent use of the reflexive, e.g. *shames me*, p. 31, l. 62 ; *dress þe, mystris þe, melle þe*, p. 37, ll. 52, 54, 55 ; *me repentys*, p. 40, l. 15 ; *hym to for-fare*, p. 142, l. 140; the employment of the infinitive, as in *to sayne*, p. 59, l. 106; *to layne*, p. 116, l. 132, &c. Also the examples of aphetic words (to use Dr. Murray's useful coinage) i. e. words that, in poetry especially, are shortened by the loss of the first syllable; such are *stroy*, p. 41/28 ; *sente*, 49/124; *closed*, 94/29 ; *dure*, 95/66 ; *legge*, 131/147; *half*, 207/192; *cordis*, 208/226 ; *langis*, 215/442; *ray, paire*, 221/38, 224/114; *saie*, 274/99.

In the two pieces (IV and XLI), copied in 1558, are, as may be expected, a few variations, *fewle* for *fowle* or *foule*, 18/13; *hais* for *has* 19/42, 438/156 ; *aige* for *age*, *haith* for *hath*, 445/387 ; &c. Both language and metre of XLI show that it was composed at a later date than the rest.

Hye, 211/329; *hus*, 439/194; *herand*, 168/233 ; *arme* for *harme*, 105/101, show the mis-placed aspirate, rare in the northern dialect.

---

[1] For examples, see pp. 279, l. 210, 280, l. 255, 294, l. 62, 339, l. 60.

The French *bewchires*, *as armes*, *belamy*, *boudisch*, *boyste*, and *duge peres*, common in Northern poetry, and elsewhere, appear to come in just as naturally as *dame*, *bewte*, and other French words which do not now seem extraordinary. No doubt they were regarded as fine words, fit for poetry and exalted persons (though not confined to these last); compare, too, the *a-diew* of Cayphas, 257/87, the *bene-venew* of Pilate, 282/281, and the address of Herod to Jesus, 297/146, 300/234.

GENERAL REMARKS. We are not told of how many stages the York pageants were made; no doubt some of the plays would require either two platforms or one stage and the street. But it is quite evident that sometimes two scenes were represented on the stage together; the alternate action of Moses and the Hebrews, Pharaoh and his men, must both have been seen by the audience (pp. 80–91); the management of the scenes in the 'Entry into Jerusalem' is only to be understood on this supposition (pp. 202, &c.); the scenes which took place in the high priest's and Pilate's halls, and before Herod, when Judas was denied by the porter, or when the prisoner was brought, depended for much of their effect on the double action being present together. Even in the later play of the Purification (pp. 436-444) it is probable that the Temple and Bethlehem were seen near together, to say nothing of Simeon's house. In the 'Descent of the Holy Spirit' two distinct scenes must have been apparent to the spectators on the stage at the same time (pp. 467–471). At Paris[1], in a MS. of the *Mistére de la Passion*, played at Valenciennes in 1547, there is a most curious picture of the stage then employed, drawn by one of the actors (H. Cailleau) himself, which helps us to realize how double and treble scenes were understood. The scenery was either painted or modeled at the back of the stage, with the name of each place written over it, beginning with Paradise at one end, Nazareth, the Temple, Jerusalem, the Palace, &c., intervening, till we arrive at Limbo and the indispensable Hell-mouth at the other. Towards the front at one side is a green tract for the sea, with a ship upon it. Our York

---

[1] Bib. Nat., MS. réservé Fr. 12536. Other pictures in the same MS. are very instructive to the student of these early dramas, e. g. on fos. 193, 294. A large model of the stage made from Cailleau's picture may be seen in the Bibliothèque of the Grand Opera, Paris.

stages, being movable, were by no means so ambitious or so advanced as this great stage where Arnoul Gréban's vast drama might be performed, but the germs of dramatic convention must have been well understood, even if the employment of 'le décor simultané [1]' had not begun.

What appear to be indications of a prompter may be noted on pp. 246, 285. The MS. of the Scriveners' Play is the only separate prompter's book now known [2]. The actors, especially in going off the stage, sometimes addressed the audience directly ; see evidences of this on p. 29, l. 15, p. 432, and at the end of XVII, XXI, and XXIV [3]. At the beginning, too, of Play XXII the Devil, entering with a bluster as usual, seems to be pushing aside some part of the audience as he enters, for there are but three other personages in the play.

As to the dress of the actors at York, we have remarkably little information; that the doctors in the Temple wore furred gowns (p. 168, l. 232) is the only indication I have noted.

An open-minded perusal of these plays will be enough to rebut the ignorant sneers that have been made (by Oliver, Warton, and others) against the earnestness or the capacity of the original dramatists of this order. Well-read in the bible, especially in the New Testament, and in the dependent legends allowed in those times, the imagination of this author had considerable play within his prescribed limits; a facile versifier (albeit aided by the conventional rules for his craft handed down from old time), he displayed not a little dramatic power in the arrangement of scenes with the means at his command (see especially Play XXV). Observant of human nature and sympathetic, his calls on the domestic affections are well worth notice, in the womanly weakness of Mary and the trustfulness of Joseph in the *Flight into Egypt*, outraged

---

[1] See the study by M. Franc. Sarcey in *Le Temps* for 6 Août, 1883. This picture has also been realized by M. M. Sepet, in chap. v. of his 'Drame chrétien au Moyen-âge,' Paris, 1878.

[2] Every craft must have had their own play-book, not only at York, but elsewhere; it was often referred to as the ' orygynall,' ' regynall ' or 'new rygenale ;' see before pp. 18, 29, and Sharp's Diss. on Cov. Mysteries, as to Coventry play-books, 36, 37 note, 48, and as to Bassingbourne, p. 34. The Goldsmiths of Newcastle mention ' oure playe-book.' Brand's Hist. ii. 371.

[3] So in Gréban's *Passion*, at the end of the first day the actor speaks to the public, ' Demain retournez, sil vous plest,' ed. MM. G. Paris et Raynaud, Paris, 1878, p. 129.

motherly affection in the *Massacre of the Innocents*, parental distress between love and duty in *Abraham's Sacrifice*[1], in the dutiful relationship of children shown by Isaac, and the sons of Noah and Pilate. The figures of Mary and Jesus stand out with simplicity and dignity, in no way grotesque. These finer touches stand in relief to the brutality of the scenes connected with the Passion which were deemed necessary to heighten the effect of the Saviour's sufferings.

Like a true artist, the dramatist called up mirth over incidents harmless enough; he allowed Noah's wife to flout her husband, the Shepherd to sing with a cracked throat, and Judas to be covered with ridicule and abuse by the Porter. The Porter or Beadle, in fact, plays an important part in several plays (XXV, XXX, &c.). The people must have fun and show, noise and light. The principal personage in a play, whether he is wanted at the beginning or not, generally comes on the stage first, with a long speech, in the case of Noah, Abraham, Deus, and Jesus, with befitting gravity and seriousness; in the case of Satan, Pharaoh, Herod, Pilate, and Caiaphas it is daring, pompous, and blustering, in that of Pilate tempered by a sense of benevolence and justice which runs through his actions. (This writer was surprisingly lenient to Pilate, and cannot have been tainted by the old legend of his gruesome fate.) We can picture the people expectant, listening with eyes and ears for the entry and the rant of the hero of the piece. Nor were the effects of music and light neglected; the Shepherds must have both heard singing and sung themselves (p. 120, l. 59); the music itself is actually written for Play XLVI, and in several places[2] we have stage directions for singing. The Transfiguration was accompanied by a cloud and a 'noys herde so hydously,' possibly for thunder[3]. Besides the star of Bethlehem bright lights were used at the Birth, Transfiguration, and Betrayal of Jesus, and in the Vision of Mary to Thomas[4].

---

[1] For pathos and tenderness of treatment the play on Abraham and Isaac in a fifteenth century MS. recently disinterred by Dr. G. H. Kingsley, at Brome in Suffolk, exceeds all others on this subject yet known. See *Anglia*, Band vii. Heft 3 (1884), where it is printed and compared.

[2] Pp. 177, 218, 493, &c.   [3] See pp. 190, 191.

[4] It may be noted that, perhaps complying with a stage necessity, the principal actors generally lay down to rest or to sleep when an angel or a vision was to appear. See pp. 110, 137, 139, 483. Not so, however, on p. 119.

Touches of current life and usage here and there stand out amid the ancient story; the carpenters' tools and measurement used by Noah, as well as those employed at the Crucifixion; the bitter cold weather at the Nativity, telling of a truly northern Christmas; the quaint offerings of the shepherds; the ruin of the poor by murrain in the account of the Ten Plagues; the drinking between Pilate and his wife; the sleeping of Herod; and the excellent representation of a heavy manual job by a set of rough workmen in the Crucifixion (pp. 354–6). Illustrative too of English custom and forms of justice are the borrowing of the town beast (p. 203); Judas offering himself as bond-man in his remorse (p. 314); the mortgage of a property (raising money by wed-set, p. 318) : and the trial scenes in Plays XXIX, XXX, XXXII, and XXXIII, in which Pilate 'in Parlament playne' (p. 308) vindicates the course of law, and puts down the eager malice of the accuser Caiaphas and the sharp pursuer Annas. Even Herod makes proclamation for the accusers to appear, and sympathizes with the oppressed,

> 'Sen þat he is dome [dumb], for to deme hym,
> Ware þis a goode lawe for a lorde?' (P. 305.)

Note too the sturdy common morality that will not tell a lie (p. 414) and that scorns a traitor's baseness (pp. 230, 231).

Opportunity is improved in Play VII to enforce the necessity of tithes, and in XXI to inculcate the virtue of baptism, repeated in XLIII, stanza 17.

The value of the religious plays and players in leading up to what is called 'the regular drama' has not yet perhaps been fully recognized. Many allusions to them in old writers, Robert of Brunne, Chaucer, Langland, Heywood, &c. have been noticed. If Chaucer[1] and Shakespeare caught at Herod, Erasmus or his translator Udall remembered Pilate's voice, 'when he heard a certain oratour speaking out of measure loude and high, and altogether in Pilate's voice[2],' and Sackville, in his Induction to the 'Mirror for Magistrates' describes the gloominess of Hell mouth. Reforming preachers very early began the crusade against them. Wiclif deprecates those 'þat kan best pleie a pagyn of the deuyl' at Christmas[3]; and an interesting witness to their effect and popularity is the

---

[1] Miller's Tale, ll. 3383–4.
[2] 'The Apothegmes of Erasmus,' Roberts' reprint 1877, p. 382.
[3] 'English Works,' Early Eng. Text Soc. p. 206.

treatise or sermon against miracle plays[1], written in the fourteenth century, showing how men and women wept at the sights before them, and gave credence to many lies as well as truths by their means. Shakespeare, in his good humoured way, laughs at the alliteration, the craftsmen players, and the stage bombast all grown conventional and out of date, as he does at the Vice of the moralities [2], but he too was not ashamed to borrow one of their prominent characters. The study of the Janitor or Porter who appears twice, needs must with a great deal of knocking, always with a voluble tongue, in several plays of this series, will, I think, add conviction to Prof. Hales' suggestion [3], that the idea of the Porter, and his action in Macbeth, Act II. Sc. 3, was an adaptation of an old familiar friend, although it happens that he does not appear here in the Harrowing of Hell. (Hell personified is the Porter in the *Cursor*, see ll. 18075–18148.) The Janitor in Play XXV is an important person, but not Shakespeare's model; it is in the Porters of XXVI (p. 226, to whom the Italian Porter, p. xxxv, *note* 2, is akin) and XXX (pp. 279, 280) that we may seek the likeness of their much discussed successor, with the knocking that accompanied him.

Ben Jonson could not get rid of the traditional entry when, as Prof. Ward points out, he sent his devil on to the stage with a bluster [4]. But by Prynne's days religious plays had indeed become 'ridiculous' if not incredible [5].

TREATMENT IN EDITING. In this print the manuscript is rendered as faithfully as possible; the text is never altered without notice: but the corruptions which became apparent on a study

---

[1] Printed in Reliquiæ Antiquæ, ii. 42, and by Mätzner, Alteng. Sprachproben, 1869, Band I, Abth. II, 224.

[2] Mids. N. Dream, I, sc. 2, V, ll. 147, 148: Hamlet, III, sc. 2, 'out-herods Herod:' Hen. V, IV, sc. 4, 'roaring devil.' Twelfth N., IV, sc. 2 (song); 2 Hen. IV, III, sc. 2, l. 298, 'Vice's dagger.'

[3] On the Porter in Macbeth. New Shak. Soc. Trans., Part ii, 1874, pp. 264-66.

[4] 'The Devil is an Asse,' Act i.

[5] 'Histriomastix,' 1633, p. 117. Yet their relics lived on, e. g. the shows at Bartholomew's Fair in the beginning of last century, one of which ('a little Opera') gave fourteen scenes, six from the Old Testament, eight from the New, but avoiding the introduction of the Passion. Another had 'Noah's Ark with all the beasts, two by two, and all the Fowls of the air seen in a prospect sitting upon the Trees.' See the original play-bills in 'Social Life in the reign of Queen Anne' by John Ashton, pp. 256, 257. And to our own day the old play of St. George survives among the Christmas mummers who still go about the country.

of the metre, rendered several suggestions necessary[1]. This corruption of the text is worse in Plays XXVIII to XXXII than the rest, so much so that in a few parts it has been impossible to recognize the stanzas, whole lines, even groups of lines, being dropt out, others, or parts of others, displaced, and once or twice interlopers admitted. The stage directions, which are few, are usually clear, but in one or two cases they are so confused with the text that it is rendered doubtful[2]. The ear of the copyist also misled him (see pp. 266, 279, 508). One source of difficulty was the exorbitant length of some of the lines, which led the copyist to divide them, irrespective of rime or of co-relative lines. I thought it better to leave these as they stand, but have coupled them with brackets as an indication of the verse. This system begins at page 219. Stray words occur in three places[3], which seem to betray a lapse of memory or comprehension.

In MS. the name of the craft is written at the head of each play, but nothing else. I have supplied the titles, and have collected the persons of the play, added a marginal analysis, a few stage directions[4], and the indications of scenes, which last, it is hoped, will aid the reader to a better idea of the representation. The numbering of the stanzas is also mine. Every play begins on a fresh page, but its lines run on continuously without blank or division. The only contractions used are þᵘ; þ', þᵗ, þⁱ, eu̇e, p, ꝑ, ꝉ=ser or sir, Ihu, Jerlm; which, being few and simple, are extended in the ordinary type; ħ and ꝺ are rendered by *ll* and *r* because in so late a MS. they have become merely conventional flourishes.

THE MUSIC has been set in modern notation by Mr. W. H. Cummings, who has kindly given it his careful attention, and has added a Note in explanation. A few words further upon the sources of these pieces I have set against his, and will now but add my warm acknowledgments to Mr. Cummings. I also wish to thank the Rev. S. S. Greatheed, Mr. H. Jenner of the British

---

[1] See pp. 119, 130, 135, 136, 209, &c. The word *hasted* should be *chasted*, p. 321, l. 33.

[2] See for the irregular or defective stanzas pages 33, 64, 109, 152, 174, 211, 213, 224, 227, 240, 244, 246, 249, 251, 254, 268, 270 *note* 3, 274, 275, 279, 285, 291, 305, 342, 412, 472.

[3] Pages 291 *note*, 292/9, 342/148.

[4] Among these the additions of the later hand have generally been followed; they were important, being written in the full tradition of the time.

Museum, the Rev. C. Wordsworth, and other correspondents, for most serviceable help in the enquiry into meaning and origin of both music and words. As the Sheremen and Taylors' play of Coventry, containing three English songs[1] (two sung by the shepherds, one by the women), the MS. of which was burnt in the disastrous fire at Birmingham in 1879, is the only one besides that has been found with music attached, the York play music is of the greater interest.

In conclusion, I sincerely wish that this work had fallen into more able hands than mine, but I can only hope that students will be indulgent to its shortcomings. Had all the difficulties of editing the manuscript (far greater than with a poem such as the *Cursor*) been apparent, when several years ago I formed the intention of undertaking it, they might have been sufficient to deter me; but, by the kind assistance of several friends, I believe that this interesting relic of our early literature and social life is now presented in a trustworthy and intelligible form. It is a grateful duty to acknowledge my obligations to Mr. E. Maunde Thompson, of the British Museum, and M. Paul Meyer, of Paris, for much friendly help; to Professor Skeat, who has read over the proof-sheets of the text; to Professor A. W. Ward, of Manchester, who revised my suggestions of scenery and stage directions; and to Dr. J. A. H. Murray, editor of the New English Dictionary, for valuable assistance with the Glossary, as well as other acts of friendship. My thanks are also due to Mr. J. Wilkinson, Town Clerk of York, for his courtesy and the ready access to the records of York accorded to me on occasion of two visits; to Mrs. Gutch, of York, and the Rev. Canon Raine, in materially aiding my enquiries; to Mr. Halliwell-Phillipps, Mr. H. Brigstocke Sheppard, and Mr. C. T. Martin; and to the Rev. Dr. Richard Morris, for his notes upon the language. The use of MSS. granted by Lord Herries and Mr. Quaritch is acknowledged elsewhere. All and each have been animated by the true gild-spirit of mutual help; and if the reader is enabled by these pages to call up any life-picture of the art and literature so essentially a product of the people, maintained by means of the old English gild-spirit, to these modern brethren let him give honour due.

---

[1] Printed at the end of the play in Sharp's Dissertation, pp. 113–118. No mention is made of rubricated notes occurring in the MS. of those songs, which are written for three voices.

APPENDICES

TO THE

INTRODUCTION.

I. COMPARATIVE TABLE OF ENGLISH CYCLES OF RELIGIOUS PLAYS. (See p. xlvi.)

YORK.	TOWNELEY.	COVENTRY.	CHESTER.
(B = *Beverley, see App. II.*)		*Prologue.*	*Banes or Prologue.*
First six Plays, on the Creation, Fall of Lucifer, Adam and Eve, and Garden of Eden, Man's Disobedience and Fall. (B. five plays.)[1]	1. Creatio.	1. Creation.	1. The Fall of Lucifer.
7. Sacrificium Cayme et Abell. (B.)[1]	2. Mactatio Abel.	2. Fall of man.	2. The Creation and Fall, and death of Abel.
8, 9. Building of the Ark, Noah and his Wife, and the Flood. (B.)	3. Processus Noe cum filiis.	3. Cain and Abel.	3. Noah's Flood.
10. Abraham's Sacrifice. (B.)	4. Abraham.	4. Noah's Flood: [Lamach kills Cain].	4. The Histories of Lot and Abraham.
	5. Isaac. 6. Jacob.	5. Abraham's Sacrifice.	5. Balaam and his Ass.
11. Departure of Israelites from Egypt; the ten plagues; and passage of Red Sea.	7. Processus Prophetarum[3]. 8. Pharao.	6. Moses and the two Tables. 7. The Prophets. 8. The Barrenness of Anna. 9. Mary in the Temple.	6. The Salutation and Nativity: [with prophecies, Octavian and the Sibyl].
12. Prologue of Prophets, Annunciation and visit to Elizabeth. (B.)	9. Cæsar Augustus (another prophecy of Christ). 10. Annunciatio.	10. Mary's Betrothment. 11. The Salutation and Conception.	
13. Joseph's trouble about Mary.	11. Salutacio Elizabeth.	12. Joseph's Return. 13. The Visit to Elizabeth. 14. The Trial of Joseph and Mary. 15. Birth of Christ.	
14. Journey to Jerusalem, birth of Jesus. (B.)	12. Prima Pagina Pastorum.		
15. The Angels and Shepherds. (B.)	13. Secunda Pagina Pastorum. 14. Oblacio Magorum.	16. The Adoration of the Shepherds. 17. Adoration of the Magi.	7. The Play of the Shepherds. 8. The three Kings come to Herod. 9. Offering of the three Kings.
16, 17. Coming of the three Kings to Herod, Adoration. (B.)	17. Purificacio Mariae.	18. The Purification.	11. The Purification.
41. Purification. (B.) 18. Flight into Egypt. (B.)	15. Fugacio in Ægyptum. 16. Magnus Herodus.	19. Slaughter of the Innocents. 20. Christ Disputing in the Temple.	10. Slaughter of the Innocents.
19. Massacre of the Innocents. (B.)	18. Pagina Doctorum.		
20. Christ with the Doctors in the Temple. (B.)			
21. Baptism of Jesus. (B.) 22. The Temptation. (B.)	19. Johannes Baptista.	21. The Baptism of Christ. 22. The Temptation.	12. The Temptation, and the Woman taken in Adultery.
23. The Transfiguration. 24. Woman taken in adultery: La-		23. The Woman taken in Adultery.	13. [Cure of blind man], Lazarus.

lame, and Zaccheus.
26. Conspiracy to take Jesus.
27. The Last Supper. (B.)
28. The Agony and Betrayal. (B.)
29. Peter's denial, Jesus before Caiaphas. (B.)
31, 32, 33. Trials before Herod (B.) and Pilate. (B.) [2]
32. Remorse of Judas.
30. Dream of Pilate's Wife. (B.) [2]
34. Christ led up to Calvary.

35. Crucifixion.
36. Mortificatio (B.): burial of Jesus. (B.)
37. Harrowing of Hell. (B.)
38. Resurrection (B.): the three Maries.

39. Christ appears to Mary Magdalene.
40. Travellers to Emmaus. (B.)

42. Incredulity of Thomas.
43. Ascension. (B.)
44. Descent of the Holy Spirit.
45. Death of Mary.
46. Appearance of Mary to Thomas.

47. Assumption and Coronation (B.) of Virgin.
48. The Judgment-day. (B.)

20. Conspiracio et Capcio.
21. Coliphizatio.
32. Suspentio Jude.
22. Flagellatio.
23. Processus crucis. Crucifixio.
24. Processus Talentorum.
25. Extractio animarum ab inferno.
26. Resurrectio Domini.
27. Peregrini.
28. Thomas Indiae (Incredulity).
29. Ascencio Domini.
30. Juditium.

14. Christ's Entry into Jerusalem.
15. Christ betrayed.
16. The Passion.
17. The Crucifixion.
18. The Harrowing of Hell.
19. The Resurrection [and the three Maries].
20. The Pilgrims of Emaus.
21. The Ascension.
22. The Emission of the Holy Ghost.
23. Ezechiel [prophecies of the end of the world and 15 signs of Doom].
24. Antichrist.
25. Doomsday.

26. Entry into Jerusalem.
25. The Council of the Jews.
27. The Last Supper.
28. Betraying of Christ.
29. King Herod.
30. Trial of Christ.
31. Pilate's Wife's Dream.
32. Condemnation and Crucifixion of Christ.
34. Burial of Christ.
33. The Descent into Hell.
35. Resurrection [and part of Desct.].
36. The Three Maries.
37. Christ appearing to Mary.
38. Pilgrim of Emaus [and incredulity of Thomas].
39. Ascension.
40. Descent of the Holy Ghost.
41. Assumption of the Virgin.
42. Domesday.

[1] The seventh Beverley play, 'Adam and Seth,' was probably on the subject of that legend which tells of Adam's old age, his sending Seth for the oil of mercy, and Seth's return with the three seeds which, sown under Adam's tongue, give rise to the holy trees. See Cursor Mundi for the best form of this legend, ll. 1237–1432; it also occurs in the Cornish plays Origo Mundi and Creation of the World (see App. II).

[2] 'Slepyng Pylate' of Beverley answers to Play 30 of York, in which Pilate is laid to bed, and 'Demying Pilate' to Play 33, in which Judgment on Jesus is given.

[3] The prophecies of Christ, plays Y. 12, T. 7, 9, Cov. 7, Ch. 5, and of Doomsday, Ch. 23, are combined in the Anglo-Norman (?) 'Drame d'Adam,' (A.D. 1150–1200.) See M. J. Bonnard's 'Traductions de la Bible en vers Franç. au moyen âge,' Paris, 1884. p. 120.

II.

LIST OF PLACES AND PLAYS IN GREAT BRITAIN.

THE following are the places and dates of performances (unless otherwise expressed), with the authorities for reference, distinguishing also whether a single play or a cycle, as far as known. An asterisk (*) denotes that a text remains, the editions being pointed out. The Morals at Manningtree, spoken of by Dekker, and express shows before royalty, as at Windsor or Bristol before Hen. VII, do not come within this list, except in the case of Winchester.

Dunstable, 12th century, (*St. Catherine.*) Mat. Paris, Vitæ S. Alb. Abb. Ed. Wats, 1684, p. 1007 (Gaufridi 16 abb. vita).

London, 12th century, (miracle plays.) W. Fitzstephen's Descriptio Londoniæ, printed at end of Stow's Survey of London, ed. 1598, p. 480.

Cambridge, cir. 1350, (*Ludus filiorum Israel.*) Masters, Hist. of C. C. College, ed. 1753, vol. i. p. 5.

London, Skinner's Well, Clerkenwell, 1391, (*Passion of our Lord and Creation of World,* lasted three days, ? cycle.) Stow's Survey, ed. 1598, p. 69.

London, ibid. 1409, (lasted eight days, '*of matter from the creation of the worlde,*' cycle.) Stow, Survey, ed. 1598, p. 69, Chronicle, ed. 1615, p. 337 ; Devon's Issues of the Exchequer, 11 July, 14 Rich. II, p. 244.

London, 1557, Grey Friars, (*Passion of Christ,* on Corpus Christi Day.) Strype, Eccl. Mem., ed. 1822, iii., Part ii. p. 6.

London, ? 14th and 15th centuries, Holy Trinity gild, St. Botolph without Aldersgate, (*Pageants of Holy Trinity, St. Fabyan, St. Sebastian, St. Botulf,* and '*the terement*' [Burial of Christ],) Hone's Ancient Mysteries, pp. 81, 85.

Canterbury, temp. Hen. VI, (Play of Corpus Christi, by the crafts.) 'Burgmote Orders' of the City, fo. 5 *b, cir.* 1500, MS. now in the Cathedral Library. J. Brent's Canterbury in the Olden Time, 1860, pp. 38, 47 ; who speaks of '40 acts,' and appears to confound the play with the gild of Corpus Christi.

Canterbury, 1501–2, (*Three Kyngs of Coleyn,* on Twelfth Day.) Mr. J. B. Sheppard in Hist. MSS. Commission, 9th Report, p. 147. [The 'Pagent of St. Thomas,' *ib.* p. 148, appears to have been a show, not a play.]

Winchester, 1487, (*Christi descensus ad inferos,* ? played by almsboys,) MS. Wulvesey[1], apud Winton, cited in Warton, ed. 1840, vol. ii. p. 394 ; see ib. iii. p. 267. (The late D. G. Rossetti quoted the 'Winchester Mysteries' on his picture, 'A Christmas Carol,' 1867, but I am informed that no authority for this is known. See Catalogue of the Burlington Fine Arts Club for 1883, p. 29.)

Worcester, 1467, ('Five pageants among the crafts ;' Corpus Christi.) Toulmin Smith's 'English Gilds,' 1870, p. 385 ; Municipal records, quoted in 'Outlines of Life of Shakespeare,' by J. O. Halliwell-Phillipps, 4th ed. 1884, pp. 390, 391.

Sleaford, 1477, Gild of Holy Trinity, ('Kyngyng,' i.e. *Three Kings of Cologne,* on Corpus Christi day, and *Play of the Ascension.*) Add. MS. 28,533, fos. 1 v⁰, 2.

Leicester, 1477, (*Passion Play,*) Wm. Kelly's Notices illust. of the Drama from Leicester records, 1865, p. 27. See also Thos. North's Church of St. Martin, Leicester, 1866, pp. 114, 115, for indications of other plays in 1546 and 1571.

Aberdeen, 1442–1531, (Candlemas play, *Offerand of Our Lady* ; also Corpus Christi play, 9, 7, and 10 pageants named.) Extracts from the Council Register of the Burgh of Aberdeen ; Spalding Club, Aberdeen, 1844, pp. 9, 432, 445, 451.

Edinburgh, 1503, Warton II, 224 ; 1554, (12 Oct.,) Record of the City, quoted in Sharp's Dissert. on Coventry Plays, p. 142 ; (the 'Play-field' where performed), Arnot's Hist. of Edinburgh, 1779, p. 76.

Bassingbourne, Cambridgeshire, 1511, (*Play of St. George.*) Churchwardens' Accounts, quoted by Warton, ed. 1871, vol. ii. p. 233 ; and the *Antiquary,* vol. vii. 1883, p. 25.

Bethersden, Kent, 1522, (*Ludi beatæ Christinæ.*) MS. Churchwardens' Accounts : for a copy of the items as to the play I am indebted to Rev. A. F. Smith, Vicar.

Heybridge, Essex, 1532. Churchwardens' Accounts, quoted in J. P. Collier's 'Five Miracle Plays,' 1836, Har. of Hell, p. 3.

---

[1] The Rev. F. T. Madge of the Cathedral Library, Winchester, tells me that all the Wolvesey MSS. are now in the hands of the Ecclesiastical Commissioners.

e

Wymondham, Norfolk, 1549.   Holinshed, ed. 1587, fo. 1028.

Reading, 1498–1557, (*Three Kings* at Whitsontyde ; *Resurrection* and *Passion Plays* at Easter and Palm Sunday ; *Adam, Cayme,* Corpus Christi plays.)   Churchwardens' Accounts, Hist. of St. Lawrence, Reading, by Rev. C. Kerry, 1883, pp. 233–238.

Lincoln, 1564, (Play of *Old Tobit.*)   Inventory of properties, quoted in Gentleman's Magazine, vol. 54, p. 103.

Shrewsbury, 1574, (A Stage-play acted in the High Street,) Fosbroke's Dict. of Antiquities, 1840, p. 665.

Tewkesbury, 1578, 1585.   Churchwardens' Accounts, cited in Collier, Ann. of Stage, ed. 1879, ii. 67.

Witney, Oxfordshire, 16th century, (*The Resurrection* ; a dumb show,) W. Lambarde's Dict. Angliæ Topographicum, p. 459.

Preston,
Lancaster,   } *Corpus Christi* plays, seen in reign of James I, by Weever, ' Funeral Monuments,' p. 405.
Kendall,

* **York,** about 1360–1579, (cycle of 48 plays, Corpus Christi.)   The present volume.   One play, *The Scriveners,* is also found in a separate MS., now at York Philosophical Society ; printed by J. Croft in Excerpta Antiqua, York 1797, p. 105, and by J. P. Collier, in Camden Miscellany, vol. iv. (see after p. 455).

York, before 1384 ; *Play of Our Lord's Prayer.*   MS. Compotus Roll, in possession of Canon Raine, Wiclif's Works, see before, pp. xxviii, xxix ; ' English Gilds,' p. 137.

York, 1446 ; *Creed Play,* performed every tenth year by gild of Corpus Christi.   Davies and Skaife, see before, p. xxx, *notes* 2, 3.

Beverley, 1407–1604, (cycle of 36 plays, Corpus Christi,) ' Beverlac,' by Geo. Poulson, 1829, pp. 268–275, 278 (gives list and details).   See also Lansd. MS. 896, fos. 133, 139–140.

* **Wakefield,** or neighbourhood, Towneley collection, (cycle of 32 plays.)   MS. undated, of 15th century, now in possession of Mr. B. Quaritch ; ed. by Rev. J. Stevenson, Surtees Society, 1836.   Also the third play is printed by E. Mätzner in Altenglische Sprachproben, Berlin, 1867, p. 360 ; the thirteenth in J. P. Collier's Five Miracle Plays, 1836 ; and the thirtieth by F. Douce for the Roxburgh Club, 1822.

* **Coventry,** 1468 [1], (cycle of 42 plays, Corpus Christi,) Cott. MS. Vesp. D. viii, ed. by J. O. Halliwell, Shakespeare Society, 1841.   Also

---

[1] I. e. date of the MS.

Dugdale, Mon. Angl. vol. vi. pt. 3, pp. 1534-44, prints the first five plays. T. Sharp, Dissertation on Cov. Myst. 1825, says that these were not the plays 'exhibited by the trading companies of the city,' p. 7. The tenth play is printed in Collier's Five Miracle Plays, 1836.

* **Coventry**, 1534, date of MS. only. The Shearmen and Taylors' Play, viz. *Birth of Christ and Offering of the Magi, with the Flight into Egypt and Murder of the Innocents.* MS. formerly in possession of Mr. Thos. Sharp, then at Longbridge House in the Staunton collection, afterwards burnt in the fire at Birmingham, 1879. Printed in Dissert. Cov. Myst. pp. 83-114, with copies of the music. Also, The Weavers' Play, *The Presentation in the Temple and Disputation with the Doctors*; ed. by Thos. Sharp, for the Abbotsford Club, 1836. See also J. O. Halliwell-Phillipps' 'Life of Shakespeare,' 4th ed. 1884, pp. 383-389.

* **Chester**, ? 15th century, (earliest MS. 1591 ;) cycle of 24 plays, Whitsuntide,) in five MS. originals ; ed. Thos. Wright, Shakespeare Society, 2 vols. 1843, 1847. The prologue, third and tenth plays also ed. by J. H. Markland, Roxburgh Club, 1818. The twenty-fourth (*Ante-Christ*) also ed. in Collier's Five Miracle Plays, 1836. A fragment of the nineteenth play was recently found in an old book cover by Mr. C. W. Sutton of the Free Library, Manchester, and is printed in the Manchester Guardian, 19 May, 1883.

* **Newcastle-on-Tyne**, 1426-1589, (cycle of plays, 16 known,) J. Brand's Hist. of Newcastle, 1789, vol. ii. pp. 370-372. The text of one play only, *Noah's Ark*, exists, printed by Brand, ii. 373-379, and by Hen. Bourne, History of Newcastle-on-Tyne, London, 1736, p. 139. See, too, Mackenzie, ii. pp. 664, 672, 674, 691, 696.

* **Dublin**, 15th century, (cycle, 14 plays known ; Corpus Christi,) Walter Harris, History of Dublin, London, 1766, pp. 142-148. The text of one play only, *Abraham and Isaac*, exists, MS. D iv. 18, Trinity College, Dublin (hand *temp.* Henry VI). Printed by Collier, Five Miracle Plays, 1836.

* **Norfolk** or **Suffolk**, 15th century[1], (*Play of Abraham and Isaac.*) MS. at Brome Hall *penes* Sir Edw. Kerrison. Printed in *Anglia* (Halle) Band VII, Heft 3, 1884, pp. 316-337, also in Mr. Walter Rye's Norfolk Antiquarian Miscellany, vol. iii. part i.

[1] Date of the MS.

* **Croxton** (? the county, perhaps Norfolk), 1461 [1]. *The Play of the Sacrament*, MS. F iv. 20, Trinity College, Dublin ; ed. by Prof. Whitley Stokes, Transactions of the Philological Society, 1860–1, Berlin, Appendix, pp. 101–152.

* **Cornwall**, 14th century [1], (*Origo Mundi, Passio Domini Nostri, Resurrexio Domini Nostri*, three plays forming the complete cycle of subjects taken by Corpus Christi plays), [2] In Cornish. Ed. and trans. by Edwin Norris, 'Ancient Cornish Drama,' Oxford, 1859.

* **Cornwall**, 1504 [1], (*Life of St. Meriasek*,) Hengwrt MS. at Peniarth. In Cornish. Ed. and trans. by Prof. Whitley Stokes, London (Trübner), 1872.

* **Cornwall**, 1611 [1], but ? older, (*The Creation of the World.*) In Cornish. Ed. and translated by Prof. Whitley Stokes, for the Philological Society, Berlin, 1863.

* Besides these, five other plays have been preserved, nothing being known of where they were performed. One of these is the oldest English play or dramatic poem, the famous *Harrowing of Hell*. MS. Harl. 2253, fo. 55 *b*, temp. Edw. II or Edw. III, in Southern dialect. Printed by Collier, 'Five Miracle Plays,' and separately by J. O. Halliwell, London, 1840. An imperfect copy, of the first half of 14th century, in the Auchinleck MS. (Edinburgh), fos. 35–37, was printed by D. Laing, in 'Owain Miles and other inedited fragments of ancient English poetry,' Edinburgh, 1837. See also 'Englische Studien,' vol. vii. part i. p. 182, and the references there given.

The others are, *The Burial of Christ* and the *Resurrection*, a group of two played at Easter ; early 16th century [1] ; Bodl. MS. E. mus. 160 ; printed by Halliwell in 'Reliquiæ Antiquæ,' 1843, vol. ii. p. 124, and re-printed by New Shakspere Society, 1882, with 'Digby Mysteries.' *The Killing of the Children* [or Candlemas Day], *Conversion of St. Paul*, and *Mary Magdalene*, in two parts ; ? 1480–90. Digby MS. 133 at Oxford. Ed. F. J. Furnivall, 'Digby Mysteries,' New Shakspere Society, 1882. Also edited by Thos. Sharp for the Abbotsford Club, 1836. The first of these was also printed by Hawkins, 'Origin of English Drama,' 1773, and by Marriott, 'English Miracle Plays,' Basel, 1838.

---

[1] Date of the MS.

[2] The Cornish plays do not include the Marian legends; on the other hand they treat the tree-legend pretty fully.

III.

NOTES ON THE DIALECT[1] AND GRAMMAR.

I. **The Dialect** in the main is that of Hampole's *Pricke of Conscience*[2]. The grammar of the Northumbrian may be found in the Introduction to Hampole. See also Hampole's Psalms, ed. Bramley[3]; and more particularly the 'Dialect of the Southern Counties of Scotland,' by Dr. J. A. H. Murray (Philological Society, 1873), pp. 5, 37–39, 150–230.

II. A Midland (literary) scribe has altered much both in the way of grammar and orthography; in neither case have the changes been methodically made. The Northumbrian, it is known, was influenced by the Midland where the two dialects were contiguous.

III. Comparison with Hampole's works, or with any good Northumbrian specimen, shows that wholesale changes have been made in the rhyme-endings as well as elsewhere. The great change is from *a* to *o, fro, moste,* p. 1 ; *onely,* p. 2 ; goes = gas, p. 3 ; cf. wa-la-way and wo, p. 5; but *ane* and *wa* are left, p. 5; cf. oondis = aandes, p. 116. In the rhyme lines the scribe has only partly altered these.

Thus, gone and mone rhyme with nane and -ane, p. 62.

Cf. gane with one ⎫
    tane with slone ⎬ pp. 90, 91.
    taste and most, p. 218. ⎭

Cf. langis ⎫
    wrong ⎬ p. 215.
    thrang ⎭

Cf. go ⎫
  fro ⎬ p. 7
  bothe ⎭

broode ⎫ p. 16
made ⎭

with ta / ga / ma / alswa — p. 101, where all the *a*'s are kept.

---

[1] Based on some remarks kindly supplied by the Rev. Dr. R. Morris.

[2] Edited, with Introduction and Notes, by Dr. Richard Morris, for the Philological Society, Berlin, 1863.

[3] The Psalms of David, with a translation and exposition in English by Richard Rolle of Hampole. Edited from manuscripts by the Rev. H. R. Bramley. Oxford, Clarendon Press, 1884. Hampole's work in the *Pricke of Conscience* is unalliterative verse in couplets; in the Psalter it is prose. Hampole was a Yorkshireman; he died Sept. 29, 1349.

Cf. more
-fore } p. 97, and others } with { þare
þore } in pp. 197, 198 }   { sare
wore }   { care } p. 103.
                                    { mare }

Cf. more
fore } p. 54, with { sare
yore }   { mare   } p. 139.
                     { ayre = are }

Cf. wore, fore, p. 170, with ware, fare, p. 171.

So holde } one *o* rhymes   So gone } p. 106.
calde } with three } p. 99.   -ane }
alde   } *a*'s.   hole } p. 263.
talde }   bale }

                                    wroþe } p. 140.
                                    skathe }

The rhymes more, -fore, þore, wore, are for *mare, are* (= before),
þ*are, ware.*

In the Northern dialect *more* (being mare) does not rhyme with
-fore.

Hence we get bad rhymes like—

werre   soo = swa } p. 211.
-fore } p. 130 (see p. 139).   to   }
-more   stone = stane } p. 212.
                                    done   }
wore } p. 170 (see p. 173).
fare }   fro = fra } p. 214.
                                    too   }
roppe = rape } p. 178.
jape   }

P. 135.   Here is a bad rhyme, which may easily be set right—

fende) *Boune* does not = *bounden* here though it does elsewhere ;
boune { bale may be taken as gen. s. ; and *bende* = bond will be
amende { the correct rhyme. (See O. E. Miscellany, p. 142 ;
kende) Gamelyn, l. 831.)

On p. 140, *olde* rhymes with *belde* ; but *olde* does not = alde, old, but
elde = age.   So correct to *elde*.

Other bad rhymes are—

goo = ga. } p. 60.   come }
-too   }   home } p. 154.
                                    gome }
fone } p. 65.
sone }

boone = bunden
sone = sone   } p. 157 (see bune, begune, p. 262).
begonne = begunnen)

were ⎱
are ⎬ p. 238.
bere ⎰

honde = hande ⎱ p. 261.
ronne ⎰

foune ⎱ p. 261.
boune ⎰

more ⎱ p. 302.
þere ⎰

IV. Peculiarities of Orthography:—

(a) We find a double letter after a long vowel, as—cesse rhymes encrese, p. 127 ; encresse rhymes chase = encrese and chese, p. 186 ; esse—plese, p. 202 ; heppe—leppe = hepe and lepe, p. 150 ; latte—abatte = late and abate, p. 148 ; cf. wotte—gate = wate and gate, p. 148 ; cf. spakke—take, p. 186 ; late—watte, p. 182 ; hette—fete, p. 181 ; sette—ette = ete, p. 234 ; latte, gatte, hatte = làte, gate, hate, p. 213 ; latt = layte, rhymes consayte, p. 208 ; fudde = fude, rhymes blude, p. 83 ; deffe = defe, p. 267/337 ; wiffe, liffe, p. 282/294, 299.

(b) u = o, fure and blure = fore and blore, p. 85 ; cf. mode and gud, hune and sone, p. 209.

(c) ay is written for a (modern o) ; layre, fayre, pp. 78, 79 ; fays = fas, p. 79. So bayle is written for bale ; i is omitted in fraste, p. 76 ; brayþe = braþe rhymes wroþe = wraþe, p. 225.

(d) Note the senseless e's in wedde, cledde, bredde = wed, cled, bred, p. 94, and many others.

(e) sight and wryte = site (sorrow) and write, p. 150.

(f) y = e ; cf. drygh and nygh, p. 298, for dregh (see dergh for dregh, p. 349/2) ; bryme = breme (fierce), and deme, p. 306.

(g) Occasional instances of gh for w, very common in Hampole—laugher = lawer, lower, p. 281/275 ; aughen = own, p. 100/202 ; saughe = saw, p. 129/86.

(h) There is a very corrupt rhyme on p. 293 ; to blowes (an inf., read 'to blawe') rhymes with lawes, knawe, and sawes. These s's are all wrong.

V. Non-Northumbrian forms are—such for swilk, p. 186/21 ; which for whilk, p. 340/98 ; as for als ; erly for arly, p. 49/114 ; farrar = ferre, pp. 72, 73 ; sterres = sternes, p. 400 ; brayne for harnes (brains), p. 333 ; euyll for ill, p. 127 (see pp. 129, 133) ; sleeis = slas, p. 141/115 ; dong = dungen, p. 331/332 ; hande = hende, p. 190 (see the rhymes on pp. 339/79, 82 and 376/73, 75, also pp. 235/56, 424/114) ; sche = scho, sho, p. 194/17, 33. Churl, chorl for carl, korl, on account of the alliteration ? p. 280/242 (cf. 338/37) ; woll for will, p. 374/328 ; bretheren for brether, p. 347/37.

VI. Grammar :—

[The following are the normal forms of Northern Middle English.

NOUNS. The *plural* is formed in *is, ys, s,* occasionally in *es.* The few exceptions are pl. in *en,* as *eghen, eghne, oxen, shoon, fan,* or *fon* = foes ; in *er, childer* ; vowel-change, as *brether, fet, hend, men, ky, mys ;* plural unchanged, as *schepe, swyne, dere, nowt, horse.*—The *genitive singular* ends usually in *es, s,* but often (especially when it had not *es* in O. E.) is quite uninflected ; '*in a worme likenes,*' 23/23, *syster sone.*

ADJECTIVES are uninflected for number, gender, or case. Relics of the O. E. genitive plural in *-ra* remain in *althermast, alderbest, allers, althers,* and with additional *-(e)s* in *bather(e)s* —The *comparison* is often in *-ar(e*[1], and *ast(e, ast,* instead of *er* and *est* ; the comparatives, *ferre, nerre* or *narre, werre* or *warre,* farther, worse, nearer, are also found.

The terminations *-lic, -like, -ly* interchange.

PRONOUNS. 1 *pers. s.,* Ic, ik, I ; 3 *pers. f. sing.,* sco, scho, sho ; pl. þai, þaim, þam. *Possessives,* ur, our, owr, ȝour, ȝowre, yhowre, thair, thayr ; ures, oures, ȝoures, thairs. *Demonstratives,* þa, þas(e, tho, those, þir, þer, these, swilk, ilka. Qua, qhua, quhether, quhilk, are Northern forms of the *interrogative,* but are not found in the plays.

VERBS. The inflexion of the *present indicative* is to be specially noted. It has two forms, the one used with the proper pronoun immediately preceding or following[2]:—

Sing. Ic, I, syng(e,	*Pl.* we syng(e,
þu synges,	ȝe syng(e,
he synges ;	þai syng(e ;

the other takes *-s* or *-es* throughout, when the subject is either absent, or is another word than the personal pronoun, e.g. a noun, relative, &c. :—

    Sing. I that synges ;
    Pl. we that synges,
      ȝe that synges.
      þe briddes synges.
      we ga hame and tas reste.

Past tense, and *past participle* of weak verbs end with *id, yd, ed, d, t.*

Past part. of strong verbs in *en, yn, in, n.*

Present or *active part.* in *and, ande.*

Gerund or verbal substantive in *ing, yng.*

The *imperative,* 2 pers. pl. ends in *is, ys, es, s,* when the pronoun is absent. *Gas hame! Ga ȝhe hame.*

---

[1] The bracket (signifies that the *e* is sometimes present, sometimes absent.
[2] Murray, *Dialect of Southern Counties of Scotland,* p. 212.

The chief PHONOLOGICAL peculiarities are,—

In certain cases *a* replaces the Southern *o*, as *gast, sang*, stan, mare[1].

k	„	„	*ch*	„ kyrke.
f	„	„	*v*	„ doufe, gif.
sc	„	„	*sh*	„ scryke (shriek).
hard *g*	„	„	soft *dg*	„ bryg.
gh	„	„	*w*	„ felagh, aghen.
ȝ	„	„	*g*	„ ȝates.

ORTHOGRAPHICALLY, ȝ was retained for *y*, as in ȝearn.

It has been shown by Dr. Murray that in the Northern dialect *-i* or *-y* was added to another vowel simply to lengthen it (like silent *e* nowe), not to make a diphthong, *gais = gās* (*gaes, gase*), *dois = dōs* (*does, dose*), *hais = has* (*hase, haes*), *stroyd = strōd* (*strood*), *rois = rōs* (*rose*). This will often explain apparent difficulties of rhyme.

Specially Northern are *thethen, hethen, whethen* ; *fra* = from, til = to, intil = into ; sall = shall, suld = shuld ; what-kyn, thus-gates, sa-gates, no-gates ; swilk, slyke = such, whilk = which.

L. T. S.]

(1) The Midland scribe has introduced -st and -th for -es or -s (verb), see pp. 99/192, 104/51, 108/180, 162/139, 228/208, 229/225, 235/57, 260/149, 351/64.

(2) Shall, shulde, sulde, for sall and salde, *passim* ; see shalle for sall, p. 15.

(3) Aren for ere, p. 63/235 ; are for ere, p. 70/29.

(4) þei, þer, þem, for þai, þair, þar, þam, þaim, *passim* ; tho for *tha, thas* those ; *hem* once, on p. 281 !!

(5) The contraction of the passive participles : boune, foune, or bone, fone, for bunden, funden, pp. 11, 56, 65, 98/155, 131/136, 135, 157, 261, 262, 263. This is common in modern northern dialects : sc. *bun'* for *bounden*, &c. See the bad rhymes, p. 261.

---

[1] Note that O. E. *á* remained in the North, while in the 13th century it became *o* in the South ; so in most of the other phonological changes, the North has the older forms.

INDEX TO INTRODUCTION AND NOTES,

WITH EXPLANATIONS OF NAMES OF THE CRAFTS[1].

[1] This Index includes all the crafts named in this volume. The edition of *Liber Albus* referred to is the Latin one; Bardsley's *History of Surnames*, also consulted, contains several errors founded on Drake's misapprehension of the part taken by the crafts in the plays and the procession.

THE PLAYS

PERFORMED BY

THE CRAFTS OF YORK.

The Creation, and the Fall of Lucifer.

(First quire is unsigned.)

[PERSONS OF THE PLAY.

DEUS.
PRIMUS ANGELUS SERAPHYN.
ANGELUS CHERABYN.
PRIMUS ANGELUS DEFICIENS, LUCIFER. } *Each changes into*
SECUNDUS ANGELUS DEFICIENS.   } diabolus in inferno.]

[SCENE I, *Heaven.*]

[**Deus.**]   *Ego sum Alpha et O. vita via*
              Veritas primus et nouissimus.

Genesis i. 1–5.
Jude 6.

1. I am gracyus and grete, god withoutyn begynnyng,
   I am maker vnmade, all mighte es in me,
   I am lyfe and way vnto welth wynnyng,
   I am formaste and fyrste, als I byd sall it be.   4
   My blyssyng o ble sall be blendyng,
   And heldand fro harme to be hydande[1],
   My body in blys ay abydande
   Vne[n]dande withoutyn any endyng.   8

The attributes of God.

2. Sen I am maker vnmade, and moste so of mighte,
   And ay sall be endeles, and noghte es but I,
   Vnto my dygnyte dere sall diewly be dyghte
   A place full of plente to my plesyng at ply,   12

The unending creator shall have a place to delight him,

---

[1] MS. has *hyndande.*

B

And therewith als wyll I haue wroght
Many dyuers doynges be-dene,
Whilke warke sall mekely contene,
And all sall be made euen of noghte.   16

3. But onely þe worthely warke of my wyll
In my sprete sall enspyre þe mighte of me,
And in þe fyrste, faythely, my thoghts to full-fyll,
Baynely in my blyssyng I byd at here be   20
A blys al-beledande abowte me ;

In þe whilke blys I byde at be here
Nyen ordres of aungels full clere,
In louyng ay lastande at lowte me.   24

Tunc cantant ang[eli][1] *Te deum [laudamus te dominum*
confitemur][1].

4. Here vndernethe me nowe a nexile I neuen,
Whilke Ile sall be erthe now, all be at ones
Erthe haly and helle, þis hegheste be heuen,
And that welth[2] sall welde sall won in þis wones.   28
Thys graunte I ȝowe mynysters myne,
To-whils ȝhe ar stabill in thoghte ;
And also to þaime þat ar noghte   31
Be put to my presone at pyne.   [*To Lucifer :*

5. Of all þe mightes I haue made moste nexte after me,
I make þe als master and merour of my mighte,
I beelde þe here baynely in blys for to be,
I name þe for Lucifer, als berar of lyghte.   36
No thyng here sall þe be derand,
In þis blis sall be ȝhour beeldyng,
And haue al welth in ȝoure weledyng,
Ay whils ȝhe ar buxumly berande.   40

---

[1] In the MS. these words are obliterated.   [2] MS. has *wethth.*

Tunc cantant angeli, Sanctus sanctus sanctus, dominus deus
sabaoth.

6. **Primus angelus seraphyn.**   A ! mercyfull maker, full
    mekill es þi mighte,
Þat all this warke at a worde worthely has wroghte,
Ay loved be þat lufly lorde of his lighte,   43
That vs thus mighty has made, þat nowe was righte noghte ;
In blys for to byde in hys blyssyng,
Ay lastande, in luf lat vs lowte hym,
At beelde vs thus baynely abowete hym,
Of myrthe neuermore to haue myssyng.   48

7. **Primus angelus deficiens Lucifere.**   All the myrth þat es
    made es markide in me,
Þe bemes of my brighthode ar byrnande so bryghte,
And I so semely in syghte my selfe now I se,   51
For lyke a lorde am I lefte to lende in þis lighte,
More fayrear be far þan my feres,
In me is no poynte þat may payre,
I fele me fetys and fayre,
My powar es passande my peres.   56

8. **Ang. cherabyn.**   Lord ! wyth a lastande luf we loue þe
    allone,
Þou mightefull maker þat markid vs and made vs,
And wroghte us thus worthely to wone in this wone [1],
Ther neuer felyng of fylth may full vs nor fade vs.   60
All blys es here beeldande a-boute vs,
To-whyls we are stabyll in thoughte
In þe worschipp of hym þat us wroghte
Of dere neuer thar vs more dowte vs.   64

9. **Prim. ang. defic.**   O ! what I am fetys and fayre and
    fygured full fytt !
Þe forme of all fayrehede apon me es feste,

---

[1] MS. *wonus.*

B 2

All welth in my weelde es, I wete be my wytte,

þe bemes of my brighthede are bygged with þe beste.   68

My schewyng es schemerande and schynande,

So bygly to blys am I broghte,

Pain will never
pine me.
Me nedes for to noy me righte noghte,

Here sall neuer payne me be pynande.   72

10. Ang. seraphyn. With all þe wytt at we welde we wyrschip
þi wyll,

þu gloryus god þat es grunde of all grace,

Angels praise
God with stead-
fast voice.
Ay with stedefaste steuen lat vs stande styll,

Lorde! to be fede with þe fode of thi fayre face.   76

In lyfe that es lely ay lastande,

lf. 3 b.
Thi dale, lorde, es ay daynetethly delande,

And who so þat fode may be felande

To se thi fayre face es noght fastande.   80

11. Prim. ang. defec. Lucifer. Owe! certes! what I am
worthely wroghte with wyrschip, i-wys!

For in a glorius gle my gleteryng it glemes,

'How splendid
and mighty I am,
I am so mightyly made my mirth may noghte mys,   83

Ay sall I byde in this blys thorowe brightnes of bemes.

Me nedes noghte of noy for to neuen,

All welth in my welde haue I weledande,

I shall dwell in
the highest
heaven.'
Abowne ȝhit sall I be beeldand,

On heghte in þe hyeste of hewuen.   88

Boasting and
pride before
a fall.
12. Ther sall I set my selfe, full semely to seyghte,

To ressayue my reuerence thorowe righte o renowne,

I sall be lyke vnto hym þat es hyeste on heghte;   91

Owe! what I am derworth and defte.—Owe! dewes! all
goes downe [1]!

The devils fall.
My mighte and my mayne es all marrande,

Helpe! felawes, in faythe I am fallande.

Sec. ang. defec. Fra heuen are we heledande on all hande,

To wo are we weendande, I warande.   96

---

[1] Line 92 is cut into two lines in the MS.

[Scene II, *Hell.*]

13. **Lucifer deiabolus in inferno.** Owte owte ! harrowe ! 'Oh ! it is so hot
    helples, slyke hote at es here,   here ! my comli-
ness is now black
and blue.'
This es a dongon of dole þat I am to-dyghte,
Whare es my kynde be-come, so cumly and clere,
Nowe am I laytheste, allas ! þat are was lighte.   100
My bryghtnes es blakkeste and blo nowe ;
My bale es ay betande and brynande,
That gares ane go gowlande and gyrnande.
Owte ! ay walaway ! I well enew in wo nowe !   104

14. **Secundus diabolus.** Owte ! owte ! I go wode for wo, my lf. 4.
    wytte es all wente nowe,
All oure fode es but filth, we fynde vs beforn,
We þat ware beelded in blys in bale are we brent nowe,
Owte ! on þe Lucifer, lurdan ! oure lyghte has þu lorne. 108 Lamentation of
the devils who
turn round and
abuse Lucifer,
their leader.
Þi dedes to þis dole nowe has dyghte us,
To spill vs þu was oure spedar,
For thow was oure lyghte and oure ledar,
Þe hegheste of heuen hade þu hyght vs.   112

15. **Lucifer in inferno.** Walaway ! wa ! es me now, nowe es
    it war thane it was.
Vnthryuandely threpe ȝhe, I sayde but a thoghte.
Secund. diab. We ! lurdane, þu lost vs.
Luc. in inf.   ȝhe ly, owte ! allas !
I wyste noghte þis wo sculde be wroghte.   116
Owte on ȝhow ! lurdans, ȝhe smore me in smoke.
Secund. diab. This wo has þu wroghte vs.
Luc. in inf.   ȝhe ly, ȝhe ly !
Secund. diab. Thou lyes, and þat sall þu by,
We lurdans haue at ȝowe, lat loke.   120

[SCENE III, *Heaven.*]

16. **Angelus cherubyn.**   A ! lorde, louid be thi name þat vs
       þis lighte lente,
     Sen Lucifer oure ledar es lighted so lawe
     For hys vnbuxumnes in bale to be brente,

     Thi rightwysnes to rewarde on rowe.   124
     Ilke warke eftyr is wroghte
     Thorowe grace of þi mercyfull myghte,
     The cause I se itt in syghte,

     Wharefore to bale he es broghte.   128

17. **Deus** [1].   Those foles for þaire fayre-hede in fantasyes fell,
     And hade mayne of mighte þat marked þam and made
       þam,

     For-thi efter þaire warkes were, in wo sall þai well,
     For sum ar fallen into fylthe þat euermore sall fade þam,
     And neuer sall haue grace for to gyrth þam.   133
     So passande of power tham thoght þam,
     Thai wolde noght me worschip þat wroghte þam,
     For-þi sall my wreth euer go with þam.   136

18. Ande all that me wyrschippe sall wone here, i-wys,

     For-thi more forthe of my warke wyrke nowe I will.
     Syn than þer mighte es for-marryde þat mente all o-mys,
     Euen to myne awne fygure þis blys to fulfyll,   140
     Mankynde of moulde will I make ;
     But fyrste wille I fourme hym before,
     All thyng that sall hym restore,
     To whilke þat his talents will take.   144

19. Ande in my fyrste makyng to mustyr my mighte,
     Sen erthe is vayne and voyde, and myrknes emel,

     I byd in my blyssyng ȝhe aungels gyf lyghte
     To þe erthe, for it faded when þe fendes fell.   148

     ---

     [1] *Ihc* inserted, apparently later, before *deus.*

In hell sall neuer myrknes be myssande,
Þe myrknes thus name I for nighte,
The day þat call I this lyghte.   let there be light
                                                   and darkness,
My after warkes sall þai be wyssande;   152
20. Ande now in my blyssyng I twyne tham in two,
The nighte euen fro þe day, so þat thai mete neuer,   day and night.
But ather in a kynde courese þaire gates for to go,
Bothe þe nighte and þe day, does dewly ȝhour deyuer. 156 lf. 5.
To all I sall wirke be ȝhe wysshyng,
This day warke es done ilke a dele,
And all þis warke lykes me ryght wele,
And baynely I gyf it my blyssyng.   160
          Explicit [1].

[1] Near the bottom of this page is written, in a later hand and ink than the text, the date 1583, enclosed in a scroll.

II. PLAYSTERERS.

The Creation, to the fifth day.

[PERSON OF THE PLAY.
DEUS.]

[SCENE, *The New World.*]

Deus. *In altissimis habito,* in the heghest heuyn my hame
          haue I,

Gen. i. 6–25.

    Eterne mentis & ego, withoutyn ende ay lastandly [1].
        Sen I haue wroght þire worldys wyde,
          heuen and ayre and erthe also,

Although fools
aspired to the
godhead,

My hegh godhede I will noght hyde,
        all yf sume foles be fallyn me fro.   4
When þai assent with syn of pride,
        vp for to trine my trone vnto,

they have fallen
into woe.

In heuen þai myght no le[n]gger byde,
        but wyghtly went to wone in wo ;
And sen þai wrange haue wroght,
        my likes to lat þam go,
To suffir sorowe on soght,
        syne þai haue seruid so.   8
        Þare mys may neuer be amendid
        sen þai a-sent me to forsake,

---

[1] In the MS. this piece is written throughout in the long lines of sixteen
or twelve syllables ; they are here divided for greater convenience. The
same kind of stanza, with a slight diversity of rimes, will be found in twelve
other plays (see Introduction), but they were usually written in the short
lines.

For all þere force non sall þame fende
    for to be fendys foule & blake.
And þo þat lykys with me to lende,
    and trewly tent to me will take,
Sall wonne in welth withoutyn ende,
    and all-way wynly with me wake.   12
Þai salle haue for þare sele
    solace þat neuer sall sclake.
Þis warke me thynkys full wele,
    and more now will I make.

They will be black fiends for ever.

Syne þat þis world es ordand euyn,
    furth well I publysch my powere,
Noght by my strenkyth but by my steuyn,
    a firmament I byd apere;   16
Emange þe waterris lyght so leuyn,
    þere cursis lely for to lere,
And þat same sall be namyd hewuyn,
    with planitys and with clowdis clere.
Þe water I will be set
    to flowe bothe fare and nere,
And þan þe firmament,
    in mydis to set þame sere;   20

Heaven is created with the firmament to teach the waters their course.

Þe firmament sal nough[t] moue,
    but be a mene, þus will I mene,
Ouir all þe worlde to halde and houe,
    And be you tow wateris be-twyne [1].
Vndir þe heuyn, and als a-boue,
    þe wateris serly sall be sene,
And so I wille my post proue,
    by creaturis of kyndis clene.   24
Þis warke is [2] to my pay
    right well [2], withoutyn wyne [1],

The firmament shall not move, but divide the waters above and beneath.

---

[1] *twyne* and *wyne* are intended to rime with *mene* and *clene*.
[2] MS. has *his* and *will*. See *his* in l. 62.

End of the
second day.

Þus sese þe secunde day
    of my doyngys bydene.

    Moo sutyll werkys asse-say I sall,
      for to be set in seruice sere;

' Let the dry
land appear.'
lf. 6.

Alle ye wateris grete and smalle
    þat vndir heuyne er ordande here,   28
Gose to-gedir and holde yow all,
    and be a flode festynde in fere,
So þat the erthe, bothe downe and dale,
    in drynesch playnly may a-pere;
Þe drynes ' lande ' sall be
    namyd, bothe ferre and nere,
And þen I name þe ' se,'
    geddryng of wateris clere.   32

' Let the earth
bring forth grass,'
herbs and trees,

    Þe erthe sall fostyr and furthe bryng,
      buxsumly as I wyle byde,
Erbys and also othyr thyng,
    well for to wax and worthe to wede;
Treys also þar-on sall spryng,
    with braunchis and with bowis on-brede,
With flouris fayr on heght to hyng,
    and fruth also to fylle and fede.   36

each ' yielding
fruit after his
kind, whose seed
is in itself,'

And þane I will þat þay
    of þem selfe haue þe sede,
And mater þat þay may
    be lastande furth in lede.

    And all þer materis es in mynde,
      for to be made of mekyl might,

that they may
bear many
bright buds.

And to be kest in dyueris kynde
    so for to bere sere burgvns bright.   40
And when þer frutys is fully fynde,
    and fayrest semande vnto syght,

The wet and
wind shall dis-
perse the seed,
that new roots
may grow.

Þane þe wedris wete and wynde
    oway I will it wende full wyght,

And of þere sede full sone,
    new rotys sall ryse vp right.
Þe third day þus is done,
    þire dedis er dewly dyght.   44

    Now sene þe erthe þus ordand es,
    mesurid and made by myn assent,
Grathely for to growe with gres,
    and wedis þat sone away bese went,
Of my gudnes now will I ges,
    so þat my werkis no harmes hent,
Two lyghtis, one more and one lesse,
    to be fest in þe firmament;   48
The more light to [the] day
    fully suthely sall be sent,
Þe lesse lyght all-way
    to þe nyght sall take entent.

'Two great lights, the greater light to rule the day, the lesser light to rule the night,'

    Þir figuris fayre þat further sun [1]
þus on sere sydys serue þai sall,
The more lyght sall be namid þe son,
    dymnes to wast be downe and be dale;   52
Erbis and treys þat er by-gune,
    all sall he gouerne, gret and smale,
With cald yf þai be closid or bun,
    thurgh hete of þe sun þai sal be hale.
Als ye I haue honours
    in alkyn welth to wale,
So sall my creaturis
    euir byde withoutyn bale.   56

lf. 6 b.

    Þe son and þe mone on fayre manere,
    now grathly gange in ȝour degre,
Als ye haue tane ȝoure curses clere
    to serue furth loke ye be fre,
For ye sall set [2] þe sesons sere,

'for signs, for seasons, for days and years.'

---

[1] The MS. looks like *sum*.   [2] MS. *ye set*.

kyndely to knowe in ilke cuntre,
Day fro day, and yere fro yere,
    by sertayne signes suthly to se.   60

He made the
stars also.
Þe heuyn sall be ouer hyld
    with sternys to stand plente.
Þe furthe day his fulfillid;
    þis werke well lykys me.

    Now sen þir werkis er wroght with wyne,
    and fundyn furth be firth and fell,

'God created
great whales,'
and other fish to
swim with fins,
greater and less;
some mild, some
fierce.
Þe see now will I set within
    whallis whikly for to dewell;   64
And othir fysch to flet with fyne,
    sum with skale and sum with skell,
Of diueris materis more and myn,
    in sere maner to make and mell;
Sum sall be milde and meke[1],
    and sum both fers and fell,
Þis world þus will I eke,
    syn I am witt of well.   68

    Also vp in þe ayre on hyght
    I byd now þat þore be ordande,

Also winged fowl
with feathers to
fly from place to
place and to
alight.
For to be foulis fayre and bright,
    dewly in þare degre dwelland[2],
With fedrys fayre to frast þer flight
    fro[3] stede to stede where þai will stande,
And also leythly for to lyght
    whore so þame lykis in ilke a londe.   72
Þane fysch and foulis sere,
    kyndely I ȝow commande,
To meng on ȝoure mannere[4],
    both be se and sande.

---

[1] MS. has *meke and milde*, but it was evidently intended as above, to
rime with *eke*.
    [2] MS. *dewlland*.   [2] MS. *for*.   [3] MS. has *manener*.

þis materis more ȝitt will I mende,
  so for to fulfill my for-thoght,
With diueris bestis in lande to lende
  to brede & be with bale furth brught:
And with bestis I wille be blende
  serpentis to be sene vn-soght,
And wormis vp-on þaire wombis sall wende,
  to wo in erth and worth to noght.
And so it sall be kende
  how all þat eme is oght,
Begynnyng mydes and ende
  I with my worde hase wrothe.
        For als I byde bus all thyng be,
  and dewly done als I will dresse ;
Now bestys ar sett in sere degre
  on molde to moue, both more & lesse.
þane foulis in ayre, and fische in see,
  and bestis on erthe of bone and flesch,
I byde ȝe wax furth fayre plente,
  and grathly growes, als I ȝow gesse.
So multeply ȝe sall
  ay furth in fayre processe,
My blyssyng haue ȝe all ;
  the fift day endyd es.

The beasts are
created, cattle,
76 and every creep-
ing thing.

80

'Be fruitful and
multiply.'

lf. 7.

84

86

III. THE CARDMAKERS[1].

God creates Adam and Eve.

[PERSONS OF THE PLAY.

DEUS. ADAM. EVE.]

[SCENE, *the World.*]

Gen. i. 26–31 ; ii.
7, 19, 21.

Five days' work
is finished,—
angels in heaven,

stars, moon, and
sun, trees, beasts,
and fishes.

Deus. IN heuyn and erthe duly be dene
Of v. daies werke, evyn vnto þe[2] ende,
I haue complete by courssis clene ;
Me thynketh þe space of þam wele spende. 4

In heuen ar aungels faire and bright,
Sternes and planetis þer[3] courses to goo,
þe mone serues vnto þe nyghte,
The sonne to lighte þe day also. 8

In erthe is trees, and gresse to springe,
Beestes and foules, bothe grete and smale,
Fisshys in flode, all other thynge,
Thryffe and haue my blissynge alle. 12

This werke is wrought nowe at my wille,
But yitte can I here[4] no beste see
That accordes by kyndly skylle[5],
And for my werke myghte worshippe me. 16

---

[1] This play is written out twice, by different hands, on leaves 7–9 (which I call A), and 10, 11 (B), from which last the above is printed, as the best copy. Collations are given where words differ, but not for spelling.
[2] þe omitted in A.   [3] þe in B.   [4] here omitted in A.
[5] *kynde and skyll* A.

For parfite werke ne were it none
But oughte wer made þat myghte it ȝeme,
For loue made I þis worlde alone,
Therfore my loue shalle in it seme. 20

To keepe þis worlde bothe more and lesse
A skylfull beeste [1] þan will y make,
Aftir my shappe and my liknesse,
The whilke shalle wirshippe to me take. 24

Of þe sympylest parte of erthe þat is here
I shalle make man, and for this skylle,
For to a-bate his hautand [2] cheere,
Both his grete pride and other ille ; 28

And also for to haue in mynde
Howe symple he is at his makynge,
For als febill I shalle hym fynde
Qwen he is dede at his endynge. 32

For þis reasonne and skille allone,
I shalle make man like vn-to me.
Rise vppe, þou erthe in bloode and bone,
In shappe of man, I comaunde þe. 36

A female shalte þou haue to feere,
Here schalle y make of thy lefte rybbe,
Allone so shall þou nought be heere,
With-outyn faithfull freende and sibbe. 40

Takis nowe here þe goste of liffe,
And ressayue bothe youre soules of me,
Þis ffemalle take þou to þi wiffe ;
Adam and Eue youre names shalle bee [3]. 44

' But there is no
beast who by rea-
son of his nature-
will worship me.

I will make a
reasonable beast,

man, he shall be
made of earth to
abate his pride.

Rise up, thou
earth !

lf. 10 b.

Take the breath
of life, man and
woman both.'

---

[1] In A a later hand has written *wyght*. [2] *haunttande* in B.
[3] ' And leyd your lyves in good degre,
Adam here make I the
a man of mykyll myght
Thys same shall thy subget be
And Eve her name shall hight.'
These lines are written in the margin in an Elizabethan hand, to be in-
serted after line 44.

Adam. A LORD! ful mekill is þy myght,
And þat is seene in ilke a side,

'What a joyful sight is this world!'

Ffor nowe is here a joifull sighte,
To see this worlde so longe and wide.   48

Many dyuerse thynges nowe here is,
Of beestis and foules, bothe wilde and tame,
ȝitte is non made to þi liknesse
But we allone, a! loued be þy name.   52

Eue. T O swilke a lorde in alle[1] degree
Be euer-more lastand louynge,

'We are made in God's likeness, praise him!'

Þat to vs such a dyngnyte,
Has geffynne before all other thynge,   56

And selcouthe thynges may we see heere,
Of þis ilke worlde so longe and broode,
With beestes and foules so many and seere,
Blyssed be hee þat hase[2] vs made.   60

'What shall we do and where dwell?'

Adam. A BLISSED lorde! nowe at þi wille
Sethen we are wrought, wouchesaffe to telle

And also saie vs two vn-tille,
Whatte we schalle do and where to dwelle?   64

Deus. F OR this skille made y you þis daye,
My name to worschippe ay where ;

'Love and praise me,

Lovis me for-thy and loues me aye
For my makyng, I aske[3] no more.   68

Bothe wyse and witty shalle þou bee,
Als man, þat y haue made of nought,

thou shalt be lord of all,

Lordshippe in erthe þan graunte y the,
Alle thynge to serue þe þat is[4] wrought.   72

dwell together in paradise.'

In paradise shalle ye same wonne,
Of erthely thyng gete ȝe no nede,

lf. 11.
A ii.

Ille and good bothe shalle ȝe konne,
I shalle you lerne youre lyffe to leede.   76

[1] *all þe degre* in A.   [2] *hase* omitted in A.   [3] *axke* in A.   [4] *I haue* in A.

Adam. A LORD! sene we shalle do no thynge,
But loue the for thy grette goodnesse,
We shalle a-beye to þi gudnesse, to þi biddyng,
And fulfille it, bothe more and lees. 80

Eue. H YS syngne sen [1] he has on vs sette,
Before al other thyng certayne,
Hym for to loue we schal not lette,
And worshippe hym with mighte and mayne. 84

Deus. A T heuene and erthe firste I be-ganne,
And vj daies wroughte or y wolde reste,
My werke is endid nowe at man[n]e,
Alle likes me wele, but þis þe [2] beste. 88

My blissynge haue they euer and ay;
Þe seuynte day shal my restyng be,
Þus wille I sese, sothly to say,
Of my doyng in þis degree. 92

To blisse I schal you brynge,
Comes forthe ȝe two with me,
ȝe shalle lyff in likyng,
My blissyng with you be. Amen [3]. 96

[1] MS. has *sone*, but *sen = sythen* seems to be meant.
[2] Is in A.
[3] At the end here was scribbled later the cue for the next piece, ' The Fullers pagyant, Adam and eve this is the place. Deus.'

Margin notes:
' We will obey, because
he has set his sign upon us.'
The sixth day's work is ended with man.
' Come with me, you two.'

IV. THE REGYNALL OF THE FULLERS' PAGYANT[1].

Gen. i. 26; ii. 8,
9, 15-17. *God puts Adam and Eve in the Garden of Eden.*

[PERSONS OF THE PLAY.

DEUS.   ADAM.   EUE.]

[SCENE, *Paradise.*]

'Here is Paradise for you to dwell in.

1. Deus. Adam and Eve, this is the place
  That I haue graunte you of my grace
   To haue your wonnyng in ;
   Erbes, spyce, frute on tree,   4
   Beastes, fewles, all that ye see,
    Shall bowe to you, more and myn.
  This place hight paradyce,
    Here shall your joys begynne,   8
  And yf that ye be wyse,
    Frome thys tharr ye never twynne.

You may live as you will, all things are your subjects.

2. All your wyll here shall ye haue,
   Lyvyng for to eate or sayff,   12
    Fyshe, fewle, or fee,
  And for to take at your owen wyll.
  All other creatours also there-tyll
    Your suggettes shall they bee ;   16

---

[1] This piece is written in a hand of the end of the 16th century, the same which wrote the addition to the play of Cain and Abell; see after, p. 37. The reason for this is found in a Chamberlain's Book of the City of York (vol. 4) under date of 1 Eliz., 1558 ; 'Item, payd to John Clerke for entryng in the Regyster the Regynall of the pagyant pertenynge to Craft of Fullars, which was never before regestred, 12d.' *Regynall,* i. e. originall; cf. p. 29.

Adam, of more and lesse
    Lordeship in erthe here graunte I the,
Thys place that worthy is,
    Kepe it in honestye.   20

3. Looke that ye ȝem ytt wetterly,   *Care for this*
    All other creatours shall multeply,   *place intelli-*
        Ylke one in tender hower.   *gently;*
Looke that ye bothe saue and sett,   24 *sow and set*
    Erbes and treys for nothyng lett,   *for all.'*
        So that ye may endower
To susteyn beast and man,
        And fewll of ylke stature.   28
Dwell here yf that ye canne,
        This shall be your endowre.

4. **Adam.**   O Lord! lovyd be thy name,
    For nowe is this a joyfull hame   32 *A joyful home,*
        That thowe hais brought vs to;   *full of happiness.*
Full of myrthe and solys saughe,
    Erbes and trees, frute on to haugh,
        Wyth spysys many one hoo.   36
Loo! Eve, nowe ar we brought   *lf.* 12.
    Bothe vnto rest and rowe,   *A iij.*
We neyd to tayke no thought,
        But loke a¹ well to doo.   40

5. **Eve.**   Lovyng be ay to suche a lord,
To vs hais geven so great reward
    To governe bothe great and small,
And mayd vs after his owen read,   44
. . . [*line wanting, but no blank in MS.*] . . .
Emonges these myrthes all.
Here is a joyfull sight
    Where that wee wonn in shall;
We love the, mooste of myght,   48
    Great god, that we on call.

¹ Perhaps the original word was *ay*, as in line 41.

'Praise me and
do my bidding.

6. Deus. Love my name with good entent,
And harken to my comaundement,
And do my byddyng buxomly.   52
Of all the Frute in parradyce,
Tayke ye therof of your best wyse,
And mayke you right merry ;

Eat not of the
tree of good
and ill,

The tree of good and yll,   56
What tyme you eates of thys
Thowe speydes thy self to spyll,
And be brought owte of blysse.

all things are
yours but this.'

7. All thynges is mayd, man, for thy prowe,   60
All creatours shall to the bowe,
That here is mayd erthly ;
In erthe I mayke the Lord of all,
And beast vnto the shall be thrall ;   64
Thy kynd shall multeply.
Therefore this tree alone,
Adam, this owte-take I,
The frute of it negh none,   68
For an ye do, then shall ye dye.

lf. 12 b.

8. Adam. Alas ! Lorde, that we shuld do so yll,
Thy blyssed byddyng we shall fulfyll,
Bothe in thought and deyd ;   72

'We will not go
near it,

We shall no negh thys tre nor the bugh,
Nor yit the fruyte that there on groweth,
There-with oure fleshe to feyd.

Eve. We shall do thy byddyng,   76
We haue none other neyd,

this forbidden
fruit shall hang.'

Thys frute full styll shall hyng,
Lorde, that thowe hays forbyd.

'Look that you
obey me,

9. Deus. Looke that ye doe as ye haue sayd,   80
Of all that there is hold you apayd,
For here is welthe at wyll ;
Thys tre that beres the Fruyte of Lyfe,

Luke nother thowe nor Eve thy wyf,   84
    Lay ye no handes there tyll,
For-why [do my byddyng,] [1]
It is knowen bothe of good and yll,
    This frute but ye lett hyng   88
Ye speyd your self to spyll.   *or be ruined.*

10. For-thy this tree that I owt-tayke,
Nowe kepe it grathly for my sayke,
    That nothyng negh it neyre ;   92
All other at your wyll shall be,
I owte-take nothyng but this tree,   *I except nothing*
    To feyd you with in feare.   *but this tree.'*
Here shall ye leyd your lyffe   96
    With dayntys that is deare ;
Adam, and Eve thy wyfe,
    My blyssyng haue ye here.   99

Fynys.

[1] Probably some such words are missing. The copyist, having got confused, put *for why* at the end of l. 85 near the margin, and *For-thy* at the end of l. 89 instead of at the beginning of l. 90, to which it evidently belongs.

V. THE COWPERS [1].

Man's disobedience and fall from Eden.

[PERSONS OF THE PLAY.

DOMINUS.

SATHANAS.   EUA.

ADAM.   ANGELUS.]

[SCENE, *Paradise.*]

Gen. iii. 1–15, 17, 23.
Satan is troubled at God's intention to take on him the nature of man,

Satanas incipit dicens,

FOR [2] woo my witte es in a were,
     That moffes me mykill in my mynde,
The godhede þat I sawe so cleere,
     And parsayued þat he shuld take kynde,   4
         of a degree

instead of angels.

That he had wrought, and I denyed þat aungell kynde
                 shuld it noȝt be;   7
And we were faire and bright,
     Þerfore me thoght þat he
The kynde of vs tane myght,
And þer-at dedeyned me.   .   11

2. The kynde of man he thoght to take,
     And theratt hadde I grete envye,

'I will hie to man's mate,

But he has made to hym a make,   14
     And harde to her I wol me hye,
             (that redy way)

[1] Many of the lines in the first five stanzas are written very confusedly in the MS.; they are corrected here, without indicating each one.
[2] *Diabolus* in margin.

That purpose proue to putte it by,
        And fande to pike fro hym þat pray. 18
My trauayle were wele sette
    Myght y hym so betraye,
His likyng for to lette,
    And sone I schalle assaye.   22

3. In a worme liknes wille y wende,   in likeness of
    And founde to feyne a lowde lesynge.   [*Calls.*   a worm.'
Eue, Eue !

        Eua. Wha es þare?

                Satanas[1] I, a frende.
And for thy gude es þe comynge,   26
                I hydir sought.
Of all þe fruyt that ye se hynge
        In paradise, why eat ye noght ?   29
Eua. We may of tham ilkane
    Take al þat vs goode þought,
Save a tree outt is tane,
    Wolde do harm to neygh it ought.   33

4. **Sat.** And why þat tree? þat wolde I witte,   He tempts Eve.
    Any more þan all othir by ?
Eua. For oure Lord god forbeedis vs itt,
    The frute þer of, Adam nor I
                to neghe it nere,   38
And yf we dide we both shuld dye,
        He saide, and sese our solace sere. 40
Sat. Yha, Eue to me take tente,   lf. 15.
    Take hede and þou shalte here,   A vj.
What þat the matere[2] mente,
    He moved on þat manere.   44

5. To ete þer-of he you defende,
    I knawe it wele, þis was his skylle,
By-cause he wolde non othir kende
    Thes grete vertues þat longes þer-till. 48

---

[1] *Diabolus* in margin.   [2] MS. has *materere*.

For will þou see,
Who etes the frute of goode and ille
            shalle haue knowyng as wele as hee.

Eua. Why what-kynne thyng art þou,   52
þat telles þis tale to me?

Sat. A worme þat wotith wele how
þat yhe may wirshipped be.   55

6. Eua. What wirshippe shulde we wynne ther-by?
To ete þer-of vs nedith it nought,
We have lordshippe to make maistrie
Of alle þynge þat in erthe is wrought.

                Sat. Woman! do way!   60
To gretter state ye may be broughte,
            and ye will do as I schall saye.

Eua. To do is vs full lothe,
þat shuld oure god myspaye.   64

Sat. Nay, certis it is no wathe,
Ete it safely ye maye.

7. For perille ryght þer none in lyes,
But worshippe and a grete wynnynge,   68
For right als god yhe shalle be wyse,
And pere to hym in all-kyn thynge.
                Ay! goddis shalle ye be!
Of ille and gode to haue knawyng,   72
                For to be als wise as he.

Eua. Is þis soth þat þou sais?

        Sat. Yhe! why trowes þou noʒt me?
I wolde be no-kynnes wayes   76
            telle noʒt but trouthe to þe.

8. Eua. Than wille I to thy techyng traste,
And fange þis frute vnto owre foode.

                    (*Et tunc debet accipere pomum.*

Sat.   Byte on boldly, be nought a-basshed,   80   'Bite on boldly, and take it to Adam, to amend his mood and his happiness.' lr. A.vi.
    And bere Adam to amende his mode,
        And eke his blisse.

           (Tunc Satanas recedet.

Eua.   Adam! have here of frute full goode.   83

       Ad.   Alas! woman, why toke þou þis?   He reproaches Eve.
Owre lorde comaunded vs bothe
    to tente þe tree of his.   86
Thy werke wille make hym wrothe,
    Allas! þou hast don a mys.

9. **Eue.**   Nay Adam, greve þe nought at it,   Eve tempts Adam.
    And I shal saie þe reasonne why,   90
A worme has done me for to witte,
    We shalle be as goddis, þou and I,
        yf þat we ete
Here of this tree ; Adam, for-thy   94
        lette noght þat worshippe for to gete.
For we shalle be als wise
    als god þat is so grete,
And als mekill of prise ;   98
    forthy ete of þis mete.

10. **Adam.**   To ete it wolde y nought eschewe,   Adam yields,
    Myght I me sure in thy saying.

Eue.   Byte on boldely, for it es trewe,   102
    We shalle be goddis and knawe al thyng.

        Adam.   To wynnne þat name,
I schalle it taste at thy techyng.   and eats.
           (Accipit et comedit.
      Allas! what haue I done, for shame!   106
Ille counsaille woo worthe the!
    A! Eue, þou art to blame,
To þis entysed þou me,   Suddenly they are ashamed of nakedness.
    me shames with my lyghame!

11. For I am naked as me thynke.　　　　　　　111

If. 16.
A vij.　　　　　　　**Eue.** Allas! Adam, right so am I.

　　　　　　　　Adam. And for sorowe sere why ne myght we synke,
　　　　　　　　For we haue greved god almyghty　　　　114
　　　　　　　　　　þat made me man.

He reproaches
Eve.　　　　　　Brokyn his bidyng bittirly,
　　　　　　　　　　allas! þat euer we it began.

　　　　　　　þis werke, Eue, hast þou wrought,
　　　　　　　and made þis bad bargayne.　　　　119

'Nay, blame me
not,　　　　　　**Eue.** Nay, Adam, wite me nought.

　　　　　　　　Adam. Do wey, lefe Eue, whame þan?

the worm is to
blame.'　　**12. Eue.** The worme to wite wele worthy were,
　　　　　　　With tales vntrewe he me be-trayed.　　123

　　　　　　　　Adam. Allas! þat I lete at thy lare,
　　　　　　　Or trowed þe trufuls þat þou me saide.
　　　　　　　　So may I byde,
　　　　　　For I may banne þat bittir brayde,　　127
　　　　　　　　And drery dede þat I it dyde.

'I am ashamed
of our naked
shapes.'　　Oure shappe for doole me defes,
　　　　　　　where with þay shalle be hydde.

They take fig-
leaves.　　　**Eue.** Late vs take there fygge leves,　　131
　　　　　　　sythen it is þus be-tydde.

　　　　　　13. Adam. Ryght as þou sais so shalle it bee,
　　　　　　　For we are naked and all bare,
　　　　　　Full wondyr fayne I wolde hyde me,　　135
　　　　　　　Fro my lordis sight, and I wiste whare,
　　　　　　　　where I ne roght.　　　　137

　　　　　　　　　　　　　　[*The Lord calls.*

　　　　　　Dom. Adam! Adam!

　　　　　　　　Adam. Lorde!

　　　　　　　　　Dom. Where art thou, yhare?

　　　　　Adam. I here þe lorde and seys the noȝt. 139

Dom. Say, wheron is it longe

þis werke, why hast þou wrought ?

'Why hast thou done this?'

Adam. Lorde, Eue garte me do wronge

and to þat bryg me brought.

'Eve brought me to this breach.'
143

14. Dom. Say, Eue, why hast þou garte thy make

Ete frute I bad þei shuld hynge stille,

And comaunded none of it to take ?

If. 16 b.

Eue. A worme lord, entysed me ther-till [1],

So wel away !

That euer I did þat dede so dill !

148

Dom. A ! wikkid worme, woo worthe þe ay,

For þou on þis maner

hast made þam swilke affraye ;

My malysonne haue þou here,

with all þe myght y may.

God curses the worm,
151

15. And on thy wombe þan shall þou glyde,

And be ay full of enmyte

To al man kynde on ilke a side,

And erthe it shalle thy sustynaunce be

to ete & drynke.

Adam and Eue, alsoo, yhe

In erthe þan shalle ye swete and swynke,

And trauayle for youre fode.

155

159

and punishes man.

Adam. Allas ! whanne myght we synke,

We that haues alle worldis goode,

ful defly may vs thynke.

163

16. Dom. Now Cherubyn, myn aungell bryght,

To middilerth tyte go dryve these twoo.

'Drive these two to middle-earth.'

Ang. Alle redy, lorde, as it is right,

Syn thy wille is þat it be soo,

and thy lykyng [2].

168

---

[1] MS. has *ther-to*.   [2] Line 159 is inserted by a later hand.

[*To Adam and Eve.*

'Go out, you
two!

of sorrow may
ye sing.'

Adam and Eue do you to goo,   171
      For here may ȝe make no dwellyng,
Goo yhe forthe faste to fare,
      of sorowe may yhe synge.

Adam.   Allas! for sorowe and care!   175
owre handis may we wryng.

                Et sic finis[1].

[1] These three words in a later hand.

VI. THE ARMOURERS.

THE ORIGENALL PERTEYNYNG TO ÞE CRAFTE OF ARMOURERS.

Adam and Eve driven from Eden.

[PERSONS OF THE PLAY.

ANGELUS.   ADAM.   EUE.]

---

1. Ang.   Alle creatures to me take tent,   *Gen.* iii. 16-19.
    Fro god of heuen now am I sent
    Vnto þe wrecchis þat wronge has went   ' I am sent to the
              thaymself to woo,   4   wretches who
    Þe joie of heuen þat thaym was lent   have lost the joy
              is lost thaym froo.   of heaven.

2.   Fro thaym is loste boþe game and glee,
    He badde þat þei schuld maistirs be   8
    Ouer alle-kynne thyng, oute-tane a tree
              he taught þem tille ;
    And þer-to wente bothe she and he,
              agayne his wille.   12

3.   Agaynst his wille þus haue they wrought,
    To greeffe grete god gaffe they right noght [1],
              þat wele wytt ye ;
    And therfore syte is to þaym sought ;   16
              as ye shalle see.

---

[1] A line seems wanting here, and in each of stanzas 7, 8, and 11.

4. The fooles þat faithe is fallen fra,

I am sent to
warn you.

Take tente to me nowe, or ye ga ;

Fro god of heuen vnto yow twa　　　　　20

　　　　　sente am I nowe,

For to warne you what-kynne wa

　　　　　is wrought for you.

5. Adam.　For vs is wrought, so welaway !　　24

Doole endurand nyghte and day,

The welthe we wende haue wonnyd in ay

　　　　　is loste vs fra.

For this myscheffe ful wele we may　　　28

　　　　　euer mornyng ma.

You, Adam,
made all this
trouble yourself.'

6. Ang.　Adam, þy selffe made al þis syte,

For to the tree þou wente full tyte,

And boldely on the frute gan byte　　　32

　　　　　my lord for-bed.

He blames his
wife.

Adam.　Yaa, allas ! my wiffe þat may I wite,

　　　　　for scho me red.

'You are punished
for believing
her tale.'

7. Ang.　Adam, for þou trowyd hir tale,　　36

He sendis þe worde and sais þou shale

　　　　　lyffe ay in sorowe,

Abide and be in bittir bale,

　　　　　tille he þe borowe.　　40

'Alas ! we had
immense bliss,
now we have
none.'

8. Ad.　Allas ! wrecchis, what haue we wrought,

To byggly blys we bothe wer brought,

　　　　　whillis we wer þare

We hadde i-nowe, nowe haue we noghte,　　44

　　　　　allas ! for care.

If. 18.
B i.

9. Eua.　Oure cares ar comen bothe kyne and colde,

With fele fandyngis many folde,

Allas ! þat tyraunte to me tolde,　　48

　　　　　thurghoute his gyle,

That we shulde haue alle welthis in walde,

　　　　　wa worthe þe whyle !

10. Ang. That while ye wrought vnwittely,   52 'For your un-
    Soo for to greue god almighty,   wise work
    And þat mon ye full dere abye
                  or þat ye go.
    And to lyffe, as is worthy,   56 you now shall
                in were and wo.   suffer.'

11. Adam! haue þis, luke howe ye thynke,
    And tille with-alle þi meete and drynke
              for euer-more.   60

Adam. Allas! for syte why myght y synke,
              so shames me sore.

12. Eue. Soore may we shame with sorowes seere,
    And felly fare we bothe in feere,   64
    Allas! þat euyr we neghed it nere,
            þat tree vn-till.
    With dole now mon we bye full dere,
            oure dedis ille.   68

13. Ang. Giffe, for þou beswyked hym swa[1],   Eve shall bear
    Trauell herto shalle þou ta,   children with
    Thy barnes to bere with mekill wa   sorrow.
            þis warne I þe.   72
    Buxom shalle þou and othir ma
            to man ay be.

14. Eue. Allas! for doole what shall y doo,
    Now mon I neuer haue rest ne roo.   76

    Adam. Nay, lo! swilke a tale is taken me too,   Adam shall
            to trauyalle tyte,   labour.
    Nowe is shente both I and shoo,
            allas! for syte.   80

15. Allas! for syte and sorowe sadde,
    Mournynge makis me mased and madde,

---

[1] A line written over this in later hand glosses it 'Eve, for þat you begylyd hym so.'

To thynke in herte what helpe y hadde,
>> and nowe has none.   84
On grounde mon I neuyr goo gladde,
>> my gamys ere gane.

16. Gone ar my games with-owten glee,
Allas ! in blisse kouthe we no3t bee,   88

For putte we were to grete plente
>> at prime of þe day;
Be tyme of none alle lost had wee,
>> sa welawaye.   92

17. Sa welaway ! for harde peyne,
Alle bestis were to my biddyng bayne,
Fisshe and fowle, they were fulle fayne
>> with me to founde.   96
And nowe is alle thynge me agayne,
>> þat gois on grounde.

18. On grounde ongayñely may y gange,
To suffre syte and peynes strange,   100
Alle is for dede I haue done wrange
>> Thurgh wykkid wyle.
On-lyve me thynkith I lyffe to lange,
>> allas ! þe whille.   104

19. A ! lord, I thynke what thynge is þis,
That me is ordayned for my mysse,
Gyffe I wirke wronge, whom should me wys
>> be any waye ?   108
How beste wille be, so haue y blisse,
>> I shalle assaye.

20. Allas ! for bale, what may þis bee,
In worlde vnwisely wrought haue wee,   112
This erthe it trembelys for this tree,
>> and dyns ilk dele.

Alle þis worlde is wroth with mee,
>> þis wote I wele.   116

21. Full wele y wote my welthe is gone,
Erthe, elementis, euer ilkane,
For my synne has sorowe tane,
    þis wele I see.   120
Was neuere wrecchis so wylle of wane
    as nowe ar wee.

22. Eue. We are fulle wele worthy i-wis
To haue þis myscheffe for oure mys,   124
For broght we were to byggely blys,
    euer in to be.
Nowe my sadde sorowe certis is þis,
    my silfe to see.   128

'We are worthy this trouble.'

23. Ad. To see it is a sytfull syghte,
We bothe þat were in blis so brighte,
We mon go nakid euery-ilke a nyght,
    and dayes by-dene.   132
Allas! what womans witte was light!
    þat was wele sene.

They grieve at their nakedness.

How witless woman was!

24. Eue. Sethyn it was so me knyth it sore,
Bot sythen[1] that woman witteles ware,
Mans maistrie shulde haue bene more
    agayns þe gilte.
 Ad. Nay, at my speche wolde þou never spare,
    þat has vs spilte.   140

136 lf. 19. B. ij.

They accuse one another.

25. Eue. Iff I hadde spoken youe oughte to spill,
Ye shulde haue taken gode tent þere tyll,
    and turnyd my þought.
 Ad. Do way, woman, and neme it nought,[2]   144

26. For at my biddyng wolde þou not be,
And therfore my woo wyte y thee,

Adam's cowardly speech.

---

[1] MS. *sēn.*
[2] Two lines seem to be missing here (though no blank); the stanza is irregular.

D

Thurgh ille counsaille þus casten ar we,

    in bittir bale.   148

'Never trust
woman more.'

Nowe god late never man aftir me

    triste woman tale.

27. For certis me rewes fulle sare,

That euere I shulde lerne at þi lare,   152

Thy counsaille has casten me in care,

    þat þou me kende.

Eve acknow-
ledges her fault.

Eue. Be stille Adam, and nemen it na mare,

    it may not mende.   156

28. For wele I wate I haue done wrange,

And therfore euere I morne emange,

Allas! the whille I leue so lange,

    dede wolde I be!   160

Ad. On grounde mon I never gladde gange,

    withowten glee.

29. Withowten glee I ga,

This sorowe wille me sla,   164

This tree vn-to me wille I ta,

    þat me is sende.

He þat vs wrought wisse vs fro wa,

    whare-som we wende.   168

Finis.

VII. THE ORIGINALL PERTEYNYNG TO THE CRAFT OF GLOUERES.

Sacrificium Cayme and Abell.[1]

[PERSONS OF THE PLAY.

ANGELUS. CAYM. ABELL.

BREWBARRET (later addition).]

[SCENE, ? *in the field.*]

Gen. iv. 8–15.

1. Ang. That Lord of Lyffe lele ay lastand,
Whos myght vn-mesured is to meyne,
He shoppe þe sonne, both see and sande, 3
And wroughte þis worlde with worde, I wene.
His Aungell cleere, as cristall clene,
Here vn-to you þus am I sente
     þis tide. 7
Abell and Cayme, þei both by-deyne,
To me enteerly takis entent,
To meve my message haue I ment,
    if þat ye bide. 11

To Cain and Abel
comes an angel.

2. Alle myghty god of myghtes moste,
When he had wrought þis world[2] so wide,
No thynge hym þoughte was wroughte in waste
But in his blissyng boune to bide. 1
Neyne ordurs for to telle, þat tyde,
Of Aungeles bryght he bad þer be,
    for pride.

There are nine
orders of angels
the tenth was
sent to hell.

---

[1] This title is in the MS. [2] MS. *wolrd.*

D 2

And sone þe tente part it was tried,   19
And wente awaye, as was worthye,
They heild to helle all þat meyne,

               þer-in to bide.   22

3. Þanne made he manne to his liknes,
That place of price for to restore,

God asks tithes in return for his goodness to man. And sithen he kyd him such kyndnes,
Som-what wille he wirke þer-fore.   26
The tente to tyne he askis, nomore,
Of alle þe goodes he haues you sent,

               full trew.

To offyr loke þat ye be yore[1],   30
And to my tale yhe take entent,
For ilke-a lede þat liffe has lente,

               shalle you ensewe[2],   33

4. **Abell.** Gramercy! god of thy goodnes,
That me on molde has marked þi man,

If. 20 b. I worshippe þe with worthynes,   36
With alle þe comforte þat I can.

Abel is very willing to obey. Me for to were fro warkes wanne,
For to fulfille thy comaundement,

               þe teynd

Of alle þe gode sen I be-ganne,   41
Thow shalle it haue, sen þow it sent.
Come, brother Cayme, I wolde we wente,

               with hert ful hende.   44

Cain is angry. 'What a wild idea! d'ye think I'll prepare home produce? I will not bow nor mutter.' 5. **Cay.** We! Whythir now in wilde waneand,
Trowes þou I thynke to trusse of towne?
Goo, iape þe, robard iangillande,   47
Me liste noȝt nowe to rouk nor rowne.

Abell. A! dere brothir, late vs be bowne
Goddis biddyng blithe to fulfille,   50

               I tell þe.

---

[1] This should be *yare*, ready, but is made *yore* to suit the rime. Frequent examples of this free use of *o* and *a* in the rimes occur in the volume.
[2] This line was first written 'So shalle you sewe.'

Caym. Ya! daunce in þe devilway, dresse þe downe,
For I wille wyrke euen as I will.
What mystris þe, in gode or ille,
      of me to melle þe? 55

6. Ab. To melle of þe myldely I may,
Bot goode brothir, go we in haste,
Gyffe god oure teynde dulye þis day,
He byddis vs þus, be nouȝt abassed. 59

Abel answers mildly.

Cay. Ya! deuell me thynkeþ þat werke were waste,
That he vs gaffe geffe hym agayne,
      to se.
Nowe fekyll frenshippe for to fraste,
Me thynkith þer is in hym sarteyne. 64
.If he be moste in myghte and mayne,
     what nede has he?

'What need has God for what he gave us?'

7. Ab. He has non nede vn-to þi goode,
But it wille please hym principall,
If þou, myldly in mayne and moode,
Grouche noȝt geue hym tente parte of all.[1]

68 Willing gifts please him.

 · · · · · ·

If shall be done evyn as ye bydd,
And that Anone.

71 lf. 21, B v.

    [*caret inde* to Mr. Cayme what shares bryng I.]

Brewb. Lo! Mr. Cayme, what shares bryng I,
Evyn of the best for to bere seyd.
And to the ffeylde I wyll me hye
To fetch you moo, if ye haue neyd.

lf. 21 b.
Cain's servant,
74 Strife-brewer,
brings corn.

Cayme. Come vp! sir knave! the devyll the speyd,
Ye will not come but ye be prayd. 78

---

[1] Here two leaves have been cut out, the two old lines at top of lf. 21 were erased and ll. 71, 72 written instead, with a reference to the back of lf. 21, where at the end of the original piece lines 73–98 were written, towards the middle of the sixteenth century. At the end of line 98 is the cue for the old lines 99, etc., which were intended to run on after the new lines.

Brewb. O! maister Caym, I haue broken my to !

Cayme. Come vp, syr, for by my thryst,

Cain invites him
to drink.

Ye shall drynke or ye goo.   [*Enter Angel.*

Ang. Thowe cursyd Came, where is Abell?   82

Where hais thowe done thy broder dere?

Cayme. What askes thowe me that taill to tell?

For yit his keper was I never.

Ang. God hais sent the his curse downe,   86

Cain hits the
angel.

Fro hevyn to hell, *maldictio* [1] *dei.*

Cayme. Take that thy self, evyn on thy crowne,

Quia non sum custos fratris mei,   To tyne.

A double curse,

Ang. God hais sent the his malyson,   90

And inwardly I geve the myne.

Cayme. The same curse light on thy crowne,

which Cain
returns.

And right so myght it worth and be,

For he that sent that gretyng downe   94

The devyll myght speyd both hym & the.

Fowll myght thowe fall!

Here is a cankerd company,

Therefore goddes curse light on you all.   98

. . . .

lf. 21.
B v.

8. **Ang.** What hast þou done? be-holde and heere,

þe voice of his bloode cryeth vengeaunce.

Fro erthe to heuen, with voice entere,

þis tyde.

That god is greved with thy greuaunce   103

Take hede, I schalle telle þe tydandis,

þerfore abide.

The whole curse
upon Cain.

9. Þou shall be curssed vppon þe grounde,

God has geffyn þe his malisonne,   107

Yff þou wolde tyll þe erthe so rounde

No frute to þe þer shalle be founde.

[1] MS. *maladictio.*

Of wikkidnesse sen þou arte sonne,
Thou shalle be waferyng here and þere,
þis day.   112
In bittir bale nowe art þou boune,
Out-castyn shal þou be for care,
No man shal rewe of thy misfare,
for þis affraie.   116

10. **Cay.** Allas! for syte, so may I saye,
My synne it passis al mercie,
For ask it[1] þe, lord, I ne maye,   'My punishment
is greater than
To haue it am I nouȝt worthy.   120 I can bear.'
Fro þe shalle I be hidde in hye,
Þou castis me, lorde, oute of my kyth
In lande.
Both here and there oute-caste am I,
For ilke a man þat metis me with,   125
They wille slee me, be ffenne or ffrith,
with dynte of hande.

11. **Ang.** Nay, Cayme nouȝt soo, haue þou no drede,
Who þat þe slees shalle ponnysshed be
Sevene sithis for doyng of þat dede;
For-thy a token shal þou see,   131 A mark set upon
Cain.
It shalle be prentyd so in þe,
That ilke aman shalle þe knowe full wele.
Caym. Thanne wolle I ffa[r]dir flee   f. 21 b.
for shame.   135
Sethen I am sette þus out of seill,
That curse that I haue for to feill,
I giffe you þe same.   138

---

[1] MS. has *askid*.

VIII. THE SHIPWRITES.

The building of the Ark.

[PERSONS OF THE PLAY.
DEUS.   NOE.]

[*Gen.* vi. 5—vii.5.]

Deus.   FYRST qwen I wrought þis worlde so wyde,
               Wode and wynde and watters wane,
Heuyn and helle was noght to hyde,
Wyth herbys and gyrse þus I be-gane,   4
In endles blysse to be and byde.

God made man lord of middle-earth,

And to my liknes made I man,
Lorde and syre on ilke-a side
Of all medill-erthe I made hym þan.   8

A woman also with hym wrought I,
Alle in lawe to lede þer lyffe,
I badde þame waxe and multiplye,
To fulfille þis worlde, with-owtyn striffe.   12

but the sin is now so rife that he repents.

Syþn hays men wroght so wofully,
And synne is nowe reynand so ryffe,
Þat me repentys and rewys for-þi
Þat euer I made outhir man or wiffe.   16

Bot sen they make me to repente
My werke I wroght so wele and trewe,
Wyth-owtyn seys will noght assente,
Bot euer is bowne more bale to brewe.   20
Bot for ther synnes þai shall be shente,
And for-done hoyly, hyde and hewe.

Of þam shall no more be mente,
Bot wirke þis werke I will al newe.

24

Al newe I will þis worlde be wroght,
And waste away þat wonnys þer-in,
A flowyd a-bove þame shall be broght,
To stroye medilerthe, both more and myn.

28

Bot Noe alon lefe shal it noght [1],
To all be sownkyn for ther synne,
He and his sones, þus is my thoght,
And with þere wyffes away sall wynne.

32

[*To Noah.*] Nooe, my seruand, sad an cleyn,
For thou art stabill in stede and stalle,
I wyll þou wyrke, with-owten weyn,
A warke to saffe þi-selfe wyth-all.

36

Noe. O! mercy lorde, quat may þis meyne?
Deus. I am þi gode of grete and small,
Is comyn to telle þe of thy teyn,
And quat ferly sall eftir fall.

40

Noe. A! lorde, I lowe þe lowde and still,
Þat vn-to me, wretche vn-worthye,
Þus with thy worde, as is þi will,
Lykis to appere þus propyrly.

44

Deus. Nooe, as I byd þe, doo fulfill.
A shippe I will haue wroght in hye;
All-yf þou can litill skyll,
Take it in hande, for helpe sall I.

48

Noe. A! worthy lorde, wolde þou take heede,
I am full olde and oute of qwarte,
Þat me liste do no daies dede,
Bot yf gret mystir me garte.

52

Deus. Be-gynne my werke behoves þe nede,
And þou wyll passe from peynes smerte,

---

[1] Over *noght* is also written *not*.

I sall þe sokoure and the spede,

'I will help you,
men must be
drowned,

And giffe þe hele in hede and hert. 56

    I se suche ire emonge mankynde,

Þat of þare werkis I will take wreke,

Þay shall be sownkyn for þare synne,

Þer-fore a shippe I wille þou make. 60

but you and your
sons shall be
saved.'

Þou and þi sonnes shall be þere-in,

They sall be sauyd for thy sake.

lf. 23 b.

Therfore go bowdly and begynne

Thy mesures and thy markis to take. 64

     Noe. A! lorde, þi wille sall euer be wrought,

Os counsell gyfys of ilka clerk,

'I know nothing
of ship-craft.'

Bot first, of shippe-craft can I right noght,

Of ther makyng haue I no merke. 68

Deus. Noe, I byd þe hartely haue no þought,

'I will instruct
you.

I sall þe wysshe in all þi werke,

And euen to itt till ende be wroght,

Ther-fore to me take hede and herke. 72

Square some high
trees, make them
into boards,

    Take high trees and hewe þame cleyne,

All be sware and noght of skwyn,

Make þame of burdes and wandes betwene,

Þus thrivandly and noght ouer thyn. 76

Luke þat þi semes be suttilly seyn,

nail them well
together.

And naylid wele þat þei noght twyne,

Þus I deuyse ilk dele be-deyne,

Þerfore do furthe, and leue thy dyne. 80

These are the
measurements,

    iij C cubyttis it sall be long,

And fyfty brode, all for thy blys,

Þe highte of thyrty cubittis strong,

Lok lely þat þou thynke on þis. 84

Þus gyffe I þe grathly or I gang,

do not miss them.'

Þi mesures þat þou do not mysse,

Luk nowe þat þou wirke noght wrang,

þus wittely sen I þe wyshe. 88

Noe. A! blistfull lord, þat al may beylde,
I thanke þe hartely both euer and ay,
Fyfe hundreth wyntres I am of elde,
Me thynk þer ȝeris as yestirday.

'I am 500 years old, I was weak, 92 lo! now I am strong.'

Ful wayke I was and all vn-welde,
My werynes is wente away,
To wyrk þis werke here in þis feylde
Al be my-selfe I will assaye.

96 If. 24. B. vij.

To hewe þis burde I will be-gynne,

He hews a board even,

But firste I wille lygge on my lyne,
Now bud[1] it be alle in like thynne,
So put it nowthyr twynne nor twyne[2].

100

Þus sall I iune it with a gynn,
And sadly sette it with symonde fyne,
Þus sall y wyrke it both more and myn[n]e,

joins it with a bolt and cement,

Thurgh techyng of god maister myne.

104

More suttelly can no man sewe,
It sall be cleyngked euer-ilka dele,

clenches it with noble nails.

With nayles þat are both noble and newe,
Þus sall I feste it fast to feele.

108

Take here a revette, and þere a rewe,
With þer bowe þer nowe wyrke I wele,
Þis werke I warand both gud and trewe,

''Tis good work, but I have been at it 100 years, my strength fails.'

.   .   [*line wanting, but no blank in MS.*]   .
Full trewe it is who will take tente.

112

Bot faste my force begynnes to fawlde,
A hundereth wyntres away is wente,
Sen I began þis werk, full grathely talde,
And in slyke trauayle for to be bente,

116

Is harde to hym þat is þus olde.
But he þat to me þis messages sent,
He will be my beylde, þus am I bowde[3].

---

[1] *must* written over *bud* in a later hand.
[2] MS. has *twyne nor twynne*.
[3] The original was *bowde,* the later hand makes the *w* into *u.*

'It is nearly
done, but it has
to be manned.

Deus. Nooe, þis werke is nere an ende,   120
And wrought right as I warned þe,
Bot yit in maner it must[1] be mende,
Þerfore þis lessoun lerne at me.
For dyuerse beestis þer-in must[1] lende,   124
And fewles also in þere degree,
And for (þat[2]) þay sall not sam blende,

Fit it with stalls
and stages,
lf. 24 b.

Dyuerse stages must[1] þer be.

And qwen þat it is ordand soo,   128
With dyuerse stawllys and stagis seere,
Of ilka kynde þou sall take twoo,
Bothe male and femalle fare in fere ;
Thy wyffe, thy sonnes, with þe sall goo,   132
And thare thre wyffes, with-owten were,

Eight men and
women shall be
saved, no more.

Þere viij bodies with-owten moo,
Sall þus be saued on this manere.

Ther-fore to my biddyng be bayne,   136
Tille all be herberd haste þe faste,
Eftir þe vij day sall it rayne

It shall rain forty
days; take gear
to keep life
together.'

Till fowrty dayes be fully paste ;
Take with þe geere, sclyk os may gayne,   140
To man and beeste þare lyffes to laste.
I sall þe socoure for certayne,
Tille alle þi care awey be kaste.

Noe. A ! lorde þat ilk a mys may mende,   144
I lowe þi lare, both lowde and stille,

'I praise thee
who shelterest
from anger.'

I thanke þe both with herte and hende,
That me wille helpe, fro angrys hille.
Abowte þis werke nowe bus me wende   148
With beestys and fewlys my shippe to fille,
He þat to me þis crafte has kende,
He wysshe vs with his worthy wille.   151

---

[1] Erased and re-written ; probably the old word was *bus*.
[2] *þat* late inserted and *e* in *same* erased.

Noah and his wife, the Flood and its waning.

[PERSONS OF THE PLAY.

NOAH.   *Noe or Noye.*
NOAH'S WIFE.   *Vxor.*
THREE SONS OF NOAH. *j⁹ filius, ij⁹ filius, iij⁹ filius.*
THREE DAUGHTERS OF NOAH. *jᵃ, ijᵃ, iijᵃ filia.*]

[SCENE I, *The Ark in the forest where it was built.*] *Gen.* v. 28-31;
vii. 6-viii. 20;
ix. 8-17.

1. Noye. T HAT Lord þat leves ay lastand lyff,
  I loue þe euer with hart and hande,
That me wolde rewle be reasonne ryffe,
Sex hundereth yere to lyffe in lande.   4
Thre semely sonnes and a worthy wiffe
I haue euer at my steven to stande ;   Noah grieves for
the trouble that
Bot nowe my cares aren keen as knyffe, is coming upon
every country.
By-cause I kenne what is commannde. 8
Thare comes to ilke contre,
    3a, cares both kene and calde.
For god has warned me,
Þis worlde wastyd shalle be,   12
And certis þe sothe I see,
    As forme ¹ ffadres has talde.
2. My ffader Lamech who likes to neven,
Heere in this worlde þus lange gon lende, 16
Seuene hundereth yere seuenty and seuene,
In swilke a space his tyme he spende.

¹ MS. has *formed.*

Old Lamech
prayed for a son,
and got a pro-
mise which re-
joiced him.

He prayed to god with stabill steuene,

Þat he to hym a sone shuld sende,   10

And at þe laste þer come from heuen

Slyke hettyng þat hym mekill amende ;

And made hym grubbe and graue,

       And ordand faste be-forne,   24

For he a sone shulde haue,

As he gon aftir crave ;

And as god vouchydsaue

       In worlde þan was I borne.   28

3. When I was borne Noye named he me,

And saide þees wordes with mekill wynne,

' Loo,' he saide, ' þis ilke is he

That shalle be comforte to man-kynne.'   32

' Sirs, my father
knew this world
should drown
because of sin,

Syrs, by þis wele witte may ye,

My ffadir knewe both more and mynne,

By sarteyne signes he couthe wele see,

That al þis worlde shuld synke for synne.   36

Howe god shulde vengeaunce take,

       As nowe is sene sertayne,

and make an end
of mankind.

And hende of mankynde make,

That synne would nouȝt for-sake   40

And howe þat it shuld slake,

       And a worlde waxe agayne.

lf. 25 b.

4. I wolde god itt wasted were,

Sa þat I shuld nott tente þer-tille.   44

Sons and daugh-
ters,

My semely sonnes and doughteres dere,

Takis ȝe entent vn-to my skylle.

1 fil.   Fader we are all redy heere,

Youre biddyng baynly to fulfille.   48

go call your
mother.   Make
haste !'

Noe.   Goos calle youre modir, and comes nere,

And spede vs faste þat we nouȝt spille.

1 fil.   Fadir we shal nouȝt fyne

       To youre biddyng be done.   52

Noe. Alle þat leues vndir lyne,
Salle sone, son,[1] passe to pyne.

[SCENE II, *Noah's home, 1st son enters.*]

1 fil. Where are ye, modir myne?   'Mother, come!
          Come to my fadir sone.   56
5. Vxor. What sais þou? sone?
          1 fil. Moder, certeyne
My ffadir thynkis to flitte full ferre.   My father is
He biddis you[2] haste with al youre mayne.   flitting, hasten.'
Vnto hym, þat no thyng you marre.   60
Vxor. Ӡa! good sone, hy þe faste agayne,
And telle hym I wol come no narre.   'Tell him I won't
1 filius. Dame, I wolde do youre biddyng fayne,   come.'
But yow bus wende, els bese it warre.   64 'You must, or
Vxor. Werre! þat wolde I witte.   it will be worse.'
         We bowrde al wrange, I wene.
1 filius. Modir, I saie you yitte,
My ffadir is bowne to flitte.   68
Vxor. Now, certis, I sall nouӡt sitte,   'I will go and
         Or I se what he mene.   see what he
                                                 wants.'

[SCENE III, *The Ark, as before.*]

6. 1 filius. Fadir, I haue done nowe as ye comaunde,   lf. 26.
                                                            C iiij.
My modir comes to you this daye.   72
Noe. Scho is welcome, I wele warrande,
This worlde sall sone be waste awaye.   [*Wife comes in.*
Vxor. Wher arte þou Noye?
         Noe. Loo! here at hande,
Come hedir faste, dame, I þe praye.   76 'Come fast,
                                                        dame.'
Vxor. Trowes þou þat I wol leue þe harde lande,   'D'ye think I'll
And tourne vp here on toure deraye?   leave dry land
                                                        and come up
                                                        there?'

---

[1] MS. has *soner*.   [2] MS. has *þou*.

Nay, Noye, I am nouȝt bowne

to fonde nowe ouer þere [1] ffellis,   80

'Children, get
ready for town.'
'Nay, you will
drown,

Doo barnes, goo we and trusse to towne.

Noe. Nay, certis, sothly þan mon ye drowne.

Vxor. In faythe þou were als goode come downe,

And go do som what ellis.   84

it has rained
nearly forty days.'

7. Noe. Dame, fowrty dayes are nerhand past,

And gone sen it be-gan to rayne,

On lyffe salle noman lenger laste

Bot we allane, is nought to layne.   88

'Noah, you are
silly. I go home
again.'

Vxor. Now Noye, in faythe þe fonnes full faste,

This fare wille I no lenger frayne,

Þou arte nere woode, I am agaste,

Fare-wele, I wille go home agayne.   92

'Woman, are you
mad?'

Noe. O! woman, arte þou woode?

Of my werkis þou not wotte,

All þat has ban or bloode

Salle be ouere flowed with þe floode.   *[Detains her.*   96

'Let me go!
Hallo!'

Vxor. In faithe, þe were als goode

to late me go my gatte.

8. We owte! herrowe!

lf. 26 b.

Noe. What now! what cheere?

Vxor. I wille no na[r]re for no kynnes nede.   100

'Hold her, sons.'

Noe. Helpe! my sonnes to holde her here,

For tille her harmes she takes no heede.

'Mother, be
happy,

2 filius. Beis mery, modir, and mende youre chere,

This worlde beis drowned with-outen drede.   104

Vxor. Allas! þat I þis lare shuld lere.

Noe. Þou spilles vs alle, ille myght þou speede!

stay with us.'

3 filius. Dere modir, wonne with vs,

þer shal no-þyng you greve.   108

'I must go home
to pack my
things.

Vxor. Nay, nedlyngis home me bus,

For I haue tolis to trusse.

[1] MS. has *yere.*

Noe.   Woman, why dois þou þus,
            To make vs more myscheue?

9. **Vxor.**   Noye, þou myght haue leteyn me wete,   You might have
                                                              let me know
Erly and late þou wente þer outte,   114   what you were
                                                            doing, Noah.'
And ay at home þou lete me sytte,

To loke þat nowhere were wele aboutte.

Noe.   Dame, þou holde me excused of itt,   ' Excuse me,
                                                             dame.'
It was goddis wille with-owten doutte.   118

Vxor.   What? wenys þou so for to go qwitte?   ' D'ye think to
                                                             go quits?
Nay, be my trouthe, þou getis a clowte.   [*Strikes him.*

Noe.   I pray þe, dame, be stille.
            Thus god wolde haue it wrought.

Vxor.   Thow shulde haue witte my wille,   You should have
                                                            asked my leave
Yf I wolde sente þer tille,   124   at first.'

And Noye, for þat same skylle,
            þis bargan sall be bought.

10.   Nowe at firste I fynde and feele   If. 27.
                                                            C v.
Wher þou hast to þe forest soght,   128

Þou shuld haue tolde me for oure seele

Whan we were to slyke bargane broght.

Noe.   Now, dame, þe thar noȝt drede adele

For till accounte it cost þe noght,   132

A hundereth wyntyr, I watte wele,   ' I worked at it
                                                            100 years, God
Is wente sen I þis werke had wrought.   gave me orders.'

And when I made endyng,
            God gaffe me mesore fayre

Of euery-ilke a thyng,   137

He bad þat I shuld bryng

Of beestis and foules ȝynge,
            Of ilke a kynde, a peyre.

11. **Vxor.**   Nowe, certis, and we shulde skape fro skathe,   ' If we are to be
                                                                saved, my gossips
And so be saffyd as ye saye here,   142   and cousins also
                                                            should come.'
My commodrys and my cosynes bathe,

Þam wolde I wente with vs in feere.

Noe.   To wende in þe watir it were wathe,

E

Loke in and loke with-outen were.   146

The wife mourns
for her friends,
but her children
comfort her.

Vxor.   Allas! my lyff me is full lath,
I lyffe ouere lange þis lare to lere.

1 filia.   Dere modir, mende youre moode,
                        For we sall wende you with.   150

Vxor.   My frendis þat I fra yoode
Are ouere flowen with floode.

2 filia.   Nowe thanke we god al goode
                        That he has grauntid grith.   154

12.   3 filia.   Modir, of þis werke nowe wolde ye noȝt wene,

lf. 27 b.

That alle shuld worthe to watres wan.

The daughters,
full of wonder,
ask questions.

2 filia.   Fadir, what may þis meruaylle mene?
Wher-to made god medilerth and man?   158

1 filia.   So selcouthe sight was never non seene,
Sen firste þat god þis worlde began.

'Shut the doors!
—This sorrow is
sent on account
of sin.

Noe.   Wendes and spers youre dores be-dene!
For bettyr counsell none I can.   162
Þis sorowe is sente for synne,
                        Therfore to god we pray,
Þat he oure bale wolde blynne.

3 filius.   The kyng of al man-kynne
Owte of þis woo vs wynne,
                        Als þou arte lorde, þat maye.

13.   1 filius.   Ȝa! lorde, as þou late vs be borne
In þis grete bale, som bote vs bede.   170

Sons, take care
of the cattle;

Noe.   My sonnes, se ȝe, myd day and morne
To thes catelles takes goode hede.
Keppes þam wele with haye and corne;

women, feed the
fowls, as long as
we live thus.

And, women, fanges þes foules and feede,
So þat þey be noȝt lightly lorne,   175
Als longe as we þis liffe sall lede.

2 filius.   Fadir, we ar full fayne
                        Youre biddyng to fulfille.

Ix monethes [1] paste er playne
Sen we wer putte to peyne.   180
3 filius. He þat is most of mayne,
    May mende it qwen he wyll.

14. Noe. O! barnes, it waxes clere aboute,   *Children, it is*
                                            growing clear.'
Þat may ȝe see ther wher ȝe sitte.   184
1 filius. I, leffe fadir ye loke þare owte,   *' Dear father, see*
                                            if the water
Yf þat þe water wane ought ȝitt.   *wanes.'*
Noe. That sall I do with-owten dowte,   *lf. 28.*
                                            C vi.
For be the wanyng may we witte.   188
A! lorde, to þe I love and lowte,
The catteraks I trowe be knytte,   *The cataracts*
                                          are knit together,
Beholde, my sonnes al three,   *the clouds are*
                                          gone.
    Þe clowdes are waxen clere.   192
2 filius. A! lorde of mercy free,
Ay louyd myght þou be.
Noe. I sall assaye þe see,
    How depe þat it is here.   196
15. Vxor. Loved be that lord þat giffes all grace,
Þat kyndly þus oure care wolde kele.
Noe. I sall caste leede and loke þe space,   *Noah finds the*
                                            water is fifteen
Howe depe þe watir is ilke a dele.   *[Casts the lead.*   200 *cubits deep.*
Fyftene cobittis of highte itt hase
Ouere ilke a hille fully to feylle,
Butte beese wel comforte in þis casse,
It is wanand, þis wate [2] I wele.   204
Ther-fore a fowle of flight
    Full sone sall I forthe sende
To seke if he haue sight,
Som lande vppon to light,   208
Þanne may we witte full right,
    When oure mornyng sall mende.

---

[1] It is difficult here (and in line 217) to see what date the author meant, unless Ix be a mistake for xi; eleven months would agree with Gen. viii. 5 and 6. But nine agrees with l. 251.
[2] MS. has *watir*.

'The raven is strong, wise, and crabbed.   Go forth.

16. Of all þe fowles þat men may fynde,

The Raven is wighte, and wyse is hee.   212

Þou arte ful crabbed and al thy kynde,

Wende forthe þi course I comaunde þe,

And werly watte andyþer þe wynd,

Yf þou fynde awdir lande or tree. [*Sends forth the raven.* 216

Ix monethes here haue we bene pyned,

But when god wyll, better mon bee.

1 filia.   Þat lorde þat lennes vs lyffe,

To lere his lawes in lande,   220

He mayd bothe man and wyffe,

He helpe to stynte oure striffe.

3 filia.   Oure cares are kene as knyffe,

God graunte vs goode tydand.   224

If. 28 b.
This bird is a long time, he must have found food on land ;

17 1 fil.   Fadir, þis foule is forthe full lange,

Vppon sum lande I trowe he lende,

His foode þerfore to fynde and fange,

That makis hym be a fayland frende.   228

Noe.   Nowe sonne, and yf he so forthe gange,

Sen he for all oure welthe gon wende,

Then be he for his werkis wrange

He shall be cursed.

Euermore weried with-owten ende.   232

And sertis for to see

Whan oure sorowe salle sesse,

A nodyr foule full free

Owre messenger salle be,   236

I will send the dove, a faithful bird.'

Þou doufe, I comaunde þe,

Owre comforte to encresse.

18. A faithfull fewle to sende art þow,

Of alle with-in þere wauys wyde,   240

Wende forthe, I pray þe, for owre prowe,

And sadly seke on ilke a side

Yf þe floodes be falland nowe,

Þat þou on þe erthe may belde and byde ;   244

Bryng vs som tokenyng þar we may trowe
What tydandes sall of vs be-tyde.   [*Sends forth the dove.*

2 filia.   Goode lorde! on vs þou luke,
    And sesse oure sorow sere,   248
Sen we al synne for-soke
And to thy lare vs toke.

3 filia.   A twelmothe bott xij weke   'We have waited
    Have we be houerand here. 252 here nine months.'

19. Noe.   Now barnes, we may be blithe and gladde,
And lowe oure lord of heuenes kyng,
My birde has done as I hym badde,   The dove brings
An olyue braunche I se hym brynge. 256 an olive branch.
Blyste be þou fewle þat neuere was fayd,
•That in thy force makis no faylyng,
Mare joie in herte never are I hadde,
We mone be saued, now may we synge! 260 lf. 29.
Come hedir my sonnes in hye,   C vij.
              'Now rejoice!
    Oure woo away is wente,
I see here certaynely[1]   I see the hills
Þe hillis of hermonye[1],   264 of Armenia.'

1 filius.   Lovyd be þat lord for-thy
    That vs oure lyffes hase lente[2].

20. Vxor.   For wrekis nowe þat we may wynne,
Oute of þis woo þat we in wore,   268
But Noye, where are nowe all oure kynne, 'Where are all
And companye we kn[e]we be-fore.   our kindred?'

Noe.   Dame, all ar drowned, late be thy dyne, 'Drowned for
              their sins. Be
And sone þei boughte þer synnes sore. 272 quiet!
Gud lewyn latte vs be-gynne   Let us begin
So þat we greue oure god nomore; living well.'
He was greved in degre,
    And gretely moved in mynde,

---

[1] These two lines are one in the MS.
[2] Added in margin, in later hand, *Tunc cantent Noe & filii sui, etc.*

For synne as men may see, 277
Dum dixit penitet me.
Full sore for-thynkyng was he
That euere he made mankynde.

21. That makis vs nowe to tole and trusse,
But sonnes he saide, I watte wele when, 282

Arcum ponam in nubibus,
He sette his bowe clerly to kenne,
As a tokenyng by-twene hym and vs
In knawlage tille all cristen men, 286
That fro þis worlde were fynyd þus,
With wattir wolde he neuere wastyd þen.
Þus has god most of myght,

Sette his senge full clere 290
Vppe in þe Ayre of heght;
The rayne-bowe it is right,
As men may se, in sight,
In seasons of þe yere [1].

22. 2 fil. Sir, nowe sen god oure souerand syre 295
Has sette his syne þus in certayne,
Than may we wytte þis worldis empire
Shall euermore laste, is noȝt to layne. 298
Noe. Nay, sonne, þat sall we nouȝt desire,
For and we do we wirke in wane,

For it sall ones be waste with fyre,
And never worþe to worlde agayne. 302
Vxor. A ! syre owre hertis are feere for þes sawes
That ȝe saye here,
That myscheffe mon be more.

Noe. Beis noȝt aferde þerfore, 306
ȝe sall noght lyffe þan yore,
Be many hundereth yhere.

23. 1 filius. Fadir, howe sall þis lyffe be ledde,
Sen non ar in þis worlde but we ? 310

[1] This line inserted later.

Noe.   Sones, with youre wiffes ȝe salle be stedde,

And multyplye youre seede salle ȝe.

ȝoure barnes sall ilkon othir wedde,

And worshippe god in gud degre ;

Beestes and foules sall forthe be bredde,

And so a worlde be-gynne to bee.

Nowe travaylle salle ȝe taste

      To wynne you brede & wyne,

For alle þis worlde is waste ;

Theȝ beestes muste be vnbraste,

And wende we hense in haste,

      In goddis blissyng & myne.

Go forth, multiply, and work.'

314

318

322

X. THE PARCHEMYNERS AND BOKEBYNDERS.

Abraham's sacrifice of Isaac.

[PERSONS OF THE PLAY.

ABRAHAM.   PRIMUS FAMULUS.
ISAAC.   SECUNDUS FAMULUS.]
ANGELUS.

[SCENE, *Abraham's abode in Beersheba.*]

Gen. xvii; xvi.
1–3, 15; xxi. 5,
33; xxii. 1–19, 23;
xxiv. 2–4.

1. Abr. GRETT god, þat alle þis world has wrought,
    And wisely wote both gud and ille,
I thanke hym thraly in my thought
Of alle his laue he lens me tille.   4
That þus fro barenhede has me broghte,

I am 100 years
old,

A hundereth wynter to fulfille,
Thou graunte me myght so þat I mowght
Ordan my werkis aftir þi wille.   8
For in þis erthely lyffe
Ar non to god more boune,
Then is I and my wyffe

and have found
great friendship.'
Gen. xviii. 8, 10.
God's promises
to Abraham.

For frenshippe we haue foune.   12
2. Vn-to me tolde god on a tyde,
Wher I was telde vnder a tree,
He saide my seede shulde multyplye [1],
Lyke to þe gravell of þe see,   16
And als þe sternes wer strewed wyde,
So saide he þat my seede shuld be ;

---

[1] The late hand added a *d*, to make a rime with *tyde*.

And bad I shulde be circumcicyd,
To fulfille þe lawe; þus lernynde he me.　20
In worlde wher-for we wonne
He sendes vs richeys ryve,
Als ferre as schynes þe sonne,
He is stynter of stryve.　24
Abram[1] first named was I,
And sythen he sette a sylypp ma,　　　A syllable added to his name.
And my wiffe hyght Sarae
And sythen was scho named Sara.　28

3. But Sara was vncertan thanne　　　Sara was barren.
That euere oure seede shulde sagates ȝelde,
Be-cause hir-selfe sho was barrane,
And we wer bothe gone in grete eelde.　32
But scho wroght as a wyse woman,
To haue a barne vs for to beelde,
Hir seruand prevely scho wan
Vn-to my bede my wille to welde.　36
Sone aftir þan be-felle
When god oure dede wolde dight,　　　If. 30 b.
Sho broght forthe Esmaell,　　　Her servant bore Ishmael.
A sone semely to sight.　40

4. Than aftirward when we waxed alde,
My wyffe sche felle in feere for same,
Oure god nedes tythynges tyll vs talde,　　　A son was promised to Sara.
Wher we wer in oure house at hame,　44
Tille haue a sone we shulde be balde,
And Isaak shulde be his name,
And his seede shulde springe many falde.
Gyff I were blythe, who wolde me blame?　　　'If I were glad, who would blame me?
And for I trowed þis tythynge,　49
That god talde to me þanne,
The grounde and þe begynnyng
Of trowthe þat tyme be-ganne.　52

　　　[1] The MS. has *Abraham*.

I owe much to God.

5. Nowe awe I gretely god to yeelde,

That so walde telle me his entente,

And noght gaynestandyng oure grete eelde,

A semely sone he has vs sente.   56

My seemly son is now strong.'

Now is he wight hym-selfe to welde,

And fra me is all wightnes wente,

Ther-fore sall he be my beelde.   59

I lowe hym þat þis lane has lente,

For he may stynte oure stryve,

And fende vs fro alle ille,

I love hym as my liffe,

With all myn herte and will.   64

6. Ang.   Abraham! Abraham!

           Abr.   Loo I am here.

' I bring you a message, take Isaac to the land of Vision, and sacrifice him.' lf. 31. D ij.

Ang.   Nowe bodeword vnto þe I brynge,

God wille assaye þi wille and cheere,

Giffe þou wille bowe tylle his byddyng ;

Isaak, þi sone, þat is the dere,   69

Whom þou loues ouer [1] alle thyng,

To þe lande of Vyssyon wende in feere,

And there of hym þou make offering.

I salle þe shewe fulle sone,   73

The stede of sacrifice,

God wille þis dede be done,

And þerfore þe avise.   76

' This is a strange thing.

7. Abr.   Lord god, þat lens ay lastand light,

This is a ferly fare to feele,

Tille haue a sone semely to sight,

Isaak, þat I loue full wele,   80

My son is more than thirty years old.

He is of eelde, to reken right,

Thyrty ȝere and more sum dele,

And vnto dede hym buse be dight,

God has saide me so for my seele.   84

[1] MS. has *our*.

And biddis me wende on all wise
To þe lande of Vysionne,
Ther to make sacryfice
Of Isaak þat is my sone.   88

8. And þat is hythyn thre daies iornay,   Mount Moriah
                                                  is three days'
   The ganeste gate þat i gane goo,—   journey hence.
   And sertis, I sall noght say hym nay,
   If god commaunde my self to sloo.   92
   Bot to my sone I will noght saye,   'I will say no-
                                                  thing to Isaac,
   Bot take hym and my seruantis twoo,   but go.
   And with our Assee wende forthe our waye,
   As god has saide, it sall be soo.   [*Enter Isaac.*
   Isaak, sone, I vndirstande   97 My son, we go
                                                  to make offering.
   To wildirnesse now wende will we,
   Thare-fore to make oure offerand,
   For so has god comaunded me.   100

9. Isaac. Fadir, I am euere at youre wille,
   As worthy is with-owten trayne,
   Goddis comaundement to fulfille
   Awe all folke forto be fayne.   104
   Abr.   Sone, þou sais me full gode skille,
   Bott all þe soth is noȝt to sayne,   lf. 31 b.
   Go we sen we sall þer-tille
   I praye god send vs wele agayne.   108
   Isaac. Childir, lede forthe oure Asse, [*To the two servants.* 'Lead forth the
                                                  ass with wood.'
   With wode þat we sall bryne,
   Euen as god ordand has,
   To wyrke we will be-gynne.   [*They set out.*

10. 1 Fam. Att youre biddyng we wille be bowne,   113
   What way in worlde þat ȝe wille wende.
   2 Fam. Why, sall we trusse ought forthe a towne   'Shall we go out
                                                  of town to a
   In any vncouthe lande to lende?   116 strange land?
   1 Fam. I hope tha haue in þis sessoune,
   Fro god of heuyn sum solayce sende.
   2 Fam. To fulfille yt is goode reasoune,

And kyndely kepe þat he has kende.   120

'I do not know
what they intend.'

1 Fam. Bott what þei mene certayne,
Haue I na knowlage clere.

'Never mind.'

2 Fam. It may noght gretely gayne,
To move of swilke matere.   124

'No, don't trouble
yourselves as to
what we do.

11. Abr. No, noye you noght in no degre
So for to deme here of oure dede,
For als god comaunded so wirke wille we,
Vn-tille his tales vs bus take hede.   128

1 Fam. Alle þos þat wille his seruandis be,
Ful specially he wille thaym spede.

Young men, I
praise the Lord.'

Isaac. Childir, with all þe myght in me.
I lowe that lorde of ilke a lede,   132
And wirshippe hym certayne,
My wille is euere vnto.

lf. 32.
D iij.

2 Fam. God giffe you myght and mayne
Right here so for to doo.   136

'Son, if God
willed it, I would
die for him.'

12. Abr. Sone, yf oure lord god almyghty,
Of my selfe walde haue his offerande.
I wolde be glade for hym to dye,
For all oure heele hyngis in his hande.

'So would I.'

Isaac. Fadir, for suth, ryght so walde I,   141
Leuer þan lange to leue in lande.

Abr. A ! sone, thu sais full wele, for-thy
God geue þe grace grathely to stande.

'Young men,
abide here.'

Childir, bide ȝe here still ;   [*To the servants.*
No ferther sall ȝe goo.   146
For ȝondir I se þe hill
That we sall wende vntoo.   148

13. Isaac. Kepe wele our Asse and all oure gere,
To tyme we come agayne you till. [*Exeunt Isaac & Abr.*

[SCENE II, *The land of Vision, near Mount Moriah.*]

Abr. My sone, þis wode behoues þe bere,

Till þou come high vppon yone hill.   152

Isaac. Fadir, þat may do no dere

Goddis comaundement to fullfyll;

For fra all wathes he will vs were,

Whar-so we wende to wirke his wille.   156

Abr. A ! sone, þat was wele saide,

Lay doune þat woode euen here,

Tille oure auter be grathide,—

14. And, my sone, make goode cheere.   160

Isaac. Fadir, I see here woode and fyre,

Bot wher-of sall oure offerand be ?

Abr. Sertis, son, gude god oure suffraynd syre

Sall ordayne it in goode degre.   164

For sone, and we do his dessyre,

Full gud rewarde thar-fore gette wee.

In heuyn ther mon we haue oure hyre,

For vnto vs so hight has hee.   168

Ther-fore sone, let vs praye,

To god, bothe þou and I,

That we may make þis daye

Oure offerand here dewly.   172

15. Grete god! þat all þis worlde has wrought,

And grathely gouernes goode and ill,

Thu graunte me myght so þat I mowght

Thy comaundementis to full-fill.   176

And gyffe my flessche groche or greue oght,

Or sertis my saule assentte þer-till,

To byrne all that I hydir broght,

I sall noght spare yf I shulde spille.   180

Isaac. Lorde god ! of grete pouste,

To wham all pepull prayes,

Isaac carries the wood up the hill,

sets it down,

and asks, where is the offering?
lf. 32 b.

The father evades the question.

Abraham prays that he may not rebel.

Graunte bothe my fadir and me
To wirke þi wille all weyes!   184

16. But fadir, nowe wolde I frayne full fayne,
Whar-of oure offerand shulde be grathid?

' Son, thou must
bear this bitter
turn.'

Abr. Sertis, sone, I may no lengar layne,
Thy-selfe shulde bide þat bittir brayde.   188

Isaac. Why! fadir, will god þat I be slayne?
Abr. ჳa, suthly sone, so has he saide.

Isaac is pleased
to obey.

Isaac. And I sall noght grouche þer agayne,
To wirke his wille I am wele payed;   192
Sen it is his desire,
I sall be bayne to be

If. 33.
D iiij.

Brittynd and brent in fyre,
And þer-fore morne noght for me.   196

' I must do it.'

17. Abr. Nay, sone, this gatis most nedis be gone,
My lord god will I noght gayne-saye,
Nor neuer make mornys nor mone,
To make offerand of þe this day.   200

Isaac. Fadir, sen god oure lorde all-ane
Vowchesaffe to sende when ჳe gon praye
A sone to you, when ye had nane,
And nowe will that he wende his waye,   204

' Father, offer me
gladly,

Therfore faynde me to fell
Tille offerand in þis place,
But firste I sall you telle
My counsaille in þis case.   2c8

but my flesh will
dread, I may
oppose you.

18. I knaw myselfe be cours of kynde,
My flessche for dede will be dredande,
I am ferde þat ჳe sall fynde
My force youre forward to withstande.   212

Therefore bind
me fast, while
I am in the mind;

Ther-fore is beste þat ye me bynde
In bandis faste, boothe fute and hande,
Nowe whillis I am in myght and mynde,
So sall ჳe saffely make offerrande.   216

For fadir, when I am boune,
My myght may not avayle,
Here sall no fawte be foune
To make youre forward faylle.   220

19. For ȝe ar alde and alle vnwelde,
And I am wighte and wilde of thoght.

Abr. To bynde hym þat shuld be my beelde!
Outtane goddis will, þat wolde I noght.   224
But loo! her sall no force be felde,
So sall god haue that he has soght.
Fare-well! my sone, I sall þe ȝelde   *[Binds him.*
Tylle hym þat all this world has wroght.
Nowe kysse me hartely, I þe pray,   229
Isaak, I take my leue for ay.
My blissyng haue þou enterly,
                   Me bus þe mys!   232
And I beseke god all-myghty
                   He giffe þe his.
Thus aren we samyn assent,
Eftir thy wordis wise,   236
Lorde god! to þis take tente,
Ressayue thy sacrifice.

20. This is to me a perles pyne,
To se myn nawe dere childe þus boune!   240
Me had well leuer my lyf to tyne
Than see þis sight, þus of my sone.
It is goddis will, it sall be myne,
Agaynste his saande sall I neuer schone;   244
To goddis cummaundement I sall enclyne,
That in me fawte non be foune.
Therfore my sone so dere,
If þou will any thyng saye,   248
Thy dede it drawes nere,
Fare-well, for anes and ay.

Side notes:

then you can offer safely, for you are old and weak, I am strong.'

'Bind him who should be my support!

If. 33 b.

Kiss me, farewell!

bless you! I must lose you.

It is a peerless sorrow, to see my dear child bound,

but I bow to God's will.'

21. Isaac. Now, my dere fadir, I wolde you praye,

Here me thre wordes, graunte me my bone!   252

Sen I fro this sall passe for ay,

I see myn houre is comen full sone.

In worde, in werke, or any waye

That I haue trespassed or oght mysdone,   256

For-giffe me fadir, or I dye þis daye,

For his luffe þat made boþe sonne and mone.

Here sen we two sall twynne,

Firste god I aske mercy,   260

And you in more and myne,

This day or euere I dy.

22. Abr. Now my grete god, Adonay!

That all þis worlde has worthely wroght,   264

For-gyffe the sone, for his mercye,

In worde, in worke, in dede, and thoght.

Nowe sone, as we ar leryd

Our tyme may not myscarie[1].   268

Isaac. Nowe fare wele, all medilerth,

My flesshe waxis faynte for ferde;

Nowe fadir, take youre swerde,

Me[2] thynke full lange ȝe tarie.   272

23. Abr. Nay, nay sone, nay, I the be-hete,

That do I noght, with-outen were,

Thy wordis makis me my wangges to wete,

And chaunges, childe, ful often my cheere.   276

Ther-fore lye downe, hande and feete,

Nowe may þou witte thyn oure is nere.

Margin notes:

'Father, I pray you

forgive my misdeeds.

I first ask God's mercy, then yours.'

If. 34.
D v.
'May God forgive thee all.'

'Farewell, my flesh grows fearful, take your sword, you tarry too long.'

'Thy words wet my cheeks, lie down!'

---

[1] Lines 267, 268 are written as one in the MS. There seem to be some lines wanting here, both to the sense and to complete the stanza, which is more irregular than any other in this play. (Four others, stanzas 2, 19, 24, 25, are irregular.) In the margin two new lines in a late hand seem to have been suggested to remedy this:

'*Abr.* Nowe haue I chose whether I had lever
My nowne swete son to slo or greve my
God for ever. Hic caret.'

[2] MS. has ȝe.

Isaac. A! dere fadir, lyff is full swete,   ' Father, life is
sweet,

The drede of dede dose all my dere.   280

As I am here youre sone,

To god I take me till,

Nowe am I laide here bone,

Do with me what ȝe will.   284

24. For fadir, I aske no more respete,   but I am ready
now.

Bot here a worde what I wolde mene,

I beseke ȝou or þat ȝe smyte,

Lay doune þis kyrcheffe on myn eghne.   288   Lay a kerchief
over my eyes.

Than may ȝoure offerand be parfite,

If ȝe wille wirke thus as I wene.

And here to god my saule I wite,

And all my body to brenne bydene.   292

Now, smite fast.'

Now fadir be noght myssyng,

But smyte fast as ȝe may.

Abr. Fare-wele, in goddis dere blissyng,   ' Farewell, in
God's blessing.'

And myn, for euer and ay.   296

That pereles prince I praye

Myn offerand here till haue it,

My sacryfice þis day,

I praye þe lorde ressayue it.   300

25. **Ang.** Abraham! Abraham!

Abr. Loo! here I wys.   lf. 34 b.

Ang. Abraham, abyde, and halde þe stille.

Sla noght thy sone, do hym no mysse,   ' Slay not thy
son! here is a
sheep.'

Take here a schepe thy offerand tyll,   [*A sheep comes in.*   304

Is sente þe fro the kyng of blisse.

That faythfull ay to þe is fone,

He biddis þe make offerrand of þis,

Here at this tyme, and saffe thy sone.   308

26. **Abr.**   I lowe þat lord with herte entier,   They praise God,

That of his luffe þis lane me lente,

To saffe my sone, my darlyng dere,

And sente þis schepe to þis entente,   312

F

and offer the
sheep instead.

That we sall offir it to the here,
So sall it be as þou has mente.
My sone, be gladde and make goode cheere,
God has till vs goode comforte sente;   316
He will noght þou be dede,
But tille his lawes take kepe,
And se, son, in thy stede,
God has sente vs a schepe.   320

27. Isaac. To make oure offerand at his wille
All for oure sake he has it sente.
To lowe þat lorde I halde grete skyll,
That tylle his menȝe þus has mente.   324
This dede I wolde haue tane me till,
Full gladly lorde, to thyn entent.

Abr. A! sone, thy bloode wolde he noght spill,
For-thy this shepe thus has he sente.   328

' Son, I am glad.
Let us go home.'

And sone I am full fayne
Of our spede in þis place,
Bot go we home agayne,
And lowe god of his grace.   *[going.*   332

28. Ang. Abraham! Abraham!
Abr. Loo! here in dede.

God's reward to
Abraham.
lf. 35.
D vj.

Harke sone! sum saluyng of our sare.
Ang. God sais þou sall haue mekill mede
For thys goode will þat þou in ware,   336
Sen þou for hym wolde do þis dede,
To spille thy sone and noght to spare;
He menes to multiplie youre seede,
On sides seere, as he saide are;   340
And yit he hight you this,
That of youre seede sall ryse,
Thurgh helpe of hym and his
Ouere hande of all enmys.   344

29. Luk ȝe hym loue, þis is his liste,
And lelly lyff eftir his laye,

For in youre seede all mon be bliste,
That ther bese borne be nyght or day.
If ȝe will in hym trowe or triste,
He will be with ȝou euere and aye.

'Live loyally,
God will ever
be with you.'

348

Abr.   Full well wer vs and we it wiste,
Howe we shulde wirke his will alwaye.

352

Isaac.   Fadir, þat sall we frayne
At wyser men þan wêe,
And fulfille it fulfayne,
In dede eftir oure degree.

'We will ask
how to do his
will from wiser
men than we.'

356

30. Abr.   Nowe sone, sen we þus wele hase spede,
That god has graunted me thy liffe,
It is my wille þat þou be wedde,
And welde a woman to thy wyffe ;
So sall thy sede springe and be spredde,
In the laweȝ of god be reasoune ryffe.
I wate in what steede sho is stede,
That þou sall wedde, withowten stryffe.
Rabek þat damysell,
Hir fayrer is none fone,
The doughter of Batwell,
That was my brothir sone.

360

364

Isaac shall wed
Rebecca, daugh-
ter of Bethuel.

368

31. Isaac.   Fadir, as þou likes my lyffe to spende,
I sall assente vnto the same.

lf. 35 b.

Abr.   One of my seruandis sone sall I sende
Vn-to þat birde to brynge hir hame.
The gaynest gates now will we wende.

372

[*Coming back finds the servants.*

My barnes, yee ar noght to blame
ȝeff ȝe thynke lang þat we her lende ;
Gedir same oure gere, in goddis name,
And go we hame agayne.
Euyn vnto Barsabe,
God þat is most of mayne
Vs wisse and with ȝou be.

376

'We go home
now quickly.'

380

XI. THE HOSEERS.[1]

---

*The departure of the Israelites from Egypt, the
ten plagues, and the passage of the Red Sea*[2].

PERSONS OF THE PLAY.

REX PHARAO.   DEUS.   MOYSES.
PRIMUS ET SECUNDUS CONSOLES (i.e. king's officers).
PRIMUS, SECUNDUS ET TERTIUS PUERI (i.e. Jews).
PRIMUS ET SECUNDUS EGYPTII.

[SCENE I, *Pharaoh's court.*]

1. Rex.　　O PEES, I bidde þat noman passe,
　　　　　　　　 But kepe þe cours þat I comaunde,
And takes gud heede to hym þat hasse
Youre liff all haly in his hande.　　　　　　4

Pharaoh pro-
claims his might
and power,

Towneley
Mysteries (Sur-
tees Society,
1836), p. 55.

Kyng Pharo my fadir was,
　　　And led þe lordshippe of this lande,

Incipit Pharao.

Pharao.　Peas, of payn that no man pas,
　　　　　　 But kepe the course that I commaunde,
　　　　　　 And take good hede of hym that has
　　　　　　 Youre helthe alle holy in hys hande;
　　　　　　 For kyng Pharro my fader was,
　　　　　　 And led thys lordshyp of thys land,

---

[1] In the MS. many of the verses in this piece are written in the old
16-syllable length, with a red line to mark the break at the inner rime
and some are written in two lines as in modern usage. The lines being
inconveniently long, and the diversity misleading, all the lines are here
broken and printed in the usual 8-syllable verse. The eighth Towneley
play runs parallel to this, and is printed at the foot.

[2] The passages in Exodus on which this play is founded are, chap. i. ver
7-16; ii. 23; iii. 1-15; iv. 1-6, 31; vii. 19—x. 27; xii. 29-31; xiv. 5-31

I am hys hayre as elde will asse,
    Euere in his steede to styrre and stande.   8
All Egippe is myne awne,
    To lede aftir my lawe,
I will my myght be knawen,
    And honnoured als it [1] awe.   12
2. Ther-fore als Kyng I commaunde pees
    To all þe pepill of þis Empire,   *and ordains peace and obedience.*
That noman putte hym fourthe in prees,
    But þat will do als we desire.   16
And of youre sawes I rede you sees,
    And sesse to me, youre sufferayne sire,
That most youre comforte may encrese,
    And at my liste lose liffe and lyre.   20
i Cons. My lorde, yf any were
    Þat walde not wirke youre will,

    I am hys hayre as age wylle has,
    Ever in stede to styr or stand.   8
    Alle Egypt is myne awne
    To leede aftyr my law,
    I wold my myghte were knowne
    And honoryd, as hit awe.   12
    Fulle low he shalle be thrawne
    That harkyns not my sawe,
    Hanged hy and drawne,
    Therfor no boste ye blaw;
    Bot as for kyng I commaund peasse,   13
    To alle the people of thys empyre.
    Looke no man put hym self in preasse,
    Bot that wylle do as I desyre,   16
    And of youre wordes look that ye seasse.
    Take tent to me, youre soferand syre,
    That may youre comfort most increasse,
    And to my lyst bowe lyfe and lyre.   20
'rimus Miles. My Lord, if any here were,
    That wold not wyrk youre wylle,

---

[1] MS. repeats *as it.*

And we wist whilke thay were,
Ful sone we sall þaym spill.   24

3. **Rex.**   Thurgh-oute my kyngdome wolde I kenn,

Thanks be to
those who tell
us of cursed foes.

And konne tham thanke þat couthe me telle,
If any wer so weryd þen
That wolde aught fande owre forse to fell.   28

A sort of men
called Jews mul-
tiply too fast in
Goshen.

ii **Con.**   My lorde, þar are a maner of men,
That mustirs grete maistris þam emell,
The Jewes þat wonnes here in Jessen
And er named the childir of Israell.   32

They multyplye so faste,
Þat suthly we suppose
Thay are like, and they laste,
Yowre lordshippe for to lose.   36

What tricks are
they doing?

4. **Rex.**   Why, devill, what gawdes haue they begonne?
Er þai of myght to make a frayse?

i **Cons.**   Tho felons folke, Sir, first was fonn
In kyng Pharo ȝoure fadyr dayse;   40

'They came in
your father's day.

Thay come of Joseph, Jacob sonn,

If we myghte com thaym nere,
Fulle soyn we shuld theym spylle.   24

Pharao.   Thrughe out my kyngdom wold I ken,
Aud kun hym thank that wold me telle,
If any were so waryd men
That wold my fors down felle.   28

Secundus Miles. My Lord, ye have a manner of men
That make great mastres us emelle;
The Jues that won in Gersen,
Thay are callyd chyldyr of Israel.   32
Thay multyplye fulle fast,
And sothly we suppose
That shalle ever last,
Oure lordshyp for to lose.   36

Pharao.   Why, how have thay syche gawdes begun?
Ar thay of myght to make sych frayes?

Primus Miles.   Yei, Lord, fulle felle folk ther was fun
In kyng Pharao, youre fader's, dayes   40
Thay cam of Josephe, was Jacob son,

That was a prince worthy to prayse,
And sithen in ryste furthe are they run,
Now ar they like to lose our layse.   44
Thay sall confounde vs clene,
Bot if þai sonner sese.
Rex.   What devill ever may it mene,
Þat they so fast encrese?   48
5. ii Cons.   Howe they encrese, full wele we kenn,   lf. 36 b.
Als oure elders be-fore vs fande,
Thay were talde but sexty and ten   From 70 they
Whan þei enterd in to þis lande.   52   have in 400 years
                                             increased to
Sithen haue they soionerd here in Jessen   300,000 strong
                                             men.'
Foure houndereth ӡere, þis we warande,
Now are they noumbered of myghty men,
Wele more þan thre hundereth thowsande,   56
With-owten wiffe and childe,
And herdes þat kepes ther fee.
Rex.   So myght we be bygillid,
But certis þat sall noght be,   60

He was a prince worthy to prayse,
In sythen in ryst have thay ay ron;
Thus ar thay lyke to lose youre layse,   44
Thay wylle confound you cleyn,
Bot if thay soner seasse.
Pharao.   What, devylle, is that thay meyn
That thay so fast incresse?   48
Secundus Miles.   How thay incres fulle welle we ken.
As oure faders dyd understand;
Thay were bot sexty and ten
When thay fyrst cam in to thys land,   52
Sythen have sojerned in Gersen
Four hundred wynter, I dar warand;
Now are thay nowmbred of myghty men
Moo then ccc thousand,   56
Wythe outen wyfe and chyld,
Or hyrdes that kepe thare fee.
Pharao.   How thus myghte we be begyled?
Bot shalle it not be;   60

'We will destroy them with cunning.

6. For with qwantise[1] we sall þam qwelle,
  Þat þei sall no farrar sprede.

We have heard that a man should grow among them who should ruin us.'

i Cons. Lorde, we have herde oure ffadres telle,
  Howe clerkis, þat ful wele couthe rede,   64
Saide, a man shulde wax þam emell,
  That suld for-do vs and owre dede.

Rex. Fy on þam ! to þe devell of helle !
  Swilke destanye sall we noght drede.   68

'Kill their men children.

We sall make mydwayes to spille þam,
  Whenne oure Ebrewes are borne,
All þat are mankynde to kille þam,
  So sall they sone be[2] lorne.   72

7. For of the other haue I non awe,

We will bid them to bondage, and keep them low.'

  Swilke bondage sall we to þam bede,
To dyke and delfe, beere and drawe,
  And do all swilke vn-honest dede.   76
Þus sall þe laddis be holden lawe,
  Als losellis ever thaire lyff to leede.

  For wythe quantyse we shalle thaym quelle,
  So that thay shalle not far sprede.

Primus Miles. My Lord, we have hard oure faders telle, 63
  And clerkes that welle couthe rede, 64
  Ther shuld a man walk us amelle
  That shuld fordo us and oure dede.

Pharao. Fy on hym, to the devylle of helle,
  Sych destyny wylle we not drede ; 68
  We shalle make mydwyfes to spylle them,
  Where any Ebrew is borne,
  And alle menkynde to kylle them,
  So shalle they soyn be lorne. 72
  And as for elder have I none awe.
  Syche bondage shalle I to theym beyde,
  To dyke and delf, bere and draw,
  And to do alle unhonest deyde ; 76
  So shalle these laddes be holden law,
  In thraldom ever thare lyfe to leyde.

---

  [1] MS. has *qwantile*.   [2] MS. has *by*.

ii Con.   Certis, lorde, þis is a sotell sawe,
　　　So sall þe folke no farrar sprede.　　　　　　　　　80
Rex.   Yaa! helpes to halde þam doune,
　　　Þat we no fantnyse[1] fynde.
i Cons.   Lorde, we sall ever be bowne,
　　　In bondage þam to bynde.　　　　　　　　　　　84

[SCENE II, *near Mount Sinai.*]

8. Moyses.   Grete god! Þat all þis grounde be-gan,
　　　And governes euere in gud degree,
That made me Moyses vn-to man,　　　　　　　　lf. 37.
　　　And saued me sythen out of þe see.　　88　　E j.
Kyng Pharo he comaunded þan　　　　　　　'God saved me
　　　So þat no sonnes shulde saued be,　　　　out of the sea.
Agayns his wille away I wan,
　　　Thus has god shewed his myght in me.　　92
Nowe am I here to kepe,　　　　　　　　I now keep
　　　Sett vndir synay syde,　　　　　　　bishop Jethro's
　　　　　　　　　　　　　　　　　　　sheep, under
　　　　　　　　　　　　　　　　　　　Sinai.

Secundus Miles.   Now, certes, thys was a sotelle saw,
　　　　　Thus shalle these folk no farthere sprede.　　80
Pharao.　　　Now help to hald theym downe,
　　　　　Look I no fayntnes fynde.
Primus Miles.   Alle redy, Lord, we shalle be bowne,
　　　　　In bondage thaym to bynde.　　　　　　84

　　　　Tunc intrat Moyses cum virgâ in manu, etc.

Moyses.　　　Gret God, that alle thys warld began,
　　　　　And growndyd it in good degre,
　　　　　Thou mayde me, Moyses, unto man,
　　　　　And sythen thou savyd me from the se,　　88
　　　　　Kyng Pharao had commawndyd than,
　　　　　Ther shuld no man chyld savyd be;
　　　　　Agans hys wylle away I wan;
　　　　　Thus has God showed hys might for me.　　92
　　　　　Now am I set to kepe,
　　　　　Under thys montayn syde,

　　　　　　　[1] MS. has *fantynse.*

The bisshoppe Jetro schepe,
So bettir bute to bide.   [*Sees the burning bush.*

9. A ! mercy, god, mekill is thy myght,   97
What man may of thy meruayles mene,

I se ȝondyr a ful selcouth syght,
Wher-of be-for no synge was seene.   100
A busk I se yondir brennand bright,
And þe leues last ay in like grene,
If it be werke of worldly wight,
I will go witte with-owten wene.   104

Deus.   Moyses ! come noght to nere,
Bot stille in þat stede dwelle,
And take hede to me here,
And tente what I þe telle.   108

10. I am thy lorde, with-outyn lak,
To lengh þi liffe euen as me list,
And the same god þat som tyme spak

Byschope Jettyr shepe,
To better may betyde ;   96
A, Lord, grete is thy myght !
What man may of yond mervelle meyn?
Yonder I se a selcowth syght,
Syche on in warld was never seyn ;   100
A bush I see burnand fulle bryght,
And ever elyke the leyfes ar greyn,
If it be wark of warldely wyght,
I wylle go wyt wythoutyn weyn.   104
Deus.   Moyses, Moyses !
Hic properat ad rubum, et dicit ei Deus,
Moyses com not to nere,
Bot stylle in that stede thou dwelle,   106
And harkyn unto me here ;
Take tent what I the telle.   108
Do of thy shoyes in fere,
Wyth mowth as I the melle,
The place thou standes in there
Forsoth, is halowd welle.
I am thy Lord, withouten lak,   10
To lengthe thi lyfe even as I lyst,
I am God that som tyme spake

Vn-to thyne elders als þei wiste;   112
But Abraham and Ysaac,
    And Jacob, saide I, suld be bliste,
And multyplye and þam to mak,
    So þat þer seede shulde noght be myste.   116
And nowe kyng Pharo,
    Fuls þare childir ful faste
If I suffir hym soo,
    Þare seede shulde sone be past.   120

11. Go, make þe message haue I mende   'Go, warn
    To hym þat þam so harmed hase,   Pharaoh to let
Go, warne hym with wordes hende,   my people pass.
    So þat he lette my pepull passe,   124
That they to wildirnesse may wende,
    And wirshippe me als whilom was.
And yf he lenger gar them lende,
    His sange ful sone sall be, 'allas!'   128

    To thyn elders, as thay wyst;   112
    To Abraham, and Isaac,
    And Jacob, I sayde shulde be blyst,
    And multytude of them to make,
    So that thare seyde shuld not be myst.   116
    Bot now thys kyng, Pharao,
    He hurtys my folk so fast,
    If that I suffre hym so,
    Thare seyde shuld soyne be past;   120
    Bot I wylle not so do,
    In me if thay wylle trast
    Bondage to brynge thaym fro.
    Therfor thou go in hast,
    To do my message have in mynde   121
    To hym, that me syche harme mase;
    Thou speke to hym wythe wordes heynde,
    So that he let my peple pas   124
    To wyldernes, that they may weynde
    To worshyp me as I wylle asse.
    Agans my wylle if that thay leynd,
    Ful soyn hys song shalle be, alas.   128

'He is afraid.   **Moyses.**   A ! lord syth, with thy leue,
                   Þat lynage loves me noght,
                   Gladly they walde me greve,
                   And I slyke boodword brought.   132

            12. Ther-fore lord, late sum othir fraste
                   Þat hase more forse þam for to feere.

                Deus.   Moyses, be noght a-baste,
                   My bidding baldely to bere,   136
                   If thai with wrang ought walde þe wrayste
                   Owte of all wothis I sall þe were.

'They will not
heed me without
a token.'   **Moyses.**   We ! lord, þai wil noght to me trayste,
                   For al the othes þat I may swere.   140
                To neven slyke note of newe
                   To folke of wykkyd will,
                With-outen taken trewe,
                   They will noght take tente þer-till.   144

If. 37 b.   13. **Deus.** And if they will noght vndirstande,
                   Ne take heede how I haue þe sente,

            Moyses.   A, Lord ! pardon me, wyth thy leyf,
                   That lynage luffes me noght,
                   Gladly thay wold me greyf,
                   If I syche bodworde broght.   132
                   Good Lord, lette som othere frast,
                   That has more fors the folke to fere.

            Deus.   Moyses, be thou nott abast,
                   My bydyng shalle thou boldly bere;   136
                   If thay with wrong away wold wrast,
                   Outt of the way I shalle the were.

            Moyses.   Good Lord, thay wylle not me trast
                   For alle the othes that I can swere;   140
                   To never sych noytes new
                   To folk of wykyd wylle,
                   Wyth outen tokyn trew,
                   Thay wylle not tent ther-tylle.   144

            Deus.   If that he wylle not understand
                   Thys tokyn trew that I shalle sent,

Before the kyng cast downe thy wande,

 & it sall seme as a serpent. 148

Sithen take the tayle in thy hande,

 And hardely vppe þou itt hente,

In the firste state als þou it fande.

 So sall it turne be myn entent. 152

Hyde thy hande in thy barme,

 And serpent it sall be like,

Sithen hale with-outen harme,

 Þi syngnes sall be slyke. 156

14. And if he wil not suffre than

 My pepull for to passe in pees,

I sall send vengeaunce ix or x.,

 To sewe hym sararre, or I sesse. 160

Bot þe Jewes þat wonnes in Jessen

 Sall noȝt be merked with þat messe,

Als lange als þai my lawes will kenne

 Þer comfort sal I euere encresse. 164

Moyses. A! lorde, lovyd be thy wille,

'Cast down thy wand, it shall seem a serpent.

Hide thy hand in thy bosom, it shall turn to a serpent,' [error, see *Exod.* iv. 6, and l. 154 below.]

Nine or ten plagues.

'I will go.

 Afore the kyng cast down thy wand,

 And it shalle turne to a serpent. 148

 Then take the taylle agane in hand,

 Boldly up look thou it hent,

 And in the state thou it fand

 Thou shal it turne by myne intent; 152

 Sythen hald thy hand soyn in thy barme,

 And as a lepre it shal be lyke,

 And hole agane with outen harme;

 Lo, my tokyns shal be slyke. 156

 And if he wylle not suffre then

 My people for to pas in peasse,

 I shalle send venyance IX or ten,

 Shalle sowe fulle sore or [I] seasse. 160

 Bot ye Ebrewes, won in Jessen,

 Shalle not be merkyd with that measse;

 As long as thay my lawes wylle ken

 Thare cormforthe shalle ever increasse. 164

Moyses. A, Lord, to luf the aght us welle

Þat makes thy folke so free,
I sall tell þam vn-till
Als þou telles vn-to me.   168

15. But to the kyng, lorde, whan I come,

But if the king
ask thy name?'

And he ask me what is thy name,
And I stande stille þan, defe and dum,
How sall I be withouten blame?   172

The answer.

Deus. I saie þus, *ego sum qui sum*,
I am he þat I am the same,
And if þou myght not meve[1] ne mum,
I sall þe saffe fro synne & shame.   176

Moyses. I vndirstande þis thyng,
With all þe myght in me.

' I will be thy
protection.'

Deus. Be bolde in my blissyng,
Thy belde ay sall I be.   180

16. **Moyses.** A ! lorde of lyffe, lere me my layre,
Þat I þere tales may trewly tell,

That makes thi folk thus free,
I shalle unto thaym telle   167
As thou has told to me.   168
Bot to the kyng, Lord, when I com.
If he aske what is thy name,
And I stand stylle, both deyf and dom,
How shuld I skake withoutten blame?   172

Deus. I say the thus "Ego sum qui sum,"
I am he that is the same;
If thou can nother muf nor mom
I shalle sheld the from shame.   176

Moyses. I understand fulle welle thys thyng,
I go, Lord, with alle the myght in me.

Deus. Be bold in my blyssyng,
Thi socoure shall I be.   180

Moyses. A, Lord of luf, leyn me thy lare,
That I may truly talys telle ;

---

[1] MS. has *meke*.

Vn-to my frendis nowe will I fayre [1],
Þe chosen childre of Israell.
To telle þam comforte of ther care,
And of þere daunger þat þei in dwell.

'I will go to my friends to comfort them.'
184

[Scene III, *Moses and the Hebrews.*]

[**Moses**]. God mayntayne you & me euermare,
And mekill myrthe be you emell.

188

i puer. A! Moyses, maistir dere,
Oure myrthe is al mornyng,
We are harde halden here
Als carls vndir þe kyng.

'We are slaves.

192

17. ii puer. Moyses, we may mourne and myne,
Þer is no man vs myrþes mase,
And sen we come al of a kynne,
Ken vs som comforte in þis case.

Give us some comfort.'

196

Moyses. Beeths of youre mornyng blyne,
God wil defende you of your fays,

To my freyndes now wylle I fare,
The chosyn childre of Israelle,
To telle theym comforthe of thare care,
In dawngere ther as thay dwelle.
God manteyn you evermare,
And mekylle myrthe be you emelle.

184

188

Primus Puer. A, master Moyses, dere !
Oure myrthe is alle mowrnyng;
Fulle hard halden ar we here,
As carls under the kyng.

192

Secundus Puer. We may mowrn, both more and myn,
Ther is no man that oure myrth mase,
Bot syn we ar alle of a kyn
God send us comforth in thys case.

196

Moyses. Brethere, of youre mowrnyng blyn ;
God wylle delyver you thrughe his grace,

---

[1] *Will I fayre* written in later hand, correcting the original word *fayne*, which is crossed through.

'God will deliver
you from this
woe.'

Oute of þis woo he will you wynne,
    To plese hym in more plener place.   200
I sall carpe to þe kyng,
    And fande to make you free.

lf. 38.
E ij.

  iii puer. God sende vs gud tythyngis,
    And all may with you be.   204

[SCENE IV, *At Pharaoh's court.*]

18. **Moyses.** Kyng Pharo! to me take tent!

    Rex. Why, what tydyngis can þou tell?

'God sends for
his folk.'

Moyses. Fro god of heuen þus am I sente,
    To fecche his folke of Israell,   208
To wildirnesse he walde thei wente.

'Go to the devil!
I do not care
for you.'

    Rex. ȝaa! wende þou to þe devell of hell,
I make no force howe þou has mente,
    For in my daunger sall þei dwelle.   212
And faytour, for thy sake,
    Þei sall be putte to pyne.

    Out of this wo he wylle you wyn,
    And put you to youre pleassyng place.   200
    For I shalle carp unto the kyng,
    And fownd fulle soyn to make you free.

Primus Puer. God grant you good weyndyng,
    And evermore with you be.   204

Moyses, Kyng Pharao to me take tent.

Pharao. Why, boy, what tythynges can thou telle?

Moyses. From God hym self hyder am I sent
    To foche the chyldre of Israelle;   208
    To wyldernes he wold thay went.

Pharao. Yei, weynd the to the devylle of helle,
    I gyf no force what he has ment,
    In my dangere, herst thou, shalle thay dwelle;   212
    And, fature, for thy sake,
    Thay shalbe pent to pyne.

Moyses. Þanne will god vengeaunce take

On þe and on al þyne. 216

Moses threatens God's vengeance.

19. Rex. Fy on the! ladde, oute of my lande!

Wenes þou with wiles to lose oure laye?

Where [1] is þis warlowe with his wande,

Þat wolde þus wynne oure folke away? 220

' Who is this wizard?'

ii Cons. It is Moyses, we wele warrand,

Agayne al Egipte is he ay.

Youre fadir grete faute in hym fande,

Nowe will he marre you if he may. 224

' Moses, who will injure you.'

Rex. Nay, nay, þat daunce is done,

Þat lordan leryd ouere late.

Moyses. God biddis þe graunte my bone,

And late me go my gate. 228

' God bids thee grant my petition.

20. Rex. Biddis god me? fals lurdayne, þou lyes;

What takyn talde he, toke þou tent?

Moyses. ȝaa! sir, he saide þou suld despise

Botht me & all his comaundement. 232

Moyses. Then wylle God venyance take

Of the, and of alle thyn. 216

Pharao, On me? fy on the lad, out of my land!

Wenys thou thus to loyse oure lay?

Say, whence is yond warlow with his wand

That thus wold wyle oure folk away? 220

Primus Myles. Yond is Moyses, I dar warand,

Agans alle Egypt has beyn ay,

Greatt defawte with hym youre fader fand;

Now wylle he mar you if he may. 224

Pharao. Fy on hym! nay, nay, that dawnce is done;

Lurdan, thou loryd to late.

Moyses. God bydes the graunt my bone,

And let me go my gate. 228

Pharao. Bydes God me? fals loselle, thou lyse!

What tokyn told he? take thou tent.

Moyses. He sayd thou shuld dyspyse

Bothe me, and hys commaundement; 232

---

[1] MS. has *when.*

In thy presence kast on this wise
  My wande he bad by his assent,
And þat þou shulde þe wele avise,
  Howe it shulde turne to a serpent.   236
And in his haly name,
  Here sal I ley it downe,
Loo! ser, se her þe same.
        Rex.   A![1] dogg! þe deuyll þe drowne!   240

21. Moyses.   He saide þat I shulde take þe tayle,
  So for to proue his poure playne,
And sone he saide it shuld not fayle
  For to turne a wande agayne.   244
Loo! sir, be-halde!

                    Rex.   Hopp illa hayle!

Now certis þis is a sotill swayne.
  But þis boyes sall byde here in oure bayle,
For all þair gaudis sall noght þam gayne;   248
  Bot warse, both morne and none,
Sall þei fare for thy sake.

Forthy, apon thys wyse,
My wand he bad, in thi present,
I shuld lay downe, and the avyse
How it shuld turne to oone serpent.   236
And in hys holy name
Here I lay it downe;
Lo, syr, here may thou se the same.
Pharao. A, ha, dog! the devylle the drowne!   240
Moyses. He bad me take it by the taylle,
For to prefe hys powere playn,
Then sayde, wythouten faylle,
Hyt shuld turne to a wand agayn.   244
Lo, sir, behold.
Pharao.   Wyth yl a haylle!
Certes this is a sotelle swayn,
Bot thyse boyes shalle abyde in baylle,   247
Alle thi gawdes shalle thaym not gayn;
Bot wars, both morne and none,
Shalle thay fare, for thi sake.

---

[1] MS. has *Al*.

Moyses. God sende sum vengeaunce sone,   lf. 38 b.
And on þi werke take wrake.   252 Vengeance
comes.

[Moses retires : enter Egyptians [1].

22.   **i Egip.** Allas ! allas ! þis lande is lorne,
On lif we may no lenger lende.

    ii Egip. So grete myscheffe is made sen morne,
Þer may no medycyne vs amende.   256

    Cons. Sir kyng, we banne þat we wer borne,   'We curse the
time we were
Oure blisse is all with bales blende.   born.'

    Rex. Why crys you swa, laddis? liste you scorne?

i Egip. Sir kyng, slyk care was neuere kende.   260 The water turned
to blood (1st
Oure watir þat was ordand   plague).
To men and beestis fudde,
Thurghoute al Egipte lande
Is turned to rede blude ;   264

23.   Full vgly and ful ill is it,
Þat was ful faire and fresshe before.

Moyses. I pray God send us venyance sone,
And on thi warkes take wrake.   252

Primus Miles. Alas, Alas ! this land is lorne !
On lyfe we may [no] longer leynd ;
Syche myschefe is fallen syn morne,
Ther may no medsyn it amend.   256

Pharao. Why cry ye so? laddes, lyst ye skorne?   259

Secundus Miles. Syr kyng, syche care was never kend,
In no mans tyme that ever was borne.

Pharao. Telle on, belyfe, and make an end.

Primus Miles. Syr, the waters that were ordand   261
For men and bestes foyd,
Thrughe outt alle Egypt land,
Ar turnyd into reede bloyde :   264
Fulle ugly and fulle ylle is hytt,
That bothe fresh and fayre was before.

---

[1] Two scenes appear to be presented at once, with Moses and his Jews
at one side, Pharaoh and his Egyptians at the other: frequent commu-
nications going on between the two. It seemed best to mark these move-
ments by white spaces in the text, though there is no such discontinuance,
or any direction, in the MS.

Rex. This is grete wondir for to witte,
Of all þe werkis þat ever wore. 268

ii Egip. Nay, lorde, þer is anothir ȝitt,
That sodenly sewes vs ful sore,

(2) Toads and frogs.
For tadys and frosshis we may not flitte,
Thare venym loses lesse and more. 272

i Egip. Lorde, grete myses bothe morn and none
(3) Swarms of lice.
Bytis vs full bittirlye,
And we hope al by done
By moyses, oure enemye. 276

24. **i Cons.** Lord, whills we [1] with þis menyhe meve,
'We shall never be happy while these folk are here.'
Mon never myrthe be vs emange.

Rex. Go, saie we salle no lenger greve ; *[Aside.*
But þai sall neuere þe tytar gang. 280

lf. 39.
E. iij.
Deceitful message from Pharaoh,
ii Egip. Moyses, my lord has grauntyd leve
At lede thy folke to likyng lande,
So þat we mende of oure myscheue.

Pharao.   O, ho! this is a wonderfulle thyng to wytt,
                 Of alle the warkes that ever were.   268
Secundus Miles. Nay, Lord, ther is anothere yit,
                 That sodanly sowys us fulle sore ;
                 For todes and froskes may no man yfit,
                 Thay venom us so, bothe les and more.   272
Primus Miles.   Greatte mystes, sir, ther is bothe morne and noyn,
                 Byte us fulle bytterly ;
                 We trow that it be done
                 Thrughe Moyses oure greatte enmy.   276
Secundus Miles. My Lord, bot if this menye may remefe
                 on never myrthe be us amang.
Pharao.   Go, say to hym we wylle not grefe,
                 Bot thay shalle never the tytter gayng.   280
Primus Miles.   Moyses, my lord geffys leyfe   281
                 To leyd thi folk to lykyng lang,
                 So that we mend of oure myschefe.

---

[1] MS. has *ve.*

Moyses.   I wate ful wele þar wordes er wrang,   284 which Moses
                                                      does not believe.
That sall ful sone be sene,

For hardely I hym heete

And he of malice mene.

Mo mervaylles mon he mett.   288

25.   **i Egip.**   Lorde, allas! for dule we dye,   *[To the king.*
We dar not loke oute at no dore.

    Rex.   What deuyll ayles yow so to crye?

ii Egip.   We fare nowe werre þan euere we fure [1].   292 Plagues of (4)
                                                  flies,
Grete loppis ouere all þis lande þei flye,

That with bytyng makis mekill blure.

    i Egip.   Lorde, oure beestis lyes dede and dry,   (5) Murrain.
Als wele on myddyng als on more;   296

    Both oxe, horse, and asse,

Fallis dede doune sodanly.

    Rex.   Ther-of no man harme has   The king may
Halfe so mekill as I.   300 have harm,

26. **ii Cons.**   3is, lorde, poure men has mekill woo   but the poor have
                                                    much woe.

Moyses.   Fulle welle, I wote, thyse wordes ar wrang   284
                       Bot hardely alle that I heytt.   286
                       Fulle sodanly it shalle be seyn,   285
                       Uncowth mervels shalbe meyt   288
                       And he of malyce meyn.   287

Secundus Miles.   A, Lord, alas, for doylle we dy.   289
                       We dar look oute at no dowre.

Pharao.   What, ragyd the dwylle of helle, alys you so to cry?

Primus Miles.   For we fare wars then ever we fowre;   292
                       Grete loppys over alle this land thay fly,
                       And where thay byte thay make grete blowre,
                       And in every place oure bestes dede ly.   295

Secundus Miles.   Hors, ox, and asse,   297
                       Thay falle downe dede, syr, sodanly.   298

Pharao.   We, lo, ther is no man that has
                       Half as myche harme as I.   300

Primus Miles. Yis, sir, poore folk have mekylle wo,

---

[1] MS. has *fare.*

To see þer catell be out cast,
    The Jewes in Jessen faren noȝt soo,
They haue al likyng in-to last.   304

    Rex. Go, saie we giffe þam leue to goo
To tyme there parellis be ouer past ;   [*Aside.*
    But, or thay flitte over farre vs froo,
We sall garre feste þam foure so fast.   308

    ii Egip. Moyses, my lord giffis leue
Thy men for to remewe.

    Moyses. He mon haue more mischeff
But if his tales be trewe.   312

27.   **i Egip.** We! lorde, we may not lede this liffe.
    •**Rex.** Why! is ther greuaunce growen agayne?
    ii Egip. Swilke pou[d]re, lord, a-pon vs dryffe,
That whare it bettis it makis a blayne.   316

    i Egip. Like mesellis makis it man and wyffe ;
Sythen ar they hurte with hayle and rayne,
    Oure wynes in mountaynes may not thryve,
So ar they threst and thondour slayne.   320

            To se thare catalle thus out cast.
            The Jues in Gessen fayre not so,
            Thay have lykyng for to last.   304
Pharao.   Then shalle we gyf theym leyf to go   305
            To tyme this perelle be on past,
            Bot, or thay flytt oght far us fro,
            We shalle them bond twyse as fast.   308
Secundus Miles. Moyses, my lord gyffes leyf
            Thi meneye to remeve.
Moyses.   Ye mon hafe more myschefe
            Bot if thyse talys be trew.   31·
Primus Miles. A, Lord, we may not leyde thyse lyfys.
Pharao.   What, dwylle, is grevance grofen agayn?
Secundus Miles. Ye, sir, sich powder apon us dryfys,
            Where it abides it makes a blayn ;
            Meselle makes it man and wyfe,   31·
            Thus ar we hurt with haylle and rayn.
            Syr, unys in montanse may not thryfe,
            So has frost and thoner thaym slayn.   3·

  Rex. How do thay in Jessen ;
Þe Jewes, can ȝe aught say ?
  ii Egip. Þis care nothyng they ken,
Þay fele no such affray.   324
28. **Rex.** No, devill! and sitte they so in pees?
And we ilke day in doute and drede.
  i Egip. My lorde, þis care will euere encrese
Tille Moyses have leve þam to lede.   328
  i Cons. Lorde, war they wente þan walde it sese, 'Unless the Jews
So shuld we save vs and oure seede,   go, we shall be
                    lost.'
Ellis [1] be we lorne; þis is no lese.
Rex. Late hym do fourth! þe devill hym spede! 332
For his folke sall no ferre
Yf he go welland woode.
  ii Cons. Þan will itt sone be warre,
ȝit war bettir þai ȝoode.   336
29. **ii Egip.** We! lorde, new harme is comon to hande. Plagues of (8)
Rex. No! devill! will itt no bettir be?   locusts.
  i Egip. Wilde wormes is laide ouere al this lande,

Pharao.   Yei, bot how do thay in Gessen,
      The Jues, can ye me say?
Primus Miles. Of alle these cares no thyng thay ken,
      Thay feylle noghte of our afray. 324
Pharao,   No? the ragyd, the dwylle, sytt thay in peasse?
      And we every day in doute and drede?
Secundus Miles. My lord, this care will ever encrese,
      To Moyses have his folk to leyd ; 328
      Els be we lorne, it is no lesse,   331
      Yit were it better that thai yede.
Pharao.   Thes folk shall flyt no far,   333
      If he go welland wode.
Primus Miles. Then wille it sone be war,
      It were better thay yode.   336
Secundus Miles. My lord, new harme is comyn in hand.
Pharao.   Yei, dwille, wille it no better be?
Primus Miles. Wyld wormes ar layd over all this land,

---

[1] MS. has *Eellis.*

þai leve no frute ne floure on tree;   340

Agayne þat storme may no thyng stande.

ii **Egip.**   Lord, ther is more myscheff thynke me,

And thre daies hase itt bene durand,

So myrke þat non myght othir see.   344

i **Egip.**   My lorde, grete pestelence [1]

Is like ful lange to last.

Rex.   Owe! come þat in oure presence?

Than is oure pride al past.   348

30. ii Egip.   My lorde, þis vengeaunce lastis lange,

And mon till Moyses haue his bone.

i **Cons.**   Lorde, late þam wende, els wirke [we] wrang,

It may not helpe to hover na hone.   352

Rex.   Go, saie we graunte þam leue to gange,

In the devill way, sen itt bus be done,

For so may fall we sall þam fang,

Thai leyf no floure, nor leyf on tre.   340

Secundus Miles.   Agans that storme may no man stand;

And mekylle more mervelle thynk me,

That thise iij dayes has bene durand

Siche myst, that no man may other se.   344

Primus Miles.   A, my Lord!

Pharao.   Haghe!

Secundus Miles.   Grete pestilence is comyn;

It is like ful long to last.   346

Pharao.   Pestilence? in the dwilys name!

Then is oure pride over past.   348

Primus Miles.   My lord, this care lastes lang.

And wille to Moyses have his bone;

Let hym go, els wyrk we wrang,

It may not help to hover ne hone.   352

Pharao.   Then wille we gif theym leyf to gang;

Syn it must nedes be doyn;

Perchauns we salle thaym fang

---

[1] *Pestilence* is inserted in a later hand; ll. 345, 346 are one line in the MS.

And marre þam or to-morne at none.   356
i Egip. Moyses, my lorde has saide,
Þou sall haue passage playne.

Moyses. And to passe am I paied,   'My friends, re-
                                                      joice, we can now
My frendes, bees nowe fayne ;   360 go to the land of
                                                      promise.'
31. For at oure will now sall we wende,
In lande of lykyng for to lende.

i puer. Kyng Pharo, that felowns fende,
Will haue grete care fro this be kende,   364 'The king will
                                                      pursue us.'
Than will he schappe hym vs to shende,
And sone his Ooste aftir vs sende.

Moyses. Beis noght aferde, god is youre frende,   'Fear not, come
                                                      forth.'
Fro alle oure fooes he will vs fende.   368
Þarfore comes furthe with me,
Haves done, and drede yow noght.

ii puer. My lorde, loved mott þou bee,
Þat þus fro bale has brought.   372

32. iii puer. Swilke frenshippe never before we fande.   lf. 40 b.

And mar them or to morne at none.   356
Secundus Miles. Moyses, my lord he says
Thou shalle have passage playn.

Moyses. Now have we lefe to pas,
My freyndes, now be ye fayn ;   360
Com furthe, now salle ye weynd
To land of lykyng you to pay.

Primus Puer. Bot kyng Pharao, that fals feynd,   363
He will us eft betray ;
Fulle soyn he wille shape us to sheynd,   365
And after us send his garray.

Moyses. Be not abast, God is oure freynd, 367
And alle oure foes wille slay ;
Therfor com on with me,
Have done and drede you noght.   370

Secundus Puer. That Lord blyst might he be,
That us from baylle has broght.

Primus Puer. Siche frenship never we fand ;   373

But in þis faire defautys may fall,

'The Red Sea is near, we must be slaves.'

Þe rede see is ryght nere at hande,

Þer bus vs bide to we be thrall.   376

Moyses.   I sall make vs way with my wande,

For god hase sayde he saue vs sall;

'The sea shall stand on either side as a wall.'

On aythir syde þe see sall stande,

Tille we be wente, right as a wall.   380

Therfore have ȝe no drede,

But faynde ay god to plese.

i puer.   Þat lorde to lande vs lede,

'We pass easily.'

Now wende we all at esse.   384

33. i Egip.   Kyng Pharro, ther folke er gane.

Rex.   Howe nowe! es ther any noyes of newe?

ii Egip.   The Ebrowes er wente ilkone.

Rex.   Now sais þou þat?   **i Egip.**   Þer talis er trewe. 388

Rex.   Horse harneys tyte, þat þei be tane,

'Harness horse and chariots instantly, follow me.'

Þis ryott radly sall þam rewe,

Bot yit I drede for perells alle,

The Reede See is here at hand.

Ther shal we byde to we be thralle.   376

Moyses.   I shalle make my way ther with my wand,

As God has sayde, to sayf us alle;

On ayther syde the see mon stand,

To we be gone, right as a walle.   380

Com on wyth me, leyf none behynde,

Lo fownd ye now youre God to pleasse.

Hic pertransient mare.

Secundus Puer.   O, Lord! this way is heynd;

Now weynd us all at easse.   384

Primus Miles.   Kyng Pharao! thyse folk ar gone.   38

Pharao.   Say, ar ther any noyes new?

Secundus Miles.   Thise Ebrews ar gone, lord, ever-ichon.

Pharao.   How says thou that?

Primus Miles.   Lord, that taylle is trew.   38

Pharao.   We, out tyte, that they were tayn;

That ryett radly shall thay rew,

We sall not sese or they be slone,
   For to þese we sall þam sew.   392
Do charge oure charyottis swithe,
   And frekly folowes me.
ii **Egip.** My lorde we are full blithe,
   At youre biddyng to be.   396
34. ii **Cons.** Lorde, to youre biddyng we er boune,
   Owre bodies baldely for to bede,
We sall noght byde, but dyng þam doune,   'We'll kill them all.'
   Tylle all be dede, with-outen drede.   400
Rex. Hefe vppe youre hartis ay to Mahownde,   'Lift up your hearts to Mahomet!
   He will be nere vs in oure nede.

[Scene V, *The Red Sea*.]

Owte! ay herrowe! devill, I drowne!   Hallo! I drown!'
  i **Egip.** Allas! we dye, for alle our dede.
  i **puer.** Now ar we wonne fra waa, and saued oute of þe see. lf. 41. E.v.
   Cantemus domino, to god a sange synge wee.   406

Finis.

    We shalle not seasse to thay be slayn,
    For to the see we shall thaym sew;   392
    So charge youre chariottes swythe,
    And ferstly look ye folow me.
Secundus Miles. Alle redy, lord, we ar fulle blythe
    At youre byddyng to be.   396
Primus Miles. Lord, at youre byddyng ar we bowne
    Oure bodys boldly for to beyd,
    We shalle not seasse, bot dyng alle downe,
    To alle be dede withouten drede.   400
Pharao. Heyf up youre hertes unto Mahowne,
    He wille be nere us in oure nede;
    Help, the raggyd dwylle, we drowne!
    Now mon we dy for alle oure dede.   404

        Tunc merget eos mare.

Moyses. Now ar we won from alle oure wo,
    And savyd out of the see;   402

                Lovyng gyf we God unto,
                Go we to land now merely.

Primus Puer. Lofe we may that Lord on hyght,
                And ever telle on this mervelle;
                Drownyd he has kyng Pharao myght,
                Lovyd be that Lord Emanuelle.

Moyses.   Heven, thou attend, I say in syght,
                And erthe my wordys; here what I telle.
                As rayn or dew on erthe doys lyght
                And waters herbys and trees fulle welle,
                Gyf lovying to Goddes mageste,
                Hys dedys ar done, hys ways ar trew,
                Honowred be he in trynyte,
                To hym be honowre and verteu.   Amen.

                                    [Explicit Pharao.

XII. THE SPICERS.

The Annunciation, and visit of Elizabeth to Mary.

[PERSONS OF THE PLAY.

PROLOGUE.   MARIA.
ANGELUS.   ELIZABETH.]

[SCENE I, *Nazareth:* PROLOGUE *in the fore-ground.*]

1.   L ORD God, grete meruell es to mene [1],
     Howe man was made with-outen mysse,
And sette whare he sulde euer haue bene
With-outen bale, bidand in blisse.   4
And howe he lost þat comforth clene,   *It is a wonder*
And was putte oute fro paradys,   *how man lost*
                                 Paradise.
And sithen what sorouse sor [2] warre sene
Sente vn-to hym and to al his.   8
And howe they lay lange space
   In helle lokyn fro lyght,
Tille god graunted þam grace
   Of helpe, als he hadde hyght.   12
2. Þan is it nedfull for to neven,   *We must tell*
How prophettis all goddis counsailes kende, *what prophets*
Als prophet Amos in his steuen,   *spoke.*
Lered whils he in his liffe gun lende.   16

---

[1] A marginal note here in 16th cent. hand says, 'Doctor, this matter is newly mayde, wherof we haue no coppy.'   [2] MS. has *for*.

Amos said God would send his son.

Deus pater disposuit salutem fieri in medio terre etce.

He sais þus, god þe fadir in heuen
Ordand in erthe man kynde to mende ;
And to grayth it with godhede euen [1],
His sone he saide þat he suld sende.   20
To take kynde of man-kyn
   In a mayden full mylde ;
So was many saued of syn
   And the foule fende be-gyled.   24

3. And for the feende suld so be fedd
Be tyne, and to no treuth take tentt,
Mary was wedded to deceive the fiend.
God made þat mayden to be wedde [2],
Or he his sone vn-to hir sentte.   28
So was the godhede closed and cledde
In wede of weddyng whare thy wente ;
And þat oure blysse sulde so be bredde,
Ful many materes may be mente.   32

Gen. xxii. 18.

Quoniam in semine tuo benedicentur omnes gentes &c.

lf. 42 b.
God hym self sayde this thynge
   To Abraham als hym liste,
Of thy sede sall vppe sprynge
   Whare in folke sall be bliste.   36

4. To proue thes prophettes ordande [wer],
Er als I say vn-to olde and yenge.
He moued oure myscheues for to merr,
For thus he prayed god for this thynge,   4c
   Orate celi desuper,
Isaac prayed for the dew of heaven,
Lord, late þou doune at thy likyng
Þe dewe to fall fro heuen so ferre,
Gen. xxvii. 28.
For than the erthe sall sprede and sprynge   4
A seede þat vs sall saue,

---

[1] MS. has *euen*.   [2] MS. has *wedded*.

Þat nowe in blisse are bente.
Of clerkis who-so will craue,
Þus may þer-gatis be mente.   48

5. Þe dewe to þe gode halygaste   which is the Holy
Ghost.
May be remeued in mannes mynde,
The erthe vnto þe mayden chaste,
By-cause sho comes of erthely kynde.   52
Þir wise wordis ware noght wroght in waste,
To waffe and wende away als wynde,
For this same prophett sone in haste
Saide forthermore, als folkes may fynde. 56

Propter hoc dabit dominus ipse vobis signum &c.   *Isa.* vii. 14.

Loo he sais þus, god sall gyffe
Here-of a syngne to see
Tille all þat lely lyffe,
And þis þare sygne salbe.   60

Ecce uirgo concipiett, et pariet filium &c.   *Isa.* vii. 14.

6. Loo ! he sais a mayden mon   A virgin shall
bear a son,
Here on this molde mankynde omell,
Ful clere consayue and bere a sonne,
And neven his name Emanuell.   64
His kyngdom þat euer is be-gonne,
Sall never sese, but dure and dwell;
On dauid sege þore sall he wonne,   he shall sit on
David's seat.
His domes to deme and trueth to telle.   68

Zelus domini faciet hoc &c.   *Isa.* ix. 7.

He says, luffe of oure Lorde,   lf. 43.
E. vij.
All þis sall ordan[1] þanne
That mennes pees and accorde
To make with erthely manne.   72

7. More of þis maiden me meves [he],
This prophett sais for oure socoure,

---

[1] MS. has *ordañ*.

Isa. xi. 1.

Egredietur virga de Jesse,

A rod shall spring from Jesse,

A wande sall brede of Jesse boure ;   76

And of þis same also sais hee,

which shall bear a flower.

Vpponne þat wande sall springe a floure,

Wher-on þe haly gast sall be,

To governe it with grete honnoure.   80

That wande meynes vntill vs

    Þis mayden, even and morne,

And þe floure is Jesus,

    Þat of þat blyst bees borne.   84

8. Þe prophet Johell, a gentill Jewe,

Joel has also foretold the maiden and Christ.

Som-tyme has saide of þe same thyng ;

He likenes criste euen als he knewe,

Like to þe dewe in doune commyng.   88

Hos. xiv. 6.

Ero quasi ros et virgo Israell germinabit sicut lilium.

Þe maiden of Israell al newe

He sais, sall bere one and forthe brynge,

Als þe lelly floure full faire of hewe,

Þis meynes sa to olde and ȝenge   92

Þat þe hegh haly gaste,

    Come oure myscheffe to mende,

In marie mayden chaste,

    When god his sone walde sende.   96

9. Þis lady is to þe lilly lyke,

Þat is by-cause of hir clene liffe,

For in þis worlde was never slyke,

One to be mayden, modir, and wyffe.   100

lf. 43 b.

And hir sonne kyng in heuen-ryke,

Als oft es red be reasoune ryfe ;

It passes worldly knowledge that in Mary should be united God-head, maiden-hood, and man.

And hir husband bath maistir and meke,

In charite to stynte all striffe.   104

Þis passed all worldly witte,

    How god had ordand þaim þanne,

In hir one to be knytte,
Godhed, maydenhed, and manne. 108

10. Bot of þis werke grete witnes was,
With forme-ffaders, all folke may tell.
Whan Jacob blyst his sone Judas, Jacob spoke of it in blessing Judah.
He told þe tale þaim two emell; 112
Non auferetur s[c]eptrum de Juda, *Gen.* xlix. 10.
Ueniat qui mittendus est.
He sais þe septer sall noght passe
Fra iuda lande of Israell,
Or he comme þat god ordand has
To be sente feendis force to fell. 116
Et ipse erit expectacio gencium. *Gen.* xlix. 10.
Hym sall alle folke abyde,
And stand vn-to his steuen,
Ther sawes wer signified
To crist goddis sone in heuen. 120

11. For howe he was sente, se we more,
And howe god wolde his place puruay,
He saide, 'sonne I sall sende by-fore John Baptist foretold.
Myne Aungell to rede þe thy way.' 124
Ecce mitto angelum meum ante faciem *Mark* i. 2.
tuam qui preparabit viam tuam ante te.
Of John Baptist he menyd þore,
For in erthe he was ordand ay,
To warne þe folke þat wilsom wore
Of Cristis comyng, and þus gon say; 128
Ego quidem baptizo in aqua vos autem *Matth.* iii. 11.
Baptizabimini[1] *spiritu sancto.*
'Eftir me sall come nowe lf. 44. E. viii.
A man of myghtist mast,
And sall baptis ȝowe
In the high haly gast.' 132

12. Þus of cristis commyng may we see,

---

[1] Error for *ipse vos baptizabit.*

H

How sainte Luke spekis in his gospell,

Luke narrates
the Annuncia-
tion.
Luke i. 26-46.

'Fro God in heuen es sent,' sais he,

'An aungell is named Gabriell   136

To Nazareth in Galale,

Where þan a mayden mylde gon dwell,

Þat with Joseph suld wedded be.

Hir name is Marie,' þus gan he telle,   140

Attend to God's
grace thus pre-
pared, and to the
angel's words.

To god his grace þan grayd,

To man in þis manere,

And how þe Aungell saide,

Takes hede, all þat will here [1].   144

[*Exit Prologue.*

Tunc cantat angelus [2].

Salutation of
Mary.

13. Ang.   Hayle! Marie! full of grace and blysse,

Oure lord god is with þe,

And has chosen þe for his,

Of all women blist mot þou be.   148

'What kind of
salute is this?'

Maria.   What maner of halsyng is þis?

Þus preuely comes to me,

For in myn herte a thoght it is,

Þe tokenyng þat I here see.   152

Tunc cantat angelus, Ne timeas [2] *Maria.*

14. Ang.   Ne drede þe noght, þou mylde marie,

For no-thyng þat may be-falle,

For þou has fun soueranly

At god a grace ouer othir all.   156

In chastite of thy bodye

'Thou shalt bear
a son called
Jesus.'

Consayue and bere a childe þou sall,

This bodword brynge I þe, for-thy

His name Jesu sall þou calle.   160

15. Mekill of myght þan sall he bee,

He sall be God and called God sonne [3].

---

[1] After this prologue of 12 stanzas, the rest of the piece seems to be
irregular in the arrangement of the 6- and 8-syllable lines.
[2] These stage directions are in a 16th cent. hand.
[3] MS. has *soñ*.

Dauid sege, his fadir free, lf. 44 b.
Sall God hym giffe to sytte vppon; 164
Als kyng for euer regne sall hee,
In Jacob house ay for to wonne.
Of his kyngdome and dignite
Shall noo man erthly knaw ne con [1]. 168

16. Maria. Þou goddis aungell, meke and mylde,
Howe sulde it be, I the praye,
That I sulde consayve a childe
Of any man by nyght or daye. 172
I knawe no man þat shulde haue fyled
My maydenhode, the sothe to saye;
With-outen will of werkis wilde,
In chastite I haue ben ay. 176

17. Ang. The Halygast in þe sall lighte,
Hegh vertue sall to þe holde,
The holy birthe of the so bright,
God sonne he sall be calde. 180
Loo, Elyzabeth, þi cosyne, ne myght
In elde consayue a childe for alde,
Þis is þe sexte moneth full ryght,
To hir þat baran has ben talde. 184

18. Maria. Thou aungell, blissid messanger,
Of goddis will I holde me payde,
I love my lorde with herte dere,
Þe grace þat he has for me layde. 188
Goddis handmayden, lo! me here, 'Behold the
handmaiden of
the Lord.'
To his wille all redy grayd,
Be done to me of all manere,
Thurgh thy worde als þou hast saide. 192 lf. 45
E. ix.[2]

---

[1] This line is written in the margin in a later hand, to make up the old scribe's deficiency.   No blank however.
[2] An extra leaf was added to this quire E; the catchwords for the next leaf, usual at the bottom of the *last* page in each quire, occur here on both 44*b* and 45*b*; they are however all written in the original hand.

'God save thee, lady, from guilt.'

19. [Ang.] Now God, þat all oure hope is in,
Thur[gh] the myght of þe haly gaste,
Saue þe, dame, fro sak of synne,
And wisse þe fro all werkis wast!   [*Exit Angel.*]   196

[SCENE II, *the house of Zacharias ; Mary visits Elizabeth.*]

[**Maria.**] Elyzabeth, myn awne cosyne,
Me thoght I coveyte alway mast
To speke with þe of all my kynne,
Therfore I comme þus in þis hast.   200

20. Eliz. Welcome! mylde Marie,
Myne aughen cosyne so dere,

Elizabeth blesses Mary.

Joyfull woman am I,
Þat I nowe see þe here.   204
Blissid be þou anely
Of all women in feere,
And þe frute of thy body
Be blissid ferre and nere.   208

21. Þis is ioyfull tydyng
Þat I may nowe here see,
Þe modyr of my lord kyng,
Thus-gate come to me.   212
Sone als þe voyce of þine haylsing
Moght myn neres entre and be,
Þe childe in my wombe so yenge,
Makes grete myrthe vnto þe¹.   216

22. Maria. Nowe lorde! blist be þou ay
For þe grace þou has me lente ;

Mary praises God.

Lorde I lofe þe god verray,
Þe sande þou hast me sente.   220
I þanke þe nyght and day,
And prayes with goode entente
Þou make me to thy paye,

If. 45 ᵇ.

To þe my wille is wentte.   22.

¹ The original has *alway to þe.*

23. Eliz. Blissed be þou grathely grayed
　　　To god thurgh chastite,
　　Þou trowed and helde þe payed
　　　Atte his wille for to bee.　　　　　　　　228
　　All þat to þe is saide,
　　　Fro my lorde so free,
　　Swilke grace is for the layde,
　　　Sall be fulfilled in þe.　　　　　　　　232

24. Maria. [T]o his grace I will me ta,
　　　With chastite to dele,
　　Þat made me þus to ga
　　　Omange his maidens fele [1].　　　　　　236
　　My saule sall louying ma
　　　Vn-to þat lorde so lele,
　　And my gast make ioye alswa
　　　In god þat es my hele.　　　　**Magnificat,**　240
　　　　　　　　　　　　　　　　[*tunc cantat* [2].

[1] MS. has *feele*.　　　　　　[2] Written in a later hand.

XIII. THE PEWTERERES AND FOUNDOURS [1].

Joseph's trouble about Mary.

[PERSONS OF THE PLAY.

JOSEPH.   PRIMA PUELLA.
MARIA.   SECUNDA PUELLA.
                ANGELUS.]

[SCENE, *Joseph wandering in the wilderness ; his house at one side.*]

Matth. i. 18-25.
Gosp. of Pseudo-M tth. x, xi.
Hist. of Joseph the Carpenter, v, vi.

1. JOS. Of grete mornyng may I me mene,   9
And walk full werily be þis way,
For nowe þan wende I best hase bene
Att ease and reste by reasonne ay.   4
For I am of grete elde,
Wayke and al vnwelde,
Als ilke man se it maye ;
I may nowder buske ne belde,   8
But owther in frith or felde ;
For shame what sall I saie

Joseph, old and weak,

is ashamed that he has wedded a young wife.

2. That þus-gates nowe on myne alde dase
Has wedded a yonge wenche to my wiff,   12

---

[1] The metre of this play changes, like a piece of music. The first seven are 10-line stanzas, four 8-syllable, six 6-syllable lines ; the eighth is irregular ; stanzas 9 to 16 are of six 8-syllable lines broken by a tag, followed by four 6-syllable lines. With stanza 17 the first measure is resumed, stanza 18 being irregular.

And may noȝt wele tryne over two strase !
Nowe lorde ! how langes all I lede þis liff,
My banes er heuy als lede,
And may noȝt stande in stede,   15
    Als kende it is full ryfe.
Now lorde ! þou me ¹ wisse and rede,
Or sone me dryue to dede,
    Þou may best stynte þis striffe.   20

3. For bittirly þan may I banne
The way I in þe temple wente,
Itt was to me a bad barganne,   *'I repent that
For reuthe I may it ay repente.   24   bad bargain.*
    For þare-in was ordande
    Vn-wedded men sulde stande,
        Al 'sembled at asent ;
    And ilke ane a drye wande   28
    On heght helde in his hand,
        And I ne wist what it ment.

4. In-mange al othir ane bare I,   *I went among
Itt florisshed faire, and floures on sprede,   others [in the
                                         32   temple], and my
And they saide to me for-thy   rod blossomed ;
Þat with a wiffe I sulde be wedde.   thus I was forced
    Þe bargayne I made þare,   to be wed.*
    Þat rewes me nowe full sare,   *Protevange-
                                         36   lium, or Gosp.
        So am I straytely sted.   of James, ix.*
    Now castes itt me in care,   *Nativity of
    For wele I myght euere mare   Mary, vii.*
        Anlepy life haue led.   *If. 46 b.*
5. Hir werkis me wyrkis my wonges to wete,   *I would have led
                                         40   a single life.*
I am begiled ; how, wate I noȝt.
My ȝonge wiffe is with childe full grete,
Þat makes me nowe sorowe vnsoght.   44
    Þat reproffe nere has slayne me !
                                        *What a reproof
                                        that my wife is
                                        with child.*

¹ MS. has *we.*

For-thy giff any man frayne me
How þis þing may be wroght,
To gabbe yf I wolde payne me,   48
Þe lawe standis harde agayne [1] me,
To dede I mon be broght.

6. And lathe me thinkeþ, on þe todir syde,
My wiff with any man to defame,   52
And whethir of there twa þat I bide
I mon noȝt scape withouten schame.
Þe childe certis is noght myne,
Þat reproffe dose me pyne,   56
And gars me fle fra hame.
My liff gif I shuld tyne,
Sho is a clene virgine
For me, withouten blame.   60

7. But wele I wate thurgh prophicie,
A maiden clene suld bere a childe,
But it is nought sho, sekirly,

I am beguiled.   For-thy I wate I am begiled.   64
And why ne walde som yonge man ta [2] her,
For certis I thynke ouer-ga hir

I will steal into   Into som wodes wilde,
the woods and
leave her,   Thus thynke I to stele fra hir,   68

(God shield her !)   God childe ther wilde bestes sla hir,
She is so meke and mylde.

but will speak to   8. Of my wendyng wil I none warne,
her first.'
Neuere þe lees it is myne entente   72
To aske hir who gate hir þat barne,
ȝitt wolde I witte fayne or I wente.   [*Enters his house*
All hayle! God be here-inne!

i Puella.   Welcome, by Goddis dere myght!   7

----
[1] The MS. has *agayns*.
[2] The MS. has *take*.

Jos. Whare is þat ȝonge virgine,
Marie, my berde so bright?

9. i Puella. Certis, Joseph, ȝe sall vndirstande,
Þat sho is not fulle farre you fra,   80
Sho sittis at hir boke full faste prayand
For ȝou and us, and for all þa
        Þat oght has nede.
But for to tell hir will I ga   84
Of youre comyng, withouten drede.   [*Goes to Mary.*
Haue done! and rise vppe, dame,
  And to me take gud hede,
Joseph, he is comen hame.   88

Mary sits at her book praying.

Maria. Welcome! als God me spede.

'Welcome! dear spouse.'

10. Dredles to me he is full dere,
Joseph my spouse, welcome er yhe!
Jos. Gramercy, Marie, saie what chere,   92
Telle me þe soth, how es't with þe?
        Wha has ben there?

'How is it with thee?'

Thy wombe is waxen grete, thynke me,
Þou arte with barne, allas! for care!   96
A! maidens, wa worthe ȝou!
    Þat lete hir lere swilke lare.

He reproaches her maidens.

ii Puella. Joseph, ȝe sall noȝt trowe,
  In hir no febill fare.   100

'Think no harm of her.'

11. Jos. Trowe it noght arme! lefe wenche, do way!
Hir sidis shewes she is with childe.
Whose is't Marie?
       Mar. Sir, Goddis and youres.

It is God's son.

Jos. Nay, nay, now wate I wele I am begiled.   104
        And resonne why
With me flesshely was þou neuere fylid,
And I forsake it here for-thy.
Say, maidens, how es þis?   108
  Tels me þe soþe, rede I,

And but ȝe do, i-wisse,
Þe bargayne sall ȝe aby.

12. ii Puella.   If ȝe threte als faste as yhe can,   112
Þare is noght to saie þere till,
For trulye her come neuer noman,
To waite her body with non ill,

                    Of this swete wight [1].   116
For we haue dwelt ay with her still,
And was neuere fro hir day nor nyght.
Hir kepars haue we bene
    and sho ay in oure sight,   120
Come here no man bytwene
    to touche þat berde so bright.

13. i Puella.   Na, here come noman in þere wanes,
And þat euere witnesse will we,   124
Saue an Aungell ilke a day anes,
With bodily foode hir fedde has he,
                    Othir come nane.
Wharfore we ne wate how it shulde be,   128
But thurgh þe haly gaste allone.
For trewly we trowe þis,
    is grace with hir is gone,
For sho wroght neuere no mys,   132
    we witnesse euere ilkane.

14. Jos.   Þanne se I wele youre menyng is,
Þe Aungell has made hir with childe.
Nay, som man in aungellis liknesse   136
With somkyn gawde has hir begiled;
                    And þat trow I.
For-thy nedes noght swilke wordis wilde
At carpe to me dissayuandly.   140
We! why gab ye me swa
    and feynes swilk fantassy,

---

[1] This additional line is here written in the margin by the 16th cent. hand.
It is evidently needed to complete the stanza.

Allas! me is full wa!
　　for dule why ne myght I dy.　　　　　　　144

15. To me þis is a carefull cas,　　　　　　　He is nearly
mad with shame.
　　Rekkeles I raffe, reste is my rede,
　　I dare loke no man in þe face,
　　Derfely for dole why ne were I dede.　　　148
　　　　　　Me lathis my liff!
　　In temple and in othir stede
　　Ilke man till hethyng will me dryff.
　　Was neuer wight sa wa,　　　　　　　　152
　　　　for ruthe I all to ryff,
　　Allas! why wrought þou swa,
　　Marie! my weddid wiffe?

16. **Mar.** To my witnesse grete God I call,　　156
　　Þat in mynde wroght neuere no mysse.
　　Jos. Whose is þe childe þou arte with-all?　　He beseeches
Mary
　　Mar. Youres sir, and þe kyngis of blisse.

　　　　　Jos. Ye, and hoo þan?　　160　lf. 48.
f. iij.
　　Na, selcouthe tythandis than is þis,
　　Excuse þam wele there women can.
　　　But Marie, all þat sese þe
　　　　may witte þi werkis ere wan,　　164
　　　Thy wombe all way it wreyes þe,
　　　þat þou has mette with man.

17. Whose is it? als faire mot ye be-fall.　　　to tell him the
truth.
　　Mar. Sir, it is youres and Goddis will.　　168
　　Jos. Nay, I ne haue noght a-do with-all.
　　Neme it na more to me, be still!
　　　Þou wate als wele as I,
　　　Þat we two same flesshly　　　　　172
　　　　Wroght neuer swilk werkis with ill.
　　Loke þou dide no folye
　　Be-fore me preuely
　　　Thy faire maydenhede to spill.　　　176

18. [1] But who is þe fader? telle me his name,

Mar.   None but youre selfe.

                                                  Jos.   Late be, for shame.

I did it neuere, þou dotist dame, by bukes and belles,   180

Full sakles shulde I bere þis blame aftir þou telles.

For I wroght neuere in worde nor dede,

Thyng þat shulde marre thy maydenhede,

                                                  To touche me till.   184

For of slyk note war litill nede,

Yhitt for myn awne I wolde it fede,

                                                  Might all be still.

19. Þarfore þe fadir tell me, Marie.   188

Mar.   But God and yhow, I knowe right none.

Jos.   A! slike sawes mase me full sarye,

With grete mornyng to make my mone.

Therfore be noȝt so balde   192

Þat no slike tales be talde,

                                                  But halde þe stille als stane.

Þou art yonge and I am alde,

Slike werkis yf I do walde,   196

                                                  Þase games fra me are gane.

20. Therfore, telle me in priuite

whos is þe childe þou is with nowe?

Sertis, þer sall non witte but we,   200

I drede þe law als wele as þou.

Mar.   Nowe grete God of his myght,

Þat all may dresse and dight,

                                                  Mekely to þe I bowe!   20

Rewe on þis wery wight,

Þat in his herte might light

                                                  Þe soth to ken and trowe.

21. Jos.   Who had thy maydenhede Marie? has þou ogh

mynde.   20

[1] This stanza seems to be irregular, unlike any other.

Mar.   For suth, I am a mayden clene.

Jos.   Nay þou spekis now agayne kynde;
Slike þing myght neuere naman of mene.

 A maiden to be with childe,   212
 Þase werkis fra þe ar wilde,
  Sho is not borne I wene.

Mar.   Joseph, yhe ar begiled,
 With synne was I neuer filid,   216
  Goddis sande is on me sene.

22. Jos. Goddis sande! yha Marie! God helpe,   *'God's messenger is seen in me.'*
Bot certis! þat childe was neuere oures two.

But woman kynde gif þat list yhelpe,   220
Yhitt walde þei naman wiste þer wo.

Mar.   Sertis, it is Goddis sande [1],
 Þat sall I neuer ga fra.

Jos.   Yha! Marie, drawe thyn hande,   224
For forther ȝitt will I frande,
 I trowe not it be swa.

23. Þe soth fra me gif þat þou layne
Þe childe bering may þou noȝt hyde,   228
But sitte stille here tille I come agayne,   *'Stay here till I return, I must go on an errand.'*
Me bus an erand here beside.

Mar.   Now, grete God! be you wisse,
 And mende you of your mysse,   232
  Of me, what so betyde.   *'God send you a true sight of this.'*
 Als he is kyng of blysse,
 Sende yhou som seand of þis,   *If. 49. f. iiij.*
  In truth þat ye might bide.   236

     [Joseph goes out again.

24. Jos. Nowe, lord God! þat all þing may
At thine owne will bothe do and dresse,
 Wisse me now som redy way   *'Lord! show me the way in this wilderness.*
 To walk here in þis wildirnesse.   240

[1] A line is here wanting, but no gap in MS. Lines 222, 223 are written s one in MS.

Bot or I passe þis hill,

Do with me what God will,

Owther more or lesse,

I am heavy, I must sleep.' Here bus me bide full stille   244

Till I haue slepid my fille.

Myn hert so heuy it is.   [*Sleeps.*

[*Enter the angel Gabriel.*]

'Awake, Joseph, take better care of Mary.' 25. **Ang.**   Waken, Joseph! and take bettir kepe

To Marie, þat is þi felawe fest.   248

'Let me sleep; **Jos.**   A! I am full werie, lefe late me slepe,

For-wandered and walked in þis forest.

Ang.   Rise vppe! and slepe na mare,

Þou makist her herte full sare.   252

Þat loues þe alther best.

I am caught everywhere; I can get no rest.' **Jos.**   We! now es þis a farly fare,

For to be cached bathe here and þare,

And nowhere may haue rest.   256

26.   Say, what arte þou? telle me this thyng.

Ang.   I Gabriell, Goddis aungell full euen,

Þat has tane Marie to my kepyng,

And sente es þe to say with steuen,   260

'Desert not your wife; In lele wedlak þou lede þe,

Leffe hir noȝt, I forbid þe,

Na syn of hir þou neuen.

But till hir fast þou spede þe,   264

And of hir noght þou drede þe,

the child is God's. It is Goddis sande of heuen.

27.   The childe þat sall be borne of her,

Itt is consayued of þe haly gast.   268

lf, 49 b. Alle joie and blisse þan sall be aftir,

And to al mankynde nowe althir mast.

Jesus his name þou calle,

For slike happe sall hym fall   272

Als þou sall se in haste.

His pepull saff he sall
Of euyllis and angris all,
   Þat þei ar nowe enbraste.   276

He shall save his people from evil and trouble.

28. Jos. And is this soth, aungell, þou saise?
Ang. Yha! and þis to taken right,
Wende forthe to Marie thy wiffe alwayse,
Brynge hir to Bedlem þis ilke nyght.   280
   Ther sall a childe borne be,
   Goddis sone of heuen is hee,
   And man ay mast of myght.

Go to Mary, bring her to Bethlehem.'

Jos. Nowe lorde god! full wele is me,   284
   That euyr þat I þis sight suld see,
   I was neuer ar so light.

'Thank God!'

29. For for I walde hir þus refused,
And sakles blame þat ay was clere,   288
Me bus pray hir halde me excused,
Als som men dose with full gud chere.

              [He re-enters his house.

Saie, Marie wiffe, how fares þou?
Mar. Þe bettir sir, for yhou.   292
   Why stande yhe þare? come nere.
Jos. My bakke fayne wolde I bowe,
And aske fo[r]gifnesse nowe,
   Wiste I þou wolde me here.   296

Joseph asks forgiveness of Mary.

30. Mar. Forgiffnesse sir! late be! for shame,
Slike wordis suld all gud women lakke.
Jos. Yha, Marie, I am to blame,
For wordis lang are I to þe spak.   300
   But gadir same now all oure gere;
   Slike poure wede as we were,
   And prike þam in a pak.
Till Bedlem bus me it bere,   304
For litill thyng will women dere.
   Helpe vp nowe on my bak!

She has nothing to forgive.

·lf. 50. f. v.

' Pack up our poor clothes, I'll carry them to Bethlehem, for a little hurts women.'

XIV. THE TILLE THEKERS[1].

The Journey to Bethlehem; the birth of Jesus.

[PERSONS OF THE PLAY.

JOSEPH.   MARIA.]

Luke ii. 5–7.   [SCENE I, *Bethlehem, a cattle shed.*]

1. **Jos.** All weldand God in Trinite,
   I praye þe, lord, for thy grete myght,
   Vnto thy symple seruand see,
   Here in þis place wher we are pight,   4
     oure self allone ;

'There is no lodging for us,

 Lord, graunte vs gode herberow þis nyght
     within þis wone.

2. For we haue sought both vppe and doune,   8
   Thurgh diuerse stretis in þis cite,

the town is so full ;

So mekill pepull is comen to towne,
   Þat we can nowhare herbered be,
     þer is slike prees ;   12

we must shelter with the beasts.

For suthe I can no socoure see,
     but belde vs with þere bestes.

3. And yf we here all nyght abide,
   We shall be stormed in þis steede ;   16

Here the wall and roof are in ruins.

Þe walles are doune on ilke a side,
   Þe ruffe is rayned aboven oure hede,
     als haue I roo,
   Say, Marie doughtir, what is thy rede ?   20
     How sall we doo ?

[1] Tille thekers, i. e. tile thatchers.

4. For in grete nede nowe are we stedde,
   As þou thy selffe the soth may see,
   For here is nowthir cloth ne bedde,   24   There is no bed
   And we are weyke and all werie,   and we are
                                                               weary; what
              and fayne wolde rest.   shall we do?'
   Now, gracious god, for thy mercie!
              wisse vs þe best.   28

5. **Mar.**   God will vs wisse, full wele witt ȝe,
   Þer-fore, Joseph, be of gud chere,
   For in þis place borne will he be   'The child will
   Þat sall vs saue fro sorowes sere,   32   be born here.'
              boþe even and morne.
   Sir, witte ȝe wele þe tyme is nere,
              hee will be borne.

6. **Jos.**   Þan behoves vs bide here stille,   36
   Here in þis same place all þis nyght.

   Mar.   Ȝa, sir, forsuth it is Goddis will.   ✓

   Jos.   Þan wolde I fayne we had sum light,
              what so befall.   40
   It waxis right myrke vnto my sight,   If. 51 b.
              and colde withall.   'It grows dark
                                                              and cold, I will
7. I will go gete vs light for-thy,   43   go and get some
   And fewell fande with me to bryng.   [*Goes out.*   light and fuel.'

   Mar.   All weldand God yow gouerne and gy,
   As he is sufferayne of all thyng
              fo[r] his grete myght,
   And lende me grace to his louyng   48
              Þat I me dight.

8. Nowe in my sawle grete ioie haue I,
   I am all cladde in comforte clere,
   Now will be borne of my body   52
   Both God and man to-gedir in feere.
              Blist mott he be!

I

The child is
born.

Jesu! my son þat is so dere,

      nowe borne is he.   56

          [Mary worships the child.

9. Hayle my lord God! hayle prince of pees !

  Hayle my fadir, and hayle my sone !

Pvalse   Hayle souereyne sege all synnes to sesse !

  Hayle God and man in erth to wonne !   60

        Hayle! thurgh whos myht

  All þis worlde was first be-gonne,

      merknes and light.

10. Sone, as I am sympill sugett of thyne,   64

  Vowchesaffe, swete sone I pray þe,

Mary takes the
child in her
arms.
  That I myght þe take in þe[r] armys of myne,

  And in þis poure wede to arraie þe ;

      Graunte me þi blisse !   68

  As I am thy modir chosen to be

      in sothfastnesse.

      [SCENE II, *Joseph outside the shed.*]

11. JOS.   A ! lorde, what the wedir is colde !

It is a killing
frost for the old
and weak.
  Þe fellest freese þat euere I felyd,   72

  I pray God helpe þam þat is alde,

  And namely þam þat is vnwelde,

      so may I saie.

  Now, gud God þou be my belde[1],   76

      as þou best may.

         [A sudden light shines.

'What light is
this?'
12. A ! lord God ! what light is þis

  Þat comes shynyng þus sodenly?

  I can not saie, als haue I blisse ;   80

  When I come home vn-to Marie

      þan sall I spirre.

  A ! here be god, for nowe come I.   *[Re-enters the shed.*

      [1] MS. has *bilde.*

[SCENE III, *interior of the shed, as before.*]

      Mar. Ʒe ar welcum sirre.   84

13. Jos. Say, Marie doghtir, what chere with þe?   'How are you?

      Mar. Right goode, Joseph, as has been ay.   If. 52.
F viij.

      Jos. O Marie! what swete thyng is þat on thy kne?   What sweet thing is on thy

      Mar. It is my sone, þe soth to saye,   88 knee?'
                þat is so gud.

      Jos. Wele is me I bade þis day
               to se þis foode!

14. Me merueles mekill of þis light   92
Þat þus-gates shynes in þis place,
For suth it is a selcouth sight!

      Mar. Þis hase he ordand of his grace, ⎱
          my sone so Ʒing,   96
A starne to be schyṅyng a space   'This light is the star at his birth.'
          at his bering.

15. For Balam tolde ful longe be-forne   [*Numb.*xxiv. 17.]
How þat a sterne shulde rise full hye,   100
And of a maiden shulde be borne
A sonne þat sall oure saffyng be
          fro caris kene.
For suth it is my sone so free,   104
          be whame Balam gon meene.

16. Jos. Nowe welcome, floure fairest of hewe,
I shall þe menske with mayne and myght.
Hayle! my maker, hayle Crist Jesu!   108 Joseph worships the child.
Hayle, riall kyng, roote of all right!
          Hayle! saueour.
Hayle, my lorde, lemer of light,
          Hayle, blessid floure!   112

17. Mar. Nowe lord! þat all þis worlde schall wynne,
To þe my sone is þat I saye,
Here is no bedde to laye the inne,   There is no bed,

þerfore my dere sone, I þe praye   116
        sen it is soo,

Here in þis cribbe I myght þe lay
        betwene þer bestis two.

18. And I sall happe þe, myn owne dere childe,   120
With such clothes as we haue here.

Jos. O Marie! beholde þes beestis mylde,
They make louyng in ther manere
        as þei wer men.   124
For-sothe it semes wele be ther chere
        þare lord þei ken.

19. **Mar.** Ther lorde þai kenne, þat wate I wele,
They worshippe hym with myght and mayne;   128
The wedir is colde, as ye may feele,
To halde hym warme þei are full fayne
        with þare warme breth,
And oondis on hym, is noght to layne,   132
        to warm hym with.

20. O! nowe slepis my sone, blist mot he be,
And lyes full warme þer bestis by-twene.

Jos. O nowe is fulfilled, for-suth I see,   136
þat Abacuc in mynde gon mene
        and preched by prophicie.
He saide oure sauyoure shall be sene
        betwene bestis lye;   140

21. And nowe I see þe same in sight.

Mar. ʒa! sir, for-suth þe same is he.

Jos. Honnoure and worshippe both day and nyght
Ay-lastand lorde, be done to þe,   144
        all way as is worthy,
And, lord, to thy seruice I oblissh me,
        with all myn herte holy.

22. **Mar.**   Þou mercyfull maker, most myghty,   148
My God, my lorde, my sone so free,
Thy hande-mayden for soth am I,
And to thi seruice I oblissh me,   lf. 53.
                                                                  G 1.
        with all myn herte entere.   152
Thy blissing, beseke I thee,
        Þou graunte vs all in feere[1].

[1] Marginal note in a late hand, 'Hic caret pastoribus sequitur postea.'

XV. THE CHAUNDELERS.

The Angels and the Shepherds.

[PERSONS OF THE PLAY.
PRIMUS, SECUNDUS, ET TERTIUS, PASTOR.]

Luke ii. 8-16.

[SCENE, *the fields near Bethlehem.*]

1.   i **Past.**   Bredir in haste, takis heede and here[1]
    What I wille speke and specifie,
    Sen we walke þus, withouten were,
    What mengis my moode nowe mevyd[2] will I.   4
    Oure forme-fadres, faythfull in fere,

The prophecies of Hosea and Isaiah.

    Bothe Osye and Isaye,
    Preued þat a[3] prins with-outen pere
    Shulde descende doune in a lady,   8
    And to make mankynde clerly,
        To leche þam þat are lorne.
    And in Bedlem here-by
        Sall þat same barne be[4] borne.   12

2.   ii **Past.**   Or he be borne in burgh hereby,

Balaam foretold a star.

    Balaham, brothir, me haue herde say,
    A sterne shulde schyne and signifie,
    With lightfull lemes like any day.   16
    And als the texte it tellis clerly
    By witty lerned men of oure lay,

---

[1] The reader will note that the form of the stanza changes after line 36, and again, with line 86, back to the first form.
  [2] Perhaps an error for *meve yt*.   MS. has *I*.   [4] MS. has *by*.

With his blissed bloode he shulde vs by,
He shulde take here al of a maye.　　　　20
I herde my syre saye,
　　When he of hir was borne,
She shulde be als clene maye
　　As euer she was by-forne.　　　　24

3. **iii Past.**　A! mercifull maker, mekill is thy myght,
That þus will to þi seruauntes see,　　　　'How glad we
Might we ones loke vppon þat light,　　　　should be if we
　　　　　　　　　　　　　　　　　　saw that light.
Gladder bretheren myght no men be!　　　　28
I haue herde say, by þat same light
The childre of Israell shulde be made free,
The force of the feende to felle in sighte,
And all his pouer excluded shulde be.　　　　32
Wherfore, brether, I rede þat wee　　　　If. 54 b.
　　Flitte faste ouere thees felles,　　　　But let us go
　　　　　　　　　　　　　　　　　　try to find our
To frayste to fynde oure fee,　　　　cattle.'
　　And talke of sumwhat ellis.　　　　36

　　　　　　　[*Vision of Angels in the sky.*

4. **i Pas.**　We! hudde!　　　　Whew!
　　　　　ii Pas.　We! howe!　　　　Oh!
　　　　　　　i Pas.　Herkyn to me!　　　　Hark!

ii Pas.　We! man, þou maddes all out of myght.

i Pas.　We! colle!　　　　Golly!

　　　　iii Pas.　What care is comen to þe?　　　　'What is the
　　　　　　　　　　　　　　　　　　matter?'

i Pas.　Steppe furth and stande by me right,　　　　40
　　　　　And tell me þan
　　　　　Yf þou sawe euere swilke a sight[1]!

iii Pas.　I? nay, certis, nor neuere no man.　　　　43

5. **ii Pas.**　Say, felowes, what! fynde yhe any feest,
Me falles for to haue parte, parde!　　　　45

---

[1] The MS. gives lines 41, 42 (written as one line) to iii Pastor, and l. 43 to
ii Pastor. But ll. 40 to 42 belong to one speech, and as l. 44 belongs to
ii Pastor, the above seems to be what was intended.

If. 55.
G vij.

'Look in the
east!'

     i Pas.   Whe! hudde! be-halde into the heste!

     A selcouthe sight þan sall þou see

                 vppon þe skye!

'What makes
you stare so?'

     ii Pas.   We! telle me men, emang vs thre,

         Whatt garres yow stare þus sturdely?   50

     6. iii Pas.   Als lange as we haue herde-men bene,

'Since we have
kept cattle in this
valley no such
sight has been
seen.'

     And kepis þis catell in þis cloghe,

     So selcouth a sight was neuere non sene.

     i Pas.   We! no colle! nowe comes it newe i-nowe,   54

         þat mon we fynde[1].

     Itt menes some meruayle vs emang,

         Full hardely I you behete.

     7. i Past.   What it shulde mene þat wate not ȝee,   58

     For all þat ȝe can gape and gone: [*Angel sings.*

     I can synge itt alls wele as hee,

     And on a-saie itt sall be sone

         proued or we passe.   62

'I can sing it;
stay, it was thus.'

     Yf ȝe will helpe, halde on! late see,

         for þus it was[2].

They sing
together.

     Et tunc cantant.

'It was a cheer-
ful song. I am
hoarse!'

     8. ii Pas.   Ha! ha! þis was a mery note,

     Be the dede þat I sall dye,   66

     I haue so crakid in my throte,

         þat my lippis are nere drye.

         iii Pas.   I trowe you royse,

'What made this
noble noise?'

     For what it was fayne witte walde I,   70

         That tille vs made þis noble noyse.

'An angel with
tidings.'

     9. i Pas.   An aungell brought vs tythandes newe,

     A babe in Bedlem shulde be borne,

     Of whom þan spake oure prophicie trewe,

     And bad us mete hym þare þis morne,   74

         þat mylde of mode.

---

[1] Probably the original word of the poet was *wete*, or perhaps *mete*, to rime with *behete*, l. 57; *fynde* is the copyist's error.

[2] Marginal note in a late hand, 'Caret nova loquela de pastore.'

I walde giffe hym bothe hatte and horne,
      And I myght fynde þat frely foode.   78

10. iii Pas. Hym for to fynde has we no drede,
I sall you telle a-chesonne why,
ȝone sterne to þat lorde sall vs lede.
ii Pas. ȝa! þou sais soth, go we for-thy   82   'Let us go with
      hym to honnour.   mirth and song
                                         to seek our
And make myrthe and melody,   Saviour.
      with sange to seke oure savyour.
      Et tunc cantant.
      [*Walking along, they come to Bethlehem.*

11. i Pas. Breder, bees all blythe and glad,   86   lf. 55 b.
Here is the burght þer we shulde be.   Here is the
ii Pas. . In þat same steede now are we stadde,   borough:
Thare-fore I will go seke and see.
Slike happe of heele neuere herde-men hadde;   90
Loo! here is the house, and here is hee.   here is the
iii Pas. ȝa! for sothe þis is the same,   [*They enter.*   house.'
      Loo! whare þat lorde is layde,
Be-twyxe two bestis tame,   94
      Right als þe aungell saide.

12. i Pas. The Aungell saide þat he shulde saue
This worlde and all þat wonnes þer-in,
Therfore yf I shulde oght aftir crave,   98
To wirshippe hym I will be-gynne[1].   [*They adore the child.*
Sen I am but a symple knave,   'I am but
Þof all I come of curtayse kynne,   simple but of
                                      courteous kin;
Loo! here slyke harnays as I haue,   102   I offer thee a
A baren broche by a belle of tynne   brooch with
At youre bosom to be,   a tin bell.
      And whenne ȝe shall welde all,
Gud sonne, for-gete noȝt me,   106   Forget me not,
      Yf any fordele falle.   if anything
                                          chance to my ad-
                                          vantage.'

---

[1] 'His caret nova loquela,' marginal note 16th cent.

13. ii Pas.   Þou sonne! þat shall saue boþe see and sande,
       Se to me sen I haue þe soght,

I am ovir poure to make presande   110
       Als myn harte wolde, and I had ought.
       Two cobill notis vppon a bande,
       'Loo! litill babe, what I haue broght,
       And when ȝe sall be lorde in lande,   114
       Dose goode agayne, for-gete me noght.

For I haue herde declared
           Of connyng clerkis and clene,

That bountith aftir [1] rewarde ;   118
           Nowe watte ȝe what I mene.

14. iii Pas.   Nowe loke on me, my lorde dere,
       Þof all I putte me noght in pres,
       Ye are a prince with-outen pere,   122
       I haue no presentte þat you may plees.

But lo! an horne spone, þat haue I here,
       And it will herbar fourty pese,
       Þis will I giffe you with gud chere,   126
       Slike novelte may noght disease.
       Fare [wele] þou swete swayne,
           God graunte vs levyng lange,
       And go we hame agayne,   130
           And make mirthe as we gange [2].

---

[1] The word intended was perhaps *askis, aftir* gives no sense.

[2] The metre in this piece, as in XIII (see before, p. 102), changes with the subject. The first three stanzas are of 12 lines (8 of four beats, 4 of three beats) in alternate rimes ; on the appearance of the star (line 37) the lines, though sometimes irregular, pass into the 7-line stanza riming a b a b c b c. When the child is found (l. 84) the shepherds in their speeches return to the original 12-line stanza.

XVI. THE MASONNS [1].

The coming of the three Kings to Herod.

[PERSONS OF THE PLAY.

HERODES.	TERTIUS REX.
FILIUS (HEROD'S SON).	NUNTIUS.
PRIMUS REX.	PRIMUS ET SECUNDUS MILITES.
SECUNDUS REX.	PRIMUS ET SECUNDUS CONSULES.]

[SCENE, *Herod's court, with his son and courtiers.*]

Herod. THE clowdes clapped in clerenes þat þer clematis   Herod boastingly
            in-closis,   sets forth his
                                       splendour.
Jubiter and Jouis, Martis & Mercury emyde,
Raykand ouere my rialte on rawe me reioyses,
Blonderande þer blastis, to blaw when I bidde.   4   'I ride on the
                                         raiking clouds,
Saturne my subgett, þat sotilly is hidde,
I list at my likyng and laies hym full lowe;
The rakke of þe rede skye full rappely I ridde,
Thondres full thrallye by thousandes I thrawe   8
                when me likis;
Venus his voice to me awe
Þat princes to play in hym pikis.

Þe prince of planetis þat proudely is pight   12   Sun and moon
                                         honour me.
Sall brace furth his bemes þat oure belde blithes,
Þe mone at my myght he mosteres his myght;
And kayssaris in castellis grete kyndynes me kythes,   Emperors show
                                         me kindness.

[1] *Mynstrells* is written after Masonns in a 16th cent. hand. See note, p. 125.

Lordis and ladis loo luffely me lithes,   16

I am fairer than glorious gulls.'

For I am fairer of face and fressher on folde

(Þe soth yf I saie sall) seuene and sexti sithis,

Þan glorius gulles þat gayer [is]¹ þan golde

in price ;   20

How thynke ȝe þer tales þat I talde,

I am worthy, witty, and wyse!

The soldiers obediently assent.

i Miles.   All kynges to youre croune may clerly comende

Youre lawe and youre lordshippe as lodsterne on hight, 24

What traytoure vn-trewe þat will not attende,

ȝe sall lay þaim full lowe, fro leeme and fro light.

ii Miles.   What faitoure, in faithe, þat dose ȝou offende,

We sall sette hym full sore, þat sotte, in youre sight.   28

W. 58.
H ij.
'I shall advise you for your welfare, worthy wights.

Herodes.   In welthe sall I wisse ȝou to wonne or I wende,

For ȝe are wightis ful worthy, both witty & wighte.

But ȝe knawe wele, ser knyghtis, in counsaill full conande,

Þat my regioun so riall is ruled her be rest ;   32

For I wate of no wighte in þis worlde þat is wonnande

Þat in forges any feloune, with force sall be fest ;

Arrest any unruly fellow who strives against law and order.

Arest ȝe þo rebaldes þat vnrewly are rownand,

Be they kyngis or knyghtis, in care ȝe þaim cast ;   36

ȝaa, and welde þam in woo to wonne, in þe wanyand,

Strike down brawlers.'

What browle þat is brawlyng his brayne loke ȝe brest,

And dynge ȝe hym doune.

i Miles.   Sir, what foode in faith will ȝou feese,   40

Þat sott full sone my selfe sall hym sesse.

ii Miles.   We sall noght here doute to do hym disesse,

But with countenaunce full cruell

We sall crake her his croune.   44

'My son, how these comely knights talk!'

Her.   My sone þat is semely, howe semes þe ther sawes?

Howe comely þer knyghtis, þei carpe in þis case !

¹ MS. has 'is' interlined in later hand.

Fil. Fadir, if þai like noght to listyn youre lawes,

As traytoures on-trewe þe sall teche þem a trace,   48   'Traitors shall be traced.'

For fadir, vnkyndnes ȝe kythe þem no cause.

Her. Faire falle þe my faire sone, so fettis of face!   'Well done, my pretty son.'

And knyghtis, I comaunde, who to dule drawes,

Þas churles as cheueleres ye chastise and chase,

And drede ȝe no doute.   53

Fil. Fadir, I sall fell þam in fight,   'Father, I will kill bad fellows.'

What renke þat reves you youre right.

i Miles. With dyntes to dede bes he dight,   If. 58 b.

Þat liste not youre lawes for to lowte

His wille.   58

[Enter messenger.]

Nunc. My lorde, ser herowde, king with croune! &c. [1]   *Matth.* ii. 1–12.

---

[1] The rest of this play, consisting of 144 lines, is identical with lines 73–216 of Play XVII. It is unnecessary to print it twice over, but in that play collations are given with this copy, omitting unimportant variations in spelling. The lines form a complete scene, to which for the Masons' play an introductory scene of the true boastful Herodic vein, bringing in also Herod's son, was prefixed. For the Goldsmiths' play this was discarded, and instead of the vaunts of Herod's power a scene of praise by the Three Kings searching the star, on the way to Jerusalem, appropriately leads to their entry before Herod; moreover, at the end of scene 2, a third is added, in which the kings having found the babe, offer their gifts.

On reference to Burton's lists of the plays (A.D. 1415, see Introduction) we see that the Masons were to play *Herod interrogans tres reges* and the Goldsmiths the *Oblation*. It is possible, therefore, that play XVII may have been intended to be performed entire when the Masons could not bring forward their play, and the second scene to be omitted if the Masons did perform. There are no marks or notes to guide us, and nearly 150 years after Burton's days we find that the Masons had been accustomed to produce the play; but at that date, 4 Elizabeth, 1561, a new gild of 'Musicians commonly called the Mynstrells' having been formed in York, the Masons' play was handed over to them, and their name was written at the head (see before, p. 123). The following is found in a book of Charters and Ordinances, marked ᴮᵧ, belonging to the Corporation of York, fo. 231 :—'Fynally it is further ordeyned and by consent of all the good men of the said mystery or craft fully aggreed that the said felawship of Mynstrelles of their proper chardges shall yerely frome hensfurth bryng forth and cause to be played the pageant of Corpus Christi, viz. the herold his sone twoo counselars and the messynger inquyryng the three kynges of the childe Jesu, sometyme accustomed to be brought forth at chardges of the late Masons of this Citie on Corpus Christi day, in suche like semely wise and ordre as other occupacions of this Citie doo their pageantes.'

XVII. GOLDE SMYTHIS.

The coming of the three Kings to Herod; the Adoration.

[PERSONS OF THE PLAY.

PRIMUS REX.	PRIMUS ET SECUNDUS MILITES.
SECUNDUS REX.	PRIMUS ET SECUNDUS CONSULES.
TERTIUS REX.	ANCILLA.
HERODUS.	MARIA.
NUNTIUS.	ANGELUS.]

Matth. ii. 1–12.
Apoc. Gospel of James, ch. xxi.

[SCENE I, *the road to Jerusalem, the three kings meeting.*]

1. i Rex.　Lorde! that levis euere-lastande lyff,
　I loue þe evir with harte and hande,
　That me has made to se this sight
　Whilke my kynrede was coveytande.　　　　　4
　Thay saide a sterne, with lemys bright,
　Owte of the Eest shulde stabely stande,
　And þat it shulde meffe mekill myght [1]
　Of I þat shulde be lorde in lande;　　　　　8
　That men of synne shulde saff [1];

'God help me
to find the right
way.'

　And certis I sall saye,
　God graunte me happe to haue
　Wissyng of redy waye.　　　　　12

2. ii Rex.　All weldand god, þat all has wroght,
　I worshippe þe als is worthye,

'I have come
from my realme
Araby to seek
what wonder the
star signifies.'

　That with thy brightnes has me broght
　Owte of my reame, rich Arabie.　　　　　16

---

[1] In the MS. *of* stands at the end of l. 7, but its place seems to be, as above, at the beginning of l. 8. The word *be* is also written after *saff* in l. 9; it is not wanted.

I shall [noght] seys tille I haue sought
What selcouth thyng it sall syngnyfie,
God graunte me happe so þat I myght
Haue grace to gete goode companye;   20
And my comforte encrese
With thy sterne schynyng schene,
For certis, I sall noght cesse,
Tille I witte what it mene.   24

3. iii Rex.   Lorde god! þat all goode has by-gonne,
And all may ende both goode and euyll[1],
That made for man both mone and sonne,
And stedde yone sterne to stande stone stille!   28
Tille I þe cause may clerly knowe,
God wisse me with his worthy wille,
I hope I haue her felaws fonde,
My yarnyng fayfully to full-fille.   32

> 'God show me the cause of this ; I think here are companions.'

[Advances and speaks to the other kings.

Sirs! god yowe saffe ande see,
And were ȝow euere fro woo.

> lf. 62 b.

i Rex.   Amen! so myght it bee,
And saffe yow, sir, also!   36

4. iii Rex.   Sirs, with youre wille, I wolde yow praye
To telle me some of youre entent,
Whedir ye wende forthe in this way,
And fro what contre ȝe are wente?   40

> 'Whence come you, and wherefore?'

ii Rex.   Full gladly sir, I shall ȝou say.
A sodayne sight was till vs sente,
A royall sterne þat rose or day
Before vs on the firmament,   44
Þat garte vs fare fro home
Som poynte ther-of to presse.

> 'A royal star was suddenly sent that made us leave home.

iii Rex.   Sertis, syrs, I sawe þe same,
Þat makis vs þus to moyfe.   48

> 'Sirs, I saw you together. Some marvel must move us.'

---

[1] The broad northern pronunciation of *euyll* was evidently nearly *ill*, iming with *stille* and *wille*.

5. For sirs, I haue herde say sertayne
    It shulde be seyne of selcowthe seere,
    And ferther ther-of I wolde freyne ;
    That makis me moffe in this manere.   52

'We are one   i Rex.   Sir, of felashippe are we fayne,
fellowship.'
                   Now sall we wende forth all in feere,
                   God graunte vs or we come agayne
                   Som gode hartyng þer-of to here.   56
                   Sir, here is Jerusalem,   [They journey on together.
                   To wisse vs als we goo,
                   And be-yonde is Bedleem,
                   Þer schall we seke alsoo.   60

'We must be   6. iii Rex.   Sirs, ȝe schall wele vndirstande,
wise, Herod is
king of this land.   For to be wise nowe were it nede,
lf. 63.   Sir Herowde is kyng of this lande
H viij.   And has his lawes her for to leede.   64
                   i Rex.   Sir, sen we neghe now þus nerhand,
                   Vn-till his helpe vs muste take heede,
                   For haue we his wille and his warande
                   Þan may we wende with-outen drede.

Let us get his   ii Rex.   To haue leve of the lorde,   69
leave.'
                   Þat is resoune and skyll.
                   iii Rex.   And ther-to we all accorde,
                   Wende we and witte his wille.   72

                   [SCENE II, *Herod's court*[1].]

7. Nun.   Mi lorde ser Herowde! kyng with croune!
    Herod.   Pees! dastard, in þe deueles dispite.
'My Lord,   Nun.   Sir, new nott is full nere þis towne.
here is a new
business.'   Herod.   What! false losell, liste þe flighte?   76

---

l. 75. Sire . . . nere] My lorde now note is nere.   l. 76. losell] harlott.

---

[1] This Scene II (ll. 73–216) completes also the Masons' Play (see note,
p. 125). The collations here given are from that play (M); G refers to this
Goldsmiths' play, the text of which is restored in some instances where that
of the Masons offers a better reading.

Go, betis yone boy and dyngis hym downe.

> 'What! go and beat him.'

ii **Mil.**   Lorde, messengers shulde no man wyte ;
It may be for youre awne rennowne.

> No one may blame messengers.

Herod.   That wolde I here, do telle on tyte.   80

Nun.   Mi lorde, I mette at morne
iij kyngis carpand to-gedir
Of One [1] þat is nowe borne,
And þai hight to come hedir.   84

> 'I met three kings talking this morning;

8. **Herod.**   Thre kyngis, forsothe !

   Nun.   Sir, so I saie,

> lf. 63 b.

For I saughe þem my-self all seere.

i **Con.**   My lorde, appose hym, we yow praye.

Herod.   Say, felowe, ar they ferre or nere ?   88

Nun.   Mi lorde, þei will be here þis day.
Þat wotte I wele, withouten were.   [*Exit messenger.*

> they will be here to-day.'

Herod.   Haue done ; dresse vs in riche array,
And ilke man make tham mery chere,   92
That no sembland be seene
But frenshippe faire and stille,
Tille we wete what þei meene,
Whedir it be gud or ill.   96

> 'Array us richly, we will seem friendly.'

[*Enter the three kings.*]

9. i **Rex.**   A ! lorde, þat lenys þis lastand light,
Whilke has vs ledde oute of oure lande,
Kepe þe, sir kyng, and comly knyght,
And all þi folke þat we here fande.   100

> God save the king !

Herod.   Mahounde, my god and most of myght,
Þat has myn hele all in his hande,
He saffe you sirs ! semely in sight ;
And telle vs nowe som new tythande.   104

> 'Mahomet save you, sirs.'

---

[1] *Sic* in MS.

K

ii **Rex.**   Sum shall we saie ȝou sir,

'A star makes
us seek one
new-born.'

A sterne stud vs by-forne,

That makis vs speke and spir

Of ane þat is nowe borne.   108

10. Herod.   Nowe borne ! þat birthe halde I badde.

And certis, vn-witty men ȝe werre

If. 64.
I j.

To lepe ouere lande to late a ladde.

Say when lost ȝe hym ? ought lange be-fore[1] ?   112

'You must be
mad to run seek-
ing a child.

All wyse men will wene ȝe madde,

And therfore moffis it neuere more.

iii **Rex.**   Ȝis certis, such hartyng haue we hadde,

We schall noȝt seys or we come thore.   116

Herod.   This were a wondir thyng !

Who is he?'

Say, what barne shulde þat be ?

'He shall be
king of Judæa.'

i **Rex.**   Sir, he shall be kyng

Of Jewes and of Jude[2].   120

Herod is angry.

11. Herod.   Kyng ! in þe deuyl way, dogges, Fy !

Now I se wele ȝe roþe and raue.

Be ony skymeryng of the skye

When ȝe shulde knawe owthir kyng or knave ?   124

Nay, I am kyng and non but I[3],

That shall ȝe kenne yff þat ȝe craue,

And I am juge of all Jury

To speke or spille, to saie or saffe.   128

Swilke gawdes may gretely greue,

To wittenesse þat neuere was.

---

l. 105. you *supplied from* M.   l. 108. new *for* nowe.   l. 109. new
for nowe ; burden *for* birthe.   l. 114. þis *for* it.   l. 115. swilke *for* such.
l. 116. will *for* schall.   l. 119. For-soth *for* Sir.   l. 121. kingis in þe deuels
name.   l. 122. roþe *may be* roye, *the letter in G may be* þ *or* y ; rase *for*
raue.   l. 123. skemeryng.   ll. 125, 127. he is *for* I am.   l. 128. of spille G.

---

[1] Line 112 is written as two lines in MS.
[2] The late hand struck out *Jude*, and wrote *all Jury* instead.
[3] A later hand has inserted here ' Filius,' as the speaker of the next six
lines, but it was evidently a mistake ; the original, as above, is right.   In M
he is . . he are substituted for *I am . . I*, Filius speaking, whence probably
arose the error.

Rex. Lorde, we aske noght but leue,
Be youre poure to passe. 132

12. **Herod.** Whedir? in þe deuyls name.
To late a ladde here in my lande?
Fals harlottis, but ʒe hye you hame,
ʒe shall be bette and boune in bande. 136

ii **Cons.** [*Aside.*] My lorde, to felle þis foule deffame,
Lattis all such wondir folle on hande,
And speres þaim sadly of þe same,
So shall ʒe stabely vndirstande 140
Þer mynde and þer menyng,
And takis gud tente þam too.

Herod. [*Aside.*] I thanke þe of þis thyng,
And certis, so will I doo. 144

13. Nowe kyngis, to cache all care away
Sen ʒe ar comen oute of youre kytht,
Loke noght ye legge agayne oure lay,
Uppon peyne to lose both lyme and litht. 148
And so þat ʒe þe soth will saye,
To come and goo I graunte yow grith,
And yf youre poynte be to my pay,
May falle my selfe shall wende you with. 152

i **Rex.** Sir kyng, we all accorde,
And says a barne is borne
Þat shall be kyng and lorde,
And leche þam þat ar lorne. 156

14. ii **Rex.** Sir, the thar[1] meruayle no-thyng,
Of þis ilke nott þat þus-gate newes,
For Balaham saide a starne shulde spring
Of Jacobe kynde, and þat is Jewes. 160

---

l. 131. Nowe lorde; noght *not in* M. l. 133. whedirward. l. 138. such wondir] þere hye wordis. l. 142. þam too] ther-to. l. 143. þis thyng] thy counsaille. l. 144. sall *for* will. l. 145. care *supplied from* M. l. 151. poyntes. l. 158. noote *for* nott.

---

[1] The late hand glosses *the thar* (=it needs thee) by *of this*, written above.

K 2

Isa. vii. 14.]

iii Rex. Sir, Isaie sais a mayden ȝenge
Shall bere a sone amonge Ebrewes,
Þat of all contrees shall be kyng,
And gouerne all þat on erthe grewes;   164
Emanuell shalbe his name,
To saie, God sone of heuen,

lf. 65 a.
I ij.

And certis þis is þe same,
Þat we now to you neuen.   168

Also Hosea
[xiv. 5].

15. i Rex¹. Sirs, þe proved prophete Osee
Full trulye talde in towne and toure,
Þat a mayden of Israell, sais he,
Shall bere one like to þe lely floure.   172
He menys a barne consayued shulde be
With-outen seede of man socour,
And his modir a mayden free,
And he both sone and saueour.   176

What these
prophets have
said none can
gainsay.

ii Rex. Þat fadirs has talde beforne
Has noman myght to marre.
Herod. Allas! þan am I lorne,
Þis waxith ay werre and werre.   180

An elder counsels
Herod to act
deceitfully.

16. i Con. [*Aside.*] My lorde, be ȝe no-thyng a-bast,
Þis bryge shall well to ende be broght,
Bidde þam go furthe and frendly frast
Þe soth of þis þat þei haue soght,   184
And telle it ȝou; so shall ȝe trast
Whedir þer tales be trew or noght.

---

l. 161. Sir *not in* M.   l. 162. barne *for* sone.   l. 165. shalbe] beithis.
l. 166. Goddis.   l. 168. now] here.   l. 171. Þat *not in* M; forsoth saide he.
l. 172. þe *not in* M.   l. 173. childe *for* barne; sall *for* shulde.
l. 174. mannys.   l. 175. G *has* is *for* his, *and for* a, *which are from* M.
l. 177. fadirs talde me.   l. 180. way *for* waxith.   l. 182. brigge, *in*
G a *is written over the* y; tille *for* to.

---

¹ The copyist of the original MS. assigned all these five speeches each to
a *Rex*, without marking which, except the present which he gave to *iii
Rex*. The late hand remedied this by adding the figures which are followed
here.

Than shall we wayte þam with a wrest,
And make all wast þat þei haue wroght.   188
Herod. [*Aside.*] Nowe, certis, þis was wele saide,
Þis matere makes me fayne.
    Sir kyngis, I halde me paide
    Of all youre purpose playne.   192
17. Wendis furth, youre forward to fulfill,
To Bedlem, it is but here at hande.
And speris grathe, both goode and ill,
Of hym þat shulde be lorde in lande.   196
And comes agayne þan me vntill,
And telle me trulye youre tythande,
To worshippe hym þat is my will,
Þus shall ȝe stabely vndirstande.   200
ii Rex. Sertis, syr, we sall you say
Alle þe soth of þat childe,
In alle þe hast we may.
ii Con. Fares wele, ȝe be bygilid ! [*Exeunt the three kings.*
18. **Her.** Nowe[1] certis, þis is a sotille trayne,   205
Nowe shall þei trewly take þer trace,
And telle me of þat litill swayne
And þer counsaill in þis case.   208
If it be soth, þei shall be slayne,
No golde shall gete þam bettir grace.
Go we nowe, till þei come agayne,
To playe vs in som othir place.   212
This halde I gud counsaill,
Yitt wolde I no man wist ;

Side notes:
'Sir Kings, I am pleased with your purpose ; go to Bethlehem, and return with tidings.'

lf. 65 b.

'Yes, we will tell you.'

Herod rejoices over the trap laid for the kings.

---

l. 187. ȝe for we. l. 189. is *for* was. l. 194. it *not in* M. l. 195. grathely.
l. 199. þat is] þan were. l. 202. Alle *not* in M ; þat same M. l. 203.
G *has* þat we. l. 207. litill] swytteron. l. 208. M *has* all *before* þer.
l. 209. Giffe *for* If. l. 211. Bot go we tille. l. 212. And *for* To.

---

[1] The name of the speaker Herod is here due to the late hand, the original having omitted it.

For sertis, we shall not faill
To loyse þam as vs list.   [*Exeunt.*]   216

[SCENE III. *Nota*, the Harrod passeth, and the iij kynges
comyth agayn to make there offerynges[1].

Bethlehem : a house there ; a star above.]

<table>
<tr><td>The three kings,
wandering, can-
not see the star.</td><td>19. i Rex. A! sirs, for sight what shall I say?
Whare is oure syne? I se it not[2].</td></tr>
</table>

The three kings, wandering, cannot see the star.

19. i Rex. A! sirs, for sight what shall I say?
Whare is oure syne? I se it not[2].

ii Rex. No more do I, nowe dar I lay
In oure wendyng som wrange is wroght.   220

iii Rex. Vn-to þat Prince I rede we praye,
That till vs sente his syngne vnsoght,
þat he wysse vs in redy way
So frendly þat we fynde hym moght.   224

'Here it is!'

i Rex. A! siris! I se it stande
A-boven where he is borne,
Lo! here is þe house at hande,
We haue noȝt myste þis morne. [*Maid opens the door.*]   228

If. 66.
I iij.
'Sirs, whom
seek ye?'

20. Anc. Whame seke ȝe syrs, be wayes wilde,
With talkyng, trauelyng to and froo?
Her wonnes a woman with her childe,
And hir husband; her ar no moo.   232

'A child and
his mother, a
maiden.'

ii Rex. We seke a barne þat all shall bylde,
His sartayne syngne hath saide vs soo,
And his modir, a mayden mylde,
Her hope we to fynde þam twoo.   236

Anc. Come nere, gud syirs, and see,
Youre way to ende is broght.

The journey's
end.

iii Rex. Behalde here, syirs, her and se[3]
þe same þat ȝe haue soght.   240

---

l. 215. noght *for* not.   l. 216. lose *for* loyse.

---

[1] Old stage direction, in later hand.   [2] MS. has *noth*.
[3] In the MS. *and se* comes at the beginning of line 240.

21. i Rex. Loved be þat lorde þat lastis aye,

Praise the Lord !

Þat vs has kydde þus curtaysely,

To wende by many a wilsom way,

And come to þis clene companye.   244

ii Rex. Late vs make nowe no more delay,

But tyte take furth oure tresurry,

'Let us take our gifts.'

And ordand giftis of gud aray

To worshippe hym, als is worthy.   248

iii Rex. He is worthy to welde

All worshippe, welthe, and wynne ;

And for honnoure and elde,

Brother, ȝe shall be-gynne.   252

22. i Rex. Hayle! þe fairest of felde folk for to fynde,

The eldest king begins.

Fro the fende and his feeres faithefully vs fende [1],

Hayll! þe best þat shall be borne to vnbynde

If. 66 b.

All þe barnes þat are borne & in bale boune [2],   256

Hayll! þou marc us [3] þi men and make vs in mynde,

Sen þi myght is on molde misseis [3] to amende.

Hayll! clene þat is comen of a kynges kynde,

And shall be kyng of þis kyth, all clergy has kende.   260

And sith it shall worþe on þis wise,

Thy selffe haue soght, sone, I say þe,

'Be pleased to accept this gold, the most worthy.'

With golde þat is grettest of price

Be paied of þis present, I pray þe.   264

23. ii Rex. Hayll! foode þat thy folke fully may fede,

Hayll! floure fairest, þat neuer shall fade,

Hayll! sone þat is sente of þis same sede,

Þat shall saue vs of synne þat oure syris had,   268

Hayll! mylde, for þou mette to marke vs to mede,

Off a may makeles þi modir þou made,

In þat gude thurgh grace of thy godhede,

Als þe gleme in þe glasse gladly þow glade,   272

The second king brings incense.

---

[1] Lines 253, 254 are each written as two in MS.

[2] To agree with the rime *boune* should be *bende*.

[3] The MS. has *marcus* and *misse is*.

And sythyn yow shall sitte to be demand,
To helle or to heuen for to haue vs,
In-sens to þi seruis is semand.
Sone! se to þi suggettis and saue vs.   276

24. iii Rex. Hayll! barne þat is best oure balys to bete,
For our boote shall þou be bounden and bett,
Hayll! frende faithtfull, we fall to thy feete,
Thy fadiris folke fro þe fende fals þe to fette[1].   280
Hayll! man þat is made to þi men meete[2],
Sen þou and thy modir with mirthis ar mette,

Hayll! duke þat dryues dede vndir fete,
But whan thy dedys ar done to dye is þi dette.   284
And sen thy body beryed shalbe,
This mirre will I giffe to þi grauyng.

The gifte is not grete of degree,
Ressayue it, and se to oure sauyng.   288

25. Mar. Sir kyngis, ȝe trauel not in vayne,
Als ȝe haue ment, hyr may ȝe fynde;
For I consayued my sone sartayne
With-outen misse of man in mynde,   292
And bare hym here with-outen payne,
Where women are wonte to be pynyd.
Goddis aungell in his gretyng playne,
Saide he shulde comforte al man kynde,   296
Thar-fore doute yow no dele,
Here for to haue youre bone,
I shall witnesse full wele,
All þat is saide and done.   300

26. i Rex. For solas ser now may we synge,
All is parformed þat we for prayde,
But gud barne, giffe vs thy blissing,
For faire happe is be-fore þe laide.   30.

ii Rex. Wende we nowe to Herowde þe kyng,

---

[1] The MS. has *free þu* for *fro þe*; *fals to thy fette* was first written, the
thy crossed out and *þe* inserted.   [2] MS. has *mette*.

For of þis poynte he will be paied,
And come hym-selffe and make offeryng
Vn-to þis same, for so he saide.   308

iii **Rex.** I rede we reste a thrawe,   *but rest a while*
                                                     first.
For to maynteyne our myght,
And than do as we awe,
Both vn-to kyng and knyght.   312

[*Enter Angel.*]

27. Ang. Nowe curtayse kynges, to me take tent, 'Do not return
                                                      to Herod, he
And turne be-tyme or ȝe be tenyd,
Fro God[1] hym selfe þus am I sent
To warne yow, als youre faithfull frende.   316 lf. 67 b.

Herowde the kyng has malise ment,   *means malice.*
And shappis with shame yow for to shende,
And for þat ȝe non harmes shulde hente,
Be othir waies God will ye wende   320
Euen to youre awne contre.
And yf ȝe aske hym bone,
Youre beelde ay will he be,
For þis þat ȝe haue done.   324

28. i Rex. A! lorde, I loue þe inwardly.
Sirs, God has gudly warned vs thre,
His Aungell her now herde haue I,
And how he saide.
                    ii **Rex.** Sir, so did we.   328
He saide Herowde is oure enmye,
And makis hym bowne oure bale to be
With feyned falsed, and for-thy
Farre fro his force I rede we flee.   332

iii **Rex.** Syrs, faste I rede we flitte,   'We'll flit back
                                                     to our own
Ilkone till oure contre,   country.'
He þat is welle of witte
Vs wisse,— and with yow be.   336

---

[1] The word *of* was written here and then crossed through.

XVIII. THE MARCHALLIS.

The Flight into Egypt.

[PERSONS OF THE PLAY.

JOSEPH.   MARIA.   ANGELUS.]

[SCENE, *Joseph's abode at Bethlehem.*]

Joseph. THOW maker þat is most of myght[1],
  To thy mercy I make my mone,
Lord! se vnto þin symple wight
That hase non helpe but þe allone.   4

Praise the Lord for his grace.

For all þis worlde I haue for-saken,
And to thy seruice I haue me taken.
With witte and will,
For to fulfill   8
  þi commaundement.
Þer-on myn herte is sette,
With grace þou has me lente,
Þare shall no lede me lette.   12

2. For all my triste, lorde, is in þe,
That made me, man, to thy liknes,
Thow myghtfull maker, haue mynde on me,
And se vnto my sympplenes.   16

'Lo! how weak I become.

I waxe wayke as any wande,
For febill me faylles both foote and hande;
What euere it mene!

---

[1] In the margin here was written in the 16th century, 'This matter is mayd of newe after anoyer forme'; the words were afterwards crossed out

Me thynke myne eyne   20
     hevye as leede.
Þer-fore I halde it best,
A whille her in þis stede
To slepe and take my reste.   [*Sleeps.*]   24   I must rest.'

3. **Mar.** [*Prays to the child apart.*] Thow luffely lord þat last
     schall ay,
My god, my lorde, my sone so dere,
To thy godhede hartely I pray
With all myn harte holy entere;   28
As þou me to thy modir chaas,
I beseke þe of thy grace
For all man-kynde,
Þat has in mynde   32
     To wirshippe þe.
Þou se thy saules to saue,   lf. 69 b.
Jesu my sone so free,
Þis bone of þe I crave.   36

[Enter Angel Gabriel.]

4. **Ang.** Wakyn, Joseph! and take entente!   'Wake up,
My sawes schall seece thy sorowe sare,   Joseph!'
Be noght heuy, þi happe is hentte,
Þare-fore I bidde þe slepe no mare.   40
Jos. A! myghtfull lorde, what euere þat mente?
So swete a voyce herde I neuere ayre.
But what arte þou with steuen so shylle,   'Who art thou?
Þus in my slepe þat spekis me till,   44
To me appere,
And late me here
     What þat[1] þou was?
Ang. Joseph, haue þou no drede,   48
Þou shalte witte or I passe
Therfore to me take hede.

     [1] The MS. has *what at þat*.

5. For I am sente to þe,

Gabriell, goddis aungell bright,   52

'Flee with Mary
and her precious
one.
Is comen to bidde þe flee

With Marie and hir worthy wight ;

For Horowde þe kyng gars doo to dede

All knave childer in ilke a stede,   56

Þat he may ta

With ȝeris twa

       Þat are of olde.

Tille he be dede away,   60

In Egypt shall
ye shelter.'
In Egipte shall ȝe beelde

Tille I witte þe for to saie.

lf. 70.
I vij.
6. Jos. Aye lastand lord loved mott þou be,

That thy swete sande wolde to me sende.   64

'What ails the
king at me?
But lorde, what ayles þe kyng at me ?

For vn-to hym I neuere offende [1].

or to kill little
young children ?'
Allas ! what ayles hym for to spille

Smale ȝonge barnes þat neuere did ille   68

In worde ne dede,

Vn-to no lede

       Be nyght nor day.

And sen he wille vs schende,   72

Dere lorde, I þe praye,

Þou wolde be oure frende.

7. For be he neuere so wode or wrothe,

For all his force þou may vs fende.   76

'Lord, keep us
from harm.'
I praye þe, lorde, kepe us fro skathe,

Thy socoure sone to vs þou sende ;

For vn-to Egipte wende we will

Thy biddyng baynly to fulfill,   80

As worthy is

Þou kyng of blisse,

       Þi will be wroght.

---

[1] The word 'didde' was written before 'offende,' and then crossed
through.

[Exit Angel, Joseph turns to Mary.]

Marie, my doughter dere,　　　　　　　　84　'Mary, my
On þe is all my þought.　　　　　　　　　　　　darling,

Mar. A ! leue Joseph, what chere ?

8. **Jos.** Þe chere of me is done for ay.

Mar. Allas ! what tythandis herde haue ȝe ?　88

Jos. Now certis, full ille to þe at saye,

Ther is noght ellis but uṣ most flee,　　　　　we must flee
　　　　　　　　　　　　　　　　　　　　　　from our kith.'
Owte of oure kyth where we are knowyn

Full wightely bus vs be withdrawen,　　　　92

Both þou and I.

Mar. Leue Ioseph, why ?　　　　　　　　If. 70 b.

　　　　　　　　Layne it noght,

To doole who has vs demed ?　　　　　　　96

Or what wronge haue we wroght,　　　　'Dear Joseph,
　　　　　　　　　　　　　　　　　　　　why must we be
Wherfore we shulde be flemyd ?　　　　　banished ?'

9. **Jos.** Wroght we harme ? nay, nay, all wrang,

Wytte þou wele it is noght soo,　　　　　　100

Þat yonge page liffe þou mon for-gange,　'We must flee
　　　　　　　　　　　　　　　　　　　　from the child's
But yf þou fast flee fro his foo.　　　　　foe.'

Mar. His foo, allas ! what is youre reede,

Wha wolde my dere barne do to dede ?　　104

I durk, I dare,　　　　　　　　　　'Alas ! I laugh,
　　　　　　　　　　　　　　　　　　I tremble. Who
Whoo may my care　　　　　　　　　　can stop my
　　　　　　　　　　　　　　　　　　trouble ?'
　　　　　　　Of balis blynne ?

To flee I wolde full fayne,　　　　　　　108

For all þis worlde to wynne

Wolde I not se hym slayne.

10. **Jos.** I warne þe he is thraly thrette.

With Herowde kyng, harde harmes to haue,　112

With þat mytyng yf þat we be mette

Þer is no salue þat hym may saue.

I warne þe wele, he sleeis all　　　　　'Herod the
　　　　　　　　　　　　　　　　　　mighty will slay
Knave childir, grete and small,　　116　all boy children,

In towne and felde,
With in þe elde
    Of two ȝere.

for thy son's
sake.

And for thy sones sake,   120
He will for-do þat dere,
May þat traytoure hym take.

If. 71.
I viij.

11. Mar. Leue Joseph, who tolde yow þis?
How hadde ȝe wittering of þis dede?   124

An angel told
me this.

Jos. An aungell bright þat come fro blisse
This tythandis tolde with-owten drede.
And wakynd me oute of my slepe,
Þat comely childe fro cares to kepe,   128
And bad me flee
With hym and þe
    On-to Egipte.

I dread the trip.'

And sertis I dred me sore   132
To make my smale trippe,
Or tyme þat I come þare.

12. Mar. What ayles þei at my barne
Slike harmes hym for to hete?   136

'Why should
I be deprived of
my son's life?'

Allas! why schulde I tharne [1]
My sone his liffe so sweete,
His harte aught to be ful sare,
On slike a foode hym to for-fare,   140
Þat nevir did ill
Hym for to spille,
    And he ne wate why.
I ware full wille of wane   144
My son and he shulde dye,
And I haue but hym allone.

'Dear Mary, be
quiet! quickly
prepare to flee.

13. Jos. We! leue Marie, do way, late be,
I pray þe, leue of thy dynne,   148
And fande þe furthe faste for to flee
Away with hym for to wynne,

---

[1] MS. has *thrane*.

That no myscheue on hym betyde,

Nor none vnhappe in nokyn side,   152

Be way nor strete,

Þat we non mete

      To slee hym.

Mar. Allas! Joseph, for care!   156   lf. 71 b.

Why shuld I for-go hym,

My dere barne þat I bare.

14. Jos. þat swete swayne yf þou saue,

Do tyte, pakke same oure gere,   160   Make haste!
    pack up our gear
    if you wish to

And such smale harnes as we haue.   save him.

Mar. A! leue Joseph, I may not bere.

Jos. Bere arme? no, I trowe but small,

But god it wote I muste care for all,   164

For bed and bak,   I must carry all
    we need for bed

And alle þe pakke   and back.

      Þat nedis vnto vs.

It fortheres to fene me   168

Þis pakald bere me bus,

Of[1] all I plege and pleyne me.

15. But god graunte grace I noght for-gete   God grant I for-
    get nothing.'

No tulles þat we shulde with vs take.   172

Mar. Allas! Joseph, for greuaunce grete!

Whan shall my sorowe slake,

For I wote noght whedir to fare.

Jos. To Egipte talde I þe lang are.   176

Mar. Whare standith itt?   'Where is
    Egypt?'

Fayne wolde I witt.

Jos.   What wate I?

I wote not where it standis.   180   'I don't know.'

Mar. Joseph, I aske mersy,   'I beg pardon,
    help me.

Helpe me oute of þis lande.

16. Jos. Nowe certis, Marie, I wolde full fayne,

Helpe þe al þat I may,   184   lf. 72.
    K j.

       [1] MS. repeats *Of.*

And at my poure me peyne
To wynne with hym and þe away.

Alas ! these wild roads ! why have we to flee?'

Mar. Allas ! what ayles þat feende
Þus wilsom wayes make vs to wende;   188
He dois grete synne,
Fro kyth and kynne
            He gares vs flee.

' Stop crying.

Jos. Leue Marie, leue thy grete !   192
Mar. Joseph, full wo is me,
For my dere sone so swete.

Wrap him up warm and softly,

17. Jos. I pray þe Marie, happe hym warme,
And sette hym softe þat he noght syle,   196
And yf þou will ought ese thyn arme,

I will carry him to ease thine arm.'

Gyff me hym, late me bere hym awhile.
Mar. I thanke you of youre grete goode dede,
          [*Gives the child to Joseph.*

' Take care of him !'

Nowe gud Joseph tille hym take hede,   200
þat fode so free !
Tille hym ʒe see
          Now in this tyde.

' If you ride ill, hold fast by the mane.'

Jos. Late me and hym allone,   204
And yf þou can ille ride
Haue and halde þe faste by þe mane.
18. Mar. Allas ! Joseph for woo,
Was neuer wight in worde so will !   208
Jos. Do way Marie ! and say nought soo,
For þou schall haue no cause ther-till.

' God is our friend,
lf. 72 b.

For witte þou wele, god is oure frende,
He will be with vs wherso we lende,   212
In all oure nede
He will vs spede,
        Þis wote I wele,
I loue my lorde of all,   216

I feel quite strong,

Such forse me thynke I fele,
I may go where I schall.

19. Are was I wayke, nowe am I wight,   *though before I was weak.'*

My lymes to welde ay at my wille,   220

I loue my maker most of myght,

That such grace has graunte me tille.

Nowe schall no hatyll do vs harme,

I haue oure helpe here in myn arme.   224

He will vs fende,

Wherso we lende,

      Fro tene and tray.

Late vs goo with goode chere,   228

Fare wele and haue gud day !

God blisse vs all in fere.

Mar. Amen as he beste may.

XIX. THE GYRDILLERS AND NAYLERS[1].

Matth. ii. 16–18.

The Massacre of the Innocents.

[PERSONS OF THE PLAY.

HERODES.   PRIMUS ET SECUNDUS MILITES.
PRIMUS ET SECUNDUS CONSULES.   PRIMA ET SECUNDA MULIERES.]

[SCENE I, *Herod's court.*]

'Beaux sires, still your voices,

1. **Her.**   POWRE bewsheris aboute,
            Peyne of lyme and lande[2],
Stente of youre steuenes stoute,
            And stille as stone ȝe stande,   4
And my carping recorde;
ȝe aught to dare and doute,
And lere you lowe to lowte
To me youre louely lorde.   8

2. ȝe awe in felde and towne

bow at my bidding.

            To bowe at my bidding,
With reuerence and renoune,
            As fallis for swilk a kyng   12
Þe lordlyest on-lyue
Who her-to is noght bowne,

---

[1] On lf. 73 is the word Mylners, crossed through; on the back of the same leaf is noted in a late hand, 'This matter of the gyrdlers agreyth not with the Couchez in no poynt, it begynneth, Lyston lordes vnto my Lawe.' It does not appear what this refers to. Play XXX is by the 'Tapiteres and Coucheres,' but it does not begin with this line. I have no mention of the Couchers among my extracts from the City records, though several as to the Tapiters, probably the Couchers were a newer craft.

[2] The first four lines are written as two in the MS.

Be all-myghty mahounde
To dede I schall hym dryue !   16

3. So bolde loke no man be,   Ask help only
   For to aske help ne helde [1]   of me or of
                         Mahomet.'
But of mahounde and me,
   Þat hase þis worlde in welde,   20
To mayntayne vs emelle,
For welle of welthe are we,
And my cheffe helpe is he ;
Her-to what can ȝe tell.   24

4. i Cons. Lord, what you likis to do
   All folke will be full fayne,   'All obey you.
To take entente þer-to,
   And none grucche þer-agayne.   28
Þat full wele witte shall ȝe,
And yf þai wolde noȝt soo,
We shulde sone worke þam woo.
Her. ȝa ! faire sirs, so shulde it bee.   32

5. ii Cons. Lorde, þe soth to saie,   If. 74 b.
   Fulle wele we undirstande,
Mahounde is god werraye,   'Mahomet is the
   And ȝe ar lorde of ilke a lande.   36 true God, and ye
                               are lord of every
                               land.'
Ther-fore, so haue I seell,
I rede we wayte all-way,
What myrthe most mend ȝou may.
Her. Certis ȝe saie ryght well.   40

6. But I am noyed of newe,   'I am annoyed,
   Þat blithe may I noȝt be,
For thre kyngis as ȝe knowe   those three kings
   That come thurgh þis contree,   44
And saide þei sought a swayne.
i Cons. Þat rewlle I hope þam rewe,
For hadde þer tales ben trewe,
They hadde comen þis waye agayne.   48 should have
                               come this way
                               again.'

          [1] MS. has *holde*.

7. ii Cons. We harde how þei ȝou hight,
 Yf they myght fynde þat childe,
For to haue tolde ȝou right,

'They have deceived you ;

  But certis þei are begilyd. 52
Swilke tales ar noght to trowe,
Full wele wotte ilke a wight,
Þer schalle neuere man haue myght
 Ne maystrie vnto ȝou. 56

they are ashamed to meet you.'

8. i Cons. Þam schamys so, for certayne,
 That they dar mete ȝou no more.
Her. Wherfore shulde þei be fayne
  To make swilke fare before ; 60
To saie a boy was borne
That schulde be moste of mayne ?
This gadlyng schall agayne
 Yf þat þe deuyll had sworne ; 64

lf. 75:
K iiij.

9. For be well neuer þei wotte,
 Whedir þei wirke wele or wrang
To frayne garte þam þus-gate,
  To seke that gedlyng gane, 68
And swilke carping to kith.
ii Cons. Nay lorde, they lered ouere latte,
Youre blisse schall neuere abatte,
 And therfore, lorde, be blithe. 72

[Enter Messenger.]

Mahomet, save the king !

10. Nunc. Mahounde with-outen pere
 My lorde ! ȝou saue ! and see.
Her. Messenger, come nere,

'Beau sire, good day !'

  And, bewcher ! wele ye be. 76
What tydyngis telles þou, any ?
Nun. ȝa ! lorde, sen I was here,
I haue sought sidis seere,
 And sene merueyllis full many. 80

11. Her. And of meruayles to move,
That were most myrthe to me.

Nunc. Lorde, euen as I haue seene,
The soth sone schall ʒe see, 84
Yf ʒe wille, here in hye.
I mette tow townes betwene
Thre kyngis with crounes clene, *' I met three
Rydand full ryally. 88 kings riding royally.'*

Her. A! my blys! boy, þou burdis to brode! *' Boy, you talk
[**Nunc.**] Sir, þer may no botment be [1]. too fast!*

12. [Her.] O we! by sonne and mone,
Þan tydis vs talis to nyght. 92
Hopes þou þei will come sone *Do you think
Hedir, as þei haue hight, they'll come soon
For to telle me tythande? to tell me tidings?'*

Nunc. Nay, lorde, þat daunce is done. 96 *lf. 75 b.*

Her. Why, whedir are þei gone?

Nunc. Ilkone in-to ther owne lande.

13. Her. How sais þou, ladde? late be.

Nunc. I saie for they are past. 100

Her. What, forthe away fro me?

Nunc. ʒa, lord, in faitht ful faste.
For I herde and toke hede
How þat þei wente, all thre, 104 *'They are gone
In to ther awne contre. to their own countries.*

Her. A! dogges, þe deuell ʒou spede.

14. Nunc. Sir, more of þer menyng
ʒitt well I undirstode 108
How þei hadde made offering *They had made
Unto þat frely foode [2] offerings to that beautiful creature.'*

[1] There seems something wanting here.
[2] Lines 107–110 are written as two lines in the MS.

Þat now of newe is borne.
Þai saie he schulde be kyng,
And welde all erthely thyng.

Her. Allas! þan am I lorne.

15. Fy on thaym! faytours, fy!
Wille þei be-gylle me þus.   116

Nunc. Lorde, by ther prophicy,
Þei named his name Jesus.

Her. Fy! on þe, ladde, þou lyes!

ii Cons. Hense! tyte, but þou þe hye,   120
With doulle her schall þou dye,
That wreyes hym on this wise.

16. Nunc. Ʒe wyte me all with wrang,
Itt is þus and wele warre.   124

Her. Thou lyes! false traytoure strange,
Loke neuere þou negh me nere.

Vppon liffe and lyme
May I þat faitour fange,   128
Full high I schall gar hym hange,
Both þe harlott and hym.

17. Nunc. I am nott worthy to wyte,
Bot fares-wele, all þe heppe!   132

i Consul. Go, in þe deueles dispite,
Or I schall gar the leppe,
And dere aby this bro.   [*Exit Messenger.*

Herodus. Alas!¹ for sorowe and sighte,   136
My woo no wighte may wryte,
What deuell is best to do.

18. ii Cons. Lorde, amende youre chere,
And takis no nedles noy,   140
We schall ʒou lely lere,
Þat ladde for to distroye,
Be counsaille if we cane.

¹ MS. has *Als.*

Margin notes:

Herod vents his anger on the messenger.

lf. 76.
K v.

'Thou liest! I'll hang both you and him.'

'I am blameless; farewell, the whole heap.'

'I'll make you run!'

Herod and his elders take counsel.

Her. Þat may ȝe noght come nere,   144
For it is past two ȝere
Sen þat þis bale be-gane.

19. i Cons. Lorde, þerfore haue no doute
    If it were foure or fyve,   148
Gars gadir in grete rowte
    Youre knyghtis kene be-lyue.
And biddis þam dynge to dede
Alle knave childir kepte in dowte,   152   *A great company of soldiers shall kill all the boys of two years old in Bethlehem and round about.*
In Bedlem and all aboute,
To layte in ilke a stede.

20. ii Cons. Lorde, saue none, for youre seell,   *If. 76 b.*
    Þat are of ii ȝere age with-inne,   156
Þan schall þat fandelyng felle
    Be-lyue his bliss schall blynne,
With bale when he shall blede.
Her. Sertis, ȝe saie right wele,   160
And as ȝe deme ilke dele,
Shall I garre do in-dede.

21. Sir knyghtis, curtayse and hende,
    Þow ne nott bees nowe all newe,   164   *' 'Tis a new business, but I will be your friend.'*
ȝe schall fynde me youre frende,
    And ȝe þis tyme be trewe.
i Cons. What saie ȝe, lorde, lette see.
Her. To Bedlehem bus ȝe wende,   168
That schrewe[1] with schame to schende
Þat menes to maistir me.

22. And a-bowte Bedlehem boght he,
    Bus yowe wele spere and spye,   172
For ellis it will be waghe
    Þat he losis þis Jury.
And certis þat were grete schame.
ii. Cons. My lorde, þat wer vs lathe,   176   *' We were loathe he should escape.'*

[1] The MS. has *schorwe*.

And he escapid it wer skathe,
And we welle worthy blame.

23. i **Miles.**   Full sone he schall be soughte,
That make I myne a-vowe.   180

i **Cons.**   I bide for him ʒow loghte,
And latte me telle yowe howe.

Go werke when ʒe come there,
By-cause ʒe kenne hym noght,   184
To dede they muste be brought,
Knave childre, lesse and more.

24. **Her.**   ʒaa, all with-inne two ʒere,
That none for speche be spared.   188

ii **Miles.**   Lord, howe ʒe vs lere
Full wele we take rewarde,
And certis we schall not rest.   [*Exeunt.*

[SCENE II, *Round about Bethlehem.*]

i **Miles.**   Comes furth, felowes, in feere ;   192

Loo ! fondelyngis fynde we here [1].

25. i **Mul.**   Owte on ʒou ! theves, I crye !
ʒe slee my semely sone.

ii **Miles.**   Ther browls schall dere abye   196

This bale þat is be-gonne,
Þer-fore lay fro þe faste.

ii **Mul.**   Allas ! for doule I dye,
To saue my son schall I,   200
Aye whils my liff may last.

26. i **Miles.**   A ! dame, þe deuyll þe spede.
And me, but itt be quytte.

i **Mul.**   To dye I haue no drede,   20
I do þe wele to witte,
To saue my sone so dere.

i **Miles.**   As armes ! for nowe is nede,

---

[1] A line is wanting here, but no blank in MS.

But yf we do yone dede,   208   'To arms !
Ther quenys will quelle us here.   these queans will
destroy us.'

27. **ii Mul.** Allas! þis lothly striffe!   lf. 77 b.
No blisse may be my bette,   Lamentation and
sorrow.
þe knyght vppon his knyffe   212
Hath slayne my sone so swette;
And I hadde but hym allone.

i Mul. Allas! I lose my liffe,
Was neuere so wofull a wyffe,   216
Ne halffe so wille of wone!

28. And certis, me were full lotht
Þat þei þus harmeles ȝede.

i Miles. Þe deuell myght spede you bothe,   220
False wicchis, are ye woode?   'False witches,
are ye mad?'
ii Mul. Nay false lurdayns, ye lye.
[**i Miles.**] Yf ȝe be woode or wrothe,
Ye schall noȝt skape fro skathe,   224
Wende we vs hense in hye.

29. **i Mul.** Allas! þat we wer wroughte,
In worlde women to be,
Þe barne þat wee dere bought,   228
Þus in oure sighte to see
Disputuously spill.

ii Mul. And certis, þer nott is noght,   Their business is
nought, they will
The same þat þei haue soughte,   232 never find him
they seek.
Schall þei neuere come till.

30. **i Miles.** Go we to þe kyng,   'We shall tell of
you to the king.'
Of all þis contek kene
I schall nott lette for no-thyng   236
To saie as we haue sene.

ii Miles. And certis, no more shall I.
We haue done his bidding,   f. 78.
K vij.
We schall saie sothfastly,   240
How so they wraste or wryng.

[SCENE III, *Herod's court.*]

31. i **Miles.**   Mahounde, oure god of myght,

    Saue þe! sir herowde þe kyng!

   i **Cons.**   Lorde, take kepe to youre knyght,   **244**

    He wille telle ȝou nowe thydingis

    Of bordis wher they haue bene.

 Her.   Ȝaa, and þei haue gone right,

    And holde þat þei vs hight,   **248**

    Þan shall solace be sene.

32. ii **Miles.**   Lorde, as ȝe demed vs to done,

    In contrees wher we come—

 Her.   Sir, by sonne and mone,   **252**

    Ȝe are welcome home,

    And worthy to haue rewarde.

    Haue ȝe geten vs þis gome?

   i **Miles.**   Wher we fande felle or fone,   **256**

    Wittenesse we will þat þer was none [1].

33. ii **Miles.**   Lord, they are dede ilkone,

    What wolde ȝe we ded more?

 Her.   I aske but aftir oone,   **260**

    Þe kyngis tolde of before,

    Þat schulde make grete maistrie;

    Telle vs if he be tane.

   i **Miles.**   Lorde, tokenyng hadde we none   **264**

    To knawe þat brothell by.

34. ii **Miles.**   In bale we haue þam brought

    A-boute all Bedleham towne.

 Her.   Ye lye, ȝoure note is nought!   **268**

    Þe deueles of helle ȝou droune!

    So may þat boy be fledde,

    For in waste haue ȝe wroght

    Or that same ladde be sought,   **27?**

    Schalle I neure byde in bedde.

---

[1] Line 257 should rime with l. 254. There is some mistake here.

35. [? i Cons.]¹   We will wende with you þan ²
　　To dynge þat dastard doune.
　　[? ii Cons.]   Asarme! euere ilke man,   276
　　That holdis of mahounde.
　　Wer they a thousand skore,
　　This bargayne schall þai banne ³
　　Comes aftir as yhe canne,   280
　　For we will wende be-fore.   [*Exeunt.*

---

¹ In the MS. two red lines mark off lines 274, 275 and ll. 276–281 as
separate speeches, but the names of the speakers are omitted.
² *Than* comes at the beginning of l. 275 in the MS.
³ MS. has *bande.*

XX. THE SPORIERS AND LORIMERS [1].

Christ with the Doctors in the Temple.

[PERSONS OF THE PLAY.

JESUS.   MARIA.   JOSEPH.
PRIMUS, SECUNDUS, TERTIUS DOCTOR.
PRIMUS, SECUNDUS, TERTIUS MAGISTER.]

Luke ii. 41-51.

[SCENE I, *The road from Jerusalem.*]

1. **JOS.**　　[M]ARIE, of mirthis we may vs mene,
　　　　　　　And trewly telle be-twixte vs twoo

'What solemn
sights we have
seen,

Of solempne sightis þat we haue sene
In þat cite were we come froo.　　　　　　　　　4

Mar.　Sertis, Joseph, ȝe will noȝt wene

what joy our son
has given us, in
Jerusalem.

What myrthis with in my harte I maie,
Sen þat oure sone with vs has bene,
And sene ther solempne sightis alswae.　　　　8

We will go home
with our friends.'

Jos.　Hamward I rede we hye
In all þe myght we maye,
Be-cause of company
þat will wende in oure waye.　　　　　　　　12

2.　For gode felawshippe haue we founde,
　　And ay so forward schall we fynde.

---

[1] This play is found also in the Towneley collection under the name of
Pagina Doctorum, p. 158. The parallel begins with l. 73 of York play, a
quite different prelude of 48 lines (the commencement is wanting) in the
Towneley taking place of the first 72 lines of York. A considerable
difference occurs, too, in the description of the ten commandments. The
Towneley version is given from l. 73 at the foot of the page.

Mar. A ! sir, where is oure semely sone ?

I trowe oure wittis be waste as wynde,   16

Allas ! in bale þus am I boone,

What ayleth vs both to be so blynde.

To go ouere fast we haue be-gonne,

And late þat louely leue be-hynde.   20

Jos. Marie, mende thy chere,

For certis whan all is done,

He comes with folke in feere,

And will ouere take vs sone.   24

3. **Mar.** Ouere take vs sone ? Sir, certis nay,

Such gabbyngis may me noȝht be-gyle,

For we haue trauelde all þis day

Fro Jerusalem many a myle.   28

Jos. I wende he hadde bene with vs aye,

A-waye fro vs how schulde he wyle ?

Mar. Hit helpis nought such sawes to saie,

My barne is lost, allas ! þe whille !   32

þat euere we wente þer oute

With him in companye,

We lokid ouere late aboute,

Full wooe is me forthy !   36

4. For he is wente som wayes wrang,

And non is worthy to wyte but wee.   38

Jos. Agaynewarde rede I þat we gang

The right way to þat same citee,   40

To spire and spie all men emang,

For hardely homward is he.

Mar. Of sorowes sere schal be my sang,

My semely sone tille I hym see,   44

He is but xij ȝere alde.

What way som euere he wendis.

Jos. Woman ! we may be balde

To fynde hym with oure frendis.   [*They turn back.*   48

' Where is our son ?'

' He will soon overtake us.'

' Nay, we are come many miles,
lf. 79 b.

he is lost.

We must blame ourselves.'
' Let us turn back.

He is sure to be with our friends.'

[SCENE II, *The Temple.*]

5. ius **Mag.**   Maistirs, takes to me in tente,
And rede youre resouns right on rawes,
And all þe pepull in þis present
Euere ilke man late see his sawes.   52

' Can any one
allege ought
against our law ?
But witte I wolde, or we hens wente,
Be clargy clere if we couthe knawe
Yf any lede þat liffe has lente,
Wolde might allegge agaynste oure lawe.   56
Owthir in more or lesse

If. 80.
L ij.
We must redress
it.'
If we defaute myght feele,
Dewly we schall gar dresse
Be dome euery ilk a dele.   60

6. iius **Mag.**   Þat was wele saide, so mot I the,
Swilke notis to neven me thynke wer nede,
For maistirs in this lande ar we,
And has þe lawes lelly to lede,   64
And doctoures also in oure degree,
Þat demyng has of ilka dede.

' Lay forth our
books ;
Laye fourthe oure bokes belyue, late see,
What mater moste were for oure mede.   68

iiius **Mag.**   We schall ordayne so wele,
Sen we all clergy knawe,
no one shall
find defects.'
Defaute shall noman fele
Nowdir in dede ne sawe.   [*Enter Jesus.*

' Joy unto you,
sirs !'
7. Jesus.   Lordingis, loue be with ȝou lentte   73
And mirthis be vn-to þis mene.

' Go away, child.'
ius **Mag.**   Sone, hense away ! I wolde þou wente,
For othir haftis in hande haue we.   76

Tunc venit Jesus.

Towneley MS.
fol. 67. Surtees
print, p. 158.
Jesus.   Masters, luf be with you lent,   73
And mensk be unto this meneȝe.
i Mag.   Son, hens away I wold thou went,
For othere haft in hand haue we.   76

ii^{us} **Mag.**   Sone, whoso þe hedir sente,
They were nouȝt wise, þat warne I þe,
For we haue othir tales to tente
Þan now with barnes bordand to be.   80

iii^{us} **Mag.**   Sone, yf þe list ought to lere   'If you like to
To lyve by Moyses laye,   learn Moyses' law,
Come hedir and þou shalle here   come here.'
Þe sawes þat we shall saye;   84

8. For in som mynde itt may þe brynge   If. 80 b.
To here oure reasouns redde by rawes.

Jesus.   To lerne of you nedis me no thing.
For I knawe both youre dedys and sawes.   88   'I know your
                                                          sayings and
i^{us} **Mag.**   Nowe herken ȝone barne with his brandyng,   doings.'
He wenes he kens more þan we knawes!
We! nay, certis sone, þou arte ouere ȝinge [1]   'You are young
By clergy ȝitt to knowe oure lawes.   92   to know our
                                                          laws.'
Jesus.   I wote als wele as yhe
Howe þat youre lawes wer wrought.

---

ii **Mag.**   Son, whosoeuer the hyder sent,
        Thay were not wyse, thus tell I the ;
        For we haue othere tayllys to tent
        Then now with barnes bowrdand to be.   80

iii **Mag.** Son, thou lyst oght lere To lyf by Moyses lay,
        Com heder, and thou shall here The sawes
                        that we wyll say;   84
        For in som mynde it may the bryng
        To here oure sawes red by rawes.

Jesus.   To lere of you nedys me no thyng
        For I knaw both youre dedys and sawes.   88

i **Mag.**   Hark, yonder barn with his bowrdyng
        He wenys he kens more then ho knawys,
        Nay, certes, son, thou art ouer ying
        By clergy yit to know oure lawes.   92

Jesus.   I wote as well as ye how that youre lawes
                        was wroght.

---

[1] MS. ȝonge.

'Come, sit down.

ii^{us} **Mag.** Cum sitte, sone schall we see,

[Jesus sits among them.

For certis so semys it noght.   96

9. Itt wer wondir þat any wight

Vn-till oure reasouns right schulde reche.

You think you
can see into our
laws?'

And þou sais þou hast insight,

Oure lawes truly to telle and teche?   100

Jesus. The holy gost has on me light,

And has anoynted me as a leche,

And geven me pleyne poure and might

The kyngdom of heuene for to preche. 104

'Whence is he?'

i^{us} **Mag.** Whens euere this barne may be

That shewes þer novellis nowe?

Jesus. Certis, I was or ȝe,

And schall be aftir ȝou.   108

10. i^{us} **Mag.** Sone, of thy sawes, als haue I cele,

'The sayings
and knowledge
of the boy are
wonderful,

And of thy witte is wondir thyng,

But neuere the lesse fully I feele

Itt may falle wele in wirkyng.   112

---

ii **Mag.** Com, sytt, soyn shall we se, For certys so
semys it noght.   96

iii **Mag.** It were wonder if any wyght

Untill oure resons right shuld reche,

And thou says thou has in sight

Oure lawes truly to tell and teche. 100

Jesus. The Holy Gost has on me lyght,

And anoynt me lyke a leche,

And gyffen to me powere and myght

The kyngdom of heuen to preche. 104

ii **Mag.** Whenseuer this barne may be

That shewys thise novels new?

Jesus. Certan, syrs, I was or ye,

And shall be after you. 108

i **Mag.** Son, of thi sawes, as we hane ceyll,

And of thi wytt is wonder thyng;

Bot neuer the les fully I feyll

That it may fayll in wyrkyng; 112

For Dauid demys of ilka dele,

And sais þus of childir ȝing,

And of ther mouthes, he wate full wele,

Oure lord has parformed loving. 116

But ȝitt, sone, schulde þou lette

Here for to speke ouere large,

For where maistiris are mette

Childre wordis are noȝt to charge. 120

11. And if þou wolde neuere so fayne

Yf all þe liste to lere þe lawe,

Þou arte nowthir of myght ne mayne

To kenne it as a clerke may knawe. 124

Jesus. Sirs, I saie ȝou for sartayne,

That suthfast schalbe all my sawe,

And poure haue playnere & playne to say,

And aunswer as me awe. 128

i^{us} **Doct.** Maistirs what may þis mene ?

Meruayle me thynke haue I,

If. 81.
L iij.

yet he should not
speak too big
before the
masters of the
law.'

'I will speak
with truth and
weight.'

For Dauid demys euer ilk deylle,

And thus he says of childer ying,

' Ex ore infancium et lactancium perfecisti laudem.'

Of thare mowthes, sayth Dauid, wele

Oure Lord he has perfourmed lovyng ; 116

Neuer the les, son, yit shuld thou lett

Herfor to speke in large,

For where masters are mett

Chylder wordys ar not to charge. 120

For, certes, if thou wold neuer so fayn

Gyf all thi lyst to lere the law,

Thou art nawther of myght ne mayn

To know it, as a clerk may knaw. 124

Jesus. Syrs, I say you in certan,

That sothfast shalle be alle my saw,

And powere have I plene and playn

To say and answere as me aw. 128

i **Mag.** Masters, what may this mene?

Meruelle me thynk have I ;

Whens euere þis barne hauę bene,

The child talks
with wisdom.

And carpis þus connandly.   132

12. iius **Doct.**   Als wyde in worlde als we haue wente,

Itt fand we neuere swilke ferly fare,

For certis I trowe þis barne be sente

Full souerandly to salue oure sare.   136

Jesus.   Sirs, I schall proue in youre present

Alle þe sawes þat I saide are.

Moses' first com-
mandment is,

iiius **Doc.**   Why, whilke callest þou þe firste comaundment,

And þe moste in Moyses lare?   140

Jesus.   Sirs, sen ȝe are sette on rowes,

And has youre bokes on brede,

If. 81 b.

Late se, sirs, in youre sawes

Howe right þat ȝe can rede.   144

Matth. xxii. 37-
40.

13. ius **Doct.**   I rede þis is þe firste bidding

Þat Moyses taught vs here vntill,

To honour God.

To honnoure god ouere all thing,

With all thy witte and all þi will;   148

Where euer this barne has bene

That carpys thus conandly.   132

ii Mag.   In warld as wyde as we haue went

Fand we neuer sich ferly fare;

Certes, I trow the barn be sent

Sufferanly to salfe oure sare.   136

Jesus.   Syrs, I shalle preue in youre present

Alle the sawes that I sayde are.

iii Mag.   Which callys thou the fyrst commaundement,

And the most in Moyses lare.   140

Jesus.   Syrs, synthen ye syt on raw,

And hase youre bookes on brede,

Let se, syrs, in youre saw

How right that ye can rede.   144

i Mag.   I rede that this is the fyrst bydyng

That Moyses told us here vntylle;

Honoure thi God ouer ilka thyng,

With alle thi wyt and alle thi wylle,   148

And all thyn harte in hym schall hyng,
Erlye and late both lowde and still.

Jesus. ȝe nedis non othir bokes to bring,
But fandis þis for to fulfill. 152
The secounde may men preve
And clerly knawe, wher by
Youre neghbours shall ȝe loue
Als youre selffe, sekirly. 156

The second, Love thy neighbour as thyself.

14. This comaunded Moyses to all men,
In his x comaundementis clere,
In þer ij biddingis, schall we kene,
Hyngis all þe lawe þat we shall lere. 160
Whoso ther two fulfilles then [1]
With mayne and myght in gode manere,
He trulye fulfillis all þe ten
Þat aftir folowes in feere. 164
Þan schulde we god honnoure,
With all youre myght and mayne,

     And alle thi hart in hym shalle hyng,
     Erly and late, both lowde and stylle.
Jesus. Ye nede none othere bookys to bryng,
     Bot fownd this to fulfylle; 152
     The seconde may men profe
     And clergy knaw therby,
     Youre neghburs shalle ye lofe
     Right as youre self truly. 156
     Thise commaunded Moyses tylle alle men
     In his commaundes clere,
     In thise two bydyngys, shalle ye ken,
     Hyngys alle the law we aght to lere. 160
     Who so fulfylles thise two then
     Withe mayn and mode and good manere,
     He fulfyllys truly alle ten
     That after thaym folows in fere. 164
     Then shuld we God honowre
     With alle our myght and mayn,

---

[1] MS. sets *then* at beginning of l. 162.

And loue wele ilkea neghboure
Right as youre selfe, certayne.   168

15. i^{us} Doct.   Nowe sone, sen þou haste tolde vs two,
Whilke ar þe viij ? can þou ought saye ?

[Jesus].   The iij biddis whare so ȝe goo,
Þat ȝe schall halowe þe halyday.   172
Than is þe fourthe for frende or foo,
That fadir and modir honnoure ay.
The v^{te} you biddis noght for to sloo
No man nor woman by any way.   176
The vj^{te}, suthly to see,
Comaundis both more and myne,
That thei schalle fande to flee
All filthes of flesshely synne.   180

And luf welle ilk neghboure
Right as oure self certayn.   168

i Mag.   Now, son, synthen thou has told us two,
Which ar the viij, can thou oght say ?

Jesus.   The thyrd bydys, where so ye go,
That ye shalle halow the holy day.   172
From bodely wark ye take youre rest,
Youre household looke the same thay do,
Both wyfe, chylde, servande, and beest.

The fourt is then in weyllie and wo   173
Thi fader, thi moder, thou shalle honowre,   174
Not only with thi reuerence,
Bot in thare nede thou thaym socoure,
And kepe ay good obedyence.

The fyft bydys the no man slo,   175
Ne harme hym neuer in word ne dede,
Ne suffre hym not to be in wo
If thou may help hym in his nede.

The sext bydys the thi wyfe to take,   177
But none othere lawfully,
Lust of lechery thou fle and fast forsake,
And drede ay God where so thou be.

16. The vij^{te} fo[r]bedis you to stele
　　3oure neghboures goodes, more or lesse,
　　Whilke faute3 nowe are founden fele
　　Emang þer folke þat ferly is.　　　　　　　　184
　　The viij^{te} lernes 3ou for to be lele,
　　Here for to bere no false witnesse.
　　3oure neghbours house, whilkis 3e haue hele,
　　The ix^{te} biddis take no3t be stresse.　　　188
　　His wiffe nor his women
　　The x^{te} biddis no3t coveyte.
　　They are þe biddingis x,
　　Whoso will lelly layte.　　　　　　　　　　192

17. ii^{us} Doct. Be-halde howe he alleggis oure lawe,
　　And lered neuere on boke to rede.
　　Full subtill sawes, me thinkeþ, he saies,
　　And also trewe, yf we take hede.　　　　196

The doctors are
full of wonder,
for he never
learned to read.

　　　　The vij bydys the be no thefe feyr,　　181
　　　　Ne nothng wyn with trechery,
　　　　Oker, ne symony, thou com not nere,
　　　　Bot conscyence clere ay kepe truly.
　　　　The viij byddes the be true in dede　　185
　　　　And fals wytnes looke thou none bere,
　　　　Looke thou not ly for freynd ne syb,
　　　　Lest to thi saulle that it do dere.
　　　　The ix byddes the not desyre　　　　188
　　　　Thi neghbur's wyfe ne his women,　　187
　　　　Bot as holy kirk wold it were
　　　　Right so thi purpose sett it in.
　　　　The x byddes the for nothyng　　　　190
　　　　Thi neghburs goodys yerne wrongwysly,
　　　　His house, his rent, ne his hafyng,
　　　　And Cristen fayth trow stedfastly.
　　　　Thus in tabyls shalle ye ken
　　　　Oure Lord to Moyses wrate.
　　　　Thise ar the commaundementes ten,　　191
　　　　Who so wille lely layt.
ii Mag.　Behald how he lege oure lawes,
　　　　And leryd neuer on booke to rede;　　194
　　　　Fulle sotelle sawes me thynk he says
　　　　And also true, if we take hede.　　　196

iii^us **Doct.**   3a! late hym wende fourth on his wayes;
For and he dwelle, withouten drede,
The pepull schall full sone hym prayse
Wele more þan vs for all oure dede.   200
i^us **Doct.**   Nay, nay, þan wer we wrang,
Such speking wille we spare.
Als he come late hym gang,
And move vs nowe nomore.   204

[Enter Mary and Joseph.]

18. **Mar.**   A! dere Joseph, what is youre rede?

lf. 82 b.

Mary is full of
sorrow, she has
sought her son
three days.

Of oure grete bale no bote may be,
Myne harte is heuy as any lede
My semely sone tille hym I see.   208
Nowe haue [we] sought in ilk a stede,
Boþe vppe and doune, ther¹ days thre,
And whedir þat he be quyk or dede
3itt wote we noght, so wo is me!   212

---

iii **Mag.**   Yei, lett hym furth on his wayes,
For if he dwelle withoutten drede
The pepylle wille ful soyn hym prayse
Welle more then vs for alle oure dede.   200
i **Mag.**   Nay, nay, then wyrk we wrang,
Sich spekyng wille we spare,
As he cam let hym gang,
And mefe vs not no mare.   204

Tunc venient Josephus et Maria, et dicet Maria:

Maria.   A dere Josephe! what is youre red?
Of oure greatt baylle no boytt may be,
My hart is heuy as any lede
My semely son to I hym se.   208
Now haue we soght in euery sted
Both vp and downe thise dayes thre,
And wheder he be whik or dede
Yit wote we not; so wo is me!   212

---

¹ MS. has *thre.*

Jos.   Mysese had neuere man more,
But mournyng may not mende ;
I rede forther we fare
Till God some socoure sende.   216

19. Aboute ȝone tempill if he be ought,   He may be in
I wolde we wiste þis ilke nyght.   the temple.

Mar.   A ! sir, I see þat we haue sought !
In worlde was neuere so semely a sight.
Lo ! where he sittis, ȝ[e] se hym noght ?   220   She sees him
Emong ȝone maistiris mekill of myght.   afar off, sitting
                                                   among the
                                                   doctors.
Jos.   Now blist be he vs hedir brought,
For in lande was neuere non so light.   224

Mar.   A ! dere Joseph, als we haue cele,   Mary wishes
Go furthe and fette youre sone and myne,   Joseph to go
This day is gone nere ilke a dele,   forward and
And we haue nede for to gang hyne.   228   fetch him,

20. Jos.   With men of myght can I not mell,
Than all my trauayle mon I tyne,

Joseph.   Sorow had neuer man mare,
          Bot mowr[n]yng, Mary, may not amende ;
          Fartherner I red we fare
          To God som socoure send.   216
          Abowtt the tempylle if he be oght
          That wold I that we wyst this nyght.

Maria.   A certes, I se that we haue soght,
          In warld was neuer so semely a sight ; 220
          Lo, where he syttes, se ye hymn noght,
          Amanges yond masters mekylle of myght ?

Joseph.   Blyssyd be he vs heder broght !
          In land now lyfes there none so light. 224

Maria.   Now dere Joseph, as have ye seylle,
          Go furthe and fetche youre son and myne ;
          This day is goyn nere ilka deylle,
          And we have nede for to go hien.   228

Joseph.   With men of myght can I not melle
          Then alle my trauelle mon I tyne ;

but he cannot
mix with such
fine folk, gay
in furs.

I can no3t with þem, þis wate þou wele,

They are so gay in furres fyne.   232

Mar.   To þam youre herand for to say

Suthly 3e thar no3t drede no dele,

They will take rewarde to you all way,

'Your age would
be respected.'

Be-cause of elde; þis wate 3e wele.   236

If. 83.
L v.
He is shame-
fast.

Jos.   When I come there what schall I saye?

I wate neuere, als haue I cele.

Sertis, Marie, þou will haue me schamed for ay,

For I can nowthir croke nor knele.   240

They go together, **21. Mar.**   Go we to-gedir, I halde it beste,

Vn-to 3one worthy wysse in wede,

And yf I see, als haue I reste,

Þat 3e will no3t, þan bus me nede.   244

Mary first.
Joseph following.

Jos.   Gange on, Marie, and telle thy tale firste,

Thy sone to þe will take goode heede ;

Wende fourth, Marie, and do thy beste,

I come be-hynde, als God me spede.   248

I can not with thaym, that wote ye welle,

Thay are so gay in furrys fyne.   232

Maria.   To thaym youre erand forto say.

Surely that thar ye drede no deylle,

Thay wille take hede to you alway

Be-cause of eld, this wote I weyll.   236

Joseph.   When I com ther what shalle I say?

For I wote not, as have I ceylle ;

Bot thou wille haue me shamyd for ay,

For I can nawthere crowke ne knele.   240

Maria.   Go we togeder, I hold it best,

Unto yond worthy wyghtes in wede,

And if I se, as I have rest,

That ye wille not then must I nede.   244

Joseph.   Go thou and telle thi taylle fyrst,

Thi son to se wille take good hede ;

Weynd furthe, Mary, and do thi beste,

I com behynd, as God me spede.   248

Mar.   A ! dere sone Jesus !   [*They come forward.*

   Sen we loue þe allone,

   Why dosse þou þus till vs,   Mary reproaches

   And gares vs make swilke mone?   252   Jesus,

22. Thy fadir and I be-twyxte vs twa

   Son for thy loue has likid ill [1],

   We haue þe sought both to & froo,

   Wepand full sore as wightis will.   256

Jesus.   Wherto shulde ȝe seke me soo ?   but he was

   Ofte tymes it hase ben tolde you till,   'about his
Father's
   My fadir werkis, for wele or woo,   business.'

   Thus am I sente for to fulfyll.   260

Mar.   There sawes, als haue I cele,

   Can I noȝt vndirstande ;

   I schall thynke on þam wele,

   To ffonde what is folowand.   264

23. Jos.   Now sothely sone, þe sight of þe

   Hath salued vs of all oure sore ;

Maria.   A, dere son, Jesus!

     Sythen we luf the alone

     Whi dos thou tylle vs thus

     And gars vs make this mone ?   252

     Thi fader and I betwix vs two,

     Son, for thi luf has lykyd ylle,

     We haue the soght both to and fro

     Wepeand sore, as wyghtis wylle.   256

Jesus.   Wherto shuld ye, moder, seke me so ?

     Oft tymes it has bene told ye tylle

     My fader warkys for wele or wo,

     Thus am I sent for to fulfylle.   260

     Thise sawes, as haue I ceylle,

     I can welle vnderstande

     I shalle thynk on them weylle

     To fownd what is folowand.   264

Joseph. Now sothtly, son, the sight of the

     Has comforthed vs of all oure care ;

---

[1] The MS. originally had *son* at the end of l. 251, the later hand places
t as above.

lf. 83 b.

Come furth, sone, with þi modir and me,
Att Nazareth I wolde we wore.   268

Jesus goes with them.

Jesus.   Be-leves wele, lordis free,
For with my frendis nowe will I fare.

i doct.   Nowe, sone, wher þou schall bide or be[1],
God make þe gode man eu*er*more !   272
No wondir if ȝone wiffe
Of his fynding be full fayne;
He schall (and he haue liff)
Proue till a praty swayne.   276

The doctors beg him to conceal the new things they have talked of, and invite him to stay with them.

24. But sone, loke þat þou layne for gud or ill
Þe note þat we haue nemed her nowe,
And if it like þe to lende her stille,
And wonne with vs, welcome art þowe.   280

Jesus.   Graunte mercy, Sirs, of youre gode will,
No lenger liste me lende with ȝou,

His obedience to friends.

My frendis thoughtis I wol fulfille
And to þer bidding baynely bowe.   284

Com furth, now with thi moder and me
At Nazareth I wold we ware.   268
Jesus.   Be leyf then, ye lordynges fre,
For with my freyndys now wylle I fare.
i Mag.   Son, where so thou shalle abyde or be
God make the good man euer mare.   272
ii Mag.   No wonder if thou, wife,
Of his fyndyng be fayn;
He shalle, if he haue lyfe,
Prefe to a fulle good swayn.   276
iii Mag.   Son, looke thou layn for good or ylle
The noyttes that we haue nevened now;
And if thou lyke to abyde here stylle,
And with us won, welcome art thou.   280
Jesus.   Gramercy, syrs, of youre good wyll!
No longer lyst I byde with you,
My freyndys thoght I shalle fulfylle,
And to thare bydyng baynly bow.   284

---

[1] The words *or be* in MS. stand at beginning of l. 272.

Mar. Full wele is vs þis tyde,
Nowe maye we make goode chere.
Jos. No lenger will we bide,
Fares wele, all folke in feere. 288

Jħc, Maria, Joseph,
Primus doctor, secundus doctor, & tercius doctor [1].

Maria.   Full welle is me this tyde,
      Now may we make good chere.
Joseph. No longer wylle we byde,
      Fare welle alle folk in fere. 288

---

[1] These names are here in the original hand.

XXI. THE BARBOURS.

The Baptism of Jesus.

[PERSONS OF THE PLAY.

JOHANNES [THE BAPTIST].   PRIMUS ANGELUS.
JESUS.   SECUNDUS ANGELUS.]

[SCENE, *by the river Jordan.*]

1. Joh. ALMIGHTY god and lord verray,
      Full woundyrfull is mannys lesyng,
For yf I preche tham day be day,
And telle tham, lorde, of thy comyng,   4
    Þat all has wrought,
Men are so dull þat my preching
    Serues of noght.

2. When I haue, lord, in the name of the   8
Baptiste þe folke in watir clere,
Þan haue I saide þat aftir me
Shall he come þat has more powere
    þan I to taste,   12
He schall giffe baptyme more entire
    in fire and gaste.

3. Þus am I comen in message right,
And be fore-reyner in certayne,   16
In witnesse-bering of þat light,
Þe wiche schall light in ilka a man
    þat is comand
In-to this worlde ; nowe whoso can   20
    may vndirstande.

Matth. iii. 1-3, 13-17.
Men are so dull that John's preaching is useless.

John is a fore-runner,

4. Theȝ folke had farly of my fare,
And what I was full faste þei spied,
They askid yf I a prophete ware,　　24
And I saide 'nay'; but sone I wreyede
high aperte.
I saide I was a voyce that cryede　　*a voice crying in*
here in deserte.　　28　　*the wilderness,*

5. 'Loke þou make þe redy,' ay saide I,
'Vn-to oure lord god most of myght,
þat is þat þou be clene haly,
In worde, in werke, ay redy dight　　32
Agayns oure lord,　　*Make ready by*
With parfite liffe þat ilke a wight　　*a perfect life.*
be well restored.

6. For if we be clene in levyng,　　36
Oure bodis are goddis tempyll þan
In the whilke he will make his dwellyng,
Ther-fore be clene, bothe wiffe and man.
þis is my reed;　　40
God will make in yowe haly þan
his wonnyng-steed.

7. And if ȝe sette all youre delyte
In luste and lykyng of þis liff,　　44
Than will he turne fro yow als tyte　　*If. 84 b.*
By-cause of synne, boyth of man & wiffe,　　*God will turn*
And fro ȝou flee,　　*from those who*
For w[i]th whome þat synne is riffe　　48　　*only love this*
Will god noght be.'　　*life.*

8. Ang.　þou John, take tente what I schall saye,
I brynge þe tythandis wondir gode,
My lorde Jesus schall come þis day,　　52　　*Jesus will come*
Fro Galylee vn-to þis flode　　*to-day to be*
ȝe Jourdane call,　　*baptized in*
Baptyme to take myldely with mode　　*Jordan.*
þis day he schall.　　56

9. John, of his sande ther-fore be gladde,
   And thanke hym hartely, both lowde and still.

John is afraid.   Joh.[1] I thanke hym euere, but I am radde!
   I am noȝt abill to full-fill   60
      þis dede certayne.

   ii Ang. John, þe aught with harte and will
      To be full bayne

10. To do his bidding, all by-dene.   64
   Bot in his baptyme, John, take tente,

The descent of
the dove foretold.   þe heuenes schalle be oppen sene,
   The holy gost schalle doune be sente
      To se in sight,   68
   The fadirs voyce with grete talent
      be herde full riȝt,

11. Þat schall saie þus to hym for-thy [2]
   ·   ·   ·   ·   ·

12. Joh. With wordes fewne   72
   I will be subgett nyght & day
      as me well awe,   74
   To serue my lord Jesu to paye
      in dede & sawe.   76

Baptism is to
cleanse man of   13. Bot wele I wote, baptyme is tane
sin, but here is
no sin.   To wasshe and clense man of synne,
   And wele I wotte þat synne is none
   In hym, with-oute ne with-inne.   80
      What nedis hym than
   For to be baptiste more or myne
      als synfull man?

lf. 85.
L viij.   14. Jesus. John, kynde of man is freele   8
   To þe whilke þat I haue me knytte,

'Man's nature is
weak,   But I shall shewe þe skyllis twa,
   Þat þou schallt knawe by kyndly witte

---

[1] Johannes is inserted by the late hand.
[2] A late side-note says here 'hic caret,' and it is evident that sever
lines are wanting: ll. 71 to 76 seem to be relics of two stanzas. There
no blank in MS., and ll. 72, 73 are in one.

By-cause why I haue ordand swa;   88
    and ane is þis,
Mankynde may noȝt vn-baptymde go   *he may not go*
    to [1] endless blys.   *unbaptized.*

15. And sithen my selffe haue taken mankynde   92
For men schall me þer myrroure make,
I haue my doyng in ther mynde,
And also I do þe baptyme take.   *I shall be a*
    I will for-thy   96   *mirror for men.*
My selfe be baptiste, for ther sake,
    full oppynly.

16. Anodir skill I schall þe tell,
My wille is þis, þat fro þis day   100
Þe vertue [2] of my baptyme dwelle
In baptyme-watir euere and ay,   *Baptismal water*
    Mankynde to taste,   *will ever after*
                                            have virtue.'
Thurgh my grace þerto to take alway   104
    þe haly gaste.

17. Joh. All myghtfull lorde, grete is þi grace,
I thanke þe of þi grete fordede.
Jesus. Cum, baptise me, John, in þis place.   108
Joh. Lorde! saue thy grace þat I for-bede   *John will not*
    Þat itt soo be;   *baptize Jesus;*
For lorde, me thynketh it wer more nede
    Þou baptised me.   112

18. Þat place þat I yarne moste of all,
Fro thens come þou, lorde, as I gesse,
How schulde I þan, þat is a thrall,   *'How should*
                                            a slave baptize
Giffe þe baptyme, þat rightwis is,   116 *the righteous?*
    And has ben euere?
For þou arte roote of rightwissenesse,
    Þat forfette neuere.

---

[1] MS. has *te*.
[2] *Vertue* is a later correction for the original *wittnesse*.

What rich man
begs from the
poor?'

19. What riche man gose from dore to dore   120
    To begge at hym þat has right noght?
    Lorde, þou arte riche and I am full poure,
    Þou may blisse all, sen þou all wrought.
        Fro heuen come all   124
    Þat helpes in erthe[1], yf soth be sought,
        fro erthe but small.

lf. 85 b.

20. Jesus. Thou sais full wele, John, certaynly,
    But suffre nowe for heuenly mede,   128
    Þat rightwisnesse be noȝt oonlye
    Fullfillid in worde, but also in dede,
        thrughe baptyme clere.
    Cum, baptise me in my manhed   132
        Appertly here.

As a true phy-
sician Christ
must himself
first take, then
he can preach.

21. Fyrst schall I take, sen schall I preche,
    For so be-hovis mankynde fulfille
    All right-wissenesse, als werray leche.   136
    Joh. Lord, I am redy at þi will,
        And will be ay.
    Thy subgett lord, both lowde and still,
        in þat I may.   140

John trembles to
touch Jesus.

22. A! lorde, I trymble þer I stande,
    So am I arow to do þat dede,
    But saue me lord, þat all ordand,
    For the to touche haue I grete drede,   144
        for doyngs dark.   145
    Now helpe me lorde, thurgh þi godhede,
        to do þis werke.

He baptizes
Jesus in the
name of the
Trinity,

23. Jesu, my lord of myghtis most,   148
    I baptise þe here in þe name
    Of the fadir and of the sone and holy gost!

----

[1] MS. has *erthes*.

But in þis dede, lorde, right no blame

 Þis day by me.

And bryngis all thase to thy home

 þat trowes in þe.

Tunc cantabant duo angeli Veni creator spiritus.

24. Jesus. John, for mannys prophyte, wit þou wele,

Take I þis baptyme, certaynely,

The dragons poure ilk a dele

Thurgh my baptyme distroyed haue I ;

 Þis is certayne ;

And saued mankynde, saule and body,

 fro endles payne.

25. What man þat trowis and baptised be

Schall saued be and come to blisse,

Who-so trowes noȝt, to payne endles

He schalbe dampned sone, trowe wele þis.

 But wende we nowe

Wher most is nede þe folke to wisse,

 both I & ȝou.

26. Joh. I loue þe lorde, as souereyne leche,

That come to salue men of þarę sore,

As þou comaundis I schall gar preche,

And lere to euery man þat lare,

 That are was thrall.

[*To the audience.*] Now sirs, þat barne þat marie bare,

 be with ȝou all [1].

---

[1] Notes in 16th century hand. ' Hic caret finem. This matter is newly mayd & devysed, wherof we haue no coppy regystred.'

Right margin notes:

and saves himself from blame.   152

This baptism is for man's profit, to destroy the dragon's power.   156

  160

If. 86. M j. He who is baptized shall be saved, he who is not shall be damned.   164

  168

  172

  175

XXII. THE SMYTHIS[1].

The Temptation of Jesus.

[PERSONS OF THE PLAY.

DIABOLUS.   PRIMUS ANGELUS.
JESUS.   SECUNDUS ANGELUS.]

[SCENE, *the Wilderness.*]

Matth. iv. 1–11.
Luke iv. 1–13.
The devil is in
a great fuss and
haste.

1. Diab. MAKE rome be-lyve, and late me gang,
Who makis here all þis þrang ?
High you hense ! high myght ȝou hang
    right with a roppe.   **4**
I drede me þat I dwelle to lang
    to do a jape.

Since he fell

2. For sithen the firste tyme þat I fell
For my pride fro heuen to hell,
Euere haue I mustered me emell
    emonge manne-kynde,   **8**
How I in dole myght gar tham dwell
    þer to be pynde.   **12**

he has plotted
against mankind,
and they have
come to him.

3. And certis, all þat hath ben sithen borne,
Has comen to me, mydday and morne,
And I haue ordayned so þam forne,
    none may þame fende ;   **16**
Þat fro all likyng ar they lorne
    withowten ende.

---

[1] The 16th century hand inserts *Lokk* before *Smythis.*

4. And nowe sum men spekis of a swayne,
   Howe he schall come and suffre payne,   20
   And with his dede to blisse agayne
               þ[e]i schulde be bought;
   But certis þis tale is but a trayne,
               I trowe it noȝt.   24

But now it is said they shall be redeemed.

5. For I wotte ilke a dele by-dene,
   Of þe mytyng þat men of mene,
   How he has in grete barett bene
               sithen he was borne;   28
   And suffered mekill traye a d tene,
               boþe even & morne.

This mighty one has been in strife since his birth.

6. And nowe it is brought so aboute,
   Þat lurdayne þat þei loue and lowte,   32
   To wildernesse he is wente owte,
               with-owtyne moo;
   To dere hym nowe haue I no doute,
               be-twyxte vs two.   36

He is now in the wilderness,

'no fear, but I can injure him,

7. Be-fore þis tyme he has bene tent,
   þat I myght gete hym with no glent,
   But now sen he allone is wente
               I schall assay,   40
   And garre hym to sum synne assente,
               If þat I may.

as he is alone.

8. He has fastid, þat marris his mode,
   Ther fourty dayes with-owten foode,   44
   If he be man in bone and bloode,
               hym hungris ill;
   In glotonye þan halde I gude
               to witt his will.   48

If. 87 b.

I will try him through gluttony.'

9. For so it schall be knowen and kidde
   If godhed be in hym hidde,
   If he will do as I hym bidde
               Whanne I come nare.   52

Þer was neuere dede þat euere he dide,
                                    þat greued hym warre.

[Approaches Jesus.]

10. Þou witty man and wise of rede,
    If þou can ought of godhede,   56
    Byd nowe þat þer stones be brede,
                                    Betwyxte vs two ;
    Þan may þei stande thy-selfe in stede,
                                    and othir moo.   60

11. For þou hast fastid longe, I wene,
    I wolde now som mete wer sene
    For olde acqueyntaunce vs by-twene,
                                    Thy-selue wote howe.   64
    Ther sall noman witte what I mene
                                    but I and þou.

12. **Jesus.**   My Fadir, þat all cytte may slake,
    Honnoure euere more to þe I make,   68
    And gladly suffir I for thy sake
                                    swilk velany ;
    And þus temptacions for to take
                                    of myn enemy.   72

13. Þou weried wight ! þi wittes are wode !
    For wrytyn it is, whoso vndirstande,
    A man lyvis noght in mayne and mode
                                    with brede allone.   76
    But goddis wordis are gostly fode
                                    to men ilkone.

14. Iff I haue fastid oute of skill,
    Wytte þou me hungris not so ill   80
    Þat I ne will wirke my fadirs will
                                    in all degre,
    Þi biddyng will I noȝt full-fill,
                                    þat warne I þe.   84

'If thou art of God, make these stones bread.

I will tell no one.'

'Thou cursed thing, man lives not by bread alone.

I shall do my Father's will.'

15. Diab. [*aside.*]   A! slyke carping neuere I kende,

Hym hungres noȝt as I wende ;

Nowe sen thy fadir may þe fende

             be sotill sleghte,   88

Late se yf þou allone may lende

             þer vppon heghte,

16 Vppon þe pynakill parfitely [1].

A! ha! nowe go we wele ther-by!   92

I schall assaye in vayne-glorie

             to garre hym falle.

And if he be goddis sone myghty,

             witte I schall.   96

17. [*To Jesus.*]   Nowe liste to me a litill space,

If þou be goddis sone, full of grace,

Shew som poynte here in þis place

             to proue þi myght.   100

Late se, falle doune vppon þi face,

             here in my sight.

18. For it is wretyn, as wele is kende,

How God schall aungellis to þe sende,   104

And they schall kepe þe in þer hande

             wher-so þou gose,

Þat þou schall on no stones descende

             to hurte þi tose.   108

19. And sen þou may with-outen wathe

Fall, and do thy selffe no skathe,

Tumbill downe to ease vs bathe

             here to my fete ;   112

And but þou do I will be wrothe,

             þat I þe hette.

20. Jesus.   Late be, warlow, thy wordis kene,

For wryten it is, with-outen wene,   116

Marginal glosses:

lf. 88.
M iij.
'Hunger does not touch him,

I shall try vain-glory.'

'Show me thy power here ;

fall, and do not hurt thyself.

---

[1] Marginal note here, ' tunc cantant angeli, veni creator,' in later hand.

'Tempt me not !

Thy god þou schall not tempte with tene,
              nor with discorde;
Ne quarell schall þou none mayntene
              agaynste þi lorde.   120

21. And þerfore trowe þou, with-outen trayne,

Be subject to thy lord.'

þat all þi gaudes schall no thyng gayne,
Be subgette to þi souereyne
              arely and late.   124
Diab. [*aside.*]   What! þis trauayle is in vayne,
              be ought I watte!

22. He proues þat he is mekill of price,
þerfore it is goode I me avise,   128
And sen I may noȝt on þis wise
              make hym my thrall,

The devil will try covetousness.

I will assaye in couetise
              to garre hym fall.   132

lf. 88 b.

23. For certis I schall noȝt leue hym ȝitt,
Who is my souereyne, þis wolde I witte.
[*To Jesus.*]   My selffe ordande þe þore to sitte,
              þis wote þou wele,   136
And right euen as I ordande itt,
              is done ilke dele.

' I am thy sovereign,

24. þan may þou se sen itt is soo
þat I am souerayne of vs two,   140
And ȝitt I graunte þe or I goo,
              withouten fayle,
þat, if þou woll assent me too,
              it schall avayle.   144

and wield this world ;

25. For I haue all þis worlde to welde,
Toure and toune, forest and felde,
If þou thyn herte will to me helde
              with wordis hende,   148
ȝitt will I baynly be thy belde,
              and faithfull frende.

26. Be-halde now, ser, and þou schalt see,
Sere kyngdomes and sere contre; 152 kingdoms are yours
Alle þis wile I giffe to þe
for euer more,
And þou falle and honour me, if thou honourest me.'
as I saide are. 156

27. Jesus. Sees of thy sawes, þou Sathanas, 'Satan, cease!
I graunte no-thyng þat þou me askis,
To pyne of helle I bide þe passe return to hell,
and wightely wende; 160
And wonne in woo, as þou are was,
with-outen ende.

28. Non othyr myght schalbe thy mede,
For wretyn it is, who right can rede, 164
Thy lord God þe aught to drede
and honoure ay;
And serue hym in worde and dede,
both nyȝt and d y. 168

29. And sen þou dose not as I þe tell,
No lenger liste me late þe dwell,
I comaunde þe þou hy to hell
and holde þe þare; 172 and stay there.
With felawschip of frendis fell
for euer mare.

30. Diab. Owte! I dar noȝt loke, allas! If. 89. M iiij.
Itt is warre þan euere it was, 176 Satan laments while returning to hell.
He musteres what myght he has,
hye mote he hang!
Folowes fast, for me bus pas
[*Angels appear.*] to paynes strang. [*Exit.* 180

31. Ang. A! mercy lorde, what may þis mene, The angel wonders at the mildness of Jesus.
Me merueyles þat ȝe thole þis tene
Of this foule fende cant and kene,
carpand ȝou till! 184

And ȝe his wickidnesse, I wene,
                    may waste at will.

32. Me thynke þat ȝe ware straytely stedde,
    Lorde, with þis fende þat nowe is fledde.   188
    Jesus.   Myn aungell dere, be noȝt adred,
                        he may not greue ;
    The haly goste me has ledde,
                        þus schal þow leue.   192

33. For whan þe fende schall folke see,
    And salus þam in sere degre,

    Þare myrroure may þei make of me,
                        for to stande still ;   196

    For ouere-come schall þei noȝt be,
                        bot yf þay will.

34. **ii Ang.**   A ! lorde, þis is a grete mekenesse,
    In yow in whome al mercy is,   200
    And at youre wille may deme or dresse
                        als is worthy ;
    And thre temptacions takes expres,
                        þus suffirrantly.   204

35. **Jesus.**   My blissing haue þei with my hande,
    Þat with swilke greffe is noȝt grucchand,
    And also þat will stiffely stande
                        agaynste þe fende.   208
    I knawe my tyme is faste command,
                        now will I wende.

XXIII. THE CORIOURS.

The Transfiguration.

[PERSONS OF THE PLAY.

DEUS PATER.   JOHANNES.
JESUS.   MOYSES.
PETRUS.   HELYAS.]
JACOBUS.

[SCENE, *first on the way to the mountain, then the mountain itself.*]

1. **Jesus.** PETIR, myne awne discipill dere,

    And James and John, my cosyns two,

    Takis hartely hede, for ʒe schall here

    þat I wille telle vnto nomoo.   4

    And als ʒe schall see sightis seere,

    Whilke none schall see bot ʒe alsoo,

    Therfore comes forth, with me in fere,

    For to ʒone mountayne will I goo.   8

    Ther schall ʒe see a sight

        Whilk ʒe haue ʒerned lange.

  Petrus. My lorde, we are full light

    And glad with þe to gange[1].   12

2. **Jesus**[2]. Longe haue ʒe coveyte for to kenne

    My fadir, for I sette hym be-fore,

    And wele ʒe wote whilke tyme and when

    In Galyle gangand we were.   16

Mark ix. 2-9.
Matth. xvii. 1-9.
Jesus with Peter,
James, and John,

go to a mountain.

---

[1] Lines 9–12 are written as two in the MS.

[2] The words *cum Moysez et Elias* are written after *Iħc* in the margin of the MS., by the 16th cent. hand.

In Galilee they
had wished to see
the Father.
John xiv. 8.

'Shewe vs thy ffadir,' þus saide ȝe then,
'Þat suffice vs with-outen more ; '
I saide to ȝou and to all men,
'Who seis me, seis my fadyr þore.'   20
Such wordis to ȝou I spakke,
   In trewthe to make ȝou bolde,
ȝe cowde noght vndyr-take
   The tales þat I ȝou tolde.   24

3. Anodir tyme, for to encresse
   ȝoure trouthe, and worldly you to wys,

Reports as to
Jesus.
Luke ix. 18–22.

I saide, *quem dicunt homines*
     esse filium hominis ?   28
I askid ȝow wham þe pepill chase
To be mannys sone, with-outen mys ?
ȝe aunswered and saide, ' sum [1] moyses,'

If. 93 b.

And sum saide þan, ' Hely it is.'   32
And sum saide, ' John Baptist ; '
   Þan more I enquered you ȝitt,
I askid ȝiff ȝe ought wiste
   Who I was, by youre witte.   36

Peter said he was
Christ.

4. You aunswered, Petir, for thy prowe,
And saide þat I was Crist, God sonne ;
Bot of thy selffe þat had noght þowe,
My Fadir hadde þat grace be-gonne.   40

' Bide now till
ye have seen
my Father.'

Þerfore bese bolde and biddis now [2]
To tyme ȝe haue my Fadir sonne.

Jacobus.   Lord, to thy byddyng will we bowe
Full buxumly, as we are bonne.   44

Johannes.   Lorde, we will wirke thy will
   All way with trewe entent,
We love God lowde and stille,
   þat vs þis layne has lente.   48

[1] MS. has *sam.*
[2] The words 'and biddis now' stand at beginning of l. 41 in MS.

5. Petrus. Full glad and blithe awe vs to be,

And thanke oure maistir, mekill of mayne,

Þat sais, we schall þe sightis see,

The whiche non othir schall see certayne. 52

Jacob. He talde vs of his Fadir free,

Of þat fare wolde we be full fayne.

Joh. All þat he hyghte vs holde will hee,

Therfore we will no forther frayne, 56

But as he ffouchesaffe

So sall we vndirstande.

[*Enter Moses and Elias ; Jesus, between them, is transfigured, a bright light shining.*]

Beholde ! her we haue nowe in hast

Som new tythandys ! 60

6. Helyas. Lord God ! I loue þe lastandly,

And highly, botht with harte and hande,

Þat me, thy poure prophett Hely,

Haue steuened me in þis stede to stande. 64

In Paradise wonnand am I,

Ay sen I lefte þis erthely lande ;

I come Cristis name to clarifie,

And god his Fadir me has ordand, 68

And for to bere witnesse

In worde to man and wyffe,

Þat þis his owne sone is

And lord of lastand liff. 72

7. Moyses. Lord god ! þat all welthis wele,

With wille and witte we wirschippe þe,

Þat vn-to me, Moyses, wolde tell

Þis grete poynte of thy pryuyte, 76

And hendly hente me oute of hell,

Þis solempne syght for I schuld see,

Whan thy dere darlynges þat þore dwell

Hase noght thy grace in swilk degree. 80

[marginal notes:]

The disciples anticipate high sights,

but ask no further.

If. 94.
N ij.

Elias thanks God for summoning him from Paradise.

Moses has been fetched out of hell

to see the sight
now shown.

Oure fforme-ffadyrs full fayne
　　Wolde se this solempne sight,
Þat[1] in þis place þus pleyne
　　Is mustered thurgh þie myght.　　84

The light is
dazzling.

8. Petrus.　Brethir, what euere ȝone brightnes be?
Swilk burdis be-forne was neuere sene,
It marres my myght, I may not see,
So selcouth thyng was neuere sene.　　88

Jacob.　What it will worthe, þat wote noȝt wee,
How wayke I waxe, ȝe will not wene,
Are was þer one, now is ther thre,

The disciples are
awe-struck
lf. 94 b.
at the splendour
of Christ.

We thynke oure maistir is be-twene.　　92

Joh.　That oure maistir is thare
　　Þat may we trewly trowe,
He was full fayre be-ffore,
　　But neuere als he is nowe.　　96

9. Petrus.　His clothyng is white as snowe,
His face schynes as þe sonne,
To speke with hym I haue grete awe,
Swilk ffaire be-fore was neuere fune.　　100

The disciples in-
quire of Elias
and Moses.

Jacob.　Þe tothir two fayne wolde I knawe,
And witte what werke þam hedir has wonne.
Joh.　I rede we aske þam all on rowe,
And grope þam how þis game is begonne.　　104
Petrus.　[*To Elias and Moses.*]　My bredir, if þat ȝe be come
　　To make clere Cristis name,
Telles here till vs thre,
　　For we seke to þe same.　　108

10. Elias.　Itt is Goddis will þat we ȝou wys
Of his werkis, as is worthy.

' My place in
Paradise is near
Enoch.

I haue my place in Paradise,
Ennok my brodyr me by.　　112
Als messenger withouten mys
Am I called to this company,

　　　　　　　　[1] MS. has *þan.*

To witnesse þat goddis sone is þis,

Euyn with hym mette and all myghty.   116

To dede we wer noght dight,

  But quyk schall we come,

With Antecrist for to fyght,

  Beffore þe day of dome.   120

I am come to bear witness to God's son. We did not die, but shall fight Antechrist before Dooms-day.'

11. Moyses. Frendis, if þat ȝe ffrayne my name,

Moyses þan may ȝe rede by rawe,

Two thousand ȝere aftir Adam

Þan gaffe God vn-to me his lawe.   124

And sythen in helle has bene oure hame,

Allas ! Adam's kynne þis schall ȝe knawe,

Vn-to crist come, þis is þe same,

Þat vs schall fro þat dongeoun drawe.   128

He schall brynge þam to blys,

  Þat nowe in bale are bonne,

This myrthe we may not mys,

  For this same is Goddis sonne.   132

lf. 95. N iij.

' I am come from hell ;

this is he who shall draw thence all Adam's kin.'

12. Jesus. My dere discipill, drede ȝou noȝt,

I am ȝoure souerayne certenly,

This wondir werke þat here is wrought

Is of my Fadir al-myghty.   136

Þire both are hydir brought,

Þe tone Moyses, þe todir Ely,

And for youre sake þus are þei sought

To saie ȝou, his sone am I.   140

So schall bothe heuen & helle

  Be demers of þis dede,

And ȝe in erth schall tell

  My name wher itt is nede.   144

' Fear not, my dear friends,

this wonder is wrought for your sake.'

13. Petrus. A ! loued be þou euere, my lord Jesus,

Þat all þis solempne sight has sent,

Þat ffouchest saffe to schew þe þus,

So þat þi myghtis may be kende.   148

The disciples worship Jesus,

Here is full faire dwellyng for vs,

lf. 95 b.

A lykand place in for to lende,

and desire to erect three tabernacles.

A! lord, late vs no forther trus,

For we will make with herte and hende   152

A taburnakill vn-to þe

    Be-lyue, and þou will bide,

One schall to Moyses be,

    And to Ely the thirde.   156

14. Jacob.   ʒa! wittirly, þat were wele done,

But vs awe noght swilk case to craue;

Þam thare but saie and haue it sone,

Such seruice and he fouchesaffe.   160

' He promises his men a lodging in heaven,

He hetis his men both morne and none

Þare herber high in heuen to haue,

Therfore is beste we bide hys bone;

Who othir reedis, rudely þei raue.   164

we will stay where he wills.'

Joh.   Such sonde as he will sende

    May mende all oure mischeue,

And where hym lykis to lende,

    We will lende, with his leue.   168

The Father descends, he rebukes their fears, and bears witness to his son; [the three are stunned; they hear a noise, but do not understand. Cf. ll. 184, 205, 217.]

Hic descendunt nubes, Pater in nube [1].

15. Pater.   ʒe ffebill of faithe! folke affraied,

Beis noʒt aferde for vs in feere,

I am ʒoure God þat gudly grayth

Both erthe and eyre wt clowdes clere.   172

Þis is my sone, as ʒe haue saide,

As he has schewed by sygnes sere;

Of all his werkis I am wele paied,

Therfore till hym takis hede and here.   176

Where he is, þare am I,

    He is myne and I am his,

Who trowis þis stedfastly

    Shall byde in endles blisse.   180

[1] Original stage direction.

16. Jesus. Petir, pees be vnto þe !

And to ȝou also, James and John !

Rise vppe and tellis me what ȝe see,

And beis no more so wille of wone. [*The marvel vanishes.*

Petrus. A ! lorde, what may [1] þis mervayle be.

Whedir is þis glorious gleme al gone ?

We saugh here pleynly persones thre,

And nowe is oure lorde lefte allone.

Þis meruayle movis my mynde,

And makis my flessh affrayed.

185

188

they are full of
amazement and
fear. ' We saw
three persons.'

Jacob. Þis brightnes made me blynde,

I bode neuere swilke a brayde.

192

17. Joh. Lorde god ! oure maker almyghty !

Þis mater euermore be ment,

We saw two bodis stande hym by,

And saide his fadir had þame sent.

196

' We saw two
stand near him,

Petrus. There come a clowde of þe skye,

Lyght als þe lemys on þame lent,

And now fares all as fantasye,

For wote noȝt [we] how þai are wente.

200

and a bright
cloud, now all go
like fancy.'

Jacob. Þat clowde cloumsed vs clene,

Þat come schynand so clere,

Such syght was never sene,

To seke all sydis seere.

204

18. Joh. Nay, nay, þat noys noyed vs more,

Þat here was herde so hydously.

Jesus. Frendis, be noght afferde afore,

I schall ȝou saye encheson why.

My ffadir wiste how þat ȝe were

In ȝoure faith fayland, and for-thy

He come to witnesse ay where,

And saide þat his sone am I.

208

212

' Nay, that
hideous noise
hurt us.'

If. 96 b.

Jesus comforts
them, the Father
knew they were
weak.

[1] MS. has *in.*

Ard also in þis stede
   To witnesse þe same,
A quyk man and a dede
   Come to make clere my name.   216

19. Petrus.   A! lord, why latest þou vs noȝt see
Thy ffadirs face in his fayrenes?
Jesus.   Petir, þou askis over grete degree,
That grace may noȝt be graunted þe, I gesse.   220
In his godhed so high is he

'No man can
live and see the
Father.'

As all ȝoure prophetis names expresse,
Þat langar of lyffe schall he noght be
Þat seys his godhede as it is.   224
Here haue ȝe sene in sight
   Poyntes of his priuite,
Als mekill als erthely wighte
   May suffre in erthe to see.   228

20. And therfore wende we nowe agayne

'Our friends will
ask how we have
fared.'

To oure meyne, and mende þer chere.
Jacob.   Oure felaws ful faste wil us frayne,
How we haue faren, al in feere.   232
Jesus.   Þis visioun lely loke ȝe layne,
Vn-to no leffand lede itt lere,

'Tell no one till
the Son of man
has suffered.'

Tille tyme mannys sone haue suffered payne,
And resen fro dede, kens it þan clere.   236
For all þat trowis þat thyng
   Of my ffadir and me,

If. 97.
N v.

Thay schall haue his blessing,
   And myne; so motte it be.   240

XXIV. THE CAPPEMAKERS, Etc.[1]

The Woman taken in Adultery. The raising of Lazarus.

[PERSONS OF THE PLAY.

JESUS.	MARIA.
MULIER.	MARTHA.
I[us], 2[us] JUDEUS.	LAZARUS.
3[us], 4[us] JUDEUS (*Lawyers.*)	I[us], 2[us] APOSTOLUS.
NUNTIUS.]	

[SCENE I, *in the temple at Jerusalem.*]

1. i Judeus. LEPPE fourth, late vs no lenger stande,
    But smertely þat oure gere wer grayde,
Þis felowe þat we with folye fande,
Late haste vs fast þat she wer flayed.   **4**

John viii. 3–11;
xi. 1–44.

ii Jud. We will bere witnesse and warande
How we hir raysed all vnarayed,
Agaynste þe lawes here of oure lande
Wher sche was with hir leman laide.   **8**

The Jews make a fierce accusation against the woman.

i Jud. ȝaa, and he a wedded manne,
Þat was a wikkid synne.
ii Jud. Þat bargayne schall sche banne,
With bale nowe or we blynne.   **12**

2. i Jud. A! ffalse stodmere and stynkand stroye,
How durste þou stele so stille away!

---

[1] 'And hatmakers' added in 16th cent. hand. This company is also written variously 'capmakers' and 'capperes' along the page-headings.

To do so vilaunce avowtry,
Þat is so grete agaynste oure lay.   16

ii Jud.   Hir bawdery schall she dere abye,
For as we sawe, so schall we saye,
And also hir wirkyng is worthy
Sho schall be demed to ded þis day.   20

i Jud.   The maistirs of þe lawe,
Are here even at oure hande.

ii Jud.   Go we reherse by rawe
Hir fawtes as we þam fande.   [*Enter Lawyers.*]   24

'God save you, masters.'

3. i Jud.   God saue ȝou, maistirs, mekill of mayne,
Þat grete clergy and counsaille can.

If. 99 b.

'What are you doing with that fair woman?'

iii Jud.   Welcome ffrendis, but I wolde frayne
How fare ȝe with þat faire woman?   28

ii Jud.   A! sirs, we schall ȝou saie certay[n]e
Of mekill sorowe sen sche began.

'We have taken her in adultery.'

We haue hir tane with putry playne,
Hir selff may noȝt gayne-saie it þan.   32

iv Jud.   What hath sche done? folye
In fornicacioun and synne?

i Jud.   Nay; Nay; in avowtery
Full bolde, and will noȝt blynne.   36

4. iii Jud.   A-vowtery! nemyn it noght, for schame!
It is so foule, opynly I it fye.

'Is it true, lady?'

Is it sothe þat þei saie þe, dame?

ii Jud.   What! sir, scho may it noȝt denye.   40

'We ought not to blame her if she were not guilty.'

We wer þan worthy for to blame
To greve hir, but sche wer gilty.

iv Jud.   Now certis, þis is a foule defame.
And mekill bale muste be þar-by.   44

iii Jud.   Ȝa! Sir, ȝe saie wele þore,
By lawe and rightwise rede,

'She must be stoned to death.'

Ther falles noght ellis þerfore,
But to be stoned to dede.   48

5. i Jud.   Sirs, sen ȝe telle þe lawe this tyde,
And knawes þe course in þis contre,
Demes hir on heght, no lenger hyde,
And aftir ȝoure wordis wirke schall we.   52
iv⁻ Jud.   Beis noght so bryme, bewsheris, abide,
A new mater nowe moues me¹.

.   .   .   .

6. iii Jud.   He shewes my mysdedis more and myne,   If. 100.
I leue ȝou here, late hym allone.   56   O iiij.

iv Jud.   Owe! here will new gaudes begynne;   "They, convicted
ȝa, grete all wele, saie þat I am gone.   by their own con-
                                                          science, went out
i Jud.   And sen ȝe are noght bolde,   one by one."
No lengar bide will I.   60

ii Jud.   Pees! late no tales be tolde,
But passe fourth preuylye.

7. Jesus.   Woman! wher are þo wighte men went
That kenely here accused þe?   64

Who hase þe dampned, toke þou entent?   'Hath no man
Mul.   Lord! no man has dampned me.   condemned
                                                  thee?'
Jesus.   And for me schall þou noȝt be schent;   'Neither do I,
Of all thy mys I make þe free,   68 sin no more.'
Loke þou nomore to synne assentte.

Mul.   A! lord, ay loued mott þou bee!
All erthely folke in feere
Loves hym and his high name,   72
Þat me on þis manere
Hath saued fro synne and schame.

8. i Apost.   A! lorde, we loue þe inwardly,   The apostles
And all þi lore, both lowde and still,   praise Jesus for
                                                    76 his mercy to the
That grauntes thy grace to þe gilty,   guilty.
And spares þam þat thy folke wolde spill.

¹ Here a leaf, O iij of the MS., is lost; it contained probably 58 lines, in
which evidently Jesus appeared, and his saying in John viii. 7 was embodied.

Jesus.   I schall ȝou saie encheson why,
I wote it is my ffadirs will,   80

And for to make þam ware þer-by,
To knawe þam-selffe haue done more ill.
And euermore of þis same
Ensample schall be sene,   84
Whoso schall othir blame,
Loke firste þam-self be clene.

9. ii Apos.   A! maistir, here may men se also,
How mekenes may full mekill amende,   88

To for-geue gladly where we goo
All folke þat hath vs oght offende.
Jesus.   He þat will noȝt for-giffe his foo,
And vse mekenesse with herte and hende,   92
The kyngdom may he noght come too
Þat ordande is with-outen ende.
And more sone schall we see,
Here or ȝe forther fare,   96
How þat my ffadir free
Will mustir myghtis more.

[Enter Messenger.]

10. Nunc.   Jesu, þat es prophett veray,
My ladys Martha & Marie,   10
If þou fouchesaffe, þai wolde þe pray
For to come vn-to Bethany.
He whom þou loues full wele alway
Es seke, and like, lord, for to dye.   1
Yf þou wolde come, amende hym þou may,
And comforte all þat cumpany.

Jesus.   I saie ȝou þat sekeness
Is noȝt onlye to dede,   1

¹ **Lazare mortus** is written in red at the top of this page.

But joie of goddis gudnesse
Schalbe schewed in þat stede [1].

11. And goddis sone schall be glorified
By þat sekenesse and signes feere,   112
Therfore brethir no lenger bide,
Two daies fully haue we ben here.
We will go soiourne here beside
In þe Jurie with frendis in feere.   116

  i Apos. A l lorde, þou wote wele ilke a tyde,
Þe Jewes þei layte þe ferre and nere,
To stone þe vn-to dede,
Or putte to pereles payne ;—   120
And þou to þat same stede
Covaites to gange agayne.

12. Jesus. Ʒe wote by cours wele for to kast,
Þe daie is now of xii oures lange,   124
And whilis light of þe day may last
It is gode þat we grathely gange.
For whan day-light is pleynly past,
Full sone þan may ʒe wende all wrang ;   128
Therfore takes hede and trauayle fast
Whills light of liffe is ʒou emang.
And to ʒou saie I more,
How þat Lazar oure frende   132
Slepes nowe, and I therfore
With ʒou to hym will wende.

13. ii Apos. We will be ruled aftir þi rede,
But and he slepe he schall be saue.   136
  Jesus. I saie to ʒou, Lazare is dede,
And for ʒou all grete joie I haue.
Ʒe wote I was noght in þat stede,
What tyme þat he was graued in graue.   140

[1] Lines 107–110 are written in two lines in MS.

Marginal notes:

If. 101.
O v.
'We have been here two days, we will go into Judea.'

The apostles fear for his life,

but he answers,

'We must work while there is the light of life.'

'Lazarus is dead,

His sisteres praye with bowsom beede,
And for comforte þei call and craue,
Therfore go we to-gedir
To make þere myrthis more.   144

i Apos.   Sen he will nedes wende þedir,
Go we and dye with hym þore.

his sisters pray and call for comfort.'

lf. 101 b.

' Let us also go that we may die with him.'

[SCENE II, *Bethany*.]

Mary mourns grievously for her brother.

14. **Maria** [*in the house*].   Allas! owtane goddis will allone,
þat I schulld sitte to see þis sight!   148
For I may morne and make my mone,
So wo in worlde was neuere wight.
þat I loued most is fro me gone,
My dere brothir þat Lazar hight,   152
And I durst saye I wolde be slone,
For nowe me fayles both mynde & myght.
My welthe is wente for euere,
No medycyne mende me may,   156
A! dede þou do thy deuer,
And haue me hense away.

Martha is also inconsolable,

15. **Martha** [*on the road*].   Allas! for ruthe, now may I raue,
And febilly fare by frith and felde,   160
Wolde god þat I wer grathed in graue!
þat dede hadde tane me vndir telde!
For hele in harte mon I neuere haue,
But if [he] helpe þat all may welde;   164
Of Crist I will som comforte craue,
For he may be my bote and belde.
To seke I schal noȝt cesse
Tille I my souereyne see.   168

until her Lord comes.

[*Jesus enters*.]

Hayle! pereles prince of pesse!
Jesu! my maistir so free.

16. Jesus. Martha, what menes þou to make such chere[1],

. . . .

This stone we schall full sone 172
Remove and sette on syde.
17. Jesus. Fadir! þat is in heuyn on highte!
I þanke þe euere ouere all thyng,
That hendely heres me day & nyght, 176
And takis hede vnto myn askyng:
Wherfore fouchesaffe of thy grete myght
So þat þis pepull, olde and ȝyng,
That standis and bidis to se þat sight, 180
May trulye trowe and haue knowyng,
This tyme here or I pas
How þat þou has me sent.
Lazar, veni foras,
Come fro thy monument.

18. Lazarus. A! pereles prince, full of pitee[2]! 186
Worshipped be þou in worlde alway,
That þus hast schewed þi myght in me,
Both dede and doluen, þis is þe fourþe day.
By certayne singnes here may men see 190
How þat þou art goddis sone verray.
All þo þat trulye trastis in þe
Schall neuere dye, þis dare I saye.
Therfore ȝe folke in fere, 194
Menske hym with mayne and myght,
His lawes luke þat ȝe lere,
Þan will he lede ȝou to his light.

19. Maria. Here may men fynde a faythfull frende 198
Þat þus has couered vs of oure care.
Martha. Jesu! my lord, and maistir hende
Of þis we thanke þe euermore.

Marginal notes:
If. 102.
O vii.
The stone is removed from the grave.
Jesus prays to God.

'Lazarus, come forth.'

'I have been buried four days.

This is God's Son: all who trust in thee shall never die.

---

[1] A leaf, O vj, is here lost from the MS.
[2] *Nota, quia non concordat; novo addicio facto,* marginal notes in two late inks. Perhaps the writers did not perceive that the two leaves were lost.

If. 102 b.

'I must now go
to Jerusalem;'

my blessing on
ye all.'

Jesus. Sisteres, I may no lenger lende, 202
To othir folke nowe bus me fare,
And to Jerusalem will I wende
For thyngis þat muste be fulfilled þere.
Therfore rede I you right, 206
My men, to wende with me ;
ȝe þat haue sene þis sight
My blissyng with ȝo be.

XXV. THE SKYNNERS.

The entry into Jerusalem upon the Ass.

[PERSONS OF THE PLAY.

JESUS.   JANITOR.
PETRUS.   OCTO BURGENSES.
PHILIPPUS.   CECUS (a blind man).
ZACHE (ZACHEUS the publican).   PAUPER, a poor man.
          CLAUDUS (a lame man).]

[SCENE II, *Bethphage, at the Mount of Olives.*]

Matth. xxi. 1-11, 14-16.
Luke xix. 28-44, *ib.* 1-9.

1. Jesus. TO me takis tent and giffis gud hede,
 My dere discipulis þat ben here,
I schalle ȝou telle þat shalbe in dede,   3
My tyme to passe hense, it drawith nere,
   And by þis skill,
Mannys sowle to saue fro sorowes sere
  þat loste was ill.   7

'My time draweth nigh,

2. From heuen to erth whan I dyssende
Rawnsom to make I made promys,
The prophicie nowe drawes to ende,   10
My fadirs wille forsoth it is,
  þat sente me hedyr.
Petir, Phelippe, I schall ȝou blisse,
  & go to-gedir   14

I promised to ransom men.'

3. Vn-to ȝone castell þat is ȝou agayne,
Gois with gud harte, and tarie noȝt,
My comaundement to do be ȝe bayne.   17
Also I ȝou charge loke it be wrought,
  þat schal ȝe fynde

'Go to yon castle, unbind the ass with her foal, and bring them.'

An asse, þis feste als ȝe had soght,
　　　ȝe hir vn-bynde　　　　　　　　　　　21

4. With hir foole, and to me hem bring,
　þat I on hir may sitte a space ;

　So þe prophicy clere menyng　　　　　　24
　May be fulfilled here in þis place,
　　　‘ Doghtyr Syon,
　Loo ! þi lorde comys rydand on an asse
　　　þe to opon.’　　　　　　　　　　28

5. Yf any man will ȝou gayne-saye,
　Say þat youre lorde has nede of þam,

　And schall restore þame þis same day,　31
　Vn-to what man will þam clayme.
　　　Do þus þis thyng,
　Go furthe ȝe both, and be ay bayne
　　　In my blissyng.　　　　　　　　35

6. Pet.　Jesu, maistir, evyn at þy wille,
　And at þi liste vs likis to doo,
　Yone beste whilke þou desires þe tille,　38
　Euen at þi will schall come þe too,
　　　Vn-to þin esse.
　Sertis, lord, we will þedyre all
　　　þe for to plese.　　　　　　　　42

7. Phil.　Lord þe to plese we are full bayne,
　Boþe nyght and day to do þi will.　　*[They go out.*

[SCENE II, *the castle, and Jerusalem near* [1].]

　Go we, broþere, with all oure mayne　　45
　My lordis desire for to fulfill ;
　　　For prophycye
　Vs bus it do to hym by skyll
　　　To do dewly.　　　　　　　　　49

---

[1] The part played by the Porter who grants the ass, declares the news to
the citizens, l. 102, and receives the ass again, still being in the city, ll.
483–489, is accounted for if we suppose that the ‘ castle ’ (‘ castellum ’ in
Vulgate, ‘ the village ’ Auth. Version, Matt. xxi. 2) and Jerusalem were
close together on the stage.

8. Pet. ȝa! brodir Phelipp, be-halde grathely,

For als he saide we shulde sone fynde,

Me-thinke ȝone bestis be-fore myn eye,   52

Þai are þe same we schulde vnbynde.

Þerfore frely

Go we to hym þat þame gan bynde,

And aske mekely.   56

9. Phil. The beestis are comen, wele I knawe,

Ther-fore vs nedis to aske lesse leue,

And oure maistir kepis þe lawe   59

We may þame take tyter, I preue,

For noght we lett.

For wele I watte oure tyme is breue,

Go we þam fett.   63

10. Jani. Saie, what are ȝe þat makis here maistrie,

To loose þes bestis with-oute leuerie?

Yow semes to bolde, sen noght þat ȝe   66

Hase here to do, þerfore rede I

such þingis to sesse,

Or ellis ȝe may falle in folye

and grette diseasse.   70

11. Pet. Sir, with þi leue hartely we praye

Þis beste þat we myght haue.

Jani. To what in-tente, firste shall ȝe saye?   73

And þan I graunte what ȝe will crave,

Be gode resoune.

Phil. Oure maistir, Sir, þat all may saue,

Aske by chesoune.   77

12. Jani. What man is þat ȝe maistir call?

Swilke priuelege dare to hym clayme.

Pet. Jesus of Jewes kyng, and ay be schall,   80

Of Nazareth prophete þe same,

Þis same is he,

Both god and man, with-outen blame,

Þis trist wele we.   84

'There are the beasts;

they are common [i.e. town] beasts.

We need not be hindered by asking leave.'

The porter asks why they make so bold,

why they want the beast,

and who is their master?

'Jesus of Nazareth, King of Jews.

13. Jani. Sirs, of þat prophette herde I haue,
But telle me firste playnly, wher is hee?

Phil. He comes at hande, so god me saue,   87
Þat lorde we lefte at Bephage,
He bidis vs þere.

Jani. Sir, take þis beste, with herte full free,
And forthe 3e fare.   91

14. And if 3ou thynke it be to done,
I schall declare playnly his comyng
To the chiffe of þe Jewes, þat þei may sone
Assemble same to his metyng.   95
What is your rede?

Pet. Þou sais full wele in thy menyng,
Do forthe þi dede.   98

15. And sone þis beste we schall þe bring,
And it restore as resoune will.

[They go away, taking the ass. The Porter goes to Jerusalem.]

Jani. This tydyngis schall haue no laynyng,
But to þe Citezens declare it till   102
of þis cyte,
I suppose fully þat þei wolle
come mete þat free.   105

16. And sen I will þei warned be,
Both 3onge & olde, in ilke a state,
For his comyng I will hym mete   10
To late þam witte, with-oute debate.
Lo! wher þei stande,
That citezens cheff, withoute debate,
Of all þis lande.   *[To the citizens.]* 11

17. He þat is rewler of all right,
And freely schoppe both sande and see [1],
He saue 3ou, lordyngis, gayly dight,   1
And kepe 3ou in 3oure semelyte
And all honoure.

---

[1] *See and sande* in the MS.

i Burg. Welcome, Porter! what novelte

Telle vs þis owre?   119

What news?

18. Jani. Sirs, novelte I can ȝou tell,

And triste þame fully as for trewe;

Her comes of kynde of Israell   122

Att hande þe prophete called Jesu,

Lo! þis same day,

Rydand on an asse; þis tydandis newe

consayue ȝe may.   126

'Jesus comes here to-day riding on an ass.'

19. ii Burg. And is þat prophette Iesu nere?

Off hym I haue herde grete ferlis tolde,

He dois grete wounderes in contrees seere,

He helys þe seke, both ȝonge and olde,   130

And þe blynde giffis þam þer sight.

Both dome and deffe, as hym selffe wolde,

He cures þam right.   133

*If. 105.
P ii.
The citizens have heard of his miracles;*

20. iii Burg. Ȝa v. thowsand men with loves fyue

He fedde, and ilkone hadde i-nowe;

Watir to wyne he turned ryue,   136

He garte corne growe with-outen plogh,

Wher are was none;

To dede men als he gaffe liffe,

Laȝar was one.   140

how he fed 5000 with 5 loaves,

made corn to grow,

raised the dead to life;

21. iv Burg. In oure tempill if he prechid

Agaynste þe pepull þat leued wrong,

And also new lawes if he teched   143

Agaynste oure lawis we vsed so lang,

And saide pleynlye,

The olde schall waste, þe new schall gang,

Þat we schall see.   147

preached in the temple,

and taught new laws.

22. v Burg. Ȝa, Moyses lawe he cowde ilke dele,

And all þe prophettis on a rowe,

He telles þam so þat ilke aman may fele,

' He knows the inner spirit of the laws.'

And what þei may interly knowe   151
Yf þei were dyme,
What þe prophettis saide in þer sawe,
All longis to hym.   154

'He is Emanuel,
fore-told by the
prophets.'
23. **vi Burg**.   Emanuell also by right
Þai calle þat prophette, by þis skill,
He is þe same þat are was hyght   157
Be Ysaye be-for vs till,
          Þus saide full cleŕe.

vii Burg.   Loo! a maydyn þat knew neuere ille
          A childe schuld bere.   161

24. Dauid spake of him I wene,
And lefte witnesse ȝe knowe ilkone,
He saide þe frute of his corse clene
Shulde royally regne vpon his trone,   165
          And þerfore he
Of Dauid kyn, and oþir none,
          Oure kyng schal be.   168

lf. 105 b.
25. **viii Burg**.   Sirs, me thynketh ȝe saie right wele,
And gud ensampelys furth ȝe bryng,
And sen we þus þis mater fele,   171
'Let us go to
meet him as our
king.
Go we hym meete as oure owne kyng,
          And kyng hym call.
What is youre counsaill in þis thyng?
          Now say ȝe all.   175

26. **i Burg**.   Agaynste resoune I will noȝt plete,
For wele I wote oure kyng he is,
Whoso agaynst his kyng liste threte,   178
He is noȝt wise, he dose amys.   [*To the Porter.*
          Porter, come nere,
Porter, what do
you know about
his coming?'
What knowlage hast þou of his comyng?
          Tels vs all here.   182

27. And þan we will go mete þat free,
And hym honnoure as we wele awe
Worthely tyll oure Citee,   185

And for oure souerayne lord hym knawe,
　　In whome we triste.
Jani. Sirs, I schall telle ʒou all on rowe,
　　And ʒe will lyste.　　　　　　　189

28. Of his discipillis ij þis day,
Where that I stode, þei faire me grette,
And on ther maistir halfe gan praye
Oure comon asse þat þei myght gete　　　193
　　bot for awhile,
Wher-on þer maistir softe myght sitte,
　　Space of a mile.　　　　　　　196

29. And all þis mater þai me tolde
Right haly as I saie to ʒou,
And þe asse þei haue right as þei wolde,
And sone will bringe agayne, I trowe,　　200
　　So þai be-heste.
What ʒe will doo avise ʒou nowe,
　　Þus thinke me beste.　　　　　203

30. **ii Burg.** Trewlye as for me I say,
I rede we make vs redy bowne,
Hym to mete gudly þis day,　　　　206
And hym ressayue with grete rennowne,
　　As worthy is ;
And þerfore, sirs, in felde and towne
　　ʒe fulfille þis.　　　　　　　210

31. **Jani.** ʒa! and ʒoure [childer] with ʒou take,
Þoff all in age þat þei be ʒonge,
ʒe may fare þe bettir for þer sake,
Thurgh þe blissing of so goode a kyng.　214
　　Þis is no dowte.

iii Burg. I kan þe thanke for thy saying,
　　We will hym lowte.　　　　　217

32. And hym to mete I am right bayne,
On þe beste maner þat I canne,
For I desire to se hym fayne,　　　　220

The Porter tells
how Peter and
Phillip came for
the town ass,

to ride a mile
(from Bethphage
to Jerusalem).

' We will make
ready to meet
him with renown.

'Take your chil-
dren with you,
blessing may
come to you
through them.'
lf. 106.
P. iii.

They are resolved
to meet and
honour Jesus.

And hym honnoure as his awne manne,
  Sen þe soth I see.
Kyng of Juuys we call hym þan,
  Oure kyng is he.   224

33. iv Burg. Oure kyng is he, þat is no lesse,
Oure awne lawe to it cordis well [1],
Þe prophettis all bare full witnesse, 227
Qwilke full of hym secrete gone felle [2];
  And þus wolde say,
'Emang youre selff schall come grete seele
  Thurgh god verray.' 231

34. v Burg. Þis same is he, þer is non othir,
Was vs be-heest full lange before,

The Law, For Moyses saide, als oure owne brothir,
A newe prophette god schulde restore. 235
  Þerfore loke ȝe
What ȝe will do, with-outen more;
  Oure kyng is he. 238

and the prophets, **35. vi Burg.** Of Juda come owre kyng so gent,
Of Jesse, Dauid, Salamon,
Also by his modir kynne take tente,
Þe Genolagye beres witnesse on; 242
  This is right playne.
Hym to honnoure right as I canne
  I am full bayne. 245

made them glad
and ready, **36. vii Burg.** Of youre clene witte and youre consayte
I am full gladde in harte and þought,
And hym to mete with-outen latt [3]
I am redy, and feyne will noght, 249
  Bot with ȝou same
To hym agayne vs blisse hath brought,
  With myrthe & game. 252

---

[1] Pronounce *weel*. The MS. has *will*.
[2] *fele*, i.e. many, seems to be the word intended.
[3] *consayte* was first written, then corrected to *latt*.

37. viii Burg. ȝoure argumentis þai are so clere

and give clear
arguments.
lf. 106 b.

    I can noȝt saie but graunte þou till,

    For whanne I of þat counsaille here,   255

    I coveyte hym with feruent wille

           Onys for to see,

    I trowe fro þens I schall

           Bettir man be.   259

38. i Burg. [1]   Go we þan with processioune

The procession
forms, with the
children in front.

    To mete þat comely as vs awe,

    With braunches, floures, and vnysoune,

    With myghtfull songes her on a rawe,   263

           Our childir schall

    Go synge before, þat men may knawe

           To þis graunte we all.   [*Exeunt.*]   266

[SCENE III, *Bethphage, and on the road to Jerusalem.*]

39. Pet.   Jhesu! lord and maistir free,

The disciples
bring Jesus the
ass.

    Als þou comaunde so haue we done,

    Þis asse here we haue brought to þe,   269

    What is þi wille þou schewe vs sone,

           And tarie noȝt.

    And þan schall we, with-outen hune,

           Fulfill þi þouȝt.   273

40. Jesus.   I þanke ȝou breþere, mylde of mode,

    Do on þis asse youre cloþis ȝe laye,

'*Lay clothes on*
the ass, and lift
me up.'

    And lifte me vppe with hertis gud,   276

    Þat I on hir may sitte þis daye,

           In my blissing.

           [*They lift Jesus on to the ass.*

Phil.   Lord þi will to do all-way

           We graunte þing.   280

---

[1] The rubricator made the speech of 1 *Burgess* to begin with line 261, but the commencement of the stanza and the sense both require it as above.

41. Jesus.   Now my breþere with gud chere,
Gyues gode entente, for ryde I will
Vn-to ȝone cyte ȝe se so nere,
ȝe shall me folowe, sam & still   284
          Als I are sayde.

Phil.   Lord! as þe lyfe we graunte þe till,
          And halde vs payde[1].   287

[*Jesus rides along towards Jerusalem.*

*Matth.*xx. 30–34.
Mark x. 46–52.
A blind man
asks ' what is
that noise? tell
me who comes?'

42. Cecus.   A lorde! þat all þis world has made,
Boþe sonne and mone, nyght & day,
What noyse is þis þat makis me gladde?
Fro whens it schulde come I can noȝt saye,   291
          Or what it mene.
Yf any man walke in þis way,
          Telle hym me be-dene.   294

A poor man
answers him.
lf. 107.
P iiij.

43. Paup.   Man! what ayles þe to crye?
Where wolde þou be? þou say me here.

' I have been
blind since birth;

Cecus.   A! sir, a blynde man am I,
And ay has bene of tendyr ȝere[2]   298
          Sen I was borne,

I heard nobl∋
cheer before me.

I harde a voyce with nobill chere
          Here me be-forne.   301

44. Paup.   Man, will þou oght þat I can do?

Cecus.   ȝa, sir, gladly wolde [I] witte,
Yf þou couþe oght declare me to,   304

What does it
mean?'

This myrþe I herde, what mene may it,
          Or vndirstande?

' Jesus full of
mercy comes,

Paup.   Jesu, þe prophite full of grace,
          Comys here at hande,   308

and the citizens
go to meet him
with melody.'

45. And all þe cetezens þay are bowne
Gose hym to mete with melodye,

---

[1] The late hand here has side note ' *tunc cantant.*'
[2] MS. has ' of tendyr ȝere bene.'

With þe fayrest processioune   311
That euere was sene in þis Jury.
      He is right nere.

Cecus. Sir, helpe me to þe strete hastely,   'Help me to the
      þat I may here   315   street, that I may
                                                                 hear, and crave
46. þat noyse, and also þat I myght thurgh grace   my sight!'
My syght of hym, to craue I wolde.

Paup. Loo! he is here at þis same place,   318   'Here he is, cry,
Crye faste on hym, loke þou be bolde,   loud!'
      With voyce righ[t] high.

Cecus. Jesu! þe son of dauid calde.   'Have mercy!
      þou haue mercy!   alas! he turns his
                                                                 ear away.'
47. Allas! I crye, he heris me noȝt,
He has no ruthe of my mysfare,
He turnes his herre, where is his þought?   325
Paup. Cry som-what lowdar, loke þou noȝt spare,   'Cry louder!'
      So may þou spye [1].

Cecus. Jesu, þe saluer of all sare,
      To me giffis gode hye.   329

48. **Phel.** Cesse man, and crye noȝt soo,   Philip tells him
The voyce of þe pepill gose þe by,   to be still.
þe ag[h]e sette still and tente giffe to,   332
Here passeȝ þe prophite of mercye.
      þou doys amys.

Cecus. A! dauid sone, to þe I crye,   He cries again.
      þe kyng of blisse.   336

49. **Pet.** Lorde! haue mercy and late hym goo,
He can noȝt cesse of his crying,   If. 107 b.
He folows vs both to and froo,   339   Philip begs
Graunte hym his boone and his askyng,   Jesus to grant
      And late hym wende.   him his peti-
We gette no reste or þat þis thyng   tion, or they
      Be broȝt to ende.   343   will get no
                                                                 rest.

---

[1] The stanza requires this line here, in the MS. it apparently runs on
after *þought*. The last half of l. 319 too stands at end of l. 318.

50. **Jesus.**   What wolde þou man I to þe dede
     In þis present, telle oppynly.

'Lord ! give me my sight.'
     Cecus.   Lorde my syght[1] is fro me hydde,   346
     Þou graunte me it, I crye mercy,
          Þis wolde I haue.

'Look up ! thy faith saves thee.'
     Jesu.   Loke vppe nowe with chere blythely,
          Þi faith shall þe saue.   350

'Praise to thee,
51. **Cecus.**   Wirschippe and honnoure ay to þe,
     With all þe seruice þat can be done,
     The kyng of blisse loued mote he be,   353
     Þat þus my sight hathe sente so sone,
          And by grete skill.
     I was are blynde as any stone ;

I now see.'
          I se at wille.   357

(?) *John* v. 6–14.
Those who can use their limbs may go with this rejoicing, the lame man cannot.
52. **Clau.**   A ! wele wer þam þat euere had liffe,
     Old or yonge whedir it were [2],
     Might welde þer lymmes withouten striffe,
     Go with þis mirthe þat I see here,   361
          And contynewe,
     For I am sette in sorowes sere
          Þat ay ar newe.   364

53. Þou lord, þat schope both nyght and day,
Lord, help me!'
     For thy mercy haue mynde on me,
     And helpe me lorde, as þou wele may [3] ;
          I may noȝt gang.   368
     For I am lame, as men may se,
          And has ben lang.   370

54. For wele I wote, as knowyn is ryffe,
     Boþe dome and deffe þou grauntist þam grace,
     And also þe dede þat þou hauyst geuen liff,
     Therfore graunte me lord, in þis place,   374
          My lymbis to welde.

---

[1] MS. has *syight*.   [2] Note here in late hand ' hic caret.'
[3] There is no blank in MS. here, but a line is evidently wanting.

Jesus.   My man, ryse and caste þe cruchys gode space

        Her in þe felde.   377

'Rise, cast your crutches far from you.'

55. And loke in trouthe þou stedfast be,

And folow me furth with gode menyng.

Claud.   Lorde! lo, my crouchis whare þei flee,

Als ferre as I may late þam flenge   381

        With bothe my hende ;

Þat euere we haue metyng

        Now I defende.   384

He flings them If. 108. P v. away ; 'may we never meet again !

56. For I was halte both lyme and lame,

And I suffered tene and sorowes i-nowe,

Ay lastand lord, loued be þi name,

I am als light as birde on bowe.   388

        Ay be þou blist,

Such grace hast þou schewed to me,

        Lorde, as þe list.   391

I was halt, I am now as light as bird on bough, bless the Lord!'

57. Zach.   Sen first þis worlde was made of noȝt,

And all thyng sette in equite,

Such ferly thyng was neuere non wroght,

As men þis tyme may see with eye.   395

        What it may mene?

I can noȝt say what it may be,

        Comforte or tene.   398

Luke xix. 2-9. Zaccheus does not understand it all ;

58. And cheffely of a prophete new,

Þat mekill is profite, and þat of latte,

Both day and nyght þai hym assewe,

Oure pepill same thurgh strete & gatte,   402

        [new lawes to lare,][1]

Oure olde lawes as nowe þei hatte,

        And his kepis ȝare.   405

a new prophet whom the people follow day and night through streets and ways,

59. Men fro deth to liffe he rayse,

The blynde and dome geve speche and sight,

who cures the blind and dumb

[1] A short line is missing here with probably this idea.

Gretely þerfore oure folke hym prayse,   408
And folowis hym both day and nyght;
    Fro towne to towne;
Thay calle hym prophite be right,
    As of renowne.   412

'I am chief of
the publicans,
yet I have not
heard of him
before.

60. And ȝit I meruayle of þat thyng,
Of puplicans sen prince am I
Of hym I cowthe haue no knowyng;   415
Yf all I wolde haue comen hym nere [1],
    Arly and late,
For I am lawe, and of myne hight

The road is full,

    Full is þe gate.   419

61. Bot sen no bettir may be-falle,
I thynke what beste is for to doo,

I am short,
I will climb
this tree.

I am schorte, ȝe knawe wele all,   422
Þerfore ȝone tre I will go too,
    And in it clyme;
Whedir he come or passe me fro,
    I schall se hym.   426

62. A nobill tree þou secomoure,

Blessed syca-
more tree !'
lf. 108 b.

I blisse hym þat þe on þe erþe brought.
Now may I see both here and þore,   429
That vndir me it may be noȝt.
        Þerfore in þe
Wille [2] I bidde in herte & þought
    Till I hym se   433

63. Vn-to þe prophete come to towne
Her will I bide what so befalle

Jesus calls
Zaccheus down,

Jesus [*looking up*].   Do Zache, do fast come downe.   436
Zach.   Lorde even at þi wille hastely I schall,
    And tarie noght.
To þe on knes lord here I schall,
    For sinne I wroght.   440

---

[1] *neȝe* = nigh seems to be the word intended.   [2] MS. has *Whiche*.

64. And welcome prophete, trast and trewe,
With all þe pepull þat to þe langis.

Jesus.   Zache, þi seruice new   443   and forgives him
Schall make þe clene of all þe wrong,   his sins.
          Þat þou haste done.

Zach.   Lorde, I lette noȝt for þis thrang
          Her to say sone,   447

65. Me schamys with sinne, but noȝt to mende,
I synne for-sake, þerfore I will
Haue my gud I have vnspendid   450
Poure folke to geue it till;
          Þis will I fayne.
Whom I begylyd to him I will[1]
          Make a-sith agayne.   454

66. Jesus.   Thy clere confessionn schall þe clense,
Þou may be sure of lastand lyffe,
Vn-to þi house, with-outen offense,   457
Is graunted pees withouten striffe.
          Fare-wele, Zache!

Zach.   Lord, þe lowte ay man and wiffe,
          Blist myght þou be.   461

67. Jesus.   My dere discipulis, beholde and see,   They arrive at
Vn-to Jerusalem we schall assende,   the city.
Man sone schall þer be-trayed be,   464
And gevyn in-to his enmys hande,
          With grete dispitte.
Ther spitting on hym þer schall þei spende
          And smertly smyte. [*Jesus dismounts.*] 468

68. Petir, take þis asse me fro,   [*Peter goes.* The ass is re-
And lede it where þou are it toke.   stored to its
I murne, I sigh, I wepe also,   place.
                                       Matt. xxiii. 37–
                                       xxiv. 2.

---

[1] MS. has *will I.*   Several of the lines in stanzas 64, 65, are written
ɔnfusedly in the MS., and are here corrected.

Jesus mourns
over Jerusalem

Jerusalem on þe to loke!   472

    And so may þou,

þat euere þou þi kyng for-suke,

    And was vn-trewe.   475

lf. 109.
P vi.
and its destruc-
tion.

69. For stone on stone schall none be lefte,

But doune to þe grounde all schalbe caste,

Thy game, þi gle, al fro þe refte,   478

And all for synne þat þou done hast.

    Þou arte vnkynde!

Agayne þi kyng þou hast trespast,

    Haue þis in mynde.   482

[Scene IV, *entrance to Jerusalem ; the Porter still
with the citizens.*]

The ass is
brought back
to the porter,
who runs to
wait for Jesus
in the road.

70. **Pet.**   Porter, take here þyn asse agayne,

At hande my lorde comys on his fette.

    Jani.   Behalde, where all þi Burgeis bayne

Comes with wirschippe hym to mete.   486

    Þerfore I will

Late hym abide here in þis strete,

    And lowte hym till.   48*

Chorus of eight
burgesses who
worship Jesus.

71. **i Burg.**   Hayll! prophette, preued withouten pere,

Hayll! prince of pees schall euere endure,

Hayll! kyng comely, curteyse and clere,

Hayll! souerayne semely to synfull sure,   49*

    To þe all bowes.

Hayll! lord louely, oure cares may cure,

    Ha[y]ll[1] kyng of Jewes.   4

72. **ii Burg.**   Hayll! florisshand floure þat neuere shall fad*

Hayll! vyolett vernand with swete odoure,

Hayll! marke of myrthe, oure medecyne made,

[1] This was written *all,* which the later hand corrected by putting
before it.

Hayll! blossome brigh[t], hayll! oure socoure. 500
   Hayll! kyng comely.
Hayll! menskfull man, with þe honnoure
   With herte frely. 503

73. iii Burg. Hayll! dauid sone, doughty in dede,
Hayll! rose ruddy, hayll birrall clere,
Hayll! welle of welthe may make vs mede.
Hayll! saluer of oure sores sere, 507
   We wirschippe þe.
Hayll! hendfull, with solas sere,
   Welcome þou be! 510

74. iv Burg. Hayll! blissfull babe, in Bedleme borne,
Hayll! boote of all oure bittir balis,
Hayll! sege þat schoppe boþe even and morne,
Hayll! talker trystefull of trew tales. 514
   Hayll! comely knyght,
Hayll! of mode þat most preuayles
   To saue þe tyght. 517

75. v Burgh. Hayll! dyamaunde with drewry dight,
Hayll! jasper gentill of Jewry,
Hayll! lylly lufsome lemyd with lyght,   If. 109 b.
Hayll! balme of boote, moyste and drye, 521
   To all has nede.
Hayll! barne most blist of mylde Marie,
   Hayll! all oure mede. 524

76. vi Burg. Hayll! conquerour, hayll, most of myght,
Hayll! rawnsoner of synfull all,
Hayll! pytefull, hayll! louely light, 527
Hayll! to vs welcome be schall.
   Hayll! kyng of Jues ;
Hayll! comely corse þat we þe call
   With mirþe þat newes. 531

77. vii Burg. Hayll! sonne ay schynand with bright bemes,
Hayll! lampe of liff schall neuere waste,

Hayll! lykand lanterne luffely lemes,   534
Hayll! texte of trewthe þe trew to taste.
    Hayll! kyng & sire,
Hayll! maydens chylde þat menskid hir most,
    We þe desire.   538

78. viii Burg. Hayll! domysman dredful, þat all schall deme,
Hayll! quyk and dede þat all schall lowte,
Hayll! whom worschippe moste will seme,   541
Hayll! whom all thyng schall drede and dowte.
    We welcome þe.
Hayll! and welcome of all abowte,
    To owre cete[1].   545

---

[1] *Tunc cantant* here added by late hand.

XXVI. THE CUTTELERES.

The conspiracy to take Jesus.

[PERSONS OF THE PLAY.

PILATUS.	JANITOR.
CAYPHAS.	PRIMUS, SECUNDUS DOCTOR.
ANNA.	PRIMUS, SECUNDUS MILES.]
JUDAS.	

[SCENE I, *Pilate's Hall.*]

1. **Pil.** VNdir þe ryallest roye of rente and renowne,
      Now am I regent of rewle þis region in reste,
Obeye vnto bidding bud busshoppis me bowne,
And bolde men þat in batayll makis brestis to breste.   4
To me be-taught is þe tent þis towre begon towne,
For traytoures tyte will I taynte, þe trewþe for to triste,
The dubbyng of my dingnite may noȝt be done downe,
Nowdir with duke nor dugeperes, my dedis are so dreste. 8
My desire muste dayly be done
With þame þat are grettest of game,
And þer agayne fynde I but fone,
Wherfore I schall bettir þer bone.   12
But he þat me greues for a grume,
Be-ware, for wystus I am.

2. { Pounce Pilatt of thre partis   15
  { Þan is my propir name [1];

Matth. xxvi. 3–9,
14–16.
Mark xiv. 1–5, 10,
11, 44.
Luke xxii. 2–6.
Pilate boastfully
proclaims his
dignity and his
power.

His name is of
three parts,

---

[1] As many of the lines in this and following plays are divided and
written as two in the MS., they are printed as they stand, coupled in
brackets.

{ I am a perelous prince,
{ To proue wher I peere

{ Emange þe philosofers firste
{ Ther fanged I my fame,

{ Wherfore I fell to affecte
{ I fynde noȝt my feere.   18

{ He schall full bittirly banne
{ Þat bide schall my blame;

{ If all my blee be as bright
{ As blossome on brere.

{ For sone his liffe shall he lose,
{ Or left be for lame,   21

{ Þar lowtes noȝt to me lowly,
{ Nor liste noȝt to leere.

And þus sen we stande in oure state,
Als lordis with all lykyng in lande,   24

Do and late vs wete if ȝe wate
Owthir, sirs, of bayle or debate,
Þat nedis for to be handeled full hate,
Sen all youre helpe hanges in my hande.   28

[Enter Caiaphas and Annas.]

3. **Caip.**   Sir, and for to certefie þe soth in youre sight,
As to ȝou for oure souerayne semely we seke.
   Pil.   Why, is þer any myscheue þat musteres his myȝt,
Or malice thurgh meene menn vs musters to meke?   3

{ **Anna.**   Ȝa, Sir, þer is a ranke swayne
{ Whos rule is noȝt right,

{ For thurgh[1] his romour in þis reme
{ Hath raysede mekill reke.

{ **Pil.**   I here wele ȝe hate hym,
{ Youre hartis are on heght,

{ And ellis if I helpe wolde
{ His harmes for to eke.

[1] *Thurgh* is repeated in the MS.

But why are ȝe barely þus brathe?
Bees rewly, and ray fourth your reasoune.

Caip. Tille vs, sir, his lore is full lothe.   39

Pil. Be-ware þat we wax noȝt to wrothe.

An. Why, sir, to skyste fro his skath
We seke for youre socoure þis sesoune.   42

4. { **Pil.** And if þat wrecche in oure warde
{ Haue wrought any wrong,
{ Sen we are warned we walde witte,
{ And wille or we wende;
{ But and his sawe be lawfull,
{ Legge noȝt to lange,
{ For we schall leue hym if us list
{ With luffe here to lende.   46

{ **i Doc.** And yf þat false faytor
{ Youre fortheraunce may fang,
{ Þan fele I wele þat oure folke
{ Mon fayle of a frende;
Sir þe streng[t]he of his steuen ay still is so strange,
That but he schortely be schent he schappe vs to schende.   50
For he kennes folke hym for to call
Grete god son, þus greues vs þat gome,
And sais þat he sittande be schall,
In high heuen, for þere is his hall.

Pil. And frendis if þat force to hym fall,
It semes noȝt ȝe schall hym consume.   56

5. { But þat hymselfe is þe same
{ ȝe saide schulde descende,
{ ȝoure seede and ȝou þen all for to socoure.
{   **Cayp.** A! softe sir, and sese,
{ For of criste when he comes
{ No kynne schall be kenned;
{ But of þis caytiffe kynreden
{ We knawe þe encrese.   60

be calm and reasonable;

we will hear if he has done wrong,

if not, we shall let him off.'

'If you hear the false scoundrel you are no friend to our folk.

If. III.
Q i.
His voice is strong to mis-lead the people; he says he is God's son.

Pilate argues that he is Christ,

but they say they know all about this man,

who says he
can release
from burdens.

He lykens hym to be lyke god

Ay lastand to lende,

To lifte vppe þe laby to lose or relesse.

Pil.   His maistreys schulde moue ȝou,

Youre mode for to amende.

An.   Nay, for swilke mys fro malice

We may noȝt vs meese,   64

For he sais he schall deme vs, þat dote,

And þat tille vs is dayne or dispite.

you desire to
harm him, but
the law is in
my hand.'

Pil.   To noye hym nowe is youre noote,   67

But ȝitt þe lawe lyes in my lotte.

i doc.   And yf ȝe will witt sir, ȝe wotte,

Þat he is wele worthy to wyte.   70

If. 111 b.
' He is blame-
worthy, for he
turned over the
money-changers'
tables.'

Matt. xxi. 12, 13.

6. For in oure temple has he taught

By tymes moo þan tenne,

Where tabillis full of tresoure lay

To telle and to trye,

Of oure cheffe mony-changers;

Butte, curstely to kenne,

He caste þam ouere, þat caytiffe,

And counted noȝt þer by.   74

' This ought to
be printed with
pen, make him
bend, kill him.'

Cay.   Loo ! sir, þis is a periurye

To prente vndir penne,

Wher-fore, make ȝe þat appostita,

We praye ȝou, to plye.

Pil.   Howe mene ȝe ?

Cay.   Sir, to mort hym for mouyng of menne.

Pil.   Þan schulde we make hym to morne

But thurgh ȝoure maistrie.   78

' Move that no
more.'

Latte be sirs, and move þat no more

But what in youre temple be-tyde.

They accuse
Jesus, Pilate
sheltering him.

i Mil.   We ! þare sir, he skelpte oute of score,

Þat stately stode selland þer store.

Pil.   Þan felte he þam fawte be-fore,

And made þe cause wele to be kydde.   84

7. { But what taught he þat tyme,
   { Swilk tales[1] as þou telles?

   { i **Mil.**   Sir, þat oure tempill is þe toure
   { Of his troned sire,
   { And þus to prayse in þat place
   { Oure prophettis compellis,
   { Tille hym þat has poste
   { Of Prince and of Empire.   88   If. 112.
                                                           Q ij.
   { And þei make *domus domini*
   { Þat derand þare dwellis,
   { Þe denn of þe derfenes
   { And ofte þat þei desire.

   { **Pil.**   Loo! is he noght a mad man   'Is not he mad
   { Þat for youre mede melles?   who meddles
                                                            with you,
   { Sen ȝe ymagyn a-mys
   { Þat makeles to myre.   92

   ȝoure rankoure is raykand full rawe.   your rancour
                                                            is raw.'

   Cay.   Nay, nay, sir, we rewle vs but right.

   Pil.   For sothe, ȝe ar ouer cruell to knawe.   95

   Cay.   Why, sir? for he wolde lose oure lawe
   Hartely we hym hate as we awe,
   And þerto schulde ȝe mayntayne oure myght.   98

8. { For why, vppon oure sabbott day   'He heals on the
   { Þe seke makes he saffe,   sabbath day,
   { And will noȝt sesse for oure sawes
   { To synke so in synne.
   { ii **Mil.**   Sir, he coueres all þat comes
   { Recoueraunce to craue,
   { But in a schorte contynuaunce
   { Þat kennes all oure kynne.   102
   { But he haldis noght oure haly dayes,
   { Harde happe myght hym haue!

---

[1] The MS. repeats *tales*.

let him be hanged
by the neck.'
And ther-fore hanged be he
And þat by þe halse.
Pil.   A! hoo sir, nowe, and holde in[1]?   104

For þoff ȝe gange þus gedy
Hym gilteles to graue,

'Stop! you
gain nothing
by groundless
accusation;
lf. 112 b.
With-outen grounde ȝow gaynes noght,
Swilke greffe to be-gynne.   106

tell me no trifles.'
And loke youre leggyng be lele,
With-owtyn any tryfils to telle.

An.   For certayne owre sawes dare we seele.   109

Pil.   And þan may we prophite oure pele.

Cay.   Sir, bot his fawtes were fele,
We mente noȝt of hym for to melle.   112

'He perverts
the people;
9. For he pervertis oure pepull
        Þat proues his prechyng,

And for þat poynte ȝe schulde prese
His pooste to paire.

ii doc.   ȝa, sir, and also þat caytiff
he calls himself
our king.'
           He callis hym oure kyng,

And for þat cause our comons are casten in care.   116

This moves
Pilate;
Pil.[2]   And if so be, þat borde to bayll will hym bryng,
And make hym boldely to banne þe bones þat hym bare.
For-why þat wrecche fro oure wretthe schal not wryng,
Or þer be wrought on hym wrake.
i doc.   So wolde we it ware.   120

For so schulde ȝe susteyne youre seele,
And myldely haue mynde for to meke ȝou.

he will make
the lad kneel.
Pil.   Wele, witte ȝe þis werke schall be wele,   123
For kende schall þat knave be to knele.

ii doc.   And so þat oure force he may feele,
All samme for þe same we beseke ȝou.   126

---

[1] This verse should perhaps read—judging by the accents and casting
out redundant words, 'Ther-fore hānged be he by the hālse. *Pil.* A! hōō
sir, hōlde in.'
[2] *Pilatus* is here added by the later hand.

[SCENE II, *Outside Pilate's hall, Judas alone.*]

10. Jud. *Ingenti pro Iniuria*, hym Jesus, þat Jewe,

    Vn-iust[1] vn-to me, Judas, I juge to be lathe ;

    For at oure soper as we satte, þe soþe to pursewe,

    { With Symond luprus full sone

    { My skiffte come to scathe.

    { Tille hym þer brought one a boyste,

    { My bale for to brewe,

    { That baynly to his bare feet

    { To bowe was full braythe.

    { Sho anoynte þam with an oynement

    { T[h]at nobill was and newe ;

    { But for þat werke þat sche wrought

    { I wexe woundir wrothe.

    And this, to discouer, was my skill,

    For of his penys purser was I,

    And what þat me taught was vntill,

    The tente parte þat stale I ay still ;

    But nowe for me wantis of my will,

    Þat bargayne with bale schall he by.

11. { Þat same oynement, I saide,

    { Might same haue bene solde

    { For siluer penys in a sowme

    { Thre hundereth, and fyne

    { Haue ben departid to poure men

    { As playne pite wolde.

    { But for þe poore ne þare parte

    { Priked me no peyne,

    { But me tened for þe tente parte,—

    { Þe trewthe to be-holde,—

    { That thirty pens of iij hundereth

    { So tyte I schulde tyne.

Marginal notes:

The grievances of Judas ;

130 his art has come to grief.

If. 113. Q iij.

He was angry at the anointing with the box of fine ointment. *John* xii. 3-6.

134

He was purser,

and was wont to steal out of it the tenth part ;

140

the loss to the poor of the price of the ointment (300 silver pence)

did not touch him,

144

but he was injured by losing his tenth part, i.e. thirty pence.

---

[1] The MS. has *vn-cust*; *unjust* seems intended.

Q

{ And for I mysse þis mony
{ I morne on þis molde,

He contrives
mischief,

{ Wherfore for to mischeue
{ Þis maistir of myne,   148

And þerfore faste forþe will I flitte
The princes of prestis vntill,

and will sell his
master for thirty
pence in revenge.

And selle hym full sone or þat I sitte,
For therty pens in a knotte knytte.
Þus-gatis full wele schall he witte,
Þat of my wretthe wreke me I will.   154

[*Knocks at the gate of Pilate's hall.*

12. Do open, porter, þe porte of þis prowde place,

If. 113 b.
He knocks at
the gate, but the
porter won't let
him in, he is so
grim.

{ That I may passe to youre princes
{ To proue for youre prowe.   [*Janitor, opening.*

{ Jani.   Go hense, þou glorand gedlyng!
{ God geue þe ille grace,

{ Thy glyfftyng is so grymly
{ Þou gars my harte growe.   158

{ Jud.   Goode sir, be toward þis tyme,
{ And tarie noght my trace,

{ For I haue tythandis to telle.

He sees treason
in his face.

{ Jani.   ȝa, som tresoune I trowe,

For I fele by a figure in youre fals face,

' No love in you,
Mars has set his
mark on you !'

It is but foly to feste affeccioun in ȝou.   162
For Mars he hath morteysed his mark,
Eftir all lynes of my lore,
And sais ȝe are wikkid of werk,
And bothe a strange theffe and a stark.

' You bark at
my beard ! you
shall rue it !'

Jud.   Sir, þus at my berde and ȝe berk
It semes it schall sitte yow full sore.   168

Strong language
by the porter.

13. { Jani.   Say, bittilbrowed bribour,
{ Why blowes þou such boste ?

Full false in thy face in faith can I fynde
{ Þou arte combered in curstnesse
{ And caris to þis coste;

  { To marre men of myght

  { Haste þou marked in thy mynde.   172

  { **Jud.** Sir, I mene of no malice   'I mean no malice.'

  { But mirthe meve I muste.

  { **Jani.** Say on, hanged harlott,   The porter, suspicious, lets him speak.

  { I holde þe vn-hende,

  { Thou lokist like a lurdayne   If. 114.

  { His liffelod hadde loste.   Q iiij.

  Woo schall I wirke þe away but þou wende !   176

Jud. A ! goode sir, take tente to my talkyng þis tyde,

For tythandis full trew can I telle.

Jani. Say, brethell, I bidde þe abide,

þou chaterist like a churle þat can chyde.   180

Jud. ȝa, sir, but and þe truthe schulde be tryed, He comes to save the nobles

Of myrthe are þer materes I mell.   182 from injury.

14. { For thurgh my dedis youre dugeperes

      { Fro dere may be drawe[n].

  { **Jani.** What ! demes þou till oure dukes The porter listens,

  { That doole schulde be dight ?

  { **Ju.** Nay, sir, so saide I noght [1],

  { If I be callid to counsaille

  { Þat cause schall be knawen

  { Emang þat comely companye,

  { To clerke and to knyght.   186

  { **Jani.** Byde me here, bewchere,   and goes to ask

  { Or more blore be blowen,

  { And I schall buske to þe benke

  { Wher baneres are bright,

  { And saie vnto oure souereynes,   (before more seed is sown)

  { Or seede more be sawen,   whether such a fellow as he

  { Þat swilke a seege as þi selff   may go in.

  { Sewes to þer sight.   *[He goes to the lords.]* 190

My lorde nowe, of witte þat is well,

I come for a cas to be kydde.   The porter explains the matter.

---

[1] The words *sir* to *noght* appear to be metrically in excess.

Pil.   We! speke on, and spare not þi spell.

Cay.   3a, and if vs mystir to ¹ mell,

Sen 3e bere of bewte þe bell,

Blythely schall we bowe as 3e bidde.   196

15. { Jani.   Sir, withoute þis abatyng,
    { Þer houes as I hope,

A hyve helte full of ire, for hasty he is.   198

{ Pil.   What comes he fore?
{ Jani.   I kenne hym noght, but he is cladde in a cope,

He cares with a kene face vncomely to kys.   200

{ Pil.   Go, gete hym þat his greffe
{ We grathely may grope,

So no oppen langage be goyng amys.

                         [*Janitor returns to Judas.*

{ Jani.   Comes on by-lyue, to my lorde,
                { And if þe liste to lepe,

{ But vttir so thy langage
{ That þou lette noght þare blys.   204

                    [*Judas enters.*]

Jud.   That lorde, sirs, myght susteyne 3oure seele

Þat floure is of fortune and fame.

Pil.   Welcome, thy wordis are but wele.

Cay.   Say, harste þou knave? can þou not knele?

Pil.   Loo, here may men faute in you fele.

[*To Cayphas.*] Late be, sir, youre scornyng, for schame.   210

16. Bot, bewshere, be no3t abayst to byde at þe bar ².

{ Ju.   Be-fore you, sirs, to be brought
{ Abowte haue I bene,

{ And allway for youre worschippe.
{ An.   Say, wotte þou any were?

{ Ju.   Of werke sir, þat hath wretthid 3ou,
                          { I wotte what I meene.   214

{ But I wolde make a marchaundyse
        { Youre myscheffe to marre.

¹ MS. has *te*.   ² MS. has *bay*.

{ **Pil.** And may þou soo?
{ **Ju.** Els madde I such maistries to mene.

{ **An.** Þan kennes þou of som comberaunce
{ Oure charge for to chere?

{ For cosyne, þou art cruell.
{ **Ju.** My cause, sir, is kene.   218   A keen case; he will sell Jesus.

For if ȝe will bargayne or by,
Jesus þis tyme will I selle ȝou.

i doc. My blissing, sone, haue þou for-thy,   The lawyers rejoice.
Loo! here is a sporte for to spye.

Jud. And hym dar I hete ȝou in hye,
If ȝe will be toward I telle ȝou.   224

· 17. { **Pil.** What hytist þou?   He is named Judas Iscariot.
               Jud. Judas scariott.
{ **Pil.** Þou art a juste mane,

{ Þat will Jesu be justified
{ By oure jugement;

{ But howe-gates bought schall he be?[1]
{ Bidde furthe thy bargayne.

{ **Jud.** But for a litill betyng
{ To bere fro þis bente.   228

{ **Pil.** Now, what schall we pay?
{ **Jud.** Sir, thirtipens and plete, no more þane.

{ **Pil.** Say, ar ȝe plesid of this price   He will do it for 30 pence.
{ He preces to present?

{ **ii doc.** Ellis contrarie we oure consciens,   lf. 115 b.
{ Consayue sen we cane   They all agree

{ Þat Judas knawes h[y]m, culpabill.
{ **Pil.** I call ȝou consent.   232

But Judas, a knott for to knytt,   and 'knit a knot.
Wilte þou to þis comenaunt accorde?

Jud. Ȝa, at a worde.

        Pil. Welcome is it.

---

[1] A red line here divides the speech, as though perhaps Anna were to speak, ll. 225, 226.

'Be off!
traitor ! tell no
one how he stakes
his master.'

ii Mil.　Take þee[1] of! a traytour, tyte !

i Mil.　Now leue sir, late noman wete,

How þis losell laykis with his lorde.　　238

*Pilate is igno-
rant,*

18. { **Pil.**　Why, dwellis he with þat dochard,
{ Whos dedis hase us drouyd ?

{ **i Mil.**　Þat hase he done sir, and dose,
{ No dowte is þis day.

*and asks why he
cursedly*

{ **Pil.**　Than wolde we knawe why þis knave
{ Þus cursidly contryued ?

{ **ii Mil.**　Enquere hym sen ȝe can best
{ Kenne if he contrarie[2].　　242

sells his master.

{ **Pil.**　Say, man, to selle þi maistir
{ What mysse hath he moved?

Ju.　For of als mekill mony he made me delay ;

Of ȝou, as I resayue, schall but right be reproued.

*Even Annas
curses him.*

{ **An.**　I rede noght þat ȝe reken vs
{ Oure rewle so to 'ray.　　246

For þat þe fales fende[3] schall þe fang,

i Mil.　When he schall wante of a wraste.

*lf. 116.
Q vj.*

i doc.　To whome wirke we wittandly wrang,

ii doc.　Tille hym bot ȝe hastely hang[4].

iii doc.　Ȝoure langage ȝe lay oute to lang,

But Judas, we trewly þe trast.　　252

*Judas must show
them how to take
Jesus, or he may
escape.*

19. { For truly þou moste lerne vs
{ That losell to lache,

{ Or of lande, thurgh a-lirte,
{ That lurdayne may lepe.

{ **Jud.**　I schall ȝou teche a token
{ Hym tyte for to take

{ Wher he is thryngand in þe thrang,
{ With-outen any threpe.　　256

[1] MS. has *þer*, contracted.　　[2] *Contraye* is perhaps intended.
[3] MS. has *frende*.
[4] MS. has *hastely hym hang*, but this second *hym* seems an error.

⎰ i **Mil.** We knawe hym noght.
⎱ **Ju.** Take kepe þan þat caytiffe to catche   'Take him whom
⎰ The whilke þat I kisse.   I kiss.'
⎱ ii **Mil.** Þat comes wele þe, corious, I cleepe !   Nice fellow !
⎰ But ȝitt to warne vs wisely,   I say, that be-
⎱ All-wayes must ȝe wacche ;   comes thee well.
⎰ Whan þou schall wende forth-with
⎱ We schall walke a wilde hepe,   260
And therfore besye loke now þou be.

Jud. Ȝis, ȝis, a space schall I spie vs,
Als sone as þe sonne is sƖtte, as ȝe see.

i **Mil.** Go forthe, for a traytoure ar ȝe.   'Go forth,
                                                        traitor !
ii **Mil.** Ȝa, and a wikkid man.
                    i **doc.** Why, what is he ?

ii **doc.** A losell sir, but lewte shuld lye vs,   266

20. He is trappid full of trayne þe truthe for to trist,   He is full of
    I holde it but folye his [? faythe] for to trowe.   deceit.
⎰ **Pil.** Abide in my blyssing,   lf. 116 b.
⎱ And late youre breste,
⎰ For it is beste for oure bote
⎱ In bayle for to bowe.   270
⎰ And Judas, for oure prophite
⎱ We praye þe be prest.
⎰ **Ju.** Ȝitt hadde I noght a peny   'I have not got
⎱ To purvey for my prowe.   the money yet.'
⎰ **Pil.** Þou schalte haue delyueraunce   'You shall have
⎱ Be-lyue at þi list,   it directly,
⎰ So þat þou schall haue liking
⎱ Oure lordschipp to loue.   274
And therfore, Judas, mende þou thy mone [1],
And take þer þi siluere all same.   take it,

Ju. Ȝa nowe is my grete greffe ouere-gone.

          [1] This line is two in the MS.

i **Mil.** Be lyght þan!

Ju. ȝis, latte me allone !

For tytte schall þat taynte be tone,

And þerto jocounde and joly I am [1].   280

keep your be-
hest, and we pro-
mise you our
help.' 21. { **Pil.** Judas, to holde þi behest

{ Be hende for oure happe,

{ And of vs helpe and vpholde

{ We hete þe to haue.

{ **Ju.** I schall be-kenne ȝou his corse

{ In care for to clappe.

They gloat over
their bargain. { **An.** And more comforte in þis case

{ We coveyte not to craue.   284

{ i **Mil.** Fro we may reche þat rekeles

{ His ribbis schall we rappe,

{ And make þat roy, or we rest,

If. 117.
Q vij. { For rennyng to raffe.

{ **Pil.** Nay, sirs, all if ȝe scourge hym

{ ȝe schende noȝt his schappe,

Pilate will save
Jesus if he is
innocent. { For if þe sotte be sakles

{ Vs sittis hym to saue.   288

Wherfore when ȝe go schall to gete hym,

Vn-to his body brew ȝe no bale.

ii **Mil.** Our liste is fro lepyng to lette hym,

But in youre sight sownde schall we [2] sette hym.

Pil. Do flitte nowe forthe till ȝe fette hym,

With solace all same to youre sale.   294

[*Exeunt Judas and soldiers.*

---

[1] A side-note here, begun by one hand, finished by another, says—'caret hic Janitor and Judas.'

[2] MS. has *ve*.

XXVII. THE BAXTERES[1].

The Last Supper.

[PERSONS OF THE PLAY.

JESUS.	JACOBUS.
MARCELLUS.	JUDAS.
ANDREAS.	THOMAS.]
PETRUS.	

[SCENE, *A chamber in Jerusalem.*]

1. Jesus. PEES be both be day and nyght   *Matt.* xxvi. 19.
        Vn-till þis house, and till all þat is here ![2]   *Mark* xiv. 16, 17.
                                         Luke xxii. 13.
Here will I holde as I haue hight,   We will hold the
The feeste of Paas with frendis in feere.   4   Paschal feast.

Marc. Maistir, we haue arayd full right
Seruise þat semes for youre sopere.
Oure lambe is roste, and redy dight,   The lamb is ready
As Moyses lawe will lely lere.   8   roast.

Jesus. That is, ilke man þat has
Pepill in his awne poste
Shall roste a lambe at paas,
To hym and his meyne.   12

2. And. Maistir, þe custome wele we knawe,
That with oure elthers euer has bene,
How ilke man with his meyne awe
To roste a lambe, and ete it clene.   16

Jesus. I thanke ʒou sothtly of youre sawe,
For ʒe saye as youre selffe has sene,
Ther-fore array ʒou all on rawe,   'Sit in a row,
My selfe schall parte itt ʒou be-twene.   20   I will share the
                                                     lamb,

---

[1] Side-note in late hand, 'caret hic principio.'
[2] The original copyist omitted *all*, and wrote þeryn for *here*. A later
hand corrected as above.

Wher-fore I will þat ȝe
Ette þerof euere ilkone,

the remnant
shall be given to
the poor.'

The remelaunt parted schall be,
To þe poure þat purueyse none.   24

3. Of Moyses lawes here make I an ende,
In som party, but noght in all,
My comaundement schall otherwise be kende
With þam þat men schall craftely call.   28

If. 119.
R j.

But þe lambe of Pasc þat here is spende,
Whilke Jewes vses grete and small,

The Paschal
lamb henceforth
forbidden to
Christians.

Euere forward nowe I itt deffende
Fro cristis folke, what so befall.   32
In þat stede schall be sette
A newe lawe vs by-twene,
But who þerof schall ette,
Behoues to be wasshed clene.   36

A new law.

John xiii. 1–15.

'Marcellus, bring
water.'

4. For þat new lawe whoso schall lere,
In harte þam bus be clene and chaste.
Marcelle, myn awne discipill dere,
Do vs haue watir here in hast.   40

'Here it is, and a
clean towel.'

Marc.   Maistir, it is all redy here,
And here a towell clene to taste.

Jesus begins to
wash the disci-
ples' feet,

Jesus.   Commes forthe with me, all in feere,
My wordis schall noght be wroght in waste.   44
Settis youre feete fourth, late see,
They schall be wasshen sone.
Pet.   A! lorde, with þi leue, of þee
þat dede schall noȝt be done.   48

Peter refuses,

5. I schall neuere make my membres mete,
Of my souerayne seruice to see.

but Jesus makes
him obedient.

Jesus.   Petir, bott if þou latte me wasshe þi feete,
þou getis no parte in blisse with me.   52
Pet.   A! mercy, lorde and maistir swete,
Owte of þat blisse þat I noght be,

Wasshe on my lorde to all be wete,
Both hede and hande, beseke I þe.   56
Jesus. Petir, þou wotiste noȝt ȝitt
What þis werke will be-mene.
Here aftir schall þou witte,   lf. 119 b.
And so schall ȝe all, be-dene.   60

Tunc lauat manus [1].

6. Ȝoure lorde and maistir ȝe me call,   'I, your master, have washed your feet,
And so I am, all welthe to welde,
Here haue I knelid vnto ȝou all,
To wasshe youre feete as ȝe haue feled.   64
Ensaumple of me take ȝe schall,   take example of meekness thereby.'
Euer for to ȝeme in ȝouþe and elde,
To be buxsome in boure and hall,
Ilkone for to bede othir belde.   68
For all if ȝe be trewe
And lele of loue ilkone,
Ȝe schall fynde othir ay newe,
To greue whan I am gone.   72

7. Jac. [*Aside.*] Now sen oure maistir sais he schall   'If he goes, which of us shall be chief?'
Wende, and will not telle vs whedir,
Whilke of vs schall be princepall,   *Mark* ix. 33-37.
Late loke now whils we dwell to-gedir.   76
Jesus. I wotte youre will, both grete and small,   'I hear your hearts,
And youre high hartis I here þam hedir,
To whilke of ȝou such fare schulde fall,
Þat myght ȝe carpe when ȝe come thedir,   80
Where it so schulde be tyde
Of such materes to melle.
But first behoues ȝou bide   but you must abide many trials.'
Fayndyngis full ferse and felle.   84
[*He sets a child before them.*]
8. Here schall I sette ȝou for to see
Þis ȝonge childe for insaumpills seere,

---

[1] Marginal note in later hand.

Both meke and mylde of harte is he,
And fro all malice mery of chere,　　　88
So meke and mylde but if ȝe be [1],
*　　*　　*　　*　　*　　*　　*

If. 120.
R iij.

[Jesus.]　*Quod facis fac cicius,*
Þat þou schall do, do sone.

John xiii. 27, 25.　9. Thom.　Allas! so wilsom wightis as we,　92
Was neuere in worlde walkand in wede,

His own people
have betrayed
him.

Oure maistir sais his awne meyne
Has be-trayed hym to synfull seede.

Jac.　A! I hope, sen þou sittist nexte his kne,　96
We pray þe spire hym for oure spede.

John asks who
will do that
dolefull deed.

Joh.　*Domine quis est qui tradit te ?*
Lord, who schall do þat doulfull dede?
Allas! oure playe is [2] paste,　　　100
Þis false forward is feste,
I may no lenger laste,
For bale myn herte may breste.

Judas slips away;
he sees he is
suspected.

10. Judas [*Aside*].　Now is tyme to me to gang,　104
For here be-gynnes noye all of newe,
My fellows momellis þame emang
Þat I schulde alle þis bargayne brewe.
And certis þai schall noȝt wene it wrang.　108
To þe prince of prestis I schall pursue,
And þei schall lere hym othir ought long
That all his sawes sore schall hym rewe.
I wotte whedir he remoues,　　　112
With his meyne ilkone,
I schall telle to þe Jewes,
And tyte he schalle be tane.　　　[*Exit*

*Matt.*xxvi.33-35.　11. Jesus.　I warne ȝou nowe my frendis free,　116
Mark xiv. 27-31.　Sese to ther sawes þat I schall say,

---

[1] Here a leaf R ij is lost, containing about 65 lines, (the MS. is here
closely written), which must have given the scene of Judas and the so
(John xiii. 21-27).
[2] MS. repeats *is*.

The fende is wrothe with ȝou and me,
And will ȝou marre if þat he may.
But Petir I haue prayed for þe,   120
So þat þou schall noȝt drede his dray ;
And comforte þou þis meyne
And wisse hem, whan I am gone away.
Petrus.   A! lorde, where wilte þou lende,   124
I schall lende in þat steede,
And with þe schall I wende
Euermore in lyffe and dede.

12. **And.**   No wordely drede schall me withdrawe,   128
That I schall with þe leue and dye.
Thom.   Certis, so schall we all on rawe,
Ellis mekill woo were we worthy.
Jesus.   Petir, I saie to þe þis sawe,   132
Þat þou schalte fynde no fantasie,
Þis ilke nyght or þe cokkys crowe,
Shall þou thre tymes my name denye,
And saye þou knewe me neuere,   136
Nor no meyne of myne.
Pet.   Allas! lorde, me were lever
Be putte to endles pyne.

13. **Jesus.**   As I yow saie, so schall it bee,   140
Ye nedis non othir recours to craue.
All þat in worlde is wretyn of me
Shall be fulfilled, for knyght or knave.
I am þe herde, þe schepe are ȝe,   144
And whane þe herde schall harmes haue,
The flokke schall be full fayne to flee,
And socoure seke þame selffe to saue.
Ȝe schall whan I am allone,   148
In grete myslykyng lende,
But whanne I ryse agayne,
Þan schall youre myrthe be mende[1].

        [1] MS. has *mened*.

Side notes:
'The fiend will mar you, but *Luke* xxii. 31-34.

lf. 120 b.

Peter must guide you.'

The disciples will stay with him.

Jesus foretells that Peter will deny him.

'I am the shepherd, ye are the sheep.' *Mark* xiv. 27.

Troubles to come,

lf. 121. R iiij.

but joy afterwards.

Luke xxii. 28-30, 36-38.

14. ȝe haue bene bowne my bale to bete,   152
Therfore youre belde ay schall I be,
And for ȝe did in drye and wete
My comaundementis in ilke contre,

The kingdom of heaven a reward to the faithful disciples :

The kyngdome of heuen I you be-hete,   156
Euen as my fadir has highte itt me ;
With gostely mete þere schall we mete,
And on twelffe seeges sitte schall ȝe,
For ȝe trewlye toke ȝeme   160
In worlde with me to dwell,
There shall ȝe sitte be-deme [1]
Xij kyndis of Israell.

but first they will be bewildered, and many dangers shall come.

15. But firste ȝe schall be wille of wone,   164
And mo wathes þen ȝe of wene
Fro tyme schall come þat I be tone,
Þan schall ȝe turne away with tene.

Each must have a sword ; even sell his coat for one.

And loke þat ȝe haue swerdis ilkone,   168
And whoso haues non ȝou by-twene,
Shall selle his cote and bye hym one,
Þus bidde I þat ȝe do be-dene.
Satcheles I will ȝe haue,   172
And stones to stynte all striffe,
Youre selffe for to saue
In lenghyng of youre liff.

16. And.   Maistir, we [2] haue here swerdis twoo,   176
Vs [3] with to saue on sidis seere.
Jesus.   Itt is i-nowe, ȝe nedis no moo,
For fro all wathis I schall ȝou were.

If. 121 b.

Butt ryse now vppe, for we will goo,   180
By þis owre enemyes ordand are,
My fadir saide it schall be soo,
His bidding will I noȝt for-bere.

[1] MS. has *by dene.*   [2] MS. has *ȝe.*
[3] The MS. has *Vis.*

Loke ȝe lere forthe þis lawe   184
Als ȝe haue herde of me,
Alle þat wele will itt knawe,
[1] Ay blessed schall þei bee.   187

[1] *Hic caret novo loquela,* marginal note in two later hands and inks.

XXVIII. THE CORDEWANERS[1].

The Agony and the Betrayal.

[PERSONS OF THE PLAY.

JESUS.	ANGELUS.	MALCUS.
PETRUS.	ANNA.	1[us], 2[us], 3[us], 4[us] MILES.
JACOBUS.	CAYPHAS.	1[us], 2[us], 3[us], 4[us] JUDEUS.]
JOHANNES.	JUDAS.	

[SCENE I, *The Mount of Olives and the Garden of Gethsemane.*]

*Matt.*xxvi.36–56.
Mark xiv. 26–50.
Luke xxii. 39–53.
' My soul is sorrowful unto death.'

1. Jesus. BEHOLDE my discipulis þat deyne is and dere[2],
My flesshe dyderis & daris for doute of my dede,
Myne enemyes will newly be neghand full nere,
With all þe myght if þei may to marre my manhede.　　4

{ But sen ȝe are for-wakid
And wanderede in were,

{ Loke ȝe sette ȝou doune rathely,
And reste ȝou I reede.

He bids his disciples rest a while.

{ Beis noȝt heuy in ȝoure hertis
But holde yow even here,

{ And bidis me a stounde
Stille in þis same steede.　　8

Beeis witty and wyse in youre wandyng,
So þat ȝe be wakand alway,

'Watch and pray.'

And lokis nowe prestely ȝe pray
To my fadir, þat ȝe falle in no fandyng.　　12

---

[1] The regular stanza of this play, in which the old copyist made more errors than usual, contains twelve lines, eight of four accents and four of three accents, riming a b a b a b a b c d d c. As several of the stanzas are imperfect and others confused, the short lines in stanzas 3, 4, 15, etc., should probably be taken as parts of missing lines, not as tags. Stanzas 6, 14 are each a line too long, while stanza 4 is short of four lines.
[2] Note in margin, 16th cent. hand, *de novo facto.*

2.   Pet. ʒis, lorde, at thy bidding
    Full baynly schall we abide,

    For þou arte boote of oure bale
    And bidis for þe best.

  Joh. Lorde! all oure helpe and oure hele,
    That is noght to hyde,

    In þe, oure faythe and oure foode,
    All hollye is feste.   *[Jesus goes from them.]* 16

  Jac. Qwat way is he willid
    In þis worlde wyde?

    Whedir is he walked,
    Estewarde or weste?

  Pet. ʒaa, sirs, I schall saye ʒou,
    Sittis vs doune on euery ilka side;

    And late vs nowe rathely here take oure reste; 20
    My lymmys are heuy as any leede.

  Joh. And I muste slepe, doune muste I lye.

  Jac. In faithe, felawes, right so fare I,
    I may no lenger holde vppe my hede. *[They lie down.]* 24

3.   Pet. Oure liffe of his lyolty
    His liffe schall he lose,

    Vnkyndely be crucified
    And naylyd to a tree.

  Jesus *[coming again]*. Baynly of my blissing,
    Youre eghen ʒe vnclose,

    So þat ʒe falle in no fandyng
    For noght þat may be,   28
        But prayes fast.

  Joh. Lorde, som prayer þou kenne vs,
    That somwhat myght mirthe vs or mende vs.

  Jac. Fro all fandyng vnfaythfull þou fende vs,
    Here in þis worlde of liffe whille we laste. 33

4.   Jesus. I schall kenne ʒou, and comforte ʒou,
    And kepe ʒou from care;

R

Side notes:

They all assent.

They must rest,

If. 122 b.

being heavy with sleep.

Jesus bids them pray not to fall into temptation.

'Teach us some prayer.'

  { ȝe schall be broughte, wete ȝe wele,
  { Fro bale vnto blisse.

  { **Pet.** ȝaa, but lorde, and youre willis were,
  { Witte wolde we more,

  Of this prayer so precious late vs noȝt mys,   37
      We beseke þe.

  Joh. For my felows and me all in feere,
  Some prayer þat is precious to lere.   40

  Jac. Vn-to thy Fadir þat moste is of poure
  Som solace of socoure to sende þe [1].   42

    *   *   *   *   *

lf. 123.
R viij.
5. { **Jesus.** Þe nowys þat me neghed
  { Hase, it nedis not to neuen ;

  { For all wate ȝe full wele
  { What wayes I haue wente ;

Jesus prays for
strength,
  { In-store me and strenghe
  { With a stille steuen,

  I pray þe interly þou take entent,   46
  Þou menske my manhed with mode.

his flesh trembles,
he sweats for
fear.
  My flessh is full dredand for drede,
  For my jorneys of my manhed,
  I swete now both watir and bloode.   50

6. Þes Jewes hase mente in þer mynde full of malice,
  { And pretende me to take
  { With-outen any trespasse,

  { But Fadir, as þou wate wele,
  { I mente neuere a-mys,

  { In worde nor in werk
  { I neuer worthy was.   54

  Als þou arte bote of all bale and belder of blisse,
  And all helpe and hele in thy hande hase,
  { Þou mensk thy manhede,
  { Þou mendar of mysse !

     [1] A leaf, R. vij, is lost here.

   { And if it possible be

   { This payne myght I ouer-passe.   58

And Fadir, if þou se it may noght,

Be it worthely wrought

Euen at thyne awne will,

Euermore both myldely and still,

With worschippe all way be it wroght.   63

'Father, if it be possible, let this cup pass from me.'

7. Vn-to my discipillis will I go agayne,

   { Kyndely to comforte þam

   { Þat kacchid are in care.   *[Goes to the disciples.*

   { What! are ȝe fallen on-slepe

   { Now euer-ilkone?

And þe passioun of me in mynde hase no more?   67

   { What! wille ȝe leue me þus lightly,

   { And latte me allone,

   { In sorowe and in sighyng

   { Þat sattillis full sore?

   { To whome may I meue me

   { And make nowe my mone,

I wolde þat ȝe wakened, and your will wore.   71

Do Petir, sitte vppe, nowe late se!

Þou arte strongly stedde in þis stoure,

Might þou noght þe space of an owre

Haue wakid nowe mildely with me?   75

He finds the disciples asleep.

lf. 123 b.

'What! you so easily forget my sorrow, and leave me alone?

Peter, could'st thou not have watched with me one hour?

8. **Pet.** Ȝis, lorde, with youre leue nowe will we lere,

Full warely to were ȝou. fro alle wandynge?

Jesus. Beeis wakand and prayes faste all in fere,

To my Fadir, þat ȝe falle in no fanding,   79

For euelle spiritis is neghand full nere,

That will ȝou tarie at þis tyme with his tentyng;

And I will wende þer I was withouten any were,

But bidis me here baynly in my blissing.   83

Agayne to þe mounte I will gang

Ȝitt efte-sones where I was ere,

Watch and pray, lest you fall into temptation, for evil spirits are near.'

But loke þat ȝe cacche ȝow no care,

For lely I schall noȝt dwelle lange.   [*He moves away.*] 87

9. Þou Fadir, þat all formed hase with fode for to fill,

I fele by my ferdnes my flesshe wolde full fayne

Be torned fro this turnement, and takyn þe vntill,

For mased is manhed in mode and in mayne.   91

But if þou se sothly þat þi sone sill[1]

With-outen surfette of synne þus sakles be slayne,

Be it worthly wroght even at thyne awne will,

For fadir, att þi bidding am I buxum and bayne.   95

Now wightely agayne will I wende,

Vn-to my discipilis so dere. [*He comes again to the disciples.*

What! slepe ȝe so faste all in fere?

I am ferde ȝe mon faile of youre frende.   99

10. But ȝitt will I leue ȝou and late you allone,

And efte-sones þere I was agayne will I wende.

[*He moves away again.*

Vn-to my fadir of myght now make I my mone,

As þou arte saluer of all sore som socoure me sende.   103

Þe passioun they purpose to putte me vppon,

My flesshe is full ferde and fayne wolde defende,

At þi wille be itt wrought worþely in wone,

Haue mynde of my manhed, my mode for to mende.   107

Some comforte me kythe in þis case,

And Fadir, I schall dede taste,

I will it noȝt deffende;

ȝitt yf thy willis be

Spare me a space[2].   [*An Angel appears.*

11. { **Ang.**[3] Vn-to þe maker vn-made

{ Þat moste is of myght,   113

Side notes (left margin):

Jesus returns to pray again to the Father for strength.

'Father, thy will be done.' If. 124. S j.

'What! ye are sleeping!'

He prays a third time to the Father,

'Send me comfort, I shall taste death, yet if it were thy will, spare me!'

The angel comes down to comfort Jesus.

---

[1] *sic.*

[2] Four (short) lines next following have been erased, and are illegible They may have been part of the error made in copying this incomplet stanza, or the two lines wanting to stanza 11.

[3] The words 'and archangels' are added after angels in a 17th cent hand.

Be louyng ay lastand in light þat is lente;

{ Thy Fadir þat in heuen is moste,
{ He vppon highte,

{ Thy sorowes for to sobir
{ To þe he hase me sente.   116

{ For dedis þat man done has
{ Thy dede schall be dight,

{ And þou with turmentis be tulyd.
{ But take nowe entente,

Thy bale schall be for þe beste,

Thurgh þat mannys mys schall be mende;   120   lf. 124 b.

Þan schall þou with-outen any ende

Rengne in thy rialte full of reste.

12. { Jesus.   Now if my flesshe ferde be,
   { Fadir, I am fayne

{ Þat myne angwisshe and my noyes   'Mine anguish is near an end,
{ Are nere at an ende;   124

Vn-to my discipilis go will I agayne,

{ Kyndely to comforte þam   I must comfort my disciples.'
{ Þat mased is in þer mynde.   [*He goes to the disciples.*

{ Do slepe 3e nowe sauely,
{ And I schall 3ou sayne,

{ Wakyns vppe wightely   'Arise, let us go hence;
{ And late vs hens wende;   128

{ For als tyte mon I be taken
{ With tresoune and with trayne,

{ My flesshe is full ferde
{ And fayne wolde deffende.

Full derfely my dede schall be dight,

And als sone as I am tane   132   as soon as I am taken you will all forsake me.'

Þan schall 3e forsake me ilkone,

And saie neuere 3e sawe me with sight.

13. Pet.   Nay, sothely, I schall neuere my souereyne forsake,

If I schulde for þe dede darfely here dye,   136

They all protest
they will not.

Joh. Nay such mobardis schall neuere man vs make,

{ Erste schulde we dye all at onys.

{ **Jac.** Nowe in faith, felows, so shulde I.

{ **Jesus.** 3a, but when tyme is be-tydde,

{ Þanne men schalle me take,

lf. 125.
S ij.

{ For all 3oure hartely hetyng

{ 3e schall hyde 3ou in hy,   140

'Like scattered
sheep ye will
run.'

{ Lyke schepe þat were scharid

{ A-way schall 3e schake,

{ Þer schall none of 3ou be balde

{ To byde me þan by.

Peter boasts his
steadfastness.

Pet. Nay, sothely, whils I may vayle þe[1],   143

I schall were þe and wake þe,

And if all othir for-sake þe,

I schall neuere fayntely defayle þe.   146

Jesus rebukes
him and says he
will deny him ere
the cock crows.

14. { **Jesus.** A! Petir, of swilke bostyng

{ I rede þou late bee,

{ Fo[r] all thy kene carpyng

{ Full kenely I knawe,

{ For ferde of myne enmyse

{ Þou schalte sone denye me,

{ Thries 3itt full thraly,

{ Or the Cokkes crowe :   150

{ For ferde of my fo-men

{ Full fayne be for to flee,

{ And for grete doute of þi dede

{ Þe to with-drawe.

---

[1] In the MS. the original copyist made two mistakes. Line 143, with 'I'
appended, stands as the second line of Jesus' previous speech, making non-
sense; and the first line given to Peter is, '3is sothly, quod Petir.' The
'I' gained from l. 143, no less than the '3is sothly' of the interloping
line, and the rime, show that the right reading is as above; the '3is sothly,
quod Petir' seems to have been the prompter's cue that the copyist unconsciously wrote down. At Coventry there was a 'keeper of the playe
book,' or prompter (Sharp's Diss. on Coventry Pageants, 1816, p. 48); at
York I have found no note of the 'keeper,' although one of the actor's
books, i. e. of the Scriveners' Play, has been preserved. See Play XLI.

[SCENE II, *The High Priest's palace.*]

An.   Sir Cayphas, of youre counsaille
Do, sone, late vs now see!
For lely it langes vs to luke
Vn-to oure lawe [1].   154

And therfore sir, prestely I pray 30u,
Sen þat we are of counsaille ilkone,
That Jesus þat traytoure wer tane,
Do sone, late se sir, I pray 30u.   158

Cayph.   In certayne sir, and sone schall I saye 30u,

15.   I wolde wene by my witte
   Þis werke wolde be wele,
   Late vs justely vs iune
   Tille Judas þe gente,
   For he kennes his dygnites
   Full duly ilke a dele,   162
   3a, and beste wote, I warande,
   What wayes þat he is wente.

An.   Now þis was wisely saide
   Als euer haue I seele,
   And sir, to youre saiyng
   I saddely will assente,
   Therfore take vs of oure knyghtis
   That is stedfast as stele,   166
   And late Judas go lede þam be-lyffe
   Wher that he last lente [2].   [*Enter Judas.*

Cay.   Full wele sir. Nowe Judas, dere neghboure, drawe
                nere vs [3],
Lo! Judas, þus in mynde haue we ment,
To take Jesus is oure entent,   170

Annas begs that Jesus may be seized soon.

lf. 125 b.

They agree to wait for Judas' help,

and prepare a force of soldiers.

' Judas, you must lead us.'

---

[1] The MS. has *lawys*.
[2] Lines 166, 167 stand in the MS. next following after l. 171.
[3] In the MS. ' Full wele sir' stands as a separate line.

For þou muste lede vs and lere vs.

{ [And also beis ware

{ Þat he wil not away ¹].   172

'I will show you **16.** { **Judas.**   Sirs, I schall wisse you þe way
the way, but have
some strong men.'   { Euen at youre awne will ;

                      { But loke þat ȝe haue

                      { Many myghty men,

lf. 126.   { That is both strang and sterand
S iij.
                      { And stedde hym stone stille.   175

'How shall we   { **An.**   ȝis, Judas, but be what knowlache
know him ?'
                     { Shall we þat corse kenne ?

                     { **Judas.**   Sirs, a tokenyng in þis tyme

                     { I schall telle ȝou vntill ;

'Do not give him   { But lokis by youre lewty
mercy : it is he
whom I kiss.'   { No liffe ȝe hym lenne, . . .   178

                     { Qwhat man som I kys,

                     { Þat corse schall ye kyll ².

'We do not mean   **Cay.**   Why, nay Judas, I schrew you all þenne,
to let him off.'
                   We purpose þe page schall not passe.

                   { Sir knyghtis, in hy !   [*Calls the soldiers.*

                   { i **Mil.**   Lorde we are here ³.   182

The soldiers are   **Cay.**   Calles fourth youre felaws in feere,
told to go with
Judas.   And gose justely with gentill Judas.   184

17. { i **Mil.**   Come, felaws, by youre faith

        { Come forthe all faste,

        { And carpis with Sir Cayphas,

        { He comaundis me to call.

        { ii **Mil.**   I schrewe hym all his liffe,

        { Þat loues to be last.

---

¹ This line is in error, redundant.

² In the MS. l. 179 stands immediately before the redundant l. 172.
Thus the order of the transposed lines in the MS. is 171, 166, 167, 179,
172, 173.

³ The rubricator placed 1 *miles* as the speaker of the first half, and
2 *miles* of the second half of l. 182, but ll. 183, 185, as well as the sense,
show that Caiaphas himself calls the first soldier, who answers. See too
l. 186.

{ iii **Mil.**   Go we hens þan in hy,   They hasten out,
{ And haste vs to þe halle.   188

{ **iv Mil.**   Lorde, of youre will worthely,   asking what they
{ Wolde I witte what wast?   are to do.

{ **Cay.**   To take Jesus, þat sawntrelle,   'To take Jesus.'
{ All same, þat ȝe schall.

{ **i Mil.**   Lorde, to þat purpose
{ I wolde þat we paste.

Anna.   ȝa, but loke þat ȝe be armed wele all,   192   lf. 126 b.
The moste gentill of þe jury schalle gyde ȝow[1].   They must go
                                                well armed.

Cay.   ȝa, and euery ilke a knyght in degre
Both armed and harneysed ȝe be,
To belde ȝou and baynely go by[de] ȝou.   196

18. **An.**   ȝa, and þerfore sir Cayphas, ȝe hye ȝou
Youre wirschippe ȝe wynne in þis cas[2].
As ȝe are a lorde, most lofsom of lyre,
Vndir sir Pilate þat lyfis in þis Empire,   200
ȝone segger þat callis hym-selffe a sire
With tresoure and tene sall we taste hym.
Of ȝone losell his bale schall [he] brewe,
Do trottes on for þat traytoure apas.   204   Annas is eager to
                                               make haste,

Cay.   Nowe, sirs, sen ȝe say my poure is most beste,   Caiaphas says
{ And hase all þis werke   that he is not
{ Þus to wirke at my will,   losing time, the
Now certayne riȝt sone I thinke not to rest,   traitor will soon
But solempnely in hast youre will to fulfille.   208   be taken.
Full tyte þe traytoure schall be tane.

---

[1] Two lines in the MS.

[2] Here the late annotator wrote ' hic caret ': he evidently was puzzled by
the confusion made by the early copyist. The whole of this passage, from
l. 197 to 240, which I believe represents three stanzas, is hopelessly confused
out of rime and reason; the rubricator did not understand it, as he intended
l. 203 to begin a new speech, but attempted no name, and put no guiding
lines to the short phrases to connect them with their rimes, as usual where
tag-phrases occur: the structure of other parts of the poem appears to
show that no such tags are intended here. I therefore print this passage as
it stands, except the transpositions of the words ' in hast,' in l. 208, which
in the MS. are written, apart, at the end of l. 203; and 'riȝt sone,' l. 207,
from the end of the line. Lines 203, 204 appear to belong to ll. 197, 198.

Sirs knyghtis, ȝe hye ȝou ilkone,
For in certayne þe losell schall be slane ;

Have done.

Sir Anna, I praye ȝou haue done.   212

An. Full redy tyte I schall be boune
Þis journay for to go till ;

Annas is still
eager in the pur-
suit ;

Als ȝe are a lorde of grete renoune,
Ȝe spare hym not to spill.   216
Þe devill hym spede! go we with oure knyghtis in fere.
Lo! þay are arrayed and armed clere.
Sir knyghtis, loke ȝe be of full gud chere.
Where ȝe hym see, on hym take hede.   220

lf. 127.
S iiij.

i Judeus. Goode tente to hym, lorde, schall we take,
He schall banne þe tyme þat he was borne,

the soldiers will
hunt for him
everywhere.

All his kynne schall come to late,
He schall noght skape withouten scorne   224
     fro vs in fere.

ii Jud. We schall hym seke both even and morne,
Erly and late, with full gode chere,
     Is oure entente.   228

iii Jud. Stye nor strete we schall spare none,
Felde nor towne, þus haue we mente,
     And boune in corde.

Malcus brings a
light to bear
before them.

Mal. [*bringing a light.*] Malcus! a ay! and I schulde be
     rewarde   232
And right, als wele worthy were,
Loo! for I bere light for my lorde.

Cay. A! sir, of youre speche lette, and late vs spede
A space, and of oure speche spare,   236
And Judas go fande þou be-fore,
And wisely þou wisse þam þe way,
For sothely sone schall we 'saye,
To make hym to marre vs nomore.   [*Exeunt.*]   240

[SCENE III, *The Garden of Gethsemane.*]

21. Jesus. Now will þis oure be neghand full nere,
That schall certefie all þe soth þat I haue saide,
[Go fecche forth þe freyke for his forfette¹].

{ **Jud.** All hayll, maistir in faith,
{ And felawes all in fere,   244 Judas meets his master, and asks from him a kiss.

{ With grete gracious gretyng
{ On grounde be he graied.

{ I wolde aske you a kysse,
{ Maistir, and youre willes were,

{ For all my loue and my likyng
{ Is holy vppon ȝou layde.

Jesus. Full hartely, Judas, haue it even here,   248   Jesus betrayed.
For with þis kissing is mans sone be-trayed.

i Mil. Whe! stande, traytoure, I telle þe for tane.   lf. 127 b.

Cay. Whe! do knyghtis, go falle on be-fore.

ii Mil. ȝis, maistir, moue þou nomore,
But lightly late vs allone. [*A light shines round Jesus.*] 253

22. iii Mil. Allas! we are loste, for leme of þis light.   The soldiers are amazed and confounded by the brilliant light from Jesus.

{ **Jesus.** Saye ȝe here, whome seke ȝe?
{ Do saye me, late see!

{ **i Jud.** One Jesus of Nazareth
{ I hope þat he hight.

{ **Jesus.** Be-holdis all hedirward, loo!
{ Here, I am hee!   257

{ **i Mil.** Stande! dastarde, so darfely
{ Thy dede schall be dight,

{ I will no more be abasshed
{ For blenke of thy blee.

{ **i Jud.** We, oute! I ame mased almost
{ In mayne and in myght.   260

---

¹ This line is an interloper, it does not belong either to Jesus' speech or
to the stanza. Perhaps it should follow l. 236.

　　{ ii Jud.　And I am ferde, be my feyth,
　　{ And fayne wolde I flee ;
　　　For such a siȝt haue I not sene.

　　iii Jud.　Þis leme it lemed so light,
　　　I saugh neuer such a siȝt,
　　　Me meruayles what it may mene.　　　　　265

Whom seek ye ?'　**23. Jesus.**　Doo[1], whame seke ȝe all same, ȝitt I saye?

　　{ i Jud.　One Jesus of Nazareth,
　　{ Hym wolde we negh nowe.

　　{ Jesus.　And I am he sothly,
　　{ And þat schall I a-saie.

lf. 128.　　{ **Mal.**　For þou schalte dye, dastard,
S v.　　　 {
Malcus　　 { Sen þat it is þowe.　　　　　　　　269
threatens Jesus,
so Peter attacks　　**Pet.**　And I schall fande be my feythe þe for to flaye,
him.　　　　Here with a lusshe, lordayne, I schalle þe allowe.

　　　　　　　　　　　　　[*Cuts off his ear.*

　　Mal.　We! oute! all my deueres are done[2].　273

　　Pet.　Nay, traytoure, but trewly I schall trappe þe I trowe.

Jesus bids Peter　**Jesus.**　Pees! Petir, I bidde þe,
not to meddle ;
　　　Melle þe nor moue þe no more,
　　　For witte þou wele, and my willis were[3],
　　　I myght haue poure grete plente :　　　　277

he could have　**24.**　{ Of aungellis full many
angels to show　　　{ To mustir my myght,
his power.
　　　{ For-thy putte vppe þi swerde
　　　{ Full goodely agayne,
　　　{ For he þat takis vengeaunce
　　　{ All rewlid schall be right,
　　　{ With purgens and vengeaunce
　　　{ Þat voydes in vayne.　　　　　　　　281

---

[1] *Doo* in MS. If it is the correct reading, it seems to be used here
interjectionally. Perhaps 'say' is omitted; compare l. 255.
[2] Probably the line ended with Peter's exclaiming 'nay!' This would
complete the rime and shorten the next line as it needs; it would begin
'Traytour.'　　　　　　　　　　　　　[3] Two lines in MS.

{ Þou man þat is þus derede
{ And doulfully dyght,

Jesus heals Malcus' ear.

{ Come hedir to me sauely,
{ And I schalle þe sayne,

Luke xxii. 51.

{ In þe name of my fadir
{ Þat in heuene is most vpon hight,
{ Of thy hurtis be þou hole
{ In hyde and in hane.   285

Thurgh vertewe þi vaynes be at vayle.

Mal.   What! ille hayle! I hope þat I be hole.

Malcus is grateful.

Nowe I schrewe hym þis tyme þat gyvis tale,
To touche þe for þi trauayle.   289

25. { i **Jud.**   Do felaws be youre faithe
    { Late vs fange on in fere,

lf. 128 b.

For I haue on þis hyne [1].

{ ii **Mil.**   And I haue a loke on hym nowe.
{ Howe! felawes, drawe nere.   292

{ iii **Mil.**   Ȝis, by þe bonys þat þis bare,
{ Þis bourde schall he banne.

The soldiers close in and seize Jesus.

{ **Jesus.**   Euen like a theffe heneusly
{ Hurle ȝe me here,

'I am taken as a thief.'

{ I taught you in youre tempill,
{ Why toke ȝe me noȝt þanne?
{ Now haues mekenes on molde
{ All his power.   296

{ i **Jud.**   Do, do, laye youre handes
{ Be-lyue on þis lourdayne.

iii **Jud.**   We haue holde þis hauk in þi handis.

Mal.   Whe! ȝis, felawes, be my faith he is fast!

iv **Jud.**   Vn-to sir Cayphas I wolde þat he past [2];

Fare-wele for I wisse we will wenden.   301

[They lead Jesus away.

---

[1] The latter part of this line, which should rime with *banne*, is wanting.
[2] *Passen* in MS.

XXIX. THE BOWERS AND FLECCHERS[1].

Peter denies Jesus. Jesus examined by Caiaphas.

[PERSONS OF THE PLAY.

CAYPHAS.	JESUS.
ANNA (ANNAS).	PRIMA, SECUNDA
PRIMUS, SECUNDUS, TERTIUS,	MULIER[2]
QUARTUS MILES.	MALCHUS.]

Matth. xxvi. 57–
75.
John xviii. 12–27.
Caiaphas pro-
claims peace !
and his authority
and learning in
the law.

Mark xiv. 53–65.
Luke xxii. 54–71.

[SCENE I, *Hall in the High Priest's palace.*]

1. **Cayp.** PEES, bewshers, I bid no jangelyng ȝe make,

And sese sone of youre sawes, & se what I saye,

And trewe tente vnto me þis tyme þat ȝe take,

For I am a lorde lerned lelly in youre lay;   4

By connyng of clergy and casting of witte

Full wisely my wordis I welde at my will,

So semely in seete me semys for to sitte,

And þe lawe for to lerne you and lede it by skill.   8

What wyte so will oght with me

Full frendly in feyth am I foune right sone[3];

Come of, do tyte, late me see

Howe graciously I schall graunte hym his bone.   12

---

[1] This poem is chiefly in long lines of four accents, riming alternately, varied occasionally by shorter lines of three, sometimes four, accents. It is difficult to find regular stanzas, partly owing no doubt to the corrupt arrangement of the lines, for the old copyist seems to have been puzzled by the length of some of them, and confused ends and beginnings together, so losing many rimes. I have remedied these as far as I could.

[2] According to *Matt.* xxvi. 69–71 there were two women. The rubricator has marked the speaker of l. 89 as *primus* (j^us) *mulier*, but has not numbered either of the other speeches given to a *mulier*. L. 136 indicates two women.

[3] These two words in the MS. stand at end of l. 7.

2. Ther is nowder lorde ne lady lerned in þe lawe,
Ne Bisshoppe ne prelate þat preued is for pris,
Nor clerke in þe courte þat connyng will knawe,
With wisdam may were hym in worlde is so wise.   16
I haue þe renke and þe rewle of all þe ryall[1],   'I rule the king-
To rewle it by right als reasoune it is,   dom;
All domesmen on dese awe for to dowte me,
That hase thaym in bandome in bale or in blis,   20
Wherfore takes tente to my tales and lowtis vnto me.
And therfore, sir knyghtis[2],
I charge you chalange youre rightis,   I charge you look
To wayte both be day and by nyghtis   out for that boy.'
Of the bringyng of a boy in-to bayle.   25

3. i Miles. Yis, lorde, we schall wayte if any wonderes walke,
And freyne howe youre folkis fare þat are furth ronne.

ii Miles. We schall be bayne at youre bidding and it not   'We will do your
        to balke,   bidding as to the
                                            boy in bonds.'
Yf þei presente you þat boy in a bande boune.   29

Anna. Why syr? and is þer a boy þat will noght lowte
        to youre biding?

Cayph. Ya, sir, and of þe coriousenesse of þat karle þer   'Yes, there is
        is carping;   talk of the
                                         cleverness of
                                       that carl.
But I haue sente for þat segge halfe for hethyng.

Anna. What wondirfull werkis workis þat wighte?   lf. 129 b.

Cayph. Seke men and sori he sendis siker helyng,   34
And to lame men and blynde he sendis þer sight;   He heals the sick,
Of croked crepillis þat we knawe,   the lame and
                                         blinde,
Itt is to here grete wondering,
How þat he helis þame all on rawe,   38   to hear is great
                                         wonder;
And all thurgh his false happenyng.

---

[1] This word should perhaps be *ryalte*, which would rime with l. 19.
In the MS. it is *Ryatt*.
[2] Here the late corrector wrote *tunc dicunt lorde*.

4. I am sorie of a sight

it edges me to ire,
the way he breaks
our laws.'

Þat egges me to ire[1],

Oure lawe he brekis with all his myght,   42

Þat is moste his desire.

Oure Sabott day he will not safe,

But is aboute to bringe it downe,

And therfore sorowe muste hym haue;   46

May he be kacched in felde or towne,

For his false stevyn !

He defamys fowly þe godhed,

And callis hym selffe God sone of hevene.   50

' I know the boy,
and his mother
and father, a
carpenter.'

5. **Anna.** I haue goode knowlache of þat knafe,

Marie me menys, his modir highte,

And Joseph his fadir, as god me safe,

Was kidde and knowen wele for a wrighte.   54

But o thyng me mervayles mekill ouere all,

Of diuerse dedis þat he has done.

' He does it by
witchcraft.'

Cayph. With wicche-crafte he fares with-all,

Sir, þat schall ȝe se full sone.   58

Oure knyghtis þai are furth wente

To take hym with a traye,

By þis I holde hym shente,

He can not wende away.   62

' Will you rest,
and take some
wine ?

6. **Anna.** Wolde ȝe, sir, take youre reste,

This day is comen on hande,

And with wyne slake youre thirste?

lf. 130.
S viij.

Þan durste I wele warande,   66

Ye schulde haue tithandis sone

we shall soon
hear of the
soldiers that
were sent after
him.'

Of þe knyghtis þat are gone,

And howe þat þei haue done

To take hym by a trayne;   70

And putte all þought away,

And late youre materes reste.

[1] Lines 40 and 41 are one in the MS.

Cayph. I will do as ȝe saie,
Do gette vs wyne of þe best [1]. 74

7. { **i Miles.** My lorde! here is wyne
{ Þat will make you to wynke,

{ Itt is licoure full delicious,
{ My lorde, and you like,

{ Wherfore I rede drely
{ A draughte þat ȝe drynke,

{ For in þis contre, þat we knawe,
{ I wisse ther is none slyke. 78

Wherfore we counsaile you
This cuppe sauerly for to kisse.

Cayph. Do on dayntely, and dresse me on dees,
And hendely hille on me happing, 82
And warne all wightis to be in pees,
For I am late layde vnto napping. [*Lies down to sleep.*

Anna. My lorde with youre leue, 85
And it like you, I passe. [*Exit.*

Cayph. A diew, be vnte,
As þe manere is. [*Sleeps.*

' Here is wine, a delicious liquor,

none like it in this country.'

' Lift me up daintily, and cover me nicely; it is late.'

' I will go.'

' Adieu be unto thee.'

[SCENE II, *the same, near a fire.*]

i Mulier. Sir knyghtys, do kepe þis boy in bande,
For I will go witte what it may mene,
Why þat yone wighte was hym folowand
Erly and late, morne and eue[n] [2]. 92
He will come nere, he will not lette,
He is a spie, I warand, full bolde.

iii Miles. It semes by his sembland he had leuere be sette,
By þe feruent fire, to fleme hym fro colde. 96

Mulier. Ya, but and ȝe wiste as wele as I,

The woman saw a fellow following this prisoner, he must be a spy.

Matt. xxvi. 69–71.

' He'd like to sit by the hot fire.'
lf. 130 b.

[1] A later hand has written here in the margin, as an addition:—
' *Hic,* For be we ones well wett
the better we will reste!'
[2] The word looks like *eue,* if however we read it *ene,* the *u* and *n* being
nearly alike, of course the suggested *n* at the end is not needed.

S

What wonders þat þis wight has wrought,
And thurgh his maistir sorssery
Full derfely schulde his deth be bought.   100

'We have got the
one we sought so
long, the other
may go.'

iv Miles.   Dame, we haue hym nowe at will
Þat we haue longe tyme soughte,
Yf othir go by vs still,
Þer-fore we haue no thought.   104

The woman jeers
Peter ; he lurks
like an ape.

Mulier.   Itt were grete skorne þat he schulde skape,
Withoute he hadde resoune and skill,
He lokis lurkand like an nape,
I hope I schall haste me hym tille.   108
[*To Peter.*] Thou caytiffe! what meves þe stande
So stabill and stille in þi thoght?
Þou hast wrought mekill wronge in londe,
And wondirfull werkis haste þou wroght.   112
A! lorell, a leder of lawe,
To sette hym and suye has þou soght.
Stande furth and threste in yone thrawe,
Thy maistry þou bryng vn-to noght.   116

He looks like a
badger, bound
for baiting,

Wayte nowe, he lokis like a brokke,
Were he in a bande for to bayte;

or like an owl in
a stump awaiting
his prey.

Or ellis like an nowele in a stok,
Full preualy his pray for to wayte.   120

Petrus.   Woman, thy wordis and thy wynde thou not
          waste;

Peter denies
Jesus.

Of his company never are I was kende.
Þou haste þe mismarkid, trewly be traste;
Wherfore of þi misse þou þe amende.   124

The woman
repeats what he
had said for
Jesus.
lf. 131.
T j.

[ii] Mulier.   Þan gayne-saies þou here þe sawes þat þou
          saide,
How he schulde clayme to be callid God sonne,
{ And with þe werkis þat he wrought
{ Whils he walketh in þis flodde,
{ Baynly at oure bydding
{ Alway to be bonne.   12

{ **Petrus.** I will consente to youre sawes;
{ What schulde I saye more?

Peter gives in because women are crabbed by nature; but still denies.

{ For women are crabbed,
{ Þat comes þem of kynde.

{ But I saye as I firste saide,
{ I sawe hym neuere are,

{ But as a frende of oure felawschippe
{ Shall ye me aye fynde.   132

{ **Malchus.** Herke! knyghtis, þat are knawen
{ In this contre as we kenne,

{ Howe yone boy with his boste
{ Has brewed mekill bale,

Malcus shows how Peter has forsaken his master,

{ He has forsaken his maistir
{ Before ȝone womenne.

{ But I schall preue to ȝou pertly,
{ And telle you my tale.   136

{ I was presente with pepull
{ Whenne prese was full prest,

{ To mete with his maistir,
{ With mayne and with myght,

{ And hurled hym hardely,
{ And hastely hym arreste,

{ And in bandis full bittirly
{ Bande hym sore all þat nyght.   140

And of tokenyng of trouth schall I telle yowe,

{ Howe yone boy with a brande
{ Brayede me full nere,—

and tells how he struck off Malcus' ear,

Do move of theȝ materes emelle yowe,—

For swiftely he swapped of my nere.   144

His maistir with his myght helyd me all hole,

That by no syne I cowthe see noman cowþe it witten,

If. 131 b.

And þan[1] badde hym bere pees in euery ilke bale,

which the master healed.

For he þat strikis with a swerd with a swerde schall be
    streken.   148

[1] MS. has þon.

S 2

Latte se whedir grauntest þou gilte,
Do speke oon and spare not to telle vs,
Or full faste I schall fonde þe flitte,
The soth but þou saie here emelle vs.   152

'Come, speak!
tell the truth.'

Come of, do tyte ! late me see nowe,
In sauyng of thy selffe fro schame,
3a, and also for beryng of blame.

Petrus. I was neuere with hym in werke þat he wroght,

Peter's third
denial.

In worde nor in werke, in will nor in dede,   157
I knawe no corse þat 3e haue hidir brought,
In no covrte of this kith, if I schulde right rede.

'Listen, sirs, he
had denied his
master thrice.'

Malchus.   Here, sirs ! howe he sais and has forsaken 160
His maistir þis woman here twyes,
And newly oure lawe has he taken,
Thus hath he denyed hym thryes.

[Enter Jesus with 3rd and 4th soldiers.]

Jesus reminds
Peter,

Jesus.   Petir, Petir, þus saide I are,   164
When you saide you wolde abide with me,
In wele and woo, in sorowe and care,
Whillis I schulde thries for-saken be.

whose heart is
now shorn with
sorrow.

Petrus.   Alas ! þe while þat I come here !   168
That euere I denyed my lorde in quarte,
The loke of his faire face so clere
With full sadde sorowe sheris my harte.

iii Miles.   Sir knyghtis, take kepe of þis karll and b
    konnand ;   17
Be-cause of Sir Cayphas we knowe wele his þoght.
He will rewarde vs full wele þat dare I wele warand,
Whan he wete of oure werkis how wele we haue wroght.

The soldiers are
taking Jesus to
Caiaphas' hall,
but have to wait
without, as
lf. 132.
T ij.
it is night and
they within may
be asleep.

iv Miles.   Sir, þis is Cayphas halle here at hande,   17
Go we boldly with þis boy þat we haue here broght.
Nay, Sirs, vs muste stalke to þat stede and full still stand
For itt is nowe of þe nyght, yf þei nappe oght.   1

i **Miles** [*within*]. Say who is here? Say who is here?

iii **Miles**[1].   I, a frende,   180   A parley,

Well knawyn in þis contre for a knyght.   181

ii **Miles** [*within*]. Gose furthe, on youre wayes may
             yee wende,

For we haue herbered enowe for to-nyght.

i **Miles** [*within*]. Gose abakke, bewscheres, ʒe both are
             to blame,   184

To bourde whenne oure Busshopp is bonne to his bedde.   the bishop is
gone to bed.

iv **Miles**. Why Sir! it were worthy to welcome vs home,

We haue gone for þis warlowe and we haue wele spedde.

ii **Miles**. Why, who is þat?

    iii **Miles**. The Jewes kyng, Jesus by name. 188

i **Miles**. A! yee be welcome, þat dare I wele wedde.

My lorde has sente for to seke hym.   Ye will be welcome, wait a
minute.

    iv **Miles**. Loo! se here þe same.

ii **Miles**. Abidde as I bidde, and be noght adreed.

            [*Calls Caiaphas from his sleep.*

My lorde! my lorde! my lorde! here is layke, and ʒou   The man calls
Caiaphas, twice;
    list!   192   he does not want
to get up.

Cayph. Pees! loselles, leste ʒe be nyse.

i **Miles**. My lorde! it is wele, and ye wiste.

Cayph. What! nemen vs nomore, for it is twyes,   195

{ Þou takist non hede to þe haste
{ That we haue here on honde,

{ Go frayne howe oure folke faris   The soldiers who
were sent out
{ That are furth ronne.   have come back
with the fellow
{ ii **Miles**. My lorde youre knyghtis has kared   bound.
{ As ye þame commaunde,

{ And thei haue fallen full faire.
{ **Cayph.** Why and is þe foole foune?   [*Rises.* 199

Ya! lorde, þei haue brought a boy in a bande boune.   If. 132 b.

---

[1] In the MS. no speaker's name is set to line 179, and line 180–81 is
given to I *miles*. But the text shows that it was the 3rd and 4th soldiers
who were out by night, while the 1st and 2nd stayed in to guard their
'bishop.' 'I, a frende,' is set at beginning of l. 181.

Cayph [*calls*].   Where nowe! sir Anna! þat is one and
able to be nere.

[*Enter Annas.*]

Anna. My lorde, with youre leue me be-houes to be here[1].

Cayph. A ! sir, come nere and sitte we bothe in fere. 203

[*They sit in court.*]

Anna. Do sir, bidde þam bring in þat boy þat is bune.

Cayph. Pese now, sir Anna, be stille and late hym stande.

And late vs grope yf þis gome be grathly be-gune.

Anna. Sir, þis game is be-gune of þe best.

Nowe hadde he no force for to flee þame.   208

Cayp.[2] Nowe in faithe I am fayne he is fast,

Do lede in þat ladde, late me se þan.

ii Miles [*To* 3 *&* 4 *soldiers*]. Lo ! sir, we haue saide to
oure souereyne,

Gose nowe and suye to hym selfe for þe same thyng. 212

iii Miles. Milorde, to youre bidding we haue[3] buxom
and bayne,

Lo, here is þe belschere broght þat ye bad bring.

iv Miles. My lorde, fandis now to fere hym.

                    Cayph. Nowe I am fayne,

And felawes, faire mott ye fall for youre fynding[4].

{ **Anna.** Sir, and ye trowe þei be trewe
{ With-owten any trayne,   217

Bidde þayme telle you þe tyme of þe takyng.

Cayph. Say, felawes, howe wente ye so nemely by nyȝt ?

iii Miles. My lorde, was þere noman to marre vs ne
mende vs.   22(

iv Miles. My lorde, we had lanternes and light,

And some of his company kende vs.

---

[1] Lines 201, 202 are written as four lines in MS.

[2] The names of this and the last six speakers were given wrong by th
original rubricator, and are corrected in the margin as they stand above.

[3] *sic.*

[4] 'And felawes' stands at end of l. 215 in MS.

{ **Anna.**   But saie, how did he, Judas?

    iii Miles.   A! sir, full wisely and wele,

He markid vs his maistir emang all his men,   224

And kyssid hym full kyndely his comforte to kele,

By-cause of a countenaunce þat karll for to kenne.

Cayph.   And þus did he his deuere?

    iv Miles.   Ya, lorde, euere ilke a dele.

{ He taughte vs to take hym

{ The tyme aftir tenne.   228

Anna.   Nowe, be my feith! a faynte frend myght he
þer fynde.

{ **iii Miles.**   Sire, ye myghte so haue saide,

{ Hadde ye hymn sene þenne.   230

iv Miles.   He sette vs to þe same þat he solde vs,

And feyned to be his frende as a faytour,

This was þe tokenyng before þat he tolde vs.

Cayph.   Nowe trewly, þis was a trante of a traytour.   234

Anna.   ȝa, be he traytour or trewe geue we neuer tale,

But takes tente at þis tyme and here what he telles.

Cayph.   Now sees þat oure howsolde be holden here hale[1],

So þat none carpe in case but þat in court dwellis.   238

iii Miles.   A! lorde, þis brethell has brewed moche bale.

Cayph.   Therfore schall we spede vs to spere of his spellis.

Sir Anna, takeis hede nowe, and here hym.   241

Anna [*To Jesus*].   Say ladde, liste þe noght lowte to a lorde?

iv Miles[2].   No sir, with youre leue, we schall lere hym.

                 [*Attempts to strike Jesus.*

Cayph.   Nay sir, noght so, no haste.

Itt is no burde to bete bestis þat are bune,

And therfore with fayrenes firste we will hym fraste,

And sithen forþer hym furth as we haue fune.   247

And telle vs som tales, truly to traste.

Marginal notes:

The behaviour of Judas.

'We took Jesus after 10 o'clock,

by a sign from that false one.'

'This was a traitor's trick!'

'Make ready the court!'

'Make obeisance, lad.

If. 133 b.

'Do not beat the beast that is bound; we will question him fairly.'

---

[1] MS. has *hole*.   The line is two in the MS.

[2] In the MS. the next line is given to 4 *Miles*.   But an old corrector writes Cayphas to the speech beginning 'Nay,' which seems to be right.

Anna. Sir, we myght als wele talke
Tille a tome tonne !

I warande hym witteles,
Or ellis he is wrang wrayste,   250
Or ellis he waitis to wirke
Als he was are wonne.   251

iii Miles. His wonne was to wirke mekill woo,
And make many maystries emelle vs.

Cayph. And some schall he graunte or he goo,
Or muste yowe tente hym and telle vs.   255

iv Miles. My lorde, to witte þe wonderes þat he has
                              wroght,
For to telle you the tente it wolde oure tonges stere.

Cayph. Sen þe boy for his boste is in-to bale broght,
We will witte, or he wende, how his werkis were.   259

iii Miles. Oure Sabott day we saye
saves he right noght,
That he schulde halowe and holde
Full dingne and full dere.

iv Miles. No, sir, in þe same feste
Als we the sotte soughte,
He salued þame of sikenesse
On many[1] sidis seere.   263

Cayph. What þan, makes he þame grathely to gange ?
iii Miles. ʒa, lorde even forthe in euery ilke a toune,
He þame lechis to liffe after lange.
Cayph. A! this makes he by the myghtis of Mahounde. 267

iv Miles. Sir, oure stiffe tempill, þat made is of stone,
That passes any paleys of price for to preyse,
And it were doune to þe erth and to þe gronde gone,
This rebalde he rowses hym it rathely to rayse.   27

iii Miles. ʒa, lorde, and othir wonderis he workis grete
                              wone,
And with his lowde lesyngis he losis oure layes.

<hr>

[1] MS. has *sere sidis seere.*

Cayp.[1] Go lowse hym, and levis þan and láte me allone, — *'Loose him, I will speak with him.'*
For my selfe schall serche hym and here what he saies. 275

Anna. Herke! Jesus of Jewes will haue joie,
To spille all thy sporte for thy spellis[2].

Cayph. Do meve, felawe, of thy frendis þat fedde þe — *'Tell me of thy friends and thy doings. He has lost his tongue!'*
    be-forne,
And sithen, felowe, of thi fare, forþer will I freyne. 279

Do neven vs lightly; his langage is lorne!

iii Miles. My lorde, with youre leve, hym likis for to layne,
But and he schulde scape skatheles, it wer a full skorne,
For he has mustered emonge vs full mekil of his mayne. 283

iv Miles. Malkus, youre man, lord, þat had his ere schorne,
This harlotte full hastely helid it agayne.

Cayph. What! and liste hym be nyse for þe nonys,
And heres howe we haste to rehete hym.

Anna. Nowe, by Beliall bloode and his bonys, 288 — *Annas wishes to beat Jesus,*
I holde it beste to go bete hym!

Cayph. Nay, sir, none haste, we schall have game or
    we goo. 290 — *lf. 134 b.*
Caiaphas will try him again.
[*To Jesus.*] Boy, be not agaste if we seme gaye;
I coniure þe kyndely, and comaunde þe also,
By grete God þat is liffand & laste schall ay,
Yf þou be Criste, Goddis sonne, telle till vs two. 294

Jesus. Sir, þou says it þi selffe, and sothly I saye,
Þat I schall go to my fadir þat I come froo,
And dwelle with hym wynly in welthe all-way.

Cayph. Why! fie on þe faitoure vn-trewe! 298 — *They are scandalized. 'He hath spoken blasphemy.'*
Thy fadir haste þou fowly defamed,
Now nedis vs no notes of newe,
Hym selfe with his sawes has he schamed.

Anna. Nowe nedis nowdir wittenesse ne counsaille to call,
But take his sawes as he saieth in þe same stede,
He sclaunderes þe godhed and greues vs all, 304

---

[1] Corrector of 16th cent. The original has 4 *Miles.*
[2] MS. here has 'hic caret' in the 16th cent. hand.

He is worthy of
death.

Wherfore he is wele worthy to be dede.

And therfore sir, saies hym þe sothe.

Cayph.   Sertis so I schall.

Heres þou not, harlott?   Ille happe on thy hede [1] !

Aunswere here grathely to grete and to small,   308

And reche vs oute rathely som resoune, I rede [2].

Jesus.   My reasouns are not to reherse,   310

Nor they þat myght helpe me are noȝt here nowe.

Anna.   Say, ladde, liste þe make verse,   312

Do tell on, be-lyffe, late vs here nowe [3].

Jesus.   Sir, if I saie þe sothe, þou schall not assente,

But hyndir, or haste me [to] hynge ;

'I taught daily
in the temple, in
public, ye laid
no hold on me.'
Mark xiv. 49.
Luke xxii. 53.

I preched wher pepull was moste in present,   316

And no poynte in priuite to olde ne ȝinge [4].

And also in youre tempill I told myne entente,

Ye myght haue tane me þat tyme for my tellyng,

Wele bettir þan bringe me with brondis vnbrente,   320

And þus to noye me be nyght, and also for no-thyng.

If. 135.
T v.

Cayph.   For nothyng ! losell, þou lies !

Thy wordis and werkis will haue a wrekyng.

Jesus answers
Caiaphas,

Jesus.   Sire, sen þou with wrong so me wreyes,   324

Go, spere þame þat herde of my spekyng.

who turns wrath
against him.

{ **Cayph.**   A ! þis traitoure has tened me
{ With tales þat he has tolde,

{ Ȝitt hadde I neuere such hething
{ as of a harlott as hee.

John xviii. 22.

{ i **Miles.**   What ! fye on þe beggarr !
{ who made þe so bolde

{ To bourde with oure Busshoppe ?
{ thy bane schall I bee.   [*He strikes Jesus.*]   329

---

[1] Line 307 is two in the MS.
[2] The late corrector here adds:—
                'Sir, my reason is not to rehers ought.'
[3] In the MS. ll. 312, 313 stand before l. 310, throwing the two speeches
together, without sense. The copyist following ear more than eye, probably
reversed the couplets (which have the same rime) unconsciously.
[4] MS. has ȝonge.

Jesus. Sir, if my wordis be wrange or werse þan þou wolde,   'If I have spoken
A wronge wittenesse I wotte nowe are ȝe,   evil bear witness
of the evil.'
And if my sawes be soth þei mon be sore solde,   'You are too
Wherfore þou bourdes to brode for to bete me.   333   quick in beating
me.'
ii Miles. My lorde, will ȝe here? for Mahounde
No more now for to neven þat it nedis.
Cayph. Gose, dresse you and dyng ȝe hym doune,   Go, strike him
down, deafen us
And deffe vs no more with his dedis.   337   no more with his
deeds.
Anna. Nay, sir, þan blemysshe yee prelatis estatis;   'You must not do
that.'
ȝe awe to deme noman, to dede for to dynge.
Cayph. Why, sir, so were bettir þan be in debate,   'Better so than
contend.'
Ye see þe boy will noȝt bowe for oure bidding.   341
Anna. Nowe sir, ye muste presente þis boy unto sir Pilate,   Pilate is judge.
For he is domysman nere and nexte to þe king,
And late hym here all þe hole, how ye hym hate,
And whedir he will helpe hym or haste hym to hyng.   345
i Miles. My lorde, late men lede hym by nyght,   'Take him away
by night.'
So schall ye beste skape oute o skornyng.
ii Miles. My lorde, it is nowe in þe nyght,
I rede ȝe abide tille þe mornyng.   349
Cayph. Bewschere, þou sais þe beste, and so schall it be,   lf. 135 b.
But lerne yone boy bettir to bende and bowe.   'Teach him
obedience.'
i Miles. We schall lerne yone ladde, be my lewte,
For to loute vn-to ilke lorde like vn-to yowe.   353
Cayph. Ȝa, and felawes, wayte þat he be ay wakand.

[SCENE III, *the soldiers buffet Jesus.*]

ii Miles. Ȝis lorde, þat warant will wee!   Certainly we
Itt were a full nedles note to bidde vs nappe nowe.   shall not nap
now.
iii Miles. Sertis, will ye sitte, and sone schall ye see
Howe we schall play papse for þe pages prowe.   358
iv Miles. Late see, who stertis for a stole?   'Fetch a stool,
here is a dress
For I have here a hatir to hyde hym.   to cover him.'

i Miles.   Lo, here is one full fitte for a foole,
Go gete it, and sette þe beside hym.   362

ii Miles.   Nay I schall sette it my-selffe and frusshe
hym also.
Lo, here a shrowde for a shrewe, and of shene shappe !

iii Miles.   Playes faire in feere, and I schall fande to
feste it [1]

With a faire flappe, and þer is one and þer is ij;   366
And ther is iij, and there is iiij.

iii Miles.   Say nowe, with an nevill happe,
Who negheth þe nowe ? not o worde, no !

{ **iv Miles.**   Dose noddil on hym with neffes
{ That he noght nappe.   370

i Miles.   Nay nowe to nappe is no nede,
{ Wassaille, Wassaylle !
{ I warande hym wakande.

ii Miles.   3a, and bot he bettir bourdis can byde,
Such buffettis schall he be takande.   374

iii Miles.   Prophete ysaie to be oute of debate,
Iniuste percussit, man rede giffe you may.

{ **iv Miles.**   Those wordes are in waste,
{ What wenes þou he wate ?

{ It semys by his wirkyng
{ His wittes were awaye.   37‹

i Miles.   Now late hym stande as he stode in a foles state
For he likis no3t þis layke, my liffe dare I laye !

ii Miles.   Sirs, vs muste presente þis page to ser Pilate,
{ But go we firste to oure souerayne,
{ And see what he saies.   3‹

[They lead him back to Caiapho

---

[1] To make lines 365, 366 into sense, and also to agree with the rin
they should perhaps be read thus :—
     'Playes faire in feere, and there is one and there is two
     I shall fande to feste it with a faire flappe.'
Pronounce *four* of the next line *fo,* to ryme with *two,* and *also* before a
no after it.

iii Miles. My lorde! we haue bourded with þis boy,
And holden hym full hote emelle vs.

Cayph. Thanne herde ye some japes of joye?

iv Miles. The devell haue þe worde, lorde, he wolde
telle vs. 386

but that he will not say a word.

Anna. Sir, bidde belyue, þei goo and bynde hym agayne,
So þat he skape noght, for þat were a skorne.

Cayph. Do telle to sir Pilate oure pleyntes all pleyne,
And saie, þis ladde with his lesyngis has oure lawes
lorne; 390
And saie þis same day muste he be slayne,
Be-cause of sabott day þat schalbe to-morne ;
And saie þat we come oure selffe for certayne,
And forto fortheren þis fare, fare yee be-forne. 394

Tell Pilate our complaints, and that this lad must be slain to-day because it is Sabbath to-morrow.

i Miles. My lorde, with youre leve, vs muste wende,
Oure message to make as we maye.

Anna. Sir, youre faire felawschippe we be-take to þe
fende[1].

Cayph. Goose onne nowe, and daunce forth in þe deuyll
way. 398

---

[1] L. 397 is two in the MS.

XXX. THE TAPITERES AND COUCHERS.

The Dream of Pilate's Wife: Jesus before Pilate.

[PERSONS OF THE PLAY.

PILATUS.	DIABOLUS.
VXOR PILATI *alias* DOMINA.	CAYPHAS.
BEDELLUS.	ANNA [ANNAS].
ANCILLA.	PRIMUS ET SECUNDUS
FILIUS [PILATI] [1].	MILITES.]

[SCENE I, *Pilate's judgment-hall.*]

1. **Pil.** YHE cursed creatures þat cruelly are cryand,

Matth. xxvii.
11-19.

    { Restreyne you for stryuyng
    { For strengh of my strakis,

Luke xxiii. 1-7.
Gosp. of Nichod.
ch. ii.
Pilate threatens
brawlers and
traitors.

    { Youre pleyntes in my presence
    { Vse plately applyand,

    { Or ellis þis brande in youre braynes
    { Schalle [2] brestis and brekis.   4

    Þis brande in his bones brekis,
    What brawle þat with brawlyng me brewis,
    That wrecche may not wrye fro my wrekis [3],

---

[1] The rubricator, in marking Filius, did not perceive that the son is the same boy throughout the piece, and gave 2 *Fil.* for scene i (ll. 116, 120), and 1 *Fil.* for scenes ii, iii.

[2] *Schalle* appears to be in error for *sone*, or a similar adverb, *brestis and brekis* being pres. indicative, not infinitive as required by the auxiliary.

[3] MS. has 'werkis.' This piece presents several difficulties; stanzas 8, 22, 30 are irregular; st. 10, 13, 15, 16, 47, 48 are imperfect; other changes I suggest in the notes. The first 18 stanzas rime a b a b b c b b b. With st. 19 a fourth rime is introduced, a b a b c d d d c.

Nor his sleyghtis noȝt slely hym slakis,
Latte þat traytour noȝt triste in my trewys.　　　9

2. { For sir Sesar was my sier
　　{ And I sothely his sonne,
　　That exelent Emperoure exaltid in hight,
　　Whylk all þis wilde worlde with wytes had wone,
　　And my modir hight Pila þat proude was o pight,　　13
　　O Pila þat prowde and Atus hir fadir he hight.
　　This pila was hadde in to Atus,
　　Nowe renkis, rede yhe it right?
　　For þus schortely I haue schewid you in sight,
　　Howe I am prowdely preued Pilatus.　　18

3. Loo! Pilate, I am proued a prince of grete pride,
　　I was putte in to Pounce þe pepill to presse,
　　And sithen Sesar hym selffe with exynatores be his side,
　　Remytte me to þe remys, þe renkes to redresse.　　22
　　And yitte am I grauntid on grounde, as I gesse
　　To justifie and juge all þe Iewes[1].
　　A! luffe! here lady! no lesse,　　[*Enter dame Percula.*
　　Lo! sirs, my worthely wiffe, þat sche is!
　　So semely, loo! certayne scho schewys.　　27

4. Vx. Pil. Was nevir juge in þis Jurie of so jocounde
　　　　generacion,
　　Nor of so joifull genolgie to gentrys enioyned,
　　As yhe, my duke doughty, demar of dampnacion,
　　{ To princes and prelatis
　　{ Þat youre preceptis perloyned.　　31
　　Who þat youre perceptis pertely perloyned[2],
　　With drede in to dede schall ye dryffe hym,
　　By my trouthe, he vntrewly is stonyd,
　　Þat agaynste youre behestis hase honed;
　　All to ragges schall ye rente hym and ryue hym.　　36

Marginal notes:

'Caesar was my sire,

Pila my mother, daughter of Atus,

whence I am Pilatus.

Cæsar and his senators sent me to these realms.

Ah! here is my love, my wife.'

lf. 138.
T viij.

Pilate's wife salutes her lord.

---

[1] Lines 23, 24 are reversed in the MS.
[2] *Pertely and perloyned* are both written with *p* contraction.

'I am dame Pro-
cula,

5. I am dame precious Percula[1], of prynces þe prise,
Wiffe to Sir Pilate here prince with-outen pere,
All welle of all womanhede I am, wittie and wise,

behold my
comely face,
and my rich
robes;

Consayue nowe my countenaunce so comly & clere.   40
The coloure of my corse is full clere,
And in richesse of robis I am rayed,

no one has a nicer
companion,
though I say it.'
' You may say so !

Ther is no lorde in þis londe as I lere,
In faith þat hath a frendlyar feere,
{ Than yhe my lorde,
{ My-selffe yof I saye itt.   45

6. { **Pil.** Nowe saye itt save may ye saffely,
{ For I will certefie þe same[2].

Vxor. Gracious lorde, gramercye, youre gode worde is
gayne.

let me kiss you.'

Pil. Yhitt for to comforte my corse, me must kisse you,
madame !

Vx. To fulfille youre forward, my fayre lorde, in faith I
am fayne.   49

Pil. Howe ! howe ! felawys, nowe in faith I am fayne
Of theis lippis, so loffely are lappid,
In bedde is full buxhome and bayne.

'There is no use
hiding it, all
ladies like to be
kissed.'

Domina. Yha, sir, it nedith not to layne,
{ All ladise we coveyte þan
{ Bothe to be kyssed and clappid.   54

[Enter Beadle (of the court).]

The beadle ob-
jects to this
behaviour
If. 138 b.
in court,

7. Bed. My liberall lorde, O leder of lawis,
O schynyng schawe þat all schames escheues,
I beseke you my souerayne, assente to my sawes,
As ye are gentill juger and justice of Jewes.   5[

---

[1] The name of Pilate's wife is here written pcula, i. e. Percula; in the
Coventry accounts it is written pcula, i. e. Procula. See Th. Sharp'
Dissertation on Coventry Mysteries, p. 30. The name does not occur i
the Coventry play itself on the Dream of Pilate's Wife. It is Procula i
the Gospel of Nichodemus, ch. ii.

[2] It may be suggested that 'saue' and 'For' are too much in l. 46, an
that l. 49 would be perfect without 'in faith.'

Dom. Do herke, howe þou, javell, jangill of Iewes!
Why, go bette, horosonne boy, when I bidde þe.

but the lady is angry.

Bed. Madame, I do but þat diewe is.

Dom. But yf þou reste of thy resoune, þou rewis,
For all is a-cursed carle, hase in, kydde þe [1]!   63

8. Pil. Do mende you, madame, and youre mode be amendand,

Pilate will listen to him;

For me semys it wer sittand to se what he sais.

Dom. Mi lorde, he tolde nevir tale þat to me was tendand,
But with wrynkis and with wiles to wend me my weys. 67

{ **Bed.** Gwisse [2] of youre wayes to be wendand,
{ Itt langis to oure lawes.

{ **Dom.** Loo! lorde, þis ladde with his lawes,
{ Howe thynke ye it prophitis wele
His prechyng to prayse?

she objects.

Pil. Yha, luffe, he knawis
All oure custome [3], I knawe wele.   72

Pilate says, 'he knows our customs.'

9. Bed. My seniour, will ye see nowe þe sonne in youre sight,
For his stately strengh he stemmys in his stremys,

' My lord, the sun is setting,

Behalde ovir youre hede how he holdis fro hight
And glydis to þe grounde with his glitterand glemys [4]. 76
To þe grounde he gois with his bemys,
And þe nyght is neghand anone;

night comes on;

Yhe may dome aftir no dremys,

{ But late my lady here
{ With all her light lemys,

let my bright lady go home,

Wightely go wende till her wone.   81

If. 139.
V j.

10. For ye muste sitte, sir, þis same nyght of lyfe and of lyme;

for you must sit in judgment this night.

{ Itt is noȝt leeffull for my lady,
{ By the lawe of this lande,

---

[1] L. 63 stands as two lines in MS., with 'þou rewis' of l. 62 as part of the first.

[2] The last section of st. 8 is evidently wrong; the rimes are lost, even if *lawes* be pronounced *layes*, as often occurs (e.g. l. 363).

[3] Lines 71 and part of 72 stand as one in MS.

[4] Lines 75, 76 are written as three in the MS.

T

The lady must
not stop at night,

$\left\{\begin{array}{l}\text{In dome for to dwelle} \\ \text{Fro þe day waxe ought dymme ;}\end{array}\right.$

she might stagger
in the street.'

$\left\{\begin{array}{l}\text{For scho may stakir in þe strete} \\ \text{But scho stalworthely stande.}\end{array}\right.$ 85

Late hir take hir leue whill þat light is [1].

Pil. Nowe wiffe, þan ye blythely be buskand.

Dom. I am here, sir, hendely at hande.

'The fellow has
said what is
right.'

Pil. Loo ! þis is renke has vs redde als right is.   90

11. Dom. Youre comaundement to kepe to kare forþe y
caste me,

'I will hinder
you no longer.'

My lorde, with youre leue, no lenger y lette yowe.

'Before you go,
you must have
some wine.'

$\left\{\begin{array}{l}\textbf{Pil.}\ \ \text{Itt were appreue to my persone} \\ \text{Þat preuely ȝe paste me,}\end{array}\right.$

$\left\{\begin{array}{l}\text{Or ye wente fro this wones} \\ \text{Or with wynne ȝe had wette yowe.}\end{array}\right.$ 94

$\left\{\begin{array}{l}\text{Ye schall wende forthe with wynne} \\ \text{Whenne þat ȝe haue wette yowe.}\end{array}\right.$

Get some drink !
Come sit down,
here it is.'

Gete drinke ! what dose þou ! haue done !   [*Calls out.*

Come semely, beside me, and sette yowe,

Loke ! nowe it is even here, þat I are behete you,

Ya, 'saie it nowe sadly & sone [2].   99

'You begin, my
lord.'

12. Dom. Itt wolde gladde me, my lorde, if ȝe gudly begynne.

Pil. Nowe I assente to youre counsaille, so comely &
clere [3];

'Drink, madam.'

Nowe drynke [ȝe], madame : to ḍeth all þis dynne !

'You need not
teach me !'

Dom. Iff it like yowe myne awne lorde, I am not to
lere ;   103

This lare I am not to lere.

If. 139 b.

Pil. Yitt efte to youre damysell, madame.

'Here is for the
damsel also.'

Dom. In thy hande, holde nowe, and haue here.

Anc. Gramarcy, my lady so dere.

Pil. Nowe fares-wele, and walke on youre way.   108

---

[1] A line (should be l. 86) is wanting here.

[2] In the MS. the words ' what does þou, haue done' are repeated after
'Loke!' l. 98, and 'þat ... you' stand at beginning of l. 99.

[3] MS. has *clene*.

13. Dom. Now fare wele, ye frendlyest, youre fomen to fende[1]. 'Farewell, my dear.'

Pil. Nowe fare wele, ye fayrest figure þat euere did fode fede, 'Farewell, ladies.

And fare wele, ye damysell, in dede.

   An. My lorde, I comande me to youre ryalte. 112

   Pil. Fayre lady, he þis schall you lede,

   [*To his son*] Sir, go with þis worthy in dede, Son, go with her obediently.

{ And what scho biddis you doo,

{ Loke þat buxsome you be. 115

14. Fil. I am prowde and preste to passe on a passe,

To go with þis gracious, hir gudly to gyde.

   Pil. Take tente to my tale, þou turne on no trayse,

Come tyte and telle me yf any tythyngis be-tyde. 119 Come and tell me if anything happens.'

   Fil. If any tythyngis my lady be-tyde,

I schall full sone sir, witte you to say.

This semely schall I schewe by hir side, The son goes.

Be-lyffe sir, no lenger we byde.

         [*Exeunt Percula, son, and damsel.*

   Pil. Nowe fares-wele, and walkes on youre way. 124

15. Nowe wente is my wiffe, yf it wer not hir will,

And scho rakis tille hir reste as of no thyng scho rought. ' My lady goes to her rest,

Tyme is, I telle þe, þou tente me vntill, it is time, friend,

And buske þe belyue, belamy, to bedde þat y wer broght. 128 that I went to bed.'

And loke I be rychely arrayed[2].

   Bed. Als youre seruaunte I haue sadly it sought, If. 140. V ij.

And þis nyght, sir, newe schall ye noght, 'All is ready, you shall not be

I dare laye, fro ye luffely be layde. 132 annoyed.'

        [*Pilate goes to his couch.*

16. Pil. I comaunde þe to come nere, for I will kare to my couche,

Haue in thy handes hendely and heue me fro hyne, ' Lift me into bed, but don't hurt me.'

But loke þat þou tene me not with þi tastyng, but tendirly me touche,

---

[1] Stanza 12 is somewhat corrupt, lines 104, 105 being imperfect; the two first lines of st. 13 are wanting.

[2] There is a line missing here, before l. 129.

'Sir, you weigh
heavy!'

{ **Bed.**   A! sir, yhe whe wele!

{ **Pil.**   Yha, I haue wette with me wyne[1].   136

'Tuck me up
evenly, I will
sleep for the
present. Let no
noise be made.

Yhit helde doune and lappe me even [here], [*Is laid down.*

For I will slelye slepe vnto synne.

Loke þat no man nor no myron of myne

With no noyse be neghand me nere.   140

17. { **Bed.**   Sir, what warlowe yow wakens

{ With wordis full wilde,

{ Þat boy for his brawlyng

{ Were bettir be vn-borne.

Chastise those
who chatter and
roar.'

{ **Pil.**   Yha, who chatteres, hym chastise,

{ Be he churle or childe,

{ For and he skape skatheles

{ Itt were to vs a grete skorne.   144

Yf skatheles he skape, it wer a skorne;

What rebalde þat redely will rore,

I schall mete with þat myron to-morne,

And for his ledir lewdenes hym lerne to be lorne.

'Sleep, sir, say
no more.'

Bed.   Whe! so sir, slepe ye, and saies nomore.   149

[SCENE II; *Chamber of dame Percula, Pilate's wife.*]

18. **Dom.**   Nowe are we at home, do helpe yf ye may,

'I will get to
rest.'

For I will make me redye and rayke to my reste.

Anc.   Yhe are werie, madame, for-wente of youre way,

'Your bed is
ready.'
lf. 140 b.

Do boune you to bedde, for þat holde I beste.   153

Fil.   Here is a bedde arayed of þe beste.

'Cover me, and
go.'

Dom.   Do happe me, and faste hense ye hye.

Anc.   Madame, anone all dewly is dressid.

'You shall not
be disturbed.'

Fil.   With no stalkyng nor no striffe be ye stressed.

Dom.   Nowe be yhe in pese, both youre carpyng and
crye.   158

---

[1] The last part of this stanza seems to be imperfect, the first four lines only are complete.

[All sleep, enter Satan.]

19. **Diab.** Owte! owte! harrowe! in-to bale am I brought,
    This bargayne may I banne,
    But yf y wirke some wile, in wo mon I wonne,
    This gentilman Jesu of cursednesse he can
    Be any syngne þat I see, þis same is goddis sonne.   162
    And he be slone, oure solace will sese,
    He will saue man saule fro oure sonde,
    And refe vs þe remys þat are rounde.
    I will on stiffely in þis stounde,
    Vnto Sir Pilate wiffe, pertely, and putte me in prese.   167
             [Whispers to Percula.

The devil will work against Jesus.

'If Jesus is slain, I lose my realms. I'll go to Pilate's wife.'

20. O woman! be wise and ware, and wonne in þi witte,
    Ther schall a gentilman, Jesu, vn-justely be juged
    Byfore thy husband in haste, and with harlottis be hytte.
    And þat doughty to-day to deth þus be dyghted,   171
    Sir Pilate, for his prechyng, and þou,
    With nede schalle ye namely be noyed,
    Your striffe and youre strenghe schal be stroyed,
    Youre richesse schal be refte you þat is rude,
    With vengeaunce, and þat dare I auowe.   176
             [Percula awakes, starting.

'Woman, if the gentleman, Jesus, is unjustly doomed, Pilate and you will be destroyed.'

21. **Dom.** A! I am drecchid with a dreme full dredfully to
        dowte,
    Say, childe! rise vppe radly, and reste for no roo,
    Thow muste launce to my lorde and lowly hym lowte,
    Comaunde me to his reuerence, as right will y doo.   180

Fil. O! what! schall I trauayle þus tymely þis tyde?
    Madame, for the drecchyng of heuen,
    Slyke note is newsome to neven,
    And it neghes vnto mydnyght full even.

Dom. Go bette, boy, I bidde no lenger þou byde,   185

22. And saie to my souereyne, þis same is soth þat I send hym.
    All naked þis nyght as I napped,

'Ah! I am tormented with a horrid dream! I say, child! get up and run to my lord.'

'Must I go so early? By God's passion it is disagreeable.'

If. 141.
V iij.

'Go, boy, tell him as I slept, naked, a dream struck me, of Jesus that just man; I beg he

may be de-
livered.

With tene and with trayne was I trapped

With a sweuene, þat swiftely me swapped,   189

Of one Iesu, þe juste man þe Iewes will vndoo;

She prayes tente to þat trewe man, with tyne be noȝt
trapped,

But als a domes man dewly to be dressand,   192

And lelye delyuere þat lede.

'Madam, I will
go, but I will
nap first.'

Fil. Madame, I am dressid to þat dede ;

But firste will I nappe in þis nede,

For he hase mystir of a morne slepe þat mydnyght is
myssand.   [*Sleeps.*] 196

[Scene III ; *On the way from the palace of Caiaphas to
Pilate's judgment-hall.*]

John xviii. 28.   **23.** { **An.** Sir Cayphas, ye kenne wele

{ This caytiffe we haue cached,

{ That ofte tymes in oure tempill

{ Hase teched vntrewly,

Annas and Caia-
phas agree to
take Jesus before
Pilate.

{ Oure meyne with myght

{ At mydnyght hym mached,

{ And hase drevyn hym till his demyng

{ For his dedis vndewly.   200

Wherfore I counsaile þat kyndely we care [1]

Vnto sir Pilate, oure prince, and pray hym

That he for oure right will arraye hym,

This faitour for his falsed to flay hym,

{ For fro we saie hym þe soth

{ I schall sitte hym full sore.   205

24. Cay. Sir Anna, þis sporte haue ye spedely aspied,

As I am pontificall prince of all prestis.

'He has hewn
our hearts from
our breasts.'

We will prese to Sir Pilate, and presente hym with pride,

With þis harlott þat has hewed owre hartis fro oure

brestis,   20

¹ MS. has *carie.*

Thurgh talkyng of tales vntrewe. And þerfor, Sir knyghtis! If. 141 b.

i Mil. Lorde¹!

Cay. Sir Knyghtis, þat are curtayse and kynde,   'Soldiers, let the
We charge you þat chorle be wele chyned,   churl be chained
Do buske you and grathely hym bynde,   and bound.'
And rugge hym in ropes, his rase till he rewe.   214

25. i Mil. Sir, youre sawes schall be serued schortely and sone,   They bind Jesus.
Yha, do felawe, be thy feith, late vs feste þis faitour full fast².

ii Mil. I am douty to þis dede, delyuer, haue done,
Latte vs pulle on with pride till his poure be paste.   218

i Mil. Do haue faste and halde at his handes.

ii Mil. For this same is he þat lightly avaunted,
And god sone he grathely hym graunted.

i Mil. He bese hurled for þe highnes he haunted;
Loo! he stonyes for vs, he stares where he standis.   223

26. ii Mil. Nowe is the brothell boune for all þe boste þat he   Now he is ready.
      blowne,
And þe laste day he lete no lordynges myзt lawe hym ³.

An. Ya, he wende þis worlde had bene haly his awne,
{ Als ye are dowtiest to-day
{ Tille his demyng ye drawe hym.   227

{ And þan schall we kenne
{ How þat he canne excuse hym.

i Mil. Here, ye gomes, gose a rome, giffe vs gate,   'Here, you
We muste steppe to yone sterne of a-state.   fellows, make
     way!

ii Mil. We muste yappely wende in at þis yate,
For he þat comes to courte, to curtesye muste vse hym. 232

27. { **i Mil.** Do rappe on the renkis,   If. 142.
    { Þat we may rayse with oure rolyng;   V iiij.

    { Come forthe, sir coward!   Come forth,
    { Why cowre ye behynde.   *[Knocks at Pilate's hall.*   coward.'

---

¹ The line must end with *vntrewe*, which rimes with *rewe* of l. 214. The opyist was perhaps thinking aloud as he wrote *and þerfor*; the following our words seem to be a prose call and answer.
² Line 216 is complete without the words *be thy feith*.   ³ MS. has *lawne*.

*Who are you with that noise?'

Bed. [*within.*] O, what javellis are ye þat jappis with
   gollyng?

'Words are but wind,

i Mil. A! goode sir, be noȝt wroth, for wordis are as þe
   wynde.   236

Bed. I saye, gedlynges, gose bakke with youre gawdes.

let us tell you.'

ii Mil. Be sufferand, I beseke you,
And more of þis matere yhe meke yow.

'You knaves, I'll kill you.'

Bed. Why, vnconand knaves, an I cleke yowe,
I schall felle yow, be my faith, for all youre false frawdes¹. 241

28. { Pil. [*within, in bed.*] Say childe, ill cheffe you!

'Who is chattering so?'

{ What churlles are so claterand?

'Ignorant knaves.'

Bed. My lorde, vn-conand knaves þei crye and þei call.

Pil. Gose baldely beliffe, and þos brethellis be battand,

'Beat and put them in prison,

And putte þam in prisoune vppon peyne þat may fall. 245
Yha, spedely spir þam yf any sporte can þei spell,
Yha, and loke what lordingis þei be.

Bed. My lorde, þat is luffull in lee,
I am boxsom and blithe to your blee.

but see if they have any tidings.'

{ Pil. And if they talke any tythyngis
{ Come tyte and me tell.   250

The beadle asks. **29.** { Bed. [*To the soldiers.*] My felawes, by youre faith,
{ Can ye talke any tythandis?²

'The priests have taken

i Mil. Yha, sir Cayphas and Anna ar come both to-gedir.
To sir Pilate o pounce and prince of oure lawe;

If. 142 b.

{ And þei haue laughte a lorell

a lawless wretch.'

{ Þat is lawles and liddir.   25.

Bed. My lorde! my lorde!   [*Runs to Pilate*

Pil. Howe!³

'My lord, get up quickly, Sir Caiaphas and Annas have brought a traitor!'

Bed. My lorde, vnlappe yow belyve wher ye lye.
Sir Cayphas to youre courte is caried,
And sir Anna, but a traytour hem taried,

---

¹ This line is two in MS.
² *Read* ' Can you talke any tythands, by your faith, my felawes?' *
correspond to l. 253.
³ The beadle's call and Pilate's answer appear to be outside the verse,
in st. 24 they do not belong to the other lines, which are complete witho
them.

Many wight of þat warlowe has waried,
They haue brought hym in a bande, his balis to bye. 259

30. **Pil.** But are thes sawes certayne in soth þat þou saies?

The priests salute Pilate.

Pilate is doubtful, but afterwards glad.

  Bed. Yha, lorde, þe states yondir standis,
  For striffe are they stonden.

  Pil. Now þan am I light as a roo,
  And ethe for to rayse,   [*He rises.*

  Go bidde þam come in both
  And the boye þey haue boune. 263

  Bed. Siris, my lorde geues leue
  Inne for to come.

The beadle bids all to enter.

[SCENE IV; *Pilate's judgment hall; enter Caiaphas and company.*]

  Cay. Hayle! prince þat is pereles in price,
Ye are leder of lawes in þis lande,
Youre helpe is full hendely at hande.

The priests salute Pilate.

  An. Hayle! stronge in youre state for to stande,
Alle þis dome muste be dressed at youre dulye deuyse. 269

31. **Pil.** Who is there[1]? my prelates?
              Cay. Yha, lorde.
  Pil. Nowe be ʒe welcome, i-wisse!

If. 143. V v.

  Cay. Gramercy, my souerayne,
  But we beseke you all-same,

  By-cause of wakand you vnwarly
  Be noght wroth with þis.

They excuse themselves for waking him.

  For we haue brought here a lorell,
  He lokis like a lambe. 273

  Pil. Come byn, you bothe, and to þe benke brayde yow.

  Cay. Nay gud sir, laugher is leffull for vs.

  Pil. A! sir, Cayphas, be curtayse yhe bus.

  An. Nay goode lorde, it may not be þus.

He bids them 'come ben,' and sit by him; they affect humility.

  Pil. Sais no more, but come sitte you beside me,
  In sorowe as I saide youe. 278

---

[1] The MS. has *thenne* or *theme*, it is uncertain which.

[Enter Pilate's son.]

32. **Fil.** Hayle! þe semelieste seeg vndir sonne sought,
           Hayle! þe derrest duke and doughtiest in dede.

' Welcome, beau sire! what message from my lady?'

    { **Pil.** Now bene-veneuew, beuscher,
    { What boodworde haste þou brought?
           Hase any langour my lady newe laught in þis hede?   282

    Fil. Sir, þat comely comaundes hir youe too,

The boy relates the dream.

           And sais, al nakid þis nyght as sche napped,
           With tene and with traye was sche trapped,
           With a sweuene þat swiftely hir swapped,
           Of one Jesu þe juste man, þe Iewes will vndo.   287

33. She beseches you as hir souerayne þat symple to saue,
    Deme hym noght to deth, for drede of vengeaunce.

' I suppose this is he that ye bring?'
lf. 143 b.

    Pil. What! I hope þis be he þat hyder harlid ȝe haue.

    { **Cay.** Ya, sir, þe same and þe selffe;
    { But þis is but a skaunce,   291

Caiaphas says Jesus has wrought the dream with witchcraft.

           He with wicchecrafte þis wile has he wrought [1],
           Some feende of his sand has he sente,
           And warned youre wiffe or he wente,
           Yowe [2]! þat schalke shuld not shamely be shente.
           Þis is sikir in certayne, and soth [3] schulde be sought.   296

Annas says he has done many wonders through devilcraft.

34. **An.** Yha, thurgh his fantome and falshed and fendes-craft,
    { He has wroght many wondir
    { Where he walked full wyde,
    { Wherfore my lorde it wer leeffull
    { His liffe were hym rafte.

Pilate sees their evil feelings;

    Pil. Be ye neuere so bryme, ye boþe bus abide,   30
           But if þe traytoure be taught for vntrewe,
           And þerfore sermones you no more;

he will judge for himself.

           I will sikirly sende hym selffe fore,

---

[1] Line 292 is two in MS.
[2] There is a dot after *yowe* in the MS., perhaps indicating a pause of e
clamation, as after ha! p. 347, l. 322. The word is either an interjectic
or an adverb.
[3] *Soh* in MS. seems to be intended for *soth.*

And se what he sais to þe sore.

{ Bedell, go brynge hyme,

{ For of þat renke haue I rewþe. 305

'Beadle, fetch him.'

35. { **Bed.** This forward to fulfille

{ Am I fayne moued in myn herte[1];

Gosp. of Nichodemus, ch. i.

{ Say, Jesu, þe juges and þe Iewes

{ Hase me enioyned

{ To bringe þe before þam,

{ Even bounden as þou arte,

{ Yone lordyngis to lose þe

{ Full longe haue þei heyned. 309

{ But firste schall I wirschippe þe

{ With witte and with will,

The beadle goes, but first worships Jesus.

This reuerence I do þe for-thy [*He bows to Jesus.*

For wytes þat wer wiser þan I,

They worshipped þe full holy on hy,

And with solempnite sange Osanna till. 314

lf. 144. V vj.

36. i Mil. My lorde þat is leder of lawes in þis lande,

All bedilis to your biding schulde be boxsome and bayne,

The soldiers are scandalised at the beadle's behaviour.

{ And ȝitt þis boy here before yowe

{ Full boldely was bowand,

{ To worschippe þis warlowe.

{ Me thynke we wirke all in vayne. 318

ii Mil. Yha, and in youre presence he prayed hym of pees,

In knelyng on knes to þis knave,

He be-soughte hym his seruaunte to saue.

Caip. Loo, lord such arrore amange þem þei haue,

It is grete sorowe to see, no seeg may it sese. 323

'Such contempt of your worship ought to be avoided in your sight.'

37. It is no menske to youre manhed þat mekill is of myght,

To for-bere such forfettis þat falsely are feyned,

Such spites in especiall wolde be eschewed in your sight.

{ **Pil.** Sirs, moves you noȝt in þis matere,

{ But bese myldely demeaned, 327

For yone curtasie I kenne had som cause.

'Calm yourselves, there must be a reason for it.'

---

[1] In the MS. *moved* stands after *herte.*

An.   In youre sight sir, þe soth schall I saye,
As ye are prince, take hede I you praye,
Such a lourdayne vnlele, dare I laye,
{ Many lordis of oure landis
{ Might lede fro oure lawes.   332

Pilate questions
the beadle,

38. { **Pil.** [*to the Beadle.*]   Saye, losell, who gaue þe leve
       { So for to lowte to yone ladde,

{ And solace hym in my sight
lf. 144 b. { So semely, þat I sawe?

{ **Bed.**   A! gracious lorde, greue you noght
{ For gude case I hadde.

{ Yhe comaunded me to care,
{ Als ye kende wele and knawe,   336
To Jerusalem on a journay, with seele;

he replies that he
saw Jesus met in
Jerusalem by the
people when
Hosanna was
sung to him.

And þan þis semely on an asse was sette,
And many men myldely hym mette,
Als a god in þat grounde þai hym grette,
Wele semand hym in waye with worschippe lele.   341

39. Osanna þei sange, þe sone of dauid,
Riche men with þare robes þei ranne to his fete,
And poure folke fecched floures of þe frith,
And made myrthe and melody þis man for to mete.   345

'What does
Hosanna mean?'

{ **Pil.**   Nowe gode sir, be þi feith,
{ What is Osanna to saie?

{ **Bed.**   Sir, constrew it we may
{ Be langage of þis lande as I leue,

The beadle
explains it.

It is als moche to me for to meve,
(Youre prelatis in þis place can it preue),
{ Als, ' oure Sauiour and souerayne,
{ Þou saue vs, we praye.'   35

Pilate appeals to
the lords,

40. { **Pil.**   Loo, senioures, how semes yow
       { Þe soþe I you saide?

Cai.   Yha, lorde, þis ladde is full liddir, be þis light!
Yf his sawes wer serchid and sadly assaied,

{ Saue youre reuerence,
His resoune þei rekenne noȝt with right.   354   *but they say the man construes wrongly,*

This caytiffe þus cursedly can construe vs.

Bed. Sirs, trulye þe trouþe I haue tolde,
Of þis wighte ȝe haue wrapped in wolde.

An. [*Rising.*] I saie, harlott, thy tonge schulde þou holde,   *lf. 145. V vij.*
And noght agaynste þi maistirs to meve þus.   359   *and angrily would silence him.*

41. Pil. Do sese of youre seggyng, and I schall examyne full   *Pilate is annoyed at their persist-ence.*
    sore.

An. Sir, demes hym to deth, or dose hym away.

Pil. Sir, haue ye saide?
          An.   Yha, lorde.
Pil. Nowe go sette you with sorowe and care,   *'Sit down, be quiet.'*
For I will lose no lede þat is lele to oure law.   363

[*To Jesus.*] But steppe furth and stonde vppe on hight,
And buske to my bidding, þou boy,   *He tells the beadle to pro-claim attention! (an Oy).*
And for þe nones þat þou neven vs anoy.

Bed. I am here at youre hande to halow a hoy,
Do move of youre maister, for I shall melle it with myȝt.   368

42. Pil. Cry, Oyas!
         Be. Oyas!
Pil. Yit efte, be þi feithe.
         Bed. Oyas! a lowde.
{ **Pil.** Pilatus, yit lowder
That ilke lede may light [1],   369   *'Cry, oyez, peace! and quiet!*
Crye pece in this prese, vppon payne þer-vppon,

---

[1] The first line of st. 42 is lost in the confusion here. Pilate would not call out his own name, and 'alowde' must be a stage direction to the Beadle, not words uttered by him; Pilate's 'yit lowder' may be the same; 'feithe' is the best rime to 'swithe.' I should therefore venture to restore the line thus—casting out 'that ilke lede may light' altogether, as irre-levant and without sense. Perhaps it belongs to st. 48.

     Pil. Cry Oyas!
         Bed. Oyas!
           Pil. Yit lowder!
             Bed. Oyas! (*a-lowde*).
              Pil. Yit efte, be þi feithe.
Cry pece in þis prese, etc.

    { Bidde them swage of þer sweying
    { Bothe swiftely and swithe,

And stynte of þer stryuyng and stande still as a stone.   3

Calle 'Jesu, þe gentill of Jacob, þe Jewe,

Come preste and appere,

To þe barre drawe þe nere,

To þi jugement here,'

To be demed for his dedis vndewe.   3

43. i Mil.   Whe! harke how þis harlott he heldis oute of harꝛ

This lotterelle liste noght my lorde to lowte.

ii Mil.   Say beggar, why brawlest þou? go boune þe to þ
barre.

i Mil.   Steppe on thy standyng so sterne and so stoute.   3

ii Mil.   Steppe on thy standyng so still.

i Mil.   Sir cowarde, to courte muste yhe care,

ii Mil.   A lessoune to lerne of oure lare [1].

i Mil.   Flitte fourthe, foule myght þou fare !

ii Mil.   Say, warlowe, þou wantist of þi will.   3

44. Junior Fil.   O Jesu vngentill, þi joie is in japes,

Þou can not be curtayse, þou caytiffe I calle þe,

No ruthe were it to rug þe and ryue þe in ropes,

Why falles þou noȝt flatte here, foule falle þe,   3

For ferde of my fadir so free ?

Þou wotte noght his wisdome i-wys,

All thyne helpe in his hande þat it is,

Howe sone he myght saue þe fro þis ;

Obeye hym, brothell, I bidde þe.   3

45. Pil.   Now, Jesu, þou art welcome ewys, as I wene,

Be noȝt abasshed, but boldely boune þe to þe barre.

What ! seyniour will sewe for þe sore, I haue sene ;

To wirke on þis warlowe, his witte is in warre [2].   3

---

[1] MS. has *lawe*.

[2] The MS. has *waste*, but *warre* may be intended. The sense of the passaꞡ
is obscure.

Come preste, of a payne, and appere,

And sir prelatis, youre pontes bes prevyng,

What cause can ye caste of accusyng?

þis mater ye marke to be mevyng,

And hendly in haste late vs here.   404

46. Cay.   Sir Pilate O Pounce, and prince of grete price,

We triste ye will trowe oure tales þei be trewe,

To deth for to deme hym with dewly device,

For cursidnesse yone knave hase in case, if ye knew,   408

In harte wolde ye hate hym in hye.

For if it wer so

We mente not to misdo;

Triste, sir, schall ye þerto,

We hadde not hym taken to þe [1].   413

47. { Pil.   Sir, youre tales wolde I trowe,

{ But þei touche none entente,

{ What cause can ye fynde

{ Nowe þis freke for to felle?

An.   Oure sabbotte he saues not, but sadly assente

To wirke full vnwisely, þis wote I riȝt wele [2];   417

He werkis whane he will, wele I wote,

And þerfore in herte we hym hate,

Itt sittis you to strenghe youre estate

Yone losell to louse for his lay.   421

48. Pil.   Ilke a lede for to louse, for his lay is not lele,

Youre lawes is leffull, but to youre lawis longis it

þis faitoure to feese wele with flappes full fele,

And woo may ye wirke hym be lawe, for he wranges it.   425

Therfore takes vn-to you full tyte,

And like as youre lawes will you lede,

Ye deme hym to deth for his dede.

Cay.   Nay, nay sir, þat dome muste vs drede [3],   429

Margin notes:

'Come! prelates, quickly appear, what are the points of accusation?'

If. 146. V viij.
'We trust you will believe us and judge him to death.'

'What cause have you to kill this fellow?'

'He does not keep our Sabbath.'

'By your law you can punish him with scourging,

or doom him to death.'
They refuse.

---

[1] These four lines are written as two in the MS.

[2] A line is wanting after l. 417, to fill up the sense, and to rime with l. 421.

[3] A line is here wanting; perhaps 'that ilk lede may light' (see note to l. 369) is the stray, it supplies both sense and rime.

49.   It longes noȝt till vs no lede for to lose.

Pilate is angry
with them, and
pities Jesus.

{ **Pil.** What wolde ye I did þanne?
 Þe deuyll motte you drawe!

Full fewe are his frendis, but fele are his fooes.

His liff for to lose þare longes no lawe ;   433

Nor no cause can I kyndely contryue

Þat why he schulde lose þus his liffe.

If. 146 b.

An. A! gude sir, it raykes full ryffe

'He has stirred
strife,

In steedis wher he has stirrid mekill striffe

Of ledis þat is lele to youre liffe.   438

he has healed the
lame, the deaf
and dumb ;

50. Cay. Sir, halte men and hurte he helid in haste,

The deffe and þe dome he delyuered fro doole,

By wicchecrafte, I warande, his wittis schall waste,

{ For þe farles þat he farith with,

the people follow
him.

 Loo! how þei folowe yone fole ;   442

Oure folke so þus he frayes in fere.

He raises the
dead and cures
the leper.'

An. The dethe he rayses anone,

Þis laȝare þat lowe lay allone

He graunte hym his gates for to gone,

And pertely þus proued he his poure.   447

51. Pil. Now goode siris, I saie, what wolde yhe?

'Do him out of
day.'
'Condemn him
because he has
done well? where
learnt ye such
law? This is no
treason.'

Cay. Sir, to dede for to do hym or dose hym a-dawe.

Pil. Yha, for he dose wele his deth for to deme?

{ Go, layke you, sir, lightly,
 Wher lerned ye such lawe?   451

This touches no tresoune, I telle you.

Yhe prelatis þat proued are for price,

Yhe schulde be boþe witty and wise,

And legge oure lawe wher it lyse,

Oure materes ye meve þus emel you.   456

52. { **An.** Misplese noȝt youre persone,
      Yhe prince with-outen pere!

'It does touch
treason : he for-
bid the tribute to
Cæsar.'

It touches to tresoune, þis tale I schall tell ;

Yone briboure, full baynly he bed to for-bere

The tribute to þe Emperoure, þus wolde he compell   460
Oure pepill þus his poyntis to applye.

Cay. The pepull, he saies he schall saue,
And Criste garres he calle hym, yone knave,
And sais he will þe high kyngdome haue.
Loke whethir he deserue to dye!   465

53. Pil. To dye he deserues yf he do þus in-dede,
But y will se my-selffe what he sais.
Speke Jesu, and spende nowe þi space for to spede [1];
þeȝ lordyngis þei legge þe þou liste noȝt leve on oure
    lawes [2].   469
They accuse þe cruelly and kene,
And þerfore, as a chiftene y charge þe,
Iff þou be Criste þat þou telle me,
And God sone þou grughe not to graunte ye,
For þis is þe matere þat y mene.   474

54. Jesus. Þou saiste so þi-selue, I am sothly þe same,
Here wonnyng in worlde to wirke al þi will,
My fadir, is faithfull to felle all þi fame;
With-outen trespas or tene am I taken þe till.   478
Pil. Loo! Busshoppis, why blame ye þis boye?
Me semys þat it is soth þat he saies,
Ye meve all þe malice ye may,
With youre wrenchis and wiles to wrythe hym away,
Vn-justely to juge hym fro joie.   483

55. Cay. Nought so, sir, his seggyng is full sothly soth,
It bryngis oure bernes in bale for to bynde.
An. Sir, douteles we deme als dewe of [3] þe deth,
Þis foole þat ye fauour, grete fautes can we fynde   487
This daye, for to deme hym to dye.
Pil. Saie, losell, þou lies be þis light!
Saie! þou rebalde! þou rekens vnright.
Cay. Avise you sir, with mayne and with myght,

Marginal notes:

'He says he will have the king-dom.'
lf. 147.
Xj.

'If he do thus he deserves to die.'

'Art thou the Christ?'

'Thou sayest.

I am taken with-out guile.'
'Bishops, why do you blame the boy?

You are mali-cious.'

'If his saying is true, it brings us harm;

doom him!'

'You lie! you reckon wrongly.'

---

[1] MS. has *speke*.
[2] Line 469 is too long, probably þe and *liste* should be omitted.
[3] MS. has *als*.

U

'Be not angry.' And wreke not youre wrethe nowe for-thy.   492

lf. 147 b.   **56. Pil.**   Me likes noȝt [t]his langage so largely for to lye.

          Cay.   A! mercy, lorde, mekely, no malice we mente.

Pilate is molli-   **Pil.**   Noo done is it douteles, balde and be blithe,
fied.

          Talke on þat traytoure and telle youre entente.   496

'Where learnt he   Yone segge is sotell ye saie,
such subtlety?'

          Gud sirs, wher lerned he such lare?

'We know not;   **Cay.**   In faith we cannot fynde whare.

          Pil.   Yhis, his fadir with some farlis gan fare,

          And has lered þis ladde of his laie [1].   501

his father was but   **57. An.**   Nay, nay, sir, we wiste þat he was but a write [2],
a wright.'

          No sotelte he schewed þat any segge saw.

          Pil.   Thanne mene yhe of malice to marre hym of myght,

          Of cursidnesse convik no cause can yhe knawe.   505

'I wonder at   Me meruellis ye malyngne o mys.
your malice.'

'His works are   **Cay.**   Sir, fro Galely hidir and hoo
known in Galilee,

          The gretteste agayne hym ganne goo,

          Yone warlowe to waken of woo,

          And of þis werke beres witnesse y-wis.   510

     58. Pil.   Why, and hase he gone in Galely, yone gedlyng on-
          gayne?

where he was   **An.**   Yha, lorde þer was he borne, yone brethelle, and
born.'

          brede [3].

          Pil.   Nowe with-outen fagyng, my frendis, in faith I am
          fayne,

          For now schall oure striffe full sternely be stede.   514

'Sir Herod is   Sir Herowde is kyng þer, ye kenne,
king in Galilee;

          His poure is preued full preste,

          To ridde hym, or reue hym of rest;

          And þerfore, to go with yone gest,

pick out some   Yhe marke vs out of þe manliest men.   519
men.'

---

[1] This word is clearly *lare* in MS., but *laie* was probably intended.
[2] Line 502, *was but a write þat we wiste*, in MS.
[3] 'And bredde' is suggested in later hand; the original has *borne*, repeated from last half-line, this being written as two lines in MS.

59. Cay. Als witte and wisdome youre will schalbe wroght,
Here is kempis full kene to þe kyng for to care.

An.[1] Nowe seniours, I saie yow sen soth schall be soght,
But if he schortely be sente it may sitte vs full sare. 523

Pil. Sir knyghtis þat are cruell and kene,
That warlowe ye warrok and wraste,
And loke þat he brymly be braste ;
And þerfore, sir knyghtis [in haste][2],
Do take on þat traytoure you be-twene. 528

60. Tille Herowde in haste with þat harlott ye hye,
Comaunde me full mekely vnto his moste myght,
Saie þe dome of þis boy, to deme hym to dye[3],
Is done vpponne hym dewly, to dresse or to dight, 532
Or liffe for to leue at his liste.
Say ought I may do hym in dede,
His awne am I worthely in wede.

i Mil. My lorde, we schall springe on a-spede, 536
Come þens to me[4] þis traitoure full tyte.

61. Pil. Bewe sirs, I bidde you ye be not to bolde,
But takes tente for oure tribute full trulye to trete.

ii Mil. Mi lorde, we schall hye þis be-heste for to halde,
And wirke it full wisely, in wille and in witte. 541

Pil. So sirs, me semys itt is sittand.

i Mil. Mahounde, sirs, he menske you with myght :

ii Mil. And saue you, sir, semely in sight.

Pil. Now in þe wilde vengeaunce ye walke with þat wight,
And fresshely ye founde to be flittand. 546

Side notes:
'Here are good soldiers to take him.'
If. 148. X ij.
'Let him be sent at once.
Soldiers, strongly bind this deceiver;
commend me to Herod, say I have sent him this boy for life or death.'
'Look after our tribute.'
'Mahomet keep you, sirs.'
'Be off at once !'

---

[1] The MS. has *Pilatus*, repeating the same at line 524. Annas or Caiaphas seems here intended.

[2] In the MS l. 527 stands next after l. 523. followed by a blank and the disconnected word 'lorde'; the copyist evidently felt he had made a blunder. Its transposition as in the text restores the sense, and the words 'in haste,' according with both rime and repeated idea (see l. 529), are probably what are lost.

[3] The words 'is done' are put at end of l. 531 in MS., evidently a mistake.

[4] *Sic*, but these words must be wrong, perhaps *to me* should be *dome*.

U 2

XXXI. THE LYTSTERES[1].

Trial before Herod.

[PERSONS OF THE PLAY.

Rex (i. e. Herod).	1, 2 Milites.
Jesus.	1, 2, 3 Filii.]
1, 2 Duces.	

[Scene, *Herod's Court.*]

Luke xxiii. 6–12.
*Gospel of Nicho-
demus (Latin),
ch.* ix.
King Herod
boastfully pro-
claims himself
and his power.

Rex. PES, ye brothellis and browlys, in þis broydenesse
    in brased,
And frekis þat are frendely your freykenesse to frayne,
Youre tounges fro tretyng of trifillis be trased,
Or þis brande þat is bright schall breste in youre brayne. 4
Plextis for no plasis, but platte you to þis playne,
And drawe to no drofyng, but dresse you to drede,
                      with dasshis.
Traueylis noȝt as traytours þat tristis in trayne,
Or by þe bloode þat mahounde bledde, with þis blad schal
    ye blede.   8
Þus schall I brittyn all youre bones on brede,   ȝae,
And lusshe all youre lymmys with lasschis.
Dragons þat are dredfull schall derke in þer denne
In wrathe when we writhe, or in wrathenesse ar wapped, 12
Agaynste jeauntis on-gentill haue we joined with ingendis [2],
And swannys þat are swymmyng to oure swetnes schall be
    suapped,

---

[1] The normal stanza of this piece appears to consist of sixteen lines, eight
long, riming alternately a b, six shorter, riming c d c c c d, and two long
(containing interwoven rimes), e e. But this is not strictly adhered to,
whether it is that there are omissions and errors, or that the original poet
indulged in considerable variety within the limits of these rimes and lines.
I have therefore only tentatively marked what appear to be stanzas or
parts of stanzas, of which but four, viz. 8, 11, 12, 15, are regular. The first
seventeen lines, strongly alliterative, do not conform.

[2] Line 13 stands after l. 14 in the MS.

And joged doune þer jolynes oure gentries engenderand ;
Who so repreue oure estate we schall choppe þam in
    cheynes.   16
All renkkis þat are renand to vs schall be reuerande.

(1) Ther-fore I bidde you sese or any bale be,
Þat no brothell be so bolde boste for to blowes,
And ȝe þat luffis youre liffis, listen to me,   20
As a lorde þat is lerned to lede you be lawes.
And ye þat are of my men and of my menȝe,
Sen we are comen fro oure kyth as ȝe wele knawe[s],
And semlys all here same in þis cyte,   24
It sittis vs in sadnesse to sette all oure sawes.

'We must gravely utter our sayings.'

i Dux. My lorde, we schall take kepe to youre call,
And stirre to no stede but ȝe steuen vs ;
No greuaunce to grete ne to small.   28

' We will take heed.'

Rex. Ya, but loke þat no fawtes be-fall.

ii Dux. Lely, my lorde, so we shall.
Ye nede not nomore for to nevyn vs !

(2) **i Dux.** Mounseniour, demene you in menske in mynde
    what I mene,   32
And boune to youre bodword, for so holde I best,
For all þe comons of þis courte bene avoyde clene.
And ilke a renke, as resoune is [1], are gone to þer reste,
Wher-fore I counsaile my lorde, ȝe comaunde you a
    drynke.   36

If. 149 b.
' My lord, all the commons are gone to rest, will you order your wine.'

Rex. Nowe certis, I assente as þou sais,
Se ych a qwy [2] is wente on his ways,
Lightly with-outen any delayes.
Giffe vs wyne wynly and late vs go wynke,   40
And se þat no durdan be done [3].

He will have wine and go wink.

i Dux. My lorde, vn-lase you to lye,
Here schall none come for to crye.

' My lord, unlace you,'

---

[1] MS. has *as.*
[2] The words ' see ilk a wy,' i. e. a man (A. S. *wíga*, a warrior), may be intended. But this is the only example in the volume of *ilk* being spelt *ych.*
[3] ' Tunc bibit Rex' here written in later hand.

Rex.   Nowe spedely loke þat þou spie,   44

'No noise.'   Þat no noyse be neghand þis none.

'Your bed is   (3) i dux.   My lorde, youre bedde is new made,
new-made.'   You nedis not for to bide it.

Rex.   Ya, but as þou luffes me hartely,   48

'Lay me softly,   Laye me doune softely,
                            For þou wotte full wele

my skin is   Þat I am full tendirly hydid.   [Lies down.
tender.'

i Dux.   Howe lye ȝe, my goode lorde?   52

Rex.   Right wele, be þis light,
                            All hole at my desire,

'Satan and   Wherfore I praye sir Satan, oure sire,
Lucifer save you!
Good night!'   And Lucifer moste luffely of lyre,   56
      •   He sauffe you all sirs, and giffe you goode nyght.

                                            [Soldiers, outside.

Soldiers at the   (4) i Miles.   Sir knyght, ye wote we ar warned to wende,
gate with Jesus.   To witte of þis warlowe what is þe kyngis will.

ii Miles.   Sir, here is Herowde all even here at oure hende, 60
                            And all oure entente tyte schall we tell hym vntill.

lf 150.   i Miles.   Who is here?   [At the door.
X iiij.
                  i Dux.   Who is there?

                  i Miles.   [Outside.]   Sir, we are knyghtis kende,
                            Is comen to youre counsaill þis carle for to kill.

'Unless your   i Dux.   Sirs, but youre message may myrthis amende, 64
message be good
stalk forth.'   Stalkis furthe be yone stretis, or stande stone still.

ii Miles.   Yis certis, sir, of myrthis we mene,
                            The kyng schall haue matteres to melle hym,
                            We brynge here a boy vs be-twene,   68
                            Wher-fore haue worschippe we wene.

                  i Dux.   Wele sirs, so þat it turne to no tene,
The duke goes to   Tentis hym and we schall go telle hym. [Goes to the king.
tell the king.
                  (5) My lorde, yondir is a boy boune, þat brought is in blame; 72
                            Haste you in hye, þei houe at youre ȝates.

Rex. What! and schall I rise nowe, in þe deuyllis name?   *He does not like it,*
To stighill amang straungeres in stales of a state.
But haue here my hande, halde nowe!   [*Rising.*]   76 *but he gets up.*
And se þat my sloppe be wele sittande.   *'See that my shirt fits.'*
i Dux. My lorde, with a goode will y wolde youe,
No wrange will I witte at my wittande.

(6) But my lorde, we can tell ȝou of vncouthe tythandes.   80 *'My lord, there is some to-do about this prisoner,*
Rex. ȝa, but loke ye telle vs no tales but trewe.
ii Dux. My lorde, þei bryng you yondir a boy boune in a bande,
Þat bodus outhir bourdyng or bales to brewe.
Rex. Þanne gete we some harrowe full hastely at hande. 84
i Dux. My lorde, þer is some note þat is nedfull to neven
you of new.
Rex. Why, hoppis þou þei haste hym to hyng?   *lf. 150 b.*
ii Dux. We wotte noght þer will nor þere wenyng.
But boodword full blithely þei bryng.   88 *but they bring you a good message.'*
Rex. Nowe do þan and late vs se of þere sayng.
ii Dux. [*Calls to the soldiers.*] Lo! sirs, ye schall carpe *'Sirs, come talk with the king.'*
with the kyng,
And telles to hym manly youre menyng.   [*Enter soldiers.*
(7) **i Miles.** Lorde, welthis and worschippis be with you alway. 92
Rex. What wolde þou?
    ii Miles. A worde, lorde, and youre willis were.
Rex. Well, saye on þan.
    i Miles. My lorde, we fare foolys to flay,
Þat[1] to you wolde forfette.
    Rex. We! faire falle you þerfore!
i Miles. My lorde, fro ȝe here what we saie,   96 *'What we say will raise your spirits.'*
Itt will heffe vppe youre hertis.
    Rex. ȝa, but saie what heynde haue ȝe þore?
ii Miles. A presente fro Pilate, lorde, þe prince of oure lay. *A present from Pilate to the king.*
Rex. Pese in my presence, and nemys hym nomore.   99
i Miles. My lorde, he woll worschippe you faine.

---

[1] MS. has *Yt*, with a distinct y; but the þ and y are frequently interchangeable.

Luke xxiii. 12.

Rex. I consayue ȝe are ful foes of hym.

ii Miles. My lorde, he wolde menske you with mayne,

And therfore he sendis you þis swayne.   103

'I don't care for him a borrowed bean.'

Rex. Gose tyte with þat gedlyng agayne,

And saie hym a borowed bene sette I noght be hym.

lf. 151.
X v.

(8) i Dux. A! my lorde, with youre leve, þei haue faren ferre;

And for to fraiste of youre fare was no folye.   107

ii Dux. My lorde, and þis gedlyng go þus it will greue werre,

For he gares growe on þis grounde grete velanye.

Rex. Why, menys þou þat þat myghtyng schulde my myghtes marre?

Herod is persuaded to listen,

i Dux. Nay lorde, but he makis on þis molde mekill maystrie.   111

Rex. Go ynne, and late vs see of þe sawes ere,

And but yf þei be to oure bordyng, þai both schall abye [1].

ii Miles. My lorde, we [were] worthy to blame,

To brynge you any message of mysse.   115

Rex. Why, þan can ye nemyn vs his name?

i Miles. Sir, Criste haue we called hym at hame.

and is glad when he hears this is Christ sent to him.

Rex. O! þis is the ilke selue and þe same!

Nowe sirs, ye be welcome y-wisse,   119

{ And in faith I am fayne he is fonne,
{ His farles to frayne and to fele,

{ Nowe þes games was grathely begonne.
{ **ii Miles.** Lorde, lely, þat likis vs wele.   121

(9) Rex. Ya, but dar ȝe hete hartely þat harlott is he?

'Are you sure he is the right man? and why sent to me?'

i Miles. My lorde takis hede, and in haste ye schall here howe.

Rex. Ya, but what menys þat þis message was made vn-to me?

ii Miles. My lorde, for it touches to tresoune, I trowe. 125

i Miles. My lorde, he is culpabill kende in oure contre,

Of many perillus poyntis, as Pilate preues nowe.

---

[1] Line 113 is written as two in the MS.

ii **Miles.** My lorde, when Pilate herde he had gone thurgh lf. 151 b.
    Galyle,   ' Pilate heard
                                                 that he came
He lerned vs þat þat lordschippe longed to ȝou,   129   from Galilee.'
And or he wiste what youre willis were,
No ferther wolde he speke for to spille hym.
Rex. Þanne knawes he þat oure myghtis are þe more?
i Miles. Ȝa, certis sir, so saie we þore.   133
Rex. Nowe sertis, and oure frenschippe þerfore
We graunte hym, and no greuaunce we will hym.
(10) And sirs, ye are welcome y-wisse, as ye wele awe,   'Yeare welcome.
                                                          I coveted to
And for to wende at youre wille y you warande;   137   know the carl;
For I haue coveite kyndely þat comely to knawe,   men say he is
                                                           wise.'
For men carpis þat þe carle schulde be konnand.
ii Miles. My lorde, wolde he saie you soth of his sawe,
Ȝe saugh nevir slik selcouth, be see nor be sande.   141
Rex. Nowe gois a-bakke both, and late þe boy blowe,   ' Stand back; let
For I hope we gete some harre hastely at hande.   him breathe.'
i Miles. Jerusalem and þe Jewes may haue joie,
And hele in ther herte for to here hym.   145
Rex. Saie! beene venew in bone fay,   Herod addresses
Ne plesew et a parle remoy.   Jesus in French.
ii Miles. Nay, my lorde, he can of no bourdyng, þis boy.   ' He cannot jest,
Rex. No sir, with þi leue we schall lere hym.   149   my lord.'
                             [Enter Herod's son.
(11) i Fil. My lorde, se ther knyghtis, þat knawe and are kene,   The son is sur-
How þai come to youre courte withoutyn any call.   prised at the
                                                    company of
Rex. Ȝa, sone, and musteris grete maistries, what may   strangers.
    þis by-mene?[1]
i Dux. My lorde, for youre myghtis are more þan ye all,   lf. 152.
                                                         X vj.
They seke you as souerayne, and sertis þat is sene.   154   It is an acknow-
Rex. Nowe certis, sen ȝe saie so, assaie hym I schall,   ledgment of
                                                         sovereignty.
For I am fayner of þat freyke þen othir fiftene.
Ȝae, and hym þat firste fande, faire myght hym fall!
i Miles. Lorde, lely we lereth you no legh,   158

    [1] Line **152** is written as two in MS.

Þis liffe þat he ledis will lose hym.

'Sirs, draw aside;
bring him near.

Rex.   Wele sirs, drawes you a-drygh,

And bewscheris, bryngis ȝe hym nygh,

For yif all þat his sleghtis be slye,   162

Ȝitte or he passe we schall appose hym.

My heart hops
for joy to see
him.'

{ O ! my harte hoppis for joie

{ To se nowe þis prophette appere,

{ We schall haue goode game with þis boy,

{ Takis hede, for in haste ȝe schall here.   165

(12) I leve we schall laugh and haue likyng

To se nowe þis lidderon her he leggis oure lawis.

The soldiers ad-
vise Jesus how
to talk to a king.

ii Dux. Harke, cosyne, þou comys to carpe with a kyng,

Take tente and be conande, and carpe as þou knowis. 169

i Dux. Ya, and loke þat þou be not a sotte of thy
saying,

But sadly and sone þou sette all þi sawes.

Rex.   Hym semys full boudisch, þat boy þat þei bryng.

Mi lorde, and of his bordyng grete bostyng men blawes.

Rex.   Whi, þerfore haue I soughte hym to see,   174

Loke bewscheris, ye be to oure bodis boune.

Jesus will not
kneel,

i Dux. Knele doune here to þe kyng on thy knee.

ii Dux. Naye, nedelyngis yt will not be.

lf. 152 b.

Rex.   Loo ! sirs, he mekis hym no more vnto me   178

Þanne it were to a man of þer awne toune.

at which all are
shocked.

{ **i Dux.** Whe ! go lawmere, and lerne þe to lowte,

{ Or þai more blame þe to bring.

Herod excuses
him.

{ **Rex.**   Nay, dredeles with-outen any doute

{ He knawes noȝt þe course of a kyng,   18?

(13) And her beeis in oure bale. Bourde or we blynne !

Saie firste at þe begynnyng withall, where was þu borne ?

Do felawe, for thy faith latte vs falle ynne

Firste of þi ferleis, who fedde þe be-forne ?   18?

Jesus deigns no
answer. Herod,
in joke, pretends
to be deafened.

What ! deynes þou not ? lo ! sirs, he dethis vs with dynne

Say, deynis þou not, whare ledde ȝe þis lidrone ? h?
langage is lorne.

i Miles. My lorde, his mervaylis to more and to myne, 188
Or musteres emange vs both mydday and morne.

ii Miles. My lorde, it were to fele
Of wonderes, he workith þam so wightely.

i Miles. Whe! man, momelyng may no thyng a-vayle, 192
Go to þe kyng, and tell hyme [1] fro toppe vnto tayle.

Rex. Do bringe vs þat boy vnto bale,
For lely we leffe hym noȝt lightly.

(14) i Dux. This [2] mop meynes þat he may marke men to þer
    mede,   196
He makis many maistries and mervayles emange.

ii Dux. V m̅. folke faire gon he feede.
With fyve looffis and two fisshis to fange.

Rex. Howe fele folke sais þou he fedde ?   200

ii Dux. V m̅. lorde, þat come to his call.

Rex. ȝa, boye, howe mekill brede he þem bedde ?

i Dux. But V looffis, dare I wele wedde.

Rex. Nowe, be þe bloode þat mahounde bledde,   204
What! þis was a wondir at all.

{ **ii Dux.** Nowe lorde, ij fisshis blissid he efte,
{ And gaffe þame and þer none was for-getyn.

{ **i Dux.** ȝa, lorde, and xij lepfull þer lefte
{ Of releue whan all men had eten.

(15) Rex. Of such anodir mangery noman mene may.   208

ii Dux. Mi lorde, but his maistries þat [3] musteris his myght,

Rex. But saie sirs, ar þer sawis soth þat þei saie ?

ii Miles. ȝa lorde, and more selcouth were schewed to
    oure sight.

One Lazar, a ladde þat in oure lande lay,
Lay loken vndir layre fro lymme and fro light,
And his sistir come rakand in rewfull arraye,   214
And lorde, for þer raryng he raysed hym full right,

Marginal notes:
The soldiers tell Herod

of the works and miracles done by Jesus, especially of the feeding five thousand folk with five loaves and two fishes.
Math. xiv. 13–21.
Mark vi. 14, 33–44.

lf. 153.
X vij.

No one may think of such another feast.

Also of the raising of Lazarus.

---

[1] The words 'tell hyme' are interlined by later hand.
[2] *Thus* in MS.   [3] The MS. repeats þat.

And fro his grath garte hym gang.

Euere forthe, with-outen any evill.

Rex.   We! such lesyngis lastis to lange.   218

i Miles.   Why lorde, wene ȝe þat wordis be wronge?

Þis same ladde lenys vs emange.

Rex.   Why, there hope y be dedis of þe deuyll.

{ Why schulde ȝe haste hym to hyng

{ That sought not newly youre newys?   222

{ **ii Miles.**   My lorde, for he callis hym a kyng,

{ And claymes to be a kyng of Jewis.

(16) Rex.   But saie, is he kyng in his kyth where he come

froo?   224

i Miles. Nay lorde, but he callis hym a kyng, his caris to kele.

Rex.   Thanne is it litill wondir yf þat he be woo,

For to be weried with wrang sen he wirkis wele.

But he schalle sitte be my-selfe sen ȝe saie soo,   228

Comes nerre, kyng, into courte, saie can ȝe not knele?

We schalle haue gaudis full goode and games or we goo.

Howe likis þa? wele, lorde? saie, what! deuyll neuere

a dele?

I faute in my reuerant in otill moy,   232

I am of fauour, loo! fairer be ferre.

Kyte oute yugilment, vta! oy! oy!

Be any witte þat y watte it will waxe werre.

Seruicia primet[1] such losellis and lurdaynes as þou, loo! 236

Respicias timet, what þe deuyll and his dame schall y

now doo?

(17) Do carpe on carle, for y can þe cure,

Say may þou not here me? oy! man, arte þou woode?

Nowe telle me faithfully before howe þou fore,   240

Forthe frende, be my faith, þou arte a fonde foode.

i Dux. My lorde it astonys hym, youre steuen is so store,

Hym had leuere haue stande stone still þer he stode.

---

[1] *Sic*; ' primet ' is clearly written with the contraction, p̄met. There seems
little attempt at sense (purposely) in this jumble of French and Latin.

Rex. And whedir þe boy be abasshid of Herrowde byg
blure, 244
That were a bourde of þe beste, be mahoundes bloode!

ii Dux. My lorde, y trowe youre fauchone hym flaies
And lettis hym.

It is a joke if he be abashed at Herod's big bluster!

    Rex. Nowe lely I leue þe,
And therfore schall y waffe it away. 248
And softely with a septoure assaie.
Nowe sir, be perte y þe pray,
For none of my gromys[1] schall greue þe[2].
Si loqueris tibi laus, pariter quoque prospera dantur,
Si loqueris tibi fraus, fell fex et bella parantur.
Mi menne, ȝe go menske hym with mayne, 254
And loke yhow þat it wolde seme.

Herod puts a sceptre in Jesus' hand,

and the men mock him.

i Dux (Dewcus[3]). Fayff sir, and sofferayne.
ii Dux (Sir vdins). Amangidre demayne.
Rex. Go, aunswer thaym grathely agayne : 258
What deuyll! whedir dote we or dremys!

(18) i Miles. Naye we gete noȝt o worde, dare y wele wedde,
For he is wraiste of his witte or will of his wone.

Rex. ȝe saie he lakkid youre lawes as ȝe þat ladde ledde.
ii Miles. ȝa, lorde, and made many gaudis as we haue gone.

lf. 154.
X viij.
They cannot get a word out of him.

Rex. Nowe sen he comes as a knave and as a knave
cledde, 264
Wherto calle ye hym a kyng?

    i Dux. Nay lorde, he is none,
But an harlotte is hee.

    Rex. What deuyll! y ame harde stedde,
A man myght as wele stere a stokke as a stone.

i Fil. My lorde, þis faitour so fouly is affrayde,
He loked neuere of lorde so langly allone. 269

The son thinks he is afraid.

[1] This word was first written *gomys*, the *r* was added above the line, apparently by the same hand.
[2] These last six lines are irregularly written as four in the MS.
[3] The copyist here wrote the names of the two speakers, as well as the rubricator. I add the brackets.

'No, he takes us
for angels with
our gay gear.'

Rex. No sone, þe rebalde seis vs so richely arayed,

He wenys we be aungelis euere ilkone.

ii Dux. My lorde, y holde hym agaste of youre gaye gere.

Rex. Grete lordis augh to be gay;   273

'No one shall
hurt thee;

whisper in my
ear.'

Here schall noman do to þe dere,

And therfore yit nemyne in my nere,

For by the grete god, and þou garre me swere

Þou had neuere dole or this day,   277

{ Do carpe on tyte, karle, of thy kynne.

{ **i Dux.** Nay, nedelyngis he neuyns you with none.

Herod is getting
angry,

{ **Rex.** Þat schalle he bye or he blynne.

{ **ii Dux.** A ! leves lorde !

(19)   **Rex.** Lattis me allone.   279

i Dux. Nowę goode lorde and ye may meue you nomore,

Itt is not faire to feght with a fonned foode,

and is advised to
retire to his
council.
lf. 154 b.

But gose to youre counsaille and comforte you þere.

Rex. Thou sais soth, we schall see yf so will be goode, 283

For certis oure sorowes are sadde.

The sons take it
up. 'What ails
the prisoner? he
must be mad or
witless.'

ii Fil. What a deuyll ayles hym ?

My lorde, I can garre you be gladde,

For in tyme oure maistir is madde,   287

He lurkis loo, and lokis like a ladde,

He is wode, lorde, or ellis his witte faylis hym.

(20) iii Fil. My lorde, ȝe haue meste you as mekill as ȝe may,

For yhe myght menske hym nomore, were he mahounde.

And sen it semys to be soo, latte vs nowe assaie.   292

Rex. Loke bewscheris, ȝe be to oure boddis boune.

i Dux. My lorde, howe schulde he dowte vs, he dredis
not youre drays.

Rex. Nowe do fourthe, þe deuyll myght hym drawe [sonne]!

And sen he freyins falsed and makis foule frayes,

'Shout at him.'

Raris on hym rudely, and loke ȝe not ronne[1].   297

i Fil. My lorde, I schall enforce my selffe sen ȝe saie soo,

---

[1] The 16th cent. hand has *nota* before l. 295 and *hic* at end of l. 297, and
again, before l. 307 and at end of 306.

Felawe, be not afferde nor feyne not þerfore,
But telle vs nowe some truffillis be-twene vs twoo,
And none of oure men schall medill þam more.

And þerfore by resoune array þe,
Do telle vs some poynte for thy prowe,   303
Heris þou not what y saie þe?
Þou mummeland myghtyng, I may þe
Helpe and turne þe fro tene, as y trowe.

The eldest son begs Jesus to tell him something in his favour.

'Do you hear? You mumbling midget! I could help you.'

(21) **ii Fil.** Loke vppe, ladde, lightly and loute to my lorde here,
For fro bale vnto blisse he may nowe þe borowe;   308
Carpe on knave cautely and caste þe to corde here,
And saie me nowe somwhat, þou sauterell with sorowe.

Why standis þou as still as a stone here?
Spare not, but speke in þis place here,   312
Þou gedlyng! it may gayne þe some grace here.

My lorde, þis faitour is so ferde in youre face here,
None aunswere in þis nede he nevyns you with none here.

The second son tries persuasion.

If. 155.
Y j.

iii Fil. Do bewscheris, for Beliall bloode and his bonys [1],
Say somwhat or it will waxe werre.

i Fil. Nay we gete nouȝt one worde in þis wonys.   318

ii Fil. Do crie we all on hym at onys, Oȝes! Oȝes! Oȝes!

Rex. O! ȝe make a foule noyse for þe nonys.

iii Fil. Nedlyng my lorde, it is neuere þe nerre.

The third is out of patience.

They all cry out together,
'Listen!'
'What a noise!

(22) **i Fil.** My lorde, all youre mutyng amendis not a myte,
To medill with a madman is meruaille to me [2],   323
Comaunde youre knyghtis to clothe hym in white,
And late hym carre as he come to youre contre.

Rex. Lo sirs, we lede you no lenger a lite,
Mi sone has saide sadly how þat it schuld be;   327
But such a poynte for a page is to parfite.

i Dux. Mi lorde, fooles þat are fonde þei falle such a fee.

Rex. What! in a white garmente to goo,

'There's no use in all your barking.'

They wish to clothe him in white, as a fool.

The king objects that it is too gay,

---

[1] The later hand gives these two lines to 'Pylatus,' the name of 'tercius dius' being inserted before l. 327 as well as here.
[2] MS. has *mene*, which does not agree with the rime.

þus gayly girde in a gowne?   331
ii Dux.   Nay lorde, but as a foole forcid hym froo.
Rex.   How saie ȝe, sirs, schulde it be soo?
Al chylder.   Ȝa, lord.
                    [**Rex.**] We! þan is þer no moo,
But boldely bidde þam be boune.

but finally con-
sents.
(23) Sir knyghtis, we caste to garre you be gladde,   336
Oure counsaile has warned vs wisely and wele,
White clothis we saie fallis for a fonned ladde,
And all his foly in faith fully we feele.

i Dux.   We will with a goode will for his wedis wende, 340
For we wotte wele anowe what wedis he schall were.

ii Dux.   Loo! here is an haterell here at youre hent,

lf. 155 b.
Here is an attire
at hand, fashion-
ed for fools.
Alle facionnd þerfore foolis to feere.

i Miles.   Loo! here a jappon of joie,   344
All such schulde be gode for a boy,

He shall be
arrayed as a
king!
i Dux.   He schalle be rayed like a Roye,
And schall be fonne in his folie.   [*They robe him.*

ii Dux.   We! thanke þam, euyll motte þou the!   348
i Miles.   Nay we gete noȝt a worde, wele y warand.
ii Miles.   Man, mustir some meruaile to me.
i Dux.   What! wene ȝe he be wiser þan we.

' Let alone, and
let the king see ;
my lord, are you
pleased ?'
Leffe we and late þe Kyng see,   352
Howe it is forcyd and farand.

{ Mi lorde, loke yf ȝe be paied,
{ For we haue getyn hym his gere.

{ **Rex.**   Why, and is þis rebalde arayed,
{ Mi blissing, bewscheris, ȝe bere.   35[5]

Go cry it in court;
if no one is ag-
grieved, let the
fellow go free.
(24) { Gose, garre crye in my courte,
       { And grathely garre write

All þe dedis þat we haue done in þis same degre.
And who fyndis hym greued late hym telle tyte[1],

{ And yf we fynde no defaute
{ Hym fallis to go free.   35[6]

---

[1] These four last words in the MS. stand at beginning of the next line.

i **Dux.** [*Crys in the court.*] O yes! if any wight with þis
    wriche any werse wate

Werkis, beris wittenesse who so wirkis wrang,

Buske boldely to þe barre, his balis to a-bate,   362 The crying is
      done and no one
For my lorde, be my lewte, will not be deland!   appears.

[*To Herod.*] My lorde, here apperes none to appeyre his estate.

Rex. Wele þanne fallis hym goo free[1].   The soldiers are
      to go back to
Sir knyghtis, þanne grathis you goodly to gange, 366 Pilate

And repaire with youre present and saie to Pilate,

We graunte hym oure frenschippe all fully to fang.   with Herod's
      friendship.
i **Miles.** My lorde, with youre leue þis way schall we lere, If. 156.
      Y ij.
Vs likis no lenger here to abide[2].   370

ii **Miles.** Mi lorde, and he worþe ought in were,

We come agayne with goode chere.

Rex. Nay bewscheris, ȝe fynde vs not here,

Oure leue will we take at þis tyde.   374 Herod goes now
      to rest; the busi-
{ And rathely[3] araye vs to reste,   ness has annoyed
      him.
{ For such notis has noyed vs or nowe.

{ i **Dux.** Ȝa, certis lorde, so holde y beste,

{ For þis gedlyng vngoodly has greued you.   376

(25) ii **Dux.** Loke ȝe bere worde as ye wotte,

Howe wele we haue quitte vs þis while[1].

i **Miles.** We! wise men will deme it we dote,

But if we make ende of oure note.   380

Rex. Wendis fourth, þe deuyll in þi throte!   Go forth with
      curses, we find
We fynde no defaute hym to slee,   no fault in him
      to kill him.
Wherfore schulde we flaye hym or fleme hym

We fynde noȝt in rollis of recorde.   384

And sen þat he is dome, for to deme hym,

Ware þis a goode lawe for a lorde?

---

[1] Line 365 seems out of place, as shown by the rime, though the sense
is good. Can it belong to l. 378, which ought to rime with l. 382? The
sentence of l. 365 agrees well with the scorn of the soldier, l. 379. The
whole passage, from l. 365 to the end, is difficult to read, both for rime
and for sense.

[2] In l. 370 *here* stands after *abide* in MS.

[3] MS. has ȝathely.

(26) Nay losellis, vn-lely ȝe lerned all to late,   387
Go lere þus lordingis of youre londe such lessons to lere.

Repaire with youre present and saie to Pilate,
We graunte hym oure poure all playne to appere,
And also oure greuaunce for-geue we algate,
And we graunte hym oure grace with a goode chere.   392
As touchyng þis brothell þat brawlis or debate,
Bidde hym wirke as he will, and wirke noght in were.

Go telle hym þis message fro me,
And lede fourth þat mytyng, euyll motte he the !   396
i Miles.   Mi lorde, with youre leue, late hym be,
For all to longe ledde hym haue we.
ii Miles.   What ! ȝe sirs, my lorde will ȝe see ?

Rex.   What ! felawes, take ȝe no tente what I telle you 400
And bid you ? þat yoman ye ȝeme.
ii Miles.   Mi lorde, we schall wage hym an ill way.

Rex.   Nay bewscheris, be not so bryme,
Fare softely, for so will it seme.   404
i Miles.   Nowe sen we schall do as ye deme,

A dewe, sir !
Rex.   Daunce on, in þe deuyll way !

XXXII. THE COKIS AND WATIR-LEDERES[1].

If. 157 b.
Y iij.

Second accusation before Pilate: remorse of Judas, and purchase of Field of Blood.

[PERSONS OF THE PLAY.

PILATUS.	1, 2 MILITES.
ANNA.	FILIUS.
KAYPHAS.	ARMIGER.]
JUDAS.	

[SCENE, *Pilate's Hall.*]

1. **Pilatus.** PEES, bewscheres, I bidde you, þat beldis
　　　here aboute me,
And loke þat 3e stirre with no striffe but stande stone still,
Or, by þe lorde þat me liffe lente, I schall garre you lowte me,
And all schall byde in my bale þat wirkis no3t my will.　4
Ye rebaldis þat regnys in þis rowte,
3e stynte of youre steuenyng so stowte,
Or with þis brande þat dere is to doute,
All to dede I schall dryue you þis day.　　8

2. For sir Pilate of pounce as prince am y preued,
As renke moste royall in richeste array,　　**To knawe.**
Þer is no berne in þis burgh has me aboute heuyd,
But he sekis me for souereyne, in certayne y saie,　12
Therfore take hede to youre lordis estate,
Þat none jangill nor jolle at my 3ate,

Matt. xxvii.1-10.
Luke xxiii. 13-15, 23.
Mark xv. 1-10.
Pilate commands peace;

as prince most royal,

all barons own him lord.

---

[1] As this piece presents three kinds of stanzas, it is perhaps no wonder that some parts are in confusion. Several lines are lost and words wrong: I have tentatively supplied a few omissions, in brackets. The *first*, a b a b c c c d, are found in stanzas 1, 2; stanzas 3 and 4 I cannot define; the *second*, a b a b c d c d, are in stanzas 5-15, and in 35-39; stanzas 16, 17, appear to be imperfect; *third*, stanzas 18-34, 40, 41, rime as the second, but with three lines added, e d e, of which one is a tag. The repetition links are of much help in studying this piece, which must have undergone some vicissitudes.

X 2

Nor no man to grath hym no gate,
Tille I haue seggid and saide all my sawe.   16

He boasts his
beauty,
For I ame þe luffeliest lappid and laide,
With feetour full faire in my face,

his broad fore-
head,
glittering eyes,
golden hair,
My forhed both brente is and brade,
And myne eyne þei glittir like þe gleme in þe glasse.   20
And þe hore þat hillis my heed
Is even like to þe golde wyre,

ruddy cheeks,
and clear colour.
My chekis are bothe ruddy and reede,
And my coloure as cristall is cleere [1].   24

Ther is no prince preuyd vndir palle
But I ame moste myghty of all,
Nor no kyng but he schall come to my call,
Nor grome þat dare greue me for golde.   28

Sir Kayphas, thurgh counsaill þi clergy is kid,
For thy counsaille is knowyn for connand and clere,
And Sir Anna, þyn aunswer aught not to be hidde,

He will settle the
claims of Caia-
phas and Annas
in Parliament.
For þou is one and is abill and aught to be nere,   32
In Parlament playne.
And I am Prince pereles, youre poyntis to enquere.
How saie ȝe, Jues, of Jesus þat swayne?
Haue done, sirs, sais on youre sawis,   36

If. 158.
Y iiij.
' By what title
will you now kill
Jesus?'
What tytill nowe haue ȝe vnto hym?
And lely ȝe loke vppon youre lawes.
Saye, why sente ȝe so sone for to spille hym?

5. **Anna.** Sir, þat is prince and lorde of oure laye,   4
That traitour vntrewe þat ye of telle vs,
Nowe certayne and sone þe soth schall I saie,
It is Jesus þat japer þat Judas ganne selle vs.

They accuse
Jesus again of
harming the
people, of show-
ing miracles, of
breaking the
Sabbath.
He marres oure men in all þat he may,
His [2] merueylis full mekill is mustered emelle vs,
He dois many derffe dedis on oure sabotte day,
Þat vn-connand conjeon he castis hym to quelle vs.

---

[1] The late hand adds *to behold* at the end of this line.
[2] The MS. has ' This,' but ' His ' seems intended.

6.   That faitoure so false [1]   48
    Fro man on to man he will compelle vs,
    And vndo you and our selffe als.
    Youre selffe he will for-do   ' He will ruin
    And he halde furth þis space,   52   you and Judea.'
    And all þis Jurie to,
    Yf þat ye graunte hym grace [2].

7. **Pilat.**   Sir Anna, þis aunswere allow I no thyng,   Pilate does not
    I holde it but hatereden, þis artikill hale,   56 allow this answer:
    And therfore, sir Busshoppe, at my biddyng,
    Do telle me nowe trewly þe texte of þis tale.
    Do termyne it trewly and tyte,   ' Tell me the
    And lely ȝe lede it by þe lawe,   60   truth, seriously.'
    Felonye or falsed euyn here I defie it,
    Saie me sadly þe soth, for loue or for awe.

8. **Kayphas.**   Sir Pilate, þe talis þe traitoure has tolde,
    It heuys vs in harte full haly to here þám,   64
    Þe warlowe with his wilis he wenys þam to wolde,
    Þe ladde with his lesyngis full lightly gan lere þam.
    Full tyte will he take þam vntill hym,   Anna is most
    And he þus forth go with his gaudis,   68   eager to kill him.
    Or speche ouer-sprede; ȝa, bettir is to spille hym,
    The faitoure is so felle with his false fraudis.

9. **Pilat.**   Youre aunsweres is hedouse and hatefull to here,   If. 158 b.
    Hadde I nowe herde hym and myselfe had hym sene,   72   ' Your answer is
    Yitt ȝe myght haue made me to trowe you intere,   hideous ; I find
    But faute in hym I fynde none, but conande & clene.   no fault in him.'
    For conande and clene can I clepe hym,
    No faute can I fynde to reffuse hym,   76
    I hope yitt in haste ȝe schall here hym,
    Whanne he comys to racleyme, þan may ȝe cuse hym.

10. **i Miles.**   Lorde, fele of his ferles in faith haue we fonne,   With hatred the
    Yone harlotte heuys oure hartis full of hate ire,   80   soldiers repeat
                                       the sayings of
                                       Jesus (*Matth.*

---

[1] Line 48 stands after l. 45 in the MS., but the rime appears to point this xxiv. 29-31).
out as the right place for it. There seems to be a line wanting before l. 48.
[2] Lines 51-54 stand as two lines in MS.

He sais hym selffe þat he is goddis sone,
And schall sitte on þe right hande beside his awne sire.

ii **Miles.**   Þer talis is full trewe þat we telle,

'He will judge
us after our
deeds.'

On þe rayne-bowe þe rebalde it redis,   84
He sais he schall haue vs to heuene or to hell
To deme vs a day aftir oure dedis.

11. { **Pilat.**   To deme vs! in þe deuyll name!
    { Say, whedir? saie whedir to þe deuyll?   87
What dastardis! wene ye be wiser þan we?

i **Miles.**   Mi lorde, with youre leue, we neuen it [1] for non ill
He has mustered his meruayles to mo þan to me.

Mi souerayne lorde, yone sauterell he sais,   91

'He will cast
down the temple
and raise it in
three days.'

He schall caste doune oure tempill, noȝt for to layne,
And dresse it vppe dewly with-in thre daies,
Als wele as it was, full goodely agayne.

12. **Anna.**   Ȝa, sir, and on oure awne sabott day,   95
Þanne werkis he werkis full wele.

Pilat.   We! fye on hym, faitour, for ay!
For þei are darke dedis of þe deuyll.

Kayph.   Sir, a noysomemare note newly is noysed,

'More noisome
than all, he calls
himself king of
the Jews.'
lf. 159.
Y v.
John xviii. 33–37.

Þat greuis me more þan any-kynne thyng,   100
He claymes hym clerly till a kyngdome of Jewes,
And callis hym selffe oure comeliest kyng.

Pilate is now
stirred to wrath;
'Where is he?'

13. **Pilat.**   Kyng! in þe deuyllis name, we! fye on hym, dastard!
What! wenys þat woode warlowe ouere-wyn vs þus lightly?
A begger of Bedlem, borne as a bastard,   105
Nowe by Lucifer lath I þat ladde, I leue hym not lightly.

Anna.   Sir, þe harlotte is at Heroudes hall, euyn her at
      your hande.

'He was sent to
Herod.'

Pilat.   I sente to þat warlowe, þe deuyll myght hym wery.

Kaiph.   It langis to youre lordschippe, be lawe of þis land,
As souerayne youre selffe, to sitte of enquery.   110

14. **Anna.**   Sir, þe traitoure has tolde vs mo trufullis truly,
Wolde tene you full tyte, and we you þam tolde :

---

[1] MS. has *neuenist.*

Pilat. Nowe, be Beliall bonis, þat boy schall abie,
And bring on his bak a burdeyne of golde.

i Filius. Mi lorde þat is ledar of lawis of þis lande, 115
ȝe sente hym youre selfe to Herowde þe kyng,
And sais, ' Þe dome of þat doge lies holy in your hande
To deme hym or lose hym, at youre likyng.'

Pilate's son re-
minds him that
as he sent Jesus
to Herod, he
must await the
king's judgment.

15. And þus ȝe comaunded youre knyghtis for to saie, 119
' For sir Heroude will serche hym full sore,
So þat he wende with no wilis away,'
And þerfore, my goode lorde, moue you nomore[1].

{ **Kaiph.** Nowe certis, þis was wele saide,
{ But sir, will ȝe sese nowe, and we schall se syne. 123

Pilat. Sir Kayphas and Anna, right so nowe I thynke,
Sittis in mahoundis blissing, and aske vs þe wyne.
ȝe knyghtis of my courte, comaundis vs to drynke[2]. 126

While they are
waiting they will
drink.

[*They drink. Enter Judas, speaking to himself.*

16. **Judas.** Allas! for woo þat I was wrought
Or euere I come be kynde or kynne,
I banne þe bonys þat me furth brought,
Woo worthe þe wombe þat I bredde ynne, 130
So may I bidde.
For I so falsely did to hym [3]
Þat vnto me grete kyndnesse kidde.

' Alas! that I was
born.'

If. 159 b.

Judas repents
having betrayed
his master.

17. Þe purse with his spens aboute I bare, 134
Þer was none trowed so wele as I,
Of me he triste no man mare,
And I be-trayed hym traytourly
With a false trayne, 138
Sakles I solde his blessid body,
Vnto Jues for to be slayne[3].

' Guiltless I sold
his blessed body.'

18. To slaa my souereyne assente I,
And tolde þem þe tyme of his takyng, 142

---

[1] Line 122 stands after l. 119 in the MS.
[2] Marginal note in late hand, ' Hic caret loquela de primo filio et aliis.'
[3] Lines 132, 133 are written as one in MS.; so are ll. 139, 140.

Shamously my selfe þus schente I
So sone for to sente to his slayng.
Nowe wiste I howe he myght passe þat payne,
To loke howe beste þat bote myght be [1]   146
Vnto þe Jues I will agayne,
To saue hym he myght passe free,
      Þis ware my will. [*Advances towards Pilate.*
Lorde, welthe and worschippe mot with yow be!   150
    Pilat. What tythandis, Judas, tellis þou vs till [2]?

19. Judas. My tydyngis are tenefull, I telle ȝou,
Sir Pilate, þerfore I you praye,
My maistir þat I gune selle ȝou,   154
Gode lorde, late hym wende on his way.
    Kaiph. Nay, nedelyngis, Judas, þat we denye,
What mynde or mater has moued þe þus?
    Judas. Sir, I haue synned full greuously,   158
Betraied þat right-wisse bloode, Jesus
        And maistir myne.

    Kaiph. Bewscher, what is þat till vs,
      Þe perill and þe plight is thyne.   162

20. Thyne is þe wronge, þou wroughte it,
Þou hight vs full trewlye to take hym,
And oures is þe bargayne, we boughte [it] [3],

Loo! we are alle sente for to slee hym.   166
    Judas [4]. Allas! þat may me rewe full ill,
Giffe ȝe assente hym for to slaa.
    Pilat. Why, what wolde þou þat we did þer-till?

    Judas. I praie you goode lorde, late hym gaa,   170
      And here is of me youre paymente [playne] [5].

    Kayph. Naie, we will noght so,
      We bought hym for he schulde be slayne;

---

[1] In the MS. l. 146 runs, 'To loke þat howe beste myght be bote,' an
it stands after l. 147.
[2] Marginal note in late hand, 'Hic caret loquela magna et diversa.'
[3] MS. has *hym*.
[4] The name *Judas* is inserted by the late hand; evidently needed.
[5] MS. has *hale*, perhaps a reminiscence of l. 197. The line is also too long

21. To slee hym þi selffe þou assente it. 174
Þis wate þou wondirly wele,
What right is nowe to repente [it],
Þou schapist þi selffe vn-seele.

Anna. Do waie, Judas, þou dose for noght. 178
Thy wordis I warne þe are in waste.
Thy selffe to selle hym whanne þou vs sought,
Þou was agaynste hym þanne þe moste,
Of vs ilkan. 182

Kayph. We schall be venged on hym in haste,
Whedir þat euere he will or none.

None of them listen to Judas;

22. Pilat. Þer wordis þat þou nenys noght nedis it,
Þou on-hanged harlott, hark what I saie, 186
Spare of thy spekyng, noght spedis it,
Or walke oute at þe dore, in þe deuill way.

Judas. Why will ye þanne noȝt latte hym passe,
And haue of me agayne youre paie? 190

Pilat. I telle þe, traytoure, I wille it noght.

Judas. Allas! þanne am I lorne [this day]
Boþe bone and bloode,
Allas þe while! so may I saie, 194
That euere I sente to spille his bloode.

he is told to walk out of the door.

23. To saue his bloode, sirs, I saie you,
And takes you þare youre payment hole,
Spare for to spille hym, I praye youe, 198
Ellis brewe ȝe me full mekill bale.

Pilat. Nay, heriste þou, Judas, þou schall agayne,
We will it nouȝt, what deuyll art þou?
When þou vs sought þou was full fayne 202
Of þis money; what aylis þe nowe
For to repente?

Judas. Agayne, sirs, here, I giffe it you,
And saue hym þat he be noȝt schent. 206

He prays them to take the money and spare Jesus. lf. 160 b.

Pilate forcibly refuses.

24. Pilat. To schende hym thy-selfe has þe schamed,
Þou may lathe with þi liffe þat þou ledis,

and taunts him with his treachery.

Fondely as a false foole þi selffe has famed,
Therfore þe deuyll þe droune for thy darfe dedis.

Judas. I knawe my trespasse and my gilte,   211
It is so grete, it garres me grise,
Me is full woo he schulde be spilte;
Might I hym saue of any wise,
   Wele were me þan   215
Saue hym, sirs, to youre seruise
   I will me bynde to be your man.

Judas offers to be
bondman to
Pilate.
25. Youre bonde-man, lorde, to be
Nowe euere will I bynde me,   219
Sir Pilate, ye may trowe me,
Full faithfull schall ȝe fynde me.

' Find thee faith-
ful ? a traitor
worthy to be
hanged and
drawn !'
Pilat. Fynde þe faithfull? a! foule mot þe falle!
Or þou come in oure companye,   223
For by mahoundes bloode, þou wolde selle vs all,
Thi seruice will we noght for-thy [1]
   Þou art unknowen
Fals tiraunte, for þi traitoury   227
   Þu art wo[r]þi to be hanged & drawen.

26. Hanged and drawen schulde þou be, knave [2],
And þou had right, by all goode reasoune,
Thi maistirs bloode þou biddist vs saue,   231
And þou was firste þat did him treasoune.

Judas. I cry ȝou mercy, lorde, on me rewe,
lf. 161.
Y vij.
Þis werryd wight þat wronge has wrought,
Haue mercy on my maistir trewe,   235
Þat I haue in youre bandome brought.
   [I cry ȝou sore].

They laugh at
the sorrow of
Judas, and jeer
him.
Pilat. Goo, jape þe, Judas, and neuen it noght,
   Nor move vs of þis matere more.

27. Anna. No more of þis matere þou move þe,   239
Þou momeland mytyng emell,

---

[1] The MS. has *for it*; and ll. 225, 226 are reversed.
[2] The MS. has *knowen*. See *knave* in l. 319.

Oure poynte expresse her reproues þe,
Of felonye falsely and felle.

   Kaiph. He grucchis noȝt to graunte his gilte,   243
Why schonnys þou noȝt to schewe þi schame?
We bought hym for he schulde be spilte,   *'We bought him from you.'*
All same we were consente to þe same,
      And þi selffe als;   247
Þou feyned noȝt for to defame,
      Þou saide he was a traytoure fals.

28. Pilat. Ȝaa, and for a false faitoure,   *'Yea, it was a traitor's trick.'*
Thy selffe full fully gon selle hym,   251
O! þat was a trante of a traytour,
So sone þou schulde goo to begile hym.
   i Miles. What, wolde þou þat we lete hym ga?
Yon weried wight, þat wrought such wronge,   255
We will not lose oure bargayne swaa,   *'We can't lose our bargain :*
So lightely for to late hym gang;
      And reson why
Latte we þat lotterell liffe ought long,
      It will be fonde, in faith, foly.   260

29. ii Miles. Yone folte for no foole schall he fynde vs,   *we are not such fools.'*
We wotte all full wele howe it was,
His maistir whanne he gune bringe vs,
He praied yow my goode lord late hym not passe.   264
   Pilat. Nay, sertis, he schalle noȝt passe free.
Þat we for oure mony has paied.
   Judas. Take it a-gayne þat ȝe toke me,   *lf. 161 b.*
And saue hym fro þat bittir braide,   268 *'Take the money.'*
      Þan were I fayne.
   Anna. Itt serues of noght þat þou has saide,
      And therfore takis it tyte agayne.

30. Pilat. Tyte agayne, traytoure, þou take it,   272 *'We will not take the money nor give him up.'*
We wille it noght welde with-in oure wolde,
Ȝitt schalte þou noȝt, sawterell, þu sune for-sake it,
For I schall sers hym my selffe sen þou has hym solde.

Kaiph. For-sake it in faith, þat he ne schall,   276
For we will halde hym þat we haue,

‘ The payment
binds the cove-
nant.’

The payment chenys þe with-all,
The thar no nodir comenaunte craue.

[Nor mercy none].

Judas. Sen ȝe assente hym for to slaa,   280
Vengeaunce I crie on you ilkone!

Judas cries
vengeance on
them all!

31. Ilkane I crie, þe deuill for-do youe[1]!
And þat myghte I both here and see,
Herde heuenyng here I wn-to youe.   284
For sorowe on-sought ye on me se.

They send him
off with hard
words.

Kaiph. Whe! fye on the, traytoure attaynte, at þis tyde ;
Of treasoune þou tyxste hym, þat triste þe for trewe.
Do buske þe henne, brothell, no lenger þou abide,   288
For if þou do, all þi respouns sare schall þe rewe.
Say wote þou noght who is I?
Nowe be my nociens, myght I negh nere þe,
In certayne, ladde, yitt schulde I lere þe   292
To lordis to speke curtaisely.

Pilat. Go thy gatis, geddlyng, and greue vs no more,
Leffe of þi talke, þe deuill mot þe hange.

Judas sets down
the money ;

Judas. Þat att ȝe toke me, take it you þere,   296
Ther with youre maistrie make yowe emange,
    And clayme it you clene,
Me lathes with my liff, so liffe I to lang.

lf. 162.
Y viij.
he loathes his
life ; his traitorous
action torments
him ; no mercy is
to be had, he will
kill himself.

    My traitourfull torne he turment my tene. 300

32. Sen for my treasoune haue I tane vnto me,
Me thare aske no mercy, for none mon y gete,
Ther-fore in haste my-selffe schall for-do me,
Allas! þe harde while þat euere ete I meete.   304
Thus schall I marke my mytyng meede,
And wirke me wreke with harte and will,

---

[1] If we take out the speech of Caiaphas, ll. 286–293, the four lines before
it and the seven after it make a perfect stanza.

To spille my selffe nowe wille I spede,
For sadly haue I seruyd þer-till;   308
    So wala way !
Þat euere I was in witte or wille,
    Þat tristy trewe for to be-traye.

'Alas ! that ever
I betrayed that
trust.

33. Allas ! who may I meue to ?   312
Shall I me take non othir reede,
Mi-selffe in haste I schall for-doo,
And take me nowe vn-to my dede.   [*Exit Judas.*] 315

In haste I will
slay myself.'

Kaiph. Haue done nowe, Sir Pilate, late se what ȝe saie,
As touchyng þis money þat we here haue,
Þat Judas in a wreth has wauyd away,
And keste vs crabbidly, þat cursed knave.
    Howe saie ȝe þer-by ?   320

They consult
what to do with
the money.

Anna. Sir, sen he it slang, we schall it saue.
    Kaiph. Tite truste it tille oure tresorie.

34. **Pilat.** Nay sir, noght soo.   323
        Kaiph. Why sir, how þan ?
Pilat. Sir, it schall not combre vs,
Nor come in oure Corbonan.

{ **Kaiph.** No, tille oure tresory certayne
{ Farther schall it nought.   327

It shall not go in
the treasury,

And se youre selffe soth certayne and skill [1]
It is price of þe bloode þat we with it boght,
Therfore some othir poynte I purpose it till.
    And þus I deuyse ;   331

it is the price of
blood.

[**Pilat.** [2]] A spotte of erthe for to by, wayte nowe I will,
    To berie in pilgrimes þat by þe wey dies.

If. 162 b.
We will buy a
spot of earth to
bury pilgrims in.

35. Pilgrimes and palmeres to putte þere,
Sir Kaiphas and Anna, assente ȝe þerto ?
And oþere false felons þat we for-fare.   336
    Anna. As ȝe deme, lorde, so wille we doo.
                [*Enter an Esquire.*

---

[1] MS. has *skall.*
[2] The rubricator forgot to insert the name of Pilate, but it seems likely
that his speech begins with l. 332.

The squire sa-
lutes Pilate ;

¹ **Armiger.** Hayle! Sir Pilate, perles and prince of þis empire,
Haile ! þe gaiest on grounde, in golde þer ȝe glide,
Haile ! þe louffeliest lorde of lyme and of lyre,   340
And all þe soferans semely þat sittith þe beside.

Pilat.   What wolde þou?

Armig.   A worde, lorde, and wende.

Pilat.   Nowe þou arte welcome i-wisse.

36. But delyuere þe lightly with-outen any lette,   344
We haue no tome all day to tente on-to þe.

he wishes to let
(i. e. set at
pledge) a place
near.
'What title have
you?'
'It is a free title.

It is called
"Calvary locus."
I will let, but not
sell it.

Armig.   A place here beside lorde, wolde I wedde-sette.

Pilat.   What title has þou þer-to? is it þyne awne free?

Armig.   Lorde, fre be my fredome me fallis it.   348
Þis tale is full trewe þat I telle ȝou,
And Caluary locus men callis it,
I wolle it wedde-sette, but not for to selle ȝou.

37. Pilat.²   What wolde þou borowe, bewshire, be-lyve, late
me se?   352

I would like you
to lend me thirty
pence on it.'

Armig.   If it ware youre lekyng, my lorde, for to lene it,
xxx pens I wolde ȝe lente on-to me.

They agree to
the sum and ask
for the deeds.
If. 163.
Z j.

Kayph.   Yis, bewshire, þat schall þou haue.

Pilat.   Shewe vs thi dedis and haue here þi mony.   356

Armig.   Haue her, gode lord, but loke ȝe þame saue.

[*Gives the deeds.*

As soon as the
deeds are given
up they defy the
squire and cheat
him of his land.

38. Pilat.   Ȝis, certis, we schall saue þame full soundely,
And ellis do we noght dewly oure deuere.
Faste, freke, for thy faith, on thy fote fonde þe !   360
For fro þis place, bewschere, I soile þe for euere³.

Armig.   Now sorowe on such socoure as I haue soght,
For all my tresoure thurgh tresoune I tyne ;

39. I tyne it vn-trewly by tresoune,   364

He goes his way
mourning.

Þer-fore nowe my way will I wende ;

¹ The late hand here writes ' Hic caret.'
² There seem to be two lines missing here, one before l. 352 riming to
'lene it,' the other before l. 355 riming to 'mony.'
³ Marginal note in late hand, 'hic caret loquela'; two lines (riming to
'soght' and 'tyne') are seen to be wanting here.

For ʒe do me no right nor no resoune,
I be-take you all to þe fende! [*Exit Esquire.* 'Go to the devil,
                                                  all of you!'
Pilat. Nowe certis, we are serued att all, 368
Þis place is purchesed full propirly,
The felde of bloode loke ʒe it call,
I you comaunde ilkone for-thy.

40. Kaiph. Sir, as ʒe comaunde vs, call it schall we soo, 372
But my lorde, with youre leue, we may lende her no lengar,
But faste late vs founde to fang on oure foo, 'Let us go;
ʒone gedlyng on-godly has brewed vs grete angir.
Anna. Do way, Sir busshoppe, and be not a-baste, 376
For loste is all oure lekyng, lepe he so light.
Kaiph. Nay, Sir, he schall not trusse so tite, and þat be
        ʒe traste,
For it wynnes vs no worschippe, þe werkis of yone wight, the doings of
                                                          that fellow win
        But grete angir. 380 us no respect.'
For-thy late vs dresse vs his deth for to dite,
        And late we þis lotterell leue her no lengar.

41. Pilat. Sir Kayphas, thurgh counsaile comaunde we our lf. 163 b.
        knyghtis,
⎰ To wacche on yone warlowe
⎱ What way þat he wendis, 384
⎰ Do dresse ʒou nowe dewly,
⎱ To yone doderon ʒou dightis,
⎰ And lette noʒt to laite hym
⎱ In lande where he lendis,
        Nor leuys hym noʒt lightly. 387
⎰ **ii Miles.** In faith we schall fette hym
⎱ Full farre fro his frendis.
⎰ **Pilat.** Nowe walkis on in þe wanyand,
⎱   And wende youre way wightely. 389

XXXIII. THE TYLLEMAKERS [1].

*The second Trial before Pilate continued;
the Judgment of Jesus.*

[PERSONS OF THE PLAY.

JESUS.	CAYPHAS.
PILATUS.	1, 2, 3, 4, 5, 6 MILITES.
ANNA.	PRECO (Beadle or Porter).

BARABBAS.]

[SCENE, *Pilate's Hall.*]

Matth. xxvii.
22-31.
Mark xv. 15-20.
John xix. 1-16.
Pilate commands
obedience from
his followers.

1. **Pil.** LORDYNGES, þat are lymett to þe lare of my
    liaunce,
3e schappely schalkes and schene for to schawe,
I charge 3ou as 3our chiftan þat 3e chatt for no chaunce,
But loke to youre lord here, and lere at my lawe.   4
As a duke I may dampne 3ou and drawe,
Many bernys bolde are aboute me,
And what knyght or knave I may knawe
Þat list no3t as a lord for to lowte me,   8
    I sall lere hym
In the deueles name, þat dastard, to dowte me.
3a, who werkis any werkes with-oute me,
    I sall charge hym in chynes to chere hym.   12

2. Tharfore 3e lusty ledes, with-in þis lenght lapped,
No noise,   Do stynte of 3oure stalkyng and of stoutnes be stalland,
What traytoures his tong with tales has trapped,   15
That fende for his flateryng full foull sall be falland.

---

[1] *Tillemakers* is crossed through, and *Mylners* is written in the later hand
as a fresh heading, on five of the pages of this piece.

What broll ouere brathely is bralland,   or quarrellings.
Or vnsoftely will sege in þer sales,
Þat cayteffe[1] þus carpand and calland
As a boy sall be broght vn-to bales.   20
      Þerfore
Talkes not nor trete not of tales,
For þat gome þat gyrnes or gales,   'He who grins or screams I will
   I myself sall hym[2] hurte full sore.   24 hurt him !'

3. **An.** Ʒe sall sytt hym full sore, what sege will assay Ʒou,   Chorus of adulation from the
If he like not youre lordshippe, þat ladde, sall Ʒe lere hym,   priests.
As a pereles prince full prestly to pay Ʒou,
Or as a derworth duke with dyntes sall Ʒe dere hym.   28

Cay. Ʒaa, in faythe Ʒe haue force for to fere hym,
Thurgh youre manhede and myght bes he marred,
No chyualrus chiftan may chere hym,
Fro that churll with charge Ʒe haue charred   32
      [and hasted ?]

Cay. In pynyng payne bees he parred,
An. Ʒaa, and with schath of skelpys yll scarred
   Fro tyme þat youre tene he haue tasted.   36

4. Now certes, as me semes, who so sadly has soght Ʒou,   lf. 164 b.
Youre praysyng is prophetable, Ʒe prelates of pees,
Gramercy, Ʒoure goode worde, and vngayne sall it noƷt you,   'Thanks for your good words and
Thaƚ Ʒe will say the sothe and for no sege cese.   40 truth-saying.'

Cay. Elles were it pite we appered in þis prees,
But consayue how Ʒoure knyghtes ere command.   'The soldiers are coming,

An. Ʒa, my[3] lord, þat leve Ʒe no lese
I can telle you, Ʒou tydes sum tythandis   44
     ful sadde.

Pil. Se, they bring Ʒoone brolle in a bande ;
We sall here nowe, hastely at hand,   we shall hear what unhap he
   What vnhappe before Herowde he had.   48 had with Herod.'

[1] The MS. has *caysteffe*.   [2] MS. has *hyn*.
   [3] The MS. repeats *my* twice.

5. i Mil. Hayll! louelyest lorde þat euere lawe led ȝitt,

Hayll! semelyest vndre on euere ilka syde,

Hayll! stateliest on stede in strenghe þat is sted ȝitt,

Hayll! liberall, hayll! lusty to lordes allied.   52

Pil. Welcome, what tydandis þis tyde,

Late no langgage lightly nowe lette ȝou.

ii Mil. Sir Herowde, sir, it is not to hyde,

As his gud frende grathely he grete yowe   56

for euere,

In what manere þat euere he mete ȝou,

By hym-selfe full sone wille he sette you,

And sais þat ȝe sall not disseuer.   60

6. Pil. I thanke hym full thraly, and sir, I saie hym þe same,

But what meruelous materes dyd þis myron þer mell?

i Mil. For all þe lordis langage his lipps, sir, wer lame,

For any spirringes in þat space no speche walde he spell.

Bot domme as a dore gon he dwell,   65

Þus no faute in hym gon he fynde,

For his dedis to deme hym to qwell,

Nor in bandis hym brathely to bynde,   68

and þus

He sente hym to youre self, and assynde

Þat we, youre knyghtis, suld be clenly enclyned,

And tyte with hym to you to trus.   72

7. Pil. Syrs, herkens! here ȝe not what we haue oppon hand,

Loo, howe þere knyghtes carpe þat to þe kyng cared!

Syr Herowde, þai say no faute in me fand,

He fest me to his frenschippe, so frendly he fared.   76

More-over sirs, he spake, and noght spared,

Full gentilly to Jesu þis iewe,

And sithen to ther knyghtis declared

How fawtes in hym fande he but fewe   80

To dye,

He taste hym, I telle ʒou for trewe,
For to dere hym he demed vndewe,
      And sirs, þe sothly saie I.   84

8. Cai. Sir Pilate oure prince, we prelatis nowe pray ʒou,

Caiaphas wishes to bring Jesus to the bar:

Sen Herowde fraysted no ferþer þis faitour to slaye,
Resayue in ʒour sall þer sawes þat I saie you,
Late bryng hym to barre, and at his berde sall we baye. 88

An. ʒa, for and he wende þus by wiles away,

he does much harm among the people, breeding blunders.

I wate wele he wirke will vs wondre,
Oure menʒe he marres þat he may,
With his seggynges he settes þam in sondre,   92
      With synne.
With his blure he bredis mekill blondre;
Whills ʒe haue hym, nowe haldes hym vndir,

'Hold him now you have him.'

      We sall wery hym away yf he wynne.   96

9. Cay. Sir, no tyme is to tarie þis traytour to taste,
Agayne Sir Cesar hym selfe he segges and saies,
All þe wightis in this world wirkis in waste,

They falsely accuse him.

Þat takis hym any tribute; þus his teching outrayes.   100
ʒitt forther he feynes slik affraies,
And sais þat hym self is God son;
And sir, oure lawe leggis and layes
In what faytour falsed is fon   104
      Suld be slayne.
Pil. For no schame hym to shende will we shon.
An. Sir, witnesse of þis wanes may be wonne,

lf. 165 b.

      Þat will tell þis with-owten any trayne.   108

10. Cayp[1]. I can reken a rable of renkes full right,

They bring forward false witnesses.

Of perte men in prese fro this place ar I pas,
Þat will witnesse, I warande, þe wordis of þis wight,
How wikkidly wrought þat þis wrecche has;   112
Simon, ʒarus, and Judas,
Datan and Gamaliell,

          [1] This name is inserted by the later hand.

Neptalim, Leui, and Lucas,
And Amys þis maters can mell   116
    to-githere ;
Þer tales for trewe can they telle,
Of this faytour þat false is and felle,
    And in legyng of lawes ful lithre.   120

Pilate sets them
aside ; this pro-
ceeding is urged
by hatred.

11. Pil.   ȝa, tussch ! for youre tales, þai touche not entente,
Þer witnesse I warande þat to witnesse ȝe wage,
Some hatred in ther hartis agaynes hym haue hent,
And purpose be this processe to putt down þis page.   124
Caip.   Sir, in faith vs fallith not to fage,
Þai are t[r]yst men and true þat we telle ȝou,
Pil.   Youre swering, seris, swiftely ȝe swage,
And no more in this maters ye mell ȝou,   128
    I charge.
An.   Sir, dispise not þis speche þat we spell you,

Pilate is dis-
pleased with the
persistent
charges,

Pil.   If ȝe feyne slike frawdis, I sall felle ȝou,
    For me likis noght youre langage so large.   132

12. Cai.   Oure langage is to large, but ȝoure lordshipp re-
    leue vs,
ȝitt we both beseke you, late brynge hym to barre,
What poyntes þat we putte forth, latt your presence
    appreue vs,
ȝe sall here how þis harlott heldes out of herre.   136

but at length is
persuaded to
send for Jesus
again.

Pil.   ȝa, butt be wise, witty, and warre.
An.   ȝis, sir, drede ȝou noȝt for no thyng we doute hym.
Fecche hym, he is noght right ferre,
Do bedell, buske þe abowte hym.   140
    Preco.   I am fayne,

lf. 166.
Z v.

My lorde, for to lede hym or lowte hym,
Vncleth hym, clappe hym, and clowte hym,
    If ȝe bid me, I am buxhome and bayne.   144
               [*Goes to the soldiers.*

13. Knyghtis, ȝe er commaundid with þis caityf to care,
And bryng hym to barre, and so my lord badd.

i Mil. Is þis thy messege? [Præco] ȝa, sir. [i Mil.] Þan
moue þe no mare,
For we ar light for to leppe and lede forthe þe ladd.   148

ii Mil. [*To Jesus.*] Do steppe furth, in striffe ert þou stadde,
I vphalde full euyll has þe happed.

The soldiers, in-
sulting, bring
Jesus in.

i Mil. O man, thy mynde is full madde,
In oure clukis to be clowted and clapped,   152
And closed.

ii Mil. Þou bes lassched, lusschyd, and lapped.

i Mil. ȝa, rowted, russhed, and rapped,
Þus thy named with noye sall be noysed.   156

14. ii Mil. [*To Pilate.*] Loo, this sege her, my souerayne, þat
ȝe for-sente.

Pil. Wele, stirre noȝt fro þat stede, but stande stille þare ;
Bot he schappe som shrewdnesse, with shame bese he shente,
And I will frayst in faith, to frayne of hir fare.   160

Caip. [*Starting.*] We, outte ! stande may I noȝt, so I stare.

The priests sud-
denly exclaim,
*Gosp. of Nicho-
demus,* ch. i.

An. ȝa, harrowe, of this traytour with tene.

Pil. Say, renkes, what rewth gars you rare ?
Er ye woode, or wittles I wene,   164
What eyles ȝou ?

'What do you
roar at, are you
mad?'

Caip. Out ! slike a sight suld be sene.

'We are con-
quered !'

An. ȝa ! allas, conquered ar we clene.

Pil.   We ! ere ȝe fonde, or youre force fayles ȝou ?   168

'Are ye silly?'

15. Cai. A ! sir, saugh ȝe noȝt þis sight, how þat þer schaftes
schuke,
And theȝ baneres to this brothell þai bowde all on brede ?

'Saw you not
how the banners
bowed to him?'

An. ȝa, ther cursed knyghtes by crafte lete them croke,
To worshippe þis warlowe vnworthy in wede.   172

If. 166 b.

Pil. Was it dewly done, þus in dede ?

Caip. ȝa, ȝa, sir, oure selfe we it sawe.

Pilate is angry
with the stan-
dard-bearers,

Pil. We! spitte on them, ill mott þai spede!

Say, dastard, þe deuyll mote ȝou drawe, 176

How dar ȝe

Þer baners on brede þat her blawe,

Lat lowte to þis lurdan so lawe?

O faytouris, with falshed how fare ȝe? 180

but they declare
they could not
hinder the
lances bowing.

16. iii Mil. We beseke you and tho seniouris beside ȝou, sir, sitte,

With none of oure gouernaunce to be greuous and gryll,

For it lay not in oure lott þer launces to lett,

And þis werke þat we haue wrought it was not oure will. 184

Pil. Þou lise, harstow, lurdan? full ille,

Wele þou watte if þóu witnes it walde.

iv Mil. Sir, oure strengh myght noȝt stabill þam stille,

They hilded for ought we couthe halde, 188

Oure vnwittyng.

v Mil. For all oure fors, in faith, did þai folde,

As þis warlowe worschippe þai wolde;

And vs semid, forsoth, it vnsittyng. 192

The priests do
not believe the
men.

17. Cai. A! vnfrendly faytours, full fals is youre fable,

Þis segge with his suttelte to his seett haþ you sesid.

vi Mil. ȝe may say what you semes, sir, bot þer standerdes to stabill

What freyke hym enforces full foull sall he be fesid. 196

An. Be þe deuyllis nese, ȝe ar doggydly diseasid,

A! henne-harte! ill happe mot ȝou hente.

Pil. For a whapp so he whyned and whesid

And ȝitt no lasshe to þe lurdan was lente, 200

foul fall ȝou!

iii Mil. Sir, i-wisse no wiles we haue wente,

Shamefully ȝou satt to be shente,

Here combred caystiffes, I call ȝou! 20

If. 167.
Z vj.
' Let the biggest

18. iv Mil. Sen ȝou lykis not, my lord, oure langage to leve,

Latte bryng the biggest men þat abides in þis land,

Propirly in youre presence þer pouste to preve,

Be-holde þat they helde nott fro þei haue þaim in hand.   208

Pil. Now ȝe er ferdest þat euere I fand,

Fy on youre faynte hertis in feere,

Stir þe, no langer þou stande,

Þou bedell, þis bodworde þou bere   212

    Thurgh þis towne ;—

Þe wyghtest men vn-to were,

And þe strangest þer standerdis to stere,

    Hider blithely bid þam be bowne.   216

men in the country come and try to hold them.'

Pilate sends for the strongest men,

19. Preco. My souerayne full sone sall be serued youre sawe,

I sall bryng to þer baneres right bigg men and strange,

A company of keuellis in this contre I knawe

That grete ere and grill, to þe gomes will I gange.   220

        [*Goes to two soldiers.*

Say, ye ledis botht lusty and lange,

ȝe most passe to sir Pilate a pace.

i Mil. If we wirke not his wille it wer wrang,

We are redy to renne on a race,   224

    And rayke.

Preco. Then tarie not, but tryne on a trace,

And folow me fast to his face.

and the beadle brings two tall soldiers.

ii Mil.[1]   Do lede vs, vs lykes wele þis lake.   228

    [*The Beadle returns with them to Pilate.*

20. Pre. Lorde, here are þe biggest bernes þat bildis in þis

      burgh,

Most stately and strange if with strenght þai be streyned,

Leve me, sir, I lie not, to loke þis lande thurgh,

Þai er myghtiest men with manhode demened.   232

---

[1] If we take this rubric as correct, the beadle goes out and fetches in he same soldiers (1st and 2nd) who had brought Jesus back from Herod to Pilate, and we may suppose had then retired. See line 157. They as well as Pilate are, however, quite unconscious of the identity (see next page), and we should probably name them seventh and eighth soldiers.

Having made
sure that they are
true,
lf. 167 b.

Pil. Wate þou wele, or ellis has þou wenyd.

Pre. Sir, I wate wele, withoute wordis moo.

Caip. In thy tale be not taynted nor tenyd.

Pre. We! nay sir, why shuld I be soo?   236

Pil.   Wele þan,
We sall frayst er they founde vs fer fro,
To what game þai be-gynne for to go,
          Sir Cayphas, declare þam ȝe can.   240

Caiaphas bids
them keep the
shafts up from
bowing, or
suffer endless
penalty.

21. **Caip.** ȝe lusty ledis, nowe lith to my lare,
Schappe ȝou to þer schaftis þat so schenely her schyne,
If ȝou barnes bowe þe brede of [1] an hare,
Platly ȝe be putte to perpetuell pyne.   244

i **Mil.** I sall holde þis as even as a lyne.

An. Who so schakis, with schames he shendes.

ii **Mil.** I certayne, I saie as for myne,
Whan it sattles or sadly discendis   248
          Whare I stande,

If it twists, turns,
or bends, hack off
my hands.

When it wryngis or wronge it wendis,
Outher bristis, barkis, or bendes,—
          Hardly lat hakke of myn hande!   252

22. **Pil.** Sirs, waites to þer wightis þat no wiles be wrought,
Þai are burely and brode, þare bost haue þai blowen.

They are threat-
ened sore if they
fail.

An. To neven of þat nowe, sir, it nedis right noght,
For who curstely hym quytes, he sone sall be knawen. 256

Cay. ȝa, þat dastard to dede sall be drawen,
Who so fautis, he fouly sall falle.

The cock has
crowed;

Pil. Nowe knyghtis, sen þe cokkis has crowen,
Haue hym hense with hast fra this halle   260
          His wayes;
Do stiffely steppe on þis stalle,
Make a crye, and cautely þou call,
          Euene like as sir Annay þe sais.   26.

---
[1] *Of* is written twice in MS.

23. An. [1] Jesu! þou rewe of gentill Jacob kynne,   cry Jesus again, to defend himself.

Þou nerthrist of Nazareth, now neuend is þi name,

Alle creatures þe accuses, we commaunde þe comme in,   If. 168.
Z vij.

And aunswer to þin enemys, deffende now thy fame.   268

Et Preco, semper post Annam, recitabit, Judicatur Jesus [2].

                    [The banners bow, and Pilate rises.

Cay. We! out, we are shente alle for shame,   All are afraid.

Þis is wrasted all wrange, as I wene.

An. For all þer boste, ȝone boyes are to blame.

Pil. Slike a sight was neuere ȝit sene!   272

    Come sytt ;

My comforth was caught fro me clene,

I vpstritt! I me [3] myght noȝt abstene   Pilate forced to rise and worship

    To wirschip hym in wark and in witte.   276 Jesus,

24. Cay. Þer-of meruayled we mekill what moued ȝou in

    mynde,

In reuerence of þis ribald so rudely to ryse.

Pil. I was past all my powre, þogh I payned me and pynd,

I wrought not as I wolde in no maner of wise.   280 in spite of himself ;

Bot syrs, my spech wele aspise,

Wightly his wayes late hym wende,

Þus my dome will dewly deuyse,

For I am ferde hym in faith to offende,   284 he is afraid to offend Jesus.

    In sightes.

An. Þan oure lawe were laght till an ende

To his tales if ȝe treuly attende ;

    He enchaunted & charmed oure knyghtis.   288

25. Cay. Be his sorcery, sir, youre selfe þe soth sawe,   'By sorcery he has charmed our soldiers and ourselves.'

He charmes oure chyualers & with myscheffe enchaunted,

To reuerence hym ryally we rase all on rowe,

Doutles we endure not of þis dastard be daunted.   292

---

[1] The later hand here adds in the margin *Oyes !*
[2] Original rubric or stage direction in the MS.
[3] MS. has *me*.

' But I know no-
thing to convict
him.'

Pil.   Why, what harmes has þis hatell here haunted?
I kenne to co[n]vyk hym no cause.

An.   To all gomes he God son hym graunted,
And liste not to leve on oure lawes.   296

' Knowest thou
why they accuse
thee ?'
lf. 168 b.

Pil. [*To Jesus.*]   Say, man
Consayues þou noȝt what comberous clause
Þat þis clargye accusyng þe knawse ?
          Speke, and excuse þe if þou can.   300

26. Jesus.   Euery man has a mouthe þat made is on molde,
In wele and in woo to welde at his will,
If he gouerne it gudly like as God wolde,

' For all the
words of his
mouth man must
account.'

For his spirituale speche hym [thar] not to spill.   304
And what gome so gouerne it ill,
Full vnhendly and ill sall he happe,
Of ilk tale þou talkis vs vntill,
Þou accounte sall, þou can not escappe.   308

Pilate finds no
points to punish,

Pil.   Sirs myne,
Ȝe foune in faithe all ȝe frappe,
For in þis lede no lese can I lappe,
          Nor no poynte to putt hym to pyne.   312

27. Cai.   With-oute cause, sir, we come not þis carle to
          accuse hym,
And þat will we ȝe witt, as wele is worthy.

but gives the
priests power to
judge him.

Pil.   Now I recorde wele þe right, ȝe will no raþere
          refuse hym,
To he be dreuen to his dede and demed to dye ;   316
But takes hym vn-to you forthy [1],
And like as youre lawe will you lere,
Deme ȝe his body to abye.

An.   O ! sir Pilate, with-outen any pere,   320
          Do way,

----

[1] *Forthe* in MS.

3e wate wele with-outen any were,   They refuse this,
Vs falles not, nor oure felowes in feere
    To slo noman[1], youre self þe soth say.   324

28. Pil. Why suld I deme to dede þan with-oute deseruyng
      in dede?
But I haue herde al haly why in hertes 3e hym hate,
He is fautles in faith, and so god mote me spede,
I graunte hym my gud will to gang on his gate.   328

Cai. Nought so, sir, for wele 3e it wate,
To be kyng he claymeth with croune,   If. 169.
And who so stoutely will steppe to þat state,   Z viij.
3e suld deme, sir, to be dong doune   332 and persuade
      And dede.   Pilate that Jesus
                                                             treasonably
                                                             claims the
                                                             crown.

Pil. Sir, trulye þat touched to tresoune,
And or I remewe, he rewe sall þat reasoune,   ' He shall rue
    And or I stalke or stirre fro þis stede.   that before I stir
                                                        336 from this place ;'
                                                             and gives orders
                                                             to scourge Jesus.

29. Sir knyghtis þat ar comly, take þis caystiff in keping,
Skelpe hym with scourges and with skathes hym scorne,
Wrayste and wryng hym to, for wo to he be wepyng,
And þan bryng hym before vs as he was be-forne.   340
i Mil. He may banne þe tyme he was borne ;
Sone sall he be serued as 3e saide vs.

An. Do wappe of his wedis þat are worne.

                                                             ' Unwrap his
ii Mil. All redy sir, we haue arayde vs,   344 clothes.'
      Haue done.
To þis broll late vs buske vs and brayde vs,
As sir Pilate has propirly prayde vs.

iii Mil. We sall sette to hym sadly sone.   348
    [They take Jesus to another part of the Hall.

30. iv Mil. Late vs gete of his gere, God giffe hym ille grace.   The soldiers
                                                                     unclothe,

          [1] MS. has *nonan.*

i **Mil.** Þai ere tytt of tite, lo ! take þer his trasshes.

iii **Mil.** Nowe knytte hym in þis corde.

ii **Mil.** I am caut in þis case.

iv **Mil.** He is bun faste, nowe bete on with bittir brasshis.

i **Mil.** Go on, lepis, har ȝe, lordyngis, with lasshes,
And enforce we þis faitoure to flay hym.

ii **Mil.** Late vs driffe to hym derfly with dasshes,
Alle rede with oure rowtes we aray hym   356
And rente hym.

iii **Mil.** For my parte I am prest for to pay hym.

iv **Mil.** Ȝa, sende hym sorow, assaye hym.

i **Mil.** Take hym þat I haue tome for to tente hym.

31. ii **Mil.** Swyng to this swyre, to swiftely he swete.   361

iii **Mil.** Swete may þis swayne for sweght of our swappes !

iv **Mil.** Russhe on this rebald and hym rathely rehete !

i **Mil.** Rehete hym I rede you with rowtes and rappes ! 364

ii **Mil.** For all oure noy, þis nygard he nappes.

iii **Mil.** We sall wakken hym with wynde of oure whippes.

iv **Mil.** Nowe flynge to þis flaterer with flappes.

i **Mil.** I sall hertely hitte on his hippes   368
and haunch.

ii **Mil.** Fra oure skelpes not scatheles he skyppes.

iii **Mil.** Ȝitt hym list not lyft vp his lippis,
And pray vs to haue pety on his paunch.   372

32. iv **Mil.** To haue petie of his paunche he propheres no
prayer.

i **Mil.** Lorde, how likis thou þis lake and þis lare þat we
lere ȝou ?

ii **Mil.** Lo, I pull at his pilche, I am prowd payer.

iii **Mil.** Thus youre cloke sall we cloute to clence yoụ
and clere ȝou.   37▪

iv **Mil.**   I am straunge in striffe for to stere ȝou.

i **Mil.**   Þus with choppes þis churll sall we chastye.

ii **Mil.**   I trowe with þis trace we sall tere you.

iii **Mil.**   All þin vntrew techyngis þus taste I,   380
      þou tarand.

iv **Mil.**   I hope I be hardy and hasty.

i **Mil.**   I wate wele my wepon not wast I.

ii **Mil.**   He swounes or sweltes, I swarand.   384   lf. 170.
         &j.

33. iii **Mil.**   Late vs louse hym lightyly, do lay on your handes.   He swoons, they
           unbind him,

iv **Mil.**   ȝa, for and he dye for this dede, vndone ere we
      all.

i **Mil.**   Nowe vnboune is þis broll, and vnbraced his bandes.

ii **Mil.**   O fule, how faris þou now, foull mott þe fall ! 388

iii **Mil.**   Nowe be-cause he oure kyng gon hym call,
We will kyndely hym croune with a brere.

iv **Mil.**   ȝa, but first þis purpure and palle,   and clothe him in
And þis worthy wede sall he were   392   purple and pall,
      for scorne.

i **Mil.**   I am prowd at þis poynte to appere.

ii **Mil.**   Latte vs clethe hym in þer clothes full clere,
As a lorde þat his lordshippe has lorne.   396

34. iii **Mil.**   Lange or þou mete slike a menȝe as þou mett with
      þis morne !

iv **Mil.**   Do sette hym in þis sete, as a semely in sales.   set him on a seat,
          and crown him

i **Mil.**   Now thryng to hym thrally with þis þikk þorne.   with thorns.

ii **Mil.**   Lo ! it heldes to his hede, þat þe harnes out hales.

iii **Mil.**   Thus we teche hym to tempre his tales,
His brayne begynnes for to blede.

iv **Mil.**   ȝa, his blondre has hym broght to þer bales.
Now reche hym and raught hym in a[1] rede   404   They put a reed
      so rounde,   for a sceptre in
For his septure it serues in dede.   his hand,

           [1] *a* is added by later hand.

i Mil. ʒa, it is gode i-nowe in þis nede,
  Late vs gudly hym grete on þis grounde.   408

35. Aue! riall roy and rex judeorum!

lf. 170 b.
and mock him
with 'Hail, king
of the Jews.'

  Hayle! comely kyng, þat no kyngdom has kende,
  Hayll! vndughty duke, þi dedis ere dom,
  Hayll! man, vnmyghty þi menʒe to mende.   412

iii Mil. Hayll! lord with-out lande for to lende,
  Hayll! kyng, hayll! knave vnconand.

iv Mil. Hayll! freyke, without forse þe to fende.
  Hayll! strang, þat may not wele stand   416
        To stryve.

i Mil. We! harlott, heve vp thy hande,
  And vs all þat þe wirschip are wirkand
        Thanke vs, þer ill mot þou þryve.   420

36. ii Mil. So late lede hym be-lyve, and lenge her no lenger,
        To Sir Pilate oure prince our pride will we prayse.

The men take
him,

iii Mil. ʒa, he may synge or he slepe of sorowe and angir,
  For many derfe dedes he has done in his dayes.   424

iv Mil. Now wightly late wende on oure wayes,
  Late vs trusse vs, no tyme is to tarie.   [They go to Pilate.

and go to tell
Pilate what they
have done.

i Mil. My lorde, will ʒe listen oure layes?
  Here þis boy is, ʒe bade vs go bary   428
        With battis.

ii Mil. We ar combered his corpus for to cary,
  Many wightis on hym wondres and wary;
        Lo! his flesh al be-be-flapped þat fat is.   432

Pilate sees how
he has suffered,

37. Pil. Wele, bringe hym be-fore vs; [They do so.] A! he
        blisshes all bloo,
  I suppose of his seggyng he will cese euermore.
  Sirs, be-holde vpon hight and ecce homoo,
  Þus bounden and bette and broght you be-fore.   436
  Me semes þat it sewes hym full sore.

and is going to
speak.

  For his gilte on this grounde is he greuyd,

If ȝou like for to listen my lore,

.   .   .   .   .   .   .¹

In race.

38. **[Pil.]** For propirly by þis processe will I preve   440
I had no force fro þís felawshippe þis freke for to lende.

Preco. Here is all, sir, þat ȝe for sende,
  Will ȝe wasshe whill þe watir is hote²?

[Barabbas is brought in.

Pil. Nowe þis Barabas bandes ȝe vnbende,   444
With grace late hym gange on his gate³
  Where ȝe will.

Bar. ȝe worthy men, þat I here wate,
God encrece all youre comely estate,   448
  For þe grace ȝe haue graunt me vn-till.

39. **Pil.** Here þe jugement of Jesu, all Jewes in þis stede,
Crucifie hym on a crosse and on Caluerye hym kill,
I dampne hym to-day to dy þis same dede,   452
Þerfore hyngis hym on hight vppon þat high hill.
And on aythir side hym I will,
Þat a harlott ȝe hyng in þis hast,
Me thynkith it both reasoune and skill   456
Emyddis, sen his malice is mast,
  ȝe hyng hym.
Þen hym turmente, som tene for to tast ;
Mo wordis I will not nowe wast,   460
  But blynne not to dede to ȝe bryng hym.

40. **Cay.** Sir, vs semys in oure sight þat ȝe sadly has saide,
Now knyghtis þat are conant with þis catyf ȝe care,
The liffe of þis losell in youre list is it laide.   464

If. 171.
& iij.
The beadle
brings water for
Pilate to wash
his hands.

'Let Barabbas
go.'

'Crucify Jesus
to-day, on the
hill of Calvary,
and on either
side hang a
harlot.'

---

¹ A leaf, & ij, is lost here. The words *In race* are written at the end
ɔf l. 439, but should follow the next line missing.
² In the margin, in later hand, 'Tunc lavat manus suas.' 'Hote' (pro-
ᵇably pronounced hâte) is intended to rime with 'gate,' as shown by the
ᵉd connecting line.
³ MS. has *gatis.*

i **Mil.**   Late vs alone, my lorde, and lere vs na lare.

Siris, sette to hym sadly and sare,

All in cordis his coorse vmbycast.

ii **Mil.**   Late vs bynde hym in bandis all bare,   468

iii **Mil.**   Here is one, full lange will it laste.

iv **Mil.**   Lay on hande here.

v **Mil.**   I powll to my poure is past.

Nowe feste is he, felawes, ful fast,   472

        Late vs stere vs, we may not long stand here.

41. An.   Drawe hym faste, hense delyuere ȝou, haue done.

Go, do se hym to dede withoute lenger delay.

For dede bus hym be nedlyng be none.   476

All myrthe bus vs move to-morne þat we may,

Itt is sothly oure grette Sabott day,

No dede bodis vnberid sall be.

vi **Mil.**   We see wele þe soth ȝe vs say.   480

We sall traylle hym tyte to his tree,

        Þus talkand.

iv **Mil.**   Fare wele, now wightely wende we.

Pil.   Nowe certis, ȝe are a manly menȝe!

        Furth in þe wylde wanyand be walkand.   485

XXXIV. THE SHERMEN.

Christ led up to Calvary.

[PERSONS OF THE PLAY.

JOHANNES.	PRIMUS MILES.
MARIA.	SECUNDUS MILES.
JESUS.	WYMOND 3 MILES.
SYMON.	SECUNDA MARIA.

TERTIA MARIA.]

[SCENE I; *The soldiers making ready for the crucifixion.*]

Luke xxiii. 26–33.
Mark xv. 21.

i **Miles.** PEES, barnes and bachillers þat beldis here
    aboute,
Stirre noȝt ones in þis stede but stonde stone stille,
Or be þe lorde þat I leue on, I schall gar you lowte,
But ȝe spare when I speke youre speche schall I spille 4
Smertely and sone;
For I am sente fro sir Pilate with pride,
To lede þis ladde oure lawes to abide,
He gettis no bettir bone. 8
Therfore I comaunde you on euere ilke a side,
Vppon payne of enprisonment þat noman appere
To suppowle þis traytoure, be tyme ne be tyde,
Noght one of þis prees; 12
Nor noght ones so hardy for to enquere,
But helpe me holly, all that are here,
Þis kaitiffe care to encrees[1].

'Peace! barons and bachelors, I am sent to lead this lad to execution,

let none support the traitor.

---

[1] These first lines appear so irregular (purposely so, perhaps) that I count the stanzas from line 16. Line 2 is divided in the MS., and four of the short lines are out of place.

z

1. Therfore make rome and rewle you nowe right,   16
   That we may with þis weried wight
      Wightely wende on oure waye[1];

He napped noght of all þis nyght,

He did not nap last night and shall be dead to-day,

And þis daye schall his deth be dight,   20
      Latte see who dare saie naye.

as to-morrow is our Sabbath.

Be-cause to-morne is prouyde
For oure dere Sabbott day,
We wille no mysse be moued,   24
But mirthe in all þat euere men may.

He has been crowned with thorns, as a fool-king.'

2. We haue bene besie all þis morne
   To clothe hym and to croune with thorne,
      As falles for a fole kyng;   28

The soldiers are impatient

And nowe me thynkith oure felawes skorne,
They highte to haue ben here þis morne,
      Þis faitour forthe to bring:
To nappe nowe is noȝt goode,   32
We! howe! high myght he hyng!
ii Miles.   Pees, man, for mahoundes bloode,
Why make ȝe such crying?

for their fellows to come and help crucify Jesus.

3. **i Miles.**   Why wotte þou noght als wele as I,   36
   Þis carle burde[2] vnto Caluery,
      And þere on crosse be done?

lf. 172 b.

ii Miles.   Sen dome is geuen þat he schall dy,
Late calle to vs more companye,   40
      And ellis we erre oure fone.
i Miles.   Oure gere be-houes to be grayde,
And felawes sammed sone,

'He must be dead by noon.

For Sir Pilate has saide   44
Hym bus be dede be none.

Where is Sir Wymond?' 'Gone to fetch a cross.'

4. Where is sir Wymond, wotte þou oght?
   ii Miles.   He wente to garre a crosse be wroght
      To bere þis cursed knave.   48

---

[1] MS. has *wayes.*
[2] *Sic* in MS., but probably *bude* = must, behoves, is intended.

i **Miles.** That wolde I sone wer hyder broght,
For sithen schall othir gere be soght,
 That vs be-houes to haffe.

ii **Miles.** Vs bus haue sties and ropes,   52 'We must have
To rugge hym tille he raue,   steps and ropes
And nayles and othir japes,   and nails.'
 If we oure selue wille saue.

5. i **Miles.** To tarie longe vs were full lathe,   56
But Wymond come, it is in wathe
 But we be blamed all three.
We! howe! Sir Wymond, wayt e[s] skathe[1].   'How now,
                Wymond?'
ii **Miles.** We, howe! Sir Wymond, howe? [*Enter Wymond.*

iii **Miles.** I am here, what saie ʒe bathe,   61
 Why crye ʒe so on me?
I haue bene garre make
Þis crosse, as yhe may see,   64 'I have been
Of þat laye ouere þe lake,   making the cross
Men called it þe kyngis tree.   out of the king's
                tree.'

6. i **Miles.** Nowe sekirly I þought þe same,
For þat balke will noman vs blame   68
 To cutte it for þe kyng.

ii **Miles.** This karle has called hym kyng at hame,   lf. 173
And sen þis tre has such a name,   & vj.
 It is accordyng thyng,   72 'It is fitting that
Þat his rigge on it may reste,   this carl who
For skorne and for hethyng.   calls himself
                king should have
iii **Miles.** Me thoughte it semyd beste   a royal tree.'
Tille þis bargayne to bryng.   76

7. i **Miles.** It is wele warred, so motte I spede,
And it be lele in lenghe and brede,   'It is the right
 þan is þis space wele spende.   ware, if the mea-
               sure be good.'
iii **Miles.** To loke þer-aftir it is no nede,   80
I toke þe mesure or I yode,   'I measured him
 Bothe for þe fette and hande.   before I went,

---

[1] These three words are run together in the MS, *wayteskathe.*

<table>
<tr><td>and it is well
bored.</td><td>

ii Miles. Be-holde howe it is boorede
Full euen at ilke an ende,
This werke will wele accorde,
It may not be amende.

</td><td>84</td></tr>
</table>

ii **Miles.** Be-holde howe it is boorede
 Full euen at ilke an ende,
 This werke will wele accorde,
 It may not be amende.   84

8. iii **Miles.** Nay, I haue ordande mekill more,
 3aa, thes theues are sente before,   88
  Þat beside hym schall hang [1];

Steps are ordered with strong steels,
And sties also are ordande þore,
 With stalworthe steeles as mystir wore,
  Bothe some schorte and some lang.   92

hammers, nails,
i **Miles.** For hameres and [for] nayles,
 Latte see sone who schall gang.

and brads.
ii **Miles.** Here are bragges þat will noght faile,
 Of irnne and stele full strange.   96

9. iii **Miles.** Þanne is it as it aweth to bee,
 But whiche of yowe schall bere [2] þis tree,
  Sen I haue broughte it hedir?

He shall bear the tree who is to be hanged on it.
i **Miles.** Be my feithe bere it schall hee   100
 Þat þer-on hanged sone schall bee,
  And we schall teeche hym whedir.

lf. 173 b.
ii **Miles.** Vppon his bakke it schalle be laide,
 For sone we schall come thedir.   104

iii **Miles.** Loke þat oure gere be grayede,
 And go we all to-gedir.

[SCENE II ; *The road to Calvary : John, Mary, and others waiting.*]

John laments the judgment passed on his master.
10. **Johannes.** Allas! for my maistir þat moste is of myght,
 That 3ister-even late, with lanternes light,   108
  Be-fore þe busshoppe was brought;
 Bothe Petir and I we saugh þat sight,
 And sithen we wente oure wayes full wight,
  When þe Jewes wondirly wrought.   11[

---

[1] The MS. has *hyng*.   [2] MS. has *beere*.

At morne þei toke to rede,
And soteltes vp soght,
And demed hym to be dede
Þat to þam trespassed noght[1].　　　116

11. Allas! for syte, what schall I saie,
My worldly welthe is wente for ay,
　　In woo euere may I wende;
My maistir, þat neuere lakke[d] in lay,　　120
Is demed to be dede þis day,
　　Ewen in hys elmys hende.
Allas! for my maistir mylde
That all mennys mysse may mende,　　124
Shulde so falsely be filed,
And no frendis hym to fende.

'Alas! my mild master has no friends to defend him.

12. Allas! for his modir and oþir moo,
Mi modir and hir sisteres alsoo,　　128
　　Sittes samen with sighyngis sore;
Þai wate no-thyng of all þis woo,
For-thy to warne þam will I goo,
　　Sen I may mende no more.　　132
Sen he schall dye as tyte,
And þei vnwarned wore,
I ware worthy to wite,
I will go faste ther-fore.　　136

His mother and others sit together sighing.'

13. But in myn herte grete drede haue I,
Þat his modir for dole schall dye,
　　When she see ones þat sight;
But certis I schal not wande for-thy,　　140
To warne þat carefull company,
　　Or he to dede be dight[2].　　142

John fears that Jesus' mother will die of grief.

*　　*　　*　　*　　*

---

[1] These four lines are written as two in the MS.
[2] A leaf, & *vij*, corresponding to & *ij*, is here lost.

lf. 174.
& viij.

14. [i Mary ?]   Sen he fro vs will twynne [1]
      I schall þe neuere for-sake.
      Allas ! þe tyme and tyde !

Mary feels that
Simeon's pro-
phecy is come
true:

      I watte wele þe day is come   146
      Þat are was specified,
      Of prophete Symeoun,   in prophicie,
      The swerde of sorowe schulde renne
      Thurgh-oute þe herte, sotelly.   150

15. ii Maria.   Allas ! þis is a sithfull sight,
      He þat was euere luffely and light,
         And lorde of high and lawe ;
      Oo ! doulfully nowe is he dight,   154
      In worlde is none so wofull a wighte,
         Ne so carefull to knawe.
      Þei þat he mended moste
      In dede and als in sawe,   158
      Now haue they full grete haste,
      To dede hym for to drawe.

                [Enter the soldiers, with Jesus bearing the cross.

'Weep not for
me, but for your-
selves and your
children.'

16. Jesus.   Doughteres of Jerusalem cytte,
      Sees, and mournes no more for me,   162
         But thynkes vppon this thyng ;
      For youre selfe mourne schall ȝee,
      And for þe sonnes þat borne schal be
         Of yowe, bothe olde and yonge ;   166
      For such fare schall be-falle,
      That ȝe schall giffe blissyng
      To barayne bodies all,
      That no barnes forthe may brynge.   17[

'For ye shall see
a sad day, when
ye shall say to the
mountains, "fall
on us."

17. For certis ȝe schall see suche a day,
      That with sore sighyng schall ȝe saye
         Vnto þe hillis on highte,

---

[1] It appears to be the Mary Mother who is speaking ; but the lines a[
evidently wrong.

'Falle on vs, mountaynes, and ȝe may,   174
And couere vs fro þat felle affraye,
   That on vs sone schall light.'
Turnes home þe toune vntill,
Sen ȝe haue þis sight,   178
   It is my fadirs will,
Alle þat is done and dighte.

lf. 174 b.
Return home.'

18. iii Maria. Allas ! þis is a cursed cas,
He þat alle hele in his hande has   182
   Shall here be sakles slayne ;
A ! lorde, be leue lete clense thy face,
Behalde howe he hath schewed his grace,
   Howe he is moste of mayne.   186
This signe schalle bere witnesse
Vnto all pepull playne,
   Howe goddes sone here gilteles
Is putte to pereles payne.   190

'God's guiltless
Son is put to
peerless pain.'

19. i Miles. Saie, wherto bide ȝe here aboute,
Thare quenys, with þer skymeryng and þer schoute,
   Wille noght þer stevenis steere?

The soldiers send
the weeping
women away,
with insults.

ii Miles. Go home, casbalde with þi clowte,   194
Or be þat lorde we loue and loute,
   Þou schall a-bye full dere.

iii Maria. This signe schall vengeaunce calle
On yowe holly in feere.   198

iii Miles. Go, hye þe hense with alle [1],
Or ille hayle come þou here.

20. Joh. Lady, youre gretyng greues me sore.

Maria Sancta. John, helpe me nowe and neuere more.   202
   That I myght come hym tille.

John and Mary
mother still stand
about on the hill,

Joh. My lady, wende we forthe be-fore,
To Caluery when ȝe come thedir [2],
   Þan schall ȝe saie what ȝe will.   206

[1] The MS. has *ille.*
[2] Perhaps 'thore' was the word originally meant. It occurs in l. 2ᴄ6
-d elsewhere. In l. 206 *þan* seems intended, in MS. *þᵘ* is written.

lf. 175.
9 i.

and the men get
angry; 'go,

i Miles.   What a deuyll is þis to saye,
How longe schall we stande stille?
Go [1] hye you hens awaye,
In þe deuylis name, doune þe hill.   210

these queans
comber us with
their clack,

21. ii Miles.   Ther quenes vs comeres with þer clakke,
He schall be serued for þer sake,
   With sorowe and with sore ;

we'll put them
in the lake!'

iii Miles.   And þei come more such noyse to make,   214
We schall garre lygge þame in þe lake,
   Yf þei were halfe a skore.   [*The women flee.*

i Miles.   Latis nowe such bourdyng be,
Sen oure tooles are before,   218
Þis traitoure and þis tree,
Wolde I full fayne were þore.

22. ii Miles.   We schall no more so stille be stedde,
For nowe þer quenes are fro vs fledde   222
   Þat falsely wolde vs feere.

Jesus has lost so
much blood that
he swoons.

iii Miles.   Me thynkith þis boy is so for-bledde,
With þis ladde may he noght be ledde,
   He swounes, þat dare I swere.   226

i Miles.   It nedis noȝt harde to harle
Sen it dose hym slike dere.

ii Miles.   I se here comes a karle,
Shall helpe hym for to bere.   230

                    [*Enter Simon the Cyrenian*

23. iii Miles.   Þat schall ȝe see sone one assaye.

'Good man,
whither away?'

Goode man, whedir is þou away?
   Þou walkis as þou were wrothe.

lf. 175 b.
'I have a long
way to go to-day.

Symon.   Sir I haue a grete jornay,   23
Þat bus be done þis same day,
   Or ellis it may do skathe.

i Miles.   Þou may with litill payne,
Eease thy selffe and vs bathe.   2

---

[1] MS. has *To.*

Symon.   Goode sirs, þat wolde I fayne,   I cannot stop.'
But to dwelle were me lathe.

24. ii Miles.   Nay, beuscher, þou shall sone be spedde,
Loo, here a ladde þat muste be ledde   242
    For his ille dedis to dye;
iii Miles.   And he is brosid and all for-bledde[1],
That makis vs here þus stille be stedde,
    We pray þe, sir, for-thy,   246   They ask him to carry the cross to Calvary.
That þou wilte take þis tree,
And bere it to Caluerye.
Symon.   Goode sirs, þat may nouȝt be,
For full grete haste haue I.   250

25.   My wayes are lang and wyde,
And I may noght abide,
    For drede I come to late;
For surete haue I hight   254   'I have promised a surety which I must keep to-night or injure my estate ;
Muste be fulfillid þis nyght,
    Or it will paire my state.
Therfore, sirs, by youre leue,
Me thynkith I dwelle full lang,   258
Me were loth you for to greue,   by your leave, let me go.'
Goode sirs, ȝe late me gang.

26.   No lenger here now may I wone.
i Miles.   Nay, certis, þou schalte noȝt go so sone,   262   They force him to stay.
    For ought þat þou can saye ;
Þis dede is moste haste to be done,
For þis boy muste be dede by none,
    And nowe is nere myddaye.   266
Go helpe hym in þis nede,
And make no more delaye.
Symon.   I praye yowe dose youre dede,   lf. 176. & ij.
And latis me wende my waye.   270   'Do your deed, I will help you on my return.'

---

[1] The late hand here writes 3 *Miles* as the speaker of the following five ꞁes. There is, however, no red line to mark off a separate speech.

27. And, sirs, I schall come sone agayne,
    To helpe þis man with all my mayne,
        And even at youre awne will.
    ii **Miles.** What ! wolde þou trusse with such a trayne !   274
    Nay, faitour, þou schalte be fayne,
        Þis forwarde to full-fille.
    Or, be myghty mahounde !

    Þou schalte rewe it full ille.   278
    iii **Miles.** Late dyng þis dastarde doune,
    But he goo tyte þer-till.

28. **Symon.** Sertis, sir, þat wer nought wisely wrought,
    To bete me, but I trespassid ought,   282
        Outhir in worde or dede.

    i **Miles.** Vppon his bakke it schall be brought,
    To bere it, whedir he wille or noght,
        What ! deuyll, whome schulde we drede ?   286
    Go, take it vppe be-lyve,
    And bere it forthe, goode spede !

    Symon. It helpis noȝt here to striue,
    Bere it be-houes me nede.   290

29. And þerfore, sirs, as ȝe haue saide,
    To bere þis crosse I holde me paied,
        Right as ȝe wolde it wore.

    ii **Miles.** Ȝaa, nowe are we right arraied,   294
    Loke þat oure gere be redy grayed,
        To wirke whanne we come þore.
    iii **Miles.** I warand all redy,
    Oure tooles bothe lesse and more,   29⁸
    Late hym goo hardely,
    Forthe with þe crosse before ¹.

30. i **Miles.** Sen he has his lade, nowe late hym gang,

    For with þis warlowe wirke we wrang,   30⁰
        And we þus with hym yode.

¹ These four lines are written as two in the MS.

ii Miles. And nowe is noght goode to tarie lang,
What schulde we done more vs emang?
     Say, sone, so motte þou spede.   306

iii Miles. Neuen vs no nodir noote,
Tille we haue done þis dede.   *'Talk of no other business till this is done.'*

i Miles. We! me [1] me-thynke we doote,
He muste be naked, nede.   310

31. All yf he called hym-selffe a kyng,   *'He shall hang naked;*
    In his clothis he schall noȝt hyng,
     But naked as a stone be stedde.

ii Miles. That calle I accordand thyng,   314
But tille his sidis I trowe þei clyng,
     For bloode þat he has bledde.

iii Miles. Wheder þei clynge or cleue,
Naked he schalle be ledde,   318
And for þe more myscheue,
Buffettis hym schall be bedde.

32. i Miles. Take of his clothis be-liffe, latte see,   *take off his clothes,*

        [They strip Jesus.

A ha! þis garment will falle wele for mee,   322
    And so I hope it schall.

ii Miles. Nay, sir, so may it noght be,   *they shall be parted amonge the soldiers.*
Þame muste be parte amonge vs thre,
     Take euen as will fall.   326

iii Miles. Ȝaa, and sir Pilate medill hym,   *unless Pilate meddle.*
Youre parte woll be but small.

i Miles. Sir, and ȝe liste, go telle hym,
Ȝitt schall he noght haue all,   330

33. Butte even his awne parte and nomore.   *lf. 177. ϑ iij.*

ii Miles. Ȝaa, late þame ligge still here in stoore,
     Vntill þis dede be done.

iii Miles. Latte bynde hym as he was before,   334   *'He shall be bound as before, and be hanged before noon.'*
And harle on harde þat he wer þore,
     And hanged or it be none.

---

[1] These two words stand *weme* in the MS.

  i Miles. He schall be feste of fee,
  And þat right sore and sone.   338
  ii Miles. So fallis hym for to be,
  He gettis no bettir bone.   [*They bind Jesus again.*

34. **iii Miles.** Þis werke is wele nowe, I warand,
  For he is boune as beeste in bande,   342
    That is demed for to dye.
  i Miles. Þanne rede I þat we no lenger stande,
  But ilke man feste on hym a hande,
    And harle hym hense in hye.   346
  ii Miles. Ȝaa, nowe is tyme to trusse,
  To alle oure companye.
  iii Miles. If anye aske aftir vs,
  Kenne þame to Caluarie.   350

XXXV. THE PYNNERES (AND PAYNTERS[1]).

Crucifixio Cristi.

[PERSONS OF THE PLAY.

JESUS.   1, 2, 3, 4 MILITES.]

[SCENE, *Golgotha, afterwards Mount Calvary.*]

1. i Miles.   SIR knyghtis, take heede hydir in hye,
     This dede on-dergh we may noght drawe,
3ee wootte youre selffe als wele as I,
Howe lordis and leders of owre lawe   4
Has geven dome þat þis doote schall dye.

ii Mil.   Sir, alle þare counsaile wele we knawe,
Sen we are comen to Caluarie,
Latte ilke man helpe nowe as hym awe.   8

iii Mil.   We are all redy, loo,
Þat forward to fullfille.

iv Mil.   Late here howe we schall doo,
And go we tyte þer tille [2].   12

2. i Mil.   It may no3t helpe her for to hone,
If we schall any worshippe wynne.

ii Mil.   He muste be dede nedelyngis by none.

iii Mil.   Þan is goode tyme þat we begynne.   16

iv Mil.   Late dynge hym doune, þan is he done,
He schall nought dere vs with his dynne.

Math. xxvii. 33–35.
Luke xxiii. 33–37.
Mark xxv. 22–32.

'We cannot carry out this death without dree (trouble).

Let all help now we are at Calvary.

Strike him down, he will make no noise.

---

[1] The words 'and Paynters' are added in later hand.
[2] These four lines are written as two in the MS.

i **Mil.**   He schall be sette and lerned sone,
With care to hym and all his kynne.   20

ii **Mil.**   Þe foulest dede of all
Shalle he dye for his dedis.

iii **Mil.**   That menes crosse hym we schall.

iv **Mil.**   Behalde so right he redis.   24

Let us take care that our work be right.'

3. i **Mil.**   Thanne to þis werke vs muste take heede,
So þat oure wirkyng be noght wronge.

ii **Mil.**   None othir noote to neven is nede,
But latte vs haste hym for to hange.   28

If. 178 b.
' Here is the gear, hammers and nails.

iii **Mil.**   And I haue gone for gere, goode speede,
Bothe hammeres and nayles large and lange.

iv **Mil.**   Þanne may we boldely do þis dede,
Commes on, late kille þis traitoure strange.   32

i **Mil.**   Faire myght ȝe falle in feere,
Þat has wrought on þis wise.

ii **Mil.**   Vs nedis nought for to lere,
Suche faitoures to chastise.   36

' As everything is ready,

4. iii **Mil.**   Sen ilke a thyng es right arrayed,
The wiselier nowe wirke may we,

the cross laid on the ground and bored [with holes],

iv **Mil.**   Þe crosse on grounde is goodely graied,
And boorede even as it awith to be.   40

the lad shall be laid on it.'

i **Mil.**   Lokis þat þe ladde on lengthe be layde,
And made me þane vnto þis tree.

ii **Mil.**   For alle his fare he schalle be flaied,
That one assaie sone schalle ye see.   4

iii **Mil.**   Come forthe, þou cursed knave,
Thy comforte sone schall kele.

iv **Mil.**   Thyne hyre here schall þou haue.

' Walk on.'

i **Mil.**   Walkes oon, now wirke we wele.   4

Jesus prays to the Father,

5. **Jesus.**   Almyghty god, my Fadir free,
Late þis materes be made in mynde,
Þou badde þat I schulde buxsome be,
For Adam plyght for to be pyned.   5

Here to dede I obblisshe me

Fro þat synne for to saue mankynde,

And soueraynely be-seke I þe,

That þai for me may fauoure fynde; 56

And fro þe fende þame fende,

So þat þer saules be saffe,

In welthe withouten ende; 60

I kepe nought ellis to craue.

he dies to save mankind from Adam's sin;

'May they find favour for my sake.'

If. 179. 9 v.

6. i Mil. We! herke, sir knyghtis, for mahoundis bloode! *'Listen!*

Of Adam-kynde is all his þoght.

ii Mil. Þe warlowe waxis werre þan woode,

Þis doulfull dede ne dredith he noght. 64

iii Mil. Þou schulde haue mynde, with mayne and moode,

Of wikkid werkis þat þou haste wrought.

he does not dread death.'

iv Mil. I hope þat he had bene as goode

Haue sesed of sawes þat he vppe sought. 68

i Mil. Thoo sawes schall rewe hym sore

For all his saunteryng sone.

ii Mil. Ille spede þame þat hym spare

Tille he to dede be done! 72

'I think he might have stopped such sayings.

7. iii Mil. Haue done belyue, boy, and make þe boune, *Have done! boy.'*

And bende þi bakke vn-to þis tree. *[Jesus lies down.*

iv Mil. Byhalde, hym-selffe has laide hym doune,

In lenghe and breede as he schulde bee. 76

Jesus, having lain down stretched out,

i Mil. This traitoure here teynted of treasoune,

Gose faste and fette hym þan, ʒe thre.

And sen he claymeth kyngdome with croune,

Even as a kyng here haue schall hee. 80

ii Mil. Nowe, certis, I schall noʒt feyne

Or his right hande be feste.

one man takes the right hand,

iii Mil. Þe lefte hande þanne is myne,

Late see who beres hym beste. 84

another the left,

8. iv Mil. Hys lymmys on lenghe þan schalle I lede, *a third the limbs*

And even vnto þe bore þame bringe,

i **Mil.**　Vnto his heede I schall take hede,

And with myne hande helpe hym to hyng.　　88

ii **Mil.**　Nowe sen we foure schall do þis dede,

And medill with þis vnthrifty thyng,

Late no man spare for speciall speede,

Tille þat we haue made endyng.　　92

iii **Mil.**　Þis forward may not faile,

Nowe are we right arraiede.

iv **Mil.**　This boy here in oure baile

Shall bide full bittir brayde.　　96

9. i **Mil.**　Sir knyghtis, saie, howe wirke we nowe?

ii **Mil.**　Ʒis, certis, I hope I holde þis hande.

iii **Mil.**　And to þe boore I haue it brought,

Full boxumly with-outen bande.　　100

? iv **Mil.**[1]　Strike on þan harde, for hym þe boght.

? i **Mil.**[1]　Ʒis, here is a stubbe will stiffely stande,

Thurgh bones and senous it schall be soght.

This werke is well, I will warande.　　104

ii **Mil.***　Saie, sir, howe do we þore,

Þis bargayne may not blynne.

iii **Mil.**　It failis a foote and more,

þe senous are so gone ynne.　　108

10. iv **Mil.**　I hope þat marke a-misse be bored.

ii **Mil.**　Þan muste he bide in bittir bale.

iii **Mil.**　In faith, it was ouere skantely scored;

Þat makis it fouly for to faile.　　112

i **Mil.**　Why carpe ʒe so? faste on a corde,

And tugge hym to, by toppe and taile.

iii **Mil.**　Ʒa, þou comaundis lightly as a lorde,

Come helpe to haale, with ille haile.　　116

---

[1] Here the rubricator put twice ii *Miles*. As the previous order of the soldiers in speaking has been 1, 2, 3, 4, I have altered these two so as to continue that order, making what was i *Miles* at * to accord with it.

i **Mil.**   Nowe certis þat schall I doo,
Full suerly as a snayle.

lf. 180.
9 vj.

iii **Mil.**   And I schall tacche hym too,
Full nemely with a nayle.

The executioners
do their horrid
work.

120

11.   Þis werke will holde, þat dar I heete,
For nowe are feste faste both his handis.

iv **Mil.**   Go we all foure þanne to his feete,
So schall oure space be spedely spende.   124

ii **Mil.**   Latte see, what bourde his bale myght beete,
Tharto my bakke nowe wolde I bende.

iv **Mil.**   Owe! þis werke is all vnmeete,
This boring muste all be amende.   128

i **Mil.**   A! pees man, for mahounde,
Latte noman wotte þat wondir,
A roope schall rugge hym doune,
Yf all his synnous go a-soundre.   132

12.   ii **Mil.**   Þat corde full kyndely can I knytte,
Þe comforte of þis karle to kele.

i **Mil.**   Feste on þanne faste þat all be fytte,
It is no force howe felle he feele.   136

They pull till
the body fits the
holes bored.

ii **Mil.**   Lugge on ȝe both a litill ȝitt.

iii **Mil.**   I schalle nought sese, as I haue seele.

iv **Mil.**   And I schall fonde hym for to hitte.

ii **Mil.**   Owe, haylle!

iv **Mil.**   Hoo nowe, I halde it wele.   140

i **Mil.**   Haue done, dryue in þat nayle,
So þat no faute be foune.

iv **Mil.**   Þis wirkyng wolde noȝt faile,
Yf foure bullis here were boune.   144

13.   i **Mil.**   Ther cordis haue evill encressed his paynes,
Or he wer tille þe booryngis brought.

lf. 180 b.

ii **Mil.**   ȝaa, assoundir are both synnous and veynis,
On ilke a side, so haue we soughte.   148

Sinews and veins
are asunder.

A a

iii Mil.   Nowe all his gaudis no thyng hym gaynes,
His sauntering schall with bale be bought.
iv Mil.   I wille goo saie to oure soueraynes
Of all þis werkis howe we haue wrought.   152

'We must now
hang him up, to
be seen;

i Mil.   Nay sirs, a nothir thyng
Fallis firste to youe me,
I badde we schulde hym hyng,
On heghte þat men myght see.   156

14. ii. Mil.   We woote wele so ther wordes wore,
But sir, þat dede will do vs dere.
i Mil.   It may not mende for to moote more,
Þis harlotte muste be hanged here.   160

the mortise is
made to fit.'

ii Mil.   The mortaise is made fitte þerfore.
iii Mil.   Feste on youre fyngeres þan, in feere.
iv Mil.   I wene it wolle neuere come þore.
We foure rayse it noȝt right, to yere.   164

Some of the men
think they four
are not enough
to lift the cross.

i Mil.   Say man, whi carpis þou soo?
Thy liftyng was but light.
ii Mil.   He menes þer muste be moo
To heve hym vppe on hight.   168

15. iii Mil.   Now certis, I hope it schall noght nede
To calle to vs more companye.

John xix. 23
('four parts').

Me-thynke we foure schulde do þis dede,
And bere hym to ȝone hille on high.   172

'It must be done;

i Mil.   It muste be done, with-outen drede,
Nomore, but loke ȝe be redy;

lf. 181.
Θ vij.

And þis parte schalle I lifte and leede,
On lenghe he schalle no lenger lie.   176
Therfore nowe makis you boune,

carry him to yon
hill.'

Late bere hym to ȝone hill.
iv Mil.   Thanne will I bere here doune,
And tente his tase vntill.   180

16. ii Mil.   We twoo schall see tille aythir side,
For ellis þis werke will wrie all wrang.

iii **Mil.** We are redy, in Gode, sirs, abide,   They are ready,
And late me first his fete vp fang.   184

ii **Mil.** Why tente ȝe so to tales þis tyde?

i **Mil.** Lifte vppe!   [*All lift the cross together.*

    iv **Mil.** Latte see!   but make a great
to-do about the
        ii **Mil.** Owe! lifte a-lang.   weight.

iii **Mil.** Fro all þis harme he schulde hym hyde,
And he war God.

    iv **Mil.** Þe deuill hym hang!   188

i **Mil.** For grete harme haue I hente,
My schuldir is in soundre.

ii **Mil.** And sertis I am nere schente,
So lange haue I borne vndir.   192

17. iii **Mil.** This crosse and I in twoo muste twynne,   'My back is
broken.' They
Ellis brekis my bakke in sondre sone.   wait a while.

iv **Mil.** Laye doune agayne and leue youre dynne,
Þis dede for vs will neuere be done. [*They lay it down.*] 196

i **Mil.** Assaie, sirs, latte se yf any gynne,
May helpe hym vppe, with-outen hone;
For here schulde wight men worschippe wynne,
And noght with gaudis al day to gone.   200

ii **Mil.** More wighter men þan we
Full fewe I hope ȝe fynde.

iii **Mil.** Þis bargayne will noght bee,   lf. 181 b.
'I am out of
For certis me wantis wynde.   204 breath.'

18. iv **Mil.** So wille of werke neuere we wore,
I hope þis carle some cautellis caste.

ii **Mil.** My bourdeyne satte me wondir soore,
Vnto þe hill I myght noght laste.   208

i **Mil.** Lifte vppe, and sone he schall be þore,
Therfore feste on youre fyngeres faste.

iii **Mil.** Owe, lifte!   [*They take up the cross again.*
    i **Mil.** We, loo!

        iv **Mil.** A litill more.
       A a 2

ii **Mil.**   Holde þanne !

i **Mil.**   Howe nowe !

ii **Mil.**   Þe werste is paste.

iii **Mil.**   He weyes a wikkid weght.

They reach the
top of the hill.

ii **Mil.**   So may we all foure saie,

Or he was heued on heght,

And raysed in þis array.   216

19. iv **Mil.**   He made vs stande as any stones,

So boustous was he for to bere.

They set it in
the mortice and
let it fall in sud-
denly, so as to
jolt.

i **Mil.**   Nowe raise hym nemely for þe nonys,

And sette hym be þis mortas heere.   220

And latte hym falle in alle at ones,

For certis þat payne schall haue no pere.

iii **Mil.**   Heue vppe !

iv **Mil.**   Latte doune, so all his bones

Are a-soundre nowe on sides seere. [*The cross is reared.*] 224

i **Mil.**   Þis fallyng was more felle,

þan all the harmes he hadde,

lf. 182.
9 viij.

Nowe may a man wele telle,

þe leste lith of þis ladde.   228

20. iii **Mil.**   Me thynkith þis crosse will noght abide,

Ne stande stille in þis mo[r]teyse ȝitt.

The hole of the
mortice being too
wide,

iv **Mil.**   Att þe firste tyme was it made ouere wyde,

Þat makis it wave, þou may wele witte.   232

i **Mil.**   Itt schall be sette on ilke a side,

So þat it schall no forther flitte,

they fix in the
cross with
wedges,

Goode wegges schall we take þis tyde,

And feste þe foote, þanne is all fitte.   236

ii **Mil.**   Here are wegges arraied

For þat, both grete and smale.

iii **Mil.**   Where are oure hameres laide,

þat we schulde wirke with all ?   240

*   hammering them 21. iv **Mil.**   We haue þem here euen atte oure hande.
     in.

ii **Mil.**   Gyffe me þis wegge, I schall it in dryue.

iv **Mil.**   Here is anodir ȝitt ordande.

iii **Mil.**   Do take it me hidir belyue.   244

i **Mil.**   Laye on þanne faste.

             iii **Mil.**   ȝis, I warrande.

I thryng þame same, so motte I thryve.

Nowe will þis crosse full stabely stande,

All yf he raue þei will noght ryve.   248

i **Mil.**   Say, sir, howe likis þou nowe,

þis werke þat we haue wrought?

iv **Mil.**   We praye youe sais vs howe,

ȝe fele, or faynte ȝe ought?   252

They jest to Jesus.

22. Jesus.   Al men þat walkis by waye or strete,

Takes tente ȝe schalle no trauayle tyne,

By-holdes myn heede, myn handis, and my feete,

And fully feele nowe or ȝe fyne,   256

Yf any mournyng may be meete

Or myscheue mesured vnto myne.

My Fadir, þat alle bales may bete,

For-giffis þes men þat dois me pyne.   260

What þai wirke wotte þai noght,

Therfore my Fadir I craue

Latte neuere þer synnys be sought,

But see þer saules to saue [1].   264

If. 182 b.
'Is any mourn-ing like unto mine?'

Luke xxiii. 34.
Father, forgive them, for they know not what they do.'

23. i Mil.   We! harke! he jangelis like a jay.

ii **Mil.**   Me thynke he patris like a py.

iii **Mil.**   He has ben doand all þis day,

And made grete meuyng of mercy.   268

iv **Mil.**   Es þis þe same þat gune vs say,

That he was Goddis sone almyghty?

i **Mil.**   Therfore he felis full felle affraye,

And demyd þis day for to dye.   272

'He jangles like a jay or a pie.'

'He said he was God's son,

---

[1] In the margin here the late hand has written, as if intended to be added—

        ' In welth without end
        I kepe noght elles to crave.'

Matth. xxvii. 40.	**ii Mil.**	Vah! qui destruis templum[1].
	iii Mil.	His sawes wer so, certayne.
	iv Mil.	And sirs, he saide to some

and that he might
raise the temple ;

He myght rayse it agayne.   276

but he has no
power to show
for all his tricks.'

24. i Mil.   To mustir þat he hadde no myght,
For all the kautelles þat he couthe kaste,
All yf he wer in worde so wight,
For all his force nowe he is feste.   280
Als Pilate demed is done and dight,
Therfore I rede þat we go reste.

ii Mil.   Þis race mon be rehersed right,
Thurgh þe worlde þoth este and weste.   284

If. 183.
xxvi J.
'Let him hang,
and make mows
on the moon.'

iii Mil.   ȝaa, late hym hynge here stille,
And make mowes on þe mone.

iv Mil.   Þanne may we wende at wille.

i Mil.   Nay goode sirs, noght so sone.   288

25.   For certis vs nedis anodir note,
Þis kirtill wolde I of you craue.

John xix. 23, 24.

ii Mil.   Nay, nay, sir, we will loke be lotte,
Whilke of vs foure fallis to to haue.   292

The men draw
lots for Jesus'
garments.

iii Mil.   I rede we drawe cutte for þis coote,
Loo, se howe sone alle sidis to saue.

iv Mil.   The schorte cutte schall wynne, þat wele ȝe woote,
Whedir itt falle to knyght or knaue.   296

i Mil.   Felowes, ȝe thar noght flyte,
For this mantell is myne.

ii Mil.   Goo we þanne hense tyte,
Þis trauayle here we tyne.   300

[1] The MS. has *Vath* and *destruit*.

XXXVI. THE BOCHERES.

Mortificacio Cristi [and burial of Jesus].

PERSONS OF THE PLAY.

PILATUS.	JOHANNES.	MILES.
CAIPHAS.	MARIA CLEOPHE.	LONGEUS LATUS.
ANNA.	LATRO A SINISTRIS.	CENTERIO.
JESUS.	LATRO A DEXTRIS.	JOSEPH [of Arimathea].
MARIA.	GARCIO.	NICHOMEDIS [1].

[SCENE I, *The way before the hill of Calvary.*]

1. **Pil.** SEES, Seniours, and see what I saie,
       Takis tente to my talkyng enteere,
Devoyde all þis dynne here þis day,
And fallis to my frenschippe in feere.   4
Sir Pilate, a Prince with-owten pere,
My name is full neuenly to neuen,
And domisman full derworth in dere [2],
Of gentillest Jewry full euen   8
      Am I.
Who makis oppressioun,
Or dose transgressioun,
Be my discressioun,   12
    Shall be demed dewly to dye.

Mark xv. 26-38
John xix. 19-37.
Gospel of Nicodemus. (Greek vers.) ch. xi.
Pilate commands peace and order.

---

[1] Nicodemus is spelt as above throughout the piece.
[2] The MS. has *dede*.

2. To dye schall I deme þame to dede,

Rebels may see
on yon hill how
they will be
treated !

Þo rebelles þat rewles þame vn-right,

Who þat to ȝone hill wille take heede,   16

May se þer þe soth in his sight,

Howe doulful to dede þei are dight

That liste noȝt owre lawes for to lere,

Lo þus be my mayne and my myght,   20

Tho churles schalle I chasteise and cheere,

Be lawe.

Ilke feloune false,

Shall hynge be þe halse,   24

Transgressors
shall be knit to
a cross.

Transgressours als,

On the crosse schalle be knytte for to knawe.

3. To knawe schall I knytte þame on crosse,

To schende þame with schame schall I shappe,   28

Ther liffis for to leese is no losse,

Suche tirrauntis with teene for to trappe.

Þus leelly þe lawe I vnlappe,

And punyssh þame pitously,   32

‘ But it is un-
happy that Jesus
is hung,

Of Jesu I holde it vnhappe,

Þat he on yone hill hyng so hye,

For gilte.

His bloode to spille,   36

he has been
killed through
spite.’

Toke ye you till

Þus was youre wille

Full spitously to spede he were spilte.

If. 184 b.
The priests ex-
cuse themselves.

4. Caip. To spille hym we spake in a speede,   40

For falsed he folowde in faie,

With fraudes oure folke gan he feede,

And laboured to lere þame his laye.

An. Sir Pilate, of pees we youe praye,   44

Oure lawe was full lyke to be lorne,

He saued noȝt oure dere Sabott daye,

And þat for to scape it were a scorne,

By lawe.   48

Pil. Sirs, be-fore youre sight,
With all my myght,
I examynde hym right,
    And cause non in hym cowthe I knawe.   52

Pilate found no harm in him.

5. Cay. ȝe knawe wele þe cause sir in cace,
It touched treasoune vntrewe,
Þe tribute to take or to trace
For-badde he, oure bale for to brewe.   56
Anna. Of japes ȝitt jangelid yone Jewe,
And cursedly he called hym a kyng,
To deme hym to dede it is diewe,
For treasoune it touches þat thyng,   60
    In dede.
Caip. ȝitt principall
And worste of all,
He garte hym call   64
    Goddes sonne, þat foulle motte hyme speede !

6. Pil. He spedis for to spille in space,
So wondirly wrought is youre will,
His bloode schall youre bodis enbrace,   68
For þat haue ȝe taken you till.

'His blood be on you.'

Anna. Þat forwarde fulfayne to fulfille,
In dede schall we dresse vs be-dene,
ȝone losell hym likis full ille,   72
For turned is his trantis all to teene,
    I trowe.

The priests accept it exultingly.

Cay. He called hym kyng,
Ille joie hym wring !   76
ȝa, late hym hyng,
    Full madly on þe mone for to mowe.

If. 185.
xxvj iij.

'Let him madly mow on the moon.'

7. An. To mowe on þe moone has he mente,
We! fye on þe, faitour in faye,   80
Who trowes þou, to þi tales toke tente.
Þou saggard, þi selffe gan þou saie,

They mock Jesus
on the cross.

Þe tempill distroie þe to-daye

Be þe thirde day ware done ilk-a-dele,   84

To rayse it þou schulde þe arraye.

Loo ! howe was þi falsed to feele,

  Foule falle þe !

For thy presumpcyoune   88

Þou haste thy warisoune,

Do faste, come doune,

  And a comely kyng schalle I calle þee.

8. Cay. I calle þe a coward to kenne,   92

Þat meruaylles and mirakills made,

Þou mustered emange many menne,

But, brothell, þou bourded to brede.

' Thou saved
others, save
thyself !'

Þou saued þame fro sorowes þai saide,   96

To saue nowe þi selffe late vs see,

God sonne if þou grathely be grayde,

Delyuere þe doune of þat tree

  Anone,   100

If þou be funne

Þou be Goddis sonne,

We schall be bonne

  To trowe on þe trewlye, ilkone.   104

The priests want
Pilate to alter
the writing that
he set above
Jesus :

9. An. Sir Pilate, youre pleasaun[c]e we praye,

Takis tente to oure talkyng þis tide,

And wipe ȝe yone writyng away,

It is not beste it abide.   108

lf. 185 b.

It sittis youe to sette it aside,

And sette þat he saide in his sawe,

As he þat was prente full of pride,

' Jewes kyng am I,' comely to knawe,   112

  Full playne.

but he will not.

Pil. *Quod scripci, scripci,*

Ȝone same wrotte I

I bide þer-by,   11

  What gedlyng will grucche there agayne.

[Scene II; *Calvary.*]

10. **Jesus.** Þou man þat of mys here has mente,
    To me tente enteerly þou take,
    On roode am I ragged and rente,   120
    Þou synfull sawle, for thy sake,
    For thy misse amendis wille I make.
    My bakke for to bende here I bide,
    Þis teene for thi trespase I take,   124
    Who couthe þe more kyndynes haue kydde
                 than I[1]?
    Þus for thy goode
    I schedde my bloode,   128
    Manne, mende thy moode,
       For full bittir þi blisse mon I by.

'Man, take heed; for thy misdeeds I make amends.'

11. **Ma.** Allas! for my swete sonne I saie,
    Þat doulfully to dede þus is diȝt,   132
    Allas! for full louely þou laye
    In my wombe, þis worthely wight.
    Allas! þat I schulde see þis sight
    Of my sone so semely to see,   136
    Allas! þat þis blossome so bright
    Vntrewly is tugged to þis tree,
             Allas!
    My lorde, my leyffe,   140
    With full grete greffe,
    Hyngis as a theffe,
       Allas! he did neuer trespasse.

Mary mourns for her son,

hung here like a thief.

12. **Jesus.** Þou woman, do way of thy wepyng,   144
    For me may þou no thyng amende,
    My fadirs wille to be wirkyng,
    For mankynde my body I bende.

'Woman, weep not; I do my Father's will.'

---

[1] These two words are written in a later hand.

lf. 186.
xxvj iiij.

Ma. Allas! þat þou likes noght to lende,   148
Howe schulde I but wepe for thy woo!
To care nowe my comforte is kende,

'Alas! why
must we part?'

Allas! why schulde we twynne þus in twoo
   For euere?   152

Jesus gives his
mother into
John's charge.

Jesus. Womanne, in stede of me,
Loo John þi sone schall bee.
John, see to þi modir free,
   For my sake do þou þi deuere.   156

13. **Ma.** Allas! sone, sorowe and siȝte,
þat me were closed in clay,
A swerde of sorowe me smyte,

She wishes she
were dead,

To dede I were done þis day.   160

Joh. A! modir, so schall ȝe noght saie,

but John tries to
comfort her.

I praye youe be pees in þis presse,
For with all þe myght þat I maye,
Youre comforte I caste to encresse   164
   In dede.
Youre sone am I,
Loo, here redy,
And nowe for-thy   168
   I praye yowe hense for to speede.

14. **Ma.** My steuen for to stede or to steere,

'How can I see
such sorrow?'

Howe schulde I such sorowe to see,
My sone þat is dereworthy and dere,   172
Thus doulfull a dede for to dye.

'Dear mother,
cease, mourning
does no good.'

Joh. A! dere modir, blynne of þis blee,
Youre mournyng it may not amende.

Ma. Cleo. A! Marie, take triste vn-to þe,   176
For socoure to þe will he sende
   þis tyde.

Joh. Fayre modir, faste
Hense latte vs caste.   180

Ma.   To he be paste,

Wille I buske here baynly to bide.

She will not go till her son has passed.

15. Jesus.   With bittirfull bale haue I bought,

Þus, man, all þi misse for to mende,   184   *If. 186 b.*

On me for to looke lette þou noȝt,

Howe baynly my body I bende.

'Man, see what bitter sorrow I suffer for thee;

No wighte in þis worlde wolde haue wende,

What sorowe I suffre for thy sake,   188

Manne, kaste þe thy kyndynesse be kende,

Trewe tente vn-to me þat þou take,

And treste.   *take heed,*

For foxis þer dennys haue þei,   192

Birdis hase ther nestis to paye,

But þe sone of man this daye,

Hase noȝt on his heed for to reste.

for foxes have holes, birds have nests, but the son of man has nowhere to rest his head.'

16. Lat. a sin.   If þou be Goddis sone so free,   196

Why hyng þou þus on þis hille?

To saffe nowe þi selffe late vs see,

And vs now, þat spedis for to spille.

The robber on the left taunts him,

Lat. a dex.   Manne, stynte of thy steuen and be stille,   200

For douteles thy God dredis þou noȝt,

Full wele are we worthy ther-till,

Vnwisely wrange haue we wrought

i-wisse.   204

but is stopt by the one on the right; 'we did wrong, he had no ill.

Noon ille did hee,

Þus for to dye;

Lord! haue mynde of me

What þou art come to þi blisse.   208

Lord, remember me.'

17. Jesus.   For sothe, sonne, to þe schall I saie,

Sen þou fro thy foly will falle,

With me schall dwelle nowe þis daye,

In paradise place principall.   212

'Son, thou repentest thy folly: thou shalt be with me this day in Paradise.

Heloy! heloy!

My God, my God, full free,

Lamaȝabatanye,

Eloi, eloi, lama sabacthani.'

Whar-to for-soke þou me [1],   216
       In care ?
And I did neuere ille
Þis dede for to go tille,
But be it at þi wille.   220

       A ! me thristis sare.

18. Gar. A drinke schalle I dresse þe in dede,
    A draughte þat is full dayntely dight,
    Full faste schall I springe for to spede,   224
    I hope I schall holde þat I haue hight.

Caip. Sir Pilate, þat moste is of myght,
    Harke ! Heely ! now harde I hym crye,
    He wenys þat þat worthely wight   228
    In haste for to helpe hym in hye
        In his nede.
Pil. If he do soo,
He schall haue woo.   232
An. He wer oure foo,
    If he dresse hym to do vs þat dede.

19. Gar. Þat dede for to dresse yf he doo,
    In sertis he schall rewe it full sore ;   236
    Neuere þe lees if he like it noght, loo,
    Full sone may he couere þat care.
Nowe swete sir, youre wille yf it ware,
    A draughte here of drinke haue I dreste,   240
    To spede for no spence þat ȝe spare [2],
    But baldely ye bib it for þe beste
        For-why;
Aysell and galle   244
Is menged with alle,
Drynke it ȝe schalle,
Youre lippis, I halde þame full drye.

---

[1] These four lines, 213–216, are written as two in the MS.
[2] MS. has *sware*.

20. Jesus. Þi drinke it schalle do me no deere, 248 'The drink will
not harm me ;
Wete þou wele þer-of will I none. I will none of it.

Nowe, fadir, þat formed alle in fere,

To thy moste myght make I my mone.

Þi wille haue I wrought in þis wone, 252

Þus ragged and rente on þis roode,

Þus doulffully to dede haue þei done,

For-giffe þame be grace þat is goode,

     Þai ne wote noȝt what it was, 256

My fadir, here my bone, Father, into thy
hands I commend
For nowe all thyng is done, my spirit.

My spirite to þee right sone

     Comende I in manus tuas. [*Jesus dies.*] 260

21. Mar. Now dere sone, Jesus so iente, Mary mourns
and sighs.
Sen my harte is heuy as leede,

O worde wolde I witte or þou wente ;

Allas ! nowe my dere sone is dede. 264 If. 187 b.

Full rewfully refte is my rede,

Allas ! for my darlyng so dere.

Joh. A modir, ȝe halde vppe youre heede, John and
Mary Cleophe
And sigh noȝt with sorowes so seere, 268 lead her away.

     I praye.

Ma. Cleo. It dose hir pyne

To see hym tyne,

Lede we her heyne, 272

     Þis mornyng helpe hir ne maye.

       [*Exit John and the two Maries.*

22. Caip. Sir Pilate, parceyue I you praye, The priests beg
Pilate to kill the
Oure costemes to kepe wele ȝe canne, crucified men,
who are now
To-morne is our dere sabott daye, 276 wan. They must
be buried before
Of mirthe muste vs meve ilke a mane. the Sabbath.

Ȝone warlous nowe waxis full wane,

And nedis muste þei beried be,

Deluyer þer dede sir, and þane 280

Shall we sewe to oure saide solempnite
　　　In dede.

Pil.　It schalle be done,
In wordis fone ;　　　　　　　　　　　　　　　284
Sir knyghtis, go sone,
　　　To ȝone harlottis you hendely take heede.

23. Þo caytiffis þou kille with þi knyffe,
Delyuere, haue done, þei were dede.　　　　　288
Mil.　Mi lorde I schall lenghe so þer liffe,
Þat þo brothelles schall neuere bite brede.

Pil.　Ser Longeus, steppe forthe in þis steede,
Þis spere, loo, haue halde in thy hande,　　　292
To Jesu þou rake fourthe I rede,
And sted nouȝt but stiffely þou stande
　　　A stounde.

In Jesu side　　　　　　　　　　　　　　　296
Schoffe it þis tyde,
No lenger bide,
　　　But grathely þou go to þe grounde.

　　　　　　　　　[Longeus pierces Jesus' side.

24. **Long. lat.**　O ! maker vnmade, full of myght,　300
O ! Jesu so jentile and jente,
Þat sodenly has lente me my sight,
Lorde ! louyng to þe be it lente.

On rode arte þou ragged and rente,　　　　　304
Mankynde for to mende of his mys,
Full spitously spilte is and spente,
Thi bloode lorde to bringe vs to blis
　　　full free.　　　　　　　　　　　　　　308

A ! mercy my socoure,
Mercy my treasoure,
Mercy my sauioure,
　　　Þi mercy be markid in me.　　　　　　　31:

25. **Cent.**　O ! wondirfull werkar i-wis,
Þis weedir is waxen full wan,

Trewe token I trowe þat it is

Þat mercy is mente vnto man.   316

Full clerly consayue þus I can,

No cause in this corse couthe þei knowe,

ȝitt doulfull þei demyd hym þan

To lose þus his liffe be þer lawe,   320

   No riȝte.

Trewly I saie,

Goddis sone verraye,

Was he þis daye,   324

   Þat doulfully to dede þus is diȝt.   [*Enter Joseph.*

26. Jos.   Þat lorde lele ay lastyng in lande,

Sir Pilate, full preste in þis presse,

He saue þe be see and be sande,   328

And all þat is derworth on deesse.

Pil.   Joseph, þis is lely no lesse,

To me arte þou welcome i-wisse,

Do saie me þe soth or þou sesse,   332

Thy worthyly wille what it is

   Anone.

Jos.   To þe I praye,

Giffe me in hye   336

Jesu bodye,

   In gree it for to graue al alone.

27. Pil.   Joseph sir, I graunte þe þat geste,

I grucche noȝt to grath hym in grave,   340

Delyuer, haue done he were dreste,

And sewe, sir, oure sabott to saffe.

Jos.   With handis and harte þat I haue,

I thanke þe in faith for my frende,   344

God kepe þe þi comforte to craue,

For wightely my way will I wende

   In hye.

To do þat dede   348

He be my speede,

Þat armys gun sprede,

   B b

thinks it a token that Jesus was judged un-righteously.

Joseph comes to Pilate

to beg the body of Jesus.

Pilate agrees.

If. 188 b.

Joseph thanks him,

and goes to bury Jesus.

Manne kynde be his bloode for to bye.

[Enter Nichodemus.

28. Nicho.   Weill mette, sir, in mynde gune [I] meffe   352
For Jesu, þat juged was vn-jente,
Ye laboured for license and leve,
To berye his body on bente.

Jos.   Full myldely þat matere I mente,   356
And þat for to do will I dresse.

Nicho.   Both same I wolde þat wente
And lette not for more ne for lesse,
      For-why   360
Oure frende was he,
Faithfull and free.

Jos.   Þerfore go we
    To berie þat body in hye.   364

[They go to the cross.

29. All mankynde may marke in his mynde
To see here þis sorowfull sight,
No falsnesse in hym couthe þei fynde,
Þat doulfully to dede þus is dight.   368

Nicho.   He was a full worthy wight,
Nowe blemysght and bolned with bloode.

Jos.   ȝa, for þat he maistered his myght,
Full falsely þei fellid þat foode   372
      I wene[1],

Bothe bakke and side,
His woundes wide ;
     For-þi þis tyde   376

    Take we hym doune vs be-twene.

30. Nicho.   Be-twene vs take we hym doune,
And laie hym on lenthe on þis lande.

Jos.   Þis reuerent and riche of rennoune,   380
Late vs halde hym and halse hym with hande.

A graue haue I garte here be ordande,

---

[1] MS. has *wyne.*

Þat neuer was in noote, it is newe.

Nicho. To þis corse it is comely accordande, 384
To dresse hym with dedis full dewe
    Þis stounde.

Jos. A sudarye
Loo here haue I, 388
Wynde hym for-thy,
    And sone schalle we graue hym in grounde.

Joseph has a winding-sheet or napkin.

31. Nicho. In grounde late vs graue hym and goo,
Do liffely, latte vs laie hym allone ; 392
Nowe sauiour of me and of moo
Þou kepe vs in clennesse ilkone.

They bury the body,

Jos. [*Prays*]. To [1] thy mercy nowe make I my moone,
As sauiour be see and be sande, 396
Þou gyde me þat my griffe be al gone,
With lele liffe to lenge in þis lande,
    And esse.

and pray.

Nicho. Seere oynementis here haue I 400
Brought for þis faire body ;
I anoynte þe for-thy
    With myrre and aloes.

Nicodemus anoints the body with several ointments.

32. Jos. Þis dede it is done ilke a dele, 404
And wroughte is þis werke wele i-wis.
To þe kyng on knes here I knele,
Þat baynly þou belde me in blisse.

If. 189 b.

Nicho. He highte me full hendely to be his. 408
A nyght whan I neghed hym full nere ;
Haue mynde lorde and mende [2] me of mys,
For done is oure dedis full dere
    Þis tyde. 412

'Lord, remember me ; forgive me my sins.'

Jos. þis lorde so goode,
Þat schedde his bloode,
He mende youre moode,
    And buske on þis blis for to bide. 416

[1] The MS. has *Do*.   [2] The MS. has *wende*.

B b 2

XXXVII. THE SADILLERES[1].

The Harrowing of Hell.

PERSONS OF THE PLAY.

ADAME.	JOHANNES BAPTISTA.	BELLIALL.
EUA.	MOYSES.	MICHILL (Archangel).
ISAIAH [Isaac in error].	BELSABUB.	PRIMUS DIABOLUS.
SYMEON.	SATTAN.	SECUNDUS DIABOLUS.
JESUS.	DAUID.	

Gospel of Nichodemus (Latin vers.), Part II, ch. ii–viii.
' Man, meekly think of me,

SCENE I, *outside the gates of Hell.*

1. Jesus. Manne on molde, be meke to me,

And haue thy maker in þi mynde,

And thynke howe I haue tholid for þe,

With pereles paynes for to be pyned. 4

I have fulfilled my Father's promise ;

The forward of my Fadir free

Haue I fulfillid, as folke may fynde,

Incipit Extractio Animarum ab Inferno.

Jesus. My fader me from blys has send

Tille erth for mankynde sake,

Adam mys for to amend,

My deth nede must I take.

I dwellyd ther thyrty yeres and two

And somdele more, the sothe to say,

In anger, pyne, and mekylle wo,

I dyde on cros this day.

---

[1] The 25th Play of the Towneley Collection (f. 97 *b* in the MS., p. 244 of Surtees print) runs nearly parallel with this piece; it is given below entire.

Þer-fore a-boute nowe woll I bee,
Þat I haue bought for to vnbynde.　　　　　8
Þe feende þame wanne with trayne
Thurgh frewte of erthely foode,
I haue þame getyn agayne
Thurgh bying with my bloode.　　　　　　**12**

I will now un-
bind those I
have bought

2. And so I schall þat steede restore,
　For [1] whilke þe feende fell for synne,
　Þare schalle mankynde wonne euermore,
　In blisse þat schall neuere blynne.　　　**16**
　All þat in werke my werkemen were
　Owte of thare woo I wol þame wynne,
　And some signe schall I sende be-fore
　Of grace to garre þer gamys be-gynne.　**20**
　A light I woll þei haue
　To schewe þame I schall come sone,
　My bodie bidis in graue,
　Tille alle thes dedis be done.　　　　　**24**

I shall restore
my workmen
to heaven.'

Jesus sends a
light as a sign
that he is coming.

Therfor tille helle now wille I go,　　　　7
To chalange that is myne,　　　　　　　　8
Adam, Eue, and othere mo,
Thay shalle no longer dwelle in pyne;
The feynde them wan withe trayn　　　　　9
Thrughe fraude of earthly fode,　　　　　10
I have theym boght agan　　　　　　　　　11
With shedyng of my blode.　　　　　　　　12
And now I wille that stede restore,　　　　13
Whiche the feynde felle fro for syn,　　　14
Som tokyn wille I send before,　　　　　　19
Withe myrth to gar thare gammes begyn.
A light I will thay haue　　　　　　　　　21
To know I wille com sone,
My body shalle abyde in graue　　　　　　23
Tille alle this dede be done.　　　　　　　24

---

[1] Read *fro.*

3. My Fadir ordand on þis wise
   Aftir his will þat I schulde wende,
   For to fulfille þe prophicye,
   And als I spake my solace to spende.   28

   My frendis þat in me faith affies,
   Nowe fro ther fois I schall þame fende,

   And on the thirde day ryght vprise,
   And so tille heuen I schall assende.   32

   Sithen schall I come agayne
   To deme bothe goode and ill,
   Tille endles joie or peyne
   Þus is my Fadris will[1].   36

[SCENE II, *Hell; at one side Limbo, enclosing the patriarchs
and prophets; a light shines across.*]

4. **Adame.**   Mi bretheren, harkens to me here,
   Swilke hope of heele neuere are we hadde,
   Foure thousande and sex hundereth ȝere
   Haue we bene heere in þis stedde.   40

   Nowe see I signe of solace seere,
   A glorious gleme to make vs gladde,
   Wher-fore I hope oure helpe is nere,
   And sone schall sesse oure sorowes sadde.   44

   Eua.   Adame, my husband hende,
   Þis menys solas certayne,

Adam.	My brether, herkyn unto me here,	37
	More hope of helth neuer we had,	
	Four thousand and six hundred yere	
	Haue we bene here in darknes stad;	40
	Now se I tokyns of solace sere,	
	A gloryous gleme to make vs glad,	
	Wherthrughe I hope that help is nere,	
	That sone shalle slake oure sorowes sad.	44
Eve.	Adam, my husband heynd,	
	This menys solace certan,	

---

[1] A late marginal note here says 'tunc cantent.'

Such light gune on vs lende
In paradise full playne. 48

5. Isaiah [1]. Adame, we schall wele vndirstande,
I, Ysaias as god me kende,
I prechid in Neptalym, þat lande,
And Zabulon even vn-till ende. 52
I spake of folke in mirke walkand,
And saide a light schulde on þame lende,
This lered I whils I was leuand,
Nowe se I God þis same hath sende. 56
Þis light comes all of Criste,
Þat seede to saue vs nowe,
Þus is my poynte puplisshid,
But Symeon, what sais þou ? 60

6. Symeon. Yhis, my tale of farleis feele,
For in þis temple his frendis me fande,

Isaiah while living prophesied a great light.
Isa. ix. 2.

It was Christ.

Simeon repeats the tale.

Siche light can on vs leynd'
In paradyse full playn. 48
Isaias. Adam, thrugh thi syn
Here were we put to dwelle
This wykyd place within,
The name of it is helle ;
Here paynes shalle neuer blyn
That wykyd ar and felle,
Loue that lord withe wyn
His lyfe for vs wold selle.

Et cantent omnes 'Salvator mundi' primum versum.

Adam thou welle vnderstand
I am Isaias, so Crist me kende.
I spake of folke in darknes walkand,
I saide a light shuld on theym lende ;
This light is alle from Crist commande
That he tille vs has hedir sende,
Thus is my poynt proved in hand,
As I before to fold it kende.
Simeon. So may I telle of farlys feylle
For in the tempylle his freyndes me fande, 61

---

[1] Isaac is written, but it is evidently a mistake for Isaiah.

I hadde delite with hym to dele,
And halsed homely with my hande.   64
I saide, " lorde, late thy seruaunt lele
Passe nowe in pesse to liffe lastand,

lf. 191 b.
For nowe my selfe has sene thy hele,
Me liste no lengar to liffe in lande."   68

He sees the
light.
Þis light þou hast purueyed
To folkes þat liffis in leede,
Þe same þat I þame saide,
I see fulfillid in dede.   72

John Baptist
recognizes
Christ's coming.
7. Joh. Bapt. Als voyce criand to folke I kende,
Þe weyes of criste als I wele kanne,
I baptiste hym with bothe my hande
Euen in þe floode of flume Jordanne.   76
Þe holy goste fro heuene discende,
Als a white dowue doune on hym þanne,
The Fadir voice, my mirthe to mende,
Was made to me euen als manne,   80

Me thoght dayntethe with hym to deylle,
I halsid hym homely with my hand,   64
I saide, Lord, let thi servandes leylle
Pas in peasse to lyf lastande,
Now that myn eeyn has sene thyn hele   67
No longer lyst I lyf in lande.   68
This light thou has purvayde
For theym that lyf in lede,   70
That I before of the haue saide
I se it is fulfillyd in dede.   72

Johannes Baptista. As a vo[i]ce cryand I kend
The wayes of Crist, as I welle can,   74
I baptisid hym with bothe myn hende
In the water of flume Jordan ;   76
The Holy Gost from heuen discende
As a white dowfe downe on me than,   78
The Fader voyce oure myrthes to amende
Was made to me lyke as a man ;   8c

This is my sone, he saide,
In whome me paies full wele,
His light is on vs laide,
He comes oure cares to kele.   84

8. Moyses. Of þat same light lernyng haue I,
To me Moyses he mustered his myght,
And also vnto anodir, Hely,
Wher we were on an hille on hight.   88
Whyte as snowe was his body,
And his face like to þe sonne to sight,
No man on molde was so myghty
Grathely to loke agaynste þat light,   92
Þat same light se I nowe,
Shynyng on vs sarteyne,
Wherfore trewly I trowe,
We schalle sone passe fro payne.   96

9. i Diab. Helpe! Belsabub! to bynde þer boyes,
Such harrowe was neuer are herde in helle.

     'Yond is my son,' he saide,
     'And whiche me pleasses fulle welle,'   82
     His light is on us layde,
     And commys oure karys to kele.   84
Moyses. Now this same nyght lernyng have I,
     To me, Moyses, he shewid his myght,   86
     And also to another oone, Hely,
     Where we stud on a hille on hyght,   88
     As whyte as snaw was his body,
     His face was like the son for bright,   90
     Noman on mold was so mighty
     Grathly durst loke agans that light,   92
     And that same lighte here se I now
     Shynyng on vs, certayn,   94
     Where thrughe truly I trow
     That we shalle sone pas fro this payn.   96
Rybald. Sen fyrst that helle was mayde, And I was
                 put therin
     Siche sorow neuer ere I had, nor hard I siche
             a dyn;

ii **Diab.** Why rooris þou soo, rebalde? þou royis,

What is be-tidde, canne þou ought telle?   100

i **Diab.** What! heris þou noȝt þis vggely noyse,

Þes lurdans þat in lymbo dwelle,

Þei make menyng of many joies,

And musteres grete mirthe þame emell.   104

ii **Diab.** Mirthe? nay, nay, þat þoynte is paste,

More hele schall þei neuere haue.

i **Diab.** Þei crie on Criste full faste,

And sais he schal þame saue.   108

'They are shut
up in a special
part, they shall
never pass out.'

10. **Belsabub.** Ȝa, if he saue þame noght, we schall,

For they are sperde in speciall space,

Whils I am prince and principall

Schall þei neuer passe oute of þis place.   112

Calle vppe Astrotte and A

To giffe þer counsaille in þis case,

My hart beginnys to brade, my wytt waxys thyn,

I drede we can not be glad, thise saules mon

fro us twyn;

How, Belsabub! bynde thise boys, sich harow

was neuer hard in helle.   98

Belzabub. Out, Rybald! thou rores, what is betyd? can

thou oght telle?   100

Rybald. Whi, herys thou not this vgly noyse!

Thise lurdans that in lymbo dwelle

They make menyng of many joyse,

And muster myrthes theym emelle.   104

Belzabub. Myrth? nay, nay! that poynt is past,

More hope of helth shalle they neuer haue.

Rybald. Thay cry on Crist fulle fast,

And says he shalle theym saue.   108

Belzabub. Yee, tho he do not I shalle

For thay ar sparyd in specyalle space,

Whils I am prynce and pryncypalle,

Thay shalle neuer pas out of this place.   112

Calle up Astarot and Anaballe

To gyf vs counselle in this case;

Bele, Berit, and Belial,
To marre þame þat swilke maistries mase. 116
Say to Satan oure sire,
And bidde þame bringe also,
Lucifer louely of lyre.

The other devils
are called to
council.

i **Diab.** Al redy, lorde, I goo. 120

11. **Jesus** [*Without*]. *Attollite portas principes*,
Oppen vppe ȝe princes of paynes sere,
Et eleuamini eternales,
Youre yendles ȝatis þat ȝe haue here. 124

'Open your
gates!'

Sattan. What page is þere þat makes prees,
And callis hym kyng of vs in fere?

'Who is it?

Dauid [*in Limbo*]. I lered leuand, with-outen lees,
He is a kyng of vertues clere. 128

David bears wit-
ness to Christ.

Telle Berith and Bellyalle
To mar theym that siche mastry mase; 116
Say to sir Satan oure syre,
And byd hym bryng also
Sir Lucyfer lufly of lyre.

Rybald. Alle redy, lord, I go. 120

Jesus. Attollite portas, principes, vestras et eleuamini
portae eternales, et introibit rex gloriae.

Rybald. Out, harro, out! what deville is he
That callys hym kyng ouer vs alle? 126
Hark Belzabub, com ne, 137
For hedusly I hard hym calle.

Belzabub. Go spar the yates, ylle mot thou the!
And set the waches on the walle, 140
If that brodelle com ne
With vs ay won he shalle;
And if he more calle or cry, 141
To make us more debate,
Lay on hym hardely,
And make hym go his gate. 144

David. Nay, withe hym may ye not fyght,
For he is kyng and conqueroure,

A ! lorde, mekill of myght,
And stronge in ilke a stoure,

In batailes ferse to fight,
And worthy to wynne honnoure.   132

12. Sattan.   Honnoure ! in þe deuelway, for what dede ?
All erthely men to me are thrall,
Þe lady þat calles hym lorde in leede,
Hadde neuer ȝit herberowe, house, ne halle.   136

i Diab.   Harke, Belsabub ! I haue grete drede,
For hydously I herde hym calle.

Belliall.   We ! spere oure ȝates, all ill mot þou spede,
And sette furthe watches on þe wall.   140
And if he call or crie
To make vs more debate,

Lay on hym þan hardely,
And garre hym gang his gate.   144

13. Sattan.   Telle me what boyes dare be so bolde,
For drede to make so mekill draye.

And of so mekille myght,   129
And styf in euery stoure ;   130
Of hym commys alle this light
That shynys in this bowre,
He is fulle fers in fight   131
Worthi to wyn honoure.   132

Belzabub.   Honoure ! harsto, harlot, for what dede
Alle erthly men to me are thralle,   134
That lad that thou callys lord in lede
He had neuer harbour, house, ne halle ;   136
How, sir Sathanas, com nar
And hark this cursid rowte !

Sathanes.   The deville you alle to-har !
What ales the so to showte ?
And me, if I com nar
Thy brayn bot I bryst owte.

Belzabub.   Thou must com help to spar,
We are beseged abowte.

Sathanes.   Besegyd aboute ! Whi who durst be so bold   145
For drede to make on vs a fray ?   146

i Diab. Itt is þe Jewe þat Judas solde
For to be dede, þis othir daye.   148

' 'Tis the Jew
that Judas sold.'

Sattan. Owe! þis tale in tyme is tolde,
Þis traytoure traues vs alway,
He schall be here full harde in holde,
Loke þat he passe noght, I þe praye.   152

ii Diab. Nay, nay, he will noȝt wende
A-way or I be ware,
He shappis hym for to schende
Alle helle or he go ferre.   156

' He will ruin
all hell.'

14. Sattan. Nay, faitour, þer-of schall he faile,
For alle his fare I hym deffie,
I knowe his trantis fro toppe to taile,
He leuys with gaudis and with gilery.   160
Þer-by he brought oute of oure bale
Nowe, 'late, Lazar of Betannye,
Þer-fore I gaffe to þe Jewes counsaille,
Þat þei schulde alway garre hym dye.   164

Satan defies him.

lf. 193.
xxvij iij.
Satan advised
the Jews and
entered into
Judas.

Belzabub. It is the Jew that Judas sold
For to be dede this othere day.   148

Sathanes. How, in tyme that tale was told,
That trature trauesses vs alle-way
He shalbe here fulle hard in hold,
Bot loke he pas not, I the pray.   152

Belzabub. Pas! nay, nay, he wille not weynde
From hens or it be war,
He shapys hym for to sheynd
Alle helle or he go far.   156

Sathanes. Fy, faturs, therof shalle he faylle,
For alle his fare I hym defy;
I know his trantes fro top to taylle,
He lyffes by gawdes and glory.   160
Therby he broght furthe of oure baylle
The lathe Lazare of Betany,
Bot to the Jues I gaf counsaylle
That thay shuld cause hym dy;   164

I entered in Judas
Þat forwarde to fulfille,
Þer-fore his hire he has,
All-way to wonne here stille.   168

15. **Belsabub.**   Sir Sattanne, sen we here þe saie,
Þat þou and ȝe Jewes wer same assente,
And wotte he wanne Lazar awaye,
Þat tille vs was tane for to tente.   172

If Satan has
done these
things he may
now conquer
Jesus.

Trowe þou þat þou marre hym maye,
To mustir myghtis what he has mente,
If he nowe depriue vs of oure praye,
We will ȝe witte whanne þei are wente.   176

' Be ready to
strike him down.'

Sattan.   I bidde ȝou be noȝt abasshed
But boldely make youe boune
With toles þat ȝe on traste
And dynge þat dastard doune.   180

Jesus enters
through hell-
gates.

16. **Jesus** [*Without*].   *Principes, portas tollite,*
Vndo youre ȝatis, ȝe princis of pryde,
Et introibit rex glorie,
Þe kyng of blisse comes in þis tyde.   184

                              [*Enters the gates of Hell.*

I enterd ther into Judas
That forward to fulfylle,
Therfor his hyere he has
Alle wayes to won here stylle.   168

Rybald.   Sir Sathan, sen we here the say
Thou and the Jues were at assent,
And wote he wan the Lazare away
That vnto vs was taken to tent,   172
Hopys thou that thou mar hym may
To muster the malyce that he has ment?
For and he refe us now oure pray
We wille ye witt or he is went.   176

Sathanas.   I byd the noght abaste,
Bot boldly make you bowne,
Withe toyles that ye intraste
And dyng that dastard downe.   180

Jesus.   Attollite portas principes vestras, etc.   181

Sattan. Owte ! harrowe [what harlot] is hee,   Satan bewails.
Þat sais his kyngdome schall be cryed.

Dauid [*in Limbo*]. Þat may þou in my sawter see
For þat poynte of prophicie.   188
I saide þat he schuld breke   David foretold
Youre barres and bandis by name,   this in his Psalm
    [xxiv. 7–9].
And on youre werkis take wreke,
Nowe schalle ȝe see þe same.   192

17. **Jesus.** Þis steede schall stonde no lenger stoken,   lf. 193 b.
Opynne vppe and latte my pepul passe.   The whole place
    is thrown open.
Diabolus. Oute ! beholdes, oure baill is brokynne,
And brosten are alle oure bandis of bras.   196

Rybald. Outt, harro! what harlot is he   185
    That sayes his kyngdom shalbe cryde?
David. That may thou in sawter se,   187
    For of this prynce thus ere I saide;
    I saide that he shuld breke   189
    Youre barres and bandes by name,
    And of youre warkes take wreke;
    Now shalle thou se the same.   192
Jesus. Ye prynces of helle open youre yate,
    And let my folk furthe gone;
    A prynce of peasse shalle enter therat
    Wheder ye wille or none.
Rybald. What art thou that spekys so?
Jesus. A king of blys that hight Jesus.
Rybald. Yee, hens fast I red thou go,
    And melle the not with vs.
Belzabub. Oure yates I trow wille last,
    Thay ar so strong I weyn,
    Bot if oure barres brast
    For the thay shalle not twyn.
Jesus. This stede shalle stand no longer stokyn,   193
    Open vp and let my pepille pas.
Rybald. Out, harro! oure baylle is brokyn,
    And brusten ar alle oure bandes of bras.   196

Telle lucifer alle is vnlokynne.

Belsabub.　What þanne, is lymbus lorne, allas !
Garre Satan, helpe þat we were wroken,
Þis werke is werse þanne euere it was.　　　200

The devils re-
criminate on each
other.

Sattan.　I badde ȝe schulde be boune
If he made maistries more,
Do dynge þat dastard doune,
And sette hym sadde and sore.　　　204

18. **Belsabub.**　ȝa, sette hym sore, þat is sone saide,
But come þi selffe and serue hym soo,
We may not bide his bittir braide,
He wille vs marre, and we wer moo.　　　208

Sattan.　What ! faitours, wherfore are ȝe ferde ?
Haue ȝe no force to flitte hym froo ?
Belyue loke þat my gere be grathed,
Mi selffe schall to þat gedlyng goo.　　　212

Belzabub.　Harro ! oure yates begyn to crak,
　　　In sonder, I trow, they go,
　　　And helle, I trow will alle-to-shak ;
　　　Alas, what I am wo !

Rybald.　Lymbo is lorne alas !　　　198
　　　Sir Sathanas com vp ;
　　　This wark is wars then it was.

Sathanas.　Yee, hangyd be thou on a cruke ;
　　　Thefys, I bad ye shuld be bowne　　　201
　　　If he maide mastres more
　　　To dyng that dastard downe,
　　　Sett hym bothe sad and sore.　　　204

Belzabub.　To sett hym sore that is sone saide
　　　Com thou thi self and serue hym so ;
　　　We may not abyde his bytter brayde,
　　　He wolde vs mar and we were mo.　　　208

Sathanas.　Fy, faturs ! Wherefor were ye flayd ?
　　　Have ye no force to flyt hym fro ?
　　　Loke in haste my gere be grayd,
　　　My self shalle to that gadlyng go.　　　212

[*To Jesus.*] Howe! belamy, a de,
With al thy booste and bere,
And telle to me þis tyde,
What maistries makes þou here ? 216

' Stay, my fine friend, what lordship do you want here ?'

19. **Jesus.** I make no maistries but for myne,
Þame wolle I saue, I telle þe nowe,
Þou hadde no poure þame to pyne,
But as my prisonne for þer prowe. 220
Here haue þei soiorned, noght as thyne,
But in thy warde, þou wote wele howe.

' I only want my people, you had no power save to imprison them for their good.

Sattan. And what deuel haste þou done ay syne
Þat neuer wolde negh þame nere, or nowe? 224

If. 194. xxvij iiij.

Jesus. Nowe is þe tyme certayne
Mi Fadir ordand be-fore,
Þat they schulde passe fro payne,
And wonne in mirthe euer more. 228

This is the time ordained to set them free.'

20. **Sattan.** Thy fadir knewe I wele be sight,
He was a write his mette to wynne,

Satan parleys with Christ.

How, thou belamy, abyde,
Withe alle thi boste and beyn 214
And telle me in this tyde
What mastres thou makes here. 216

Jesus. I make no mastry bot for myne,
I wille theym saue, that shalle the sow,
Thou has no powere theym to pyne,
Bot in my pryson for thare prow 220
Here haue thay soiornyd, noght as thyne
Bot in thi wayrd, thou wote as how.

Sathanas. Why, where has thou bene ay syn
That neuer wold neghe theym nere or now. 222

Jesus. Now is the tyme certan
My Fader ordaned her-for,
That thay shuld pas fro payn,
In blys to dwelle for euer more. 228

Sathanas. Thy fader knew I welle by syght,
He was a wright his meett to wyn,

And Marie me menys þi modir hight,
Þe vttiremeste ende of all þi kynne. 232
Who made þe be so mekill of myght?
Jesus.   Þou wikid feende, latte be thy dynne,

' My Father dwells in heaven.

Mi Fadir wonnys in heuen on hight,
With blisse þat schall neuere blynne. 236
I am his awne sone,
His forward to fulfille [1].
And same ay schall we wonne,
And sundir whan we wolle. 240

21. **Sattan.**   God sonne, þanne schulde þou be ful gladde,
Aftir no catel neyd thowe crave [2],
But þou has leued ay like a ladde,

Jesus lived in sorrow

And in sorowe as a symple knave. 244
Jesus.   Þat was for hartely loue I hadde

in order to save man.

Vnto mannis soule it for to saue;
And for to make þe mased and madde,
And by þat resoune þus dewly to haue, 248

Mary me mynnys thi moder hight,
The utmast ende of alle thy kyn, 232
Say who made the so mekille of myght?
Jesus.   Thou wykyd feynde lett be thi dy[n],
My Fader wonnes in heven on hight
In blys that neuer more shalle blyn; 236
I am his oonly son his forward to fulfylle,
Togeder wille we won in sonder when we wylle. 240
Sathanas.   Goddes son! nay then myght thou be glad,
For no catell thurt the craue;
Bot thou has lyffed ay lyke a lad,
In sorow and as a sympille knaue. 244
Jesus.   That was for the hartly luf I had
Vnto man's saulle it forto saue,
And forto make the masyd and mad,
And for that reson rufully to rafe. 248

---

[1] Lines 237, 238 are written as one in MS.
[2] This line was first written ' Aftir no catel þus þe I telle,' but was corrected as above by the Elizabethan hand, which also in l. 244 inserted *as* and wrote *knave* for *braide*.

Mi godhede here I hidde
In Marie modir myne,
For it schulde noȝt be kidde,
To þe nor to none of thyne.　　　252

22. Sattan. A! þis wolde I were tolde in ilk a toune.
So sen þou sais God is thy sire,　　　If. 194 b.
I schall þe proue be right resoune,
Þou motes his men in to þe myre.　　　256　Satan reproaches
To breke his bidding were thei boune,　　Christ, for that
And, for they did at my desire,　　　men were
　　　　　　　　　　　　　　　　obliged to break
Fro paradise he putte þame doune　　　God's bidding.
In helle here to have þer hyre.　　　260
And thy selfe, day and nyght,
Has taught al men emang,
To do resoune and right,
And here workis þou all wrang.　　　264

23. Jesus. I wirke noght wrang, þat schal þow witte,
If I my men fro woo will wynne,
Mi prophetis playnly prechid it,

　　　　My Godhede here I hyd
　　　　In Mary moder myne,
　　　　Where it shalle neuer be kyd
　　　　To the ne none of thyne.　　　252
Sathanas. How now? this wold I were told in towne,
　　　　Thou says God is thi syre;
　　　　I shalle the prove by good reson
　　　　Thou meyttes as man dos into myre.　　　256
　　　　To breke thi byddyng they were full bowne,
　　　　And soyn they wroght at my desyre,
　　　　From Paradise thou putt theym downe,
　　　　In helle here to haue thare hyre:　　　260
　　　　And thou thi self by day and nyght,
　　　　Taght euer alle men emang,
　　　　Euer to do reson and right,
　　　　And here thou wyrkys alle wrang.　　　264
Jesus. I wyrk no wrang, that shall thou wytt,
　　　　If I my men fro wo wille wyn;
　　　　My prophettes playnly prechyd it,
　　　　　　　C C 2

All þis note þat nowe be-gynne. 268
Þai saide þat I schulde be obitte,
To hell þat I schulde entre in,
And saue my seruauntis fro þat pitte,
Wher dampned saulis schall sitte for synne. 272
And ilke trewe prophettis tale
Muste be fulfillid in mee,
I haue þame broughte with bale,
And in blisse schal þei be. 276

24. Sattan. Nowe sen þe liste allegge þe lawes,

Þou schalte be atteynted, or we twynne,
For þo þat þou to wittenesse drawes,
Full even agaynste þe will be-gynne. 280

Salamon saide in his sawes,
Þat whoso enteres helle withynne,
Shall neuer come oute, þus clerkis knawes,—
And þerfore felowe, leue þi dynne. 284

Job, þi seruaunte also,
Þus in his tyme gune telle,

  Alle the noytes that I begyn; 268
  They saide that I shuld be that ilke
  In helle where I shuld intre in,
  To saue my seruandes fro that pytt
  Where dampnyd saullys shalle syt for syn. 272
  And ilke true prophete taylle
  Shalbe fulfillid in me,
  I haue thaym boght fro baylle,
  In blis now shalle they be. 276

Sathanas. Now sen thou lyst to legge the lawes
  Thou shalbe tenyd or we twyn,
  For those that thou to witnes drawes
  Fulle euen agans the shalle begyn; 280
  As Salamon saide in his sawes,
  Who that ones commys helle within
  He shalle neuer owte, as clerkes knawes,
  Therfor, belamy, let be thy dyn. 284
  Job thi seruande also
  In his tyme can telle

Þat nowthir frende nor foo
Shulde fynde reles in helle.   288

If. 195.
xxvij v.

25. **Jesus.**   He saide full soth, þat schall þou see,
Þat in helle may be no reles,
But of þat place þan preched he,
Where synffull care schall euere encrees.   292
And in þat bale ay schall þou be,
Whare sorowes sere schall neuer sesse,
And for my folke þer fro wer free,
Nowe schall þei passe to þe place of pees.   296
Þai were here with my wille,
And so schall þei fourthe wende,
And þi selue schall fulfille,
Þer wooe with-outen ende.   300

26. **Sattan.**   Owe ! þanne se I howe þou mouys emang,

Job says the
truth,

thou shalt stay in
hell for ever,

but my folk shall
pass forth.

'Oh ! there is a
limit to the
harm,

That nawder freynde nor fo
Shalle fynde relese in helle.   288
Jesus.   He sayde fulle soythe, that shalle thou se,
In helle shalbe no relese,
Bot of that place then ment he
Where synfulle care shalle euer encrese.   292
In that baylle ay shalle thou be,
Where sorowes seyr shall never sesse,
And my folk that wer most fre
Shalle pas vnto the place of peasse ;   296
For thay were here with my wille,
And so thay shalle furth weynde,
Thou shalle thiself fulfylle,
Euer wo withoutten ende.   300
Sathanas.   Whi, and wille thou take theym alle me fro?
Then thynk me thou art vnkynde ;
Nay I pray the do not so,
Vmthynke the better in thy mynde.
Or els let me with the go,
I pray the leyfe me not behynde.
Jesus.   Nay tratur, thou shalle won in wo,
And tille a stake I shalle the bynde.
Sathanas.   Now here I how thou menys emang.   301

Some mesure with malice to melle,
Sen þou sais all schall noȝt gang,
But some schalle alway with vs dwelle.   304

Jesus.   Ȝaa, witte þou wele, ellis were it wrang,
Als cursed Cayme þat slewe Abell,
And all þat hastis hem selue to hange,
Als Judas and Archedefell,   308
Datan and Abiron,
And alle of þare assente,

Als tyrantis euerilkone
Þat me and myne turmente.   312

27. And all þat liste noght to lere my lawe,
Þat I haue lefte in lande nowe newe,
Þat is my comyng for to knawe,
And to my sacramente pursewe.   316

Mi dede, my rysing, rede be rawe,
Who will noght trowe þei are noght trewe,

Vnto my dome I schall þame drawe,
And juge þame worse þanne any Jewe.   320

With mesure and malyce for to melle,
Bot sen thou says it shalbe lang,
Yit som let alle-wayes with vs dwelle.   304

Jesus.   Yis wytt thou welle, els were greatt wrang,
Thou shalle haue Caym that slo Abelle,
And alle that hastes theym self to hang,
As dyd Judas and Architophelle;   308
And Daton and Abaron and alle of thare assent,
Cursyd tyranttes euer ilkon that me and myn
                                   tormente.   312
And alle that wille not lere my law
That I haue left in land for new
That makes my commyng knaw,
And alle my sacramentes persew;   316
My deth, my rysyng, red by raw,
Who trow thaym not thay ar vntrewe,
Vnto my dome I shalle theym draw,
And juge theym wars than any Jew.   320

And all þat likis to leere
My lawe and leue þer bye,
Shall neuere haue harmes heere,
But welthe as is worthy.   324

All who live by
Christ's law will
get no harm in
hell.

28. Sattan.   Nowe here my hande, I halde me paied,
Þis poynte is playnly for oure prowe,
If þis be soth þat þou hast saide,
We schall haue moo þanne we haue nowe.   328
Þis lawe þat þou nowe late has laide
I schall lere men noȝt to allowe,
Iff þei it take þei be be-traied,
For I schall turne þame tyte, I trowe.   332
I schall walke este and weste,
And garre þame werke wele werre.

Satan is content,
and thinks he will
have enough.

He will walk
east and west
and make men
work badly.

Jesus.   Naye, feende, þou schall be feste,
Þat þou schalte flitte not ferre.   336

29. Sattan.   Feste! þat were a foule reasoune,
Nay, bellamy, þou bus be smytte.

And thay that lyst to lere my law and lyf therby,
Shalle neuer have harmes here, bot welth as is
                                        worthy.   324

Sathanas.   Now here my hand. I hold me payde,
Thise poyntes are playnly for my prow,
If this be trew as thou has saide
We shall haue mo then we haue now,   328
Thies lawes that thou has late here laide
I shalle theym lere not to alow,
If thay myn take thay ar betraide,
And I shalle turne theym tytt I trowe.   332
I shalle walk eest, I shalle walk west,
And gar theym wyrk welle war.

Jesus.   Nay feynde, thou shalbe fest,
That thou shalle flyt no far.   336

Sathanas.   Feste? fy! that were a wykyd treson!
Belamy, thou shalbe smytt.   338

But Jesus calls
Michael to chain
the devil into his
cell.

Jesus. Mighill! myne Aungell, make þe boune,

And feste yone fende, þat he not flitte.   340

And deuyll, I comaunde þe go doune,

In-to thy selle where þou schalte sitte.   [*Satan sinks.*

'Help, Mahomet!
I go mad!'

Sattan. Owt, ay! herrowe! helpe mahounde!

Nowe wex I woode oute of my witte.   344

Belsabub. Sattan, þis saide we are,

Nowe schall þou fele þi fitte.

Sattan. Allas! for dole, and care,

He falls into the
pit of hell.

I synke in to helle pitte.   [*Falls into the pit.*   348

30. **Adame.** A! Jesu lorde, mekill is þi myght,

If. 196.
xxvij vi.
Adam rejoices
and praises
Jesus,

That mekis þi-selffe in þis manere.

Vs for to helpe as þou has hight,

Whanne both forfette I and my feere.   352

Here haue we leuyd with-outen light,

Foure thousand and vi c ȝere,

Now se I be þis solempne sight,

Howe thy mercy hath made vs clere [1].   356

Jesus.	Deville, I commaunde the to go downe	341
	Into thi sete where thou shalle syt.	342
Sathanas.	Alas for doylle and care	347
	I synk into helle pyt.	348
Rybald.	Sir Sathanas, so saide I are,	345
	Now shalle thou haue a fytt.	346
Jesus.	Com now furthe my childer alle,	
	I forgyf you youre mys;	
	Withe me now go ye shalle	
	To joy and endles blys.	
Adam.	Lord thou art fulle mekylle of myght,	34
	That mekys thi self on this manere,	
	To help vs alle as thou had vs hight,	
	When bothe forfett I and my fere;	35
	Here haue we dwelt withoutten light,	
	iiiiM. and vi hundreth yere,	
	Now se we by this solempne sight	
	How that thi mercy makes vs dere.	3!

---

[1] The MS. has *clene.*

Eue. A ! lorde, we were worthy 　　　　　　followed by Eve.
Mo turmentis for to taste,
But mende vs with mercye
Als þou of myght is moste. 　　　　　　　360

31. **[John] Baptista.** A l lorde I loue þe inwardly,. 　　and John the Baptist,
That me wolde make þi messengere,
Thy comyng in erth for to crye,
And teche þi faith to folke in feere. 　　　　364
And sithen be-fore þe for to dye,
And bringe boodworde to þame here,
How þai schulde haue thyne helpe in hye,
Nowe se I all þi poyntis appere. 　　　　368　who sees all come true.
Als dauid prophete trewe
Ofte tymes tolde vntill vs,
Of þis comyng he knewe,
And saide it schulde be þus. 　　　　　372

32. **Dauid.** Als I haue saide, ȝitt saie I soo,
Ne derelinquas, domine, 　　　　　　Ps. xvi. 10.
Animam meam [in] inferno,

Eua. Lord we were worthy more tornamentes to tast,
　　　　Thou help vs Lord with thy mercy, as thou of
　　　　　　　　　myght is mast. 　　360
Joh. Lord, I loue the inwardly
　　　　That me wold make thi messyngere,
　　　　Thi commyng in erthe to cry,
　　　　And teche thi fayth to folk in fere, 　　364
　　　　Sythen before the forto dy,
　　　　To bryng theym bodword that be here,
　　　　How they shuld haue thi help in hy,
　　　　Now se I alle those poyntes appere. 　　368
Moyses. David, thi prophette trew
　　　　Oft tymes told vnto vs ;
　　　　Of thi commyng he knew,
　　　　And saide it shuld be thus. 　　372
Dauid. As I saide ere yit say I so,
　　　　Ne derelinquas, domine,
　　　　Animam meam in inferno ;

'Thou wilt not
leave my soul in
hell.' *Ps.* xvi. 10.

Leffe noght my saule, lorde, aftir þe,   376
In depe helle where dampned schall goo,
Ne suffre neuere saules fro þe be,
The sorowe of þame þat wonnes in woo
Ay full of filthe, þat may repleye.   380

Adame. We thanke his grete goodnesse
He fette vs fro þis place,

If. 196 b.

Makes joie nowe more and lesse,
Omnis we laude god of his grace[1].   384

Jesus calls Adam
and his friends to
come forth, and
tells Michael to
lead them to
Paradise,

33. Jesus. Adame and my frendis in feere,
Fro all youre fooes come fourth with me,
ʒe schalle be sette in solas seere,
Wher ʒe schall neuere of sorowes see.   388
And Mighill, myn aungell clere,
Ressayue þes saules all vnto þe,
And lede þame als I schall þe lere
To Paradise with playe and plente.   392

[They come out of Limbo.

while he returns
to the grave,
ready to rise.

Mi graue I woll go till,
Redy to rise vppe-right,
And so I schall fulfille
That I be-fore haue highte.   396

Michael asks for
a saving blessing,

34. Mich. Lord, wende we schall aftir þi sawe,
To solace sere þai schall be sende,
But þat þer deuelis no draught vs drawe,
Lorde, blisse vs with þi holy hende[2].   400

which Jesus
gives.

Jesus. Mi blissing haue ʒe all on rawe,
I schall be with youe wher ʒe wende,

Leyfe neuer my saulle, lord, after the,   376
In depe helle wheder dampned shalle go;
Suffre thou neuer thi sayntes to se
The sorowe of thaym that won in wo,
Ay fulle of fylthe and may not fle.   380

---

[1] The late hand here writes 'tunc cantent.'
[2] A later pen has altered it to *honde.*

And all þat lelly luffes my lawe,
Þai schall be blissid with-owten ende.   404

Adame.   To þe lorde, be louyng,
Þat vs has wonne fro waa,
For solas will we syng,
Laus tibi cum gloria.   [*Exeunt.*   408   Praise the Lord.

Moyses.   Make myrthe bothe more and les,
And loue oure lord we may,
That has broght vs fro bytternes
In blys to abyde for ay.

Ysaias.   Therfor now let vs syng
To loue oure lord Jesus,
Vnto his blys he wille vs bryng,
Te Deum laudamus.

XXXVIII. THE CARPENTERES[1].

The Resurrection; fright of the Jews.

[PERSONS OF THE PLAY.

PILATUS.	ANGELUS.
ANNA.	1 MARIA [Magdalene].
CAYPHAS.	2 MARIA [mother of James and Joses].
CENTURIO.	3 MARIA [Salome]. 1, 2, 3, 4 MILITES.]

Matt. xxvii. 45,
51-54, 61-66 ;
xxviii. 1-15.
Mark xv. 33, 38,
39, 44 ; xvi. 1-8.
Gosp. of Nichod.
ch. xiii.

[SCENE I; *?in Pilate's Hall.*]

1. Pil.[1] LORDINGIS, listenys nowe vnto me,
    I comaunde ȝou in ilke degre
Als domesman chiffe in þis contre,
    For counsaill kende,   4
Atte my bidding ȝou awe to be
    And baynly bende.

Pilate and
Caiaphas declare
they will stand by
their deed in the
death of Jesus.

2. And sir Cayphas, chiffe of clergye,
Of youre counsaill late here in hye,   8
By oure assente sen we dyd dye
    Ihesus þis day ;
Þat we mayntayne and stand þerby
    Þat werke all-way.   12

---

[1] The 26th Towneley Play, 'Resurrectio Domini' (fo. 101 b of the MS.,
p. 254 of Surtees print), is in part parallel. The first forty-five lines differ
entirely; it is here given from that point.
[2] This name, forgotten by the rubricator, was added in later.

3. **Cayph.** ʒis, sir, þat dede schall we mayntayne,
By lawe it was done all be-dene,
ʒe wotte youre selue, with-outen wene,
    Als wele as we.   16
His sawes are nowe vppon hym sene,
    And ay schall be.

It was lawfully done.

4. **Anna.** Þe pepull, sirs, in þis same steede,
Be-fore ʒou saide with a hole hede,
Þat he was worthy to be dede
    And þerto sware,
Sen all was rewlid by rightis rede
    Nevyn it nomore.   24

Annas confirms it, say no more.

(line 20 marker)

5. **Pil.** To neuyn me thinketh it nedfull thyng,
Sen he was hadde to beriyng,
Herde we nowthir of olde ne ʒing
    Thithynges be-twene.   28
    Cayph. Centurio, sir, will bringe thidingis
      Of all be-dene.

' I must speak of it, we have heard nothing since his burial.'

6. We lefte hym þere for man moste wise,
If any rebelles wolde ought rise
Oure rightwise dome for to dispise,
    Or it offende,
To sese þame till þe nexte assise,
    And þan make ende.   36
             [Enter Centurion.

The centurion will tell you if there is rebellion against our judgment.

(line 32 marker)

7. **Cent.** [*To himself.*] A! blissid lorde, Adonay,
What may þes meruayles signifie,
Þat her was schewed so oppinly
    Vn-to oure sight?   40

What wonders came the day of Jesus' death!

Tunc veniet Centurio velut miles equitans.

Centurio. A blyssyd lord, Adonay, what may this
             meruelle sygnyfy   38
    That here was showyd so openly vnto oure sight,

Þis day whanne þat þe man gune dye
Þat Ihesus highte.

If. 197 b. 8. Itt is a misty thyng to mene,
So selcouth a sight was neuere sene   44
Þat oure princes and prestis be-dene
Of þis affray;
I woll go weten, with-outen wene,
What þei can saye.   48

He salutes Pilate
and the priests. 9. [*To Pilate, &c.*]   God saue ȝou, sirs, on ilke a side,
Worschippe and welthe in worldis wide
With mekill mirthe myght ȝe abide,
Boght day and nyght[1]!   52
Pil.   Centurio, welcome this tide,
Oure comely knyght!

10. ȝe haue bene miste vs here among.
Cent.   God giffe you grace grathely to gang.   56
Pil.   Centurio, ure frende full lang,
What is your will?

He fears they
have done great
wrong. **Cent.**   I drede me þat ȝe haue done wrang
And wondir ill.   60

When the rightwys man can dy that Jesus hight?   42
[Here occur 25 lines not in York Play.]
God saue you, syrs, on euery syde,   49
Worship and welth in warld so wyde.   5
Pilatus.   Centurio, welcom this tyde,   5
Oure comly knyght.   5
Cent.   God graunt you grace welle for to gyde,   5
And rewlle you right.
Pil.   Centurio, welcom, draw nere hand,
Tell vs som tythynges here emang,
For ye haue gone thrughoutt oure land,
Ye know ilk dele.
Cent.   Sir, I drede me ye haue done wrang
And wonder ylle.

---

[1] This line is written in a late hand.

11. **Cayph.**   Wondir ill? I pray þe, why?
      Declare it to þis company.

    Cent.   So schall I, sirs, telle ȝou trewly;
          With-owten trayne.   64
    Þe rightwise mane þanne mene I by
          Þat ȝe haue slayne.

                                            'Ye have slain a righteous man.'

12. **Pil.**   Centurio, sesse of such sawe,
    Þou arte a lered man in þe lawe,   68
    And if we schulde any witnes drawe
          Vs to excuse,
    To mayntayne vs euermore þe awe,
          And noȝt reffuse.   72

'Cease, you ought to support us, not oppose.'

13. **Cent.**   To mayntayne trouthe is wele worþi,
    I saide ȝou, whanne I sawe hym dy,
    Þat he was Goddis sone almyghty,
          Þat hangeth þore;   76
    Ȝitt saie I soo, and stande þerby
          For euermore.

'Truth ought to be supported. I said he was God's son, and still say so.'

    Caip.   Wonder ylle? I pray the why?   61
        Declare that to this company.
    Cent.   So shalle I, sir, fulle securly,
           With alle my mayn,   64
      The rightwys man, I meyn, hym by
           That ye haue slayn.
    Pil.   Centurio sese of sich saw,   67
      Ye ar a greatt man of oure law,
      And if we shuld any wytnes draw
           To vs excuse,   70
      To mayntene vs euermore ye aw,
           And noght refuse.   72
    Cent.   To mayntene trowthe is welle worthy,
      I saide when I saghe hym dy,
      That it was Godes son almyghty,
           That hang thore;   76
      So say I yit and abydes therby,
          For euermore.

If. 198.
xxviij i.

'Have you any
true signs?'

The elements
made mourning;

the sun grew pale
for woe;

the earth shook,
stones brake
asunder, and
dead men rose.'

14. Cayph. ʒa, sir, such reasouns may ʒe rewe,
ʒe schulde noght neueyn such note enewe,   80
But ʒe couthe any tokenyngis trewe
    Vnto vs tell.
Cent. Such woundirfull cas neuere ʒit ʒe knewe
    As now befell.   84

15. Anna. We praye þe telle vs of what thyng.
Cent. All elementis, both olde and ʒing,
In ther maneres þai made mornyng,
    In ilke a stede;   88
And knewe be countenaunce þat þer kyng
    Was done to dede.

16. Þe sonne for woo he waxed all wanne,
Þe mone and sterres of schynyng blanne,   92
Þe erthe tremeled, and also manne
    be-gan to speke;
Þe stones þat neuer was stered or þanne
    gune a-sondir breke.   96

Anna. Yee, sir, siche resons may ye rew,
Thou shuld not neuen sich notes new,   80
Bot thou couthe any tokyns trew,
    Vntille vs telle.   82
Cent. Sich wonderfulle case neuer ere ye knew
    As then befelle.   84
Cayp. We pray the telle vs of what thyng.
Cent. The elymentes, both old and ying,
In thare manere maide greatt mowrnyng,
    In ilka stede;   88
Thay knew by contenaunce that thare kyng
    Was done to dede.
The son for wo it waxed alle wan,
The moyn and starnes of shynyng blan,   92
And erthe it tremlyd as a man
    Began to speke;
The stone that neuer was styrryd or than
    In sonder brast and breke;   96

17. And dede-men rose, both grete and small.

    Pil. Centurio, be-ware with-all,

    ȝe wote oure clerkis þe clipsis þei call

        Such sodayne sight,   100 *Such sights of sun and moon are called eclipses.*

    Both sonne and mone þat sesonne schall   *Gosp. of Nichodemus, ch. xj.*

        lak of þer light.

18. **Cayph.** ȝa, and if dede men rose bodily,   *' And dead men might rise*

    Þat myght be done thurgh socery,   104 *through sorcery.*

    Þerfore we sette no thyng þerby

        To be abaiste.

    Cent. All þat I tell for trewthe schall I

        euermore traste.   108

19. In this ilke werke þat ȝe did wirke,

    Nought allone þe sonne was mirke,

    But howe youre vaile raffe in youre kirke,   *How was the veil in the temple torn?*

        That witte I wolde.   112

    Pil. Swilke tales full sone will make vs irke   *' These tales will do us harm.'*

        And þei be talde.

    And dede men rose up bodely bothe greatt and smalle.

    Pil. Centurio, bewar withe alle,

    Ye wote the clerkes the clyppes it calle

        Siche sodan sight;   100

    That son and moyne a seson shalle

        Lak of thare light.

    Cayp. Sir, and if that dede men ryse vp bodely,

    That may be done thrughe socery,   104

    Therfor nothyng we sett therby,

        That be thou bast.

    Cent. Sir, that I saw truly,

        That shalle I euermore trast.   108

    Not for that ilk warke that ye dyd wyrke,

    Not oonly for the son wex myrke,

    Bot how the vaylle rofe in the kyrke,

        Fayn wyt I wold.   112

    Pil. A! siche tayles fulle sone wold make vs yrke,

        If thay were told.   114

        D d

402   XXXVIII. THE CARPENTERES.

'We don't want
to hear you.'

20. Anna. Centurio, such speche withdrawe,
Of all þes wordes we haue none awe.   116

Cent. Nowe sen ȝe sette noght be my sawe,

'Sirs, good day.'
Sirs, haue gode day!
graunte you grace þat ȝe may knawe
þe soth alway.   120

Annas sends him
off, but Pilate
muses on his
sayings.

21. Anna. With-drawe þe faste, sen þou þe dredis,
For we schall wele mayntayne oure dedis. [*Exit Centurion.*

Pil. Such wondir reasouns as he redis
Was neuere beforne.   124

If. 198 b.

Caiph. To neven þis noote no more vs nedis,
Nowþere even ne morne.

22. Þerfore loke nomanne make ilke chere,
All þis doyng may do no dere,   128
But to be-ware ȝitt of more were
Þat folke may fele;
We praye you, sirs, of þes sawes sere
Avise ȝou wele.   132

Harlot, wherto commys thou vs emang
Withe siche lesynges vs to fang?
Weynd furthe, hy myght thou hang,
Vyle fatur!

Cayp. Weynd furthe, in the wenyande,
And hold stylle thy clattur.

Cent. Sirs, sen ye set not by my saw, haues now good day,   117
God lene you grace to knaw the sothe alle way.   120

Anna. Withe draw the fast, sen thou the dredys,
For we shalle welle mayntene oure dedes.

Pil. Siche wonderfulle resons as now redes
Were neuer beforne.   124

Cayp. To neuen this note nomore us nedes,
Nawder euen nor morne,
Bot forto be war of more were
That afterward myght do vs dere.   128
Therfor, sir, whils ye are here.
Vs alle emang,
Avyse you of thise sawes sere
How thay wille stand.   132

23. And to þis tale takes hede in hye,
  For Iesu saide even opynly
  A thyng þat greues all þis Jury,
    And riȝte so may,—   136
  Þat he schulde rise vppe bodily
    With-in þe thirde day.

24. And be it so, als motte I spede,
  His lattar deede is more to drede 140
  Þan is the firste, if we take hede
    Or tente þerto.
  To neuyn þis noote me thynke moste nede
    and beste to do.   144

25. **Anna.** Ȝa, Sir, if all þat he saide soo,
  He has no myght to rise and goo,
  But if his mennestele hym vs froo
    And bere away;   148
  Þat were tille us and oþer moo
    A foule ffraye.

Side notes:
' Take heed of this tale,

for Jesus said he should rise on the third day;

his latter death is more to be feared than the first.'

If his men steal him away

  For Jesus saide fulle openly   134
  Vnto the men that yode hym by,
  A thyng that grevys alle Jury,   135
    And right so may,
  That he shuld ryse up bodely
    Within the thryde day.   138
  If it be so as myght I spede,
  The latter dede is more to drede 140
  Then was the fyrst, if we take hede
    And tend therto;
  Avyse you, sir, for it is nede
    The best to do.   144
Anna. Sir, neuer the les if he saide so
  He hase no myght to ryse and go
  Bot his dyscypyls steylle his cors vs fro
    And bere away;   148
  That were tille vs, and othere mo,
    A fowlle enfray.

they will say that he rose.

26. For þanne wolde þei saie, euere ilkone,
    Þat he roose by hym selffe allone ;   152
    Therfore latte hym be kepte anone
        With knyghtes hende.
    Vnto thre daies be comen and gone
        and broght till ende.   156

27. **Pil.** In certayne, sirs, right wele ȝe saie,
    For þis ilke poynte nowe [to] purvaye,

Pilate allows a watch to be set,

    I schall ordayne if I may
        He schall not ryse.   160
    Nor none schalle wynne hym þens away
        On no-kyns wise.   *[To the soldiers.*

28. Sir knyghtis [1], þat are in dedis dowty,
    Chosen for chiffe of cheualrye,   164
    As we ay in youre force affie
        Boþe day and nyght,
    Wendis and kepis Jesu body
        With all youre myghte ;   168

    Then wold the pepylle say euerilkon
    That he were rysen hym self alon,   152
    Therfor ordan to kepe that stone
        Withe knyghtes heynd,
    To thise iij dayes be com nen and gone
        And broght tille ende.   156
Pil. Now, certes, sir, fulle welle ye say,
    And for this ilk poynt to purvay
    I schalle, if that I may,
        He shalle not ryse,   160
    Nor none shalle wyn hym thens away,
        Of nokyns wyse.
    Sir knyghtes, that ar of dedes dughty,
    And chosen for chefe of cheualry,   164
    As I may me in you affy,
        By day and nyght,
    Ye go and kepe Jesus' body
        Withe alle youre myghte,   168

---

[1] The late hand has here interlined the word 'lorde,' it does not appear why.

29. And for thyng þat euere be maye
    Kepis hym wele to þe thirde day,
    And latis noman takis hym away
        Oute of þat stede.   172
    For and þei do, suthly I saie
        ӡe schall be dede.

telling the soldiers to watch him till the third day.

30. i Mil. Lordingis, we saie ӡou for certayne,
    We schall kepe hym with myghtis and mayne,   176
    Þer schall no traitoures with no trayne
        Stele hym vs froo.
    Sir knyghtis, takis gere þat moste may gayne,
        And lates vs goo.   [*Exeunt.*] 180

If. 199. xxviij ij.

They go, declaring no traitors shall steal him.

[SCENE II, *near the Sepulchre.*]

• 31. ii Mil. Ӡis, certis, we are all redy bowne,
    We schall hym kepe till oure rennowne;
    On ilke a side latte vs sitte doune,
        Nowe all in fere,   184
    And sone we schall crake his croune
        Whoso comes here.
            [*The soldiers sit down and fall asleep.*

      And for thyng that be may,
      Kepe hym welle vnto the thryd day,
      That no tratur steylle his cors you fray,
        Out of that sted,   172
      For if ther do, truly I say,
        Ye shalle be dede.

i Miles. Yis, Sir Pilate, in certan,
      We shall hym kepe withe alle oure mayn,   176
      Ther shalle no tratur with no trayn
        Steylle hym vs fro;
      Sir knyghtys, take gere that best may gayn,
        And let vs go.   180

ii Miles. Yis, certes, we are alle redy bowne,
      We shalle hym kepe tille youre renowne,
      On euery syde lett us sytt downe,
        We alle in fere;   184
      And I shalle fownde to crak his crowne,
        Who so commys here.   186

[Here Towneley play has 122 lines, chiefly a monologue by Jesus.]

Tunc Iesu resurgente[1].

[Enter the three Maries going to the tomb.

<table>
<tr><td>Christ is dead,</td><td>32. i Mar.</td><td>Allas! to dede I wolde be dight,</td><td></td></tr>
<tr><td></td><td></td><td>So woo in werke was neuere wight,</td><td>188</td></tr>
<tr><td></td><td></td><td>Mi sorowe is all for þat sight</td><td></td></tr>
<tr><td></td><td></td><td>þat I gune see ;</td><td></td></tr>
<tr><td></td><td></td><td>Howe Criste my maistir, moste of myght,</td><td></td></tr>
<tr><td></td><td></td><td>Is dede fro me.</td><td>192</td></tr>
</table>

33. Allas! þat I schulde se his pyne,
    Or yit þat I his liffe schulde tyne ;

who is medicine of all ills.

Of ilke a myscheue he is medicyne
      And bote of all,   196
Helpe and halde to ilke a hyne
    þat on hym on wolde call [2].

34. ii Mar.   Allas! who schall my balis bete
    Whanne I thynke on his woundes wete ;   200
    Jesu, þat was of loue so swete,
      and neuere did ill,

Maria Magdalene.   Alas, to dy with doylle am I dyght,   187
    In warld was neuer a wofuller wight,
    I drope, I dare, for seyng of sight
      That I can se ;   190
    My lord, that mekelle was of might,
      Is ded fro me.   192
    Alas, that I shuld se hys pyne
    Or that I shuld his lyfe tyne,
    For to iche sore he was medecyne
      And boytte of alle ;   196
    Help and hold to euer ilk hyne
      To hym wold calle.
Maria Jacobi.   Alas, how stand I on my feete
    When I thynk on his woundes wete,   200
    Jesus, that was on luf so swete,
      And neuer dyd ylle,

---

[1] The marginal note in later hand here, 'tunc angelus cantat Resurgens See lines 383–386.
[2] *Sic,* but probably the line should read, 'on hym wolde call.'

Es dede and grauen vnder þe grete
    With-outen skill.

He is dead,
slain without
204 reason by the
Jews.

35. iii Mar.   With-owten skill þe Jewes ilkone
Þat louely lorde has newly slayne,
And trespasse did he neuere none
    In no-kyn steede.

208

To whome nowe schall I make my mone
    Sen he is dede?

36. i Mar.   Sen he is dede, my sisteres dere,
Wende we will on mylde manere
With oure a-noynementis faire & clere
    Þat we haue broght
To noynte his wondis on sides sere,
    Þat Jewes hym wroght.

They go to anoint
the body.

212

216

37. ii Mar.[1]   Goo we same my sisteres free,
Full faire vs longis his corse to see,
But I wotte noght howe beste may be,
    Helpe haue we none.

If. 199 b.
' Let us go
together,

220

[They approach the sepulchre.

Is dede and grafen vnder the grete,
    Withoutten skylle.

204

Maria Salomee.   Withoutten skylle thise Jues ilkon
That lufly lord they haue hym slone,
And trespas dyd he neuer none,
    In nokyn sted;

208

To whom shalle we now make oure mone?
    Oure Lord is ded.

Maria Magdalene.   Sen he is ded, my systers dere,
Weynd we wille with fulle good chere,
With oure anoyntmentes fare and clere
    That we haue broght
For to anoyntt his woundes sere,
    That Jues hym wroght.

212

216

Maria J.   Go we then, my systers fre,
For sore me longis his cors to see,
Bot I wote neuer how best may be,
    Help haue we none;

220

---

[1] The MS. has *Prima* Maria, but this seems to be a mistake.

but who will
remove the
stone ?'
And who schall nowe here of vs thre
          remove þe stone?

38. iii Mar.   Þat do we noght but we wer moo,
For it is huge and heuy also.   224

They see a young
child clothed in
white.
i Mar.   Sisteris ! a ȝonge child as we goo
          Makand mornyng,
I see it sitte wher we wende to,
          In white clothyng.   228

39. ii Mar.   Sisters, sertis, it is noght to hide,

The stone is
gone !
Þe heuy stone is putte beside !
iii Mar.   Sertis ! for thyng þat may be-tyde
          Nere will we wende,   232
To layte þat luffely and with hym bide,
          Þat was oure ffrende.

          [*They look in, an angel is beside them.*

40. Ang.   Ȝe mournand women in youre þought,
Here in þis place whome haue ȝe sought?   236
i Mar.   Jesu, þat to dede is brought,
          Oure lorde so free.

And whiche shalle of vs systers thre
          Remefe the stone?
Maria S.   That do we not bot we were mo,
For it is hoghe and heuy also.   22
Maria M.   Systers, we thar no farther go
          Ne make mowrnyng;
I se two syt where we weynd to,
          In whyte clothyng.   22
Maria J.   Certes, the sothe is not to hyde,
The graue stone is put besyde.
Maria S.   Certes, for thyng that may betyde,
          Now wille we weynde   2
To late the luf, and with hym byde,
          That was oure freynde.
i Ang.   Ye mowrnyng women in youre thoght,
Here in this place whome haue ye soght?
Maria M.   Jesus, that vnto ded was broght   2
          Oure lord so fre.

Ang. Women, certayne here is he noght,
　　　Come nere and see.　　　　　　　240

The angel tells
them Jesus is not
there,

41. He is noght here, þe soth to saie,
　　Þe place is voide þat he in laye,
　　Þe sudary here se ȝe may
　　　　Was on hym laide.　　　　　244
　　He is resen and wente his [1] way,
　　　　As he ȝou saide.

and shows them
the napkin.

42. Euen as he saide so done has hee,
　　He is resen thurgh grete poostee,　248
　　He schall be foune in Galile
　　　　In flesshe and fell.
　　To his discipilis nowe wende ȝe
　　　　and þus þame tell.　　　　　252

'He is risen and
gone to Galilee;

tell his disciples.

43. i **Mar.** Mi sisteres dere, sen it is soo,
　　Þat he is resen dede þus froo,
　　As þe Aungell tolde me and yow too,—
　　　　Oure lorde so fre,—　　　　256

Mary Magdalene
remains while the
other two go.
[*Mark* xvi. 9.]

---

ii Ang. Certes, women, here is he noght,
　　　　Com nere and se.　　　　　240
i Ang. He is not here the sothe to say,
　　The place is voyde ther in he lay,
　　The sudary here se ye may
　　　　Was on hym layde;　　　　244
　　He is rysen and gone his way,
　　　　As he you sayde.
ii Ang. Euen as he saide so done has he,
　　He is rysen thrughe his pauste,　248
　　He shalbe fon in Galale,
　　　　In fleshe and felle;
　　To his dycypyls now weynd ye
　　　　And thus thaym telle.　　　252
Maria M. My systers fre, sen it is so
　　That he is resyn the dethe thus fro,
　　As saide tille vs thise angels two,
　　　　Oure lord and leche,　　　256

---

[1] MS. repeats *his*.

Hens will I neuer goo
Or I hym see.

44. ii Mar. Marie, vs thare no lenger layne [1],   260
To Galile nowe late vs wende.

i Mar. Nought tille I see þat faithfull frende,
Mi lorde & leche,

' Tell all ye have seen.'

Þerfore all þis my sisteres hende,
Þat ȝe forth preche.   264

45. iii Mar. As we haue herde, so schall we saie,

' Good day, Mary.'

Marie oure sistir, haue goode daye!

i Mar. Nowe verray god as he wele maye

' God be with you.

He wisse you sisteres wele in youre waye   268
and rewle ȝou right [2].

[*Exeunt 2nd and 3rd Maries.*

46. Allas! what schall nowe worþe on me,

Alas! my wretched heart will break.'

Mi kaytiffe herte will breke in three,
Whenne I thynke on þat body free   272
How it was spilte!
Both feete and handes nayled tille a tre,
Withouten gilte.

As ye haue hard where that ye go,
Loke that ye preche.   264
Maria J. As we haue hard so shalle we say,   265
Mare, oure syster, haue good day.
Maria M. Now veray God, as he welle may,
Man most of myght,   267*
He wyshe you systers welle in youre way,
And rewle you right.   26·
Alas what shalle now worth on me?
My catyf hart wylle breke in thre
When that I thynk on that ilk bodye
How it was spylt;   27·
Thrughe feete and handes nalyd was he—
Withoutten gylt.

---

[1] *Lende* must have been intended.
[2] The copyist made an error in this stanza, as a short line is missing; the late hand supplied in the margin 'a weryed wight,' but the Townele play supplies the true line, 267*.

47. With-outen gilte þe trewe was tane,   276
For trespas did he neuere none,
Þe woundes he suffered many one
        Was for my misse.
It was my dede he was for-slayne   280
        And no-thyng his.

48. How might I but I loued þat swete,—
Þat for my loue tholed woundes wete,
And sithen be grauen vndir þe grete—   284
        Such kyndnes kithe.
Þer is no-thing to þat we mete   *There is no joy now.*
        May make me blithe.   [*The soldiers awaken.*

49. i Mil.   What! oute allas! what schall I saie,   *The soldiers wake up one after the other,*
Where is þe corse þat here in laye?   289
ii Mil.   What ayles þe man? is he awaye
        Þat we schulde tent?
i Mil.   Rise vppe, and see.   **ii Mil.**   Harrowe! for ay;   *shouting and swearing, for they find the grave empty.*
        I telle vs schente.   293

Withoutten gylt then was he tayn,   276
That lufly lord, thay haue hym slayn,
And tryspas dyd he neuer nane,
        Ne yit no mys;
It was my gylt he was fortayn,   280
        And nothing his.
How myght I bot I lufyd that swete
That for me suffred woundes wete,
Sythen to be grafen vnder the grete,   284
        Siche kyndnes kythe;
There is nothyng tille that we mete
        May make me blythe.
i Miles.   Outt, alas! what shalle I say?   288
Where is the cors that here in lay?
ii Miles.   What alys the man? he is away
        That we shuld tent.
i Miles.   Ryse vp and se.
ii Miles.   Harrow thefe for ay,   292
        I cownte vs shent!

50. iii Mil.   What deuill is þis, what aylis ȝou twoo?
Such noyse and crye þus for to make too.
i Mil.   Why is he gone?   296
iii Mil.   Allas! whare is he þat here laye?
iv Mil.   Whe! harrowe! deuill, whare is he away[1]?

If. 200 b.

51. ii Mil.[2]   What! is he þus-gatis fro vs wente,
þat fals traitour þat here was lente,   300
And we trewly here for to tente
        Had vndir tane?
'We are ruined!   Sekirlie, I telle vs schente,
        Holy ilkane.   304

52. iii Mil.   Allas! what schall we do þis day,
þat þus þis warlowe is wente his waye,
I dare say he
really rose alone.   And sauely sirs, I dare wele saie
        He rose allone.   308
We had better
not tell Pilate,   **ii. Mil.**   Witte sir pilate of þis affraye,
        We mon be slone.

---

iii Miles.   What devylle alys you two?
Sich no[y]se and cry thus for to may?   295
ii Miles.   For he is gone.
iii Miles.   Alas! wha?
ii Miles.   He that here lay.
iii Miles.   Harrow, deville, how swa gat he away?
iv Miles.   What, is he thus-gates from us went?
The fals tratur that here was lentt,   300
That we truly to tent
        Had undertane?
Certanly I telle vs sheynt
        Holly ilkane.   304
i Miles.   Alas, what shalle I do this day,
Sen this tratur is won away?
And safely, syrs, I dar welle say,
        He rose alon.   305
ii Miles.   Wytt sir Pilate of this enfray
        We mon be slone.

---

[1] This stanza is imperfect.
[2] The rubricator gave this to the 3 Mil., but he has the next speech.

53. iii Mil. Why, canne none of vs no bettir rede?

iv. Mil. Þer is not ellis, but we be dede.   312

ii Mil. Whanne þat he stered oute of þis steede
　　　　None couthe it kenne.

i Mil. Allas! harde happe was on my hede,
　　　　Amonge all menne.   316

54. Fro sir Pilate witte of þis dede,
　　Þat we were slepande whanne he ȝede,
　　He will forfette with-outen drede
　　　　All that we haue.   320

if he knows we were asleep, we shall lose all we have.'

ii Mil. Vs muste make lies, for þat is nede,
　　　　Oure-selue to saue.

They propose to lie,

55. iii Mil. Ȝa, that I rede I wele, also motte I goo.

iv Mil. And I assente þerto alsoo.   324

ii Mil. An hundereth, schall I saie, and moo,
　　　　Armed ilkone,
　　Come and toke his corse vs froo
　　　　And vs nere slayne.   328

and to say that 100 armed men took Jesus.

---

iv Miles. Wote ye welle he rose in dede.

ii Miles. I sa[g]h my self when that he yede.   312

i Miles. When that he styrryd out of the stede
　　　　None couthe it ken.

iv Miles. Alas, hard hap was on my hede
　　　　Emang alle men.   316

iii Miles. Ye, bot wyt sir Pilate of this dede,
　　That we were slepand when he yede,
　　We mon forfett, withoutten drede,
　　　　Alle that we haue.   320

iv Miles. We must make lees, for that is nede,
　　　　Oure self to saue.

i Miles. That red I welle, so myght I go.

ii Miles. And I assent therto also.   324

iii Miles. A thousand shalle I assay and mo,
　　　　Welle armed ilkon,
　　Com and toke his cors vs fro,
　　　　Had vs nere slone.   328

56. i Mil.   Nay, certis, I halde þere none so goode
As saie þe soth even as it stoode,
Howe þat he rose with mayne and mode
            And wente his way.   332
To sir Pilate if he be wode
            Þis dar I saie.

57. ii Mil.   Why, dare þou to sir Pilate goo
With thes tydingis and saie hym soo?   336
i Mil.   So rede I, if he vs sloo

            We dye but onys.

iii Mil.   Nowe, he þat wrought vs all þis woo,
            Woo worthe his bonys!   340

58. iv Mil.   Go we þanne, sir knyghtis hende,
Sen þat we schall to sir Pilate wende,
I trowe þat we shall parte no frendes
            Or þat we passe.   344

i Mil.[1]   And I schall hym saie ilke worde tille ende,
            Even as it was.   [*They go to Pilate.*

---

iv Miles.   Nay, certes, I hold ther none so good
As say the sothe right as it stude,
How that he rose with mayn and mode,
            And went his way;   332
To Sir Pilate, if he be wode,
            Thus dar I say.
i Miles.   Why and dar thou to Sir Pilate go
With thise tythynges, and telle hym so?   336
ii Miles.   So red I that we do also,
            We dy bot oones.
iii Miles et Omnes.   Now he that wroght vs alle this wo
            Wo worth his bones!   340
iv Miles.   Go we sam, sir knyghtes heynd,
Sen we shalle to sir Pilate weynd,
I trow that we shalle parte no freynd,
            Er that we pas.   344
i Miles.   Now and I shalle telle ilka word tille ende,
Right as it was.

---

[1] This speaker added by late hand.

[SCENE III, *Pilate's Hall; enter the soldiers.*]

59. Sir Pilate, prince withouten pere,
  Sir Cayphas and Anna in fere,   348
  And all ȝe lordyngis þat are here
     To neven by name,
  God saue ȝou all, on sidis sere,
     Fro synne and schame !   352

They salute Pilate and the others.

60. Pil. ȝe are welcome, oure knyghtis kene,
  Of mekill mirthe nowe may ȝe mene,
  Therfore some tales telle vs be-twene
     Howe ȝe haue wroght.   356

 i Mil. Oure wakyng lorde with-outen wene
     Is worthed to noȝt.

'Our watching has come to nought,

61. Cayph. To noght ? allas ! sesse of such sawe.
 ii Mil. Þe prophete Jesu þat ȝe wele knawe   360
 Is resen and gone, for all oure awe,
     With mayne and myght.

Jesus has risen.'

 Pil. Þerfore þe deuill hym selffe þe drawe,
     Fals recrayed knyght !   364

'False recreants !

  Sir Pilate, prynce withoutten peyr,
  Sir Cayphas and Anna bothe in fere,   348
  And alle the lordes aboute you there,
     To neuen by name;
  Mahowne you saue on sydes sere
     Fro syn and shame.   352

 Pil. Ye ar welcom, oure knyghtes so keyn,
  A mekille myrth now may we meyn,
  Bot telle vs som talkyng us betwene,
     How ye haue wroght.   356

 i Miles. Oure walkyng, lord, withoutten wene,
     Is worthe to noght.

 Cayp. To noght ? alas, seasse of siche saw.
 ii Miles. The prophete Jesus, that ye welle knaw,   360
  Is rysen and went fro vs on raw,
     With mayn and myght.

 Pil. Therfor the deuille the alle to-draw,
     Vyle recrayd knyght !   364

cowards !

62. Combered cowardis I you call,
Haue ȝe latten hym goo fro you all?

iii Mil. Sir, þer was none þat did but small
When þat he ȝede. 368

iv Mil. We wer so ferde downe ganne we falle,
And dared for drede.

had ye no strength to bind him?'

63. Anna. Hadde ȝe no strenghe hym to gayne stande?
Traitoures! ȝe myght haue boune in bande 372
Bothe hym and þame þat ȝe þer fande,
And sessid þame sone.

i Mil. Þat dede all erthely men leuand
Myght noȝt haue done. 376

'We were so frightened we durst not stir.

64. ii Mil. We wer so radde euer-ilkone,
Whanne þat he putte beside þe stone,
We wer so stonyd we durste stirre none
And so abasshed. 380

He rose alone.'

Pil. What! rose he by hym selfe allone?

i Mil. Ȝa, sir, þat be ȝe traste.

65. iv Mil. We herde never sen we were borne,

lf. 201 b. Nor all oure faderes vs be-forne, 384

What! combred cowardes I you calle,
Let ye hym pas fro you alle?

iii Miles. Sir, ther was none that durst do bot smalle
When that he yede. 368

iv Miles. We were so ferde we can downe falle,
And qwoke for drede. 370

i Miles. We were so rad euerilkon 377
When that he put besyde the stone,
We qwoke for ferd, and durst styr none,
And sore we were abast. 380

Pil. Whi, bot rose he bi hymself alone?

ii Miles. Ye, lord, that be ye trast,
We hard neuer on euen ne morne,
Nor yit oure faders vs beforne, 384

Suche melodie, mydday ne morne,

    As was made þere.

Melody at the time.

Cayph. Allas! þanne is oure lawes lorne

    for euere-mare.

388

66. ii **Mil.** What tyme he rose good tente I toke,

Þe erthe þat tyme tremylled and quoke,

All kyndely force þan me for-soke

    Tille he was gone.

392

iii **Mil.** I was a-ferde, I durste not loke,

    ne myght had none,

67. I myght not stande, so was I starke.

Pil. Sir Cayphas, ȝe are a connyng clerke,

If we amisse haue tane oure merke

    I trowe same faile,

Þerfore what schalle worþe nowe of þis werke?

    Sais your counsaille.

396

Pilate asks Caiaphas' counsel, ' we must fail together if we have aimed amiss.'

400

68. **Cayph.** To saie þe beste forsothe I schall,

That schall be prophete to vs all,

Ȝone knyghtis behoues þere wordis agayne call

    Howe he is miste.

404

Siche melody, myd-day ne morne,

    As was maide thore.

Pil. Alas, then ar oure lawes forlorne

    For euer more!

A deuille, what shalle now worthe of this?

This warld farys with quantys,

I pray you, Cayphas, ye vs wys

    Of this enfray.

388

Cayp. Sir and I couth oght by my clergys

    Fayn wold I say.

Anna. To say the best for sothe I shalle,

It shalbe profett for vs alle,

Yond knyghtes behovys thare wordes agane calle,

    How he is myst;

401

404

E e

We nolde for thyng þat myght be-fall
Þat no man wiste.

69. Anna. Now, sir Pilate, sen þat it is soo,
Þat he is resynne dede us froo, 408

'Tell the soldiers
to say that he
was taken by
20,000 men,
Comaundis youre knyghtis to saie wher þei goo,
Þat he was tane
With xx^{ti} m^{l}. men and mo,
And þame nere slayne. 412

70. And therto of our tresorie
Giffe to þame a rewarde for-thy.

Pil. Nowe of þis purpose wele plesed am I,
and forther þus; 416
[*To the soldiers.*] Sir knyghtis, þat are in dedis dowty,
takes tente to vs,

71. And herkenes what þat ȝe shall saie,
To ilke aman both nyȝt and daye, 420
That ten m^{l}. men in goode araye
Come ȝou vntill,
'It is well,
soldiers, say this
in every land,
With forse of armys bare hym awaye
Agaynst your will. 424

We wold not for thyng that myght befalle
That no man wyst. 406
And therfor of youre curtessie 413
Gyf theym a rewarde for-thy. 414

Pil. Of this counselle welle paide am I,
It shalbe thus. 416
Sir knyghtes, that ar of dedes doghty,
Take tent tille vs;
Herkyns now how ye shalle say,
Where so ye go by nyght or day, 420
Ten thousand men of good aray
Cam you vntille,
And thefyshly toke his cors you fray,
Agans youre wille. 424

72. Thus schall ȝe saie in ilke a lande,
    And þerto on þat same comenaunde,
    A thousande pounde haue in youre hande   *here is £1000 reward.'*
            To your rewarde;   428
    And frenschippe, sirs, ȝe vndirstande,
            Schall not be spared.

73. **Caiph.**[1] Ilkone youre state we schall amende,
    And loke ȝe saie as we ȝou kende.   432 *If. 202. xxviij v.*
    i Mil. In what contre so ȝe vs sende
            Be nyght or daye,
    Wherso we come, wherso we wende,
            So schal we saie.   436

74. **Pil.** Ȝa, and where-so ȝe tarie in ilke contre,
    Of oure doyng in no degre
    Dois þat nomanne þe wiser be,   *'Say nothing of what you have seen and heard.'*
            Ne freyne be-forne,   440
    Ne of þe sight þat ȝe gonne see
            Nevynnes it nowþere even ne morne.

75. For we schall mayntayne ȝou alwaye,
    And to þe pepull schall we saie,   444

	Loke ye say thus in euery land,	
	And therto on this couande	
	Ten thousand pounds haue in youre hande	
	To youre rewarde,	428
	And my frenship I understande	
	Shalle not be sparde;	430
	Bot loke ye say as we haue kende.	432
i Miles.	Yis, sir, as Mahowne me mende,	431
	In ilk contree where so we lende	433
	By nyght or day,	
	Where so we go, where so we weynd,	
	Thus shalle we say.	436

---

[1] *Cayphas* inserted by the late hand.

It is gretely agaynste oure lay
    To trowe such thing.
So schall þei deme, both nyght and day,
    All is lesyng.   448

'Truth shall be bought and sold.'

76. Thus schall þe sothe be bought and solde,
And treasoune schall for trewthe be tolde,
    Þerfore ay in youre hartis ȝe holde
      Þis counsaile clene.   452
And fares nowe wele, both younge and olde,
    Haly be-dene.

Fil. The blyssyng of Mahowne be with you
      Nyght and day.

[Seventy-six lines follow this in Towneley, on the subject of York play XXXIX; they are not parallel.]

XXXIX. THE WYNEDRAWERS[1].

Jesus appears to Mary Magdalene after the Resurrection.

[PERSONS OF THE PLAY.

JESUS.   MARIA MAGDALENE.]

[SCENE, *near the holy sepulchre.*]

1. **Maria.** ALLAS, in þis worlde was neuere no wight
Walkand with so mekill woo,
Thou dredfull dede, drawen hythir and dight
And marre me, as þou haste done moo.   4
In lame is it loken all my light,
For-thy on grounde on-glad I goo,
Jesus of Nazareth he hight,
The false Jewes slewe hym me froo.   8

2. Mi witte is waste nowe in wede,
I walowe, I walke, nowe woo is me,
For laide nowe is þat lufsome in lede,
The Jewes hym nayled vntill a tree.   12

John xx. 11–18.
Matth. xxviii. 10.
None had ever such woe, my light is locked in clay, I go unglad.

My wits are lost, I totter.

---

[1] 'The Wynedrawers' runs along the top of every page of this piece except the first, where it has been scratched out and the following written, 'Wevers assygnyd in aº. dñi m¹ c liijᵗⁱ, Willm. Cowplande then maire.' On the left hand margin is written 'Sledmen,' while in the right hand corner at top is the word 'Palmers,' the latter in a later hand. Along the top of every page of the next piece XL the original copyist also wrote 'The wynedraweres,' but it has been crossed through and 'Sledmen' written instead, on the first page (fo. 206), in the same hand that wrote 'Sledmen' on fo. 203 vº. It seems therefore that the original copyist made the mistake of writing 'The Wynedrawers' over the two plays, that a contemporary in correcting it himself wrote 'Sledmen' to Play XXXIX in error for XL (there is a faint line across the word which may mean a stroke of his pen), but then went on to correct the first page of XL (the rest are done in a different hand). And Play XXXIX, originally performed by the Winedrawers, was assigned to the Weavers in 1553, and at some other time, perhaps late in their history, it was assigned to the Palmers. See after, p. 433, *note*.

My doulfull herte is euere in drede,
To grounde nowe gone is all my glee,
I sporne þer I was wonte to spede,

O God, help me ! Nowe helpe me God in persones three.   16

3. Thou lufsome lede in ilke a lande,
As þou schope both day and nyght,
Sonne and mone both bright schynand,

let me see my
lord or his mes-
senger. Þou graunte me grace to haue a sight   20
Of my lorde, or ellis his sande[1].

4. **Jesus** [*as a gardener*].   Thou wilfull woman in þis waye,
Why wepis þou soo als þou wolde wede,

'Why weepest
thou so? whom
seekest thou?' Als þou on felde wolde falle doune faie?
Do way, and do nomore þat dede.   25
Whome sekist þou þis longe daye?
Say me þe sothe, als Criste þe rede.

'My lord Jesus.' **Maria.**   Mi lorde Jesu and God verray,
Þat suffered for synnes his sides bleede.   29

5. **Jesus.**   I schall þe saie, will þou me here,
Þe soth of hym þat þou hast sought,

'Thou faithful
friend, he is near.'
lf. 204.
xxviij vii. With-owten drede, þou faithfull fere,
He is full nere þat mankynde bought.   33

Maria.   Sir, I wolde loke both ferre and nere
To fynde my lorde, I se hym noght.

Jesus.   Womane, wepe noght, but mende thy chere,
I wotte wele whedir þat he was brought.   37

'Sir, if you have
borne him away,
tell me for the
sake of the
prophets where
the body may be, 6. **Maria.**   Swete Sir, yf þou hym bare awaye,
Saie me þe sothe and thedir me leede,
Where þou hym didde with-outen delay
I schall hym seke agayne, goode speede.   41
Therfore, goode gardener, saie þou me,
I praye þe for the prophetis sake,
Of ther tythyngis þat I aske þe.
For it wolde do my sorowe to slake,   45

[1] Lines 17–21 seem to belong to an imperfect stanza. Stanzas 6 and 7
have twelve lines each, the rest have eight lines, of varying length though
regular as to rime.

Wher Goddis body founden myght be
Þat Joseph of þe crose gonne take,
Might I hym fange vnto my fee,
Of all my woo he wolde me wrake.

could I have him in my keeping it might comfort me.'

49

7. **Jesus.** What wolde þou doo with þat body bare
Þat beried was with balefull chere?
Þou may noght salue hym of his sare,
His peynes were so sadde and seere.

' What couldest thou do with the bare body?'

53

But he schall cover mankynde of care,
Þat clowded was he schall make clere,
And þe folke wele for to fare
Þat fyled were all in feere.

57

Maria. A! might I euere with þat man mete
Þe whiche þat is so mekill of myght,
Drye schulde I wype þat nowe is wete,
I am but sorowe of worldly sight.

' I only sorrow for the worldly sight.'

61

8. **Jesus.** Marie, of mournyng amende thy moode,
And be-holde my woundes wyde,
Þus for mannys synnes I schedde my bloode,
And all þis bittir bale gonne bide.

65 If. 204 b.

Þus was I rased on þe roode
With spere and nayles that were vnrude,
Trowe it wele, it turnes to goode,
Whanne men in erthe þer flessh schall hyde.

'Dry up thy tears, feel my wounds, I am he.'

69

9. **Maria.** A! Rabony, I haue þe sought,
Mi maistir dere full faste þis day.

She recognizes, and would clasp him.

Jesus. Goo awaye, Marie, and touche me noȝt,
But take goode kepe what I schall saie.

'Touch me not, Mary,

73

I ame hee þat all thyng wroght,
Þat þou callis þi lorde and God verraye,
With bittir dede I mankynde boght,
And I am resen as þou se may.

77

10. And therfore, Marie, speke nowe with me,
And latte þou nowe be thy grette.

but speak to me, and stay thy sorrow.'

Maria. Mi lorde Jesu, I knowe nowe þe,

' I know thee.'

Þi woundes þai are nowe wette.   81

'Touch me not,
my love, I ascend
not yet.'

Jesus.   Negh me noght, my loue, latte be!

Marie, my doughtir swete.

To my fadir in Trinite

Forþe I stigh noȝt yette [1].   85

'Comely con-
queror, thou hast
overcome death,
thy love is
sweeter than
honey.'

11. Maria.   A! mercy, comely conquerour,

Thurgh þi myght þou haste ouercome dede :

Mercy, Jesu! man and saueour,

Thi loue is swetter þanne þe mede.   89

Mercy! myghty confortour,

For are I was full wille of rede.

Welcome lorde, all myn honnoure,

Mi joie, my luffe, in ilke a stede.   93

If. 205.
xxviij viij.
The figure of
Christ's armour ;
his leather jacket
was man's flesh,

12. Jesus.   Marie, in thyne harte þou write,

Myne armoure riche and goode,

Myne actone couered all with white,

Als cors of man be-hewede   97

With stuffe goode and parfite

Of maydenes flessh and bloode.

Whan thei ganne thirle and smyte

his hauberk was
his head, his
[breast] plate was
his out-spread
body, his helm
was his man-
hood ;

Mi heede for hawberke stoode.   101

13. Mi plates wer spredde all on-brede,

Þat was my body vppon a tree ;

Myne helme couered all with manhede,

Þe strengh þer-of may no man see ;   105

the crown of
thorns betokens
dignity ;

Þe croune of thorne þat garte me blede,

Itt be-menes my dignite.

his diadem, ever-
lasting life.

Mi diademe sais, with-outen drede,

Þat dede schall I neuere be.   109

14. Maria.   A! blessid body, þat bale wolde beete,

Dere haste þou bought man-kynne,

Thy woundes hath made þi body wete,

'Thou hast
bought mankind
dearly,

With bloode þat was þe with-inne.   113

Nayled þou was thurgh hande and feete,

---

[1] Here a late side-note says 'Hic deficit.'

And all was for oure synne.
Full grissely muste we caitiffis grete,
Of bale howe schulde I blynne? 117

15. To see þis ferly foode
Þus ruffully dight,
Rugged and rente on a roode,
Þis is a rewfull sight. 121
And all is for oure goode,
And no-thyng for his plight, *all for our good,*
not for thy fault.'
Spilte þus is his bloode,
For ilke a synfull wight. 125

16. Jesus. To my god and my Fadir dere, *If. 205 b.*
To hym als swithe I schall assende,
For I schall nowe noȝt longe dwelle here, *'I shall soon*
ascend to my
I haue done als my Fadir me kende, 129 *Father,*
And therfore loke þat ilke man lere,
Howe þat in erthe þer liffe may mende.
All þat me loues I schall drawe nere, *I shall be near*
all who love me.'
Mi Fadirs blisse þat neuere schall ende. 133

17. Maria. Alle for joie me likes to synge,
Myne herte is gladder þanne þe glee,
And all for joie of thy risyng
That suffered dede vpponne a tree. 137 *Mary rejoices.*
Of luffe nowe is þou crouned kyng,
Is none so trewe levand more free,
Thy loue passis all erthely thyng,
Lorde, blissed motte þou euere bee! 141

18. Jesus. To Galile schall þou wende, *'Go, tell my*
brethren in
Marie, my doghtir dere, *Galilee all these*
words.'
Vnto my brethir hende,
Þer þei are all in fere. 145
Telle þame ilke word to ende
Þat þou spake with me here.
Mi blissing on þe lende,
And all þat we leffe here. 149

XL. THE SLEDMEN[1].

The Travellers to Emmaus meet Jesus.

[PERSONS OF THE PLAY.

JESUS.
PRIMUS PEREGRINUS.
SECUNDUS PEREGRINUS[2].]

Luke xxiv. 13-33.

[SCENE, *The road near Emmaus* (*Emax*). *Enter two*
travellers, who meet.]

Two travellers
lamenting the
death of Jesus,

1. i Pereg.   T HAT lorde me lente þis liffe for to lede,
       In my wayes þou me wisse þus will of wone,
Qwen othir men halfe moste mirthe to þer mede,
Þanne als a mornand manne make I my mone[3].   4
For douteles nowe may we drede vs,
Allas! þei haue refte vs oure rede,
With doole haue þei dight hym to dede,
Þat lorde þat was leeffe for to lede vs.   8

2. ii Pereg.   He ledde vs full lelly þat lorde, now allas,
Mi lorde for his lewte his liffe has he lorne[3].

meet and frater-
nize.

i Pereg.   Saye, who comes þere claterand?
ii Pereg.   Sir, I, Cleophas.
Abide my leffe broþere, to bale am I borne.   12
But telle me whedir þou bounes?

---

[1] *Wynedrawers* was written first, then crossed through, and *Sledmen*
written above in contemporary hand. See note on p. 421.
[2] In the MS. *peregrinus* is spelt throughout *perigrinus*, in the contracted
form pign?.
[3] A stroke is drawn after this line, and the words 'hic de novo facto'
written in the margin. The same words are repeated after lines 10, 11.

i **Pereg.**   To Emax, þis castell beside vs,

Ther may we bothe herber and hyde vs,

Þerfore late vs tarie at no townes.   16

They are going to
Emmaus castle,

3. ii **Pereg.**   Atte townes for to tarie take we no tent,

But take vs tome at þis tyme to talke of sume tales,

And jangle of þe Jewes and of Jesu so gente,

Howe þei bette þat body was bote of all bales.   20

With buffetis þei bete hym full barely,

In Sir Cayphas hall garte þei hym call,

And hym be-fore sir Pilate in his hall,

On þe morne þan aftir, full arely.   24

and they leisurely
talk of Jesus
and the late pro-
ceedings before
Pilate.

4. i **Pereg.**   Full arely þe juggemen demed hym to dye,

Both prestis and prelatis to Pilate made preysing,

And alls cursid caytiffis and kene on criste gan þei crie,

And on þat lele lorde made many a lesyng.   28

Þei spitte in his face to dispise hym,

To spoile hym no thyng þei spared hym,

But natheles baynly þei bared hym,

With scourges smertly goyng þei smote hym.   32

If. 206 b.

5. ii **Pereg.**   Þei smotte hym full smertely þat þe bloode
                            oute braste,

Þat all his hyde in hurth was hastely hidde,

A croune of thorne on his heede full thraly þei thraste,

Itt is grete dole for to deme þe dedis þei hym dide.   36

With byndyng vn-baynly and betyng,

Þane on his bakke bare he þame by,

A crosse vnto Caluery,

Þat swettyng was swemyed for swetyng.   40

The cruelties
they made him
suffer were most
grievous.

6. i **Pereg.**   For all þe swette þat he swete with swyngis þei
                            hym swang,

And raffe hym full rewfully with rapes on a rode,

Þan heuyd þei hym highly on hight for to hang,

With-outen misse of þis man, þus mensked þei his mode, 44

Þat euere has bene trewest in trastyng.

'My heart breaks when I think of the sorrow of such a friend.'

Me thynkith myn herte is boune for to breke
Of his pitefull paynes when we here speke,
So frendfull we fonde hym in fraistyng.　　　48

7. ii Pereg.　In frasting we fonde hym full faithfull and free,
And his mynde mente he neuere mysse to no man ;
Itt was a sorowe, for-soth, in sight for to see

They rehearse his death,

Whanne þat a spetyffull spere vn-to his harte ranne.　52
In baill þus his body was beltid,
In to his harte thraly þei thraste,
Whan his piteffull paynes were paste,
Þat swetthyng full swiftely he swelted.　　　56

and burial.

8. i Pereg.　He sweltid full swithe in swonyng þat swette,
Allas! for þat luffely þat laide is so lowe,

lf. 207:
xxix ii.

With granyng full grissely on grounde may we grette,
For so comely a corse canne I none knowe.　　60
With dole vnto dede þei did hym
For his wise werkis þat he wrought þame ;
Þes false folke whan þei be-þoughte þame,
Þat grette vnkyndynesse þei kidde hym.　　64

9. ii Pereg.　Vnkyndynesse þei kidde hym, þo caitiffis so kene,
And als vn-witty wightis, wrought þei hym wreke.
　　　　　　　[*Jesus approaches and joins them.*

Jesus asks what wonders they are speaking of.

Jesus.　What are þes meruailes þat ȝe of mene,
And þus mekill mournyng in mynde þat ȝe make,　68
Walkyng þus wille by þes wayes?

They are surprised he does not know.

ii Pereg.　Why arte þou a pilgryme, and haste bene
At Jerusalem, and haste þou noght sene
What dole has ben done in þes daies?　　　72

10. Jesus.　In ther daies, dere sir? what dole was þer done?
Of þat werke wolde I witte, and youre will were ;

'I pray you tell me.'

And therfore I pray you telle me now sone,
Was þer any hurlyng in hande? nowe late me here.　7(

i **Pereg.**   Why herde þou no carpyng nor crying,
Att Jerusalem þer þou haste bene?
Whenne Jesu of Nazarene
Was doulfully dight to þe dying.   80

11. **ii Pereg.**   To þe dying þei dight hym, þat defte was & dere,
Thurgh prokering of princes þat were þer in prees,
For-thy¹ as wightis þat are will þus walke we in were,
For pechyng als pilgrymes þat putte are to pees.   84
For mornyng of oure maistir þus morne wee,
As wightis þat are wilsome þus walke we,
Of Jesus in telling þus talke we²,
Fro townes for takyng þus turne we.   88

12. **i Pereg.**   Þus turne we fro townes, but take we entent
How þei mourthered þat man þat we of mene,
Full rewfully with ropis on rode þei hym rente,
And takkid³ hym þer-till full tyte in a tene,   92
Vppe-rightis full rudely þei raised hym;
Þanne myghtely to noye hym withall,
In a mortaise faste lete hym fall,
To pynne hym þei putte hym and peysed hym⁴.   96

13. **ii Pereg.**   Thei peysed hym to pynne hym, þat pereles
                 of pese,
Þus on þat wight þat was wise wroȝt þei grete wondir,
Ȝitt with þat sorowe wolde þei noȝt sesse,
They schogged hym and schotte hym his lymes all in
                 sondir.   100
His braynes þus brake þei and braste hym,
A blynde knyght, such was his happe,
Inne with a spere-poynte atte þe pappe
To þe harte full thraly he thraste hym.   104

---

¹ MS. has *For they*.
² The rubricator placed i *Peregrinus* to this line, as well as to line 89,
evidently by mistake.
³ MS. has *talkid*.
⁴ MS. has *and peysed hym* before *þei*.

14. i Pereg. Thei thaste hym full thraly, þan was þer no threpyng,
þus with dole was þat dere vn-to dede dight,
His bak and his body was bolned for betyng,
Itt was, I saie þe for soth, a sorowfull sight.　　108

' We have oft
heard that he
would ransom
Israel. Now is
the third day.'

But oft sithes haue we herde saie,
And we trowe as we herde telle,
That he was to rawsonne I[s]raell;
But nowe is þis þe thirde daye.　　112

15. ii Pereg. Þes dayes newe owre wittis are waxen in were,
For some of oure women for certayne þei saide

lf. 208.
xxix iii.
' The women have
told us they saw
a light and a
vision of angels,
and that the Lord
is alive;

That þai sawe in þer sightis solas full seere,
Howe all was lemand light wher he was laide.　　116
Þei called vs, as euer myght þei thriffe,
For certayne þei saugh it in sight,
A visioune of aungellis bright,
And tolde þame þer lorde was a-lyue.　　120

16. i Pereg. On-lyue tolde þei þat lorde leued hir in lande,
Þer women come lightly to warne, I wene,

some of our folk
found what they
said was true.'

Some of oure folke hyed forthe and faste þei it fande,
Þat all was soth þat þei saide þat sight had þei sene.　　124
For lely þei loked þer he laye,
Þei wende þer þat foode to haue fonne,
Þanne was his toumbe tome as a tonne,
Þanne wiste þei þat wight was away.　　128

17. ii Pereg. Awaye is þat wight þat wonte was vs for to wisse.
Jesus. A! fooles, þat are fauty and failes of youre feithe,

Jesus reproaches
them for want of
faith, he talks of
the law and the
prophets.

Þis bale bud hym bide and belde þame in blisse;
But ӡe be lele of youre laye, youre liffe holde I laith.　　132
To prophetis he proued it and preched,
And also to Moyses gan he saie
Þat he muste nedis die on a day,
And Moyses forth talde it and teched[1].　　136

---

[1] Lines 135, 136 are transposed in the MS.

18. And talde it and teched it many tymes þan.

    i Pereg. A! more of þis talking we pray you to telle vs.

They beg him to go on talking thus.

    ii Pereg. ȝa, sir, be youre carping full kyndely we kenne,

ȝe meene of oure maistir of whome þat we melle vs.   140

    i Pereg. ȝa, goode sir, see what I saie ȝou,

Se ȝe þis castell beside here?

All nyght we thynke for to bide here,

If. 208 b.

Bide with vs, sir pilgrime, we praye ȝou,   144

19. We praye ȝou, sir pilgrime, ȝe presse noȝt to passe.

They beg Jesus to stay with them all night at Emmaus castle.

    Jesus. ȝis sir, me bus nede.

    i Pereg.   Naye, sir, þe nyght is ovir nere.

    Jesus. And I haue ferre for to founde.

    ii Pereg.   I hope wele þou has.

    i Pereg. We praye þe sir, hartely, all nyght holde þe

here.   148

    Jesus. I thanke youe of þis kyndinesse ȝe kydde me.

After hesitation he consents.

    i Pereg. Go in, sir, sadly, and sone. [*They enter the castle.*

    ii Pereg. Sir, daunger dowe noȝt, haue done.

Courtesies.

    Jesus. Sir, I muste nedis do as ȝe bid me,   152

20. ȝe bidde me so baynly I bide for þe beste.

They invite him to sit down and to take of what food they have.

    i Pereg. Lo her is a sege, goode sir, I saie ȝou.

    ii Pereg. With such goode as we haue, glad we oure geste.

    i Pereg. Sir, of þis poure pitaunce take parte now we pray yow.

    Jesus. Nowe blisse I þis brede þat brought is on þe borde,

He blesses the bread.

Fraste þer-on faithfully, my frendis, you to feede.   158

[*Jesus vanishes.*

21. **i Pereg.** [To feed þer-on] vnterly haue we tane entent,—[1]

Ow! I trowe some torfoyr is be-tidde vs!

'Oh! what disaster has befallen us; where is he?'

Saie! wher is þis man?

    ii Pereg.   Away is he wente,

Right now satte he beside vs!   162

22. **i Pereg.** Beside vs we both sawe him sitte!

If. 209. xxix iv. 'I did not see him go!'

And by no poynte couthe I parceyue hym passe.

[1] See *note*, p. 432.

ii **Pereg.**   Nay be þe werkis þat he wrought full wele
    myght we witte,
Itt was Jesus hym selffe, I wiste who it was.   166

23. i **Pereg.**   Itt was Jesus þus wisely þat wrought,
    Þat raised was and rewfully rente on þe rode,
    Of bale and of bittirnesse has he vs boght,
    Boune was and betyn þat all braste on bloode.   170

They recognise that it was Jesus.

24. ii **Pereg.**   All braste on bloode, so sore was he bette,
    With þer wickid Jewes þat wrethfull was euere,
    With scourges and scharpe thornes on his heede sette,
    Suche torfoyr and torment of-telle herde I neuere.   174

25. i **Pereg.**   Of-telle herde I neuere of so pitefull peynes
    As suffered oure souerayne, hyngand on highte,
    Nowe is he resen with myght and with mayne,
    I telle for sikir, we saugh hym in sight.   178

'He is risen; we have seen him.'

26. ii **Pereg.**   We saugh hym in sight, nowe take we entent,
    Be þe brede þat he brake vs so baynly betwene,
    Such wondirfull wais as we haue wente
    Of Jesus þe gente was neuere none seene.   182

'Of Jesus the gentle

27. i **Pereg.**   Sene was þer neuere so wondirfull werkes,
    Be see ne be sande, in þis worlde so wide,
    Menskfully in mynde þes materes now merkis,
    And preche we it prestly on euery ilke side.   186

let us go preach the wonderful works.'

28. ii **Pereg.**   On euery ilke side prestely prech it we,
    Go we to Jerusaleme þes tydingis to telle,
    Oure felawes fro fandyng nowe fraste we,
    More of þis mater her may we not melle.   190

If. 209 b.
'We can do no more about this now, because other plays have to come.'

29. i **Pereg.**   Here may we notte melle [of] more at þis tyde,
    For prossesse of plaies þat precis in plight,
    He bringe to his blisse on euery ilke side,
    Þat sofferayne lorde þat moste is of myght[1].   194

---

[1] The first portion of this play is in regular 8-line stanzas, riming a b a b c d d c; but at l. 158, the point where Jesus vanishes, the metre changes into one of alternate rimes and 4-line stanzas. Lines 160, 161 are reversed in the MS., it is one of the blunders of the old copyist.

XLI.[1] HATMAKERS, MASONS, AND LABORERS.

The Purification of Mary: Simeon and Anna prophesy.

[PERSONS OF THE PLAY.

MARIA.	ANNA PROPHETISSA.
JOSEPH.	SYMEON.
ANGELUS.	PRISBETER.]

[SCENE I, *The Temple at Jerusalem.*]

Prisb. ALMYGHTY God in heven so hy,

The maker of all heven and erth,

He ordenyd here all thynges evenly,

For man he ment to mend his myrth.   4

In nomber, weight, and mesure fyne

God creat here althyng, I say,

His lawes he bad men shulde not tyne,

But kepe his commandmentes all way.   8

In the mount of Syney full fayre,

And in two tabyls to you to tell,

His lawes to Moyses tuke God there

To geve to the chylder of Israell.   12

God created all and bade men keep his laws.

---

[1] This play is written on the blank leaves at the end of quire xxix, in the same hand of the middle of the 16th century which wrote the Fullers' play (p. 18). The rubrication (which is not nearly so bright as that of an earlier date) carefully joins the rimes and the combined verse throughout the piece. The words 'explicit liber' at the end seem to show that this was the concluding piece in a book from which it was copied. On leaf 68 (the proper place for this play), otherwise blank, is written in the same hand, 'Hatmakers, Maysons, and Laborers, purificacio Marie; the Laborers is assigned to bryng furth this pagyant. It is entryd in the latter end of this boke, next after the Sledmen c3 [i. e. caret] Palmers, and it begynnyth (by the preest), All myghty god in heven so hye.' See notes, pp. 421, 446.

(The play should, rightly, have been numbered XVIII and have been placed between the *Adoration* and the *Flight into Egypt*.)

F f

That Moyses shull theme gyde alway,
And lerne theme lely to knowe Goddes wyll,
And that he shulde not it denay,
But kepe his lawes stable and styll,   16
For payn that he hadd putt therefore,
To stone all theme that kepis it nott
Vtterly to death, both lesse and moore.
There shulde no marcy for them be soght,   20

Keep God's command or you will be lost.

Therefore kepe well Goddes commandement,
And leyd your lyf after his lawes,
Or ells surely ye mon be shent
Bothe lesse and moore, ylkone on rawes.   24
This is his wyll after Moyses lawe.
That ye shulde bryng your beistes good,
And offer theme here your God to knawe,
And frome your synns to turne your moode.   28

lf. 210.
xxix v.

God's will by Moses' law is that after certain sicknesses, beasts should be offered up.

Suche beestes as God hais marked here,
Vnto Moyses he spake full yell[1],
And bad hyme boldly with good chere,
To say to the chylder of Israell,   32
That after that dyvers seknes seer,
And after that dyvers synes alsoo,
Go bryng your beestes to the preest even here
To offer theme vp in Goddes sight, loo.   36
The woman that hais borne her chylde,
She shall comme hether at the forty day
To be puryfied where she was fylde,

A woman after child-birth must offer a lamb and two turtle-doves.

And bryng with her a lame, I say,   40
And two dove byrdes for her offerand,
And take them to the preest of lay
To offer theme vp with his holy hand:
There shulde no man to this say nay.   44
The lame is offeryd for Goddes honour

---

[1] Corrected by the same hand to ' To Moyses he spake as I yow tell;'
yell perhaps an error for *well.*

In sacrefyes all onely dight,
And the preistes prayer purchace secure,
For the woman that was fylyd in God sight.   48
And yf so be that she be power,
And have no lame to offer, than
Two tyrtle doves to Godes honoure
To bryng with her for her offrand.   52
Loo! here am I, preest present alway,
To resave all offerandes that hydder is broght,
And for the people to God to pray,
That helth and lyfe to theme be wroght.   56

I, a priest, am here to receive all such offerings.

Anna. Here in this holy playce I say,
Is my full purpose to abyde,
To serve my God bothe nyght and day,
With prayer and fastyng in ever ylk a tyde.   60
For I haue beyn a wyddo this threscore yere
And foure yere to, the truthe to tell,
And here I haue terryed with full good chere,
For the redempcyon of Israell.   64
And so for my holy conversacion,
Grete grace to me hais nowe God sent,
To tell by profecy for mans redempcion,
What shall befall by Goddes entent.   68
I tell you all here in this place,
By Goddes vertue in prophecy,
That one is borne to oure solace,
Here to be present securely   72
                    within short space ;
Of his owen mother a madyn free,
Of all vyrgens moost chaist suthly,
The well of mekenes, blyssed myght she be   76
                    moost full of grace !
And Symeon, that senyour,
That is so semely in Godes sight,   79

Anna abides in the temple night and day.

She has been a widow sixty-four years,

and has the grace of prophecy.

lf. 210 b.

The child Jesus will soon be here,

and old Simeon shall see him, and take him in his arms ;

He shall hyme se and do honour,
And in his armes he shall hym plight,
                    that worthy leyd.   82
Of the holy goost he shall suthly

he shall be in-
spired and go
to the temple.
Take strength, and answere when he shall hy
Furth to this temple and place holy
                    to do þat deyd.   86

[Scene II, *Simeon's house at Jerusalem*.]

Simeon bewails
his age and
feebleness,
Symeon.   A! blyssed God, thowe be my beylde,
And beat my baill bothe nyght and day,
In hevynes my hart is hylde,
Vnto my self, loo thus I say.   90
For I ame wayke and all vnwelde,
My welth ay wayns and passeth away,
Where so I fayre in fyrth or feylde
I fall ay downe, for febyll, in fay;   94
In fay I fall where so I fayre,
In hayre and hewe and hyde, I say.
he wishes for
death as he grows
worse.
Owte of this worlde I wolde I were!
Thus wax I warr and warr alway,   98
And my myscheyf growes in all that may.
Bot thowe, myghty Lorde, my mornyng mar!
Mar ye, for it shulde me well pay,
So happy to se hyme yf I warr.   102
But it would
rejoice him to
see the blessed
babe foretold by
the prophets.
Nowe certys then shulde my gamme begynne,
And I myght se hyme, of hyme to tell,
That one is borne withouten synne,
And for mans kynde mans myrth to mell.   106
Borne of a woman and madyn fre,
As wytnesse Davyt and Danyell,
Withouten synne or velanye,
                    As said also Isacheell.   110

And Melachiell, that proffett snell,
Hais tolde vs of that babb so bright,
That he shulde come with vs to dwell
    In our temple as leme of light. 114
And other proffettes prophesieth,
And of this blyssed babb dyd mell,
And of his mother, a madyn bright,
    In prophecy the truth gan tell,— 118 ' He is to harrow
                      hell
That he shulde comme and harro hell   lf. 211.
As a gyant grathly to glyde,   xxix vj.
And fersly the feyndes malles to fell,   and fell the
                      malice of the
    And putt there poors all on syde. 122 fiend,
The worthyest wight in this worlde so wyde!
His vertues seer no tong can tell,
He sendes all succour in ylke tyde,
As redemption of Israell,   126 and redeem
                      Israel.
    thus say they all,—
There patryarkes and ther prophettes clere,—
' A babb is borne to be oure fere,
Knytt in oure kynde for all our chere   130
    to grete and small.'
Ay! well were me for ever and ay,
If I myght se that babb so bright,
Or I were buryed here in clay,   134
Then wolde my cors here mend in myght
    Right faithfully.
Nowe lorde! thowe grant to me thy grace, Grant me life to
                    see him ere I
To lyf here in this worlde a space,   138 die.'
That I myght se that babb in his face
    here or I dy.
A! lorde God, I thynke, may I endure,
Trowe we that babb shall fynde me here, 142
Nowe certys with aige I ame so power
    that evir it abaites my chere.
Yet yf kynde fale for aige in me,

God yett may length my lyfe, suthely,   146
Tyll I that babb and foode so free
                    haue seyn in sight.
For trewly, yf I wyst reverce (?)
Thare shulde nothyng my hart dyseas,   150
Lorde! len me grace yf that thowe pleas,
                    and make me light.

When wyll thowe comme, babb? let se, haue done;
Nay comme on tyte and tarry nott,   154
For certys my lyf days are nere done,
                    for aige to me grete wo hais wroght.
Great wo is wroght vnto mans harte,
Whan he muste want that he wolde haue;   158

I kepe no longar to haue quarte,
                    for I haue seen that I for crave.
A! trowes thowe these ij eyes shall see
That blyssed babb, or they be owte?   162
Ye, I pray God so myght it be.
                    then were I putt all owte of dowte.
                    [*Enter Angel.*]
Ang.   Olde Symeon, Godes seruaunt right,

Bolde worde to the I bryng, I say,   166
For the holy goost, moost of myght,
He says thowe shall not dye away
                    to thowe haue seen
Jesu the babb that Mary bare,   170
For all mankynde to slake there care.
He shall do comforth to lesse and mayr,
                    both morne and even.

Symeon.   A! lorde, gramarcy, nowe I say!   174
That thowe this grace hais to me hight,
Or I be buryed here in clay
                    to see that semely beam so bright.
No man of molde may haue more happ   178
To my solace and myrth allway,

Than for to se that Mary lapp,
Jesu, my joy and savyour ay,
    Blyssyd be hys name!   182
Loo, nowe mon I se, the truth to tell,
The redempcion of Israell,
Jesu, my lorde Emanuell,
    withouten blame.   186

[SCENE III, *Mary and Joseph at Bethlehem* [1].]

Mary. Joseph, my husbonde and my feer,
Ye take to me grathely entent,
I wyll you showe in this manere,
What I wyll do, thus haue I ment.   190
Full xl days is comme and went
Sens that my babb Jesu was borne,
Therefore I wolde he were present,
As Moyses lawes sais hus beforne,   194
Here in this temple before Goddes sight,
As other women doith in feer,
So me thynke good skyll and right
The same to do nowe with good chere,   198
    after Goddes sawe.

Jos. Mary, my spowse and madyn clene,
This matter that thowe moves to me
Is for all these women, bedene,   202
That hais conceyved with syn fleshely
    to bere a chylde.
The lawe is hedgyd for theme right playn,
That they muste be puryfied agayne,   206
For in mans pleasoure for certayn
    before were they fylyd.
But Mary byrde, thowe neyd not soo,

Luke ii. 22–38.
Mary tells
Joseph that as her
babe is forty days
old she will pre-
sent him in the
temple, as others
do.

Joseph replies
that she is differ-
ent from other
women and need
not do so.

[1] I place this scene thus, notwithstanding l. 195, which is probably a slip
due to the fact that Bethlehem and the temple were near together on the
stage. Cf. the passage ll. 248–274.

For this cause to bee puryfiede, loo,   210
             in Goddes temple.

For certys, thowe arte a clene vyrgyn,
For any thoght thy harte within,
Nor never wroght no flesly synne   214
             nor never yll.

Mary. That I my madenheade hais kept styll
It is onely throgh Goddes wyll,
             that be ye bold.   218

She would do it as an example of meekness to the law.

Yett to fulfyll the lawe, ewysse,
That God almyghty gon expresse,
And for a sample of mekenesse,
             offer I wolde.   222

Jos. A! Mary, blyssed be thowe ay,
Thowe thynkes to do after Goddes wyll,

Joseph freely consents.

As thowe haist said Mary, I say,
I will hartely consent there-tyll   226
             withouten dowte.

lf. 212. xxix vij.

Wherefore we dresse vs furth oure way,
And make offerand to God this day,
Even lykwyse as thy self gon say   230
             with hartes devowte.

Mar. Therto am I full redy dight,

She hesitates

But one thyng, Joseph I wolde you meyve.

Jos. Mary, my spouse and madyn bright,   234
Tell on hartely, what is your greyf?

about the lamb and two doves;

Mar. Both beest and fewll hus muste neydes haue,
As a lambe and ij dove byrdes also,

they have no lamb, what shall they do?

Lame haue we none nor none we crave,   238
Therefore Joseph what shall we do,
             what is your read?

And we do not as custome is,
We are worth to be blamyd, i-wysse,   242
I wolde we dyd nothing amys
             as God me speyd.

Jos. A! good Mary, the lawe is this,
To riche to offer bothe the lame and the byrd,   246
And the ij tyrtles, i-wys,
Or two doyf-byrdes shall not be fyrd
    for our offerand;
And Mary, we haue doyf byrdes two,   250 *Joseph has two doves ready in a basket.*
As falls for hus therefore we goo,
They ar here in a panyer, loo,
    Reddy at hand.
And yf we haue not both in feer,   254
The lame, the burd, as ryche men haue,
Thynke that vs muste present here
Oure babb Jesus, as we voutsaue
    before Godes sight.   258 *Jesus is their lamb!*
He is our lame, Mary, kare the not,
For riche and power none better soght;
Full well thowe have hym hither broght
    this our offerand dight.   262 *He is the lamb of God also.*
He is the lame of God, I say,
That all our syns shall take away
    of this worlde here.
He is the lame of God verray,   266
That muste hus fend frome all our fray,
Borne of thy wombe, all for our pay [1],
    and for our chere.

Mar. Joseph, my spowse, ye say full trewe,   270 *Mary assents;*
Than lett vs dresse hus furth our way.

Jos. Go we than Mary, and do oure dewe,
And make meekly offerand this day.   [*They set forth.* *they go to the priest in the temple,*
Lo, here is the tempyll on this hyll,   274
And also preest ordand by skyll,
    power havand.

---

[1] MS. has *pray.*

And Mary, go we thyther forthy,
And lett vs both knele devowtly,   278
And offre we vp to God meekly
     our dewe offrand.

[SCENE IV, *The Temple, as before. Enter to the Priest, Joseph
and Mary with the Babe.*]

Mar. Vnto my God highest in heven,
And to this preest ordand by skyll,

Jesu my babb, I offer hyme,
Here with my harte and my good wyll   284
     right hartely.
Thowé pray for hus to God on hyght,
Thowe preest, present here in his myght,
At this deyd may be in his sight   288
     accept goodly.

Jos. Loo sir? and two doyf-byrddes ar here,
Receyve them with your holy handes,
We ar no better of power,   292
For we haue neyther rentes ne landes
     trewely.
Bott good sir, pray to God of myght
To accepte this at we have dight,   296
That we haue offeryd as we arr hight
     here hartely.

Presb. O God, and graunter of all grace,
Blyst be thy name both nyght and day,   300
Accepte there offerand in this place
That be here present to the alway.
A! blyssed lorde, say never nay,
But lett thy offerand be boot and beylde   304
Tyll all such folke lyvand in clay,
That thus to the mekly wyll heyld,
That this babb, lord, present in thy sight,

Borne of a madyns wombe vnfylde ;   308
Accepte, [lord,] for there specyall gyft
Gevyn to mankynde, both man and chylde,
        so specyally.

And this babb borne and here present   312   A prayer of
May beylde vs, that we be not shent,   worship and
           welcome.
But ever reddy his grace to hent
        here verely.

A blyssed babb! welcome thowe be,   316
Borne of a madyn in chaistety,
Thowe art our beylde, babb, our gamme and our glee
        ever sothly.

Welcome! oure wytt and our wysdome,   320
Welcome! our joy all and somme,
Welcome! redemptour omnium
        tyll hus hartely.
                [Enter Anna.

Anna.   Welcome ! blyssed Mary and madyn ay,   324   Anna welcomes
Welcome! mooste meke in thyne array,   *[To the Babe.* the bright star,
Welcome! bright starne that shyneth bright as day,
        all for our blys.

Welcome ! the blyssed beam so bryght,   328
Welcome ! the leym of all oure light,
Welcome ! that all pleasour hais plight
        to man and wyfe.

Welcome ! thowe blyssed babb so free,   332   lf. 213.
Welcome ! oure welfayre wyelly,   xxix viij.
And welcome all our seall, suthly,   our welfare and
           bliss.
        to grete and small.

Babb, welcome to thy beyldly boure,   336
Babb, welcome nowe for our soccoure,
And babb, welcome with all honour
        here in this hall.

[SCENE V, *Simeon's house as before : enter Angel.*]

The angel tells
Simeon to get
ready.

Ang.   Olde Symeon, I say to the,   340
Dresse the furth in thyne array,
Come to the temple, there shall þu see,
Jesus, that babb that Mary barre,
     that be thowe bolde.   344

Simeon rejoices,
as light as a leaf,
he feels young
again.

Sym.   A! lorde, I thanke þe ever and ay,
Nowe am I light as leyf on tree,
My age is went, I feyll no fray,
Me thynke for this that is tolde me   348
    I ame not olde.
Nowe wyll I to yon temple goo
To se the babb that Mary bare,
He is my helth in well and woo,   352
And helps me ever frome great care.   [*Exit.*

[SCENE VI, *The Temple, as before : enter Simeon.*]

Simeon hails the
babe and the
mother.

Haill! blyssed babb, that Mary bare,
And blyssed be thy mother, Mary mylde,
Whose wombe that yeildyd fresh and fayr,   356
And she a clean vyrgen ay vnfyld.
Haill babb, the Father of Heven own chylde,
Chosen to chere vs for our myschance;
No erthly tong can tell fylyd   360
What thy myght is in every chance.

'Shield us from
ill.

Haill! the moost worthy to enhance,
Boldly thowe beylde [us] frome all yll,
Withoute thy beylde we gytt grevance,   364
And for our deydes here shulde we spyll.

Hail, rose of
Sharon!
(*Cant. cant.* cap.
ii. 1.)

Haill! floscampy, and flower vyrgynall,
The odour of thy goodnes reflars to vs all.
Haill! moost happy to great and to small   368
    for our weyll.

Haill! ryall roose, moost ruddy of hewe.   *Royal rose !*
Haill! flower vnfadyng, both freshe ay and newe,
Haill the kyndest in comforth that ever man knewe,   372
         for grete heyll.

And mekly I beseke the here where I kneyll,
To suffre thy servant to take the in hand,   *Let me take thee*
                                        in mine arms.
And in my narmes for to heue the here for my weyll,   376
And where I bound am in bayll to bait all my bandes.
           [*Takes the babe in his arms.*

Now come to me, lorde of all landes,   lf. 213 b.
Come myghtyest by see and by sandes,
Come myrth by strete and by strandes   380
         on moolde.

Come halse me, the babb that is best born,   *Embrace me, or*
Come halse me, the myrth of our morne,   *else I am lost.'*
Come halse me, for elles I ame lorne   384
         for olde.

I thanke the lord God of thy greet grace,   *Simeon thanks*
That thus haith sparyd me a space,   *and praises God.*
This babb in my narmes for to inbrace   388
         as the prophecy tell[es].

I thanke the that me my lyfe lent,
I thanke the that me thus seyll sent,
That this sweyt babb, that I in armes hent,   392
         With myrth my myght alwais melles.

Mellyd are my myndes ay with myrth,
Full fresh nowe I feyll is my force,
Of thy grace thowe gave me this gyrth,   396
Thus comly to catch here thy corse
         moost semely in sight.

Of helpe thus thy freynd never faills,   *God's mercy*
Thy marcy as every man avaylls,   *never fails.*
Both by downes and by daylls,   400
         Thus mervelous and muche is thy myght.

A ! babb, be thowe blyssed for ay,
For thowe art my savyour, I say,   404
And thowe here rewles me in fay,
        In all my lyfe.

Nowe blist be þi name !
For thowe saves hus fro shame,   408
And here thou beyld vs fro blame,
        And frome all stryfe.

Nowe care I no moore for my lyfe,
Sen I have seen here this ryall so ryfe,   412
My strength and my stynter of stryfe,
        I you say,

'Let me depart in peace, for mine eyes have seen thy salvation.'

In peace lorde, nowe leyf thy servand,
For myne eys haith seyn that is ordand,   416
The helth for all men that be levand,
        here for ay.

That helth lorde hais thowe ordand, I say,
Here before the face of thy people,   420
And thy light hais thowe shynyd this day,
        for evermore

To be knowe of thy folke that was febyll.
And thy glory for the chylder of Israell,
That with the in thy kyngdome shall dwell,   424
Whan the damnyd shall be drevyn to hell
        than with great care.

Mary and Joseph marvel at what they hear said.

Jos. Mary, my spowse and madyn mylde,
In hart I marvell here greatly   428
Howe these folke spekes of our chylde ;
They say and tells of great maistry,
        that he shall doo.

lf. 214. xxix ix [1].

Mar. Yea, certes, Joseph I marvell also,   432
But I shall bere it full styll in mynde.

---

[1] An extra leaf added to this quire, on which to finish the play. See *note*, p. 433.

Jos. God geve hyme grace here well to do,
For he is come of gentyll kynde.
Sym. Harke! Mary, I shall tell the þe truth or I goo,   436
This was putt here to welde vs fro,
In redemption of many and recover also,
        I the say.
And the sworde of sorro thy hart shal thyrll,   440
Whan thowe shall se sothly thy son soffer yll,
For the well of all wrytches þat shall be his wyll
        here in fay.

'He is for the redemption of many, and a sword shall thrill thy heart when he suffers.

But to be comforth agayn right well thowe may,   444
And in harte to be fayne the suth, I the say,
For his myght is so muche thare can no tong say nay,
        here to his wyll.

But thou shalt be comforted.

For this babb as a gyant[1], full graythly shall glyde,   448
And the myghtiest mayster shall meve on ylke syde,
To all the wightes that wons in this worlde wyde,
        for good or for yll.

Tharefore babb, beylde vs, that we here not spyll.   452
And fayrwell, the former of all at thy wyll,
Fayrwell! starne stabylyst by lowde and be styll,
        in suthfastnes.

Farewell!

Fayrwell! the ryolest roose that is renyng,   456
Fayrwell! the babb best in thy beryng,
Fayrwell! God son, thowe grant vs thy blyssyng
        to fynd our dystresse.

Explicit Liber.

[1] MS. has *gyane.*

XLII. THE ESCREUENERES.

The Incredulity of Thomas.

[PERSONS OF THE PLAY.

DEUS (i. e. Jesus).   JACOBUS.
PETRUS.   THOMAS.]
JOHANNES.

John xx. 19-29.   [SCENE I, *A chamber with doors shut : the disciples assembled.*]

The disciples are
grieving;

1. Petrus.   ALLAS! to woo þat we wer wrought,
　　　　Hadde never no men so mekill þought
　　　　Sen that oure lorde to dede was brought   3
　　　　　　　　with Jewes fell;
　　　　Oute of þis steede ne durst we noght,
　　　　　　　　but here ay dwelle.   6

they fear the
Jews,

2. Joh.   Here haue we dwelte with peynes strang,
　　　　Of oure liffe vs lothis, we leve to lange,
　　　　For sen the Jewes wrought vs þat wrong   9
　　　　　　　　Oure lorde to sloo,
　　　　Durste we neuere come þame emang,
　　　　　　　　ne hense to goo.   12

and therefore
remain still.

3. Jac.   Þe wikkid Jewes hatis vs full ille,
　　　　And bittir paynes wolde putte vs till,
　　　　Therfore I rede þat we dwelle stille   15
　　　　　　　　Here þer we lende,
　　　　Unto þat Criste oure lorde vs wille
　　　　　　　　some socoure sende.   18

Collations with the Sykes MS. of this play at York ; see p. 455.

l. 1. to] the ; wer] are.   l. 5. ne] sens.   l. 6. ay] a.   l. 8. And
with our lyvys owe lath we lyff so longe.   l. 9. Sen that thes Jewys
wroght this.   l. 11. Sens drust.   l. 12. ne hyne goo.   l. 13. þes.
l. 14. wolde] thay.   l. 15. *omit* þat.   ll. 17, 18. *These lines stand
as one*, tyll that cryst vs some socor send.

[*Jesus appears.*   Jesus appears to
                    them for an in-
4. **Deus.**   Pees and reste be with yowe !   [*He vanishes.*   stant.

Petrus.   A ! brethir dere, what may we trowe,

What was this sight þat we saughe nowe   21

    Shynand so bright?

And vanysshed þus and we ne wote how,

    Oute of oure sight?   24

5. **Johes.**   Oute of youre sight nowe is it soghte,

Itt makith vs madde, þe light it broght.

Jacobus.   Sertis I wotte noght but sekirly   27   It must have
                                                                been fancy !
    What may it be ;

Itt was vanyte in oure þought,   29

    Nought ellis trowe I it be.   30

     [*Jesus re-appears.*   Jesus appears
                                                      again. 'Fearnot.'
6. **Deus.**   Pees vnto yowe euermore myght be,

Drede you noȝt, for I am hee.

Petrus.   On goddis name, benedicite,   33

    What may þis mene ?

Jacobus.   Itt is a sperite, for sothe thynketh me,   They think it is
                                                               a spirite,
    Þat dose vs tene.   36

7. **Johannes.**   A sperite it is, þat trowe I right,   If. 215 b.

All þus appered here to oure sight,

Itt makis vs madde of mayne and myght,   39   they are afraid.

    Dois vs flaied,

Ȝone is þe same þat broughte þe light,

    Þat vs affraied.   42

8. **Deus.**   What thynke ȝe, madmen, in youre thought?   'Why are ye
                                                             afraid ? I am
What mournyng in youre hertis is brought ?   Christ ;

I ame Criste, ne drede ȝou noght,   45

    her may [1] ȝe se

---

l. 19. Deus] Jesus ; with] vnto. l. 21. this] the. l. 23. þus ys
vanysshed we wayt not. l. 25. youre] our. l. 26. makes. l. 27.
whole line *omitted*. l. 29. Ẏt ys some vanytes. l. 31. Deus] Jesus.
l. 35. A sprett for soth so thynke me. l. 38. þat þus. l. 40. flaied]
frayd. l. 41. ȝone] yt. l. 46. may.

---

[1] MS. has *nay*.

Þe same body þat has you bought

vppon a tre.   48

9. Þat I am comen ʒou here to mete,

see my hands
and feet, and feel
my wounds.

Be-halde and se myn handis and feete,   50

And grathely gropes my woundes wete

Al þat here is,   52

Þus was I dight youre bales to beete,

and bring to blis.   54

10. For yowe þusgatis þanne haue I gone,

Folous me grathely euerilkone,   56

And se þat I haue flessh and bone,

Gropes me nowe.   58

Feel and believe,
I am no spirit ;

For so ne has sperite none,

Þat schall ʒe trowe.   60

for further proof

11. To garre ʒou kenne and knowe me clere,

I schall you schewe ensaumpillis sere,

bring to me meat,
if ye have aught
to eat.'

Bringe nowe forthe vnto me here   63

some of youre mette,

If ʒe amange you all in-fere

haue ought to ete.   66

12. Jacobus. Þou luffand lorde þat laste schall ay,

Loo here is mette þat þou ete may,

They bring
honeycomb and
some roast fish.

A hony kombe þe soth to saye,

Roste fecche þertill ;   70

To ete þerof here we þe praie,

with full goode will.   72

' To make your
faith steady and
your despair for-
gotten I now eat
with you.'

13. Deus. Nowe sen ʒe haue broughte me þis mete,

To make youre trouthe stedfast and grete,

And for ʒe schall wanhope for-gete,   75

and trowe in me,

With youe þan here wol I ete,

Þat ʒe schalle see.   78

---

l. 50. behold.   l. 55. þanne] þus.   l. 56. felys.   l. 70. Roch fych.
l. 71. here we] we wold.   l. 77. þan] now ; þen woll.

14. Nowe haue I done, ȝe haue sene howe,
Boldely etyng here with youe,
Stedfastly loke þat ȝe trowe
   yitt in me efte,
And takis þe remenaunte sone to you
   þat her is lefte.   84

15. For ȝoue þus was I reuyn and dreste,
Þerfore some of my peyne ȝe taste,   86
And spekis now no whare my worde waste,
   þat schall ȝe lere,
And vnto ȝou þe holy goste   89
   Releffe yow here.

*If. 216.
xxx. ij.*

16. Beis now trewe and trowes in me,   91
And here I graunte youe in youre poste,
Whome þat ȝe bynde bounden schall be   93
   Right at youre steuene,
And whome þat ȝe lesid losed schalbe   95
   Euer more in heuene. [*Exit.* 96

'I grant that whom ye bind shall be bound, and whom ye loose shall be loosed in heaven.'

   [*Thomas outside the chamber.*

17. **Thomas.** Allas for sight and sorowes sadde,
Mornyng makis me mased and madde,
On grounde nowe may I gang vngladde   99
   Boþe even and morne.   100
Þat hende þat I my helpe of hadde
   his liffe has lorne.   102

Thomas is mourning for Jesus,

18. Lorne I haue þat louely light,   103
Þat was my maistir moste of myght,
So doulfully as he was dight   105
   was neuere no man ;
Such woo was wrought of þat worthy wighte
   with wondis wan.

he rehearses his master's wrongs.

---

l. 81. Now stedfastly.   l. 83. remland.   l. 85. reuyn and
dreste] rent and rayst.   l. 87. now *omitted*; your wordes I wayst.
88. here that ye lere   90. releffe] resave.   l. 100. even] eyn.
101. hende] hynd.

19. Whan lo ! as his wondis and wondis wette,

<ins>With skelpis sore was he swongen, þat swette,</ins>   110

All naked nailed thurgh hande and feete,   111

allas ! for pyne,   112

Þat bliste, þat beste my bale myght bete,   113

his liffe schulde tyne !   114

He is so cast
down with
sorrow that he
will seek his
brethren.

20. Allas ! for sorowe my selffe I schende,   115

When I thynke hartely on þat hende,

I fande hym ay a faithfull frende,   117

Trulie to telle ;   118

To my brethir nowe wille I wende   119

wher so þei dwell.

[*Enters the chamber.*

' All our joy is
gone. God bless
you, brethren.'

21. A ! blistfull sight was neuere none,   121

Oure joie and comforte is all gone,

Of mournyng may we make oure mone

In ilka lande ;   124

God blisse you, brether ! bloode and bone,

same þer ȝe stande.

' Welcome, we
have seen our
lord.'

22. Petrus.   Welcome Thomas, where has þou bene ?

Wete þou wele withouten wene   128

Jesu oure lorde þan haue we sene,

on grounde her gang.

Thomas.   What saie ȝe men ? allas ! for tene,

I trowe ȝe mang.   132

lf. 216 b.

23. Johannes[1].   Thomas, trewly it is noght to layne,

Jesu oure lorde is resen agayne.

---

l. 109. Whan lo as] wan was.   l. 110. skelpis] swapis.   l. 113. bale
balles.   l. 119. To] Vnto.   l. 120. wher some.
l. 121. A . . . sight] so wofull wyghtis.   l. 122. and] owr.

---

[1] Johannes supplied from Sykes MS., the name is wanting in Ashburnham.

Thomas.   Do waie, these tales is but attrayne

of fooles vnwise.   136

For he þat was so fully slayne,   137

howe schulde he rise ?   138

Thomas will not
believe that
Jesus is risen.

24. Jacobus.   Thomas, trewly he is on-lyue,

Þat tholede þe Jewes his flessh to riffe,   140

He lete vs fele his woundes fyue,   141

Oure lorde verray.   142

Thomas.   That trowe I nought, so motte I thryue,

what so ȝe saie.   144

' Truly he is
alive, we felt his
wounds.'

25. Petrus.   Thomas we saugh his woundes wette,

How he was nayled thurgh hande and feete,   146

Hony and fisshe with vs he eette,   147

þat body free.

Thomas [1].   I laye my liff it was some sperit   149

ȝe wende wer hee.

' It was a spirit.'

26. Johannes.   Nay Thomas, þou haste misgone,

For-why he bad vs euerilkon   152

To grope hym grathely, bloode and bone

And flessh to feele,   154

Such thyngis, Thomas, hase sperite none,

þat wote ȝe wele.   156

' We felt his
blood, bones, and
flesh ; spirits
have none.'

27. Thomas.   What ! leue felawes, late be youre fare,

Till þat I see his body bare,   158

And sithen my fyngir putte in thare

within his hyde,   160

And fele the wound þe spere did schere

riȝt in his syde ;   162

Thomas will not
believe till he
has felt the
wound of the
spear.

---

l. 135. a trayne.   l. 137. For *supplied from Sykes MS.*
l. 139. trewly] lely.   l. 144. what so] why sa.   l. 155. spretes.
l. 157. What leue] now.   l. 158. his] þat.   l. 161. þe ... did]
this sper.

---

[1] Thomas supplied from Sykes MS.

28. Are schalle I trowe no tales be-twene.

Jacobus.   Thomas, þat wounde haue we seene.

Thomas.   ȝa, ȝe wotte neuere what ȝe mene,

youre witte it wantis,   166

'Ye play tricks upon me.'

Ye muste thynke sen ȝe me þus tene

and tule with trantis.   168

Jesus appears again.

[Jesus reappears.

29. Deus.   Pees! brethir, be vn-to you,

'Thomas, see and feel me,

And, Thomas, tente to me takis þou,   170

Putte forthe thy fingir to me nowe,

myn handis þou see;   172

Howe I was nayled for mannys prowe

vppon a tree.   174

30. Beholde my woundis are bledand,   175

lf. 217.
xxx. iij.

put your hand in my side and believe.'

Here in my side putte in þi hande,

And fele my woundis and vndirstande

þat þis is I,   178

And be no more so mistrowand,

But trowe trewly.   180

[Thomas touches the side of Jesus.

Thomas believes and asks grace.

31. Thomas.   Mi lorde, my god, full wele is me,

A! blode of price! blessid mote þou be,   182

Mankynd in erth, be-hold and see   183

þis blessid blode.   184

Mercy nowe lorde ax I the,

with mayne and mode.   186

'Thomas, you believe because you have seen, but blessed are those who believe without seeing.

32. Deus.   Thomas, for þou haste sene þis sight,

Þat I am resen as I you hight,   188

Þerfore þou trowes it; but ilka wight,   189

Blissed be þou euere,   190

---

l. 166. wyttis ye wantis.   l. 167. thynke no syne thus me to tene.
168. tule] tyll; trawntes.   l. 169. brethir] and rest.   l. 178. þis] yt.
l. 179. so *from Sykes MS.*   l. 183. *this line from Sykes MS., wholly
wanting in Ashburnham.*   l. 188. resyng; you] þe.   l. 189. *omit* þou;
but ilka] euerylk.   l. 190. þou] they.

Þat trowis haly in my rising right, 191

    And saw it neuere. 192

33. My brethir, fonde nowe forthe in fere, 193 Go forth, and

Ouere all in ilke a contre clere,   preach my rising.'

My rising both ferre and nere, 195

    And preche it schall 3e,

And my blissyng I giffe 3ou here, 197

    And my men3e. 198

---

l. 193. fandes. 194. clere] sere. l. 196. Preached shall be. l. 198. my] this.

The MS. of the Skryveners' play, now in the possession of the York Philosophical Society, to which it has been presented by Dr. Sykes of Doncaster, consists of four leaves of parchment, sewn in a parchment cover with a flap, the whole doubled lengthwise, the flap folding over, as though intended for the pocket. It is endorsed ' Skryveners' only, no other marks indicate the object of this duplicate ; the hand is of about the beginning of the 16th cent., and is not the regular clerkly hand of the Ashburnham MS. ; the spelling differs considerably, and the short lines are often confused with the long ones. This cannot have been copied *from* the Ashburnham, as it supplies a line and several important words wanting in that MS. ; on the other hand the Ashburnham is a better text in some points. Both were probably copied from another original.

The collations given are those of variants from the Ashburnham text found in the Sykes MS. Notice is not taken of different spelling merely, which may be seen by consulting Mr. Collier's print of the Sykes MS., Camden Miscellany, vol. iv.

XLIII. THE TAILOURES [1].

lf. 218 b.
xxx. iiij b.

The Ascension.

[PERSONS OF THE PLAY.

JESUS.	JACOBUS.
MARIA.	ANDREAS.
PETRUS.	1 ANGELUS.
JOHANNES.	2 ANGELUS.]

Luke xxiv. 49-53.
Acts i. 4-14.

[SCENE, *The Mount of Olives, near Bethany : the disciples with
Mary are assembled.*]

The disciples are
in doubt when
Jesus will leave
them.

1. Petrus. O MIGHTFULL god, how standis it nowe,
      In worlde þus will was I neuere are,—
Butte he apperes,—bot I ne wo¹e howe
He fro vs twynnes whanne he will fare.   4
And ȝitt may falle þat for oure prowe,
And alle his wirkyng lesse and mare,
A ! kyng of comforte ! gudde arte þou,
And lele and likand is thy lare [2].   8

John mourns the
loss and want of
his company.

2. Johannes. The missing of my maistir trewe,
That lenghis not with vs lastandly,
Makis me to morne ilke a day newe,
For tharnyng of his company.   12
His peere of gudnes neuere I knewe,
Of myght ne wisdome it anly.
    Petrus. That we hym tharne, sore may vs rewe,
For he luffed vs full faithfully.   16

---

[1] An early hand wrote 'Potters' on this page after 'Tailoures,' but the
pen was struck through it. The Potters play the next piece.
[2] In the MS. *and lele* was originally written at end of l. 7; but the
Elizabethan hand corrected it as above.

3. Bot ȝitt in all my mysselykyng,
   A worde þat Criste saide comfortis me,
   Oure heuynes and oure mournyng,
   He saide to joie turned schuld be.   20
   Þat joie he saide in his hetyng,
   To reue vs none schulde haue no poste,
   Wherfore abouen all othir thyng
   That joie me longis to knowe & see.   24

A word of comfort, our mourning shall be turned to joy. John xvi. 20.

4. **Maria.** Þou Petir, whanne my sone was slayne,
   And laide in graue, ȝe wer in were
   Whedir he schulde rise, al moste ilkane,
   But nowe ȝe wotte thurgh knowyng clere.   28
   Come þat he saide schulde is gane,
   And some to come, but ilkane sere,
   Whedir it be to come or none,
   Vs awe to knowe it all in fere.   [*Jesus appears.*]   32

' Whatever is to come, let us all be together.' lf. 219. xxx. v.

5. **Jesus.** Almyghty god, my Fadir free,
   In erthe þi bidding haue I done,
   And clarified þe name of þe,
   To thy selffe clarifie þe sone.   36
   Als þou haste geuen me pleyne poste,
   Of ilke a flesh graunte me my bone,
   Þat þou me gaffe myght lyffand be
   In endles liffe and with þe wonne.   40

John xvii. 4–23. ' Father, I have glorified thy name.

Glorify thy son.

Grant life eternal to those thou givest me,

6. Þat liffe is þis þat hath none ende,
   To knawe the Fadir, moste of myght,
   And me thy sone, whanne þou gon sende
   To dye for man with-outen plight,   44
   Mankynde was thyne whome þu be-kende
   And toke me to þi ȝemyng right.
   I died for man, mannes misse to mende,
   And vnto spitous dede was dight.   48

mankind, given me to rule.

7. Thy wille vn-to þem taughte haue I,
   Þat wolde vn-to my lare enclyne,

Mi lare haue they tane buxsomly,

Schall none of them þer trauaile tyne.   52

Þou gaffe þem me but noght for-thy

Ȝitt are they thyne als wele as myne,

Fleme þem not fro oure companye,

Sen thyne are myne and myne er thyne.   56

8. Sen they are oures, if þame nede ought

Þou helpe þem, if it be thy will,

And als þou wate þat I þame boght,

For faute of helpe latte þem not spill.   60

Fro þe worlde to take þem pray I noght,

But þat þou kepe þame ay fro ill.

All þois also þat settis þare þoght

In erthe my techyng to fulfill.   64

9. Mi tythandis tane has my menȝe

To teche þe pepull wher they fare ;

In erthe schall þei leue aftir me,

And suffir sorowes sadde and sare.   68

Dispised and hatted schall þei be,

Als I haue bene, with lesse and mare,

And suffer [1] dede in sere degre

For sothfastnesse schall none þem spare.   72

10. Þou halowe þame, fadir, for-thy,

In sothfastnes so þat þei may

Be ane as we ar, yowe and I,

In will and werke, both nyght and day,   76

And knawe þat I ame verilye

Both sothfastnes and liffe alway ;

Be the whilke ilke man þat is willy

May wynne þe liffe þat laste schall ay.   80

11. Bot ȝe, my postelis all be-dene,

Þat lange has wente a-bowte with me,

In grete wanne-trowing haue ȝe bene,

And wondir harde of hartis ar ȝe,   8

[1] MS. has *suffered.*

Worthy to be reproued, I wene,
Ar ȝe forsothe, and ȝe will see,
In als mekill als ȝe haue sene
My wirkyng proued and my poste.   88

12. Whan I was dede and laide in graue,
Of myne vpryse ȝe were in doute,
And some for myne vprysing straue,
When I was laide als vndir-lowte   92
So depe in erthe ; but sithen I haue
Ben walkand fourty daies aboute,
Eten with ȝou, youre trouthe to saue,
Comand emange ȝou inne and oute.   96

13. And þerfore beis nomore in were
Of myne vppe-rysing, day nor nyght,
Youre misbeleue leues ilkone seere,
For witte ȝe wele, als man of myght   100
Over whome no dede may haue poure,
I schall be endles liffe and right.
But for to schewe you figure clere,
Schewe I me þus-gatis to youre sight,   104

14. Howe man by cours of kynde schall ryse,
All þogh he be roten on-till noȝt,
Oute of his graue in þis same [1] wise
At þe daye of dome schall he be broght   108
Wher I schall sitte as trewe justise,
And deme man aftir he has wroght ;
Þe wikkid to wende with þer enmyse,
Þe gode to blisse þei schall be broght.   112

15. A-nodir skill for-soth is þis,
In a tre man was traied thurgh trayne,
I man, for-thy, to mende þat misse
On a tree boght mankynde agayne.   116
In confusioune of hym and his
Þat falsely to forge þat frawde was fayne,

[1] MS. has *sane*.

---

they quarrelled about Christ's uprising.

lf. 220. xxx. vj.
He has been with them forty days since then,

they must cast away unbelief.

Man shall rise from the grave in course of nature, although he be rotten, at dooms-day.

Through a tree man was be-trayed, Christ redeemed him on a tree,

Mankynde to bringe agayne to blisse
His foo þe fende till endles peyne.   120

16. Þe thirde skille is, trewly to telle,
Right als I wende als wele will seme,

Christ will come again in the flesh at doomsday.

So schall I come in flessh and fell
Atte þe day of dome ; whan I schal deme   124
Þe goode in endles blisse to dwell,
Mi fomen fro me for to fleme,
With-outen ende in woo to well.

lf. 220 b.

Ilke leuand man, here to take yeme.   128

17. But in-till all þe worlde weldand
Þe Gospell trewly preche schall ȝe,
Tille ilke a creatoure liffand.

He who believes, and is baptized, shall be saved;

Who trowes, if that he baptised be   132
He schall, als yhe schall vndirstande,
Be saued, and of all thraldome free ;

the unbeliever is damned.

Who trowis it not, as mistrowand
For faute of trouth dampned is he,   136

The powers given to those who believe.

18. But all þer tokenyngis be-dene
Schall folowe þam þat trowis it right,
In my name deuellis crewell and kene,
Schall þei oute-caste of ilk-a wight ;   140
With newe tongis speke ; serpentis vnclene
For-do ; and if þei day or nyght
Drinke venym wik, with-outen wene,
To noye þame schall it haue no myght.   146

19. On seke folke schall þei handes lay,
And wele schall þei haue sone at welde ;
Þis poure schall þei haue alway,
My menȝhe, bothe in towne and felde.   15⸱

'They who do my will shall abide with me in bliss.

John xiv. 2.

And witte ȝe wele, so schall þei
Þat wirkis my wille in youthe or elde,
A place for þame I schall purveye
In blisse with me ay in to belde.   15⸱

20. Nowe is my jornay brought till ende,
Mi tyme þat me to lang was lente[1],
To my Fadir nowe vppe I wende,
And youre Fadir þat me doune sente. 158
Mi God, youre God, and ilke mannes frende,
That till his techyng will consente,
Till synneres þat no synne þame schende,
Þat mys amendis and will repente. 162

My time is at an end, I go to my Father and your Father. *John* xiv. 27, 28.

21. But for I speke þes wordis nowe
To you, youre hartis hase heuynes,
Full-ffillid all be it for youre prowe,
Þat I hense wende, als nedful is. 166
And butte I wende, comes noght to yowe
Þe comfortoure[2] of comforteles ;
And if I wende, ȝe schall fynde howe
I schall hym sende, of my goodnesse. 170

Ye are sorrowful, If. 221. xxx. vij.

but unless I go the Comforter will not come to you. *John* xvi. 7.

22. Mi Fadirs will full-fillid haue I,
Therfore fareswele, ilkone seere,
I goo make youe a stede redye
Endles to wonne with me in feere. 174
Sende doune a clowde, fadir ! for-thy
I come to þe, my fadir deere.
Þe Fadir blissing moste myghty
Giffe I you all þat leffe here[3]. *[Jesus ascends.* 178

Farewell, I go to make a place ready for you. Father, I come.'

A cloud descends.

23. Maria. A ! myghtfull god, ay moste of myght,
A selcouth sight is þis to see,
Mi sone þus to be ravisshed right
In a clowde wendande vppe fro me. 182
Bothe is my harte heuy and light,
Heuy for swilke twynnyng schulde be,
And light for he haldis þat he hight,
And þus vppe wendis in grette poste. 186

Mary is sad at parting, joyful that he keeps his promise.

---

[1] MS. has *lende*. [2] MS. has *comforte oure*.
[3] In the margin is here written in the late corrector's hand, 'Ascendo ad ·atrem meum. Tunc cantent angeli.'

24. His hetyngis haldis he all be-dene,
Þat comfortis me in all my care,
But vnto whome schall I me mene,
Þus will in worlde was I neuere.   190

She fears to stay among the Jews.

To dwelle amonge þes Jewes kene,
Me to dispise will þei not spare.
Joh.   All be he noght in presens seene,
Ʒitt is he salue of ilk a sare,   194

John will serve her as her son

25. But lady, sen þat he be-toke
Me for to serue you as youre sonne,
Ʒou nedis no-thyng, lady, but loke

lf. 221 b.

What thyng in erthe ʒe will haue done.   198
I ware to blame if I for-soke
To wirke youre wille, midday or none,

at all times.

Or any tyme ʒitt of þe woke.
Maria.   I thanke þe, John, with wordis fune,   202

She will give John her mother-hood.

26. Mi modirhed, John, schall þou haue,
And for my sone I wolle þe take.
Joh.   Þat grace, dere lady, wolde I craue.

'We must not go contrary to my son's wish,

Maria.   Mi sone sawes will I neuere for-sake.   206
Itt were not semand þat we straue
Ne contraried noʒt þat he spake.
But John, tille I be broght in graue,

but my sorrow will never lessen.'

Schall þou never see my sorowe slake.   210

27. Jacob.   Owre worthy lorde, sen he is wente
For vs, lady, als is his will,
We thanke hym þat vs þe hath lente

James and Andrew will do all her desire.

With vs on[1] lyue to lenge her stille.   214
I saie for me with full concente,
Þi likyng all will I fulfille.
Andreas.   So wille we all with grete talent,
For-thy, lady, giffe þe noght ill.   218

[1] MS. has *no*.

[Enter Angels.

28. i Angelus. ȝe men of þe lande of Galile,

What wondir ȝe to heuene lokand?

Þis Jesus whome ȝe fro youe see

Vppe-tane, ȝe schall well vndirstande,   222

Right so agayne come doune schall he,

When he so comes with woundes bledand,

Who wele has wrought full gladde may be,

Who ill has leved full sore dredand.   226

The angels explain that as Christ has ascended, so he shall descend.

29. ii Angel. ȝe þat has bene his seruauntis trewe,

And with hym lengand, nyght and day,

Slike wirkyng als ȝe with hym knew,

Loke þat ȝe preche it fourthe alway.   230

Youre mede in heuene beis ilke day newe,

And all þat seruis hym wele to paye,

Who trowes you noght, it schall þame rewe,

Þei mon haue peyne encresànd ay.   234

*If. 222.
xxx. viij.*

'Preach him forth, your reward is in heaven.'

30. Jacobus. Loued be þou lorde ay, moste of myght,

Þat þus, in all oure grete disease,

Vs comfortist with thyne aungellis bright;

Nowe might þer Jewes þare malise meese,   238

Þat sawe þame-selue þis wondir sight,

Þus nere þame wroght vndir þer nese [1].

And we haue mater day and nyght,

Oure god more for to preyse and plese.   242

James gives praise for this comfort.

31. Andreas. Nowe may þer Jewes be all confused

If þai on-thinke þame inwardly,

Howe falsely þei haue hym accused,

And sakles schente thurgh þer envy.   246

Þer falsed, þat þei longe haue vsed,

Nowe is it proued here opynly,

And they were of þis mater mused,

Itt schulde þame stirre to aske mercy.   250

The Jews ought now to be confounded and to ask mercy.

[1] MS. has *nose.*

'They will not
do that, as there
is no profit in
staying; let us
go to many
countries.'

32. Petrus. Þat wille þei noȝt, Andrewe, late be!
For þei are full of pompe and pride,
Itt may noȝt availe to þe ne me,
Ne none of vs with þame to chide.   254
Prophite to dwelle can I none see,
For-thy late us no lenger bide,
But wende we vnto seere contre,
To preche thurgh all þis worlde so wide.   258

33. Joh. Þat is oure charge, for þat is beste,
Þat we lenge nowe no lenger here,
For here gete we no place of reste,
To lenge so nere þe Jewes poure.   262

If. 222 b.

John takes Mary
away,

Vs for to do þei will þame caste,
For-thy come forthe my lady dere,
And wende vs hense, I am full preste
With you to wende with full goode chere[1].   266

34. Mi triste is nowe euer ilk a dele
In yowe to wirke aftir youre counsaill.

James will never
fail her.

Jacob. Mi lady dere, þat schall ȝe fele
In oght þat euere vs may availe,   270
Oure comforte, youre care to kele,
Whill we may leue we schall not faile.
Maria. Mi brethir dere, I traste itt wele,
Mi sone schall quyte ȝou youre trauaile.   274

'Now to Jerusa-
lem.'

35. Petrus. To Jerusalem go we agayne,
And loke what fayre so aftir fall,
Oure lorde and maistir moste of mayne,
He wisse youe, and be with youe all.   278

---

[1] These two lines are written as three in the MS.

XLIV. THE POTTERES.

The Descent of the Holy Spirit.

[PERSONS OF THE PLAY.]

MARIA.	4 APOSTOLUS.
PETRUS [1 Apos.].	5 APOSTOLUS.
JOHANNES [2 Apos.].	1 DOCTOR.
JACOBUS [3 Apos.].	2 DOCTOR.]

[SCENE, *A chamber in Jerusalem ; Mary and the Apostles are assembled in it : the Jews, headed by their Doctors, are outside.*]

1. Peter[1].   BRETHIR, takes tente vnto my steuen,   *Acts,* ch. ii.
        Þanne schall ȝe stabily vndirstande,
Oure maistir hende is hence to heuyn,
To reste þere on his fadirs right hande.   4
And we are leued a-lyue, elleuyn,
To lere his lawes lely in lande,   The apostles meet
Or we begynne vs muste be even,   to choose another
                      to make their
Ellis are owre werkis noght to warande. 8 number perfect ;
For parfite noumbre it is none,
Off elleuen for to lere,
Twelue may be a-soundir tone,   twelve can be
And settis in parties seere.   12 divided in
                      several.
Nobis precepit dominus predicare populo et   *Acts* x. 42.
testificare quia prope est iudex[2] *viuorum et mortuorum.*

[1] The rubricator forgot to write the first speaker's name here; a later hand wrote *Deus,* which was struck out, and *Petrus* substituted.
[2] The word *iudex* is interlined in later hand, the rubricator of these two Latin lines having omitted it. In the margin the late corrector wrote ' nota, a newe clause mayd for the eleuen, of an apostle to make the nomber of xij.'

Our Lord bade
us preach.

2. Oure lord comaunded vs, more and lesse,

To rewle vs right aftir his rede,

He badde vs preche and bere wittenesse

That he schulde deme bothe quike and dede.   16

To hym all prophettis preuys expresse,

All þo þat trowis in his godhede,

Off synnes þei schall haue forgiffenesse,

So schall we say mekill rede.   20

Since we publish
his counsel we
must not say
differently.'

And senne we on þis wise

Schall his counsaile discrie,

Itt nedis we vs avise,

Þat we saye noȝt serely.   24

3. Joh.   Serely he saide þat we schulde wende

In all þis worlde his will to wirke,

And be his counsaile to be kende

He saide he schulde sette haly kirke.   28

He said he
should establish
holy church, but
first his mes-
senger, the Holy
Ghost, should
come.
If. 223 b.

But firste he saide he schulde doune sende

His sande, þat we schuld noȝt be irke,

His haly gaste on vs to lende,

And make vs to melle of materes mirke.   32

Vs menis he saide vs þus,

Whan þat he fared vs fra [1],

John xiv. 26;
xv. 26.

iii Apos.   *Cum venerit paraclitus*

Docebit vos omnia.   36

4. Jacob.   Ȝa certaynely, he saide vs soo.

And mekill more þanne we of mene,

Nisi ego abiero,

James repeats
the promises as
to the Holy
Ghost.

Þus tolde he ofte tymes vs be-twene,

He saide forsoth, but if I goo,   40

Þe holy goste schall not be sene,

Et dum assumptus fuero,

Þanne schall I sende ȝou comforte clene.   44

Þus tolde he holy howe

Þat oure dedis schulde be dight,

---

[1] MS. has *froo.*

So schall we trewly trowe,
He will holde þat he vs highte.   48

5. iv Apos. He highte vs fro harme for to hyde,
And holde in hele both hede and hende,
Whanne we take þat he talde þat tyde,
Fro all oure foois it schall vs fende.   52

But þus in bayle behoues vs bide,
To tyme þat sande till vs be sende ;
Þe Jewis besettis vs in ilke aside
Þat we may nowdir walke nor wende.   56

v Apos. We dare noȝt walke for drede,
Or comforte come vs till,
Itt is moste for oure spede,
Here to be stokyn still.   60

6. Maria. Brethir, what mene ȝe ȝou emelle,
To make mournyng at ilk a mele ?
My sone, þat of all welthe is well,
He will ȝou wisse to wirke full wele.   64

For þe tente day is þis to telle,
Sen he saide we schull fauoure fele,
Leuys wele þat lange schall it not dwell,
And therfore drede you neuere a dele ;   68

But prayes with harte and hende,
Þat we his helpe may haue,
Þanne schall it sone be sende,
Þe sande þat schall vs saue.   72

7. i Doctor. Harke, maistir, for Mahoundes peyne,
Howe þat þes mobbardis maddis nowe,
Þer maistir þat oure men haue slayne
Hase garte þame on his trifullis trowe.   76

ii Doc. Þe lurdayne sais he leffis agayne,
Þat mater may þei neuere avowe,
For as þei herde his prechyng pleyne,
He was away, þai wiste noȝt howe.   80

H h 2

Side notes:

'He promised to shield us from harm ; but we must wait in sorrow till it comes.'

'It is best to stop here.'

lf. 224.
xxxj. ij.
Mary asks why they mourn, her Son will show them what to do.

The Jews, outside the chamber, hear them talking.

i Doc. They wiste noȝt whenne he wente,
Þerfore fully þei faile,
And sais þam schall be sente
Grete helpe thurgh his counsaille. 84

' Let us give a great shout ; no, they'll die for fear ;

8. ii Doc. He myghte nowdir sende clothe nor clowte,
He was neuere but a wrecche alway,
But samme oure men and make a schowte,
So schall we beste yone foolis flaye. 88

i Doc. Nay, nay, þan will þei dye for doute,
I rede we make noȝt mekill dray,

we will way-lay them as they come out.'

But warly wayte when þai come oute,
And marre þame þanne, if þat we may. 92

lf. 224 b.

ii Doc. Now, certis, I assente þer-tille,
Yitt wolde I noght þei wiste,
Ȝone carles þan schall we kill
But þei liffe als vs liste. 96

[The Holy Ghost descends among the Apostles in the chamber.]

Angelus tunc cantare.[1]

Mary praises her Son for this deed.

9. Maria[2]. Honnoure and blisse be euer nowe,
With worschippe in þis worlde alwaye,
To my souerayne sone, Jesu,
Oure lorde allone þat laste schall ay, 100
Nowe may we triste his talis ar trewe,
Be dedis þat here is done þis day.
Als lange as ȝe his pase pursue,
Þe fende ne fendis yow for to flay. 104
For his high haligaste
He lattis here on ȝou lende
Mirthis and trewthe to taste,
And all misse to aménde. 108

---

[1] 'Veni creator spiritus' is added in the margin by a later hand.
[2] The rubricator omitted this name, which was supplied by the late hand.

10. Pet. All mys to mende nowe haue we myght,

Þis is þe mirthe oure maistir of mente,

I myght noȝt loke, so was it light,

A ! loued be þat lorde þat itt vs lente.   112

Now hase he holden þat he vs highte,

His holygoste here haue we hente,

Like to þe sonne itt semed in sight,

And sodenly þanne was itt sente.   116

ii Apos. Hitt was sente for oure sele,

Hitt giffis vs happe and hele,

Me thynke slike forse I fele,

I myght felle folke full feele.   120

11. iii Apos. We haue force for to fighte in felde,

And ffauour of all folke in feere,

With wisdome in þis worlde to welde,

Be knowing of all clergye clere.   124

iv Apos. We haue bewteis to be oure belde,

And langage nedis vs none to lere,

Þat lorde vs awe ȝappely to ȝelde,

Þat vs has ȝemed vnto þis ȝere.   128

v Apos. This is þe ȝere of grace

Þat musteris vs emang,

As aungellis in þis place,

Þat sais þus in þer sange.   132

12. i Apos. In þare sigging saide þei þus,

And tolde þer talis be-twene þem two,

Veni creator spiritus,

mentes tuorum visita [1].   136

Þei praied þe spirite come till vs,

And mende oure myndis with mirthis ma,

Þat lered þei of oure lorde Jesus,

For he saide þat itt schulde be swa.   140

[1] These two are written as one line in the MS.

Marginal notes:

The apostles rejoice at the coming of the Holy Ghost.

It seemed like the sun.

' It has made me so strong I could fell many folk.'

If. 225. xxxj. iij.
' It has given us strength, learning, and languages.'

This is the year of grace.

' The angels, singing, prayed the Spirit to come to us.'

ii **Apos.**   He saide he schulde vs sende
His holygoste fro heuyn,
Oure myndis with mirthe to mende,
Nowe is all ordand euyn.   144

13. iii **Apos.**   Euen als he saide schulde to vs come,
So has bene schewid vn-to oure sight,

John xvi, 6, 20.
' Sadness is
turned into joy.'

Tristicia impleuit cor vestrum,
Firste sorowe in herte he vs hight;   148
Sed conuertetur in gaudium,
Sen saide he þat he schulde be light,
Nowe þat he saide vs, all & summe,
Is mefid emange vs thurgh his myght.   152

iv **Apos.**   His myght with mayne and mode

lf. 225 b.

May comforte all man-kynde.

The Jews shout,
' these men are
mad, they talk
many tongues,

Doctor [*outside*].   Harke man, for Mahoundes bloode,
Þer men maddis oute of mynde.   156

14. Þei make carpyng of ilke contre,
And leris langage of ilk a lande.

ii **Doct.**   They speke oure speche als wele as we,
And in ilke a steede it vndirstande.   160

i **Doct.**   And all are noȝt of Galilee

they are
drunken with
wine.'

Þat takis þis hardinesse on hande;
Butt þei are drounken, all þes menȝe,
Of muste or wyne, I wolle warande.   164

ii **Doct.**   Nowe certis þis was wele saide,
þat makis þer mynde to marre,
Ȝone faitours schall be flaied,
Or þat þei flitte aught ferre.   168

' Take care,
brethren, the
Jews are strong
against us.'

15. iv **Apos.** [*within.*]   Harke, brethir, waites wele aboute,
For in oure fayre we ffynde no frende,
Þe Jewes with strengh are sterne and stoute,
And scharpely schapes þem vs to schende.   172

i **Apos.**   Oure maistir has putte alle perellis oute,

And fellid þe falsed of þe fende,
Vndo youre dores, and haues no doute,
For to ʒone warlowes will we wende. 176

'Have no fear, open the doors, we will go to yon fiends.'

ii Apos. To wende haue we no drede,
Noght for to do oure dette,
For to neuyn þat is nede
Shall none on-lyve vs lette. *[They open the doors.* 180

'We will do our duty.'

16. **Pet.** ʒe Jewez þat in Jerusalem dwelle,
Youre tales are false, þat schall ʒe fynde ;
Þat we are dronken we here you telle,
Be-cause ʒe hope we haue bene pynnyd. 184
A prophette preued, his name is Johell,
A gentill Jewe of youre awne kynde,
He spekis þus in his speciall spell,
And of þis matere makis he mynde. 188
Be poyntis of prophicie
He tolde fulle ferre be-fore,
Þis may ʒe noʒt denye,
For þus his wordis wore, 192
Et erit in nouissimus diebus, dicit dominus,
effundam de spiritu meo super omnem carnem.

Peter addresses the Jews ;

Joel prophesied all these things.

If. 226. xxxj. iiij.

Acts ii. 17. *Joel* ii. 28.

17. **iii Apos.** Loo, losellis, loo, þus may ye lere,
Howe youre elders wrotte alway,
Þe holygoste have we tane here,
As youre awne prophettis prechid ay. 196
iv Apos. Hitt is þe myght of oure maistir dere,
All dedis þat here are done þis daye,
He giffis vs myght and playne power
To conclude all þat ʒe can saie. 200
i Doct. There men hase mekill myght,
Thurgh happe þei here haue tone.
ii Doct. Wende we oute of þer sight,
And latte þem even allone. *[Exeunt.* 204

'Ye wretches, the Holy Spirit has come to us, as your prophets preached. Our Master gives us power.'

The Jews shrink away and let them alone.

18. i Apos.   Nowe, brethir myne, sen we all meffe,
To teche þe feithe to foo and frende,
Oure tarying may turne vs to mischeffe,
Wherfore I counsaille þat we wende   208

Vntille oure lady, and take oure leue.
ii Apos.   Sertis so woll we with wordis hende.
[*To Mary.*] Mi lady, takis it noȝt to greue,
I may no lenger with you lende[1].   212

19. Maria.   Nowe Petir, sen itt schall be soo,
Þat ȝe haue diuerse gatis to gang,

Ther schall none dere you for to doo,
Whils my sone musteris you emang.   216
Butt John and Jamys, my cosyns twoo,
Loke þat ȝe lenge not fro me lange.
Johan.   Lady, youre wille in wele and woo,
Itt schall be wroght, ellis wirke we wrang.   220
Jacob.   Lady, we bothe are boune
Atte youre biddyng to be.
Maria.   The blissing of my sone
Be boith with you and me[2].   224

---

[1] This stanza is short of the four 2-accented lines.
[2] Here is a side-note, ' loquela de novo facta,' and in a more recent ink
is written at the end,

> ' That with his grace ye may endewe,
> And bryng yowe to his Companye.'

XLV. THE DRAPERES.

The Death of Mary.

[PERSONS OF THE PLAY.

GABRIELL.	JACOBUS.
MARIA.	ANDREAS.
JOHANNES.	PRIMA ET SECUNDA ANCILLA.
PETRUS.	PRIMUS ET SECUNDUS JUDAEUS.
JESUS.	1, 2, 3, 4 ANGELUS.]
VNUS DIABOLUS.	

[SCENE I, *Mary's dwelling-place.*]

1. Gab. HAYLE ! myghfull Marie, Godis modir so mylde !

Hayle ! be þou roote of all reste, hayle be þou ryall,

Hayle ! floure and frewte noȝt fadid nor filyd,

Haile ! salue to all synnefull ; nowe saie þe I schall, 4

Thy sone to þi selue me has sente,

His sande, and sothly he saies,

No lenger þan þer thre dayes

Here lefte þe þis liffe þat is lente[1]. 8

2. And þerfore he biddis þe loke þat þou blithe be,

For to þat bigly blisse þat berde will þe bring,

There to sitte with hym-selue, all solas to see,

And to be crowned for his quene and he hym-selue

  kyng. 12

In mirthe þat euere schall be newe[2],

He sendis to þe worþely, i-wis,

Þis palme oute of Paradise,

In tokenyng þat it schall be trewe. 16

Transitus Mariæ, Tischendorf, Text A. pp. 114–118; Text B. pp. 124–129.

Gabriel salutes Mary, and tells her she has but three days to live.

Her Son will take her to bliss, and have her crowned queen. As a token he brings a palm from Paradise.

[1] MS. has *lentthe.* [2] Lines 12–15 are run into three lines in MS.

3. Mar. I thanke my sone semely of all his sandis sere,
Vn-to hym lastandly be ay louyng,
Þat me þus worþely wolde menske on þis manere,
And to his bigly blisse my bones for to bringe.   20
But gode sir, neuenes me þi name?
Gab. Gabriell, þat baynely ganne bringe
Þe boodworde of his bering,
For sothe, lady, I ame þe same.   24

Mary thanks
Gabriel for his
message,

4. Mar. Nowe Gabriell, þat sothly is fro my sone sent,
I thanke þe þer tythyngis þou tellis me vntill,
And loued be þat lorde of the lane þat has me lente[1],   27
And dere sone, I beseke þe,
Grete God, þou graunte me þi grace,

and prays that
the apostles may
be at her burying.

Thyne appostelis to haue in þis place,
Þat þei at my bering may be[2].   31

5. Gab. Nowe foode faireste of face, most faithfull and fre,
Þyne askyng þi sone has graunte of his grace ;

'They shall all
appear together,
lf. 228.
xxxj. vj.

And saies all same in sight ȝe schall see
All his appostelis appere in þis place,   35
To wirke all þi will at þi wending,

and thy pains be
soon over.'

And sone schall þi peynes be paste,
And þou to be in liffe þat schall laste
Euermore with-outen any ending.   39

[Enter John.]

6. Joh. Marie, my modir, þat mylde is and meke,
And cheffe chosen for chaste, nowe telle me, what chere?

Mary tells John
she is sick, and
will die in three
days.

Mar. John, sone, I say þe forsothe I am seke,
Mi swete sone sonde I hete, right nowe it was here,   43
And douteles he saies I schall dye,
Within thre daies i-wis,
I schall be belded in blisse,
And come to his awne company[3].   47

[1] Evidently a line is wanting here, probably it ended in 'will.'   But no
blank in MS.
[2] Lines 28–31 are written as two in MS.
[3] Lines 44–47 are run into three in MS.

7. **Joh.** A! with þi leue, lady, þou neuene it me noght,
Ne telle me no tydingis to twynne vs in two!
For be þou, blissid birde, vnto bere broght,
Euermore whils I wonne in þis worlde will me be full
woo [1].
Therfore lete it stynte, and be still.   52

Mar. Nay, John sone, my selue nowe I see,
Atte Goddis will moste it nedis be,
Þer-fore be it wroght at his will.

8. **Joh.** A! worthy, when þou art wente will me be full
woo!   56

But God giffe þe appostelis wiste of þi wending.

Mar. Ʒis, John sone, for certayne schall it be so,
All schall þei hardely be here at myne ending.
The sonde of my sone saide me þus [2],   60
Þat sone schall my penaunce be paste,
And I to be in liffe þat euere schall laste,
Than baynly to belde in þat blisse.

[*Enter Peter, James, and Andrew, suddenly.*]

9. **Pet.** O God! omnipotent, þe giffer of all grace,   64
Benedicite dominus, a clowde now full clere
Vmbelappid [3] me in Jude prechand as I was,
And I haue mekill meruayle how þat I come here.

Jac. A! sesse, of þis assemelyng can I noʒt saie   68
Howe and in what wise þat we are here mette,
For sodenly in sight here sone was I sette,
Owthir myrþe or of mornyng mene wele it maye [4].

10. **And.** A! bredir, be my wetand and i-wisse so wer we,   72
In diuerse landes lely I wotte we were lente,
And how we are semelid þus can I noʒt see,
But as God of his sande has vs same sente.

Joh. A! felawes, late be youre fare,   76

Marginal notes:

'Tell me nothing to part us two, be still.'

John mourns, but hopes the apostles may come.

They all appear, miraculously.

'A cloud covered me as I was preaching in Judea.'

lf. 228 b.

They are all astonished but think God has sent them.

---

[1] Two lines in MS.
[2] Perhaps *þisse* is intended.
[3] MS. has *Vnbelappid*.
[4] Lines 70, 71, are reversed in MS.

For as God will it moste nedis be,
Þat pereles is of poste
His myȝt is to do mekill mare [1]   79

John tells them
it is to be near
Mary.

11. For Marie, þat worthy, schall wende nowe, I wene,
Vnto þat bigly blisse þat high barne baynly vs boght,
þat we in hir [2] sight all same myght be sene,
Or sche disseuer vs froo, hir sone sche be-soght.
And þus has he wroght atte hir will,   84
Whanne sche shalbe broght on a bere,
That we may be neghand hir nere
This tyme for to tente hir vn-till.

Mary thanks her
Son for his grace.

12. Mar. Jesu, my darlyng þat ding is, and dere,
I thanke þe my dere sone of þi grete grace,   89
Þat I all þis faire felawschip atte hande nowe has here,
Þat þei me some comforte may kythe in þis case.
Þis sikenes it sittis me full sare,   92
My maidens, take kepe nowe on me!
And caste some watir vppon me,

She faints.

I faynte! so febill I fare.   *[She faints.*   95

13. i Ancilla. Allas! for my lady þat lemed so light,

Her maidens
weep and cry,
help!

That euere I leued in þis lede þus longe for to lende,
That I on þis semely schulde se such a sight.
ii Ancilla. Allas! helpe! sche dyes in oure hende.
A! Marie, of me haue þou mynde,   100
Some comforte vs two for to kythe [3],
Þou knowes we are comen of þi kynde.   102

Mary scolds
them for their
noise.
lf. 229.
xxxj. vij.
'We must
all die. John,
make them be
quiet.'

14. Mar. What ayles yow women, for wo þus wynly to wepe?
Yhe do me dere with youre dynne, fo[r] me muste nedis dye.
Yhe schulde, whenne ȝe saw me so slippe and slepe,
Haue lefte all youre late and lette me lye.   106
John! cosyne, garre þame stynte and be still.
Joh. A! Marie, þat mylde is of mode,

---

[1] Lines 76-79 are two in MS.   [2] MS. has *high.*
[3] A line is wanting here.

When þi sone was raised on a rode,

To tente þe he toke me þe till,   110

'Thy Son gave thee to me on the rood,

15. And þerfore at þi bidding full bayne will I be.

Iff þer be oght, modir, þat I amende may,

I pray þe, myldest of mode, meue þe to me ;

And I schall, dere-worþi dame, do it ilke a daye.   114

if I can do aught, dearest lady, I will.'

Mar. A! John sone, þat þis peyne were ouere paste !

With goode harte ȝe alle þat are here

Praies for me faithfully in feere,

For I mon wende fro you as faste.   118

'All pray for me, I must go fast.'

16. i Judeus. A! foode fairest of face, most faithfull to fynde,

Þou mayden and modir þat mylde is and meke,

As þou arte curtaise and comen of oure kynde,

All our synnes for to sesse þi sone þou be-seke,   122

With mercy to mende vs of mys.

The Jews pray her to help them to heaven.

ii Judeus. Sen þou lady come of oure kynne,

Þou helpe vs nowe, þou veray virginne,

Þat we may be broght vnto blisse.   126

17. Mar. Jesu, my sone, for my sake beseke I þe þis,

As þou arte gracious and grete God, þou graunte me my

   grace !

Þei þat is comen of my kynde and amende will þere mys,

Nowe specially þou þame spede and spare þame a space, 130

And be þer belde, if þi willis be.

And dere sone, whane I schall dye,

I pray þe þan, for þi mercy,

Þe fende þou latte me noȝt see.   134

Mary beseeches her Son for her kinsfolk ;

and that she may not see the devil when she dies.

18. And also my blissid barne, if þi will be,

I sadly beseke þe, my sone, for my sake,

Men þat are stedde stiffely in stormes or in see,

And are in will wittirly my worschippe to awake,   138

And þanne nevenes my name in þat nede,

lf. 229 b.

'Grant mercy to all who call on me in storms, at sea,

Þou late þame not perissh nor spille;
Of þis bone, my sone, at þi will,
Þou graunte me specially to spede!   142

help those who
are oppressed or
in need,

19. Also, my bliste barne, þou graunte me my bone,
     All þat are in newe or in nede and nevenes me be name,
     I praie þe sone, for my sake, þou socoure þame sone,
     In alle þer schoures þat are scharpe þou shelde þame fro
         schame.   146

and especially
women in child-
birth.'

And women also in þere chylding,
Nowe speciall þou þame spede,
And if so be þei die in þat drede,
To þi blisse þane baynly þou þame bringe.   150

                         [*Jesus appears.*

Jesus grants her
asking;

20. Jesus.   Marie, my modir, thurgh þe myght nowe of me,
     For to make þe in mynde with mirthe to be mending,
     Þyne asking all haly here heete I nowe þe.

'but the devil,
hideous, must be
there,

But modir, þe fende muste be nedis at þyne endyng,
In figoure full foule for to fere þe;   155
Myne aungelis schall þan be a-boute þe.

yet fear not, my
angels will be
round thee.'

And þerfore, dere dame, þou thar noȝt doute þe,
For douteles þi dede schall noȝt dere þe;   158

21. And þerfore, my modir, come myldely to me,
     For aftir þe sonne my sande will I sende,
     And to sitte with my selfe all solas to se,
     In ay lastand liffe in likyng to lende.   162

Thou shalt abide
with me in ever-
lasting bliss.

In þis blisse schall be þi bilding,
Of mirth schall þou neuere haue missing,
But euermore abide in my blissing.   166
All þis schall þou haue at þi welding [1].   167

If. 230.
xxxj. viij.
Mary gives
thanks and gives
up her spirit.

22. Mar.   I thanke þe my swete sone, for certis I am seke,
     I may noȝt now meve me, for mercie,—almoste,—
     To þe [2], sone myne þat made me, þi maiden so meke,

---

[1] In the MS., line 167 stands before l. 165.
[2] The MS. has *þie*, but it is a little indistinct.

Here thurgh þi grace, god sone, I giffe þe my goste.   170
Mi sely saule I þe sende
To heuene þat is highest on heghte,
To þe, sone myne, þat moste is of myght,
Ressayue it here in-to þyne hande.   [*Dies.*   174

[SCENE II, *Heaven.*]

23. Jesus. Myne aungellis louely of late, lighter þan þe levene,
In-to þe erþe wightly I will þat ȝe wende,
And bringe me my modir to þe highest of heuene,
With mirthe and with melody hir mode for to mende.
For here schall hir blisse neuer be blynnande,
My modir schall myldely be me   180
Sitte nexte þe high Trinite,
And neuere in two to be twynnand.

Jesus sends his angels to fetch his mother into heaven.

24. i Ang. Lorde! atte þi bidding full bayne will I be,
Þat floure þat neuere was fadid full fayne will we fette.
ii Ang. And atte þi will, gode lorde, wirke will we
With solace in ilke side þat semely vmsitte.   186
iii Ang. Latte vs fonde to hir faste fors hir to deffende,
Þat birde for to bringe vnto þis blis bright,
Body and sawle we schall hir assende,
To regne in þis regally, be regentte full right.   190
iv Ang. To bliss þat birde for to bringe,
Nowe Gabriell, late vs wightly be wendand[1];
This maiden mirthe to be mendand,
A semely song latte vs sing[2].   194

Chorus of angels singing.

Cum vno diabolo.

Et cantant antiphona scilicet Aue regina celorum.

---

[1] In the MS. l. 191 stands after l. 186, and is spoken by ii **Ang.**, the
iv **Ang.** beginning with l. 192. Probably four lines are missing after
l. 186.
[2] MS. has *see.*

XLVI. THE WEFFERES [WEAVERS].

The Appearance of our Lady to Thomas.

[PERSONS OF THE PLAY.

THOMAS APOSTOLUS.　　　JACOBUS.
MARIA.　　　　　　　　ANDREAS.
PETRUS.　　　　　　　　JOHANNES.
TWELVE ANGELS, SINGING.]

[SCENE, *on the way from India ; afterwards the Vale of Jehoshaphat.*]

Transitus Mariæ, Tischendorf, Text A. pp. 119-121.

Thomas mourns the cruel death of Jesus.

1. **Thom.**　In waylyng and weping, in woo am I wapped,
In site and in sorowe, in sighing full sadde,
Mi lorde and my luffe loo full lowe is he lapped,
Þat makes me to mourne nowe full mate and full madde.　4
What harling and what hurlyng þat hedesman he hadde!
What breking of braunches ware brosten a-boute hym,
What bolnyng with betyng of brothellis full badde!
Itt leres me full lely to loue hym and lowte hym.　8
That comely to kenne,
Goddis sone Jesus
He died for vs,
Þat makes me þus　12
To mourne amange many men.

2. Emange men may I mourne, for þe malice þei mente
To Jesu, þe gentillest of Jewes generacioun,
Of wisdome and witte were þe waies þat he wente,   16
Þat drewe all þo domesmen derffe indignacioun ;
For douteles full dere was his diewe dominacioun.
Vnkyndely þei kidde þem þer kyng for to kenne,
With carefull comforth and colde recreacioun,   20
For he mustered his miracles amonge many men,
And to þe pepull he preched,
But þe Pharases fers
All his resouns revers,   24
And to þer hedesmen rehers
Þat vntrewe were þe tales þat he teched.

3. He teched full trewe, but þe tirauntes were tened,
For he reproued þer pride, þai purposed þame preste,   28
To mischeue hym with malis in þere mynde haue þei menyd,
And to accuse hym of cursednesse þe caistiffis has caste.
Ther rancoure was raised, no renke might it reste,
Þei toke hym with treasoune, þat turtill of treuthe,   32
Þei fedde hym with flappes, with fersnesse hym feste,
To rugge hym, to riffe hym, þer reyned no rewthe.
Vndewly þei demed hym,
Þei dusshed hym, þei dasshed hym,   36
Þei lusshed hym, þei lasshed hym,
Þei pusshed hym, þei passhed hym,
All sorowe þei saide þat it semed hym.

4. Itt semed hym all sorowe, þe saide in þe seggyng,   40
Þei skippid and scourged hym, he skapid not with scornes,
Þat he was leder and lorde in þere lawe lay no leggyng,
But thrange on and thristed a croune of thik thornes.
Ilk tag of þat turtill so tatterid and torne es,   44
That þat blissid body blo is and bolned for betyng,
ȝitt þe hedesmen to hynge hym with huge hydous hornes,
As brothellis or bribours we[re] belyng and bletyng.

'Crucifie hym!' þei cried.   48
Sone Pilate in parlement
Of Jesu gaffe jugement[1],
To hynge hym þe harlottis hym hente;
Þer was no deide of þat domesman denyed.   52

5. Denyed not þat domesman to deme hym to dede,

That friendly
fair creature was
doomed to death.

Þat frendly faire foode þat neuere offended,
Þei hied þame in haste þan to hynge vppe þere heede,
What woo þat þei wroghte hym no wyȝt wolde haue
    wende it.   56
His true titill þei toke þame no tome for to attende it,

As a traitor he
was pulled about
and lashed to the
cross.

But as a traytour atteynted þei toled hym and tugged hym,
Þei schonte for no schoutis his schappe for to schende it,
Þei rasid hym on rode als full rasely þei rugged hym.   60
Þei persed hym with a spere,

His royal blood
fell to the ground.

Þat the blode riall
To the erþe gun fall,
In redemption of all   64
Þat his lele lawes likis to lere.

He that learns of
Him will find him
a faithful friend.

6. To lere he þat likis of his lawe, þat is lele,
Mai fynde in oure frende here full faithfull feste,
Þat wolde hynge þus on hight to enhaunce vs in hele,   68
And by vs fro bondage by his bloode þat is beste.
Þan þe comforte of oure companye in kares were keste,
But þat lorde so allone wolde not leffe vs full longe,

He rose on the
third day,

On þe thirde day he rose riȝt with his renkis to reste;   72
Both flessh and fell fersly þ.t figour gon fange,
And to my brethir gonne appere;

If. 232.
xxxij. ij.
'My brethren told
me, but I would
not believe it.

Þai tolde me of þis,
Bot I leued a-mys,   76
To rise flesshly, i-wis,
Me thought þat it paste mans pou[e]re.

---

[1] Lines 49, 50, are one in MS.

7. But þe poure of þat prince was presiously previd,
   Whan þat souerayne schewed hym selffe to my siȝt, 80
   To mene of his manhode my mynde was all meued,
   But þat reuerent redused me be resoune and be riȝt.
   Þe woundes full wide of þat worthy wight,
   He frayned me to fele þame, my faith for to feste, 84
   And so I did douteless, and doune I me diȝt,
   I bende my bak for to bowe and obeyed hym for beste.
   So sone he assendid
   Mi felaus in feere 88
   Ware sondered sere.
   If þai were here
   Mi myrthe were mekill amended.

Jesus made me believe,

I felt his wounds and bowed down.

If my companions were here I should be happier, I shall go seek them.

8. Amendid were my mirthe with þat meyne to mete, 92
   Mi felaus in fere for to fynde woll I fonde,
   I schall nott stedde in no stede but in stall and in strete,
   Grath me be gydis to gette þame on grounde.
        [*The Vale of Jehoshaphat suddenly appears.*
   O souerayne! how sone am I sette here so sounde! 96
   Þis is þe Vale of Josophat, in Jury so gente.
   I will steme of my steuene and sted here a stounde,
   For I am wery for walkyng þe waies þat I wente,
   Full wilsome and wide. 100
   Þerfore I kaste
   Here for to reste,
   I halde it beste
   To buske on þis banke for to bide.   [*He lies down.* 104

Transitus Mariæ, Tischendorf, Text A, pp. 119-121.

O wonder! I am suddenly in Judea!

I will rest, for I am weary.'

[This page is occupied with music, the words to which are, *Surge proxima mea columba mea tabernaculum glorie vasculum vite templum celeste.*]

If. 232 b.
(?) *Transitus Mariæ*, Text B.
p. 135.

[*Vision of Mary, and Angels singing before her.*]

9. i Ang. Rise, Marie, þou maiden and modir so milde.
   ii Ang. Rise, lilly full lusty, þi luffe is full likand.
   iii Ang. Rise, chefteyne of chastite, in cheriŋg þi childe.

If. 233.
xxxij. iij.

The angels call upon Mary,—
rose, dove, turtle,

seemly and goodly,—to rise and come to the king to be crowned.

iv Ang. Rise, rose ripe redolent, in reste to be reyn-
and.   108

v Ang. Rise, douffe of þat domesman, all dedis is demand.

vi Ang. Rise, turtour, tabernacle, and tempull full trewe.

vii Ang. Rise, semely in sight, of þi sone to be semande.

viii Ang. Rise, grathed full goodely in grace for to
grewe.   112

ix Ang. Rise vppe þis stounde.

x Ang. Come chosen childe!

xi Ang. Come Marie milde!

xii Ang. Come floure vnfiled!   116

viii Ang. Come vppe to þe kyng to be crouned.

Song of Solomon iii. 8. [The rest of the page, about half, is occupied with more music, of which
the words are, *Veni de libano sponsa veni coronaberis.*]

lf. 233 b.

Thomas sees a bright light and a vision of Mary, borne aloft by angels.

10. Thom. O glorious god, what glemes ar glydand!
I meve in my mynde what may þis be-mene?
I see a babbe[1] borne in blisse to be bidand,   120
With aungelus companye, comely and clene.
Many selcouth sitis in sertis haue I sene,
But þis mirthe and þis melody mengis my mode.

Mar. Thomas, do way all þi doutes be-dene,   124
For I ame foundynge fourthe to my faire fode,
I telle þe þis tyde.

Thom. Who, my souerayne lady?

Mar. ʒa! sertis I saie þe.   128

Thom. Whedir wendes þou, I praye þe?

Mar. To blisse with my barne for to bide.

Thomas praises Mary, the gentle courteous, and beloved,

11. Thom. To bide with thy barne in blisse to be bidand!
Hayle! jentilest of Jesse in Jewes generacion,   132
Haile! welthe of þis worlde all welthis is weldand,
Haile! hendest enhaunsed to high habitacion.
Haile! derworth and dere is þi diewe dominacion.

[1] MS. has *babbe*, but *berde* or *burde* (i. e. lady) was surely intended.

Haile! floure fresshe florisshed, þi frewte is full felesome. 136
Haile! sete of oure saveour and sege of saluacion,
Haile! happy to helde to, þi helpe is full helesome.
Haile! pereles in plesaunce,
Haile! precious and pure,   140
Haile! salue þat is sure,
Haile! lettir of langure,
Haile! bote of oure bale in obeyesaunce.

the peerless and
pure, the help for
all our ills.

12. **Mar.** Go to þi brethir þat in bale are abiding,   144
And of what wise to welthe I ame wendande,
With-oute taryng þou telle þame þis tithynge,
Þer mirthe so besse mekill amendande.
For Thomas, to me were þei tendande,   148
Whanne I drewe to þe dede, all but þou.

Thom. Bot I, lady! whillis in lande I ame lendande,
Obeye þe full baynly my bones will I bowe.
Bot I! allas!   152
Whare was I þanne
When þat barette beganne?
An vnhappy manne
Both nowe and euere I was.   156

lf. 234.
xxxij. iv.
Mary tells
Thomas to go
tell his brethren
what he now sees.

'But, unhappily,
they will not
believe me.'

13. Vnhappy, vnhende, am I holden at home,
What drerye destonye me drew fro þat dede!

Mar. Thomas, sesse of thy sorowe, for I am sothly the
same.

Thom. Þat wote I wele, þe worthiest þat wrapped is in
wede!   160

Mar. Þanne spare nott a space nowe my speche for to
spede,
Go saie þem sothely, þou sawe me assendinge.

Thom. Now douteles, derworthy, I dare not for drede,
For to my tales þat I telle þei are not attendinge,   164
For no spelle þat is spoken.

'Delay not, say
you saw me
ascending,

Maria. I schall þe schewe
A token trewe,

Full fresshe of hewe,   168
Mi girdill, loo, take þame þis tokyn.

14. Thom. I thanke þe as reuerent rote of oure reste,
I thanke þe as stedfast stokke for to stande,
I thanke þe as tristy tre for to treste,   172

I thanke þe as buxsom bough to þe bande,
I thanke þe as leeffe þe lustiest in lande,
I thanke þe as bewteuous braunche for to bere,
I thanke þe as floure þat neuere is fadande,   176
I thanke þe as frewte þat has fedde vs in fere.
I thanke þe for euere,
If they repreue me,

Now schall þei leue me !   180
Þi blissinge giffe me,
And douteles I schall do my deuere.

15. Mar. Thomas, to do þanne thy deuere be dressand,
He bid þe his blissinge þat beldis aboven,   184
And in siȝtte of my sone þer is sittand,
Shall I knele to þat comely with croune ;
Þat what dispaire be dale or be doune

With pitevous playnte in perellis will pray me,   188
If he synke or swete, in swelte or in swoune,
I schall sewe to my souerayne sone for to say me.
He schall graunte þame þer grace,
Be it manne in his mournyng,   192
Or womanne in childinge,
All þes to be helpinge,
Þat prince schall I praye in þat place.

16. Thom. Gramercy ! þe goodliest grounded in grace,   196
Gramercy ! þe lufliest lady of lire,
Gramercy ! þe fairest in figure and face,
Gramercy ! þe derrest to do oure desire.

Mar. Farewele, nowe I passe to þe pereles empire,   200

Farewele, Thomas, I tarie no tyde here.

Mary passes aloft,

Thom. Farewele, þou schynyng schappe þat schyniste so schire,

Thomas bids farewell to the belle of all beauties.

Farewele, þe belle of all bewtes to bide here ;

Farewele þou faire foode,   204

Farewele þe keye of counsaile,

If. 235. xxxij. v.

Farewele all þis worldes wele,

Farewele, our hape and oure hele,

Farewele nowe, both gracious and goode.   208

[*The Vision vanishes.*

[Four staves of music here occupy about half the page, the words are,
Veni electa mea et ponam in te tronum meum Quia concupiuit rex speciem tuam [1].]

17. **Thom.** That I mette with þis may here my mirtheis amend,

I will hy me in haste and holde þat I haue hight,

Thomas hastens by hill and valley to find his fellowship.

To bere my brethir þis boodeword my bak schall I bende,

And saie þame in certayne þe soth of þis sight.   212

Be dale and be doune schall I dresse me to diȝt,

To I fynde of þis felawschippe faithfull in fere,

I schall renne and reste not to ransake full right.

Lo ! þe menȝe I mente of I mete þam euen here at hande. 216

If. 235 b.

[*Meets the other Apostles.*

He greets them they are surly.

God saffe ȝou in feere,

Say breþir, what chere ?

Pet. What dois þou here ?

Þou may nowe of þi gatis be gangand.   220

18. **Thom.** Why dere brethir, what bale is be-gune ?

Pet. Thomas, I telle þe, þat tene is be-tidde vs.

Thom. Me for-thinkith for my frendis þat faithfull are foune.

He thought his friends were true.

Jacob. ȝa, but in care litill kyndnes þou kid vs.   224

Andr. His bragge and his boste is he besie to bid vs,

They upbraid him as a boaster,

But and þer come any cares he kepis not to kenne,

---

[1] See the Frontispiece.

We may renne till we raue, or any ruth rid vs,

For þe frenschippe he fecched vs be frith or be fenne.   228

Thom.   Sirs, me meruailes, I saie yowe,

What mevis in youre mynde.

and unkind,   Joh.   We can wele fynde

Þou art vnkynde.   232

Thom.   Nowe pees þanne, and preue it, I pray yowe.

because he did
not come to
Mary's burial.   19. Pet.   Þat þou come not to courte here vnkyndynes þou
kid vs,

Oure treuth of has turned vs to tene and to traye,

Þis yere haste þou rakid, þi reuth wolde not ridde vs,   236

For witte þou wele þat worthy is wente on hir waye.

In a depe denne dede is scho doluen þis daye,

lf. 236.
xxxij. vj.
Thomas knows
about it.   Marie, þat maiden and modir so milde.

Thom.   I wate wele i-wis.

Jacob.   Thomas, do way.   240

Andr.   Itt forse noȝt to frayne hym, he will not be filde.

Thom.   Sirs, with hir haue I spoken

Lattar þanne yee.

Joh.   Þat may not bee.   244

Thom.   Yis, knelyng on kne.

Pet.   Þanne tite, can þou telle us some token?

He shows the
girdle to them,
who still do not
believe him.   20. Thom.   Lo! þis token full tristy scho toke me to take youe.

[Shows the girdle.]

Jacob.   A! Thomas, whare gate þou þat girdill so gode?   248

Thom.   Sirs, my messages is meuand some mirthe for to
make youe,

For founding flesshly I fande hir till hir faire foode,

And when I mette with þat maiden, it mengid my mode.

Hir sande has scho sente youe, so semely to see.   252

And.   Ya, Thomas, vnstedfaste full staring þou stode,

Þat makis þi mynde nowe full madde for to be.

But herken and here nowe [1]   255

---

[1] This line is placed after l. 257 in the MS.

Late vs loke where we laid hir,
If any folke haue affraied hir.

Joh. Go we groppe wher we graued hir, 258
If we fynde ouȝte þat faire one in fere nowe.

[*They go to Mary's grave.*

21. **Pet.** Be-halde nowe, hidir youre hedis in haste,
Þis glorious and goddely is gone fro þis graue.

Thom. Loo! to my talking ye toke youe no tente for to
traste. 262

Jacob. A! Thomas, vntrewly nowe trespassed we haue,
Mercy, full kyndely we crie and we craue.

Andr. Mercye, for foule haue we fautid in faye.

Joh. Mercye, we praye þe, we will not de-praue. 266

Pet. Mercye, for dedis we did þe þis daye.

Thom. Oure saueour so swete
For-giffe you all,
And so I schall. 270
Þis tokyn tall
Haue I brought yowe, youre bales to beete.

22. **Pet.** Itt is welcome, i-wis, fro þat worthy wight,
For it was wonte for to wappe þat worthy virgine. 274

Jacob. Itt is welcome, i-wis, fro þat lady so light,
For hir wombe wolde scho wrappe with it and were it with
wynne.

Andr. Itt is welcome i-wis, fro þat saluer of synne,
For scho bende it aboute hir with blossom so bright. 278

Joh. Itt is welcome i-wis, fro þe kepe of oure kynne,
For aboute þat reuerent it rechid full right.

Pet. Nowe knele we ilkone
Vpponne oure kne. 282

Jacob. To þat lady free.

Andr. Blissid motte sche be!
ȝa, for scho is lady lufsome allone.

They look in the
grave and find
she is gone ;

they all beg
pardon for not
believing
Thomas.
lf. 236 b.

The girdle is
welcome for the
sake of its wearer.

They kneel to
Mary.

Thomas returns to India, **23. Thom.**   Nowe brethir, bese besie and buske to be bow-

                nand,   286

    To Ynde will I torne me and trauell to teche.

Peter goes to Rome, **Pet.**   And to Romans so royall þo renkis to be rownand,

    Will I passe fro þis place, my pepull to preche.

James to Samaria, **Jac.**   And I schall Samaritanus so sadly enserche,   290

    To were þam be wisdome þei wirke not in waste,

lf. 237.
xxxii. vij.
Andrew to Achaia, **Andr.**   And to Achaia full lely þat lede for to leche,

    Will hy me to helpe þame and hele þame in haste.

John to Asia. **Joh.**   Þis comenaunt accordis,   294

    Sirs, sen ȝe will soo,

    Me muste nedis parte youe froo

    To Assia will I goo.

    He lede ȝou, þat lorde of all lordis !   298

' Pray God may bless our labours.' **24. Thom.**   The lorde of all lordis in lande schall he lede youe,

    Whillis ȝe trauell in trouble, þe trewthe for to teche,

    With frewte of oure feithe in firthe schall we fede youe,

    For þat laboure is lufsome, ilke lede for to leche.   302

    Nowe I passe fro youre presence þe pepull to preche,

    To lede þame and lere þame þe lawe of oure lorde ;

    As I saide, vs muste a-soundre and sadly enserche,

    Ilke contre to kepe clene and knytte in o corde   306

    Off oure faithe.

    Þat frelye foode

    Þat died on rode,

    With mayne and moode,   310

    He grath yowe be gydis full grath !

[The rest of leaf 237 and back are blank. Both sides of leaf 238 are filled with music ; see the facsimiles.]

XLVII. THE OSTELERES [1].

The Assumption and Coronation of the Virgin.

[PERSONS OF THE PLAY.

JESUS.   1, 2, 3, 4, 5, 6 ANGELUS.]
MARIA.

[SCENE I, *The heights of Heaven.*]

Jesus.

MYNE aungellis þat are bright and schene,
    On my message take ye þe waye
Vnto Marie, my modir clene,
Þat berde is brighter þan þe daye.   4
Grete hir wele haly be-dene,
An to þat semely schall ȝe saye,
Off heuene I haue hir chosen quene,
In joie and blisse þat laste schall aye.   8
I wille ȝou saie what I haue þoughte,
And why þat ȝe schall tille hir wende,
I will hir body to me be brought,
To beilde in blisse with-outen ende.   12
Mi flesshe of hir in erþe was tone,
Vnkindely thing it were, i-wis
Þat scho schulde bide be hire allone,
And I beilde here so high in blis.   16
For-thy tille hir þan schall ȝe fare,
Full frendlye for to fecche hir hedir,
Þere is no thyng þat I loue more,
In blisse þanne schall we belde to-gedir.   20

*Transitus
Mariæ,* Tischen-
dorf, Text B,
p. 135.
Jesus sends his
angels to burd
Mary,

to say he has
chosen her queen
of heaven;

she was his
mother, it were
unnatural she
should be left
alone, while he is
high in bliss.

---

[1] 'Alias Inholders,' and 'caret' beneath, is written immediately after
Osteleres, in the late hand.

i Angelus. O ! blissfull lorde, nowe moste of myght,
We are redye with all oure myght
Thy bidding to fulfille,   23

To þi modir, þat maiden free,
Chosen cheffe of chastite,
As it is thy wille.   26

ii Angelus. Off þis message we are ful fayne,
We are redy with myght and mayne,
Bothe be day and be nyght;   29
Heuene and erþe nowe gladde may be,
Þat frely foode nowe for to see,

In whome þat þou did light[1].   32

iii Angelus. Lorde ! Jesu Criste, oure gouernoure,
We are all boune att þi bidding,
With joie and blisse and grete honnoure,
We schall þi modir to þe bringe.   36

[Scene II, *Near Mary's grave.*]

iv Angelus. Hayle ! þe doughtir of blissid Anne,

Þe whiche consayued thurgh þe holy goste,
And þou brought forthe both god and manne,
The whiche felled doune þe fendis boste.   40

v Angelus. Haile ! roote of risse, þat fourthe brought

Þat blissid floure oure saueoure,
The whiche þat made mankynde of noght,
And brought hym vppe in to his toure.   44

vi Angelus. Of þe allone he wolde be borne
In-to þis worlde of wrecchidnesse,
To saue mankynde þat was for-lorne,
And bringe þame oute of grete distresse.   48

i Angelus. Þou may be gladde, bothe day and nyght,
To se thy sone oure saueoure,

---

[1] These two 6-line stanzas are the only two that occur in this piece.

He will þe croune nowe, lady bright,

Þou blissid modir and faire floure.　　　　　52

ii **Angelus.**　Marie modir, and mayden clene,

Chosen cheffe vn-to þi childe,

Of heuene and erþe þou arte quene,

Come vppe nowe, lady, meke and mylde.　　56

iii **Angelus.**　Þi sone has sente vs aftir þe

To bringe þe nowe vnto his blisse,

Þer schall þou belde and blithe be,

Of joie and mirthe schall þou noȝt misse.　　60

iv **Angelus.**　For in his blisse with-outen ende,

Þere schall þou alkynne solas see,

Þi liffe in likyng for to lende,

With þi dere sone in Trinite.　　　　　64

Maria [*rising*].　A! blissid be god, Fadir all weldand,

Hym selffe wottith best what is to doo,

I thanke hym with harte and hande,

Þat þus his blisse wolde take me too :　　68

And ȝou also his aungellis bright,

Þat fro my sone to me is sente,

I am redy with all my myght,

For to fulfille his comaundement.　　　　72

v Angelus.　Go we nowe, þou worþi wight,

Vnto þi sone þat is so gente,

We schall þe bringe in-to his sight,

To croune þe quene, þus hase he mente.　　76

vi Angelus.　Alle heuene and erþe schall worschippe þe,

And baynnely be at þi biddinge,

Thy joie schall euere incressid be,

Of solas sere þan schall þou synge.　　　*Cantando*

[Scene III, *The heights of Heaven.*]

i Angelus.　Jesu, lorde and heuene-is kyng,　　81

Here is þi modir þou aftir sente,

---

¹ Original direction.

Marginal notes:

He will crown thee.

Come up, now, lady,

thy son sends us for thee,

lf. 240.
xxxiij. ij.

thou shalt live in all kinds of joy.'

Mary thanks the Father and the angels.

She is ready.

' Let us go to thy gentle son.'

We haue her brought at þi biddynge,

Take hir to þe as þou haste mente.   84

Maria.   Jesu, my sone, loved motte þou be,

I thanke þe hartely in my þought

Þat þis wise ordandis for me,

And to þis blisse þou haste me broght.   88

Jesus.   Haile ! be þou Marie, maiden bright,

Þou arte my modir and I thy sone,

With grace and goodnesse arte þou dight,

With me in blisse ay schall þou wonne.   92

Nowe schall þou haue þat I þe hight,

Thy tyme is paste of all þi care,

Wirschippe schall þe aungellis bright,

Of newe schall þou witte neuere more.   96

Maria.   Jesu my sone, loued motte þou be,

I thanke þe hartely in my þoȝt,

Þat on þis wise ordandis for me,

And to this blisse þou has me broght.   100

Jesus.   Come forth with me, my modir bright,

In-to my blisse we schall assende,

To wonne in welthe, þou worþi wight,

That neuere more schall it haue ende.   104

Thi newis, modir, to neuen þame nowe,

Are turned to joie, and soth it is,

All aungellis bright þei schall þe bowe,

And worschippe þe worþely i-wis.   108

For mekill joie, modir, had þou,

Whan Gabriell grette þe wele be þis,

And tolde þe tristely for to trowe,

Þou schulde consayue þe kyng of blisse.   112

i Angelus.   Nowe maiden meke and modir myne [1],

Itt was full mekill myrþe to þe,

Þat I schulde ligge in wombe of þine,

Thurgh gretyng of an aungell free.   116

[1] See note on next page.

ii Angelus.   The secounde joie modir was syne,
With-outen payne whan þou bare me.

The birth of Jesus.

iii Angelus.   The thirde aftir my bittir peyne,
Fro dede on lyve þou sawe me be.

120   *The resurrection.*

iv Angelus.   The fourthe was when I stied vppe right,
To heuene vnto my fadir dere,
My modir, when þou saugh þat sight,
To þe it was a solas seere.

Christ's ascension into heaven.

124

v Angelus.   Þis is þe fifte, þou worthy wight,
Of þe jois þis has no pere,
Nowe schall þou belde in blisse so bright,
For euer and ay, I highte þe here.

Her own assumption.

128

vi Angelus.   For þou arte cheffe of chastite,
Off all women þou beris þe floure,
Nowe schalle þou, lady, belde with me,
In blisse þat schall euere in-dowre.

132

i Angelus.   Full high on highte in mageste,
With all worschippe and all honnoures,
Wher we schall euere samen be,
Beldand in oure bigly boures [1].

'We will dwell together in our delightful bowers of bliss.

136

ii Ang.   Alle kynnys swetnesse is þer-in,
Þat manne vppon may thynke, or wiffe,
With joie and blisse þat neuere schall blynne,
Þer schall þou, lady, lede thy liffe.

140

iii Angelus.   Þou schalte be worshipped with honnoure
In heuene blisse þat is so bright,
With martiris and with confessouris,
With all virginis, þat worthy wight.

144   f. 241 b.

[Jesus.]   Be-fore all oþere creatours
I schall þe giffe both grace and might,
In heuene and erþe to sende socoure,

Jesus grants her grace above all other creatures, and mercy to all who call on her.

[1] The rubricator has made the *Angels* tell the five joys of Mary, but
t is clear from the pronouns used that ll. 113–136 are spoken by Jesus,
n continuation of his previous speech.   Jesus also should begin again at
ine 145, or rather l. 129.

To all þat seruis þe day and nyght.　　148
I graunte þame grace with all my myght,
Thurgh askyng of þi praier,
Þat to þe call be day or nyght,
In what disease so þat þei are.　　152
Þou arte my liffe and my lekyng,
Mi modir and my mayden schene,

> [*Placing the crown on Mary's head.*

Mary is crowned.

Ressayue þis croune, my dere darlyng,
Þer I am kyng, þou schalte be quene.　　156
Myne aungellis bright, a songe ȝe singe,
In þe honnoure of my modir dere,
And here I giffe ȝou my blissing,
Haly nowe, all in fere.　　160

XLVIII. THE MERCERES [1].

The Judgment Day.

[PERSONS OF THE PLAY.

DEUS.
1, 2, 3 ANGELUS.
1, 2 ANIMA BONA.

1, 2 ANIMA MALA.
1, 2 APOSTOLUS.
1, 2, 3 DIABOLUS.]

[SCENE I, *Heaven.*]

Deus incipit.

1. FIRSTE when I þis worlde hadde wroght,
Woode and wynde and wateris wan,
And all-kynne thyng þat nowe is oght,
Fulle wele me þoght þat I did þanne.   4
Whenne þei were made goode me þame þoght,
Sethen to my liknes made I man,
And man to greue me gaffe he noght,
Þerfore me rewis þat I þe worlde began.   8

God rehearses his creation of the world,

2. Whanne I had made man at my will,
I gaffe hym wittis hym selue to wisse,
And paradise I putte hym till,
And bad hym halde it all as his.   12
But of þe tree of goode and ill,
I saide, "what tyme þou etis of þis,
Manne, þou spedes þi selue to spill,
Þou arte broght oute of all blisse."   16

how he placed man therein in Paradise,

3. Belyue brak manne my bidding,
He wende haue bene a god þerby,
He wende haue wittyne of all-kynne thyng,
In worlde to haue bene als wise as I.   20

how man broke God's bidding.

---

[1] The 30th Towneley Play, 'Juditium' (fo. 122 of MS., p. 305, of Surtees print), is in part parallel; the beginning is lost, the first existing 16 lines and other parts differ. It is here given from line 17 (York 1. 145).

K k

He ete the appill I badde schulde hyng,
Þus was he begilid thurgh glotony,
Sithen both hym and his ospring,
To pyne I putte þame all for-thy.   24

God sent his Son
to save man from
sorrow, who shed
his blood, and

4. To lange and late me þoghte it goode,
   To catche þois caitiffis oute of care,
   I sente my sone with full blithe moode
   Till erþe, to salue þame of þare sare.   28
   For rewþe of þame he reste on roode,
   And boughte þame with his body bare,
   For þame he shedde his harte and bloode,
   What kyndinesse myght I do þame mare?   32

afterwards
harrowed hell.

5. Sethen aftirwarde he heryed hell,
   And toke oute þois wrechis þat ware þare-inne.
   Þer faughte þat free with feendis feele

lf. 242 b.

   For þame þat ware sounkyn for synne.   36
   Sethen in erthe þan gonne he dwelle,
   Ensaumpill he gaue þame heuene to wynne,
   In tempill hym-selffe to teche and tell,
   To by þame blisse þat neuere may blynne.   40

' Man has found
me full of mercy
and forgiveness,

6. Sethen haue þei founde me full of mercye,
   Full of grace and for-giffenesse,
   And þei als wrecchis, wittirly,
   Has ledde þer liffe in lithirnesse.   44
   Ofte haue þei greued me greuously,

but they have
grieved me oft,

   Þus have þei quitte me my kyndinesse,
   Þer-fore no lenger, sekirlye,

I will suffer their
wickedness no
more.

   Thole will I þare wikkidnesse.   48

7. Men seis þe worlde but vanite,
   Ȝitt will no-manne be ware þer-by,
   Ilke a day þer mirroure may þei se,
   Ȝitt thynke þei noȝt þat þei schall dye.   52
   All þat euere I saide schulde be
   Is nowe fulfillid thurgh prophicie,

Ther-fore nowe is it tyme to me
To make endyng of mannes folie. 56

8. I haue tholed mankynde many a ȝere,
In luste and likyng for to lende,
And vnethis fynde I ferre or nere
A man þat will his misse amende. 60

In erthe I see butte synnes seere,
Therfore myne aungellis will I sende
To blawe þer bemys, þat all may here
The tyme is comen I will make ende. 64

9. Aungellis! blawes youre bemys belyue!
Ilke a creatoure for to call,
Leerid and lewde, both man and wiffe,
Ressayue þer dome þis day þei schall; 68

Ilke a leede þat euere hadde liffe,
Bese none for-getyn, grete ne small.
Ther schall þei see þe woundes fyve
Þat my sone suffered for þem all. 72

10. And sounderes þame be-fore my sight,
All same in blisse schall þei not be,
Mi blissid childre, as I haue hight,
On my right hande I schall þame see: 76

Sethen schall ilke a weried wight
On my lifte side for ferdnesse flee.
Þis day þer domys þus haue I dight,
To ilke a man as he hath serued me. 80

11. **Primus Ang.** Loued be þou, lorde of myghtis moste,
Þat aungell made to messengere,
Thy will schall be fulfillid in haste,
Þat heuene and erthe and helle schalle here. 84

Goode and ill euery ilke agaste,
Rise and fecche youre flessh þat was youre feere,
For all þis worlde is broght to waste,
Drawes to youre dome, it neghes nere. 88

Far or near I scarcely find a man who repents.

Matth. xxiv. 31 ;
xxv. 31–46.

Angels, blow your trumpets to call all to the day of doom.'

lf. 243.
xxxiij. vj.

The five wounds that Christ suffered will be seen.

' Set the good men on the right,

the cursed on the left hand.'

He summons to justice.

12. ii Angel. Ilke a creature, bothe olde and yhing,
Be-lyue I bidde ʒou þat ʒe ryse,
Body and sawle with ʒou ʒe bring,
And comes be-fore þe high justise.   92

Matth. xvi. 27.

For I am sente fro heuene kyng
To calle ʒou to þis grette assise,
Þerfore rise vppe and geue rekenyng,
How ʒe hym serued vppon sere wise. [*The Souls rise up.*] 96

13. Prima anima bona. Loued be þou lorde, þat is so schene,

They rise, body and soul together.

Þat on þis manere made vs to rise
Body and sawle to-gedir, clene,
To come before þe high justise.   100

The good souls pray mercy for their sins,

Of oure ill dedis, lorde, þou not mene,
That we haue wroght vppon sere wise,
But graunte vs for thy grace be-dene
Þat we may wonne in paradise.   104

lf. 243 b.

14. ii An. bona. A ! loued be þou, lorde of all !
Þat heuene and erthe and all has wroght,
Þat with þyne aungellis wolde vs call,
Oute of oure graues hidir to be broght.   108

they have often grieved God.

Ofte haue we greued þe, grette and small,
Þer aftir lorde þou deme vs noght !
Ne suffir vs neuere to feñdis to be thrall,
Þat ofte in erþe with synne vs soght.   112

The bad souls shudder at the horn,

15. i An. mala. Allas ! allas ! þat we were borne,
So may we synfull kaytiffis say,
I here wele be þis hydous horne
Itt drawes full nere to domesday.   116
Allas ! we wrecchis þat ar for-lorne,
Þat never ʒitt serued God to paye,
But ofte we haue his flessh for-sworne,
Allas ! allas ! and welaway.   120

they are in terror what can they do?

16. What schall we wrecchis do for drede,
Or whedir for ferdnes may we flee ?

When we may bringe forthe no goode dede,
Before hym þat oure juge schall be. 124
To aske mercy vs is no nede,
For wele I wotte dampned be we,
Allas! þat we swilke liffe schulde lede,
Þat dighte vs has þis destonye. 128

17. Oure wikkid werkis þei will vs wreye,
Þat we wende never schuld haue bene weten,
Þat we did ofte full pryuely,
Appertely may we se þem wreten. 132
Allas! wrecchis, dere mon we by,
Full smerte with helle fyre be we smetyn,
Nowe mon neuere saule ne body dye,
But with wikkid peynes euermore be betyne. 136

' Our wicked works will destroy us, we see them written openly.

18. Allas! for drede sore may we quake,
Oure dedis beis oure dampnacioune,
For oure mys-meuyng mon we make,
Helpe may none excusacioune. 140
We mon be sette for our synnes sake
For euere fro oure saluacioune,
In helle to dwelle with feendes blake,
Wher neuer schall be redempcioune. 144

If. 244. xxxiij. vij.

The bad must stay in hell with black devils.

19. ii An. mala. Als carefull caitiffis may we ryse,
Sore may we ringe oure handis and wepe,
For cursidnesse and for covetise,
Dampned be we to helle full depe. 148
Rought we neuere of goddis seruise,
His comaundementis wolde we noȝt kepe,

Well may they wring their hands and weep.

---

iii **Malus.** Alas carefulle catyfes may we ryse 145
Sore may we wryng oure handes and wepe, 653
For cursid and sore covytyse
Dampned be we in helle fulle depe; 148
Roght we neuer of Godes seruyce,
His commaundements wold we not kepe,

But ofte þan made we sacrafise,
To Satanas, when othir slepe.   152

'We must bear
our wicked works
on our backs. **20.** Allas! now wakens all oure were,
Oure wikkid werkis may we not hide,
But on oure bakkis vs muste þem bere,
Thei wille vs wreye on ilke a side.   156
I see foule feendis þat wille vs feere,
And all for pompe of wikkid pride,
Wepe we may with many a teere,
Allas! þat we þis day schulde bide.   160

All our deeds that
will damn us are
plainly brought
forth.' **21**[1]. Before vs playnly bese fourth brought
Þe dedis þat vs schall dame be-dene,
Þat eres has herde, or harte has þoght,
Sen any tyme þat we may mene,   164
Þat fote has gone or hande has wroght,
That mouthe has spoken or ey has sene,
Þis day full dere þanne bese it boght.
Allas! vnborne and we hadde bene.   168

Bot oft tymes maide we sacrifice
To Sathanas when othere can slepe.   152
Alas, now wakyns alle oure were,
Oure wykyd warkes can we not hide,
Bot on oure bakes we must theym bere,
That wille vs soroo on ilka syde.   156
Oure dedys this day wille do vs dere,
Oure domysman here we must abide,
And feyndes, that wille vs felly fere,   157
Thare pray to haue vs for thare pride.   158
Brymly before vs be thai broght,   161
Oure dedes that shalle dam vs bidene;   162
That eyre has harde, or harte thoght,   163
That mowthe has spokyn, or ee sene,   166
That foote has gone, or hande wroght,   112
In any tyme that we may mene,   164
Fulle dere this day now bees it boght.   167
Alas, vnborne then had I bene!   168

---

[1] In the MS. this stanza was omitted by the scribe in its right place and
added at the end.

22. iii Angel. Standis noght to-gedir, parte you in two,

All sam schall ȝe noght be in blisse,

Mi fadir of heuene woll it be soo,

For many of yowe has wroght amys.   172

Þe goode on his right hande ȝe goe,

Þe way till heuene he will you wisse;

Ȝe weryed wightis, ȝe flee hym froo,

On his lefte hande as none of his.   176

23. Deus [1]. Þis woffull worlde is brought till ende,

Mi fadir of heuene he woll it be,

Þerfore till erþe nowe will I wende,

Mi-selue to sitte in mageste.   180

To deme my domes I woll descende,

Þis body will I bere with me,

Howe it was dight, mannes mys to mende,

All mankynde þere schall it see.   *[Descends to earth.]* 184

The angels separate the good from the bad.

lf. 244 b.

Jesus goes to earth in the flesh to sit in judgment.

[Thirty-two lines intervene here, spoken by 4ᵘˢ malus.]

i Angelus cum gladio. Stand not togeder, parte in two,   169

Alle sam shalle ye not be in blys,   654

Oure lord of heven wille it be so,   171

For many of you has done amys;

On his right hande ye good shalle go,   173

The way till heuen he shall you wys;

Ye wykyd saules ye weynd hym fro,

On his left hande as none of his.   176

Jesus. The tyme is commen, I wille make ende,

My Fader of heuen wille it so be,   178

Therfor tille erthe now wille I weynde,

My self to sytt in maieste;   180

To dele my dome I wille discende,

This body wille I bere with me,   182

How it was dight man's mys to amende

Alle man's kynde ther shalle it se.   184

[A long satiro-comic scene between the devils and Tutivillus follows, fo. 123, after which the piece continues as at l. 229.]

---

[1] i. e. Jesus.

[SCENE II, *The Seat of Judgment.*]

24. Deus.　Mi postelis and my darlyngis dere,

Þe dredfull dome þis day is dight.

Both heuen and erthe and hell schall here,

Howe I schall holde þat I haue hight,　　　　188

That ȝe schall sitte on seetis sere,

Be-side my selffe to se þat sight.

And for to deme folke ferre and nere,

Aftir þer werkyng, wronge or right.　　　　192

25.　I saide also whan I you sente

To suffre sorowe for my sake,

All þo þat wolde þame right repente

Schulde with you wende and wynly wake ;　　　196

And to youre tales who toke no tente,

Shulde fare to fyre with fendis blake,

Of mercy nowe may noȝt be mente,

Butt aftir wirkyng, welth or wrake.　　　　200

26.　My hetyng haly schall I fullfille.

Therfore comes furth and sittis me by

To here þe dome of goode and ill.

i Apost.　[1] I loue þe, lord god all myghty,　　　204

Late and herely, lowde and still,

To do thy bidding bayne am I,

I obblissh me to do þi will,

With all my myght, als is worthy.　　　　208

27. ii Apost.　[2] A ! myghtfull god, here is it sene,

Þou will fulfille þi forward right,

And all þi sawes þou will maynteyne ;

I loue þe, lorde, with all my myght.　　　　212

Þer-fore vs þat has erthely bene,

Swilke dingnitees has dressed and dight.

Deus.　Comes fourthe, I schall sitte ȝou betwene,

And all fulfille þat I haue hight.　　　　216

---

[1] In the margin to this stanza, 'Hic caret O soverand Savyoᵣ de novo facto.'　　　　[2] In margin 'de novo facto.'

Hic ad sedem iudicij cum cantu angelorum.

28. i Diab. Felas, arraye vs for to fight,

And go we faste oure fee to fange,

Þe dredefull dome þis day is dight,

I drede me þat we dwelle full longe. 220

ii Diab. We schall be sene euere in þer sight,

And warly waite, ellis wirke we wrange,

For if þe domisman do vs right,

Full grete partie with vs schall gang. 224

29. iii Diab. He schall do right to foo and frende,

For nowe schall all þe soth be sought,

All weried wightis with vs schall wende,

To payne endles þei schall be broght[1]. 228

30. Deus. Ilke a creature, takes entent,

What bodworde I to you bringe,

Þis wofull worlde away is wente,

And I am come as crouned kynge. 232

Mi fadir of heuene, he has me sente,

To deme youre dedis and make ending,

Comen is þe day of jugement,

Of sorowe may ilke a synfull synge. 236

31. The day is comen of kaydyfnes,

The devils make ready to fight for their property.

'Every creature, heed my message! My father has sent me to judge your deeds.'

[Towneley, see before, l. 184.]

Jesus. Ilka creatoure take tente 229

What bodworde I shalle you bryng,

This wykyd warld away is wente,

And I am commyn as crownyd kyng, 232

Mi fader of heuen has me downe sent,

To deme youre dedes and make endyng.

Commen is the day of Iugemente,

Of sorow may euery synfulle syng. 236

The day is commen of catyfne,

---

[1] Here in the margin is written, 'Hic caret de novo facto, Alas that I was borne, dixit prima anima mala et ij[da] anima mala, de novo facto.' And indeed four lines are wanting to the stanza, as shown by the rimes, though there is no blank.

All þam to care þat are vnclene,

This day of sorrow and dread, long expected, has come.

Þe day of bale and bittirnes,

Full longe abedyn has it bene,   240

Þe day of drede to more and lesse,

Of care [1], of trymbelyng and of tene.

lf. 245 b.

Þat ilke a wight þat weried is

May say, allas! þis daye is sene!   244

Christ shows the wounds he suffered;

32. Here may ȝe see my woundes wide,

Þe whilke I tholed for youre mysdede,

Thurgh harte and heed, foote, hande, and hide,

Nought for my gilte, butt for youre nede.   248

Beholdis both body, bak, and side,

how dearly he bought man's brotherhood!

How dere I bought youre brotherhede.

Þes bittir peynes I wolde abide

To bye you blisse, þus wolde I bleede.   252

33. Mi body was scourged with-outen skill,

As theffe full thraly was [I] thrette,

On crosse þei hanged me, on a hill,

Alle those to care that ar vncleyn,

The day of batelle and bitternes,

Fulle long abiden has it beyn;   240

The day of drede to more and les,

Of ioy of tremlyng and of teyn,

Ilka wight that wikyd is

May say, alas! this day is seyn.   244

Tunc expandit manus suas et ostendit eis vulnera sua.

Here may ye se my woundes wide

That I suffred for youre mysdede,

Thrughe harte, hede, fote, hande, and syde,   247

Not for my gilte bot for youre nede.   248

Behold both bak, body, and syde,

How dere I boght youre broder-hede,

These bitter paynes I wold abide,

To by you blys thus wold I blede.   252

Mi body was skowrgid withoutten skille,

Also ther fulle throly was I thrett,

On crosse thai hang me on a hille,

---

[1] The copyist first wrote *ire* (a reminiscence of *dies iræ*), *care* is written above it by way of correction.

Blody and bloo, as I was bette. 256

The tale of the crucifixion and passion repeated.

With croune of thorne throsten full ill,
Þis spere vnto my side was sette,
Myne harte bloode spared noght þei for to spill,
Manne for thy loue wolde I not lette. 260

34. Þe Jewes spitte on me spitously,
Þei spared me nomore þan a theffe,
Whan þei me strake I stode full stilly [1],
Agaynste þam did I no thyng greve. 264
Behalde mankynde, þis ilke is I,
Þat for þe suffered swilke mischeue,
Þus was I dight for thy folye,
Man, loke thy liffe was to me full leffe [1]. 268

35. Þus was I dight þi sorowe to slake,
Manne, þus behoued þe to borowed be,
In all my woo toke I no wrake,
Mi will itt was for þe loue of þe. 272
Man, sore aught þe for to quake,
Þis dredfull day þis sight to see,

Blo and blody thus was I bett, 256
With crowne of thorne thrastyn fulle ille,
A spere vnto my harte thai sett.
Mi harte blode sparid thai not to spille,
Man, for thi luf wold I not lett. 260
The Jues spytt on me spitusly,
Thai sparid me no more then a thefe,
When thai me smote I stud stilly.
Agans thaym did I nokyns grefe: 264
Behalde, mankynde, this ilk am I,
That for the suffred sich myschefe,
Thus was I dight for thi foly,
Man, loke thi luf was me fulle lefe. 268
Thus was I dight thi sorow to slake,
Man thus behovid the borud to be,
In alle my wo tooke I no wrake,
Mi wille it was for luf of the; 272
Man for sorow aght the to qwake,
This dredful day this sight to se,

[1] The words *full* in l. 263 and *to* in l. 268 are redundant.

'I suffered all
this for man,
what didst thou
for me?

lf. 246.
xxxiiij. j.
My children on
the right, dread
not;

come to the king-
dom prepared for
you.

Ye fed me when
hungry, clad me,

had pity on me,

comforted me,
and lodged me.

All þis I suffered for þi sake,
Say man, what suffered þou for me?   276

36. Mi blissid childre on my right hande,
Youre dome þis day ȝe thar not drede,
For all youre comforte is command,
Youre liffe in likyng schall ȝe lede.   280

Commes to þe kyngdome ay lastand,
Þat ȝou is dight for youre goode dede,
Full blithe may ȝe be where ȝe stande,
For mekill in heuene schall be youre mede.   284

37. Whenne I was hungery ȝe me fedde,
To slake my thirste youre harte was free,
Whanne I was clothles ȝe me cledde,
ȝe wolde no sorowe vppon me see.   288

In harde presse whan I was stedde,
Of my paynes[1] ȝe hadde pitee,
Full seke whan I was brought in bedde
Kyndely ȝe come to coumforte me.   292

Alle this suffred I for thi sake,
Say, man, What suffred thou for me?   276
Tunc vertens se ad bonos, dicit illis,
Mi blissid barnes on my right hande,
Youre dome this day thar ye not drede,
For alle youre joy is now commande,
Youre life in lykyng shalle ye lede;   280
Commes to the kyngdom ay lastande,
That you in dight for youre good dede,
Fulle blithe may ye be there ye stand,
For mekille in heuen bees youre mede.   284
When I was hungre ye me fed,
To slek my thrist ye war fulle fre,
When I was clothles ye me cled,
Ye wold no sorowe on me se;   288
In hard prison when I was sted
On my penance ye had pyte,
Fulle seke when I was broght in bed
Kyndly ye cam to comforth me.   292

Here the copyist first wrote *penaunce* instead of *paynes*, evidently an
ear-blunder.

38. Whanne I was wikke and werieste
ȝe herbered me full hartefully,
Full gladde þanne were ȝe of youre geste,
And pleyned my pouerte piteuously. 296
Be-lyue ȝe brought me of þe beste,
And made my bedde full esyly; *Ye made my bed easy.'*
Þerfore in heuene schall be youre reste,
In joie and blisse to be me by. 300

39. i an. bona. Whanne hadde we, lorde, þat all has wroght, *'When did we all these things, Lord?'*
Meete and drinke þe with to feede?
Sen we in erþe hadde neuere noght
But thurgh þe grace of thy godhede. 304

ii an. bona. Whanne waste þat we þe clothes brought,
Or visite þe in any nede?
Or in þi sikenes we þe sought, *lf. 246 b.*
Lorde, when did we þe þis dede? 308

40. Deus. Mi blissid childir, I schall ȝou saye, *'When you helped the needy;*
What tyme þis dede was to me done,
When any þat nede hadde, nyght or day,

When I was wille and weriest
Ye harberd me fulle esely,
Fulle glad then were ye of youre gest,
Ye plenyd my pouerte full pitusly, 296
Belife ye broght me of the best,
And maide my bed there I shuld ly,
Therfor in heuen shalle be youre rest,
In joy and blys to beld me by. 300

i Bonus. Lord, when had thou so mekille nede?
Hungre or thrusty, how myght it be?
ii Bonus. When was oure harte fre the to feede?
In prison when myght we the se?
iii Bonus. When was thou seke or wantyd wede?
To harboure the when helpid we?
iv Bonus. When had thou nede of oure fordede?
When did we alle this dede to the? 308
Jesus. Mi blissid barnes, I shalle you say
What tyme this dede was to me done,
When any that nede had, nyght or day,

Askid ȝou helpe and hadde it sone.　　　312

you never refused their petition.

Youre fre hartis saide þem neuere nay,

Erely ne late, mydday ne none,

But als ofte sithis as þei wolde praye,

Þame thurte but bide, and haue þer bone.　　　316

But from the caitiffs of Cain's kin I will part for ever.

41. ȝe cursid caytiffis of Kaymes kynne,

Þat neuere me comforte in my care,

I and ȝe for euer will twynne,

In dole to dwelle for euermare ;　　　320

Youre bittir bales schall neuere blynne,

Þat ȝe schall haue whan ȝe come þare.

Þus haue ȝe serued for youre synne,

For derffe dedis ȝe haue done are.　　　324

When I had need ye expelled me, when ye sat as lords I stood outside weary and wet ;

42. Whanne I had mistir of mete and drynke,

Caytiffis, ȝe cacched me fro youre ȝate,

Whanne ȝe were sette as sirs on benke,

I stode þer-oute, werie and wette,　　　328

Was none of yowe wolde on me thynke

Pyte to haue of my poure state ;

Askyd you help and had it sone ;　　　312²

Youre fre harte saide theym neuer nay,

Erly ne late, myd-day ne noyn,

As oft-sithes as thai wold pray,

Thai thurte bot aske and haue thare boyn.　　　316

Tunc dicet malis,

Ye cursid catyfs of Kames kyn,

That neuer me comforthid in my care,

Now I and ye for euer shalle twyn,

In doylle to dwelle for euer mare ;　　　320

Youre bitter bayles shalle neuer blyn.

That ye shalle thole when ye com. thare,

Thus haue ye seruyd for youre syn,

For derfe dedes ye haue doyn are.　　　324

When I had myster of mete and drynke,

Catyfs ye chaste me from youre yate,

When ye were set as syres on bynke

I stode ther oute wery and wate,　　　328

Yet none of you wold on me thynke,

To haue pite on my poore astate,

Þer-fore till hell I schall you synke,
Weele are 3e worthy to go þat gate. 332

43. Whanne I was seke and soriest,
3e visitte me noght, for I was poure,
In prisoune faste whan I was feste,
Was none of you loked howe I fore. 336
Whenne I wiste neuere where for to reste,
With dyntes 3e draffe me fro your dore,
Butte euer to pride þanne were 3e preste,
Mi flessh, my bloode ofte 3e for-swore. 340

ye visited me
not, poor or in
prison.

lf. 247.
xxxiiij. ij.

Ye drove me
with blows from
your door,

44. Clothles whanne I was ofte, and colde,
At nede of you 3ede I full naked,
House ne herborow, helpe ne holde,
Hadde I none of you, þof I quaked. 344
Mi mischeffe sawe ye many-folde,
Was none of you my sorowe slaked,
Butt euere for-soke me, yonge and alde,
Þerfore schall 3e nowe be for-saked. 348

none of you
lessened my
sorrow,

therefore I now
forsake you.'

45. i aia. mala. Whan had þou, lorde þat all thyng has,
Hungir or thirste? sen þou god is,

Therfor to helle I shalle you synke,
Welle are ye worthy to go that gate. 332
When I was seke and soryest
Ye viset me noght, for I was poore,
In prison fast when I was fest
Wold none of you loke how I foore; 336
When I wist neuer where to rest
With dyntes ye drofe me from youre doore,
Bot euer to pride them were ye prest,
Mi flesh, my blooðe, ye ofte for-swore. 340
Clothles, when that I was cold
That nerehande for you yode I nakyd, 342
Mi myschefe saghe ye many-folde, 345
Was none of you my sorow slakyd;
Bot euer forsoke me, yong and olde,
Therfor shalle ye now be forsakyd. 348

i Malus. Lorde, when had thou, that alle has,
Hunger or thriste, sen thou God is?

The bad souls disclaim these sins.

Whan was þou in prisonne was,

Whan was þou naked or herberles?   352

ii aia. mala.   Whan was it we sawe þe seke, allas!

Whan kid we þe þis vnkyndinesse,

Werie or wette to late þe passe,

When did we þe þis wikkidnesse?   356

They were done to the needy; 'ye hid your ears, your help to them was not at home.'

46. **Deus.**   Caistiffis, als ofte als it be-tidde

Þat nedfull aught askid in my name,

Ʒe herde þem noght, youre eris ʒe hidde,

Youre helpe to þame was noʒt at hame.   360

To me was þat vnkyndines kyd,—

Þere-fore bere þis bittir blame,

lf. 247 b.

To leste or moste whan ʒe it did,

To me ʒe did þe selue and þe same.   364

Jesus calls his chosen ones to him,

47. Mi chosen childir, comes vnto me,

With me to wonne nowe schall ʒe wende,

When was that thou in prison was?

When was thou nakyd or harberles?   352

ii **Malus.**   When myght we se the seke, alas!

And kyd the alle this vnkyndnes?

iii **Malus.**   When was we let the helples pas?

When dyd we the this wikydnes?   359

iv **Malus.**   Alas, for doylle this day!

Alas, that euer I it abode!

Now am I dampned for ay,

This dome may I not avoyde.

Jesus.   Catyfs, as ofte as it betyde   357

That nedefulle oght askyd in my name,

Ye harde thaym noght, youre eeres was hid,

Youre help to thaym was not at hame;   360

To me was that vnkyndnes kyd,

Therfor ye bere this bitter blame,

To the lest of myne when ye oght dyd,

To me ye did the self and same.   364

Tunc dicet bonis,

Mi chosyn childer, commes to me,

With me to dwelle now shalle ye weynde,

Þere joie and blisse schall euer be,
Youre liffe in lyking schall ȝe lende, 368
ȝe cursed kaitiffis, fro me ȝe flee,

he sends the
cursed to hell.

In helle to dwelle with-outen ende,
Þer ȝe schall neuere butt sorowe see
¹ And sitte be Satanas þe fende. 372

48. Nowe is fulfillid all my for-þoght,
For endid is all erthely thyng,
All worldly wightis þat I haue wroght,
Aftir þer werkis haue nowe wonnyng, 376
Thei þat wolde synne and sessid noght,
Of sorowes sere now schall þei syng,
And þei þat mendid þame whils þei moght,
Schall belde and bide in my blissing. 380

*Et sic facit finem cum melodia
angelorum transiens a loco ad locum.*

Ther joy and blys euer shalle be,
Youre life in lykyng for to leynde. 368
Tunc dicet malis,
Ye warid wightes, from me ye fle,
In helle to dwelle withoutten ende,
Ther shalle ye noght bot sorow se,
And sit bi Sathanas the feynde.

[Another scene between the demons and Tutivillus, with eight closing
lines spoken by a Good soul, complete the Towneley play.]

---

¹ In margin here 'nota, miseremini mei, etc.'

THE INHOLDERS.

[*The Coronation of our Lady.*]

[Fragment in another hand, ? end of 15th cent.]

HAYLE! fulgent Phebus and fader eternall,
Parfite plasmator and god omnipotent,
Be whos will and power perpetuall,   3
All thinges hath influence and beyng verament.
To the I giffe louyng and laude right excellent,
And to the sperite also, graunter of all grace,   6
Whilke by thi woorde and thi warke omnipotent,
I am thi sonne and equale in that case.
O! sapor suauitatis, O! succour and solace,   9
O life eternall and luffer of chastite,
Whome aungels abowne and þe erthe in his grete space,
And all thinges create loues in mageste.   1
Remembre fader meke, in thi solempnyte,
The woundes of thi sonne, whilke by thy providence
þou made discende frome thyne equalite   1
Into the wombe of Marye, be meke obedience.
Of a virgin inviolate for mans iniquyte,
Whilke for his synne stoode mekill fro þi grace,
Be hoole assente of thi solempnite,
þou made me incarnate, and trulie man I was.
Wherefore too spede me here in this space,
þou here me fader hertely, I the praye,
As for my moder truely in this case,
þou here þi sonne, and herk what I shall saye.

Me semes my silfe it is right grete offence
My moder wombe in erthe sulde putrifye,
Sen her flessh and myne were bothe oone in escence,   27
I had none othir bot of hir truely.
She is my moder to whome *legem adimpleui*.
Whilke þou has ordinate as by thi prouidence,   30
Graunte me thi grace, I the beseke hertely,
As for the tyme of hir meke innocence   If. 248 b.
In woorde ne dede thoght the neuer to offende,   33
Sho myght be assumpt, I pray thyn excellence,
Vnto thi troone, and so to be commende,
In bodye and saule euer withoutyn ende   36
With the to reyne in thyne eternyte,
Fro sorrowe and sadnesse synners to offende.
O flagraunt fader! graunte yt myght so be!   39

Responcio Patris ad Filium.

O lampe of light! O lumen eternall!
O coequale sonne! O verrey sapience!
O mediator ande meen, and lyfe perpetuall,   42
In whome of derk clowedes may haue none accidence!
Thoue knawes right wele by thy providence,
I haue commyt my powere generall,   45
Tibi data potestas ande plenall influence,
Thou ert my sonne.   .   .   .

[The piece breaks off here, unfinished. See *Innholders*, in Introduction.]

SURGE PROXIMA MEA.

Ashburnham MS. 137, *leaf* 232 *v°; see before, p.* 483.

VENI DE LIBANO SPONSA.

Ashburnham MS. 137, leaf 233 ; see before, p. 484.

VENI ELECTA MEA.

Ashburnham MS. 137, *leaf* 235. *See facsimile in frontispiece, and p.* 487.

Ve - - - - - - ni e - lec - ta me - - - a, et po - nam in te tro - - num me - - um, qui - a con-cu-pi- - - - - vit rex spe - ci - em - tu - - - - - - - - - - - - - am.

NOTE ON THE MUSIC.

Edited by WILLIAM H. CUMMINGS, F.S.A.

THE difficulties attendant on an attempt to translate ancient manuscript music into modern notation are many. The scribe of the day probably wrote down from dictation some well-known melodies, which were usually orally transmitted from singer to singer; and even had he been desirous of representing the traditional tunes with accuracy, the system for indicating musical sounds by written signs was in such an indefinite and chaotic condition, that with the best and most faithful endeavours, the result would have produced merely an approximation of the music sung.

In the present case some pages of the manuscript seem to have been penned by an indifferent or careless writer; see facsimiles of fol. 238–238 v° (Plates II, III). The music here is two-part composition like the other tunes; the parts are not written in score, but each at length, the second after the first.[1]

---

[1] Mr. Cummings finds that these two leaves are written in so confused a manner as to make their rendering into modern notation extremely doubtful; instead of attempting it, therefore, the two leaves are presented to the reader in black facsimile, the only variation from the original MS. being that the red notes, and the stave-lines and clefs (all of which are red in the original) are here black. For the sake of any student who may wish to colour his copy, the following enumeration is given, by which he can identify them. Leaf 238: in the first stave, counting from top, are four red notes:—

	Stave.	Red Notes.	Identification, beginning at left hand.
Leaf 238.	1	4	7th, 13th, 14th. and 15th notes.
	2	5	12th, 15th, 16th, 17th. 18th notes.
	3	8	2nd, 3rd, 11th, 21st, 22nd, 30th, 31st, 33rd notes.
	4	4	28th, 31st–33rd notes.
	5	None.	
	6	4	9th, 24th–26th notes.
	7	1	4th note.
	8	5	4th, 15th, 16th, 31st, 32nd notes.
	9	None.	
Leaf 238,	1	15	[41st, 42nd, 45th notes. 9th, 10th, 27th–32nd, 34th, 35th, 37th, 40th,
verso.	2	4	1st, 2nd (double note, and the ♭), 13th, 29th notes. [40th, 41st notes.
	3	8	4th, 7th, 8th, 9th, 28th, 29th (double note),
	4	3	34th, 35th, 36th notes.
	5	4	7th, 8th, 22nd, 40th notes.
	6	9	2nd, 7th–10th, 22nd, 23rd, 40th, 41st notes.
	7	3	5th, 6th, 33rd notes.
	8	4	2nd, 3rd, 4th, 8th notes.
	9	2	23rd, 24th notes.

L. T. S.

The traditional memory of this music has long since passed away, and we are therefore unable to do more than guess at the probable rectification of apparent errors. Even in 1597 that learned theorist and composer, Thomas Morley, speaking of the notation found in ancient written music, said : 'That order of pricking is gone out of vse now, so that wee vse the blacke voides as they vsed their black fulles, and the blacke fulles as they vsed the redde fulles. The redde is gone almost quite out of memorie, so that *none vse it, and fewe knowe what it meaneth*[1].'

It should also be remembered that the arbitrary division of music into bars is comparatively a modern invention; in ancient music there was no such thing dreamt of as strict time; the music was entirely subordinated to the accent of the words, the very notes themselves had no absolute fixed measure, and to translate the old notation into modern signs of semibreves, minims, etc., is opposed to the spirit of ancient church song. Such music demanded and received very free declamation; a modern writer has affirmed with truth, that in the old *cantus* 'the text is the master, the notes the slaves.'

In barring these tunes we are to a considerable extent placing them in fetters, and we must not therefore always insist on making bars of equal length.

The facsimile of leaf 235 (see frontispiece), the least complex and best written of all the pages, shows very clearly the condition of the manuscript; in all cases the lines are red, some of the notes are also in that colour, but the major part are black.

The words appear to have been inserted in a very loose and pro-miscuous manner, intended, like the musical notes, simply as an aid to memory. The flat at the commencement of the tune on fol. 232 v⁰ exists in the original MS.; and the natural in the thirteenth bar of the same melody is written a sharp, at that time the usual mode of indicating that a note was to be raised a semitone.

WILLIAM H. CUMMINGS.

ADDITIONAL NOTE.

One would have been glad to find that this music—responsoria or sequences—were of any considerable beauty or value ; but truth com-pels us to say that it is not so. Reminiscences of old church music, itself now imperfectly understood, they are not even so intelligible as the songs found among the Coventry Plays, nor give us a beautiful

---

[1] 'A Plaine and easie Introdvction to practicall Mvsicke.'—London, 1597. 'Annotations' at the end, sign. ¶ 4.

melody, like the song of Chaucer's child recently discovered in the
MS. Arundel 248. Yet several points of interest arise in connection
with these musical fragments, such as the employment of red notes,
a staff of five lines, and the arrangement in two parts ; English
manuscripts containing *written* descant or counterpoint being rare at
this date, though the use of descant or improvisation upon a given
theme dates back much earlier. With regard to the red notes, the
Rev. S. S. Greatheed suggests that the red breves may be so coloured
in order to call to the attention of the singer that he is to hold them
on against the two or more corresponding notes in the other part.
The stave in the 15th and 16th centuries was of four, five, or six
lines ; that 'of four lines was used exclusively for plain chaunt,' that
'of five lines was used for all vocal music, except plain chaunt[1],'
with which this accords.

It seemed probable that these pieces of music, being attached to the
play on the Assumption, and occurring in the Vision of Mary and the
Angels seen by Thomas, might have been taken from the special
church service for that feast[2]; and particularly it seemed likely that
their original source might be found in the Breviary according to
the Use of York. After diligent search, however, the problem
appears to resolve itself in this, that the playwright did not quote
textually from any office, but wished to remind his audience in a
general way of words with which they were familiar enough in church.
The plays, themselves religious in origin, were being secularized; the
music partook of the same character. Possibly a well-known musical
phrase or theme was caught, and its descant attempted to the well-
known words. These words were naturally some of those used in the
office for the Assumption; part come from the Song of Solomon, the
mediæval biblical storehouse for imaginative language concerning
Mary. The first versicle, however, *Surge proxima mea*, &c., p. 517,
which may be referred to Cant. ii. 10, is not found there as it stands.
Examining the York Breviary, in the antiphon to the Magnificat of
the Third Day in the Octave of the Assumption[3], occur the words
' tota speciosa es proxima mea, et macula non est in te: veni a lybano:
sponsa: veni a lybano,' taken from Cant. iv. 7, and ii. 13; the word
proxima (probably a recollection from the *Transitus Mariæ*, ' ait
dominus; Exsurge amica mea et proxima mea'[4]) being substituted

---

[1] W. S. Rockstro in Grove's ' Dictionary of Music,' v. *Stave.*

[2] There is and was no festival for the Coronation of the Virgin, but that
for her Assumption was of considerable importance.

[3] York Breviary. Edited for the Surtees Society, by Mr. Lawley. Vol. II.
1882 (Surtees, vol. 75), col. 490. It may be remarked that this antiphon is
not found in the Sarum Breviary.

[4] Tischendorf, Text B. cap. 16 (17), p. 135.

for *amica* of the Vulgate. The versicle appears in its correct form, 'tota pulchra es amica mea,' at the beginning[1] of the third antiphon of the First Vespers of the Assumption; the same antiphon ending with 'surge, propera, amica mea ; veni de libano : veni coronaberis[2]' from Cant. ii. 10, and iv. 8[3]. In the feast of the Visitation the versicle from Cant. ii. 10 is used in its exact form (York Breviary, ii. col. 750). Looking now at our versicles it appears evident that the first and fourth pieces (leaves 232 v⁰ and 238 of the MS.) were made up in part from these two antiphons,—*Surge, proxima mea, columba mea*, or *Surge propera mea columba mea* (the latinity being somewhat thrown out in the last). The latter words—

> *tabernaculum glorie,*
> *vasculum vite,*
> *templum celeste—*

are probably a quotation or a recollection from some sequence, which I have been unable to trace. The short lines and the repetition of such rimes were favourite forms in these compositions, of which an example may be referred to in a York sequence printed (from a MS. in Sion College) at the end of the York Missal, edited for the Surtees Society by Dr. Henderson[4].

It has also been suggested by Mr. E. Bishop, that the second antiphon in the second nocturne of the feast of the Visitation of Mary, printed at end of the York Breviary, vol. ii. col. 742) may have left its echo on the ear of the writer of our first and fourth pieces. It runs—

> Dei tabernaculum
> quod ipse sacravit
> ex te vite fluvium
> cunctis derivavit.

From the same antiphons also come our second and fifth pieces (leaves 233, 238 v⁰ of MS.), the word *sponsa* marking the recollection of that belonging to the Third Day of the Octave, before referred to.

The third versicle (leaf 235 of MS.), the original source of which I am unable to find (it does not appear to be taken from the Scriptures), was much used in services for virgins and female saints ; in

---

[1] York Breviary, col. 476.

[2] This antiphon also occurs in the York Missal (Surtees Soc. ed. Dr. Henderson, 1874, p. 193) for the Sundays after Trinity. It is also in the Sarum Breviary, *in festo Ass. Mariæ*, and other places.

[3] The verses as they stand in *Cant. cant.* are as follow :—

Cap. ii. 10 : '. . surge, propera, amica mea, columba mea, formosa mea, et veni.'
Cap. ii. 13 : '. . . Surge, amica mea, speciosa mea, et veni.'
Cap. iv. 7 : 'Tota pulchra es, amica mea, et macula non est in te.'
Cap. iv. 8 : 'Veni de Libano, sponsa mea, veni de Libano, veni : coronaberis de capite Amana, de vertice,' &c.

[4] Vol. ii. p. 322 ; vol. 60 of the Surtees Society, 1874.

the feast of the Assumption at York it stands as a responsorium to the fourth lesson at matins [1]. Besides this, it is found in the York Breviary in the Common of Virgins, and as an antiphon in the Common of Matrons [2]; and in the Missal as part of a gradual for the feast of a Virgin and Martyr [3]. It was doubtless therefore well known, and was appropriate as the close of the vision, when Mary 'passes to the peerless empire' (p. 487, l. 200).

To determine whence came the tunes to these versicles is, however, very difficult, perhaps impossible. The only liturgical book for York containing music that I have heard of is a fine MS. Antiphonal of the 15th century, written for the cathedral church of York, belonging to Lord Herries, of Everingham Park, York. There are no books of this description in the British Museum; York breviaries, &c., being in fact rare, and York music particularly so. Lord Herries most kindly placed his valuable Antiphonal at my disposal, but in none of the antiphons in the feast of the Assumption do I find any resemblance between the music and that of the plays. And as in this Antiphonal the part known as the *Commune Sanctorum* is wanting, I am unable to see whether the 'Common of a Virgin,' or 'of a Matron,' would have yielded our tunes; it is probable they would not. Those which I can find in the Sarum Breviary give the same answer, and it seems useless looking further afield. Such as they are, the pieces are to the best of my belief unknown at the present day outside this collection of plays.

L. T. S.

[1] York Breviary, Surt. Soc. II, p. 481.　　　[2] Ibid., pp. 63, 77.
[3] York Missal, Surt. Soc. II, p. 155. Mr. Cummings also finds it in a Roman Pontifical, Venice, 1572,—in the service for consecration of a Virgin; in a Processional, Paris, 1671, in the Procession-service for a Virgin and Martyr; and in a Processional, Madrid, 1672, in the service for S. Clara, and in the service on taking the Veil.

REFERENCES TO THE MUSIC.

The Manuscript contains five pieces; three are rendered into modern notation, two are only given by photo-lithography.

1. On p. 517, and see p. 483.
2. On p. 519, and see p. 484.
3. On p. 521, see pp. 487, 524, 526, and facsimile in frontispiece.
4. Plate II, and see pp. 490, 523, 526.
5. Plate III, and see pp. 490, 523, 526.

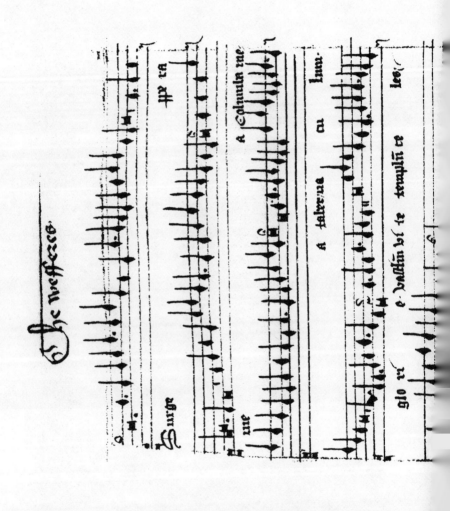

PLATE II.

ASHBURNHAM MS. 127.   *Leaf 238.*

PLATE III.

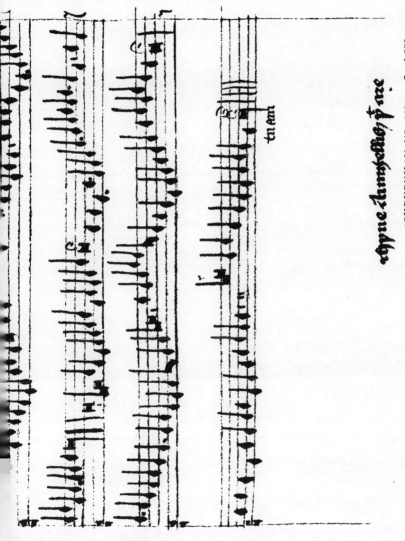

ASHBURNHAM MS. 137.   Lenf 238 ro.

GLOSSARY.

s. = substantive.
v. = verb.
v. s. = verbal substantive.
pa. p. = past participle.
pr. p. = present participle.

past t. = past tense.
adj. = adjective.
adv. = adverb.
conj. = conjunction.
pron. = pronoun.

The letter y is treated as *i*, initial ʒ as *y*, and þ as *th*.

A, 3/42, 371/409, *adj.* one.
Abaiste, 401/106 ; Abayst, 228/211 ;
 Abassed, 37/59, *pa. p.* cast down, de-
 pressed.
Abowne, 4/87, *prep.* above.
Abye, 31/54 ; Aby, 106/111, *v.* abide.
A-chesoune, 121/80, *s.* reason.
Actone, 424/96, *s.* leather jerkin or
 jacket.
Adele, 49/131, a bit.
Adreed, 261/191, *adj.* afraid.
A-drygh, 298/160, *adv.* aside, away, off.
Aferde, 190/170, *adj.* afraid.
Affles, 374/29, *v.* trust, confide.
Affraied, 190/169, *adj.* frightened.
Ayle (a person), *v.* to ail, be the matter
 with, 140/65, 67 ; 157/18.
Ay, 2/40 ; 3/43, *adv.* ever.
Ay lastand, 35/1, everlasting.
Ayre, 139/42 ; Are, 143/176, *adv.* ere,
 before : *see* Or.
Aysell, 366/244, *s.* vinegar.
Al-beledande, 2/21, *pr. p.* all-shelter-
 ing, all-protecting : *see* Belde.
Alde, 63/221, *adj.* old.
A-lirte, 230/254: *see* Lirte.
All-be, 2/26, *conj.* although.
Allegge, 158/56, 165/193, 388/277;
 v. allege, set forth.
All-kyn, 24/70 ; Alkynne, 493/62,
 adj. all kinds of, all sorts of.
All-mightfull, 175/106, *adj.* almighty.
All to, 107/153, *adv.* entirely, altogether.
All-yf, 8/4, 41/47, *conj.* although.

Als, *adv.* as.
Alther best, 110/253, *adj.* best of all.
And, 41/54, 61/165, *conj.* if.
ndyþer, 52/215, should be read as
 two words, and hither; the line
 would run thus, *And werly watte,
 and yper þe wynd,* i. e. And warily
 know, and hither wend thee.
Anes, 63/250, *adv.* once.
Angris, 111/275, *s.* troubles, afflictions.
Anlepy, 103/40, *adj.* single, alone.
A-nodyr, 52/235, *adj.* another.
A-noynementis, 407/213, *s.* ointments.
Apayd, 20/81, *pt. p.* pleased, satisfied.
Aperte, 173/26 ; Appertly, 176/133,
 adv. openly, manifestly, publicly : *see*
 Pertly.
Appose, 129/87, 298/163, *v.* to examine,
 interrogate.
Appostita, 222/76, *s.* apostate.
Appreue, 274/93, *adj.* satisfactory,
 pleasing.
Arest, 124/35, *v.* arrest, stay.
Arme, 105/101, *s.* harme.
Arow, 176/142, *adj.* averse, reluctant.
Arrore, 283/322, *s.* error.
As arms, 152/207, 155/276, to arms !
Asith, 215/454, *s.* satisfaction, amends
 for injury.
Aspise, 329/281, *v.* espy, look into;
 Aspied, 278/206, *pa. p.*
Asse, 69/7, *v.* ask ; *elde will asse,*
 seniority requires.
Assemelyng, 475/68, *s.* assembling.

M m

Assewe, 213/401, v. follow after.

Assumpt, 515/36, pa. p. taken into heaven.

At, prep. to.

Ather, 7/155, pron. either.

Atteynted, 388/278, pa. p. convicted.

Awdir, 52/216, adj. either.

Awe, 72/73, s. fear, dread.

Awe, 69/12, v. ought.

Aughen, 100/202, adj. own.

Avise, 207/202, v. consider.

Avowtry, 194/15, s. adultery.

Baill, 428/53, 436/88, s. bale, sorrow.

Baill, 383/195, s. part of a defence in fortification.

Bayne, 32/94, 174/63, adj. obedient.

Baynely, 2/20, 35, 3/47, 7/160, adv. near, closely, directly; straightly; bein Icel. (Linc. Gloss.).

Bait: see Bete.

Balde, 157/47, adj. bold.

Baldely, 91/397, adv. boldly.

Bale, 5/102, 30/39, s. sorrow.

Balke, 339/68, s. a large beam of wood.

Ban, 48/95, s. bone.

Bande, 122/112, s. a ribbon or string.

Bandome, 255/20, s. for bandon, subjection, disposal, discretion.

Banne, 26/127, 155/279, v. to curse.

Baran, 99/184, adj. barren.

Barenhede, 56/5, s. childhood.

Barett, 179/27, s. strife, struggle, trouble.

Bargayne, bargane, 26/119, 49/126, 130, s. strife, combat; 103/23, bargain, arrangement, affair.

Bary, 334/428, v. thrash or thresh (Icel. berja).

Barme, 77/153, s. bosom.

Barnes, 67/374, s. children.

Battis, 334/429, s. batt, a beating.

Bede, 50/170, 91/398, v. to bid, offer, proffer.

Be-dene, 2/14, presently, immediately, forthwith, but often a mere expletive to fill up a line or make a rime (see Mätzner).

Bedilis, 283/316, s. beadles.

Beede, 198/141, s. prayers.

Beeldand, 4/87, pr. p. building, constructing.

Beelde, 2/35, 3/47, v. to build, form; make.

Beeld: see Belde.

Beeldyng, 2/38, v. s. shelter, protection.

Beere, 72/75. v. bear, carry.

Beeths, 79/197, v. imper. be: see Bese.

Begylyd, 215/453, v. deceived, injured.

Be-heest, 208/233, v. promised.

Behete, 64/272, 120/57, v. promise, assure.

Be-hewede, 424/97, pa. p. coloured.

Behoves, 41/53, v. pr. s. must; behoves þe nede, thou needs must.

Beylde, 43/89, v. protect: see Belde.

Beyldly, 443/336, adj. protecting.

Be-kenne, 232/283, v. to give, commit, deliver; pa. p. Bekende, 457/45: see Kende.

Belamy, 275/128, 391/338, s. good friend (familiar expression).

Belde, 102/8, 112/14, 307/1, v. to protect, shelter, come under cover: see Beeld, Beylde, Bylde.

Belyng, 481/47, v. roaring, bellowing.

Belyue, 231/273, 497/17, adv. immediately, quickly, at once.

Belle, 228/195, 487/203, s. prize.

Belschere, 262/214, s. belsire, grandfather.

Be-mene, 235/58, v. mean, betoken.

Be-menes, 424/107, v. betokens, points out.

Bemes, 3/50, s. beams, rays.

Bemys, 499/63, s. trumpets.

Benke, 227/188, 510/327, s. bench.

Bente, 229/228, s. field, place.

Berande, 2/40, pr. p. bearing, behaving.

Berar, 2/36, s. bearer.

Berde, s. 105/78, 106/122, s. lady; sometimes applied to a man, 473/10.

Bere, 475/50, s. bier.

Bere, 25/81, v. persuade, induce.

Bere, 143/162, v. bear, carry.

Bering, 115/98, s. birth.

Bering, 474/31, s. burial.

Berne, 289/485, 307/11, s. a baron, knight.

Beseke, 65/287, v. beseech.

Bese, 11/46, 67/348; Bees, 96/84, v.
(3 *pers. pl. pres.*) are.

Beswyked, 31/69, *pa. p.* cheated, be-
trayed.

Be-taught, 219/5, *pa. p.* given up,
delivered : *see* Teche.

Bete, *v.* to amend, remedy; Beete, 353/
125, 424/110; Bait, 445/377.

Bete, 136/277, *v.* to beat; Bettis, 86/
316, beats; Bett, 136/278; Bette,
131/136, *pa. p.* beaten.

Be-tidde, 487/222, *pa. p.* befallen, hap-
pened to.

Betyng, 229/228, *s.* amends, satisfaction, *fig.* payment ; or possibly fuel,
kindling, *used fig.*

Bette, 153/211, *s. for* bete, bote, i.e.
help, remedy.

Bettir, 219/12, *v.* improve, amend.

Bewe, 291/538, *adj.* beau.

Bewsheris, 146/1, *s.* pl. beausires.
Bewcher, 148/76, sing.

Bewte, 228/195, *s.* beauty, fairness,
splendour.

Bewteis, 469/125, *s.* ? beauties.

Bib, 366/242, *v.* to drink.

Biddingis, 163/159, *s.* commandments.

Bide, 113/36, *v.* stay, abide, remain;
Bidand, 93/4, *pr. p.*

By, 119/19, *v.* buy.

By, 5/119; Bye, 281/259, *for* abye,
v. to abide, suffer for.

Bygged, 4/68, *pa. p.* built, made.

Byggly, 30/42, 473/10, *adj.* big-like,
commodious, immense, great, powerful.

Bygilid, 133/204, beguiled, deceived.

Bylde, 134/233, *v. for* bield, to protect.

Byn, 281/274, *prep.* be in, ben, within.

Byrde, 439/209, *s.* lady : *see* Berde.

Byrnande, 3/50, *pr. p.* burning.

Birrall, 217/505, *s.* beryl, a precious
stone.

Blayne, 86/316, *s.* blain, sore.

Blakkeste, 5/101, *adj.* most black.

Blanne : *see* Blynne.

Blee, 1/5, 220/20, 251/259, *s.* colour,
complexion.

Blenke, 251/259, *s.* blench.

Blynne, 50/165, 335/461, 352/106, *v.*

cease, stop, hold, stay ; Blanne,
400/92, *pa. t.*; Blynnande, 479/179,
pr. p.

Blisshes, 334/433, *v.* blushes.

Blyst, 96/84, *s.* blest, i.e. blest creature.

Blithes, 123/13. *v.* enjoys.

Blonderande, 123/4, *pr. p.* stirring up.

Blondre, 333/403, *s.* blustering, disturbance.

Bloo, 334/433, 507/256, *s.* blue, livid
(applied to flesh after it is beaten).

Blore, 227/187, Blure, 85/294, *s.* blast,
noise, bluster.

Blowe, 297/142, *v.* to breathe.

Boddis, 302/293, *s.* orders, bidding.

Bodeword, 58/66, *s.* command, message.

Boght he, 151/171, *s. error for*
Borghe, (borough or town).

Boyste, 225/131, *s.* box.

Bolned, 370/370, *pa. p.* swollen.

Bone, for boune, 65/283, *adj.* ready.

Bone, 64/252; 88/350, *s.* boon, petition, asking.

Boodword, 76/132, *s.* message, command.

Boore (*for* Bore), 352/99; Booryngis, 353/146, bores, holes for nails.

Bordand, 159/80, *v.* jesting, talking.

Bordis, 154/246, *s.* jests; *see* Bourde.

Borowe, 30/40, 303/308, *v.* to lay a
pledge for ; 318/352, 507/270, to
obtain upon a pledge.

Bote, 50/170, *s.* help, remedy, healing.

Botment, 149/90, *s. for* abatement, lessening.

Bott, 234/51, *conj. for* but, unless.

Boudisch, 298/172, *adj.* sulky.

Boune, 286/380, *v.* to go, advance,
with a sense of limit (to be bound for
a place).

Boune, 35/15, *adj.* ready ; 39/113,
done, ready.

Bountith, 122/118, *s.* bounty.

Bourde, 266/329; Bowrde, 47/66, *v.*
to jest, parry words.

Bourded to brede, 267/333, 362/95,
spoke or jested too broadly, i. e.
boastingly.

Boure, 96/76, *s.* bower, chamber.

Boustous, 356/218, mighty-big, huge;

'This cros is large in lengthe and also bustus,' Towneley M., p. 212 (*see* Mätzner): boastful, Hampole's Psalter, ed. Bramley.

Bowde, 43/119, *adj.* bold.

Bowe, 43/110, *s.* bow or arch, the arched frame on which the ship is built. Cf. 'a bowe of a bryge,' in *Catholicon Anglicum*, ed. E.E.T.S.

Bowis, 10/35, *s.* boughs.

Bowrde, 47/66, *v.* to jest.

Bowsom, 198/141, *v.* buxom, obedient.

Brace furth, 123/13, to press or squeeze forth.

Bragges, 340/95, *s.* ? brads, short strong nails.

Brayde, 26/127, 62/188, 352/96, *s.* hasty action, sudden start, or blow.

Brayed, 259/142, *v. for* abrayed, suddenly drew (a sword).

Bralland, 321/17, *pr. p.* brawling, shrieking, shouting.

Brande, 259/142, *s.* sword.

Brandyng, 159/89, *error for* bourding, jesting.

Braste, 291/526, *pa. p.* braced.

Brathe, 221/37, 225/132, *adj.* fierce, excessive.

Brede, 162/142, *s.* broad, *on-brede*, abroad, extended : *see* **Brode**.

Brede, 180/57, *s.* bread.

Breder, 121/86, *s.* brothers.

Brent, 5/107, *pa. p.* burnt.

Brere, 220/20, *s.* briar.

Breste, 219/4, 236/103, *v.* burst.

Brethell, 263/239, *s.* wretch.

Breue, 203/62, *adj.* brief, short.

Brewe, 236/107, *v.* brew, boil, stir up.

Bryge, 27/143, 132/182, *s.* strife, contention, trouble.

Brighthode, 3/50, *s.* brightness.

Bryme, 195/53, 282/300, *adj.* fierce.

Bryne, 5 /110, *v.* burn : *see* **Brent**.

Brittyn, 292/9, *v.* to break or cut up (with a sword) ; **Brittynd**, 62/195, *pa. p.*

Bro, 150/135, *s.* broth, anything brewed or boiled, hence figuratively a brew or a stir.

Brode, 149/89, *adj.* broad : *see* **Brede**.

Brode, 267/333, *adv.* broadly, widely.

Broydenesse, 292/1, *s.* breadth.

Brokke, 258/117, *s.* badger.

Brondis vnbrent, 266/320, unburnt swords, i. e. staves.

Brosid, 345/244, *v.* bruised.

Brothell, 154/265, *s.* wretch, bad fellow : *see* **Brethell.**

Browle, 124/38, 152/196, *s.* brat, child (contemptuously).

Bud, 43/99, 219/3 ; **Bus**, 47/64, *pres. t.* must, behoves.

Bun, 11/54, *adj.* bound.

Burde, 263/245, *s.* jest, joke.

Burdes, 42/75, *s.* boards, planks.

Burdis, 149/89, *v.* talkest ; 188/86, *s.* speech, talking ; *same as* **Bourde**, *which see.*

Burely, 328/254, *adj.* burly, big, strong.

Burgeis, 216/485, *s.* burgesses.

Burguns, 10/40, *s.* buds.

Bus, 47/64, *v.* pres. pl. must : *see* **Behoves.**

Busk, 74/101, *s.* bush.

Busk 102/8, *v.* to attire ; to bustle.

Buskand, 274/87, *pr. p.* making ready.

Bute, 74/96, *v.* behoved, was obliged.

Butte, 499/61, *adv.* only.

Buxumly, 2/40, *adv.* obediently, humbly : *see* **Bowsom.**

Cache, 131/145, *v.* to catch ; **Cached, Cacched**, 110/255, *pa. p.* caught ; 510/326, caught away, expelled.

Caistiffis, 481/30, *s.* caitiffs.

Can, 42/67, *v.* know.

Care, 124/36, *s.* grief, vexation.

Care, 274/91, 275/133, 278/201, 284/335, *v.* turn, wend ; **Caried**, *pa. p.* 280/257.

Carefull, 107/145, 481/20, *adj.* grievous, full of trouble.

Carls, 79/192, *s.* bond-men.

Carpe, 80/201, 106/140, 124/46, *v.* say, tell, talk, speak.

Carping, 148/69, *s.* talking, speech.

Casbalde, 343/194, *s.* bald-head, term of reproach.

Case, 284/335, *s.* cause.

Catel, 386/242, *s.* chattels, property.

Catteraks, 51/190, *s.* cataracts.

Caut, 183/183, 332/351, *adj.* artful, cautious.

Cautely, 303/309, *adv.* artfully.

Cautellis, 355/206, 358/278, *s.* cunning tricks, devices.

Cele, 160/109, *s. for* seel, bliss.

Chaas, 139/29, *v.* chose.

Charred, 321/32, *v.* ? stayed, turned aside.

Cheere, 15/27, 48/103, 58/67, 64/276, *s.* countenance, temper, behaviour.

Cheffe, 280/242, *v.* to arrive, to happen.

Chenys, 316/278, *v.* chains, binds.

Chesoune, 203/77, *s.* a reason, aphetic from *acheson* or *encheson.*

Cheveleres, 125/52, *s.* knights.

Chiffe, 204/94, *s.* chief.

Childe, 104/69, ? shield; God-childe, God shield, God forbid.

Chylding, 478/147, *s.* child-birth.

Childir, 59/109, 60/131, *s.* children.

Chyned, 279/212, *pa. p.* chained.

Chyualrus, 321/31, *adj.* chivalrous.

Choppe, 293/16, *v.* to put in (prison or chains).

Churles, 125/52, 280/242, *s.* low fellows, wretches.

Cyte, 210/283, *s.* city.

Cytte, 180/67, *s. for* syte, i. e. sorrow, grief.

Clakke, 344/211, *s.* clack, chattering.

Clappe, 324/143, *v.* to slap, to strike.

Clappe, 232/283, *v.* to enclose, to put in.

Clapped, 123/1, *pa. p.* couched, laid in or enclosed.

Clargy, 158/54, *s.* science, knowledge.

Clarifie, 187/67, 457/36, *v.* to glorify, make clear.

Cledde, 508/287, *v.* clothed, clad.

Cleepe, 231/258, *for* clepe, *v.* to call, name, say.

Cleyngked, 43/106, *v.* clenched.

Cleke, 280/240, *v.* clutch.

Clematis, 123/1, *s.* climates.

Clence, 332/376, *v.* to cleanse.

Clene, 9/24, 149/87, 309/75, *adj.* clean, pure, good, clear, separate.

Clerenes, 123/1, *s.* brightness, glory.

Clergy, 135/260, 308/29, *s.* science, learning.

Clipsis, 401/99, *s.* eclipses.

Cloghe, 120/52, *s.* clough or valley.

Closed, 94/29, *v.* enclosed.

Cloumsed, 191/201, *v.* shrunk or contracted (with fear), fixed, stupefied.

Clowte, 324/143, *v.* to clothe; Clowted, 325/152.

Clowte, 343/194, *s.* kerchief or napkin for the head; 49/120, a blow, a cuff.

Cobill, 122/112, *adj.* cobble, round nuts or stones. A string of nuts for the old game of cobnut may be intended in this line, 'two cobill notis vppon a bande.'

Cobittis, 51/201, *s.* cubits.

Colle, 119/39, we! colle! *interj.* of surprise.

Comberaunce, 229/217, *s.* hindrance.

Combered, 226/171, *v.* cumbered, hindered; Comeres, 344/211, *pr. t.*

Comenaunt, 229/234, 316/279, *s.* covenant, agreement.

Comende, 124/23, *v.* commend, praise.

Commodrys, 49/143, *s.* commothers, i. e. gossips, companions, (*see* Jamieson's Dict. s. v. Cummer).

Con, 99/168, *v.* to know: *see* Can.

Conant, 335/463, covenant.

Conjeon, 308/47, *s.* a dwarf or humpback, a term of contempt (*see* full discussion of this word in Dr. Skeat's Notes to Piers Plowman, Part IV, p. 241).

Connandly, 162/132; Conande, 124/31, *adv.* cunningly, with knowledge.

Consayte, 208/246, *s.* thought.

Consayue, 272/40, *v.* think, imagine.

Contek, 153/235, *s.* strife, quarrel.

Conversacion, 435/65, *s.* deportment, behaviour.

Convik, 290/505, 330/294, *adj.* convict, convinced.

Cope, 228/199, *s.* a cloak or cape.

Corde, 303/309, *v.* to accord.

Coriousenesse, 255/31, queerness, strangeness.

Corse, 206/164, 272/41, 48, *s.* body.

Coueres, 223/101, *v.* to recover, cure, aphetic for *acover,* to regain health.

Couthe, 70/26, 72/64, *v.* could, were able.

Covaites, 197/122; Coveyte, 209/256, *v.* greatly desire.

Couetise, 182/131, s. covetousness.

Cowde, 205/148, v. could *for* could tell, knew.

Crafte, 44/150, s. knowledge.

Crakid, 120/67, *pa. p.* cracked.

Craue, 95/47, v. to crave, ask earnestly, demand; 130/126, to inquire.

Crepillis, 255/36, s. cripple.

Croke, 168/240, v. crook, bow.

Cruchys, 213/376; Crouchis, 213/380, s. crutches.

Curses, 11/58, s. courses.

Curstely, 222/73, adv. cursedly.

Curtayse, 121/101, adv. courteous.

Daynetethly, 4/78, adv. daintily, with delight.

Dale, 4/78, s. dole, that which is dealt.

Dame, 502/162, v. condemn.

Dampned, 195/65, v. condemned.

Dare, 141/106, 146/6, v. to lie hid, to crouch with fear, to be in dismay; 240/2, daris, shrinks.

Dared for drede, 416/370, trembled, shrank for fear.

Darfely, 245/136, adv. cruelly, fiercely; Derfely, 245/131.

Dase, 102/11, s. days.

Daunger, 79/186, 80/212, s. feudal power, dominion, subjection; 431/151, delay, hesitation, *cf. Rom. of the Rose*, 2318.

Dawe, 288/449, s. day; *dose a-dawe*, put to death, kill.

Dede, 62/210, 350/21, s. death.

Dede, 64/266, 350/31, s. deed, action.

Dedeyned, 22/11, v. disdained.

Dees, 257/81; Dese, 255/19, s. dais.

Defayle, 246/146, v. to be wanting to.

Defaute, 158/58, 71, s. defect.

Deffame, 131/137, s. infamy.

Defende, 23/45, 213/384, v. forbid.

Defes, 26/129, v. deaves, to deafen, stun.

Defly, 27/165, adv. probably should be read *derfly*, grievously.

Defte, 4/92, adj. clever, dexterous.

Deyne, 240/1, adj. worthy.

Deyuer, 7/156, s. duty: *see* Deuer.

Delande, 4/78, 305/363, *pr. p.* dealing, distributing.

Dele, 51/200, 58/82, s. deal, i.e. a bit or piece; *sum dele*, somewhat.

Delfe, 72/75, v. delve.

Delyuer, 279/217, an exclamation of impatience, make haste!

Deme, 60/126, deem, judge; Demand, 136/273, *pr. p.*

Demers, 189/142, s. judges.

Denne, 488/238, s. valley.

Deraye, 47/78; Dray, 468/90, s. disorder, confusion.

Dere, 3/64, 61/153, s. harm, hurt, injury.

Dere, 1/11, 367/276, adj. precious.

Dere, 179/35, 323/83, v. to injure, hurt; Derand, 2/37, 223/89, *pr. p.*; Derede, 253/282, *pa. p.*

Derfely, 107 / 148, adv. grievously, heavily.

Derfenes, 223/90, s. badness, boldness, severity, gravity, trouble.

Derffe, 481/17, fierce, severe.

Derrest, 282/280, 486/199, adj. dearest, noblest, most warlike.

Derworth, 4/92, 321/28, adj. worthy of honour, precious.

Dese, 255/19, s. dais: *see* Dees.

Dette, 471/178, s. debt, duty.

Devell haue þe worde, 269/386, devil a word.

Deuer, 198/157, 364/156: Deyuer, 7/156, s. duty.

Deuyse, 42/79, v. arrange, set out.

Dewes, 4/92, interj. deuce! the deuce!

Dyamaunde, 217/518, s. diamond.

Dyder, 240/2, v. dither, tremble.

Dye, 396/9, v. kill.

Diewe, 273/61, v. due.

Diewly, 1/11, adv. duely.

Dight, 57/38, v. infin. dispose, make ready; Dight, 173/32, 503/183, Dyghte, 1/11, *pa. p.* dressed, made ready, prepared.

Dyke, 72/75, v. dig.

Dill, 27/138, adj. stupid, foolish.

Dyme, 206/152, adj. dim, difficult to understand.

Dyne, 42/80, s. noise; 142/148, *leue thy dyne*, stop thy noise.

Dyng, 91/399, v. to knock, strike.

Ding, 476/88, adj. worthy.

Dyngnyte, 16/55; Dynyte, 1/11, *s.* dignity.

Dyns, 32/114, *v.* resounds; *dyns ilk dele*, every part makes a noise.

Dynte, 39/127, *s.* a blow.

Discrie, 466/22, *v.* discover, make known openly.

Disease, 122/127, *v.* to hurt.

Disesse, 124/42, 496/152, *s.* discomfort, harm, hurt.

Dispitte, 215/466, *s.* anger, defiance.

Disputuously, 153/230, *adv.* angrily, cruelly, spitefully.

Dite, 319/381, *v.* to dispose, prepare: *see* Dight.

Doo, 41/45, make or cause; *doo fulfill*, cause to be done; Does, *imper.* 7/156; Done, *pa. p.* 291/532.

Doo to dede, 140/55, to do to death, to kill.

Doo, 252/266, ? an interjection.

Do, 253/297, 265/280, *v. intensive (auxiliary).*

Do telle, 129/80, speak.

Do way, 422/25, put away! have done! leave off!

Dochard, 230/239, *s.* fool, dotard.

Doderon, 319/385, *s.* doddering, totterer, stumbler, trembler.

Doyf-byrdes, 441/248, doves.

Dole, 5/98, 107, 26/129, *s.* grief.

Doluen, 199/189, *v.* dug (*from* delve).

Dome, 305/385, *adj.* dumb.

Doote, dote, 347/309, Dotist, 108/180, *v.* to be foolish, to doat, speak or act foolishly, as the aged.

Dote, 222/65, Doote, 349/5, *s.* fool.

Doufe, 52/237, *s.* dove: *see* Dowue, Doyf.

Doune commyng, 96/88, coming down, falling.

Doute, 87/326, 471/175, *s.* fear.

Doute, 124/42. 146/6, *v.* to fear.

Dowe, 431/151, *v.* to avail, be of use.

Downe, 10/30, *s.* hill.

Dowue, 376/78, *s.* dove.

Draffe, 511/338, *past t.* drove.

Dray, 468/90, *s. for* deray, disturbance, confusion.

Drays, 302/294, *s. for* draws, attempts.

Draught, 394/399, *s.* stratagem, artful scheme.

Drecchid, 277/177, *v.* tormented.

Drecchyng, 277/182, *s.* tormenting, suffering, passion, affliction.

Dredles, 105/90, without doubt.

Drely, 257/77, *adv.* slowly, continuously.

Dresse, 184/201, *v.* punish.

Dresse, 257/81, *v.* to make ready; *dresse pe boune*, 37/52.

Drewry, 217/518, *s.* ornament or jewel.

Dryff, 107/151; Draffe, *pa. t.* 511/338, *v.* drive.

Drynesch, 10/30, *s.* dryness.

Drofyng, 292/6, *s.* dregs, refuse.

Dubbyng, 219/7, *s.* ornamenting, clothing.

Dugeperes, 219/8, *s.* douze pairs, the twelve peers of France, *hence* great lords or knights.

Dule, 107/144, *s.* grief.

Dulye, 281/269; Dewly, 287/407, *adj.* due, fitting.

Durdan, 293/41, *s.* noise, uproar.

Dure, 95/66, *v.* last, endure.

Durk, 141/105, *v.* to hide, conceal oneself, i. e. in a dark place.

Dussh, 481/36, *v.* to push violently.

Dwelle, 166/198, *v.* remain, tarry; Dwellyng, 28/172, *pr. p.*

Efte, 274/105, *adv.* after.

Efte-sones, 244/101, *adv.* soon after, immediately.

Eftyr, 6/125, *adv.* after.

Egge, 256/40, *v.* to urge, incite.

Eghne, 65/288, *s.* eyes.

Eke, 12/68, 220/36, *v.* to increase, add to.

Elde, 43/91; Eelde, 57/32, *s.* age.

Elmys, 341/122, *s. perhaps for* almis = alms (but more probably a corruption).

Eme, 13/79, *s. for* ʒeme, care, attention; *how all pat eme is oght* (oght, due or owing to), how everything that care is owing to, i. e. how everything that ought to be done has been done.

Emel, emell, 6 / 146, 70 / 30, *prep.* among, amidst.

Enbraste, 111/276, *pa. p.* held by, surrounded by.

Encheson, 191/208, *s.* reason: *see* **A-chesoune.**

Endower, 19/26; **Endowre,** 19/30, *s.* endeavour.

Enew, 5/104, *adj.* enough.

Ensampelys, 206/170, *s.* examples, quotations.

Enserche, 490/290, 305, *v.* search out.

Ensewe, 36/33, *v.* follow after.

Entent, 11/50, 35/9, 210/282, 245/118, *s.* attention, heed; take tent, *or* entent, take heed, have regard to.

Entere, 38/101, *adj.* whole, entire.

Enterly, 35/9, 63/231, *adv.* wholly.

Equite, 213/393, *s.* equity.

Es, 3/41, is.

Euere ilkane, 106/133, *pron.* every one.

Eyre, 190/172, *s.* air.

Exynatores, 271/21, *s.* senators.

Fade, 6/132, *v.* to make foul.

Faded, 6/148, lost colour or light.

Fage, 324/125, *v.* to lie.

Fagyng, 290/513, *s.* lying, deceiving.

Fay, 436/94, 446/405, faith; *in fay,* i' faith.

Faie, 422/24, *adj.* fey, the state near death, fated to die.

Faynde, 62/205, *v.* go, set about, try: *see* **Fande.**

Fayndyngis, 235/84, *s.* trials.

Fayne, 89/360, 128/53, *adj.* glad.

Faynte, 263/229, *adj.* faint, poor, weak.

Fayntely, 246/146, *adv.* weakly.

Faire, 90/374; **Fayre,** 470/170, *for* fare, *s.* doing: *see* **Fare.**

Fayrear, 3/53, *adj.* fairer.

Fayre-hede, 6/129, *s.* fairness.

Fays, 79/198, *s.* foes.

Faythely, 2/19, *adv.* (=faytely), fitly, featly, properly, aptly. Fr. *faite.*

Faytour, 80/213, 124/27, 310/97, *s.* a conjuror, a quack and pretender, liar, deceiver.

Falle, 131/152, *v.* happen; *may-falle,* may-hap; *fallis,* 146/12, is due to.

Fande, 23/18, 80/202, 142/149, *v.* to attempt, try: *see* **Fonde.**

Fandelyng, 151/157, *s.* foñdelyngis, 152/193, fond or silly ones; sometimes a term of endearment, sometimes of contempt (*read* fondlings *in margin*).

Fandyng, 30/47, 240/12, 241/31, *s.* temptation, trial.

Fange, 24/79, 50/174, 88/355, 423/48, *v.* take, lay hold of, catch.

Fantassy, 106/142, *s.* fancy.

Fantome, 282/297, *s.* spirit, imagination.

Fare, 48/90, 58/78, *s.* doing, proceeding, action.

Faren, 86/303, *v.* (3 *pers. pl. pres.*) fare, experience, feel; **Fore,** 511/336, *pa. t.*

Farly, 173/22, *s.* a wonder; **Farles,** 288/442, *pl.* wonders, miracles.

Farre, 86/307, *adv.* far.

Fauchone, 301/246, *s.* falchion.

Fauty, 430/130, *adj.* faulty, defect.

Fawlde, 43/113, *v.* to fold, bend: here strained to mean break down, fail.

Fecche, 450/70, *s.* fish.

Fedd, 94/25, *pa. p.* fed; *fedd be tyne,* fed with vexation, deceived; *cf.* to fode out with words, to deceive, Halliwell's Dict. ; *s. v. fode.*

Fede, 108/186, *v.* feed, nourish, bring up.

Fee, 71/58, *s.* cattle; 423/48, *s.* property; *fange unto my fee,* take as my own property.

Feele, 43/108, 58/78, *v. pass.* to be felt, to be perceived.

Feylle, 51/202, ? to feel.

Feere, 58/71, *s.* company.

Feese, 287/424, 124/40, *v.* harass, worry, punish; **Fesid,** *pa. p.* 326/196.

Feest, 119/44, *s.* feast, good thing.

Feetour, 308/18, *s.* elegance, neatness.

Fekyll, 37/63, *adj.* fickle.

Felawe, 110/248, *s.* companion.

Fele, *adj.* many.

Felesome, 485/136, *adj.* tasty, agreeable.

Fell, 482/73, *s.* skin.

Fell, 12/63, 119/34, *s.* a hill, an upland pasture.

Fell, 220/18; **Felle,** 151/157, *v.* feel.

Felle, 353/136; **Fellest,** 114/72, *superl.* cruel, sharp; **Felly,** 31/64, *adv.* cruelly, badly, sharply.

Feloune, 124/34, *s.* wickedness.
Felowe, 193/3, *s.* fellow, applied to a woman.
Fende, **feende**, 94/24, 25, 269/396, *s.* fiend; **Feendis**, 97/116, the enemy, i. e. Satan.
Fende, 9/10, *v.* defend, prevent.
Fendes-craft, 282/297, *s.* devilry.
Fene me, 143/168, *for* feyne, to feign, pretend (reflexive).
Fenne, 39/126, *s.* marsh.
Ferde, 62/211, *adj.* feared, afraid.
Ferdnes, **ferdnesse**, 244/89, 499/78, *s.* fear, terror.
Fere, *s.* companion, 10/29, *in fere*, in company.
Fere, 478/155, *v.* to frighten.
Ferly, 41/40, *s.* wonder; 58/78, *adj.* wondrous, strange.
Ferre, 87/333, 86/307, *adv.* farther.
Fersly, 482/73, *adv.* freshly, a-new.
Fervent, 257/96, *adj.* hot.
Fesid, 326/196, *pa. p.* harassed, worried: *see* **Feese**.
Feste, 202/20, *s.* feast.
Feste, 392/340, *v.* bind; 391/335, *pa. p.* bound.
Festynde, 10/29, *pres. p.* fastening, joining.
Fett, 203/63; **Fette**, 136/280, 394/382, *v.* to fetch, fetched.
Fettis, 125/50; **Fetys**, 3/55, 65, *adj.* neat, pretty, elegant.
Fewell, 113/44, *s.* fuel.
Fewle, 18/5, 13, 19/28, 44/125, *s.* fowls.
Fewne, 174/72, *adj.* few.
Fygure, 6/140; **Figour**, 482/73, face, image.
Fygured, 3/65, *pa. pt.* formed, shaped.
Filde, 488/241, *adj.* polite.
Filed, 341/125, *v.* defiled.
Fyne, 46/51, *v.* to stay, end: **Fynyd**, 54/287, *pa. p.*
Fyrd, 441/248, *probably for* fered, i. e. frightened away, rejected.
Firth, 12/63, *s.* a wood or coppice.
Fitte, 392/346, *s.* match, equal.
Fytt, 3/65, *adj.* fit, pretty (*see* **Faytely** and **Fetys**).
Flaye, 252/270, 295/94, *v.* to frighten.
Fleme, 257/96, to flee, get away;

305/383, to banish; **flemyd**, 141/98, *pa. p.*
Flet, 12/64, *v.* to swim.
Flighte, 128/76, *s.* a scolding.
Flyte, 358/297, *v.* to scold.
Flitte, 47/58, 119/34, 137/333, to remove, leave house.
Flodde, 258/127, *s.* ? *for* fold, i. e. ground, earth, world. Perhaps it is a corruption, we expect here a word beginning with w.
Flowyd, 41/27, *s.* flood.
Flume, 376/76, *s.* river.
Fode, 4/76, 79, 5/106, *s.* food, victuals.
Fode, 275/110, 474/32, *s.*: *see* **Foode**.
Fole, 6/129, *s.* fool.
Folle, 131/138, *v. for* falle.
Folte, 315/261, *s.* stupid one, fool.
Fonde, 303/329; **Fonned**, 304/338, *adj.* silly.
Fonde, 479/187, *v.* to go : *see* **Founde**.
Fonde, 48/80, 169/264, *v.* to try, to inquire, discover: *see* **Fande**.
Fone, 219/11, 368/284; **Fune**, 462/202; **Fewne**, 174/72, *adj.* few.
Fonnes, 48/89, *v.* grows silly or foolish.
Foode, 115/91, 373/10, 474/32, *s.* creature, being, whether man, woman, girl, or boy; *frely foode*, noble creature.
Foole, 202/22, *s.* foal.
For, 31/69, 57/49, *conj.* because.
For, sometimes = fro.
For-bere, 283/325, *v.* to forbear, be over mild with.
For-bledde, 344/224, 345/244, *pa. p.* exhausted with bleeding.
Force, 221/55, *s.* power, dignity.
Force, 80/211, *s.* care, argument; *I make no force*, I do not care; 353/136, *no force*, no matter.
Fordede, 175/107, *s.* a deed beforehand, preparation.
Fordele, 121/107, *s.* advantage.
For-do, 142/121, *v.* kill; 316/282, to ruin.
Fore, 511/336, *past t.* fared.
Fore-reyner, 172/16, *s.* fore-runner.
For-fare, 142/140, *v.* to perish, to destroy.
Forfettis, 283/325, *s.* transgressions, crimes.

Forfette, 295/95, *v.* to transgress.

For-gange, 141/101, *v.* for-go.

Forges, 124/34, 459/118, *v.* commit, fabricate.

For-marryde, 6/139, *pa. p.* completely marred, spoilt.

Formaste, 1/4, sup. of *forme*, first.

Forme, 45/14, 97/110, *adj.* first, fore; *forme ffadres,* first parents, ancestors; 3/66, ? chiefest.

Forsake, 105/107, *v.* to deny; Forsaken, 260/167; Forsaked, 511/348, *pa. p.*; Forsuke, 216/474, *past t.* forsook.

Fortheren, 143/168, 269/394, *v.* to further, advance.

For-thy, 21/90, 53/265, *conj.* therefore.

For-wakid, 240/5, *pa. p.* over-watched, have watched very long.

For-wandered, 110/250, having much wandered.

Forward, 62/212, 133/193, *s.* promise, paction, agreement; 283/306, order, command.

Forward, 156/14, *adv.* henceforth.

For-wente, 276/152, *adj.* over-done.

Fouchesaffe, 196/101, *v.* vouchsafe.

Founde, 23/24, 32/96, 291/546, *v.* to go, go forward, set out; Foune, 56/12, *pa. p.* Foundynge, 484/125, *pres. pt.*

Foure, 86/308, ? *error for* fare.

Frayne, 48/90, 62/185; Freyne, 128/51; Frande, 109/225, *v.* to ask, inquire.

Frappe, 330/310, *v.* to brag, to talk violently.

Fraste, fraiste, frayste, 12/71, 428/48, 431/158, *v.* to try, prove, taste.

Free, 170/269, 409/256, *adj.* fine, noble, open, clear; *lordis free,* a polite address; 206/183, *adj. as s.* fine fellow.

Freele, 174/84, *adj.* frail.

Freese, 114/72, *s.* frost.

Freykenesse, 292/2, *s.* boldness, courage.

Freyne : *see* Frayne.

Freke, 287/415, 292/2, *s.* a bold man, hero, fellow.

Frekly, 91/394, *adv.* hastily, bravely.

Frely, 121/78, *adj.* noble, fair.

Frely foode, 492/31, noble creature.

Fresshely, 291/546, *adv.* briskly, quickly: *see* Fersly.

Frith, 39/126, *s.* a wood or coppice; 284/344, field, open space.

Fro, 89/364, *adv.* when.

Frosshis, 84/271, *s.* frogs.

Frusshe, 268/363, *v.* to bruise, knock, or hurt.

Fudde, 83/262, *s.* food.

Fulfille, 40/12, *v.* to fill full.

Full, 3/60, *v.* to foul.

Fune, 188/100; Fun, 98/155, *pa. p.* found, tried: *see* Fande.

Gabbe, 104/48, 106/141, *v.* to lie, to jest.

Gabbyngis, 157/26, *s.* chatterings, idle talk.

Gadling, 148/63; Gedling, 148/68, *s.* vagabond.

Gaffe, 29/14, *pa. t.* of give; *gaffe they noght,* &c., they did not hesitate to grieve God.

Gayne, 44/140, 405/179, *v.* gain, be useful or suitable.

Gaynestandyng, 58/55, withstanding; *noght gaynestandyng,* notwithstanding.

Gales, 321/23, *v.* screams.

Galylee, 173/53.

Ganeste, 59/90; Gaynest, 67/373, *adj. sup.* directest, nearest.

Gange, 34/161, *v.* to go.

Gar, 75/127; Garre, 86/308; Gares, 5/103, *v. pres. t.* make, cause; Garte, 27/142, 127/45, 370/382, *pa. p.* made, caused.

Gast, 101/239, *s.* spirit.

Gate, 511/332, *s.* road or way.

Gate, 279/229; Gatte, 48/98, *s.* way, road; *go my gatte,* go away.

Gawdes, 70/37, 82/248, *s.* tricks.

Gedy, 224/105, *adj.* giddy, heedless.

Gedling : *see* Gadling.

Genolgie, 271/29; Genolagye, 208/242, *s.* genealogy.

Gente, 247/161, 427/19, *adj.* gentle, courteous.

Gere, 111/301, 143/160, *s.* gear, personal things, clothing.

Ges, 11/47, v. guess; here perhaps resolve, hit upon, or decide upon.

Gesse, 13/84, 192/220, v. guess.

Geste, 369/339, s. deed or action.

Gyffe, 32/107, 58/68, conj. if.

Gyffe, 378/114, v. give: see Gaffe.

Gilery, 381/160, s. deceit.

Gynn, 43/101; Gynne, 355/197, s. a catch or contrivance.

Gyrne, 321/23, v. to grin; Gyr-nande, 5/103, pres. p. grinning.

Gyrse, 40/4, s. grass.

Gyrth = grith, 6/133, v. to protect; 50/154, s. safety, protection.

Gyrth, 445/396, s. for gryth, grace, peace.

Glade, 135/272, v. glided.

Glee, 4/82, 34/162, s. joy, happiness.

Gleme, 135/272, 191/186, s. gleam, brightness.

Glent, 179/38, s. start, glance.

Gleteryng, 4/82, v. s. glittering.

Glyfftyng, 226/158, s. glance, look.

Glorand, 226/157, v. staring.

Gloueres, 35, s. glovers.

Golling, 280/235, s. rushing and violence.

Gome, 154/255, 221/52, s. man, fellow.

Gowlande, 5/103, pres. p. howling.

Grayth, 94/19, v. to prepare; 190/171, prepares, frames; grayth euen, to make even, to at-one; grath hym no gate, 308/15, make ready to go; Grathid, 62/186, Graied, 251/245, Grayd, 98/141, 99/190, pa. p. prepared.

Gramercy, 105/92, great thanks.

Granyng, 428/59, s. groaning.

Grathe, 133/195, adv. directly.

Grathely, 11/46, 42/85, 61/174, 101/225, adv. properly, strictly, ready, straightly, exactly.

Graue, 369/338, v. to bury; Graued, 197/140, pa. p. buried.

Grauyng, 136/286, s. burial.

Gree, 369/338, in gree, in or under favour.

Gres, 11/46, s. grass.

Grete, 407/203, 411/284, s. grit, gravel, earth.

Grete, 144/192, s. weeping, crying.

Grette, 207/191, 494/110, s. greeted.

Greve, 194/42, v. to vex, injure.

Grewes, 132/164, v. grows.

Grill, 327/220, adj. stern, cruel, horrible.

Grise, 314/212, s. horror.

Grissely, 425/116, adv. frightfully.

Grith, 131/150, s. peace, safe conduct.

Groche, 61/177, v. grumble, murmur.

Gromys, 301/251, s. men.

Grope, 188/104, v. to feel, search, sound. (See Geneva Test., Acts xxiv.)

Grouche, 37/70, v. to grudge, grumble, murmur; Grucchand, 184/206, part. pres.

Growe, 226/158, v. become frightened, troubled.

Grughe, 289/473, = Grouche.

Grume, 219/13, s. a man.

Gud, 215/450, s. goods, money.

Gulles, 124/19, s. probably read gules, the heraldic term for red, which is here set off against gold. (In margin read gules.)

Gun, gune, for begun, 369/350, 370/352.

Gwisse, 273/68, for iwiss, certainly.

Haale, 352/116, v. to haul.

Haftis, 158/76, s. heft; affairs, matters, same as heft, chief part of one's business.

Haile, 352/116, s. salute.

Hayre, 69/7, s. heir.

Hale, 11 / 54, 77 / 155, adj. whole, healthy.

Hales out, 333/400, v. falls, draws out.

Halfe, 207/192, s. behalf.

Halfe, 426/3, for v. have.

Haly, 2/27, adv. wholly.

Halse, 224/104, s. neck.

Halse, 376/64, 445/382, v. to embrace.

Halsyng, 98/149, 100/213, s. salutation.

Hane, 253/285, s. ? error for bane = bone (but the alliteration requires hane).

Happe, 121/90, 469/118, s. chance, fortune, good luck.

Happe, 116/120, 144/195, v. to wrap up, to clothe.

Happenyng, 255/39, s. chance, luck.

Happing, 257/82, s. a coverlet, covering.

Har, 332/353, v. hear.

Hardely, 85/286, adv. boldly, certainly.

Harle, 344/227, v. to drag; Harlid, 282/290, pa. p.; Harling, 480/5, v. s.

Harnes, 333/400, s. brain.

Harnes, 143/161; Harnays, 121/102, s. ornament, household things, or clothes.

Harre, 286/378, 297/143, 324/136, s. (O. E. heorr) a hinge; figuratively, cardinal point, important matter; out of harre, out of joint, out of order.

Harro, 437/119, v. to harry = Herry; Heryd, 498/33, pa. t.

Harrowe, 295/84, 377/98, s. shouting, disturbance, cry, uproar.

Harrowe! 5/97, 383/185, 392/343, interj. a cry for help; 325/162, hallo! Harstow, 326/185; Harste, 228/208, hearest thou.

Hartely, 42/69, 43/90, adv. heartily; 185/3, closely, to heart.

Hartely, 246/140, adj. hearty, professing.

Hartyng, 128/56, 130/115, s. encouragement.

Hate, 220/27, adj. hot.

Hatereden, 309/56, s. hatred.

Haterell, 304/342, s. dress, attire.

Hatyll, 145/223; Hatell, 330/293, s. nobleman, prince, or knight (O. E. aethel).

Hatir, 267/360, s. a dress, garment, vestment.

Hatte, 213/404, v. hate.

Haues, 36/28, v. pres. has; Hais, 38/83, pres. s. hast; 38/86, has (16th cent. piece); Hays, 40/13, pres. pl. have: see Halfe.

Haugh, 19/35, s. river-side meadow.

Hauk, 253/298, s. hawk.

Hautand, 15/27, adj. haughty, proud.

Hede, 397/20, s. head; with a hole hede, with one voice.

Hedesman, 480/5, 481/25, s. chief man, chieftain.

Hedgyd, 439/205, v. closed in, limited, shown.

Heele, 60/140, 121/90, s. health, salvation.

Heete, 85/286, v. promise.

Hefe, 91/401, v. heave, lift.

Hegh, 8/4, adj. high.

Heynde, 295/97, s. hind, low fellow.

Heyne, 367/272, adv. hence.

Heyned, 283/309, v. tarried, waited.

Heldand, 1/6; Heledande, 4/95, pres. p. going down, descending: see Helde.

Helde, 182/147, ; Heyld, 442/306, v. yield, move; Heild, 36/21; Hilded, 326/188, past t.

Hele, 129/102, s. health, safety.

Helesome, 485/138, adj. full of healing, helpful.

Helte full, 228/198, for hilte-full, i. e. full to the hilt.

Hende, 36/44, 75/123, adj. gentle, well-disposed, civil, polite; as sb. 451/101.

Hendly, 187/77, adv. with kindness, gently.

Henne-harte, 326/198, adj. chicken-hearted.

Hente, 11/47, 77/150, v. seize, take hold of, catch.

Hepe, heppe, 150/132, 231/260, s. a company, troop, lot.

Herand, 168/233, s. errand.

Herbar, 122/125, v. harbour, contain.

Herbered, 44/137, 112/11, pa. p. harboured, lodged.

Herberles, 512/352, adj. without shelter.

Herberow, 112/6, s. harbour, lodging.

Herdes, 71/58, s. herdsmen.

Here, 118/1, 139/46, v. hear; Heriste, 313/200, hearest.

Heryed: see Harro.

Hermonye, 53/264, Armenia.

Herre: see Harre.

Herre, 211/325, s. ear.

Herrowe! 48/99, interj. halloo! see Harrowe.

Heste, 120/47, s. east.

Hete, 229/223, Hette, 181/114, v. promise.

Hethyng, 107/151, 255/32, s. scorn, mockery, derision, contempt.

Hettyng, 46/22; Hetyngis, 462/187, pl. s. promise.

Heuenyng, 316/284, s. vengeance.

Heuen-ryke, 96/101, s. the kingdom of heaven.

Hewuyn, 9/17, s. heaven.

Hydande, 1/6, *pr. p.* hiding.

Hyde and hewe, 40/22, skin and colour.

Hye, high; *in hye, on hye,* expression frequently used to emphasize a sentence or fill up a line, 41/46, 53/261, 366/229.

Hye, 211/329, *s.* eye.

Hy, hye, *v.* to make haste.

High, 173/26, *adj.* loud.

Hight, 129/84, 461/185, *pa. p.* promised; *also* called, named (O.E. *hátan*).

Hilded, 326/188, *v.* yielded, inclined, bowed: *see* Helde.

Hille, 257/82, 308/21, *v.* to cover, shelter.

Hyne, 167/228, *adv.* hence.

Hyne, 253/291, 406/197, *s.* servant, hind.

Hyre, 61/167, 387/260, *s.* payment, reward.

Hythyn, 59/89, *adv.* hence.

Hytist (þou), 229/225, *v.* art thou named, called: *see* Hight.

Hyve, 228/198, *s.*, probably a corruption for *hyne,* i.e. servant, fellow, the old copyist reading *n* as *u,* and by ear writing *v.*

Hoyly, 40/22, *adv.* wholly.

Hold, hald, 461/185, *v.* to keep; 469/113, perform (a promise).

Hone, 88/352, 349/13, *v.* delay, wait; Honed, 271/35.

Hoo, 19/36, *s.* a height, hill; *many one hoo,* many on hill, in opposition to the haugh or level ground of the previous line.

Hoo, 290/507, ?*for* oo, i. e. ever, continually.

Hope, 84/275, 147/46, 149/93, *v.* to think, opine, expect, consider.

Hopp illa hayle! 82/245, ejaculation of surprise.

Hore, 308/21, *s.* hair.

Hover, 88/352, *v.* to stop, wait, hover; Houerand, 53/252, *pr. p.*

Houe, 294/73, *v.* stop, wait.

Howe, 152/182, 189, *adv.* in what manner.

Howe-gates, 229/227, *adv.* in what manner.

Hudde: *see* We!

Hune, Hone, 209/272, *s.* delay.

Hurled, 259/139, *pa. p. for* harled, dragged.

Hurth, 427/34, *s.* hurt.

Jangill, 273/59, 307/14, *s.* prating.

Iangillande, 36/47, *adj.* jangling, quarrelsome.

Jape, 36/47, 178/6, *s.* trick, jest, or mock.

Jappis, 280/235, *v.* chatter.

Jappon, 304/344, *s.* a jest, gibe.

Javell, 273 / 59, *v.* to contend, to wrangle.

Javellis, 280/235, *s.* contentions.

Jeauntis, 292/13, *s.* giants.

Jessen, 86/303, 87/321, = Gessen, Goshen.

If all, 220/20, *conj.* although.

Ile, 2/26, isle.

Ille hayle! 253/287, exclamation of aversion or surprise: *see* Hopp!

Ingendis, 292/13, *s.* engines, machines.

In like, 43/99, alike.

In-mange, 103/31 *prep.* among.

Insens, 136/275, *s.* incense.

Instore, 242/45, *v.* to renovate, to strengthen.

Jolle, 307/14, *v.* to knock about.

Jorneys, 242/49, days, day's work.

Jourdane, 173/54, Jordan.

Ire, 42/57, *s.* anger.

Irke, 401/113, *adj.* tired, oppressed.

Itt, *pron.* 6/127; It, 43/100.

Itt, 162/134, *conj.* yet.

Juggemen, 427/25, *s.* judges, domesmen.

Iune, 43/101, 247/161, *v.* to join.

Jury, 130/127, 211/312, *s.* Jewry, Judea.

I-wys = Ʒewiss, certainly, surely; generally used as an expletive.

Kacchid, 243/65, *v.* caught.

Kaydyfnes, 505/237, *s.* wretchedness, captivity.

Kayssaris, 123/15, *s.* emperors.

Kele, 51/198, 300/225, *v.* cool, assuage.

Kempis, 291/521, *s.* knights, soldiers.

Kende, 34/154, 425/129, *v.* taught, gave, delivered to.

Kene, 151/150, *adj.* keen, eager : *see* Kyne.

Kenne, 70/25, 241/29, 32, *v.* to teach, give in hand ; 45/8, to know : *see* Can.

Kepe, 110/247, 423/73, *s.* care, heed ; *take kepe*, take care.

Keste, 317/319, *pa. p.* of cast.

Keuellis, 327/219, *s.* poles, staves.

Kyd : *see* Kythe.

Kynde, 62/209, 94/21, *s.* nature.

Kynde, 7/155, *adj.* natural.

Kyndynes, 123/15, *s.* feeling of kindred.

Kyndis, 9/24, *pl.*, 238/163, tribes.

-Kyn = kind, *adj. suffix* : *see* All-kyn, What-kynne, No-kynne.

Kyne, 30/46, *adj.* keen.

Kynne, 121/101, *s.* kindred, family.

Kynreden, 221/60, *s.* kindred.

Kythe, 123/15, *v.* show ; Kyd, 36/25 ; Kydde, 227/192, 135/242, *pa. p.* shown, discovered.

Kyth, 39/122, 135/260, 141/91, *s.* kith, race, kindred, own people.

Knave, 121/100, 140/56, 301/264, *s.* boy, lad, young fellow.

Knyght, 151/150, 154/244, *s.* soldier.

Knyth, 33 / 135, *v. for* gnith, contracted form of gnideth (like graydeth, grayth), gnide, to rub, fret, or irritate.

Knytte, 360/26, *v.* tied, bound.

Knowynge, *s.* knowledge.

Konne, 70/25, 16/75, *v.* to know, can, able.

Lache, 230/253, *v.* to catch, take ; Laughte, 280/254, *pa. p.*

Ladde, 344/225, *s.* load, burden.

Ladde, 81/217, 83/259, *s.* common person, young fellow (used depreciatorily), young serving man.

Laght, 329/286, *v.* drawn, taken.

Laye, 66/346, 308/40 ; Laie, 290/501, *s.* law ; Layse, 71/44, 273 *note, pl.* laws.

Layke, 261/192, *s.* game, play, pleasure.

Laykis, 230/238, *v.* to play, make game or fun of.

Layne, 186/48, *s.* loan.

Layne, 62/187, 109/227, *v.* hide, conceal ; 48/88, *passive.*

Laynyng, 204/101, *s.* concealment.

Layre, 299/213, *s.* soil, ground.

Layre, 78/181, *s.* lore, lesson.

Layte, 151/154, 408/233, *v.* to seek.

Laith, 430/132, *adj.* loath.

Laytheste, 5/100, *adj.* most loathly.

Lak, 74/109, *s.* lack, defect, want, fail ; *withouten lak*, without fail.

Lakke, 111/298, *v.* lack, want, be without.

Lame, 441/246, *s.* lamb.

Lame, 421/5, *s.* loam, clay.

Lane, 56/4, 58/60, *s.* loan.

Lange, 221/45, *adv.* long, much ; *to lange*, too much ; Lengar, 62/187, longer.

Lang are, 111/300, *adv.* long ago.

Lang, 461/156, *v.* to stay.

Lang, 215/442, *v.* to belong.

Lappe, 330/311, *v.* to lap ; *fig.* to lay hold of ; Lappid, 272/51, *pa. p.* wrapped round, embraced ; 480/3, supported, held.

Lare, 48/105 ; Layre, 78/181, *s.* lore, learning.

Largely (large), 290/493, *adj.* big, presumptuous (applied to language).

Lat = let, 5/120, *v.* ; *lat loke*, do look.

Late, 130/111, 131/134, 476/106, *v.* to seek, endeavour.

Lath, 50/147, *adj.* loath ; *full lath*, loathfull.

Lathis, 107/149, *v.* loathes.

Laugher, 281/275, *adj.* lower.

Laughte, 280/254, *pa. p.* taken, caught : *see* Lache.

Lawe, 214/418, *adj.* low (in height).

Lawe, 279/225, *v.* to humble, bring low.

Lawmere, 298/180, *s.* a term of reproach, sluggard, lown-like man : *see lowmyshe* in Prompt. Parv. ; *loamy* in Jamieson ; (Skeat's Dict., *s. v. loon*).

Leche, 160/102, *s.* doctor, physician.

Leche, 131/156, 264/266, *v.* to cure, to heal, doctor.

Lede, 36/32, 140/70, 192/234, *s.* person, man ; 422/17, being.

Lede, 10/38, *s.* ; 376/70, 476/97, people, country : ' land and lede,' Arthur and Merlin, p. 4.

Ledir, 276/148, 280/254; *adj.* lither, bad.

Lee, 280/248, s. pleasure, delight.

Leede, 139/21, s. lead.

Leeffe, 486/174, s. leaf.

Leere, 391/321, v. learn.

Lefe, 41/29, 105/101, v. leave, stop!

Lefe, 110/249, adv. soon, willingly;
Lever, 237/138, comp. rather.

Leffand, 192/234, adj. living.

Leffe, leeffe, 51/185, 426/8, 12, adj.
dear, pleasant.

Legge, 131/147, 221/45, v. allege.

Legh, 297/158, s. for lygh (see ll. 161,
162), lie.

Leythly, 12/72, adv. lightly, easily.

Lele, 165/185, adj. leal, true.

Lely, 9/17, 158/64, adv. lealy, loyally,
truly.

Lelly, 96/91, s. lilly.

Leman, 193/8, s. lover.

Lemed, 476/96, v. shone.

Lemer, 115/111, s. beamer, formed on
leme, a flame, ray, or beam; lemer
of light, shedder of light.

Lemes, 118/16, s. rays.

Lende, 3/52, 44/124, 375/54, v. to
stay, to remain, dwell, tarry; 513/
368, to pass.

Lenghis, 456/10, v. stays.

Lenne, 56/4, 248/178, v. to grant, to
lend, give; Lente, 138/11, pa. p.

Lepe, 130/111, v. to leap, to spring,
run; Leppe, 150/134, 325/148, 230/
254, 232/291, to escape.

Lepfull, 299/207, s. baskets full.

Lere, 78/181, 93/16, to teach; 48/105,
Leere, 391/321, learn; Leryd, 64/
267, pa. p.

Lerne, 16/76, 254/8, v. to teach.

Lese, 87/331, 330/311, s. lies, deceit.

Lesynge, 23/24, 172/2, s. a lie, false-
hood; Lesyngis, 264/273.

Leste, 261/193, pres. s. subj., if it please
you: see Liste : cf. l. 286, p. 265.

Lete, 26/124, 105/98, v. let, permit.

Lette, 23/21, 161/117, v. hinder, stay,
refrain.

Lettir, 485/142, s. hinderer.

Leue, 157/20, v. read lene = lende, tarry.

Leve, 289/469, 327/231, v. aphetic for
bileue, believe.

Leue, 34/159, v. to live.

Lever, 237/138, adv. sooner, rather: see
Lefe.

Leverie, 203/65, s. delivery.

Leuyn, 9/17, s. lightning.

Levis, 126/1, perhaps read lenis, givest:
cf. with 129/97.

Lewyn, 53/273, s. living.

Lewte, 231/266; Lewty, 248/178, s.
loyalty.

Lidderon, 298/167, s. weak or lazy
fellow; Lidrone, 298/187.

Liddir : see Ledir and Lithre.

Ligge, lygge, 43/98, 347/332, v. to
lay or lie.

Lyghame, 25/110, s. the body.

Light, 167/224, 213/388, adj. happy,
joyful.

Lykand, 190/150, adj. pleasant.

Lykes me, 7/159, verb impers. 8/7, me
likes, I like; 12/72, þame likes (it
likes them), they like: see Liste.

Likid ill, 169/254, v. been sorrowful,
ill-pleased.

Likyng, 84/282, 86/304, s. pleasure,
delight; likyng lande, land of delight,
the Promised land.

Limbo, 378/102, s. a special enclosed
part of hell, a prison.

Lyme, 131/148, s. limb.

Lynage, 76/130, s. lineage, people.

Lyolty, 241/25, ? for lyalty, loyalty.

Lyre, lire, 69/20, 249/199, 379/119,
s. face, countenance, flesh.

Lirte, 230/254, s. ? deception, trick
(dele the hyphen in text). Stratmann
has lurten, also bilurten, bilirten, to
deceive.

Liste, 41/51, 128/76, 265/286, v. impersonal, to like, to please; me list, it
pleases me.

Liste, 66/345, s. desire.

Lite, 303/326, s. strife, contest.

Lith, 328/241, v. listen; Lithes,
124/16.

Lithernesse, 498/44, s. idleness.

Lithre, 324/120, adj. lither, easy,
pliant, hence bad: see Ledir.

Litht, 131/148, s. joint.

Lyvyng, 18/12, s. food, victual.

Lodsterne, 124/24, s. load-star.

Lofsom, 249/199, adj. loveable, beautiful.

Loghte, 152/181, *v.* ?=lout, lurk, lie in ambush (to catch).

Loyse, 134/216, *v.* destroy: *see* **Lose.**

Lokyn, 93/10, *pa. p.* locked.

Longes, 23/48, *v.* belongs.

Loppis, 85/293, *s.* fleas (the note *flies* in the margin is an error, though according to Exod. viii. the fourth plague was of flies. The description in ll. 293, 294, suits better *locusts* than *fleas*, but they do not appear to be intended. Cf. ll. 339, 340).

Lordan, 81/226, *s.* a stupid, worthless fellow: *see* **Lurdan.**

Lorel, 258 / 113, *s.* bad, worthless fellow.

Lorne, 5/108, 50/175, *pa. p.* lost.

Lose, 70/36, 71/44, 84/272, *v.* extinguish, destroy; **Losis,** 264/273.

Losellis, 72/78, *s.* rascals, bad, worthless men.

Lothe, 221/39, *adj.* loath, disagreeable, hateful.

Lott, 326/183, 222/68, *s.* portion, choice.

Lotterell, 315/259, 319/382, *s.* ?scoundrel, a term of opprobrium.

Loves, 205/134, *s.* loaves.

Louying, 2/24, 101/237, *s.* praise, love.

Loue, 51/189; **Lowe,** 41/42, 44/145, *v.* to praise; **Louyd,** *pa. p.* 51/194.

Lowte, 1/24, 267/353, *v.* to bow, bend, reverence.

Luf, 3/46, *s.* praise.

Lufly, 3/43, *adj.* lovely; **Luffely,** 124/16.

Lufsome, 217/520; **Lofsom,** 249/199, *adj.* loveable, beautiful.

-Lurdan, 5/108, **Lurdayne,** 81/229, 467/77, *s.* sluggard, worthless or idle fellow: general term of opprobrium (Fr. *lourd, lourderie*).

Lusshe, 252/271, *s.* a slash.

Lusshe, 292/10, 481/37, *v.* to slash, cut at.

Mached, 278/199, *v.* matched, found his equal.

Madde, 119/38, *v.* to grow mad or wild.

Mahounde, Mahownde, 91/401, 147/15, 37, 148/73, Mahomet.

Maye, 119/20, *s.* maid.

Mayne, 51/181, 148/62, *s.* might, strength.

Maistrie, 203/64, *s.* mastery, i. e. right or power of a master; **Maistreys,** 222/63; **Maistries,** 385/216.

Make, 22/14, *s.* mate.

Makeles, 135/270, *adj.* without a match, unequalled; as *sub* 223/92.

Malyngne, 290/506, *v.* to malign, act spitefully.

Malysonne, 27/153, *s.* curse.

Mang, 452/132, *v.* ?*for* meng, are stupefied.

Mangery, 299/208, *s.* eating, feast.

Markid, 3/49, 58, *v.* designed, noted.

Marrande, 4/93, *pr. p.* marring.

Marre, 81/224, 89/356, 179/43, *v.* to spoil, damage, destroy.

Mased, 31/82, 245/126, *adj.* confounded, giddy.

Mase, 79/194, *v.* makes.

Mate, 480/4, *adj.* dejected, confounded, stupefied.

Matere, 23/43, *s.* matter, story.

Me, 102/1, myself, me; *me mene,* bemoan myself.

Mede, 66/335, 426/3; **Meed,** 135/269, *s.* portion, reward.

Mede, 424/89, *s.* mead, a drink made from honey.

Medill, 347/327, *v. for* mell, meddle.

Medill-erthe, 40/8, 41/28, *s.* the world.

Meene, 220/32, *adj.* low.

Meese, 222/64, 463/238, *v.* to soothe, mitigate, diminish.

Meete, 136/281, *adj.* even, on a level with: *see* **Mette.**

Mefid, 470/152; **Mefte,** 302/290, *pa.p.* moved, taken place.

Meyne, 35/2, *v.* to be spoken of: *see* **Mene.**

Meyne, 36/21, *s.* company = menée: *see* **Menȝe.**

Mekenesse, 196/88, 92, *s.* mildness, humility.

Mekill, 3/41, 74/97, *adj.* great.

Mele, 467/62, *s.* time, occasion.

Mell, 12/66, 37/55, *v.* to mingle, meddle; *to make and mell,* to work and act.

Mende : *see* Mene.

Mende, 94/18, *v.* to amend, reform,
make better; *mende your mode,* -73/
64, soften your temper, be not angry.

Mene, 93/1, 65/286, 122/119, *v.* to
tell, speak, mean, think; Menyd,
97/125 ; Mende, 75 / 121, *pa. t.* ;
Mente, *pa. p.* 66/314, 94/32, 103/30;
Meyne, *passive,* 35/2.

Meng, 12/74, 366/245, *v.* mingle, mix,
stir up; Mengis, 118/4; *menged in
mood,* disturbed in temper.

Menȝe, 66/324, *s.* company, people.

Menyng, 378/103, *s.* talking.

Menske, 115/107, 243/47, *v.* honour,
worship.

Menskfull, 217/502, *adj.* worshipfull.

Mente, 6/139, *pa. p.* meant, spoke or
intended: *see* Mene.

Mercy, 170/281, 368/309, *s.* thanks,
grace; Mersy, 143/181, *s.* mercy,
pardon.

Mercye, 489/265, *interj.* grace.

Merour, 2/34, *s.* mirror.

Merr, 94/39, *v.* to mar, destroy: *see*
Marre.

Mesellis, 86/317, *s. pl.* lepers.

Mesore, 49/136, *s.* measure.

Messe, 77/162, *s.* measure, bound, *cf.*
M. E. *meþe,* pl. *meþes.*

Meste, 302/290, *v.* error, read (as in
MS.) *mefte,* moved.

Mett, 85/288, *v.* meet.

Mette, 189/116, 135/269, *v.* measured;
euyn with hym mette, Christ measured
even with God: *see* Meete.

Metyng, 204/95, 213/383, *s.* meeting.

Myddyng,.85/296, *s.* dung-hill.

Mydwayes, 72/69, seems to be an
error for mid-wives.

Myghfull, 473/1, *? for* mightfull.

Mightefull, 3/58, *adj.* powerful.

Mightes, 2/33, *s.* powers.

Myn, 41/28, *adj.* less; *more and myn,*
greater and less.

Mynde, 471/188, *s.* remembrance.

Myre, 387/256, *s.* mire, bog (here figuratively).

Myrke, 88/344, 113/41, *adj.* dark.

Myrknes, 6/146, *s.* darkness.

Myron, 276/139, 147, 322/62, *s.,* appears to mean a subordinate or servant.

Myrroure, 175/93, 184/195, *s.* mirror,
example, pattern.

Myrthe, 79/188, 227/123; Myrþes,
79/194. *s.* pleasure, happiness, profit,
advantage.

Mys, 8/9 ; Mysse, 93/2, 106/132, *s.*
fault.

Mys, 63/232, *v.* lose, want; Miste,
398/55, *pa. p.* missed.

Myses, 84/273, *s.* ? lice. In Towneley
Myst. the word is *mystes.*

Mysfare, 211/324, *s.* misfortune.

Mismarkid, 258/123, mistaken.

Mis-paye, 24/64, *v.* displease.

Misse, 427/44, *s.* fault.

Misseis, 135/258 ; Mysese, 167/213,
s. evil, care, anxiety.

Myssyng, 3/48, *v. s.* want, lack.

Misty, 398/43, *adj.* ? sad, dreary.

Mystir, 41/52, 278/196, *s.* need.

Mystris, 37/54, *v. pres. s.* needs; *what
mystris þe,* why needest thou.

Mistrowand, 454/179, *adj.* unbelieving.

Mytyng, 141/113, 179/26, 296/110,
303/305, s. a mite, little fellow, midget,
a darling, term of endearment for
a child ; ' praty mytyng,' Towneley
Mysteries, p. 96. In margin on p. 179
read 'mite' for 'myghty one.'

Mytyng, 316/305, *adj.* tiny, very small.

Mobardis, 246/137, 467/74, *s.* clowns,
a term of contempt.

Mode, 179 / 43, 484 / 123, *s.* mood,
temper.

Moffe, 22/2, 128/52; Moyfe, 127/48,
v. to move : *see* Mefid.

Molde, 36/35, *s.* mould, earth.

Momell, 236/106, *v.* mumble, mutter ;
Mummeland, *pres. p.* 303/305.

Mon, 31/54, 67, 33/131, *aux. v.* must.

Mone, 123/14, *s.* moon. (Note, of mas-
culine gender.)

Mone, 231/275, *s.* moan.

Mop, 299/196, *s.* a fool.

More, 11/48, *adj.* greater.

More, 85/296, *s.* moor, waste.

Morne, 62/196, *v.* mourn.

N n

Mornys, 62/199; Mornyng, 79/190, *s.* mourning.

Mort, 222/77, *v. aphetic form of* amort, put to death.

Morteysed, 226/163, *pa. p.* mortised.

Moster, 123/14, *v.* show.

Mot, 158/61; Mote, 183/178, *v.* may, might.

Mote, 387/256; Moote, 354/159, *v.* to moot, plead, argue, discuss.

Moulde, 6/141, *s.* earth : *see* Molde.

Mowe, 361/78, *v.* to make faces.

Mowes, 358/286, *s. pl.* faces, grimaces.

Mum, 78/175, *v.* mutter.

Muste, 470/164, *s.* new wine.

Muster, 472/216, *v.* to show; Mustyr, 6/145; Mustirs, 70/30; Musteres, 183/177; Mustered me, 178/9.

Namely, 114/74, 277/173, *adv.* especially.

Nare, 179/52, *adj.* near; Narre, 47/62; Nerre, 303/321, nearer.

Nawe, *for* awe, 63/240, *adj.* own.

Ne, 468/104, *read* he.

Nedelyngis, 302/278, *adv.* necessarily.

Nedes, 57/43, *adv.* of necessity.

Neffes, 268/370, *s.* fists.

Neghe, 128/65; Neygh, 23/33, 38, *v.* come near to, approach.

Nemely, 262 / 219, 353 / 120, *adv.* quickly, nimbly.

Nemen, nemyn, neme, 33/144, 107/170, 194/37, *v.* name, mention.

Nenys, 313/185, ?*for* nevenys.

Nerre, 303/321, *adj.* nearer.

Nerthrist, 329/266, (?).

Neuen, 45/15, 310/89, *v.* to name, to mention ; 285/366, to call, proclaim.

Newe, 76/141, of newe = a-new ; *here* for the first time.

Newe, 478/144, 494/96, 105, *s.* noye, harm, hurt, annoyance.

Newe, 275/131, *v.* to annoy.

Newes, 217/531, *v.* renews.

Newesome, 277/183, *adj.* annoying.

Nexile (an exile), 2/25, *s.* aisle, from Lat. *axilla*, a detached part of the structure of the world ; here seems to be confounded with *isle*.

Nyse, 261/193, 265/286, *adj.* nice, good, fastidious, particular.

Noble, 43/107, 225/133; Nobill, 210/300, *adj.* glorious, notable, grand, fine, splendid.

Nociens, 316/291, *s.* ? usefulness.

Noddil, 268/370, *v.* to strike with the closed fist, to rap.

Noghte, 2/16, 30/44; Nouȝt, 37/59, nothing.

Noy, 4/71, *v. aphetic for* annoy.

Noyes, 90/386, 150/140, *s.* hurts, annoyances : *see* Newe.

Nokyn, 143/152, *adj.*; No-kynnes, 24/76, 48/100, *adj.* no kind of.

Nolde, 418/405, *v.* would not.

Nones, 285/366, *s.* nonce; *þe nones,* for *then ones,* that once, the nonce, once at least.

Note, 76/141, 154/268; Nott, 128/75, *s.* affair, business, matter; Noote, 371/383, *s.* use, occupation.

Note, 120/65, *s.* song, sound.

Notis, 122/112, *s.* nuts.

Nouȝt, 37/59, *adv.* not (nothing).

Novellis, 160/102, *s.* news.

Novelte, 122/127, 205/118, *s.* novelty, new thing, news.

Nowele, 358/119, *s.* owl (a nowele = an owele).

Obitte, 388/269, dead (Lat. *obitus*).

Oblissh, 117/151, *v.* to oblige, compel.

Of, 144/216, *prep.* for.

Of heght, 54/291, on high.

Omell, 95/62, *prep.* amidst.

On-brede, 10/35, abroad.

Ondergh, 349/2, *adj.* undree, without sorrow or trouble.

Ongayne, 290/511, *adj.* ungainly.

Ongaynely, 32/99, *adv.* with trouble.

On-glad, 421/6, *adj.* sorrowful.

On-hande, 131/138, *adv.* on one hand, aside.

On lif, 83/254; On-lyve, 32/103, 146/13, *adv.* alive.

Oondis, 116/132, *v. pr. p.* breathe, from *ande, onde,* to breathe.

Or, 31/55, *adv.* before : *see* Ayre.

Ordandis, 494/87, *v.* ordains.

Os, 42/66, 44/140, *conj.* as.

Ospring, 498/23, s. offspring.

Othir, 236/110, prep. for or, i.e. ere, before.

Ouere-wyn, 310/104, v. overcome.

Oure vnwittyng, 326/189, unknown to us.

Ought, 23/33, s. anything.

Oute-tane, 29/9; Outtane, 63/224; Owtane, 198/147, except, excepted.

Outhir, 40/16; Owthir, 130/124, adj. either.

Outrayes, 323/100, v. outrages.

Over, 86/307, adv. over, too; Oure foue, 338/41, over foolishly.

Owe! 4/81, 93, interj. oh!

Owte-take, 20/67, v. to except.

Oyas! 285/569, v. oyez, hear!

Paas, 233/4, 11; Pasc, 234/29, s. pasque, Passover.

Page, 141/101, 267/358, s. a boy child, lad.

Pay, 9/25, 131/151, s. pleasure.

Paye, 500/188, v. to please; Payed, 62/192; Paied, 89/359, pleased.

Payer, 332/375, s. ? beater, striker.

Paire, 224/114, 345/256, v. aphetic form of appair, impair.

Pak, 111/303; Pakke, 143/160, s. package or bundle.

Palle, 308/25, s. a cloth covering.

Pappe, 429/103, s. teat, breast.

Papse, 267/358, apparently the name of a game.

Parellis, 86/306, s. perils.

Parlament, 308/33, s. a discussion, a speaking.

Parred, 321/34, pa. p. inclosed.

Pase, 468/103, s. pace, steps.

Passande = Passing, 3/56, 6/134. pr. p. excessive, exceeding.

-Passe, 275/116 (second), adv. pace, A-passe, apace.

Passh, 481/38, v. to strike with violence.

Patris, 357/266, v. patters, chatters.

Peching, 429/84, pr. p. panting, breathing hard (guttural ch).

Pees, 429/84, s. silence, putte are to pees.

Peysed, 429/96, v. weighed down.

Pele, 224/110, s. stir, fuss.

Perelous, 220/16; Perles, 63/239, adj. peerless, unequalled.

Perloyned, 271/31, 32, removed, set away.

Pertly, 259/136, adv. aphetic for apertly, openly, boldly.

Pight, 112/4, pa. p. pitched, set.

Pike, 23/18; Pikis, 123/11, v. to pluck, pick, choose.

Pilche, 332/375, s. woollen or fur pelisse or coat.

Pynakill, 181/91, s. pinnacle.

Pyne, 2/32, v. to torture, to starve; Pynde, 178/12; Pynyd, 136/294; Pynnyd, 471/184, pa. p.

Pyne, 47/54, 104/56, s. pain, grief, punishment.

Playne, full, open, 161/127, 471/199.

Playnere, 161/127, adj. plenary.

Plasmator, 514/2, maker, creator.

Plately, 270/3, 328/244, adv. plainly, perfectly.

Platte, 292/5, v. sit down, sit flat.

Plege, 143/170, v. to pledge, be surety for; Of all I plege, of all I am responsible for.

Pleyne, 160/103, adj. full; Plener, 80/200, comp. fuller, larger; more fuller place, a greater, larger place: see Playne.

Pleyned, 509/296, v. plained, pitied.

Plesyng, 1/12, s. pleasure.

Plete, 229/230, ? exclamation, flat, done!

Plete, 206/176, v. plead, argue.

Plextis, 292/5, ? for pleytis, pletis, argue, quarrel (ye).

Ply, 1/12, v. to bend or turn.

Plight, 432/192, s. promise.

Plight, 312/162, 457/44, s. danger, guilt, fault.

Poynte, 127/46, 131/151, 181/99, s. business, matter, instance.

Post, Poste, 223/88; Pooste, 224/114, Pouste, 61/181, s. power, might.

Pounce, 271/20, s. Pontius.

Poure, 82/242, 144/185, s. power.

Poure, 122/110, adj. poor.

Pouste, 61/181, s. power, might.

Preces, 229/230, v. presses.

Prees, 112/12, 338/12; Prese, 285/370, s. press, crowd, surrounding.

Prente, 222/75, 362/111, *v.* to print, impress.
Presande, 122/110, *s.* a present.
Present, 162/137, *s.* presence.
Prestely, 240/11, 247/155, *adv.* readily, quickly, presently.
Pretend, 242/52, *v.* intend.
Preuys, 466/17, *v.* prove, establish; **Preued,** 307/9, 308/25, *pa. p.*
Price, 182/127, *s.* value.
Prike, 111/303, *v.* to pin, fasten.
Prime, 32/90, *s.* the first hour of the day.
Priuite, 192/226, *s.* privacy.
Processe, 324/124, *v.* law-suit.
Prokering, 429/82, *s.* procuring.
Propheres, 332/373, *v.* profers.
Prophyte, 177/155, *s.* profit.
Prossesse, 432/192, *s.* process, succession.
Proue, 23/17, *v.* try.
Prowe, 20/60, 186/37, *s.* profit, honour.
Publisshed, 375/59, openly seen, publicly known.
Pursue, 236/109, *v.* follow after, go to.
Purvey, 231/272, 234/24, *v.* to provide for oneself, make provision.

Qwantise, 72/61, *s.* cunning, device (O. Fr. *cointise*).
Qwarte, 41/50, 260/169, 438/159, *s.* health, activity, lithe condition; *out of qwarte*, infirm.
Quat, 41/40, *adj.* what.
Qwelle, 72/61, 153/209, *v.* to kill, destroy.
Qwen, *adv.* when.
Quenys, 153/209, 343/192, *s.* queans, scolds.
Quyk, 166/211, *adj.* alive.

Racleyme, 309/78, *s.* a call to return, (a term used in falconry). Cf. "Cam with him a reclayme," Rich. the Redeless, Pass. II, l. 182, and Dr. Skeat's note; *Whanne he comes to racleyme,* when he returns to the call.
Radde, 174/59, 416/377, *adj.* frightened, afraid.
Radly, 90/390, 277/178, *adv.* speedily.

Raffe, 107/146, *v.* to rave.
Raffe, 401/111, *past t.* of rive, tear: see **Refe.**
Ragged, 363/120, *pa. p. for* rugged, pulled.
Ray, 230/246, *v. for* array (*aphetic form*).
Rayke, 276/151; **Rakis,** 275/126, *v.* to move, go; **Raykand,** 123/3, 223/93, *pr. p.* raiking, a rapid irregular movement (Icel. *reika*, to wander).
Rayned, 112/18, *v.* rained.
Rakke, 123/7, *s.* rack, course or road.
Rappely, 123/7, *adv.* quickly, speedily.
Raryng, 299/215, *s.* roaring, mourning.
Rase, 279/214, *s.* course, race.
Rasely, 482/60, *adv.* angrily.
Rathely, 240/6, *adv.* soon, speedily.
Rawes, 158/50, *s.* rows, *on rawes* in order.
Read, 19/44, *s.* counsel, advice.
Reame, 126/16, *s.* realm.
Rebaldes, 124/35, *s.* scamps.
Reche, 232/283, *v.* reach.
Recorde, 330/315, *v.* to witness.
Recours, 237/141, recourse, i.e. resource, expedient.
Recoveraunce, 223/101, *s.* cure or recovery: see **Coveres.**
Recrayed, 415/364, *adj.* recreant, coward.
Recreacioun, 481/20, *colde recreacioun,* poor amusement.
Rede, 158/50, 159/86, 162/145, *v.* read.
Rede, 69/17, 97/124, *v.* to counsel, advise; **Red,** 30/35, *pa. p.*
Redy, 126/12, 134/223, *adj.* near, short.
Refe, 277/165, *v.* to rive, tear from; **Ryff,** 107/153, *pr. t.*; **Raffe,** 401/111, *pa. t.*; **Rafte,** *pa. p.* 282/299.
Reflars, 444/367, *s.* blows back.
Refuse, 330/315, *v.* to deny.
Rehete, 265/287, 332/363, *v.* to cheer, to revive, encourage.
Reyned, 481/34, *v.* reigned; **Reynand,** 40/14, *pr. p.* reigning.
Reke, 220/34, smoke; *figuratively* tumult, uproar.
Rekkeles, 107/146, *adj.* careless, not recking anything.

Releffe, 451/90, *v.* (I) leave behind.

Reles, 389/288, *s.* release.

Releue, 299/207, *s.* remains, left over.

Reme, 220/34, *s.* kingdom.

Remeued, 95/50, *error for* remened, reminded.

Remewe, 86/310, 331/335, *v.* move back, remove.

Rengne, 245/122, *v.* reign.

Renke, 255/17, *s.* ranging, setting in order.

Renke, 125/55, *s.* a strong man, a knight.

Repleye, 304/380, this seems to be a corruption; see the reading below.

Reproffe, 103/45, 104/56, *s.* reproach.

Reproued, 230/245, 459/85, *pa. p.* redressed, corrected.

Reproues, 315/241, *v.* proves back.

Resouns, 159/86, 266/309, 387/255, *s.* speeches, discourses, argument, reason.

Respete, 65/285, *s.* respite.

Reste, 481/31, *v.* quieten, appease.

Restore, 6/143, *v.* to refresh : *see* In-store.

Revette, 43/109, *s.* rivet.

Reward, 19/42, 168/235, *s.* regard, respect.

Rewe, 39/115, 273/62, *v.* to suffer, *often impersonal* ; Rewes me, 103/36, it repents me.

Rewe, 43/109, *s.* (? rule), a carpenter's tool.

Rewlle, 147/46, *s.* rule, order.

Rewly, 221/38, *adj.* ruly, calm.

Rewpe, 283/305, *s.* pity.

Riall, 124/32, *adj.* royal.

Rialte, 123/3, *s.* regality, royalty.

Ryff, 107/153, *v.* rive, tear : *see* Refe.

Rigge, 339/73, *s.* back.

Rightwysnes, Rightwissenesse,175/ 118, *s.* righteousness.

Ryott, 90/390, *s.* riot, 'row,' insurrection, stir, uproar.

Risse, 492/41, *s.* a branch.

Ryste, 71/43, *s.* rise, increase.

Ryve, 57/22 ; Ryue, 205/136, *adj.* rife, abounding.

Robard, 36/47, *s.* robber, thief, perhaps shortened from *Roberdsmen* or *rober-*

des knaves, gangs of lawless men in the fourteenth century, *see* statutes 5 Edw. III. c. 14, and 7 Rich. II c. 5 ; also the name Robert was early explained to mean robber or thief, *see* references in Dr. Skeat's notes to *Piers Plowman* (E.E.T.Soc.) Part IV, *Pass.* I, pp. 8, 125.

Roght, 26/137 ; Rought, 275/126, 501/149, *pa. p.* recked, cared : *see* Rekkeles.

Roye, 219/1, *s.* king.

Royse, 120/69, *v.* to praise oneself, to boast : *see* Rowse, Rude.

Rome, 178/1, 279/229, *s.* room ; *gose a rome*, give room.

Romour, 220/34, *s.* report.

Roo, 31/76, 277/188, *s.* rest.

Rope, 130/122, *for* roy, swagger, boast.

Rouk, 36/48, *v.* to bow or bend.

Rowe, 19/38, *s.* rest, peace : *see* Roo.

Rowe, 6/124, *s.* order, line : *see* Rawes.

Rownand, 124/35, *pr. p.* whispering, muttering.

Rowne, 36/48, *v.* to mutter or whisper.

Rowse, 264/271, *v.* boast.

Rude, 277/175, *pa. p. for* royed, boasted.

Ruffe, 112/18, *s.* roof.

Rugge, 279/214, *v.* to pull roughly ; Ragged, *pa. p.*

Saande, 63/244, *s.* sending, what is sent.

Sad, 41/33, *adj.* grave, quiet.

Sadly, 43/102, 284/353, *adv.* gravely, seriously.

Saffyng, 115/100, *s.* saving, salvation.

Sagates, 57/30, so-gates = thus-gates in this manner.

Saggard, 361/82, *s. formed from* sag, to fall or bulge by weight of parts unattached, applied to the body on the cross, sinking by its weight.

Saie, 274/99, *v. aphetic for* assay, try.

Sayff, 18/12, *v.* save, store up.

Saise, 111/277, *v.* says.

Sak, 100/195, *s.* blame, guilt.

Sakles, 108/181, *adj.* blameless.

Sales, 321/18, 333/398, *s.* halls, rooms.

Sall, 323/87, *s.* hall or chamber.

Salue, 177 / 170, *v.* to salve, heal; Salued, 264/263, *past t.*

Saluyng, 66/334, *s.* salving, healing.

Salus, 184/194, *v.* salutes.

Sam, Same, 44/126, 111/301; Samyn, 63/235, *adv.* together.

Samme, 468/87, *v.* assemble, gather together; Sammed, 338/43.

Sande, 109/217, *s.* message.

Sararre, 77/160, *adj. comp.* of sare, sore, sorer, worse.

Sattles, 328/248, *v.* settles, sinks.

Sauerly, 257/80, *adv.* tastily.

Saughe, 129/86, *v.* saw.

Saughe, 19/34, ? for saught, *adj.* peaceful, quiet : *see* **Vnsoght**.

Saunterynge, 351/70, 354/150, *s.* sauntering, strolling. Prof. Skeat tells me this is the earliest instance yet found of the word *saunter*.

Sauterell, 303/310, 310/91 ; Sawterell, 315/274, *s.* ? transgressor, trespasser (leaper over bounds). Cf. Fr. *sauterelle*, grass-hopper.

Savely, 412/307, *adv.* safely.

Sawes, 69/17, 97/119, *s.* words, sayings.

Sawntrelle, 249/190, *s.* saunterer or stroller. Cf. *gangerll* and *haverel*.

Seand, 109/235, *s.* sight, perception.

Secomoure, 214/427, *s.* sycamore tree.

Seece, 139/38, *v.* act, stay, stop.

Seege, Sege, 114/59, 227/190, 325/157, *s.* warrior, knight, man, fellow.

Seele, 49/129 ; Seill, 39/136 ; Cele, 160/109 ; Sele, 9/13 ; *s.* happiness, bliss.

Seere, 128/50, 217/519, *adj.* many, several.

Sees, 69/17, *v.* cease.

Seete, 254/7, *s.* seat.

Sege, 99/163, *s* seat.

Seggid, 308/16, *pa. p.* said.

Seggyng, 285/360, *s.* saying, nagging.

Seill, 39/136, *s.* bliss, happiness.

Seyn, 42/77, *pa. p.* ? seen, looked to.

Seys, 40/19, *s.* cease.

Sekirly, 104/63, *adv.* surely.

Selcouth, 50/159, 127/18, *adj.* wondrous, wonderful.

Sele, 9/13, *s.* happiness.

Selle, 392/342, *s.* cell.

Sembland, 129/93, *s.* semblance, appearance.

Seme, 15/20, *v.* to appear, be seen, 232/6 ; Semes, seems, is fitting ; Semand, 284/341, *pr. p.*

Semely, 4/89, 124/45, *adj.* seemly, handsome.

Semelyte, 204/116, *s.* seemliness.

Sen, 203/66, 341/132, *adv. for* sithen, since : *see* **Syn**.

Senge, 54/290, *s.* sign.

Seniour, 273/73, *s.* seigniour, lord.

Senous, 352/108 ; Synnous, 353/132, *s.* sinews.

Sente, 312/144, 166, *aphetic for* assent or consent; *see* l. 168 and 315/246.

Ser, 183/151, *s.* sir.

Sere, 10/26, *adj.* several, diverse, many, 9/20, apart, separate.

Serely, Serly, 466/24, *adv.* separately

Sermon, 282/302, *v.* to sermonize.

Sers, 315/275, *v.* to search.

Servid, 8/8, *pa. p.* deserved.

Sese, 17/91, *v.* cease.

Sethen, 16/62; Sene, 17/77; Sythen, 57/26, *conj.* since.

Sette, 23/19, *pa. p.* bestowed, placed.

Sewe, 77/160, *v.* follow, pursue.

Schalke, 282/295, 320/2, *s.* a soldier, a servant.

Shame, 137/318, *s.* bad conduct.

Shame, 31/62, 63, *v. reflex, and impers.* to be ashamed.

Shamously, 312/143, *adv.* shamefully.

Shape, 137/318, *v.* to plan, intend, prepare; Shoppe, 35/3, *past t.*: *see* **Schoppe**.

Scharid, 246/141, *pa. p.* scared.

Schawe, 272/56, *s.* show, appearance.

Schemerande, 4/69, *pr. p.* shimmering.

Schene, 127/22, 496/154, *adj.* bright, shining.

Shende, 89/365, *v.* to ruin, disgrace ; Shente, 31/79, *pa. p.*

Shere, 260/171, *v.* cut.

Schewyng, 4/69, *v.s.* appearance.

Shyll, 139/43, *adj.* shrill.

Shippe-craft, 42/67, *s.* the art of making ships.

Schire, 487/202, *adj.* sheer, pure.

Sho, 106/120, *pron.* she.

Schoffe, 368/297, *v.* shove, push.

Schogged, 429/100, *v.* jogged, shook.

Schone, 64/244, *v.* shun, escape.

Schonte, 482/59, *v.* shunned.

Schoppe, 204/114, 212/365, *v.* shaped, formed: *see* Shape.

Schoures, 478/146, *s.* showers, *figuratively,* assaults of fortune.

Schrewe, 151/169, *s.* clever, sharp, bad person.

Schrew, 248/180, 187, *v.* to curse: *? for* beshrew.

Shrowde, 268/364, *s.* a garment.

Sigging, 469/133, *s.* saying: *see* Seggyng.

Siʒte, 364/157: *see* Syte.

Syle, 144/196, *v.* to drop, glide away.

Sill, 244/92, *? for* sall, shall.

Sylypp, 57/26, *s.* syllable.

Symonde, 43/102, *s.* cæment.

Simple, 15/30, 121/100, 282/288, *adj.* innocent, weak, mean, lowly, of little value.

Syn, 6/139, *adv.* since: *see* Sen.

Syne, 54/296; Synge, 74/100; Syngnes, 77/156, *s.* sign.

Syne, Synne, 276 / 138, *adv.* since, later, by and bye.

Synke, 46/36, *v.* drown: *see* Sounkyn.

Syte, 29/16, *s.* sorrow, disgrace, shame.

Sythen, 57/26, *conj.* since.

Sithfull, 342/151; Sytfull, 33/129, *adj.* sorrowful.

Sithis, 39/130, *s.* times.

Sittis, 232/288, 287/420, *v. impers.* it becomes us (Fr. *il nous sied*).

Skape, 49/141, *v.* escape (*aphetic*).

Skathe, 49/141, 140/77, *s.* harm, damage.

Skaunce, 282/291, *s.* a chance, an accident. O. F. *escance*. *See* Towneley M. pp. 17, 199.

Skell, 12/65, *s.* shell.

Skelpte, 222/81, 321/35, *v. past t.* to strike with anything flat, as a leather strap, &c.; *skelpte out of score,* drove out of bounds.

Skemeryng, Skymeryng. 130/123, *s.* shining: *see* Schemerande.

Skyffte, 225/130, *s.* shift, trick, art.

Skylfull, 15/22, *adj.* having reason or understanding.

Skill, 459/113; Skylle, 15/26, *s.* reason, understanding, motive.

Skymeryng, 343/192, *v.* skirming, skirmishing.

Skippid, 481/41, *v.* grazed (skin).

Skyste, 221/41, *v. sometimes so written for* skyft, to `shift, divide, change, separate.

Skwyn, 42/74, *s.* skew, oblique, twisted; *of skwyn,* askew.

Slake, 46/41 ; Sclake, 9/13, *v.* abate, grow less, lessen.

Sleghte, 181/88, 271/8, *s.* sleight, contrivance, cunning.

Slely, 271/8, *adv.* cunningly.

Slyke, Slike, 46/22, 142/140; Sclyk, 44/140 (earlier *sa-lyke*), *adj.* such : *see* Swilke.

Slippe, 476/105, *adj.* sleepy, drowsy.

Slo, 331/324; Sloo, 164/175, *v.* to slay, kill.

Sloppe, 295/77, *s.* over-garment, a robe (rather than a shirt, as in margin).

Smerte, 41/54, *adj.* smart, sharp.

Smore, 5/117, *v.* to smother.

Snell, 437/111, *adj.* sharp, keen.

Softe, 144/196, *adv.* gently, easily.

Soght, 449/25, *pa. p.* of seek, attributed, fetch to ; 49/128, went ; 135/262, sought, paid homage to.

Soile, 318/361, *v. aphetic for* assoil, absolve.

Solas, 136/301, 217/509, *s.* solace, comfort, joy ; *solace sere,* 23/40, many pleasures.

Sorouse, 93/7, *s.* sorrows.

Sorowe, 103/44, *adv.* sorrowfully, sadly.

Sotell, 73/79, *adj.* subtle, clever.

Sotte, 124/28, *s.* fool.

Sounkyn, 498/36; Sownkyn, 41/30, *pa. p.* sunken, drowned, 42/59.

Spared, 419/430, *pa. p.* closed, shut up.

Spedar, 5/110, *s.* helper, promoter.

Spede, 236/92; Speed, 66/330, *s.* success.

Spede, 422/15, *v.* to succeed, go well ; Spedde, 261/187, *pa. p.*

Spell, 471 / 187, s. discourse, book
Spellis, 263/240, pl. sayings, fa-
bles.

Spence, 366/241 ; Spens, 311/134, s.
aphetic for ex ence.

Spere, 380 / 139, v. to shut, close;
Spers, 50/161, imperat. : see Spared.

Spere : see Spire.

Spill, 5/110, 46/50, 130/128, v. to
ruin, destroy, to perish ; Spyll,
21/89 ; Spilte, 33/140.

Spire, 236/97; Spirre, 114/82; Spere,
263/240, v. to ask, inquire.

Spirringes, 322/64, s. questionings.

Spites, 283/326, s. contempt.

Sporne, 422/15, v. to stumble.

Stabely, 126/6, 131/140, adv. firmly,
truly.

Stabyll, 3/62, adj. stable.

Stadde : see Stedde.

Stages, 44/127, 129, steps or floors.

Stakir, 274/85, v. stagger.

Stales, 295/75, s. deceits, slyness, hence
conspiracies.

Stalke, 331/336, v. to walk stealthily.

Stalkyng, 276/157, s. stepping softly
or slowly.

Stalland, 320/14, pr. p. forbearing.

Stark, 417/395, adj. stiff, rigid.

State, 220/23, s. pomp, high condition.

Stately, 222/82, adv. in proper posi-
tion.

States, 281/261, s. personages of high
rank, estates.

Stawllys, 44/129, s. stalls, places.

Stedde, 483/94, v. to stay, tarry.

Stedde, 67/363, 113/22, pa. p. placed,
set.

Stedde, 508/289, pressed, put to it;
stedde stiffely, 477/137, hard pressed,
in danger.

Stede, 58 / 74 ; Steede, 121/88, s.
stead, place.

Stente, 146/3, v. to still, restrain.

Sterand, 248/175, pres. p. stirring,
active, agile.

Sterne, 127/28, s. star.

Steuyn, Steven, Steuen, 9/16, 45/6,
s. voice, call.

Steuened, 187/64, v. called.

Stevenyng, 307/6, s. shouting.

Stye, 250/229, s. an ascending lane or
path.

Sties, 339/52, s. steps.

Stigh, 424/85, v. to rise or ascend ;
Stied, 495/121, past t. rose.

Stighill, 295/75, v. to decide, to establish, order, to part combatants.

Stynt, 52/222, v. to shorten, stop, stay :
see Stente.

Stodmere, 193/13, s. stud-mare.

Stoken, 383/193, 467/60, pa. p. fastened, stuck.

Stonyes, 279/223, v. for astonies, is astonished (aphetic).

Store, 300/242, adj. big, powerful,
strong.

Stormed, 112/16, pa. p. taken by the
storms of weather.

Stounde, 240/8, s. a short time.

Stoure, 243/73, s. conflict, struggle.

Straytely, 184/187, adv. closely.

Stresse, 165/188, s. force.

Stryve, 57/24, s. strife.

Sudary, 371/387, 409/243, s. napkin,
winding-sheet.

Sufferayne, 113/46, s. sovereign.

Suffraynd, 61/163, adj. sovereign.

Sugett, 114/64, s. subject.

Suye, 258/114, 262/212, v. sue, follow.

Suppowle, 338/11, v. to support.

Suttilly, Suttelly, 42/77, 43/105,
cleverly.

Swa, 83/259, so.

Swayne, 122/128, 133/207, s. youth,
boy.

Swapped, 259/144, 282/286, v. struck,
cut off quickly.

Swarand, 333/384, I swarand, Is' (for
I sall = shall) warrant, (provincialism
still in use).

Sware, 42/74, s. square.

Sweght, 332/362, s. force.

Sweying, 286/371, s. noise.

Swelte, 333/384, 428/56, v. to faint.

Swemyed, 427/40, pa. p. seized with
swimming in the head, giddy.

Swete, 332/361, v. sweat.

Swetyng, 427/40, s. sweating.

Swettyng, 427/40, 428/56, s. sweeting,
darling.

Sweuene, 278/189, s. dream.
Swilke, 16/53, adj. such : see Slyke.
Swynke, 27/161, v. labour.
Swyre, 332/361, s. a pillar.
Swithe, 91/393, 425/127, adv. soon, quickly, immediately.

Ta, 104/65, 140/57, v. take.
Tacche, 353/119, v. tack, fasten ; Takkid, 429/92, fastened.
Tadys, 84/271, s. toads.
Taynte, 219/6, v. for attaint.
Taken, 76/143, 111/278, s. token.
Talde, 99/184, v. told, reckoned.
Talent, 174/69, 462/217, s. desire, pleasure, inclination.
Tales, 60/128, s. sayings.
Tase, 354/180, s. toes.
Taste, 55/317, 218/535, 393/358, v. to touch, try, feel.
Taught, 29/10, 225/137, v. pa. p. of teche, to deliver, give in charge, commit ; 263/228, showed.
Teche, 230/255, 393/364, v. to give, deliver, teach ; 125/48, show.
Teyn, 41/39, s. sorrow, trouble.
Teynd, 36/40 ; Tente, 36/27, s. tenth.
Telde, 198/162, s. cover or habitation.
Telde, 56/14, v. tented, pitched, set up.
Tene, 213/386, 398, s. sorrow, trouble, grief.
Tenefull, 312/152, adv. sorrowful.
Tenyd, 137/314, pa. p. grieved.
Tent, 9/11, s. heed, attention ; 29/1, take tent : see Entent.
Tente, 412/301, v. to heed, attend to.
Tente, 36/27, s. tenth.
Texte, 218/535, s. text.
Thaym, 29/7 ; þaime, 2/31, pron. them.
Tharne, 142/137, 456/15, v. to be deprived of, lack, want (Icel. tharnan, a want).
Tharning, 456/12, s. lacking, want.
Tharr, 18/10 ; Thar, 168/234, v. impers. it needs ; Thurte, 510/316, pa. t.
The, 158/61, v. thrive; so mot I the, so may I thrive.
þedyre, 202/41, adv. thither.
Ther, 3/60 ; þere, 512/367, adv. where.

There, 86/306; þer, 43/92, 90/388, 460/137, adj. these: see þire.
þer-gatis, 95/48, adv. in those ways, those things.
þire, 8/3 ; þir, 95/53, pron. these.
Thirle, 424/100, v. thrill, pierce.
Thithynges, Thidingis, 397/28, 29, tidings, news.
Tho, 70/39 ; þo, 9/11, adj. those.
þof, 511/344, conj. though.
þof all, 121/101, 122/121, although.
Thole, 183/182, v. suffer, bear.
Thondour, 86/320, s. thunder.
Thore, þore, 12/69, 130/116, adv. there.
Thraly, 56/3, 123/8, 322/61, adv. eagerly, earnestly, obediently, dutifully.
þrang, 178/2, s. throng, crowd.
Thrange, 481/43, v., pa. t. pressed.
Thrawe, 137/309, 258/115, s. while, time.
Threpe, 230/256, s. threat, dispute.
Threpe, 5/114, v. to chide, dispute.
Threpyng, 430/105, v. s. disputing.
Threste, 258/115, v. to thrust.
Threst, 86/320, pa. p. thrust, beaten down.
Thrette, 141/111, pa. p. threatened.
Thristed, 481/43, v. thrust.
Thrivandly, 42/76, adv. prosperously.
Thurte, 510/316, past t. of Thar.
Tyde, 149/92, v. betide, happen.
Till, 65/282, 298, prep. to.
Tille, 31/59, v. to obtain, procure.
Tyne, 63/241, 318/363, v. lose.
Tyne, 94/26, s. for teyne, teen, vexation.
Tyraunte, 30/48, s. said of Satan.
Tirraunt, 314/227, 360/30, s. usurper.
Tyte, 90/389, 135/246, adv. quickly, speedily, directly ; Tytar, 84 / 280, comp. quicker, sooner.
Tytt, 332/350, pa. p. snatched or pulled off.
Tyxste, 316/287, v. accusest. O. E. tíhan, M. E. tiȝe.
To, 38/79, s. toe.
To, prep. 65/304, 348/348, for.
To-dyghte, 5/98, pa. p. committed to.
To-morne, 89/356, s. to-morrow.
To-whils, 2/30, adv. whilst.

Tole, 54/281, 482/58, *v.* to work, labour at, pull about: *see* **Tule.**

Toles, 48/110, 382/179, *s.* tools, methods, instruments, utensils.

Tome, 318/345, 428/18, *s.* leisure; *adj.* 430/127, empty.

Tone, 471/202, 491/13, *pa. p. for* tane, taken.

Tonne, 264/249, 430/127, *s.* tun, barrel.

Torfoyr, 431/160, 432/174, *s.* disaster, hardship, difficulty.

Towne, 36/46, *s.* an enclosed place, as opposed to wild open country, field; home farm.

Trace, 125/48, *s.* step, path, way.

Traye, 279/29, *s.* trouble, vexation.

Traye, 256/60, *s. for* trayne, deceit, trick.

Trayne, 59/102, 133/205, 179/23, *s.* plot, device; *withouten trayne,* a phrase to fill up a line.

Trayse, 275/118, *s.* trace, path, way.

Trante, 263/234, 315/251, 454/168, *s.* trick.

Trappid, 231/267, *v.* pinched or squeezed.

Traste, 24/78; **Trayste,** 76/139, *v.* trust; **Trast,** 132/185, be assured.

Trauayle, 197/129, *v.* work.

Traues, 381/150, *v.* crosses.

Trembelys, 32/113, *v.* trembles, quakes.

Tresurry, 135/246, *s.* treasury.

Trewys, 271/9, *s. pl.*; *trewe, truwe,* faith, fidelity.

Trine, Tryne, 8/5, 103/13, 327/226, *v.* to go, step, walk.

Triste, 67/349, 364/176; **Treste,** 365/191, trust, faith.

Trystefull, 217/514, *adj.* to be trusted.

Trowe, 24/75, 148/53, *v.* to believe.

Trufullis, 26/125, 303/300, 310/111, trifles, incidents, idle stories.

Trus, Truss, Trusse, 190/151, 348/347, 346/274, *v.* pack up, prepare, make ready.

Tule, 454/168, *v.* to work or labour (a thing), pull about; **Tulyed,** 245/118, 482/58, *pa. p.* (Scotch *tulye,* a struggle; Fr. *toullier,* to mingle in confusion.)

Tulles, 143/172, *s.* tools, things: *see* **Toles.**

Turnement, 244/91, *s.* ? *for* torment.

Twyne, 42/78, 364/151; **Twynne,** 43/100, *v.* to sunder, divide.

Twyne, 43/100, *v. for* tine, to perish.

Vayle, 246/143, *v. aphetic for* avail.

Vayne, 6/146, empty.

Vaynes, 253/286, *s.* veins.

Vernand, 216/498, *adj.* vernal, of the spring.

Verray, 100/219, *adj.* true.

Vilaunce, 194/15, vile.

Vyolet, 216/498, *s.* violet.

Vmbelappid, 475/66, *v.* covered around, surrounded.

Vmbycast, 336/467, *v.* bound about.

Vmsitte, 479/186, *s.* set around, surround.

Vnbraste, 55/320, unloosed.

Vnbuxumnes, 6/123, *s.* disobedience.

Vnconand, 280/244, *adj.* ignorant.

Vncouthe, 59/116, *adj.* unknown.

Vndir-lowte, 459/92, *s.* a subject, one stooping beneath subjection.

Vndirstand, 76/145, 78/177, 105/79, *v.* to hear.

Vndir-take, 186/23, *v.* to receive.

Vndre, 322/50, *meaning doubtful, perhaps corrupt.*

Vndughty, 334/411, cowardly.

Vnethis, 499/59, *adv.* scarcely.

Vngladde, sorry.

Vnhende, 485/155, *adj.* uncourteous.

Vnysoune, 209/262, *s.* unison, singing in one voice or part.

Vnlappe, 280/256, *v.* to uncover.

Vnmeete, 352/127, *adj.* unfit.

Vnrude = unride, 423/67, *adj.* harsh, large. (See Stratmann.)

Vnseele, 313/177, *s.* misfortune.

Vnsittyng, 326/192, *adj.* unbecoming.

Vnsoght, 13/77, 103/44, *adj.* unquiet, troubled, disturbed.

Vnthrifty, 352/90, *adj.* ill-thriving, unsuccessful.

Vnthryuandely = unthrivingly, 5/114, *adv.* unprosperously, in vain.

Vn-welde, 43/93, 63/221, *adj.* infirm.

Vnwittely, 31/52, *adv.* foolishly.

Vnwitty, 130/110, *adj.* unwise.

Vphald, 325/150, *v.* warrant, vouch for.

Vpholde, 232/282, *s.* support.

Vppe sought, 351/68, *v.* fetcht up, brought up.

Vpryse, 459/90; Vprysing, 459/91, *s.* resurrection.

Vpstritt, 329/275, *pa. t.* of upstert, started up.

Vttiremeste, 386/232, *adj.* last, utmost.

Wa, 107/143, *s.* woe.

Waferyng, 39/111, wavering, wandering.

Waffe, 95/54, 301/248, *v.* to waft, to wave, move, throw; Wauyd, *pa. p.* 317/318.

Waghe, 151/173, *adj.* and *s.* evil, wrong.

Way, 142/147, *do way!* *see* Do.

Wayke, 43/93, *adj.* weak.

Waite, 328/253, 470/169, *v.* watch.

Wake, 9/12, 504/196, *v.* to watch.

Wakynge, 415/357, *s.* watching.

Wale, 11/55, *v.* to choose, select.

Walowe, 421/10, *v.* to wither, to faint, die away.

Wanand, 51/204, *v.* waning, lessening.

Wandes, 42/75, *s.* rods or slats.

Wandynge, 243/77, *verb. s.* failing with fear, blenching.

Wane, 54/300, vain, *in wane,* in vain.

Wane, 51/186, *v.* lessen.

Wane, 40/2, 367/278, *adj.* wan pale; *see* Wanne.

Wane, 33/121, 142/144; Wone, 153/217; Waneand, 36/45, *s.* thought, meaning; (sc. *wane,* O. E. *wén,* opinion): *see* Wille.

Wanes, 106 / 123, *s.* dwellings: *see* Wones.

Wanyand, 124/37, *s.* curse, vengeance; *in the wanyand,* an imprecation, with a curse or vengeance; *in wilde waneand,* 36/45, may possibly mean the same.

Wangges, 64/275, *s.* cheeks.

Wanhope, 450/75, *s.* despair.

Wanne *for* Wan, 36/38, 50/156, *adj.* gloomy, filthy, evil.

Wanne-trowing, 458/83, *s.* mistrust, faint faith.

Want, 454/166, *v.* to lack.

Wapped, 292/12, 480/1, 489/274, *pa. p.* wrapped, enclosed.

Wappe of, 331/343, *v.* unwrap.

War, 87/329, *v. subj. imp.* were; *war they wente,* were they gone.

Warande, 128/67, *s.* warrant.

Warde, 221/43, *s.* custody, guard.

Ware, 196/31, *adj.* aware.

Warisoune, 362/89, *s.* final reward.

Warly, 468/91, *adj.* warily.

Warlow, 276/141, 281/258, 471/176, a wizard, one who has made compact with the devil, hence a wicked man, a fiendish person.

Warre, 286/399; Were, 22/1, *s.* war, doubt, confusion; *his witte is in warre,* his wits are at war, confused.

Warre, 324/137, *adj.* ware.

Warred, 339/77, *v.* purchased, spent, provided.

Warrok, 291/525, *v.* to restrain, bind.

Wast, 11/52, *v.* to rob, to waste.

Waste, 100/196, 154/271, *adj.* vain, useless, *in waste,* in vain.

Waste, 451/87, *adv.* wastefully, extravagantly.

Wathe, 24/65, 49/145, 181/109, *s.* danger, evil, injury.

Wax, 113/41, *v.* to grow; Waxen, 51/192, *pa. p.* grown.

We! 76/139, *interj.* oh! (*from the impatient* why!) We! how! We! hudde! 119/37, 120/47, interjections of surprise.

Wedde, 261/189, *v.* to pledge, to wager.

Wedde-sette, 318/346, *v.* to put in pledge, to wedset, to let.

Wede, 10/34, 94/30, 236/93, *s.* dress, raiment, clothing.

Wede, 421/9, *s.* passion, fury; 422/23, *v.* to rage, act furiously.

Wedlak, 110/261, *s.* wedlock.

Weelde, 4/67, *s.* wield, power: *see* Wolde.

Weendande, 4/96, *pr. p.* wending.

Wegge, 356/242, *s.* wedge.

Welaway ! 27/148, 32/93, *interj.* Alas !

Weldand, 112/1, *adj.* mighty; *all weldand,* all mighty, all wielding.

Welde, 212/360, 124/37, 315/273, *v.* to use, wield, exercise.

Weledyng, 2/39, *v. s.* wielding.

Weyke, 113/25, *adj.* weak.

Well, 6/131, *v.* to boil, bubble.

Welland, 87/334, *adj.* boiling, furiously.

Welthe, 2/39, 33/117, 198/155, *s.* well-being, weal.

Wende, 10/42, *v.* to turn, put ; 11/46, *away bese went,* are put away ; 29/3, went, *pa. p.* turned, done ; 444/347, gone.

Wendes, 50/161, *v. imperat.* go.

Wene, 156/5, *v.* to think ; **Wenys,** 49/119, weenest, thinkest; **Wende,** 157/29, *past t.*

Wene, 74/104, *s.* doubt, supposition.

Were, 36/38, 127/34, *v.* to defend, guard, protect.

Were, 243/82, *s.* defence, shield.

Were, 111/302, *v.* to wear.

Were, 22/1, 228/213, *s.* doubt, uncertainty, confusion ; 50/146, doubt, fear : *see* **Warre.**

Wery, 310/108, *v.* to curse; **Weried,** 52/232; **Weryed,** 70/27; **Werryed,** *pa. p.* cursed.

Werie, 110/249, 510/328. *adj.* weary; **Wery,** 108/205, worried, vexed.

Werraye, 147/35, *for* verray, *adj.* true.

Werre, 296/108, *adj.* worse.

Wetand, 475/72, *pr. p.* (? *error for* wetyng, *s.*) thinking, knowing.

Wete, 411/283, 450/51, *adj.* wet, i. e. bleeding.

Wete, 4/67, 129/95, *v.* to wit, to know ; **Weten,** 501/130, *pa. p.*

Wetterly, 19/21, *adv.* wisely, with knowledge : *see* **Vnwittely, Wittirly.**

Whapp, 326/199, *s.* a whop, a blow.

Whare-som, 34/168, *adv.* wherever.

What ! 4/81, 33/133, 114/71, *interj.* how !

What-kynne, 24/52, *adj.* what sort of.

Whe ! 251/250, *interj.* Ho !

Whedir, 236/112, *adv.* whither.

Whethir, 104/53, *pron.* which.

Whikly, 12/64, *adv.* alive (cf. quick), in activity.

Whyle, 30/51 ; **While,** 31/52, *s.* time.

Whilke, 15/24, 165/183, *pron.* which.

Whilom, 75/126, *adv.* once, formerly.

Whore, 12/72, *adv.* where.

Wicchis, 153/221, *s.* witches.

Wyelly, 443/333, *adv.* ? manlike, in form of man, from A. S. *wy.*

Wyffe, 153/216, 173/39, *s.* woman.

Wight, 140/54, *s.* child; 144/208, person, anybody.

Wighte, 52/212 ; **Wight,** 145/219, *adj.* active, strong.

Wightly, Wyght, 8/6, 10/42, 141/92, *adv.* actively, quickly, energetically.

Wightnes, 58/58, *s.* activity, strength.

Wille, 144/208, 508/293, *adj.* wild, wandering, bewildered ; **Wille of rede,** 424/91, at a loss (*see* **Rede**) ; **Wille of wane,** 142/144, 153/217, 191/184, at a loss, bewildered (wild of thought or weening) : *see* **Wane.**

Willid, 241/17, *v.* wandered, strayed.

Willy, 458/79, *adj.* willing, choosing.

Wilsom, 135/243, 144/188, 236/92, *adj.* wild, devious, wandering.

Wymond, 339, *proper name :* cf. *Rauf Coilyear,* l. 315, &c.

Wyne, 9/25, 12/63; **Wynne,** 489/276, *s.* pleasure, joy.

Wynly, 9/12, *adv.* profitably, 504/196, joyfully ; 476/103, ? *for* wanly.

Wynne, 81/220, 142/150, *v.* to gain, draw away, get, fetch ; **Wynne away,** 41/32, go away : *see* **Wonne.**

Wynnyng, 1/3, 24/68, *v. s.* attaining, reaching, gain.

Wys, wisse, wysshe, 42/70, 109/239, 237/123, *v.* teach, direct, guide.

Wyss-ande, 7/152, *pr. p.*; **Wysshyng,** 7/157, *s.* guiding, leading.

Wyrke, 41/35, *v.* to work.

Wirshippe, 24/56, *s.* (worth-ship), honour, respect.

Wyste, 5/116, *v.* knew.

Wystus, 219/14, *probably for* wyscus, i. e. vicious, angry, cruel.

Wite, 30/34, 129/78, v. blame; Witte, 382/176.

Witte, 51/209, v. to know.

Wittering, 142/124, s. hint, inkling.

Witty, 124/22, adj. full of knowledge.

Wittirly, 190/157; Wittely, 42/88, adv. wisely, surely : see Wetterly.

Wode, 140/75, adj. mad.

Wolde, 344/220, v. would.

Wolde, 30/50, 285/357, 315/273, s. power, might, authority : see Weelde.

Won, wone, wonne, 2/28, 70/31, v. to dwell; Wonnande, 124/33, pr. p.

Wondir, wondirly, 398/60, adv. marvellously, excessively.

Wones, 2/28, s. abode, dwelling-place : see Wanes.

Wonges, 103 / 41, s. cheeks : see Wanges.

Wonne, 91/405, pa. p. won, brought from.

Wonne, 264/252, s. custom.

Wonne, 264/251, pa. p. accustomed.

Wonnyng, 18/3, s. dwelling.

Wonnyng-steed, 173/42, s. dwellingplace.

Woode, 87/334, adj. mad.

Worde, 144/208, for world.

Wordely, 237/128, adj. worldly.

Worme, 23/23, 25/91, s. reptile, serpent.

Wormes, 87/339, s. wild wormes, locusts, or caterpillars.

Worth, worthe, 10/34, 50/156 ; Worbe, 135/261, v. to become ; Worthed, 415/358, pa. p.

Worthyly, 2/17, 369/333, adj. worthy.

Worthy to wyte, 150/131, blameworthy.

Wothis, 76/138, s. injuries: see Wathe.

Wraiste = Wreste, 76/137, 301/261, pa. p. wrested.

Wreye, 501/129, v. destroy, turn.

Wreyede, 173/25, v. revealed, discovered.

Wrekyng, 266/323, s. vengeance.

Wrest, 133/187, s. a twist, a deceit, trick.

Wretthe, 226/154, s. wrath, anger.

Wrye, 270/7, v. for wreye.

Wrynkis, 273/67, s. wrenches, twists.

Wrothe, 153/223, adj. angry.

Ya ! 37/52, 60, interj. yes.

Yare, 36/30; Yhare, 26/138; ȝare, 213/405, adj. or adv. active, ready.

Yarne, 175/113, v. desire, yearn for ; ȝerned, pa. p.

Yarnyng, 127/32, s. yearning, desire.

Yappely, 279/231 ; ȝappely, 469/127 adv. readily, fitly, eagerly.

Ych, 293/38, ? for ilk.

ȝede, 511/342, v. went: see Yode, Yoode.

ȝelde, 57/30; Yeelde, 58/53, v. to give, pay.

Yeme, 460/128, s. heed, care : see Eme.

ȝeme, 15/18, 235/66, v. to rule, govern, care for.

ȝemed, 469/128, v. guarded.

ȝemyng, 457/46, s. caring for, governing.

Yere, 354/164, to yere, this year. See Towneley Mysteries, p. 231.

ȝerned, 185/10, pa. p. desired.

ȝhe, 5/114, pron. ye.

ȝhit, 4/87, conj. yet.

ȝhour, 2/38, your.

ȝhow, 5/117, pron. you.

ȝynge, 49/139, adj. young.

ȝo, 200/209, pron. you.

Yode, Yoode, 50/151 ; ȝoode, 87/ 336 = Yede, v. went.

Yof, 272/45 ; for þof, conj. though.

Yore, 54/307, yet, for a long time.

Youe me, 354/154, this appears to be a corruption. Query, read ' you and me.'

Yowe ! 282/295, ? an exclamation.

THE END.